(*continued on back*)

PEER RELATIONSHIPS
IN CHILD DEVELOPMENT

Peer Relationships in Child Development

Edited by

THOMAS J. BERNDT
GARY W. LADD
Purdue University

WILEY

A WILEY-INTERSCIENCE PUBLICATION

JOHN WILEY & SONS

New York • Chichester • Brisbane • Toronto • Singapore

Copyright © 1989 by John Wiley & Sons, Inc.

All rights reserved. Published simultaneously in Canada.

Reproduction or translation of any part of this work
beyond that permitted by Section 107 or 108 of the
1976 United States Copyright Act without the permission
of the copyright owner is unlawful. Requests for
permission or further information should be addressed to
the Permissions Department, John Wiley & Sons, Inc.

This publication is designed to provide accurate and
authoritative information in regard to the subject
matter covered. It is sold with the understanding that
the publisher is not engaged in rendering legal, accounting,
or other professional service. If legal advice or other
expert assistance is required, the services of a competent
professional person should be sought. *From a Declaration
of Principles jointly adopted by a Committee of the
American Bar Association and a Committee of Publishers.*

Library of Congress Cataloging-in-Publication Data

Peer relationships in child development / edited by Thomas J. Berndt, Gary W. Ladd.
      p.   cm.—(Wiley series in personality processes)
  "A Wiley-Interscience publication."
  Bibliography: p.
  ISBN 0-471-85131-0
    1. Interpersonal relations in children.   2. Childhood friendship.
3. Interpersonal relations in adolescence.   I. Berndt, Thomas J.,
1949–   .   II. Ladd, Gary W., 1950– .   III. Series.
BF723.I646P44   1988
305.2'3—dc19   88-5779
                                                  CIP

ISBN 0-471-85131-0

Printed in the United States of America

10 9 8 7 6 5 4 3 2 1

Contributors

THOMAS J. BERNDT, PhD
Professor
Department of Psychological
 Sciences
Purdue University
West Lafayette, Indiana

B. BRADFORD BROWN, PhD
Associate Professor
Department of Educational
 Psychology
University of Wisconsin at
 Madison
Madison, Wisconsin

WILLIAM M. BUKOWSKI, PhD
Assistant Professor
Department of Psychology
University of Maine at Orono
Orono, Maine

WILLIAM DAMON, PhD
Professor of Psychology
Clark University
Worcester, Massachusetts

KENNETH A. DODGE, PhD
Associate Professor
Department of Psychology and
 Human Development
Vanderbilt University
Nashville, Tennessee

JOYCE L. EPSTEIN, PhD
Principal Research Scientist
The Johns Hopkins University
 Center for Research on
 Elementary and Middle Schools
The Johns Hopkins University
Baltimore, Maryland

CANDICE FEIRING, PhD
Associate Professor
Robert Wood Johnson Medical
 School
University of Medicine and
 Dentistry of New Jersey
New Brunswick, New Jersey

WYNDOL FURMAN, PhD
Associate Professor
Department of Psychology
University of Denver
Denver, Colorado

LESLIE A. GAVIN, MA
Doctoral Student
Department of Psychology
University of Denver
Denver, Colorado

JOHN M. GOTTMAN, PhD
Professor
Department of Psychology
University of Washington
Seattle, Washington

WILLARD W. HARTUP, EDD
Professor
Institute of Child Development
University of Minnesota
Minneapolis, Minnesota

CATHY J. HOBART, MA
Graduate Student
Department of Psychology
Wayne State University
Detroit, Michigan

BETSY HOZA, MA
Doctoral Student
Department of Psychology
University of Maine at Orono
Orono, Maine

GARY W. LADD, EDD
Associate Professor
Department of Child Development
   and Family Studies
Purdue University
West Lafayette, Indiana

MICHAEL E. LAMB, PHD
Chief
Section on Social and Emotional
   Development
National Institute of Child Health
   and Human Development
Bethesda, Maryland

MICHAEL LEWIS, PHD
Professor
Institute for the Study of Child
   Development
University of Medicine and
   Dentistry of New Jersey
New Brunswick, New Jersey

ALISON NASH, PHD
Assistant Professor
Psychology Department
State University of New York at
   New Paltz
New Paltz, New York

JEFFREY G. PARKER, MA
Doctoral Student
Department of Psychology
University of Illinois
Champaign, Illinois

ERIN PHELPS, EDD
Senior Research Associate
Radcliffe College
Cambridge, Massachusetts

JOSEPH M. PRICE, PHD
Research Associate
Department of Psychology and
   Human Development
Vanderbilt University
Nashville, Tennessee

DAVID C. ROWE, PHD
Associate Professor
School of Family and Consumer
   Studies
University of Arizona
Tucson, Arizona

LYNN HICKEY SCHULTZ, MA
Research Associate
Graduate School of Education
Harvard University
Cambridge, Massachusetts

ROBERT L. SELMAN, PHD
Associate Professor
Graduate School of Education
Harvard University
Cambridge, Massachusetts

CAROLYN U. SHANTZ, PHD
Professor
Department of Psychology
Wayne State University
Detroit, Michigan

JACQUELINE SMOLLAR, PhD
Research Associate
Youth Research Center
Catholic University of America
Washington, District of Columbia

JAMES YOUNISS, PhD
Professor
Youth Research Center
Catholic University of America
Washington, District of Columbia

Series Preface

This series of books is addressed to behavioral scientists interested in the nature of human personality. Its scope should prove pertinent to personality theorists and researchers as well as to clinicians concerned with applying an understanding of personality processes to the amelioration of emotional difficulties in living. To this end, the series provides a scholarly integration of theoretical formulations, empirical data, and practical recommendations.

Six major aspects of studying and learning about human personality can be designated: personality theory, personality structure and dynamics, personality development, personality assessment, personality change, and personality adjustment. In exploring these aspects of personality, the books in the series discuss a number of distinct but related subject areas: the nature and implications of various theories of personality; personality characteristics that account for consistencies and variations in human behavior; the emergence of personality processes in children and adolescents; the use of interviewing and testing procedures to evaluate individual differences in personality; efforts to modify personality styles through psychotherapy, counseling, behavior therapy, and other methods of influence; and patterns of abnormal personality functioning that impair individual competence.

IRVING B. WEINER

Fairleigh Dickinson University
Rutherford, New Jersey

Preface

In recent years, a considerable amount of research has been conducted on children's and adolescents' relationships with their peers. One focus of this research has been the nature and correlates of popularity with peers. Another focus has been the features of children's friendships and the changes in friendships between childhood and adolescence. Although hypotheses about the consequences of peer relationships for children's development have served as the foundation for much of the research, direct assessments of the impact of peer relationships on children's personality, social behavior, or cognition have rarely been done.

The primary aims of this volume are to identify the central issues and to present the major findings of research on the contributions of peer relationships to development during childhood and adolescence. It was our intention to create a forum in which researchers from many backgrounds could examine this question in greater detail and define and address issues needing further investigation. To do this, we have solicited chapters from a distinguished group of researchers, who have agreed to share both their thinking on this subject and their research findings.

Because of the diversity of orientations and approaches represented, the volume should be useful to a broad range of readers. Developmental psychologists may be most interested in the analyses of the processes that operate in peer relationships and the connections between parents and peers. Educational psychologists and educators may be most interested in the descriptions and evaluations of peer-learning programs and other peer-based interventions in schools. Clinical psychologists and other mental health professionals may find the section on intervention most helpful for their work. We expect that all readers will benefit, however, from the inclusion of the full range of issues relevant to peer relationships in one volume. Moreover, we hope that the ideas presented in the volume will motivate many readers to undertake their own research on the contributions of peer relationships.

Finally, during the preparation of this volume we benefited from the advice and counsel of many individuals. Although we cannot name them all, we especially want to thank Herb Reich, our Editor at John Wiley and Sons, for his enthusiastic support of the volume and for his careful handling of the manuscript. We also want to acknowledge the financial assistance of the

William T. Grant Foundation, the Spencer Foundation, and the Foundation for Child Development, who supported some of our own research and writing on peer relationships. Lastly, we thank the colleagues and students with whom we have so frequently shared our ideas about peer relationships.

THOMAS J. BERNDT
GARY W. LADD

West Lafayette, Indiana
November 1988

Contents

INTRODUCTION

Toward a Further Understanding of Peer Relationships and Their Contributions to Child Development

GARY W. LADD

Research on peer relationships in childhood and adolescence has blossomed in the past decade. Many investigators have explored the correlates of popularity in peer groups (see Coie and Kupersmidt, 1983; Dodge, 1983; Ladd, 1983; Masters & Furman, 1981; Putallaz, 1983; Renshaw & Asher, 1983; Rubin & Daniels-Bierness, 1983; Vaughn & Waters, 1981) and the features of the friendships between pairs of children (e.g., Berndt, Hawkins & Hoyle, 1986; Berndt & Hoyle, 1985; Gottman, 1983; Hinde, Titmus, Easton & Tamplin, 1985; Howes, 1983; Newcomb & Brady, 1982; Parker, 1986). Much of this research has been motivated by general hypotheses about the significance of peer relationships for children's development. Nevertheless, few studies have assessed directly the influence of peer relationships on children's personality, social behavior, and cognition. In light of this void, the purpose of this book is to consider some key issues and current evidence regarding the contributions of peer relationships to children's development.

Areas in Need of Investigation

Researchers who wish to understand how peer relationships contribute to children's development are faced with a number of conceptual and methodological hurdles. To begin, there is a need to define and describe the types of relationships children form with peers. Children's relationships with peers may take many different forms, such as friend, acquaintance, classmate, and teammate. Moreover, the form of relationship children develop with peers may change over time or differ depending on their age or length of acquaintance. For example, popularity among classmates may appreciate or decline as children move from grade to grade (see Coie & Dodge, 1983; Newcomb & Bukowski, 1984); friendships may be gained or lost as children's interests change, or grow in intimacy over time and acquaintanceship (Berndt, 1987; Berndt et al., 1986; Berndt & Hoyle, 1985). Thus, efforts to identify

1

peer influences are partly dependent on the investigator's ability to describe the types of peer relationships children form and the ways in which they evolve and change with development.

It is also likely that different types of peer relationships serve different functions in child development (see Asher, 1978; Hartup, 1983; Price & Ladd, 1986; Putallaz & Gottman, 1982). However, at present, our knowledge about the potential effects of different types of peer relationships is limited. This void exists in part, because researchers often fail to differentiate between the various forms or features of children's peer relationships when studying the contributions of agemates. For example, the distinction between dyadic and group-oriented relationships (e.g., friendship and popularity) has often been blurred in the peer relations literature, and little has been done to determine whether these two types of relationships have differential effects on children's socialization and development. It seems likely that dyadic and group relationships may offer children different opportunities for learning and development (e.g., close companionships vs. group belongingness) and may also differ in adaptive significance (e.g., the ability to protect children from disorder or place them at risk, depending on the form, availability, and quality of the relationships). In the present volume, children's friendships and popularity are viewed as two key facets of their relationships with peers that deserve further research attention.

In examining the functions of agemates in development, it is also important for researchers to identify the specific types of cognitive and behavioral processes that tend to occur in children's peer relationships and to determine the potential effects of these experiences on the individual child. Many processes that foster relationship formation, maintenance, and termination may directly or indirectly influence children's development and well-being. For example, the quarrels (see Shantz, 1987) and conversations (see Gottman & Parker, 1986) that occur in friendships may provide important lessons in autonomy and intimacy that, in turn, may influence children's later self-perceptions and relationships. In larger group settings, children's behaviors toward peers (see Coie & Kupersmidt, 1983; Dodge, 1983; Ladd, Price & Hart, in press) and peers' interpretations of these acts (Coie, Dodge & Coppotelli, 1982; Hymel, 1986; Hymel, Wagner & Butler, in press; Ladd & Mars, 1986) may foster lasting social reputations. Once formed, children's reputations in the peer group may enhance or inhibit their sense of belongingness and self-efficacy.

Peer relationships occur within a larger social ecology, and their potential contributions to children's development must be understood in relation to other socialization contexts, such as families (see Parke, MacDonald, Beitel, & Bhavnagri, 1988; Putallaz & Heflin, in press) and schools (see Damon, 1984; Epstein, 1983; Hallinan & Sorensen, 1985; and *Child Development*, Vol. 58 [5], 1987). By comparing the functions of peers with those of other socialization agents, investigators may better understand the significance of agemates in children's development. It is possible, as researchers such as

Hartup (1979) and Mueller (1979) have argued, that peers play unique roles in children's socialization by providing learning opportunities and experiences that cannot be duplicated by other socializers. Conversely, it may be that other socialization agents, such as parents, siblings, and teachers, make peers' contributions largely redundant. Were this the case, the primary function of peer relations might be to elaborate or extend the influence of other socialization agents and contexts.

If peers play unique roles in children's socialization, it is possible that their contributions may enhance or impede developments in other contexts and relationships. For example, children's peer relations in school settings can be a source of support (e.g., Berndt, 1987; Ladd & Price, 1987) and learning (e.g., Damon, 1984; Slavin, 1987) or a source of distress (Asher & Wheeler, 1985; Asher & Williams, 1987) and continuing rejection (e.g., Coie & Dodge, 1983; Newcomb & Bukowski, 1984). Developments that occur in the peer group may complement parental teachings or may conflict with family values (see Berndt, 1979; Youniss, 1980; Youniss & Smollar, 1985). Moreover, the nature of the interface between socialization agents and contexts may affect children's development. Cross-pressures between contexts may lead to different developmental outcomes than confluence. Therefore, to understand the significance of peer relations in children's development, investigators must also consider the ways in which children's experiences in the peer culture affect their socialization in other contexts, and vice versa.

Conversely, children's experiences in the peer culture can be seen as extensions and elaborations of their family history and socialization. Processes that originate in primary socialization contexts (e.g., parent-child relationships), and heritable child characteristics (e.g., general sociability, temperament) may contribute to children's successes and failures in peer relations. Recent research suggests that a number of factors associated with early family relationships and socialization are associated with the quality of children's subsequent peer relationships, including parents' perceptions (e.g., Ladd & Price, 1986), pathology (e.g., Baldwin, Cole, & Baldwin, 1982), attachment styles (e.g., Waters, Wippman, & Sroufe, 1979), disciplinary orientations (see Maccoby & Martin, 1983), interpersonal behaviors (e.g., MacDonald & Parke, 1984; Puttalaz, 1987), and management of children's peer relations (e.g., Ladd & Golter, 1988). Other investigators emphasize the importance of heritable child characteristics and constitutional factors, such as child sociability (see Buss & Plomin, 1984; Vandell, 1985) and temperament (e.g., Daniels, 1986; Olweus, 1980).

Important information about the contributions of peers to children's development may also be gleaned from the study of exceptional peer relationships. Currently, very little is known about children who are especially successful or competent at forming and developing peer relationships, and even less is known about the effects of peer relationships on exceptionally competent or skillful children. Research on interpersonally competent children may offer important clues about the origins and maintenance of healthy peer relationships. Moreover, by studying children who demonstrate the ability to sustain satisfying peer relationships, we may learn more about the means by which children successfully adapt to change and resolve relationship-threatening problems and transitions.

Many investigators (e.g., Berndt, 1982; Fine, 1981; Hartup, 1983; Ladd & Asher, 1985) have argued that peer relationships provide a context or "staging area" for the development of interpersonal competencies, including advanced forms of social reasoning and behavioral skills. Yet, few have studied the potential impact of peers on children's strengths or have attempted to determine whether peer relations provide an arena for competent children to express and refine their existing skills and abilities.

Conversely, by studying disordered peer relations, investigators may learn more about the processes that precipitate or maintain social difficulties and, in turn, place children at risk for developmental deviations or other forms of maladjustment. There is a growing body of evidence indicating that the origins and maintenance of problem peer relationships (e.g., peer rejection, friendlessness) are complex (see Coie, in press). Among the factors that deserve further research are children's antisocial behaviors (e.g., Coie & Kupersmidt, 1983; Dodge, 1983; Olweus, 1977), social cognitions and information-processing patterns (see Dodge, Pettit, McClaskey, & Brown, 1987; Ladd & Crick, in press; Rubin & Krasnor, 1986), and self-perceptions, attributions, and emotions (see Gottman, 1986; Hymel & Franke, 1985; Hymel, Franke, & Freigang, 1985; Ladd & Crick, in press). Moreover, studies of the contexts in which children experience social difficulties, such as friendship dyads and peer groups, may help to identify factors that contribute to or exacerbate negative outcomes, such as peer rejection. For example, factors such as partner expectations and knowledge in friendships (e.g., Diaz & Berndt, 1984; Ladd & Emerson, 1984; Selman, 1980, 1981) and impression formation and stereotypes in peer groups (e.g., Hymel, 1986; Hymel, Wagner & Butler, in press) are not well understood, and yet both factors may be relevant to children's social successes and difficulties in peer relationships.

Studies that explore planned variations in children's experiences with agemates may also provide important clues about the impact and significance of peer relations (for reviews, see Conger & Keane, 1981; Damon, 1984; Furman & Robbins, 1985; Ladd, 1985; Ladd & Mize, 1983; Slavin, 1987). Typically, in intervention research, investigators attempt to manipulate children's interpersonal or academic experiences with peers and then document changes in their behavior and development. Manipulations may consist of procedures designed to induce various forms of social interaction, to foster achievement, to improve peer relationships, and to modify children's social cognitions and behaviors toward peers. The value of these investigations, beyond their potential salutary effects, lies in their ability to show that peers can affect children's development and adjustment.

Specific Aims of This Book

Our motivation for constructing this volume came from a basic interest in peer relationships and a desire to understand the potential contributions of peers to development during childhood and adolescence. We have been struck by the frequency with which researchers refer to the importance of peers in child development and by how little evidence has been assembled to support this claim. The present volume is intended to remedy this situation by marshaling the findings and observations of a group of leading researchers in this field.

The content is broad in scope, incorporating a number of areas of investigation that may help to illuminate the nature and significance of peers' contributions to children's development. Although diverse, the chapters are organized around the same general questions: What do we know about the contributions of peer relationships, and how could we learn more about the role of peers in development? This focus provides a common theme that serves to organize and integrate the book.

Within this volume, the concept of peer relations is broadly defined. Generally, peers are characterized as individuals who are similar to the child in age and/or developmental level. Typically, peers are seen as individuals who do not share kinship or reside within the same family. We recognize, however, that many of the issues relevant to the study of peer relations may also apply to research on sibling relations, and the interface between these two domains is of considerable interest. Also included in the concept of peer relations is the form of the relationship or type of association children develop with near-age companions. Peer relations may refer to children's efforts to interact with agemates, their position or role in same-age groups or cliques, and their participation in various forms of alliances and relationships. In the chapters that follow, particular attention is given to friendships, popularity or sociometric status, and the place of peer relationships in the overall social networks of children and adolescents.

Central to the aims of this book are theory and research on the potential effects of peer relations on the development of the individual child. Of particular interest are the processes that occur within the context of children's peer relations. In this volume, processes refer to the types of cognitive and behavioral events that occur between children and their peers which, in turn, may be used to define the character or quality of their relations. Research on processes can be used to achieve both descriptive and predictive aims. For example, a descriptive aim would include efforts to classify the forms of interaction that differentiate friends from nonfriends. Predictive aims, in contrast, can be understood as attempts to define the functions of particular forms of interactions in relation to specific developmental outcomes. In this case, interaction patterns and social cognitions may be studied more as a means of determining how, when, and under what conditions children are likely to become friends, develop debilitating reputations, learn from peers in school, and so forth. This volume was conceived with the latter type of research in mind.

We also recognize that peer relations occur in a variety of contexts during childhood and adolescence and that it is important to consider the effects of context on peer relations, as well as the impact of peer relations on other socialization agents and contexts. Because families and schools are among the most pervasive and influential socialization contexts for children and adolescents, they are awarded a position of central importance in this book. By including research and theory on family and school contexts, we hope to learn more about how children's peer relations operate within these settings and to what ends they are beneficial or harmful to the individual. Equally important are the ways in which children's peer relations interface with the demands of school or their experiences within the family, and vice versa.

Also relevant to the aims of this volume are programs of research in which investigators study the development and course of disordered peer relationships and attempt to experimentally manipulate children's experiences with peers. Especially pertinent to this issue are frameworks and investigations that promise to shed further light on the pathways through which potentially debilitating social difficulties and disordered peer relationships develop and evolve. Findings from recent intervention research indicating that peers influence children's learning and behavior (see Bierman, 1986; Ladd, 1985; Slavin, 1987) also reflect on the questions addressed in this book and, therefore, receive careful consideration.

Content and Structure of This Book

Due to the focus and aims of this book, each chapter is constructed to be more than a review of the existing research literature. Instead, authors discuss current ideas about the effects of peer relationships, present their own conceptual frameworks for understanding and specifying these effects, and illustrate these frameworks with existing research and findings from ongoing investigations. Furthermore, each author provides a look forward and considers important directions for future research. Each chapter, therefore, reflects the state of the art and also paves the way for future studies.

Moreover, the issues and topics addressed in this volume are explored from diverse and interdisciplinary perspectives. The contributors represent many different disciplines within the social sciences, including developmental and clinical psychology, education, and sociology, and they draw upon a variety of frameworks and methods to address their questions. As a consequence, they also explore a broad range of peer relationships and developmental outcomes. For example, attention is given to both the positive contributions of close and satisfying peer relationships and to the potentially negative influences of peers on children's behavior. A broad range of outcomes are considered, spanning such dimensions as self-esteem, academic achievement, and parent-child relationships.

Overall, this book is divided into four major parts, each of which is unified by a focus on a major theme or context. Consistent with the aims of the book, the parts are entitled *Processes, Peer Relationships in the School Context, Family Relationships and Peer Relationships,* and *Intervention.* A brief description of the content of these sections is provided below.

PROCESSES. The chapters in Part One will explore various processes that may lead to specific peer relationship outcomes. Information about the qualities of children's peer relationships will serve as a foundation for describing the functions these relationships are likely to serve in children's development. Many researchers have examined the processes that occur in peer relationships without attending to their potential outcomes, or vice versa. The chapters in this section will emphasize the importance of considering a range of potential processes and outcomes and the possible relations between them.

PEER RELATIONSHIPS IN THE SCHOOL CONTEXT. All of the chapters in Part Two will be concerned with peer relationships in the school context. In some chapters, the potential influences of peers on learning in school will be emphasized. In other chapters, the influence of the school environment on peer relationships and, in turn, on individual children will be stressed.

FAMILY RELATIONSHIPS AND PEER RELATIONSHIPS. Part Three will be devoted to the interplay between changes in peer relationships and changes in parent-child relationships during early childhood, middle childhood, and adolescence. The positive contributions of peer relationships to changes in relationships with parents, and the circumstances leading to conflict between parent and peer influences will be considered.

INTERVENTION. Part Four will focus on the utilization of peers in therapy with troubled children and adolescents. The authors, all researchers with clinical experience and expertise, will discuss current intervention programs that utilize peer relationships for therapeutic purposes. They will consider the dynamics of disordered peer relationships and the ways in which peers may foster, maintain, or aid in the resolution of children's social difficulties. Attention will also be devoted to the potential effects of problem peer relations on children's later development and to the usefulness of broad-based peer interventions for preventing psychological problems.

Finally, an overview of the major themes and the contents of the individual chapters that compose this book can be found at the beginning of each of the four substantive sections. A concluding chapter summarizes common themes and addresses discrepant findings and perspectives.

REFERENCES

Asher, S. R., & Wheeler, V. A. (1985). Children's loneliness: A comparison of rejected and neglected peer status. *Journal of Consulting and Clinical Psychology, 53,* 500–505.

Asher, S. R., & Williams, G. A. (1987, April). New approaches to identifying rejected children in school settings. In G. W. Ladd (Chair), *Identification and treatment of socially rejected children.* Symposium conducted at the meeting of the American Educational Research Association, Washington, DC.

Baldwin, A. L., Cole, R. E., & Baldwin, C. P. (1982). Parental pathology, family interaction, and competence of the child in school. *Monographs of the Society for Research in Child Development, 47*(5, Serial No. 197).

Berndt, T. J. (1979). Developmental changes in conformity to peers and parents. *Developmental Psychology, 15,* 608–616.

Berndt, T. J. (1982). The features and effects of friendship in early adolescence. *Child Development, 53,* 1447–1460.

Berndt, T. J. (1987, April). Changes in friendship and school adjustment after the transition to junior high school. In G. W. Ladd (Chair), *Entering and leaving elementary school: Consequences for social and school adjustment.* Symposium presented at the biennial meeting of the Society for Research in Child Development, Baltimore.

Berndt, T. J., Hawkins, J. A., & Hoyle, S. G. (1986). Changes in friendship during a school year: Effects of children's and adolescent's impressions of friendships and sharing with friends. *Child Development, 57,* 1284–1297.

Berndt, T. J., & Hoyle, S. G. (1985). Stability and change in childhood and adolescent friendships. *Developmental Psychology, 21,* 1007–1015.

Bierman, K. L. (1986). Process of change during social skills training with preadolescents and its relationship to treatment outcome. *Child Development, 57,* 230–240.

Buss, A. H., & Plomin, R. (1984). *Temperment: Early developing personality traits.* Hillsdale, NJ: Lawrence Erlbaum.

Coie, J. D. (in press). Toward a theory of peer rejection. In S. R. Asher & J. D. Coie (Eds.), *Peer rejection in childhood,* New York, Cambridge University Press.

Coie, J. D., & Dodge, K. A. (1983). Continuities and changes in children's social status: A five-year longitudinal study. *Merrill-Palmer Quarterly, 29,* 261–282.

Coie, J. D., Dodge, K. A., & Coppotelli, H. (1982). Dimensions and types of social status: A cross-age perspective. *Developmental Psychology, 18,* 557–570.

Coie, J. D., & Kupersmidt, J. B. (1983). A behavioral analysis of emerging social status in boys' groups. *Child Development, 54,* 1400–1416.

Conger, J. C., & Keane, S. P. (1981). Social skills intervention in the treatment of isolated or withdrawn children. *Psychology Bulletin, 90,* 478–495.

Damon, W. (1984). Peer education: The untapped potential. *Journal of Applied Developmental Psychology, 5,* 331–343.

Daniels, D. (1986). Differential experiences of siblings in the same family as predictors of adolescent sibling personality differences. *Journal of Personality and Social Psychology, 51,* 339–346.

Diaz, R. M., Berndt, T. J. (1984). Children's knowledge of a friend: Fact or fancy? *Developmental Psychology, 18,* 787–794.

Dodge, K. A. (1983). Behavioral antecedent of peer social status. *Child Development, 54,* 1386–1399.

Dodge, K. A., Pettit, G. S., McClaskey, C. L., & Brown, M. M. (1987). Social competence in children. *Monographs of the Society for Research in Child Development, 51*(2, Serial No. 213).

Entwisle, D., & Stevenson, H. W. (1987). Special issue on schools and development. *Child Development, 58,* 1149–1401.

Epstein, J. L. (1983). Selection of friends in differently organized schools and classrooms. In J. L. Epstein & N Karweit (Eds.), *Friends in school: Patterns of selection and influence in secondary schools* (pp. 73–92). New York: Academic Press.

Fine, G. A. (1981). Friends, impression management, and preadolescent behavior. In S. R. Asher & J. M. Gottman (Eds.), *The development of children's friendships* (pp. 29–52). New York: Cambridge University Press.

Furman, W., & Robbins, P. (1985). What's the point? Issues in the selection of treatment objectives. In B. Schneider, K. Rubin, & J. Ledingham (Eds.), *Children's peer relations: Issues in assessment and intervention* (pp. 41–54). New York: Springer-Verlag.

Gottman, J. M. (1983). How children become friends. *Monographs of the Society for Research in Child Development, 48*(3, Serial No. 201).

Gottman, J. M. (1986). Merging social cognition and behavior. Commentary in K. A. Dodge, et al., Social competence in children. *Monographs of the Society for Research in Child Development, 51*(2, Serial No. 213).

Gottman, J. M., & Parker, J. G. (1986). *The conversations of friends.* New York: Cambridge University Press.

Hallinan, M. T., & Sorensen, A. B. (1985). Ability grouping and student friendships. *American Educational Research Journal, 22,* 485–499.

Hartup, W. W. (1979). The social worlds of childhood. *American Psychologist, 34,* 944–950.

Hartup, W. W. (1983). Peer relations. In E. M. Hetherington (Ed.) & P. H. Mussen (Series Ed.), *Handbook of child psychology: Vol. 4. Socialization, personality, and social development* (pp. 103–196). New York: Wiley.

Hinde, R. A., Titmus, G., Easton, D., & Tamplin, A. (1985). Incidence of "friendship" and behavior toward strong associates versus nonassociates in preschoolers. *Child Development, 56,* 234–245.

Howes, C. (1983). Patterns of friendship. *Child Development, 54,* 1041–1053.

Hymel, S. (1986). Interpretations of peer behavior: Affective bias in childhood and adolescence. *Child Development, 57,* 431–445.

Hymel, S., & Franke, S. (1985). Children's peer relations: Assessing self-perceptions. In B. H. Schneider, K. H. Rubin, & J. E. Ledingham (Eds.), *Children's peer relations: Issues in assessment and intervention* (pp. 75–92). New York: Springer-Verlag.

Hymel, S., Franke, S., & Freigang, R. (1985). Peer relationships and their dysfunction: Considering the child's perspective. *Journal of Social and Clinical Psychology, 3,* 405–415.

Hymel, S., Wagner, E., & Butler, L. J. (in press). Reputational bias: View from the peer group. In S. R. Asher & J. D. Coie (Eds.), *Peer rejection in childhood.* New York: Cambridge University Press.

Ladd, G. W. (1983). Social networks of popular, average, and rejected children in school settings. *Merrill-Palmer Quarterly, 29,* 283–307.

Ladd, G. W. (1985). Documenting the effects of social skill training with children. In B. Schneider, K. Rubin, & J. Ledingham (Eds.), *Children's peer relations: Issues in assessment and intervention* (pp. 243–269). New York: Springer-Verlag.

Ladd, G. W., & Asher, S. R. (1985). Social skill training and children's peer relations. In L. L'Abate & M. Milan (Eds.), *Handbook of social skills training* (pp. 219–244). New York: Wiley.

Ladd, G. W., & Crick, N. R. (in press). Probing the psychological environment: Children's cognitions, perceptions, and feelings in the peer culture. In C. Ames & M. Maehr (Eds.), *Advances in motivation and achievement* (Vol. 6). Greenwich, CT: JAI Press.

Ladd, G. W., & Emerson, E. S. (1984). Shared knowledge in children's friendships. *Developmental Psychology, 20*, 932–940.

Ladd, G. W., & Golter, B. S. (1988). Parents' initiation and monitoring of children's peer contacts: Predictive of children's peer relations in nonschool and school settings? *Developmental Psychology, 24*, 109–117.

Ladd G. W., & Mars, K. T. (1986). Reliability and validity of preschooler's perceptions of peer behavior. *Journal of Clinical Child Psychology, 15*, 16–25.

Ladd, G. W., & Mize, J. (1983). A cognitive-social learning model of social skill training. *Psychological Review, 90*, 127–157.

Ladd, G. W., & Price, J. M. (1986). Promoting children's cognitive and social competence: The relations between parent's perceptions of task difficulty and children's perceived and actual competence. *Child Development, 57*, 446–460.

Ladd, G. W., & Price, J. M. (1987). Predicting children's social and school adjustment following the transition from preschool to kindergarten. *Child Development, 58*, 1168–1189.

Ladd, G. W., Price, J. M., & Hart, C. H. (in press). Predicting preschoolers' peer status from their playground behaviors. *Child Development*.

Maccoby, E. E., & Martin, J. A. (1983). Socialization in the context of the family: Parent-child interaction. In E. M. Hetherington (Ed.) & P. H. Mussen (Series Ed.), *Handbook of child psychology: Vol. 4. Socialization, personality, and social development* (pp. 1–101). New York: Wiley.

MacDonald, K., & Parke, R. (1984). Bridging the gap: Parent-child play interaction and peer interactive competence. *Child Development, 55*, 1265–1277.

Masters, J. C., & Furman, W. (1981). Popularity, individual friendship selection, and specific peer interaction among children. *Developmental Psychology, 17*, 344–350.

Mueller, E. (1979). (Toddlers + toys) = (an autonomous social system). In M. Lewis & L. Rosenblum (Eds.), *The child and its family* (pp. 169–194). New York: Plenum.

Newcomb, A. F., & Brady, J. E. (1982). Mutality in boys' friendship relations. *Child Development, 53*, 392–395.

Newcomb, A. F., & Bukowski, W. M. (1984). A longitudinal study of the utility of social preference and social impact sociometric classification schemes. *Child Development, 55*, 1434–1447.

Olweus, D. (1977). Aggression and peer acceptance in adolescent boys: Two short term longitudinal studies of ratings. *Child Development, 48*, 1301–1313.

Olweus, D. (1980). Familial and temperamental determinants of aggressive behavior in adolescent boys: A casual analysis. *Developmental Psychology, 16*, 644–660.

Parke, R. D., MacDonald, K. B., Beitel, A., & Bhavnagri, N. (1988). The role of the family in the development of peer relationships. In R. DeV. Peters & R. J. McMahan (Eds.), *Marriages and families: Behavioral treatments and processes.* (pp. 17–44). New York: Brunner/Mazel.

Parker, J. G., (1986). Becoming friends: Conversational skills for friendship formation in young children. In J. M. Gottman & J. G. Parker (Eds.), *The conversations of friends* (pp 103–138). New York: Cambridge University Press.

Price, J. M., & Ladd, G. W. (1986). Assessment of children's friendships: Implications for social competence and social adjustment. In R. Prinz (Ed.), *Advances in behavioral assessment of children and families* (Vol. 2, pp. 121–149). Greenwich, CT: JAI Press.

Putallaz, M. (1983). Predicting children's sociometric status from their behavior. *Child Development, 54*, 1417–1426.

Putallaz, M. (1987). Maternal behavior and children's sociometric status. *Child Development*, *58*, 324–340.

Putallaz, M., & Gottman, J. M. (1982). Conceptualizing social competence in children. In P. Karoly & J. J. Steffen (Eds.), *Improving children's competence: Advances in child behavior analysis and theory* (pp. 1–37). Lexington, MA: Lexington Books.

Putallaz, M., & Heflin, A. H. (in press). Parent-child interaction. In S. R. Asher & J. D. Coie (Eds.), *Peer rejection during childhood: Origins, maintenance, and intervention*. New York: Cambridge University Press.

Renshaw, P. D., & Asher, S. R. (1983). Children's goals and strategies for social interaction. *Merrill-Palmer Quarterly*, *29*, 353–374.

Rubin, K. H., & Daniels-Beirness, T. (1983). Concurrent and predictive correlates of sociometric status in kindergarten and grade one children. *Merrill-Palmer Quarterly, 29*, 337–352.

Rubin, K. H., & Krasnor, L. R. (1986). Social-cognitive and social behavioral perspectives on problem solving. In M. Perlmutter (Ed.), *The Minnesota symposia on child psychology, 18* (pp. 1–68). Hillsdale, NJ: Lawrence Erlbaum.

Selman, R. L. (1980). *The growth of interpersonal understanding: Clinical and developmental analyses*. New York: Academic Press.

Selman, R. L. (1981). The child as a friendship philosopher. In S. R. Asher & J. M. Gottman (Eds.), *The development of children's friendships* (pp. 242–272). New York: Cambridge University Press.

Shantz, C. U. (1987). Conflicts between children. *Child Development, 58*, 283–305.

Slavin, R. E. (1987). Developmental and motivational perspectives on cooperative learning: A reconciliation. *Child Development, 58*, 1161–1167.

Vandell, D. L. (1985, April). *Relations between infant-peer and infant-mother interactions: What we have learned*. Paper presented at the biennial meeting of the Society for Research in Child Development, Toronto.

Vaughn, B. E., & Waters, E. (1981). Attention structure, sociometric status and dominance: Interrelations, behavioral correlates and relationships to social competence. *Developmental Psychology, 17*, 275–288.

Waters, E., Wippman, J., & Sroufe, A. (1979). Attachment, positive affect, and competence in the peer group: Two studies in construct validation. *Child Development, 50*, 821–829.

Youniss, J. (1980). *Parents and peers in social development: A Sullivan-Piaget perspective*. Chicago: University of Chicago Press.

Youniss, J., & Smollar, J. (1985). *Adolescent relationships with mothers, fathers, and friends*. Chicago: University of Chicago Press.

PART ONE

Processes

This section is organized around the premise that it is possible to identify specific "processes" that influence not only the development, form, and stability of peer relationships, but also the potential benefits or risks that children may accrue from their participation in these relationships. Processes are cognitive and behavioral events that are both antecedents to relationship formation and aspects of existing relationships. Processes may produce various outcomes for relationships and individuals; they may foster or discourage relationship formation; they may drive or discourage the maintenance and elaboration of existing relationships; and they may affect the development of the individual children who establish and participate in peer relationships.

In the first chapter of this section, William Bukowski and Betsy Hoza consider the potential contributions of group-oriented and dyadic peer relations to the development of the individual child. They propose that efforts to identify important types of relationships and their potential contributions should be guided by theoretical as well as empirical concerns. Accordingly, the authors conduct a theoretical and empirical analysis of friendship and popularity and debate the value of various relationship definitions and measures. Based on this analysis and data from a recent longitudinal investigation, Bukowski and Hoza conclude that these two forms of relationship develop from different processes, engender different types of experiences, and make differential contributions to children's self-perceptions.

In the second chapter, Willard Hartup explicates the "referents" for various friendship processes, especially those that are demonstrated in children's behaviors with peers. Drawing upon a broad base of empirical literature, Hartup targets a number of behavioral processes as potential manifestations of friendship (e.g., time spent with friends, cooperation and competition, conflict between peers) and considers the potential functions of these behaviors for both relationship outcomes (i.e., friendship formation and maintenance) and the development of the individual child. A critical analysis of current findings is used to generate research questions and strategies that may help to illuminate how specific behavioral processes influence friendship formation and maintenance, change in function with age, differ across individual children, and vary as a function of environmental contexts.

Further analysis of children's conflicts is undertaken in the third chapter, by Carolyn Shantz and Cathy Hobart. Shantz and Hobart view interpersonal conflict as a process, rather than an outcome of child socialization, and define it in terms of behavioral episodes (as opposed to cognitive or intrapsychic events) that are aimed at producing changes in children's relationships with peers and siblings. The authors provide an empirically documented description of the conflict process in both peer and sibling relationships and offer a theoretical analysis of its potential contributions to children's relationships and their individual development. In the latter context, conflict is seen as a process that may allow the individual to establish and maintain a sense of self (i.e., autonomy or individuation) and involvement (e.g., connectedness, intimacy) in relationships.

In the last chapter of this section, Jeffrey Parker and John Gottman describe an extensive program of research on the dynamics of children's friendships. From the content of friends' conversations, Parker and Gottman construct a developmental model of the features and functions of children's friendships during each of three developmental periods (early childhood, middle childhood, and adolescence). In addition to describing the nature of children's conversational processes, the authors discuss the types of social concerns that appear to motivate friendships and speculate about the types of affective developments that may occur during each developmental period. The authors also consider the value of interactive data (e.g., conversations) as a means of understanding the functions of children's friendships and identify areas in need of further investigation.

CHAPTER 1

Popularity and Friendship

Issues in Theory, Measurement, and Outcome

WILLIAM M. BUKOWSKI AND BETSY HOZA

University of Maine

Western Psychiatric Institute and Clinic

A fundamental and widely accepted premise of the social-developmental literature is the proposal that childhood peer relationships contribute uniquely to social and emotional development (Hartup, 1983). This premise has been embraced by both developmental and child-clinical psychologists such that references to it appear with considerable frequency in the peer relations literature. In spite of the attention that has been devoted to this proposal, the particular components of peer relations, and their relative contributions to adjustment and development, are poorly understood.

In this chapter, we focus on several conceptual and empirical issues related to the premise that peer relations affect children's social and emotional development. Our point of departure for this discussion is Parker and Asher's (1987) recent review of the literature regarding the degree to which poor peer relations are associated with extreme, maladaptive outcomes. According to Parker and Asher, the literature is generally supportive of the "at risk" hypothesis because it demonstrates that measures of peer relations can significantly predict subsequent indices of maladjustment (i.e., dropping out of school, criminality, and psychiatric disturbance). Nevertheless, as Parker and Asher have argued, this body of research needs to be interpreted cautiously for a number of reasons. As these reasons are pertinent to the discussion that follows, we would like to reiterate and expand upon several of them.

First, in the studies reviewed by Parker and Asher (1987), the strength of the observed relationships varied as a function of the particular criterion used to identify "at risk" children and the specific outcome under examination. For example, whereas low acceptance by peers was highly predictive of school dropout, it was less strongly associated with criminality and psychological disturbance. On the other hand, aggressiveness was highly predictive of criminality and was less strongly related to the other two outcomes.

Second, given that the outcome measures used in these studies were all indicative of rather severe maladjustment, these studies shed light on only the lowest end of the adjustment continuum. Consequently, unlike most of the research discussed in this volume, these studies are not immediately relevant to the question of how peer relations contribute to normal/healthy development. Third, in the studies reviewed by Parker and Asher, and in the peer relations literature generally, a plethora of methods have been used to assess children's peer relations. The use of a wide variety of measures is especially problematic considering that many of these measures appear to have been chosen arbitrarily, or at least without much regard for the particular aspect of peer relations that the measure may represent. Most importantly, given that different measures (e.g., sociometrics, peer assessments of behavior, teacher ratings on questionnaires, teachers' comments in school records) are likely to represent different aspects of children's peer experiences, an unsystematic selection of measures makes comparisons between studies very difficult and also limits their generalizability. Moreover, the use of a wide variety of methods in a seemingly arbitrary manner does little to facilitate the development of theory regarding how particular types of peer experiences contribute to specific aspects of adjustment.

In light of the constraints on the current literature, we have adopted a "back to basics" approach in our consideration of the current status of studies regarding how peer relations affect adjustment. In particular, we believe that in order to overcome the problems stated previously, more attention needs to be devoted to the integration of theory and research. Our position is that this can best be achieved by (a) giving more consideration to the theoretical foundations of hypotheses regarding the association between peer relations and adjustment, (b) distinguishing more carefully between the particular social constructs that can be placed under the superordinate heading "peer relations," and (c) devoting greater attention to measures that reflect individual differences across the entire range of adjustment.

This chapter is organized in the following way: First, we discuss several theoretical perspectives regarding the association between peer relations and subsequent adjustment. Much of our discussion is focused on the self-concept, although attention is devoted to other developmental outcomes as well. In the second section of the chapter, we direct our attention to theoretical issues related to the distinction between popularity and friendship. This discussion is based upon the writings of Bronfenbrenner (1979), Furman and Robbins (1985), Moreno (1934/1978), and Sullivan (1953). Specifically, we argue that popularity and friendship have distinct theoretical origins and make differential contributions to development. Third, in light of these theoretical works, we argue that popularity and friendship present different measurement demands, and we outline measurement criteria for each. We then evaluate the currently available methods for measuring popularity and friendship in terms of these criteria and in regard to empirical evidence pertinent to the establishment of their validity. In the fourth section, we make recommendations for future research. In this section, we illustrate our points by citing preliminary findings from our 5-year longitudinal study of popularity, friendship, and the self-concept (i.e., Bukowski, Hoza, & Newcomb, 1987). Results from this study are also cited elsewhere in this chapter.

THEORETICAL ISSUES

The proposal that the nature of children's relations with peers affects adjustment appears in three distinct areas of the theoretical literature. First, it has been argued that experiences with peers are an important, if not necessary, context for the development of several fundamental skills required for successful social interaction. This perspective is clearly apparent in Hartup's (1977) argument that "without an opportunity to encounter individuals who are co-equals, children do not learn effective communication skills, do not acquire the competencies needed to modulate their aggressive actions, have difficulties with sexual socialization, and are disadvantaged with respect to the formation [of] moral values" (p. 1). Piaget (1932) similarly proposed that the conflicts that arise in children's interactions with peers lead to the development of social perspective-taking skills and to the acquisition of skills required for cooperative social exchange. He argued specifically that discussions and disputes among peers are necessary for the development of moral judgment. Along these same lines, Garvey (1987) proposed that the conversational experiences that young children have with peers provide a unique arena in which certain linguistic skills needed for social exchange (e.g., methods of conflict resolution) are acquired and refined.

Second, as Berndt (1982) has noted, several writers have argued that peer relations contribute to a child's sense of social support and security. He pointed, for example, to Douvan and Adelson's (1966) proposal that the friendships of preadolescents and early adolescents are important sources of social support that function to reduce anxieties and fears about changes occurring in these developmental periods. In this same vein of thought, Eichorn (1980) claimed that during the alleged emotional uncertainty of preadolescence, friendship experiences can be "a catalyst for the development of security" (p. 65). Similarly, Fine (1981) has proposed that peer relations provide a secure context in which new modes of social expression can be tested, thus facilitating the development of social skills. He added that "having a friend with whom one can feel secure, provides a solid base from which interpersonal confidence can be built" (p. 34).

Third, it has been argued that children's experiences with peers contribute to development of the self-concept. This proposal, in fact, can be found in works dating back as far as the earliest days of American psychology. Indeed, as Hoza (1987) has noted, William James (1890), in writing about the adult self, placed considerable emphasis upon social relations. In his seminal treatise, James argued, "We have an innate propensity to get ourselves noticed, and noticed favorably, by our kind" (p. 293). He added that persons will question their own worthiness when they receive little or no attention from others.

Ideas similar to those of James (1890) are apparent in the writings of a group of thinkers known collectively as the symbolic interactionists (i.e., Cooley, 1909; Mead, 1934). Cooley, for example, argued that at all developmental levels, persons define themselves in terms of their experiences in social situations. He placed particular emphasis on the family, the neighborhood, and the peer group, because he identified these contexts as the most universal and basic social arenas. In regard to the actual processes that underlie the link between social experience and the conception of self, the symbolic interactionists proposed that in social interaction, persons acquire information about how they are perceived by others. They argued that this information is then used to form the basis of the self. According to this perspective, social interaction is fundamental to the formation of the self-concept as it is through social interaction that one learns about the self.

Emphasis on the importance of social relations for the development of the self-concept is especially evident in the work of Harry Stack Sullivan (1953). More than any other developmental theorist, Sullivan focused on the importance of interpersonal relations, especially those between peers during the school-age and early adolescent years. Sullivan specifically believed that adequate peer relations during these periods were requisite for the formation of a healthy self-concept. In particular, he identified two types of peer experience that he believed to be related to the self. First, he argued that during the juvenile period (i.e., from roughly age 7 to age 9), the experience of being isolated from the group would lead to feelings of inferiority that would not be "tributary to good self-esteem" (p. 236). According to this idea, the critical aspect of peer relations during the juvenile period would be the experience of being accepted by the group. The second type of peer experience discussed by Sullivan was the "chumship." Sullivan defined a chumship as a close, intimate, mutual relation with a same-sex peer. As a relation among "co-equals," Sullivan regarded the chumship relation to be distinct from other kinds of social experience (e.g., relations with parents). Specifically, he believed it was the first opportunity for an individual to see "oneself through the other's eyes" (p. 248), and to experience true intimacy with another. He argued that it was within the context of the chumship relation that preadolescents (a) acquire interpersonal sensitivity, and, more importantly, (b) receive validation of the components of their self-worth. According to Sullivan, preadolescents come to experience this self-validation as they recognize the positive regard that a chum holds for them. Sullivan ascribed such importance to the features of chumship that he perceived the chumship relation to be (a) a fundamental determinant of the self, and (b) a potential context in which an unfortunate preadolescent might overcome the negative effects of prior social experiences.

From these theoretical perspectives regarding the importance of peer relations to development, two distinct, broadly stated hypotheses can be derived. First, considering the emphasis that has been placed on peer relations as a secure context for skill acquisition, measures of childhood peer relations would be expected to predict subsequent indices of social adjustment that are reflective of one's ability to engage effectively and cooperatively in both group and dyadic interaction. Second, theory pertaining to the contribution of peer relations to the self-concept would support an expectation that peer relations variables would be related to children's self-feelings and self-perceptions. In regard to the latter hypothesis, Sullivan's (1953) theory would indicate further that it is necessary to consider at least two distinct dimensions of peer relations, namely the extent to which a child is an accepted member of the peer group, and whether or not a child has a chum.

In summary, a substantial theoretical literature suggests that peer relations contribute uniquely to children's development of (a) skills in the social domain, (b) their sense of security, and (c) their conception of and feelings about the self. Moreover, a portion of this theory suggests that different aspects of peer relations make differential contributions to development. In the next section, two theoretically distinct aspects of peer relations, namely popularity and friendship, are discussed.

POPULARITY AND FRIENDSHIP: CONCEPTUAL DISTINCTIONS

The term "peer relations," like many other expressions used by psychologists (e.g., social cognition, social competence), refers not to just one type of process or experience, but rather to many of them. In contemporary studies of peer relations (e.g., Bukowski & Newcomb, 1984; Masters & Furman, 1981), a distinction has been drawn between two aspects of children's experiences with their peers: (a) popularity, which is the experience of being liked or accepted by the members of one's peer group; and (b) friendship, which is the experience of having a close, mutual, dyadic relation. According to this conceptualization, popularity is a general, group-oriented, unilateral construct that represents the view of the group toward an individual, whereas friendship is a specific, dyadic, bilateral construct that refers to a particular type of experience that takes place between two individuals.

The idea that social relationships can be conceptualized in terms of different levels of experience is not unique to the literature on peers. Indeed, such a conceptualization forms the cornerstone of Bronfenbrenner's (1979) ecological model of human development. According to Bronfenbrenner's perspective, any analysis of human functioning requires the consideration of several separate, but related, spheres of experience. For example, just as one could study children's experiences with their fathers, one could also consider their experiences in a broader social sphere, such as the total family unit. In other words, one may consider simultaneously experiences on both the dyadic and group levels, although one relationship (i.e., the dyad) may be embedded within the other (i.e., the group).

This approach to the study of social relations is hardly new. Indeed, such a view is apparent in Moreno's (1934/1978) complex and seminal book titled *Who Shall Survive?* Although much of Moreno's theorizing may be better suited to other branches of the social sciences (e.g., sociology) than to psychology, his perspective is nevertheless pertinent to the study of peer relations because it suggests that multiple levels of social interaction need to be examined. In Moreno's work, as in Bronfenbrenner's (1979), attention is devoted to the nature of one's relations within both the larger group and dyadic contexts. With regard to one's larger group relations, for example, Moreno referred to a person's position in the group as a leader (i.e., a role that is by definition interpersonal), and he noted that some persons are more likely than others to receive attention from group members. On the dyadic level, Moreno focused on the structure of the relation, especially on whether or not feelings of attraction are reciprocated. In these respects, Moreno's work is part of a theoretical foundation regarding the importance of considering an individual in terms of multiple levels of social experience. Indeed, a major premise of his approach to the conceptualization and measurement of the relations among the individuals within a group is the belief that individuals cannot be understood in isolation from others. For this reason, he argued that the most basic unit of analysis (i.e., "the social atom" [p. 52]) should be the dyad, not the individual.

As noted earlier, this emphasis on social relations within both the group and dyadic contexts is apparent also in Sullivan's (1953) argument that different aspects of children's peer relations are important at different ages. Specifically, Sullivan argued that the general treatment that a child receives from the peer group is especially important during the juvenile period. Indeed, Sullivan noted that children who are ostracized by the peer group show "pretty durable evidences" (p. 236) of having had such an experience. On the other hand, he argued that interaction on a dyadic level, that is, the experience of having a chum, is more important for preadolescents and early adolescents. In his description of the properties that characterize the chumship relation, Sullivan clearly implied that this relation is unique, as it presents opportunities for experiences (e.g., intimacy, closeness, and reciprocity) that are not available in other types of peer relations. Even so, Sullivan clearly recognized that preadolescent chumships exist within a larger group context. This is evident in his statement that preadolescent "two-groups tend to interlock" (p. 249), thus forming larger social entities such as gangs.

This fundamental distinction between various "levels" or types of social relationships, evident in the work of Bronfenbrenner (1979), Moreno (1934/1978), and Sullivan (1953), has been further developed in a recent essay by Furman and Robbins (1985). Based largely upon the work of Weiss (1974), Furman and Robbins outlined a theory of the "social provisions" (p. 42) that they believe to be differentially available to the child in intimate friendships versus peer relations generally. Furman and Robbins proposed that of the eight social provisions that are believed to be sought (and given) by children in their peer relationships, three (affection, intimacy, reliable alliance) are more characteristically obtained in close friendships than in other peer relations, four (instrumental aid, nurturance, companionship, enhancement of worth) can be derived from either type of relationship, and one (sense of inclusion) is predominantly derived from general peer relations. This theoretical model is important as it explicitly delineates a set of properties that distinguish dyadic relations from the more group-oriented aspect of peer experience. In doing so, this model also provides a well-defined set of dimensions on which these different types of peer relations can be compared.

In summary, theory pertinent to children's peer relationships suggests that group and dyadic interactions with peers represent distinct realms of experience and that both need to be included in a conceptualization of children's peer relationships. The term popularity was used to refer to the group aspect of peer experience and was defined as a global construct pertaining to how well regarded children are by the members of their overall peer group. On the other hand, the term friendship was used to refer to a particular type of dyadic peer relation, specifically, an intense, mutual relation that develops between individual children.

MEASUREMENT OF POPULARITY AND FRIENDSHIP

Despite the dual consideration of both group and dyadic levels of social relations in the theoretical literature, the empirical literature, with few exceptions, has been rather singularly focused on group variables (i.e., popularity).[1] As Furman and Robbins (1985) have previously commented, this state of affairs is surprising and rather problematic, not only in its failure to represent the whole realm of peer experience, but also in its failure to allow for an examination of the relative contribution to development of each of

---

[1]In a recent paper, Buhrmester and Furman (1987) adopted a multilevel approach to the measurement of social relations in the sense that they assessed social experience on both a global and a dyadic level. Although the terms they use to describe their levels are very similar to the terms we use, their approach differs in many ways from what we have recommended. First, their global level represents the view of a particular person toward his/her relationships in general, whereas the global construct described in this chapter has to do with the view of the group toward the individual. Second, whereas their global ratings were based on the constructs of intimacy and companionship, the one we propose is more in keeping with the construct of acceptance or liking. Third, in terms of dyadic ratings, the measures we advocate are focused on peer relations only, whereas theirs are oriented toward a much larger set of relationships. Moreover, as the reader will see later, we advocate the use of bilateral measures (e.g., the reciprocated friendship choice measure), whereas all of Buhrmester and Furman's measures are unilateral in nature.

these realms of experience, thus leaving many important questions unanswered. "To what extent are children without close friends at risk? Are they at greater risk than those who are unpopular? Can the presence of a close friendship or two buffer children from the deleterious effects of peer isolation or rejection?" (p. 46)

It is conceivable that at least part of the reason that investigators have failed to employ measures of both group and dyadic relations is the absence of clear guidelines as to how to differentially operationalize them. The following discussion is an attempt to "translate theory into practice" by delineating criteria for the measurement of popularity and friendship. We first specify general criteria for the measurement of each construct, and then we discuss the measurement of each construct separately with regard to a number of issues. In considering popularity, we first describe the currently available measurement procedures and evaluate each according to our criteria. Then, we evaluate the validity of these popularity measures by examining their relationships to theoretically chosen variables. Finally, we review the conceptual and empirical properties of sociometric classification systems based on popularity variables. In our discussion of friendship, we first propose a hierarchical model for the measurement of friendship. Next we evaluate extant friendship measures in terms of this model and in regard to their validity.

The primary emphasis in this discussion of popularity and friendship is on the most widely used techniques for measuring children's peer relations, namely, sociometric methods. Our discussion of sociometric methods is limited to the nomination and rating scale procedures, given that the time-consuming administration procedure of the paired-comparisons method typically precludes its usage. In the latter part of our discussion, recently developed measures of friendship quality will be considered. As other writers have already presented the psychometric properties of these sociometric (Asher & Hymel, 1981; Gresham, 1981a) and friendship quality (Berndt, Hawkins, & Hoyle, 1986; Berndt & Perry, 1986; Bukowski et al., 1987; Furman & Buhrmester, 1985) measures, we devote little attention to issues of reliability.

Criteria

Our interpretation of theory pertaining to children's peer relations is that measures of popularity and friendship should differ with regard to (a) the unit of analysis (the group versus the dyad), (b) the structure of the judgments under consideration (unilateral versus bilateral), and (c) the nature of the judgments being made (general versus specific). In particular, we suggest that an adequate popularity measure must focus on the group's perception of each child as the basic unit of analysis and must involve general, unilateral judgments of the group about individual children. In essence, popularity measures need only answer one question: "To what degree is the child liked or valued by his/her peer group?" Thus, popularity measures may be said to reflect the "majority opinion" of the group about a given child. In contrast, we suggest that a satisfactory measure of friendship must be dyadic in nature, focusing on pairs of children (i.e., the chumship) as the unit of analysis, and must involve structurally bilateral judgments. Furthermore, these bilateral judgments must reflect both global feelings of liking or regard (indeed, such feelings are prerequisite to friendship) and also specific, qualitative, relational characteristics, such as loyalty or intimacy, that distinguish friendships from other dyadic relations (e.g., acquaintanceships).[2]

Measurement of Popularity

To date, the primary methods used to measure peer relations have been nomination and rating scale sociometrics. Although the specific administration procedures vary from study to study, all nomination sociometrics involve having each child nominate grademates for given interpersonal criteria. The criteria can be either positive (e.g., best friend, someone you like to play with) or negative (e.g., someone you don't like to play with). Generally, a child's score on any given criteria is simply the number of nominations obtained from peers. Rating scales, on the other hand, typically involve having each child rate all of his or her classmates on a Likert-type scale with regard to a specified criterion (e.g., degree of liking). Scores are then computed by summing or averaging the ratings received from peers. Thus, rating scale, positive nomination, and negative nomination measures have all traditionally been employed in a quantitative, unilateral manner, to represent *how much* positive (or negative) regard a child *receives* from peers. As such, our position is that all of these methods may be considered operationalizations of the popularity construct.

In a recent review, however, Asher and Hymel (1981) took a position substantially different from our own. Specifically, they drew a distinction between positive nominations and rating scales, suggesting that whereas positive nominations measure friendship, that is, "how many peers regard a child as a best friend or high-priority playmate," rating scales measure "a child's overall level of acceptability or likability among peers" (p. 132). Two

---

[2]Children, of course, may be involved in multiple dyads, thus forming triads, quads, and so on. Even these larger friendship groups, however, are primarily dyadic in nature, since bilateral feelings of strong affection must exist between members of each twosome within the larger group, in order for each dyad to be described as friends. Furthermore, it is conceivable that three or more children may be involved in the same friendship group without all group members being equally attracted to one another. This situation makes the necessity of defining friendship in terms of both the unit of analysis (the dyad) and the structure of this unit (bilateral, unilateral, or neither) all the more evident. Specifically, considering both the unit of analysis and the structure of this unit enables one to distinguish the group that is composed entirely of mutual friendships from groups involving one or more unilateral or nonexistent relationships. For example, if A and B, B and C, and A and C are mutual friends, there are three dyadic units, all of which have the same bilateral structure. If, however, A and B, and B and C are mutual friends, but A and C are either unilateral friends or not friends at all, there are still three dyadic units, but only two of the three have a bilateral structure.

criticisms, one conceptual and one empirical, can be made with regard to their position. First, on a conceptual level, it does not appear as though "friendship" is an appropriate label for a construct measured by unilateral positive nominations. As noted above, theory (e.g., Sullivan, 1953) suggests that an adequate measure of the friendship construct must be both dyadic in nature and sensitive to the measurement of specific qualities that distinguish friendships from other types of relationships. Positive nomination sociometrics, as they have traditionally been employed, meet neither of these criteria.

Second, Hoza, Bukowski, and Gold (1987) recently reexamined the statistical evidence that has been cited in the literature to support the argument that positive nomination and rating scale sociometrics tap distinct dimensions of peer relations. A variety of different types of studies were examined (e.g., Gresham, 1981b; Hymel & Asher, 1977), including correlational, factor analytic, and classification studies. Consistent with Berndt's (1984) suggestion, Hoza et al. concluded that the evidence to support the distinction between positive nomination and rating scale measures is not compelling. Hoza et al. argued, for example, that when correlations between nomination and rating scale sociometrics are corrected for attenuation due to measurement error, the relationships between these measures appear to be remarkably strong.

But what about the relationship between negative nomination scores and rating scale scores? This question has not been given much attention in the sociometric literature, although data pertinent to it have been reported. In the studies reviewed by Hoza et al. (1987), for example, the correlations between negative nomination and rating scale scores were strikingly similar in magnitude, but opposite in sign, to those reported for the relationship between positive nominations and rating scales. In the majority of cases, in fact, the correlations between negative nomination and rating scale scores were slightly higher than those between positive nominations and rating scales. At the same time, however, it appears to be well established that positive nomination and negative nomination scores do not simply reflect extremes of a singular dimension of liking/disliking. Indeed, correlations of low to moderate magnitude are typically observed between them, and they appear to have different behavioral and nonbehavioral correlates (see Asher & Hymel, 1981, and Hartup, 1983, for reviews). Thus, we concur with previous writers (Asher & Hymel; Hartup) who have argued that acceptance (as measured by positive nominations) and rejection (as indexed by negative nominations) are distinct aspects of popularity. At the same time, however, we propose that rating scales are a type of composite measure of popularity, which simultaneously represents both the acceptance and rejection dimensions of the popularity construct. This conceptualization of the rating scale sociometric as a composite of acceptance and rejection will be discussed later in regard to classification issues.

In summary, we have argued that positive nomination, negative nomination, and rating scale sociometric procedures are all measures of the popularity construct, because all three types of measures meet the conceptual criteria for the measurement of popularity as outlined above. Furthermore, in our discussion, we attempted to clarify the nature of the relationship among these measures; we proposed that whereas positive nominations and negative nominations tap different aspects of popularity, the rating scale is a composite index that reflects both the acceptance and rejection aspects of the popularity construct.

Thus far, this discussion has been limited to a consideration of popularity measures in regard to both conceptual criteria and the associations among these measures. We now turn to a discussion of the validity of these instruments in terms of measurable, external criteria. In this discussion, we focus only on studies that are immediately relevant to determining whether popularity measures are tapping the theoretical construct that they were intended to measure. In other words, attention will be given only to studies that consider the relationship between popularity measures and indices of social behavior that reflect the conceptual properties used to define popularity.

Validity of Popularity Measures

Considering our argument that popularity measures are unilateral indices of the overall degree of positive (or negative) regard that children receive from peers, one would expect that if nomination and rating scale sociometric scores truly represent popularity, then children who receive many liked (or disliked) nominations or ratings from peers should also receive much positive (or negative) attention from peers. Studies that might offer this type of evidence for the validity of popularity measures are in surprisingly short supply. Indeed, although there is a very large literature regarding the characteristics (e.g., behavioral tendencies or traits) of popular and unpopular children, only a few studies could be found that examined the behavior of peer group members *toward* children of differing levels of popularity. In other words, the primary focus of research on popularity and social behavior has been on how children of varying levels of popularity behave toward others, rather than on how others behave toward them. Nonetheless, the available evidence appears to support the validity of the popularity measures. For example, Gottman, Gonso, and Rasmussen (1975) and Masters and Furman (1981) have reported that popular children receive more positive reinforcement from peers than do unpopular children. In another investigation, Vaughn and Waters (1981) reported that children who received many liked-peer nominations also received more visual attention from peers than did children who received few nominations. With respect to disliking, Masters and Furman found a moderately strong correlation ($r = .41$) between the number of times a child was chosen as disliked and the amount of punishment the child received from peers. Hymel, Tinsley, Geraci, and Asher (cited in Asher & Hymel, 1981) reported an analogous finding: Children who received many nominations as disliked peers were also the recipients of negative acts from peers.

Regarding the rating scale sociometric, data pertaining to its validity is scarce. In fact, we were unable to find any studies reporting how children behave *toward* peers of varying levels of popularity, as indexed by a rating scale sociometric. Thus, to our knowledge, the only studies indicating that rating scale sociometrics are valid measures of popularity are those that indicate a strong association between scores derived from a rating scale and those based on nomination techniques (see Hoza et al., 1987). That is, given the evidence that measures derived from nomination procedures are valid, the evidence of a strong association between rating scale-based measures and nomination-based measures can be regarded as evidence for the validity of rating scales.

Classification Using Popularity Variables

Given the evidence suggesting that positive and negative nominations represent distinct dimensions of popularity, a prominent issue in the sociometric literature has been a concern with the importance of simultaneously considering the constructs of acceptance and rejection (see Asher & Hymel, 1981; Newcomb & Bukowski, 1984). Indeed, as Newcomb and Bukowski have shown, ever since the 1940s it has been recognized widely that consideration of the acceptance dimension alone is inadequate as this variable does not distinguish between children who are rejected (i.e., children who have few if any friends and are generally disliked by others) and those who are neglected (i.e., children who are neither liked nor disliked by peers). Although attempts to alleviate this problem initially involved consideration of the difference between acceptance and rejection scores, it soon became clear that this method, too, was inadequate. These difference scores failed to distinguish persons with high scores on both acceptance and rejection from those with low scores on both of these variables. Indeed, as a composite measure of acceptance and rejection, the rating scale sociometric suffers from a similar problem. Specifically, because averaged or summed scores make it impossible to distinguish among various types of children who fall in the middle range, the usefulness of rating scale data in the classification of children's social status is very limited.[3] In other words, children who receive positive and negative ratings to approximately the same degree are indistinguishable from those who are rated neutrally by everyone.

In light of these issues, pioneering investigators (e.g., Bronfenbrenner, 1943, 1944), concerned with developing schemes to fully represent the ecology of children's social groups, proposed methods of assigning individuals

---

[3]It should be recognized that although the Asher and Dodge (1986) classification system depends, in part, on rating scale data, this technique is not subject to these criticisms. Specifically, considering that with the Asher and Dodge procedure, rating scale data are treated as if they were sociometric nominations, this system should, for the most part, be regarded as a nomination-based method rather than as a rating scale technique.

to sociometric categories based on two variables, namely likableness and visibility. Whereas likableness, or *preference* as it is currently known, represents the balance between acceptance and rejection, visibility, or what is currently called *impact,* is an index of how frequently one is either accepted or rejected by peers. Emphasis on these constructs has been seen in the sociometric literature throughout the past five decades (see Newcomb & Bukowski, 1983) and is particularly apparent in the two-dimensional schemes proposed by Coie, Dodge, and Coppotelli (1982), Newcomb and Bukowski (1983, 1984), and, more recently, Asher and Dodge (1986). Based on values derived from either standardization procedures or probabilistic expectations, these classification systems can be used to assign children to groups known as popular (highly visible and well liked), rejected (highly visible and poorly liked), controversial (highly visible and both liked and disliked), neglected (low visibility and neither liked nor disliked) and average (at or about the mean on both visibility and likableness).

These two-dimensional classification systems have become widely accepted as appropriate techniques for identifying children who differ in terms of their positions within a peer network. It is likely that the widespread use of these techniques is related to the fact that they represent a significant improvement over previously employed one-dimensional procedures. In spite of this improvement, however, we point out next that even the most up-to-date methods should be used with caution, as these techniques are still limited by both conceptual and empirical drawbacks.

Conceptual Limitations

The development of sociometric procedures appears to have been guided by an interest in (a) accurately measuring the social structure of groups and (b) identifying the positions of individuals within this structure. In other words, the development of current sociometric schemes seems to have been motivated and directed by measurement concerns. Consequently, very little consideration has been given to theoretical perspectives regarding the aspects of social experience that are most likely to contribute to subsequent adjustment. In light of this, it appears that sociometric methods may not provide an entirely adequate framework for the evaluation of theoretical perspectives regarding the effects of peer relations on adjustment.

This line of reasoning resembles the arguments regarding classification made by the late French philosopher Michel Foucault. In his collection of essays on the association between language, science, and technology, titled *The Order of Things* (1966/1970), Foucault argued that any practical classificatory technique, whether it is found within the natural or social sciences, will have limitations. In order to be practical, a classification procedure must be based on a finite number of factors, and consequently it cannot represent all the factors that are relevant to the phenomena it is designed to classify. For example, Linnaeus's botanical system does not take into account all the characteristics that could be used to distinguish one plant from another. For this reason, Foucault wrote that any system of classification tends to be "arbitrary in its basis since it deliberately ignores all differences and all identities not related to the selected structure" (p. 140). As an example, he pointed to Jonston's 1657 system of classifying quadrupeds and argued that this system, like others, is not problematic for what it represents, but rather for what it leaves out. This argument can be applied easily to current methods of sociometric classification: It is not that these methods fail to resolve several fundamental sociometric problems (in fact, they appear to do this very nicely), but that in doing so several aspects of children's peer experiences (e.g., the extent of reciprocity in friendship choices) are neglected.

In a similar vein of thought, Foucault (1966/1970) argued that an additional, and much more important, reason to approach systems of classification carefully is that their appearance of being comprehensive and meaningful can lead to their "becoming" the phenomena that they were intended to represent. Foucault argued that a well-structured set of constructs and terms can give such clarity and order to a set of phenomena that the constructs become indistinguishable from the phenomena themselves. This process is problematic, Foucault pointed out, as persons may begin to use arbitrary, or even artificial, constructs as if they were true representations of a natural order. Applied to sociometric methods, this argument would indicate that persons should not infer that because we can assign children to groups known as neglected, rejected, controversial, and so on, these categories represent natural, or even particularly meaningful, classifications.

Empirical Limitations

In regard to empirical concerns, it has been demonstrated by Newcomb and Bukowski (1984) that current sociometric classification systems produce groups whose membership is neither stable nor homogeneous. In considering the stability of classification, Newcomb and Bukowski reported that over a variety of time intervals, including 6, 12, 18, and 24 months, only a limited proportion of the children initially assigned to one of the extreme popularity groups subsequently remained in the same category. They noted, for example, that the stable membership of the rejected group over one year was as low as 15%. The long-term stability of classification groups as defined by the Asher and Dodge (1986) procedure has not yet been examined. Short-term stability of the Asher and Dodge method, however, is similar to that reported for Newcomb and Bukowski's probability method. The figures reported for both the overall stability of classification according to the Asher and Dodge method over a 5-month interval, and for the stability of the rejected group in particular over the same interval, are within the range of the stability figures reported by Newcomb and Bukowski for the probability method over numerous 6-month intervals. Unfortunately, the stability figures from any of these methods are not overwhelmingly impressive. This classificatory instability suggests that, to some extent, "at risk" sociometric status may be either a rather temporary phenomenon, or it may not be adequately measured by current sociometric methods.

The groups defined by the standard score and probability methods have also been evaluated with respect to the degree of homogeneity within groups and the extent of differences between groups. Newcomb and Bukowski (1984) examined the reputational profiles, derived from a class play peer assessment measure, of the children from the five sociometric groups. These profiles consisted of the subjects' scores on four dimensions of social behavior: Aggression, Immaturity, Observable Prominence, and Classroom Competence. Both considerable overlap between groups (i.e., persons from different groups had similar profiles) and considerable heterogeneity within groups (i.e., persons in the same group had different role profiles) were observed. These findings suggest that, on the basis of peer assessments of social behavior, these groups are neither especially distinct from one another nor internally consistent. The homogeneity of the groups based on the Asher and Dodge (1986) method has yet to be examined.

One could argue, of course, that homogeneity within groups and clear differences between groups on these measures may not be important. Nevertheless, recent research by Bierman (1987) suggests that these within-group differences deserve attention. Specifically, she has shown that for purposes of developing treatment procedures for rejected children, considering subtypes within this sociometric group is critically important. In light of this, it appears that sociometric methods may be a good starting point for the identification of children "at risk", but these methods may need to be supplemented by techniques that assess other aspects of children's interactions with peers.

Hierarchical Friendship Model

Thus far, this discussion of the measurement of peer relations has focused almost exclusively on the assessment of the popularity construct. Indeed, we have argued that, given the unilateral framework within which nominations and rating scales have typically been employed, they provide an inadequate measure of the dyadic phenomenon of friendship. In what follows, we would like to propose a framework for the assessment of friendship that involves bilateral usage of the sociometric methods described above in conjunction with recently developed measures of friendship quality.

In order for a child's friendship relations to be adequately assessed, we propose that three questions must be asked. These questions, which may be conceptualized as "levels" in a hierarchy are: First, does dyadic friendship exist for the target child? Second, given that at least one dyadic friendship exists for the target child, in how many friendships is he/she involved? Finally, what is the quality of the target child's dyadic friendships? Each of these levels of assessment will be described in more detail below.

LEVEL 1.   At the first level of assessment, the primary concern is with determining whether reciprocated, positive feelings exist between a given child and at least one specific peer. Thus, at Level 1, measurement must focus on the dyad, involve bilateral judgments, and pertain to global judgments of intense liking. Do any of our current measurement techniques satisfy these criteria? Certain nontraditional methods of employing nomination and rating scale techniques do seem to meet these requirements. Mutual positive nominations, for example, represent reciprocated, positive judgments of a target child and peer about each other. Reciprocated high ratings on a rating scale sociometric are another potential operationalization of this aspect of friendship, although, to our knowledge, rating scales have not been used in this manner. Finally, Berndt (e.g., 1984; Berndt, Hawkins, & Hoyle, 1986; Berndt & Hoyle, 1985; Berndt & Perry, 1986) has used positive nominations and rating scales in combination to represent friendship. His method for identifying close friendship between two children involves determining that "Either one or both of them nominated the other as a best friend, and their ratings of liking average 4.0 or better on the 5-point scale" (1984, p. 34). Although we agree that the joint use of positive nominations and ratings has potential as an operationalization of friendship, it seems that the criteria Berndt used to define friendship have conceptual drawbacks. Specifically, according to Berndt's method, it is possible for two children to be considered friends on the basis of strong unilateral liking of one child for the other and only neutral feelings of the second child toward the first. For example, Berndt's criteria for friendship will be met in the case where one child nominates the other as a best friend *and* gives him the highest possible rating on the rating scale sociometric, while the other child does not nominate the first as a best friend and assigns him or her only a neutral rating. In such cases, Berndt's measure does not capture the essential features of the construct of friendship, that is, intense, reciprocated liking. For this reason, we would recommend that Jones's (1985) revision of Berndt's criteria be employed. Specifically, Jones considered two children to be friends only if one or both of them had nominated the other as a best friend, and if both of them were given ratings by the other of either "4" or "5" on a 5-point scale.

LEVEL 2.   Once it has been determined that dyadic friendship is a feature of a child's relations with peers, we propose that the next level of assessment deal with the number of friendships that a child has. This extensivity variable might be operationalized as the number of mutual positive nominations, the number of reciprocated "5" ratings, or the number of combination method (Berndt's criteria) friends a child has. It is important to recognize that this level serves to expand, not replicate, information gained at the first level of assessment. Indeed, the second level of assessment can only be carried out for those children who were determined at Level 1 to have dyadic relations in their network.

It is important to note, however, that the value of the second level of assessment has not yet been established. Indeed, little attention has been devoted in either the theoretical or empirical literature to the issue of whether the positive effects of friendship (defined in bilateral terms) are cumulative, increasing as one's friendship network increases, or whether the effects are an "all-or-none" phenomenon. Furthermore, the few studies we are aware of that have addressed this issue provide somewhat different results. Specifically, in Bukowski et al.'s (1987) study of popularity, friendship, and the self-concept during early adolescence, no differences were observed for either boys or girls among subjects who had one, two, three, or more mutual friends when the effects of popularity were eliminated via a covariance procedure. On the other hand, Cauce (1986, 1987) reported that among early adolescents the number of mutual friends a child had was related to several outcome measures including indices of self-perceived competence and perceived emotional support. Unfortunately, however, Cauce's results are not directly applicable to the evaluation of the Level 2 assessment because she included in her analyses all subjects, not just those who had at least one mutual friend. As a consequence, it is difficult to determine whether her results reflect a difference that lies at Level 1 or Level 2. Nevertheless, studies documenting sex differences in the exclusivity of children's friendships (e.g., Eder & Hallinan, 1978), suggest that this level of assessment may be critical to understanding gender-related differences in friendship networks.

LEVEL 3.   Finally, once it has been established that a child has friends, and once the extent to which a child has friends has been determined, the third level of assessing friendship is concerned with examining the quality of a child's friendships. Friendship quality has been investigated both by asking children open-ended questions about their friendships during interview sessions (Berndt et al., 1986; Berndt & Perry, 1986) and by having children evaluate certain features of their friendships on a rating scale, in either interview sessions (Berndt et al.; Berndt & Perry) or on questionnaires (Bukowski et al., 1987; Furman & Buhrmester, 1985). Whereas an interview comprised of open-ended questions provides a richer, more comprehensive data base and also allows the interviewer the opportunity to ask for clarification or elaboration, it relies entirely on nominal data. As such, the resultant data may, in some cases, be a relatively insensitive index of individual differences and also may not be amenable to many higher level statistical procedures. An attempt by Berndt and Perry to combine such data into scales in order to convert the data to a more sophisticated scale of measurement was largely unsuccessful because the resultant internal consistency of the scales was poor (*alphas* ranged in value from − .08 to .49). The closed-ended procedures, on the other hand, may be more sensitive, and consequently more reliable, measures of variability and are rather highly correlated with the open-ended measures (Berndt & Perry), suggesting that the two types of measures would yield similar results. Nonetheless, the closed-ended procedures provide information only about features of friendship that were designated a priori as being important. Berndt and his colleagues (Berndt et al.; Berndt & Perry) have employed open-ended and closed-ended questions jointly; where time and personnel constraints do not preclude it, the adoption of this approach appears to be desirable. Where only one approach is possible, the greater sensitivity of the closed-ended format may be preferable, although both types of measures appear to tap the qualitative friendship features that theory suggests are important.

One additional methodological difference between the work of Berndt (e.g., Berndt et al., 1986; Berndt & Perry, 1986) and other investigators (Bukowski et al., 1987; Furman & Buhrmester, 1985) warrants attention in our discussion of Level 3 assessment. Berndt and his colleagues asked the children in their studies to describe and rate *specific* relationships; that is, using their criteria for friendship outlined earlier, they paired each child with a specific peer a priori, based on the children's responses to previously administered nomination and rating scale sociometrics. Thus, in Berndt's studies, only friendships existing between pairs of participating subjects were considered. In contrast, both Bukowski et al. and Furman and Buhrmester simply instructed children to rate their "best friend" relationship, without limiting the potential relationship partners to other participating subjects and without establishing that the relationship was actually reciprocated. Both approaches have strengths and limitations. Whereas Berndt's method assures, through actual verification, that the relationship being rated is bilateral, it introduces the possibility that the child is not actually rating his/her most valued peer relationship. On the other hand, because Bukowski et al. and Furman and Buhrmester give the child the freedom to make ratings about whatever peer relationship he/she perceives as most important, in some cases, the chosen child may not be a participant. In this instance, there is no means to verify that the relationship rated is a friendship, in the sense of being a bilateral phenomenon. We have no answer to the question regarding which is the lesser of these two "evils." We do feel, however, that researchers should be mindful of the limitations inherent in each approach.[4]

---

[4]This consideration of friendship quality measures does not include a discussion of Mannarino's "Chumship Checklist" (1976) for two reasons. First, unlike the other techniques we review, this scale is based upon a unidimensional conceptualization of friendship quality. That is, given its single factor structure, this scale reflects an assumption that friendship quality is a single entity. In light of the considerable emphasis in the literature on the multidimensionality of friendship (e.g., Furman and Robbins, 1985), this scale appears to be of limited value. Second, in a pilot study of the Bukowski et al. (1987) investigation, no evidence was found in support of the validity of the Chumship Checklist. Specifically, scores from this scale could not discriminate mutual and nonmutual friends, or stable and unstable friends.

SUMMARY.   In our discussion of the measurement demands of the friend-ship construct, we have suggested that a multilevel approach to assessment be employed. Specifically, we proposed that a comprehensive assessment of friendship requires considering three levels. At Level 1, whether or not a child has at least one mutual, dyadic friendship is determined. Given that the child has at least one friend, at Level 2, the extent to which dyadic friendships comprise the child's peer network is assessed. Finally, Level 3 assessment involves the examination of the specific, qualitative features of these dyadic friendships.

Of course, by proposing a hierarchical approach to the measurement of friendship, we are suggesting that each level has something unique to con-tribute to our understanding of children's friendships. According to this proposed hierarchy, an assessment of friendship that fails to consider all three levels will thus be incomplete. Unfortunately, to date, investigators have typically not captured all three levels of assessment in their research designs. A few, however, have come close to doing so. Berndt and his colleagues (Berndt et al., 1986; Berndt & Perry, 1986), for example, capture Levels 1 and 3 in their studies of the friendship quality of verified, recip-rocated friendships, but they do not consider Level 2 variables in these studies. In addition, as noted earlier, we would recommend that Jones's (1985) revision of Berndt's criteria be used in assessing friendship at Level 1. Bukowski et al. (1987), on the other hand, included measures representing each of the three levels of friendship assessment in a recent study of the effects of popularity and friendship on the self-concept. As just noted, how-ever, their Level 3 friendship quality assessment procedure did not include verification that the rated relationship was a reciprocated one.

Validity of Friendship Measures

Considering that the study of children's dyadic friendships is a fairly recent phenomenon, an examination of the validity of friendship measures is highly warranted. In this section, we note that although the amount of data germane to this point is rather small, it nevertheless supports the validity of the extant friendship measurement techniques.

In regard to Level 1 assessment, evidence from empirical studies indicates that one measurement, that is, a reciprocated friendship nomination mea-sure, is a valid measure of friendship. This evidence is as follows. First, there are studies demonstrating that reciprocated friendship selections are significantly more stable (i.e., enduring) than unreciprocated selections. The greater stability of these selections has been observed among preschoolers (Gershman & Hayes, 1983) and early adolescents (Bukowski & Newcomb, 1984), indicating that this measure of friendship is likely to be valid for the whole range of childhood and adolescent years. The Bukowski and New-comb data are especially convincing considering that their observations were made across a potentially disruptive school transition. Other studies have revealed higher levels of shared interpersonal knowledge among reciprocally chosen peers than among pairs of children characterized by a unilateral choice only (Ladd & Emerson, 1984). In addition, Hayes, Gershman, & Bolin (1980) reported that preschool children have different conceptions of their mutual versus nonmutual relations. These differences were apparent on the dimensions labeled evaluation (e.g., "He is nice") and common activities (e.g., "We do things together"), indicating that mutual relations may be more affectively based and more likely to feature reciprocal interaction. Direct evidence of higher levels of behavioral reciprocity among mutual versus nonmutual friends can be taken from the results of Newcomb and Brady's (1982) study of actual behavioral interaction in pairs of boys who were either friends (i.e., reciprocally chosen friends) or acquaintances (nonfriends who were willing to play together). Newcomb and Brady reported that among both the second and sixth graders in their study, higher levels of behavioral mutuality and responsivity were apparent in the friend pairs than in the acquaintance pairs. Furthermore, the lack of developmental effects in this study supports the claim stated above that the choice reciprocity measure may be valid across the childhood years.

Considering that Level 2 measures are essentially concatenations of Level 1 measures, any evidence pertinent to the validity of a given Level 1 measure is pertinent also to the corresponding Level 2 measure. Thus, given the evidence for the validity of mutual positive nominations as measures of friendship at Level 1, the extensivity measure at Level 2 that is based on mutual positive nominations might also be considered to be valid. Beyond this evidence, we know of no data that are relevant to the establishment of the validity of Level 2 measures.

Although evidence regarding the validity of techniques for assessing children's impressions of the quality of their friendship relations appears to be scarce (we know of only three studies), the studies that do exist support the validity of these procedures. First, using a structured interview format, Berndt et al. (1986) assessed children's impressions of their best friend relationships. According to their results, children rated nonstable friendships differently from stable friendships on dimensions reflecting intimacy and mutual responsiveness. Second, as previously noted, Berndt and Perry (1986) used an interview format to collect school-age children's and early adolescents' impressions of their relationships with specific peers on six dimensions: play and association, prosocial behavior, loyalty, intimacy, attachment, and absence of conflicts. They reported that, at several grade levels, the ratings on each of these dimensions, except absence of conflicts, easily differentiated between friends and acquaintances. That is, children's responses to the items in Berndt and Perry's rating scale differed according to whether a friend or an acquaintance was being described. Third, the results reported by Berndt et al. were recently replicated by Bukowski et al. (1987) with a paper-and-pencil technique. Specifically, children's ratings of liked peers on the same six dimensions considered by Berndt et al. differentiated between mutual and nonmutual friends. In another part of the study, Bukowski et al. assessed children's impressions of liked peers according to the dimensions of interpersonal support and closeness, again using a written rating scale format. Each of these scales distinguished mutual from nonmutual friends, and stable friendship choices from unstable choices. Taken together, these studies indicate clearly that ratings of friendship quality, whether collected in interviews or with paper-and-pencil techniques, can be used to differentiate peer relationships of varying intensity.

STUDIES OF POPULARITY, FRIENDSHIP, AND ADJUSTMENT: CURRENT LITERATURE AND RECOMMENDATIONS

Up to this point, this chapter has consisted of an overview of theoretical and measurement considerations regarding the study of popularity, friendship, and adjustment. In this section, we turn our attention to research regarding the association between peer relations and variations in adjustment across a broadly defined normal range. We first consider the extant research and then make recommendations for future research. Due to our own interest in the self-concept, our discussion will be limited to studies of this construct. This exclusive focus on studies of the self-concept is not particularly restrictive, however, as measures of the self have been used frequently in studies of "normal" individual differences in adjustment. Moreover, although our recommendations are expressed in terms of the self-concept, they are applicable to other outcome measures as well.

Extant Research

To date, nearly all the studies regarding the association between peer relations and the self-concept have operationalized peer relations according to unilateral, group-oriented measures, that is, in terms of popularity. Wylie's (1979) thorough review of these studies revealed that 23 of 34 studies conducted to assess the association between popularity and the self-concept found a small, but significant, relationship between these variables. According to her review, measures of popularity account for approximately 4% of the variance in self-concept measures (i.e., the correlation between these measures is roughly .2).

To our knowledge, the only exception to this exclusive emphasis on the effects of popularity on the self-concept is Mannarino's (1978) study of chumship and self-esteem in a sample of preadolescent boys. Mannarino identified groups of boys with and without a chum according to several indices. He then compared the self-esteem scores of these two groups and found that the scores of boys with a chum were higher than those without a chum.

The preliminary findings of the Bukowski et al. (1987) study also indicate that friendship is related to the self-concept. As space considerations preclude a complete description of the results of this study, we have chosen to highlight specific findings from this study in the following sections.

Recommendations: Back to the Future?

Given the issues we have discussed already in this chapter, we now make recommendations for future research. The basis of these recommendations is our belief that the study of the association between peer relations and adjustment would benefit from an application of the "new" to the "old." In this case, the new includes recently developed concepts and measurement procedures designed to assess children's peer relations, as well as state-of-the-art research designs and statistical procedures (e.g., structural equation modeling). The old, on the other hand, is the hypothesis that peer relations affect both social and emotional adjustment. Consistent with the issues already developed in this chapter, our recommendations are organized around the following themes: (a) that the validity and utility of extant procedures for assessing popularity and friendship should be examined further; (b) that investigators should attempt to identify the relative and unique contributions to adjustment made by different dimensions of peer relationships; and (c) that research hypotheses need to be more strongly based in theory, in order to clarify important aspects of theory that have received little or no empirical attention.

VALIDITY ISSUES. As already indicated, evidence concerning the validity of techniques to measure peer relations is, in some instances, rather limited, especially in regard to the extensivity measure and the recently developed friendship quality measures. Nevertheless, adequate validation of these techniques is necessary to justify their use. With regard to friendship quality measures, for example, examining behavioral differences (e.g., in terms of behavioral reciprocity) among friendship pairs that differ on dimensions such as those examined by Berndt et al. (1986) might be one approach to establishing the validity of friendship quality measures. At the same time, however, there may be at least two important drawbacks to studying behavioral correlates of friendship quality measures. First, given that many of the qualities operationalized by these rating scales are by their very nature subjective (e.g., feelings of intimacy), a search for behavioral indicants of them may be conceptually misguided. Second, it is conceivable that children's reports about the quality of their friendships may be influenced by infrequent events. Indeed, Asher and Hymel (1981) have raised this point previously in regard to studying behavioral correlates of popularity. Consistent with their recommendation, we suggest that researchers work to ameliorate this problem by using behavioral sampling procedures that can be implemented over long periods of time. In addition, we note that asking subjects to keep diaries regarding their interactions with particular peers may be an alternative means of tackling this problem.

Just as the validity of individual measurement techniques needs to be evaluated, the hierarchical model we have proposed should be evaluated also. The first step in evaluating the model, of course, is establishing the validity of the techniques employed at each level. Some progress toward this goal has been made already, primarily at Level 1, but also at Level 3. Once this goal has been accomplished, the central question that remains is whether the hierarchical organization of the model is needed. In other words, although the individual parts of the model may be valid and although its organization may be either intuitively or conceptually pleasing, the hierarchical aspect of the model should be evaluated functionally. The evaluation should rest upon this argument: If the hierarchy is necessary, each successive step will add to the prediction of a theoretically chosen criterion variable, for example, an outcome variable such as the self-concept. Assuming that the self-concept is an adequate criterion, one would expect each level of the model to account for additional variance in the self-concept scores.

In our recent research (Bukowski et al., 1987), this type of approach was adopted. Our study supported the validity of Level 3 measurements; the results of a stepwise, hierarchical, multiple regression procedure indicated that, after the effects of friendship mutuality and extensivity had been taken into account, friendship quality measures (of interpersonal support and closeness) added significantly to the prediction of the subjects' feelings of general self-worth, and, to a smaller extent, social competence. The measure of extensivity did not add significantly, however, to the variance already accounted for by the Level 1 variable. At Level 1, the friendship choice mutuality variable was a significant predictor of the self-concept. As this is the only study known to us in which variables from all three levels of the hierarchical friendship model were considered simultaneously, additional work is clearly needed in order to evaluate the validity of the model.

We recommend also that attention be given to the long-term predictive utility of the sociometric classification systems. Considering that they have been regarded as a valid technique for targeting children who are at risk for maladaptive outcomes, these methods should be assessed according to whether they actually do this adequately. The need for this evaluation is especially warranted, given that many persons have studied the correlates of sociometric status, assuming that children who fall into the rejected and neglected groups are, or are likely to be, maladjusted. That these systems have empirical and conceptual drawbacks makes this need only more pressing. The assessment of these groups would actually be fairly straightforward: Using a longitudinal design, one would make comparisons among the sociometric groups on the basis of a criterion index of adjustment at a later time, for example, 1 year or 5 years later.

We (Bukowski et al., 1987) recently made comparisons in this manner among the subjects in the five traditional sociometric groups (i.e., popular, rejected, neglected, controversial, and average) using measures of self-concept as our criterion (see Harter, 1982, for a discussion of the scales). We made measurements of both sociometric status and the self-concept at each of two points in time, separated by a 1-year interval, and then examined the relationship between sociometric status from the first time and the self-concept scores from the second time. Our analyses revealed clear differences between the sociometric groups, especially on the measure of perceived social competence.

These results suggest that sociometric classifications, in spite of their conceptual and empirical drawbacks, can be used to identify groups of children who generally score lower than their peers on one index of adjustment, namely the self-concept. This appears to be especially true for children's self-perceived social competence. Finally, the observation of clear differences between groups, not only at a single point in time, but also across a 1-year interval, is consistent with the argument that these methods can be used to target children who are potentially at risk for maladaptive outcomes. Our data suggest that both the rejected and neglected groups may be "at risk" categories.

CONTRIBUTIONS OF POPULARITY AND FRIENDSHIP.   Obviously, the development of valid and useful measures of peer relations is of little value unless these measures are then used to increase our understanding of these relations. Indeed, elegant methods do nothing until they are applied to the resolution of meaningful problems. As we noted at the outset of this chapter, one such question, and in fact one of the major "unknowns" of the peer relations literature, is how particular aspects of peer relations, that is, popularity and friendship, are related to adjustment. In light of this lacuna in the literature, we recommend that increased attention be devoted to uncovering the relative and unique contributions that popularity and friendship make to adjustment. We use the word *relative* in order to acknowledge that each of these constructs may be differentially related to particular aspects of adjustment; we refer to *unique* contributions in light of the fact that these constructs are conceptually distinct. We recognize, however, that although popularity and friendship are conceptually distinct, they may not be functionally independent; and, as a consequence, their effects may be overlapping. Due to this nonindependence, an inquiry into the relative and unique effects of popularity and friendship is possible only when these constructs are considered simultaneously. To our knowledge, there are three ways that this goal can be accomplished.

First, one can select children who fit the particular factorial combinations of popularity and friendship variables. This approach can be seen in research conducted by McGuire and Weisz (1982) and by ourselves (Bukowski et al., 1987). McGuire and Weisz, for example, conceptualized popularity and friendship as independent, dichotomous variables and, based on this conceptualization, selected subjects to fit the cells (i.e., popular/friend, unpopular/friend, popular/no friend, and unpopular/no friend) in a factorial model. These cells were also divided according to the dimension of gender, thus creating a 2 × 2 × 2 design. In contrast, in our research, the levels of the popularity variable were the five traditional sociometric groups, and the friendship variable was the dichotomous mutual nomination variable from Level 1 of the hierarchical friendship model. The strengths of the designs are these: (a) Because observations on each level of one independent variable have been collapsed across all levels of the other, observations of popularity are unconfounded by the effects of friendship, and vice versa; and (b) because popularity and friendship are considered simultaneously, one can assess the relative association of each to the dependent measure by simply determining how strongly each one is independently related to it. Unfortunately, however, the major weakness of this type of design derives from one of its strengths. Specifically, the procrustean assignment of subjects to cells requires that one treat the variables as if they were independent. Although this strategy has clear statistical and conceptual advantages, these variables may not be functionally independent. Thus, the resultant groups may represent rather artificial classifications, severely limiting the generalizability and meaningfulness of the findings.

A second method for simultaneously considering the effects of popularity and friendship resolves the problem associated with the nonindependence of these constructs in a very different way. This approach deals with the problem of nonindependence through the adoption of covariance techniques. Specifically, with this approach, the effects attributable to one aspect of peer relations, for example, popularity, are identified while the effects of the other aspect, that is, friendship, are eliminated or "partialed out." Whereas the technique described in the previous paragraph would provide information about the relative effects of popularity and friendship, this method provides information about the unique effects of one of these dimensions. For example, we (Bukowski et al., 1987) have used the analysis of covariance to compare the self-concept of preadolescents with a mutual friend to those without one, while holding the effects of popularity constant. Because the effects of the popularity measure were controlled, our results could be interpreted as indicating effects that were unique to the friendship variable.

Although the use of a covariance procedure is advantageous in that it isolates the effects uniquely attributable to one variable, it is also problematic as it does not reveal the totality of the variable's effects. That is, by measuring effects in terms of nonshared variance only, the effects of a variable may be underestimated. Of course, this procedure is adequate if one is specifically interested in a variable's unique effects; if, however, one wants to know about a variable's overall effects, then another approach should be adopted.

As a third possible approach to the simultaneous examination of the effects of popularity and friendship, we recommend that investigators consider using the recently developed research techniques known as structural equation modeling (see Martin, 1987). The major advantage of these methods is their usefulness in simultaneously identifying the individual effects of several variables on multiple outcome measures. Specifically, structural equation modeling procedures (e.g., LISREL) provide estimates of how strongly individual predictor variables are related to specified dependent measures, while taking the relationships among the predictors into consideration. Also, structural equation modeling procedures provide an index of the adequacy of an entire model. For example, we (Bukowski et al., 1987) have used these procedures to simultaneously examine the effects of several popularity and friendship variables on the self-concept. Our results have revealed differential patterns of association between the popularity and friendship measures and have also indicated the total extent to which the outcome measures are related to the peer measures. For example, we found that a measure of general self-worth was more strongly predicted by friendship measures than by popularity measures, whereas popularity measures were more strongly related to self-perceived competence measures, especially the social competence scale. The important point of this discussion is that structural equation modeling techniques can be used to identify the relative and total effects of numerous dimensions of peer relations on outcome variables, without being limited by the problems inherent in the approaches discussed above.

THEORETICAL CONSIDERATIONS REVISITED.   Our final set of recommendations pertains to theoretical matters concerning the proposal that peer relations affect adjustment. First, given that a major theme of this chapter has been the importance of recognizing both the group and dyadic components of children's peer relationships, we propose that investigators of peer relations expand the scope of their studies so as to consider both friendship and popularity.

Second, we recommend that investigators consider the effects of having an extensive network of friends. As mentioned earlier in this chapter, theoretical accounts of friendship have not addressed the question of whether the positive effects of friendship are cumulative or an "all-or-none" phenomenon. To investigate this issue, investigators would need to depart from the current practice of collecting information about only one of a child's friendships and instead collect information about two or more. This question has important clinical implications because it has a direct bearing on the determination of appropriate intervention strategies for children who have no friends. If it is the case that "all you need is one," then practitioners may choose to use very different goals and procedures in their treatment programs.

Our third recommendation is concerned with the differential effects of peer experiences across the childhood and adolescent years. In light of Sullivan's (1953) proposal that group and dyadic experiences are of primary importance during the juvenile and preadolescent periods, respectively, one would expect that popularity and friendship variables would show different relative associations with measures of adjustment for children of different ages. According to this proposal, one would expect the correlation between popularity and the self-concept to peak during the school-age years, whereas the correlation between friendship and the self would be expected to increase as children enter early adolescence.

Our fourth recommendation is also focused on a time-related factor. As Golob and Reichardt (1987) recently noted, "It takes time for a cause to exert an effect" (p. 80). Thus, in order to adequately assess the effect that a cause has on an outcome, one must study the causal process across the appropriate period of time. Knowing exactly what this period is (e.g., a day, a week, a month, a year), however, can be very difficult, especially when the literature offers little guidance. Consequently, investigators need to be more cognizant of the limited generalizability of findings when only a single time interval is considered.

Fifth, and finally, we recommend that investigators need to study the effects of peer relationships via designs that are amenable to causal analysis. To our knowledge, none of the extant studies regarding peer relations and adjustment can be interpreted as indicating a causal relationship because the designs of these studies do not provide results that meet all the requirements necessary for causal inference. As Kenny (1979) has noted, it is well known that in order to demonstrate a causal relationship between two variables, three conditions must be met: (a) time precedence, i.e., "For X to cause Y, X must precede Y in time" (p. 3); (b) the presence of a functional relationship, i.e., differences on one variable must be shown to vary systematically with differences on the other; and (c) nonspuriousness, i.e., "There must not be a Z that causes both X and Y such that the relationship between X and Y vanishes once Z is controlled" (p. 4).

Although one could try to use experimental procedures to meet these conditions, popularity and friendship are not constructs that can be easily manipulated. Thus, in order to satisfy these requirements, we recommend the use of structural modeling techniques. As Mulaik (1987) has shown, investigators can use these procedures to examine causal hypotheses without having to rely on explicitly experimental procedures. By using these techniques in conjunction with a longitudinal data set, the strength of direct links between causes and outcomes can be assessed, while taking into account the effects of indirect or spurious links. That is, by eliminating or accounting for indirect or spurious effects, one can directly assess the strength of the causal links. As noted earlier in this chapter, an advantage of these methods is that they provide statistics to indicate (a) how well a model fits a particular data set and (b) how important each specific element is within the model. In light of these advantages, Connell (1987) has argued that the judicious use of these techniques would contribute greatly to the examination of causal hypotheses. (In-depth discussions of structural modeling can be found in Anderson, 1987, Bentler and Bonett, 1980, Biddle and Marlin, 1987, and Joreskog, 1979.)

CONCLUSIONS

This chapter has addressed several conceptual and methodological issues pertaining to the premise that childhood peer relations contribute uniquely to social and emotional development. A major goal of this chapter was to promote greater integration of theory and research in (a) deriving hypotheses about peer relations and adjustment, (b) distinguishing peer relations constructs, and (c) determining appropriate methods of measuring peer relations. We reviewed the theoretical literature that appears to be most immediately relevant to the premise that peer relations affect adjustment and that we feel forms a strong basis for research hypotheses. We also turned to theory for guidance in distinguishing peer relations constructs, noting that theoretical descriptions of social relations typically focus on both group and dyadic levels of analysis. Within this multilevel framework, we identified the constructs of popularity and friendship, outlining criteria for the measurement of each. As we did not feel that any particular measure single-handedly captures the essence of friendship, we proposed a hierarchical model for its measurement. Data pertinent to the validity of the popularity and friendship measures were reviewed, and gaps in the validity literature were identified. Finally, based on our conceptualizations of popularity and friendship, and in light of our goal of promoting greater integration between theory and research, we outlined possible avenues for future investigations.

REFERENCES

Anderson, J. G. (1987). Structural equation models in the social sciences: Model building. *Child Development, 58,* 49–64.

Asher, S. R., & Dodge, K. A. (1986). Identifying children who are rejected by their peers. *Developmental Psychology, 22,* 444–449.

Asher, S. R., & Hymel, S. (1981). Children's social competence in peer relations: Sociometric and behavioral assessment. In J. D. Wine & M. D. Smye (Eds.), *Social competence* (pp. 125–157). New York: Guilford Press.

Bentler, P. M., & Bonett, D. G. (1980). Significance tests and goodness of fit in the analysis of covariance structures. *Psychological Bulletin, 88,* 588–606.

Berndt, T. J. (1982). The features and effects of friendship in early adolescence. *Child Development, 53,* 1447–1460.

Berndt, T. J. (1984). Sociometric, social-cognitive, and behavioral measures for the study of friendship and popularity. In T. Field, J. L. Roopnarine, & M. Segal (Eds.), *Friendships in normal and handicapped children* (pp. 31–52). Norwood, NJ: Ablex.

Berndt, T. J., Hawkins, J. A., & Hoyle, S. G. (1986). Changes in friendship during a school year: Effects on children's and adolescents' impressions of friendship and sharing with friends. *Child Development, 57,* 1284–1297.

Berndt, T. J., & Hoyle, S. G. (1985). Stability and change in childhood and adolescent friendships. *Developmental Psychology, 21,* 1007–1015.

Berndt, T. J., & Perry, T. B. (1986). Children's perceptions of friendships as supportive relationships. *Developmental Psychology, 22,* 640–648.

Biddle, B. J., & Marlin, M. J. (1987). Causality, confirmation, credulity, and structural equation modeling. *Child Development, 58,* 4–17.

Bierman, K. L. (1987, April). Distinguishing characteristics of aggressive-rejected, aggressive (non-rejected), and rejected (non-aggressive) boys. In J. D. Coie (Chair), *Types of aggression and peer status: The social functions and consequences of children's aggression.* Symposium conducted at the biennial meeting of the Society for Research in Child Development, Baltimore.

Bronfenbrenner, U. (1943). A constant frame of reference for sociometric research: Pt. I. Theory and technique. *Sociometry, 6,* 363–397.

Bronfenbrenner, U. (1944). A constant frame of reference for sociometric research: Pt. II. Experiment and inference. *Sociometry, 7,* 40–75.

Bronfenbrenner, U. (1979). *The ecology of human development: Experiments by nature and design.* Cambridge, MA: Harvard University Press.

Buhrmester, D., & Furman, W. (1987). The development of companiship and intimacy. *Child Development, 58,* 1101–1113.

Bukowski, W. M., Hoza, B., & Newcomb, A. F. (1987). *Friendship, popularity, and the "self" during early adolescence.* Unpublished manuscript.

Bukowski, W. M., & Newcomb, A. F. (1984). The stability and determinants of sociometric status and friendship choice: A longitudinal perspective. *Developmental Psychology, 20,* 265–274.

Cauce, A. M. (1986). Social networks and social competence: Exploring the effects of early adolescent friendships. *American Journal of Community Psychology, 14,* 607–628.

Cauce, A. M. (1987). School and peer competence in early adolescence: A test of domain-specific self-perceived competence. *Developmental Psychology, 23,* 287–291.

Coie, J. D., Dodge, K. A., & Coppotelli, H. (1982). Dimensions and types of social status: A cross-age perspective. *Developmental Psychology, 18,* 557–570.

Connell, J. P. (1987). Structural equation modeling and the study of child development: A question of goodness of fit. *Child Development, 58,* 167–175.

Cooley, C. H. (1909). *Social organization.* New York: Scribner's.

Douvan, E., & Adelson, J. (1966). *The adolescent experience.* New York: Wiley.

Eder, D., & Hallinan, M. T. (1978). Sex differences in children's friendships. *American Sociological Review, 43,* 237–250.

Eichorn, D. (1980). The school. In M. Johnson (Ed.), *Toward adolescence: The middle school years* (pp. 56–73). Chicago: National Society for the Study of Education.

Fine, G. A. (1981). Friends, impression management, and preadolescent behavior. In S. R. Asher & J. M. Gottman (Eds.), *The development of children's friendships* (pp. 29–52). New York: Cambridge University Press.

Foucault, M. (1970). *The order of things.* New York: Pantheon Books. (Original work published in French, 1966, under the title *Les mots et les choses.*)

Furman, W., & Buhrmester, D. (1985). Children's perceptions of the personal relationships in their social networks. *Developmental Psychology, 21,* 1016–1024.

Furman, W., & Robbins, P. (1985). What's the point? Issues in the selection of treatment objectives. In B. H. Schneider, K. H. Rubin, & J. E. Ledingham (Eds.), *Children's peer relations: Issues in assessment and intervention* (pp. 41–54). New York: Springer-Verlag.

Garvey, C. J. (1987, April). *Creation and avoidance of conflict.* Paper presented at the biennial meeting of the Society for Research in Child Development, Baltimore.

Gershman, E. S., & Hayes, D. S. (1983). Differential stability of reciprocal friendships and unilateral relationships among preschool children. *Merrill-Palmer Quarterly, 29,* 169–177.

Golob, H. F., & Reichardt, C. S. (1987). Taking account of time lags in causal models. *Child Development, 58,* 80–92.

Gottman, J., Gonso, J., & Rasmussen, B. (1975). Social interaction, social competence, and friendship in children. *Child Development, 46,* 709–718.

Gresham, F. M. (1981a). Assessment of children's social skills. *Journal of School Psychology, 19,* 120–133.

Gresham, F. M. (1981b). Validity of social skills measures for assessing social competence in low-status children: A multivariate investigation. *Developmental Psychology, 17,* 390–398.

Harter, S. (1982). The perceived competence scale for children. *Child Development, 53,* 87–97.

Hartup, W. W. (1977, Fall). Peers, play, and pathology: A new look at the social behavior of children. *Newsletter, SRCD, Inc.,* pp. 1–3.

Hartup, W. W. (1983). Peer relations. In E. M. Hetherington (Ed.) & P. H. Mussen (Series Ed.), *Handbook of child psychology: Vol. 4. Socialization, personality, and social development* (pp. 103–196). New York: Wiley.

Hayes, D. S., Gershman, E., & Bolin, L. J. (1980). Friends and enemies: Cognitive bases for preschool children's unilateral and reciprocal relationships. *Child Development, 51,* 1276–1279.

Hoza, B. (1987, April). *James and Rosenberg compared: A meta-theoretical analysis of two self theories.* Paper presented at the biennial meeting of the Society for Research in Child Development, Baltimore.

Hoza, B., Bukowski, W. M., & Gold, J. A. (1987). *A reexamination of the association between nomination and rating-scale sociometric techniques.* Unpublished manuscript.

Hymel, S., & Asher, S. R. (1977, March). *Assessment and training of isolated children's social skills.* Paper presented at the biennial meeting of the Society for Research in Child Development, New Orleans. (ERIC Document Reproduction Service No. ED 136 930)

James, W. (1890). *The principles of psychology.* New York: Henry Holt.

Jones, D. C. (1985). Persuasive appeals and responses to appeals among friends and acquaintances. *Child Development, 56,* 757–763.

Joreskog, K. G. (1979). Statistical estimation of structural models in longitudinal-developmental investigations. In J. R. Nesselroade & P. B. Baltes (Eds.), *Longitudinal research in the study of behavior and development.* New York: Academic Press.

Kenny, D. A. (1979). *Correlation and causality.* New York: Wiley.

Ladd, G. W., & Emerson, E. S. (1984). Shared knowledge in children's friendships. *Developmental Psychology, 20,* 932–940.

Mannarino, A. P. (1976). Friendship patterns and altruistic behavior in preadolescent boys. *Developmental Psychology, 12,* 555–556.

Mannarino, A. P. (1978). Friendship patterns and self-concept in preadolescent males. *Journal of Genetic Psychology, 133,* 105–110.

Martin, J. A. (1987). Structural equation modeling: A guide for the perplexed. *Child Development, 58,* 33–37.

Masters, J. C., & Furman, W. (1981). Popularity, individual friendship selection, and specific peer interaction among children. *Developmental Psychology, 17,* 344–350.

McGuire, K. D., & Weisz, J. R. (1982). Social cognition and behavior correlates of preadolescent chumship. *Child Development, 53,* 1478–1484.

Mead, G. H. (1934). *Mind, self, and society*. Chicago: University of Chicago Press.

Moreno, J. L. (1934). *Who shall survive? A new approach to the problem of human interrelations*. Washington, DC: Nervous and Mental Disease Publishing.

Moreno, J. L. (1978). *Who shall survive? Foundations of sociometry, group psychotherapy, and sociodrama* (3rd ed.). Beacon, NY: Beacon House, Inc.

Mulaik, S. A. (1987). Toward a conception of causality applicable to experimentation and causal modeling. *Child Development, 58*, 18–32.

Newcomb, A. F., & Brady, J. E. (1982). Mutuality in boys' friendship relations. *Child Development, 53*, 392–395.

Newcomb, A. F., & Bukowski, W. M. (1983). Social impact and social preference as determinants of children's peer group status. *Developmental Psychology, 19*, 856–867.

Newcomb, A. F., & Bukowski, W. M. (1984). A longitudinal study of the utility of social preference and social impact sociometric classification schemes. *Child Development, 55*, 1434–1447.

Parker, J. G., & Asher, S. R. (1986, April). Predicting long term outcomes from peer rejection: Studies of dropping out, delinquency, and adult psychopathology. In S. R. Asher (Chair), *Peer rejection in childhood: Origins and long-term outcomes*. Symposium conducted at the annual meeting of the American Educational Research Association, San Francisco.

Parker, J. G., & Asher, S. R. (1987). Peer relations and later personal adjustment: Are low-accepted children "at risk"? *Psychological Bulletin, 102*, 357–389.

Piaget, J. (1965). *The moral judgment of the child*. New York: Free Press. (Original work published 1932.)

Sullivan, H. S. (1953). *The interpersonal theory of psychiatry*. New York: Norton.

Vaughn, B. E., & Waters, E. (1981). Attention structure, sociometric status, and dominance: Interrelations, behavioral correlates, and relationships to social competence. *Developmental Psychology, 17*, 275–288.

Weiss, R. S. (1974). The provisions of social relationships. In Z. Rubin (Ed.), *Doing unto others*. Englewood Cliffs, NJ: Prentice-Hall.

Wylie, R. (1979). *The self concept (Vol. 2): Theory and research on selected topics*. Lincoln: University of Nebraska Press.

CHAPTER 2

Behavioral Manifestations of Children's Friendships

WILLARD W. HARTUP

University of Minnesota

This chapter deals with the ways in which children's interactions with their friends differ from their interactions with nonfriends. The time that children spend with friends and nonfriends is considered; cooperation and competition are examined in relation to both friendship formation and friendship maintenance; conflicts among children and their friends are also discussed. Before examining these manifestations, however, children's expectations of their friends and what they think about their friendships are briefly considered.

To most of us, the essentials of friendship are reciprocity and commitment between individuals who see themselves more or less as equals. Our friends are "intimate associates." Children begin to use the word "friend" during the early preschool years (usually sometime during the 4th year) but can seldom articulate the mutuality and commitment that adults believe are essential in "being friends." With increasing age, friendship expectations undergo a series of transformations and elaborations, largely as a function of changes in the child's understanding of social reciprocity and its implications. Early expectations stress participation in common pursuits and concrete reciprocities. To ask a 4-year-old, "Why is Dylan your friend?" will elicit something like the following response: "We play." Later, children expect friends to manifest mutual understanding, loyalty, and self-disclosure ("A friend is someone you can talk to who sort of has the same ideas as you have but has got different things that they introduce you to as well"; "You tell them all your secrets and they tell you theirs"). Older children also believe that friends have a special commitment to one another in the management of conflict: "A friend is someone you fight with, but not forever."

These developments in children's understandings about friendship are extensively documented (Bigelow & LaGaipa, 1975; Youniss, 1980; Selman, 1980; Berndt, 1981b; Furman & Bierman, 1984; Berndt & Perry, 1986). Certain questions, however, have not been completely resolved. Some investigators, for example, have argued that the development of children's friendship expectations is largely the elaboration and extension of the child's understanding of reciprocity (Youniss) or that these changes occur in a series of hierarchical stages: from a "reward-cost" stage marked by common activities and expectations about them to an "empathic stage" in which understanding, self-disclosure, and shared interests are seen to be the hallmarks of friendship (Bigelow, 1977), or from notions of friendship as "momentary interactions" to older children's notions that friendships entail stable, intimate conditions marked by trust and commitment (Selman). Other investigators have taken issue with the conclusion that the child's understanding of these relationships changes in a stagelike manner because early notions about play and mutual association are not abandoned when the importance of intimacy and loyalty is finally recognized (Berndt, 1981b). According to this view, the child's understanding of friendship changes cumulatively rather than hierarchically, not seeming to follow a stagelike progression.

Nevertheless, children's ideas about friends and friendship clearly indicate that, beginning in early childhood, the social world is cognitively differentiated, becoming more so as time goes on (Berndt & Perry, 1986). That is, children recognize that close relationships with other children serve as *resources* and *contexts* which differ from conditions prevailing with children who are not one's friends. But to what extent is the child's behavior with other children differentiated concordantly? When are such differentiations evident? Does behavioral differentiation with other children become more evident with increasing age? Do children's interactions with their friends differ from their interactions with nonfriends both qualitatively and quantitatively? This chapter is devoted to a discussion of what is known about these matters and to issues connected with studying them further.

TIME SPENT WITH FRIENDS

Specifying an age when friendships first become visible in social interaction is extremely difficult. Mothers sometimes insist that their infants or toddlers have "best friends"—usually meaning a regular playmate with whom the child interacts harmoniously. This may or may not be semantically appropriate since the babies have not chosen one another from among many different associates. But interaction that occurs between infants on a regular basis is known to increase the quantity, complexity, and degree of their social engagement (Becker, 1977). And, among preschool children, familiarity increases both the quantity and cognitive maturity of play interactions (Doyle, Connolly, & Rivest, 1980).

Stable differences in the amounts of time that children spend together are evident among preschool children, so that some can be called "strong associates," some "weak associates," and some "nonassociates." Various criteria have been used to distinguish among these relationships but, in one investigation (Hinde, Titmus, Easton, & Tamplin, 1985), a strong associate was specified as a child with whom the subject spends 30% or more of the time that both are present in the nursery school. At 42 months of age, 80% of the children had at least one strong associate; at 50 months, 74% had them.[1] Altogether, these associations accounted for about 10% of the children's social contacts and tended to endure from day to day. In due course, the mothers were asked to name their children's best friends at home. Considerable concordance was evident between these nominations and the observations. Of the children whose best friends were also available at school, 53% of the 42-month-olds and 69% of the children at 50 months had a strong association with that child. Finally, the differentiation among these children, in terms of the time they spent with each other, changed with age. The variation in time spent with different companions was significantly greater at 50 months than at 42 months, indicating that the children distinguished among their companions more sharply as they grew older. Thus, children's companion preferences are visible in very early childhood and become more clear-cut as time progresses. Moreover, time spent with other children defines relationships having at least modest stability and which, in most cases (but not all), mothers and teachers validate as "friendships."

The concordance between sociometric choices (associates named by a child as "best friends" or "preferred play companions") and social interaction has been assessed less frequently than one might imagine. Results are somewhat variable, depending on the children's ages and the sociometric methods used. At least seven investigators have examined this concordance among preschool children. Hagman (1933) used a sociometric test in which children were encouraged to pick celluloid fish out of a bowl to give to the "boys and girls you like best in your preschool," a procedure that was repeated on three successive days. From the choices of fourteen 3-year-olds, 32% who were named once (12 children), 47% of those named twice (9 children), and 73% of those named three times (16 children) were among the children's five most frequently observed companions. Among the choices of nineteen 4-year-olds, 28% who were named once, 38% who were named twice, and 46% who were named three times were most frequent companions. Since the observations were obtained over a period of several months, it is possible that the children's playmate choices may have changed, thus not providing a good basis on which to predict sociometric choice. Even so, greater-than-chance concordance seems to have been demonstrated between choices in the sociometric task and social interaction.

Subsequent investigators used more conventional sociometric assess-

---

[1]Defining "preferred partners" as recipients of at least 10% of the subject's other-directed behaviors, Attili, Hold, and Schleidt (1986) found that 100% of the children in an Italian nursery and 50% of those in a German nursery had strong associates, respectively. Using a 25% criterion, 85% of the children in three United States nursery school classes were observed to have strong associates (Hartup, Laursen, Stewart, & Eastenson, 1988).

ments. Biehler (1954) reported that 80% of the children's most preferred companions, as determined by observations, were also named as either first or second choices on a picture sociometric test calling for the children to name the classmates whom they "like best." One month later, this concordance rate was 88% among the 25 children who participated in the investigation. Marshall and McCandless (1957) asked whether preschool children's choices of best friends (actually "Whom do you like to play with outdoors?") agreed with those observed in play to an extent that was greater than chance. Frequencies were not reported, but probabilities of the obtained agreement were computed for each child, converted into chi-squares, which were then summed to provide the chi-squares used as tests of agreement. By this test, the probability of the agreement obtained was highly significant in both one group of nineteen 4-year-olds and one group of nineteen 5-year-olds.

Similar concordances between orally designated friendships and the amount of time spent between individuals was demonstrated in two other studies of preschool children. In one investigation (Chapman, Smith, Foot, & Pritchard, 1979), only 27% of 4-year-olds interacted most with their stated "best friend" in the classroom. But, in another instance (Hymel, Hayvren, & Lollis, 1982), 47% of the children's preferred playmates were also among the three peers with whom interaction was most frequently initiated. While social overtures were *never* made by the children to 33% of their preferred playmates, the average amount of social interaction was nevertheless considerably greater with preferred companions than with disliked ones.

More recently, two other investigations have demonstrated a concordance between friendship status and social interaction. Vespo (1987) established the existence of friendships by sociometric interviews with children in eight nursery school classes; these friendships were then confirmed by both teacher and parent nominations. Social interaction was observed over 6 weeks, and the target children were found to interact significantly more often with those identified as "friends" than with other children. Finally, Hartup and his co-workers (1988) compared the average percentage of time children spent with their three most preferred companions with the average percentage spent with their remaining same-sex classmates. Significantly greater proportions of time were spent with the sociometric nominees than with the "neutral associates" by children in three classrooms. The weight of the evidence, then, suggests that young children spend more time with those classmates whom they designate as friends than with other children, although this concordance may not be evident for every child.

Observations of schoolchildren are scarce, and it may be the case that sociometric choices are not closely related to classroom or playground interaction (Chapman et al., 1979). Social interaction in these settings is heavily constrained—in classrooms, for example, by seating arrangements (which are usually not self-determined), classroom activities, teacher-child relations, and myriad other conditions. On playgrounds, games and sports activities reduce the extent to which a child may have contact with those individuals who are considered to be friends. Time-use studies, however, indicate that, when on their own and out of school, children clearly spend their time with their friends and not with neutral associates (Barker & Wright, 1951; Medrich, Rosen, Rubin, & Buckley, 1982). Out-of-school friends may be different from in-school friends, depending on the social and geographic structure of neighborhoods and whether a child, indeed, attends a neighborhood school. But no one doubts that schoolchildren spend large amounts of time with their friends; the occurrence is so obvious in everyday life that it does not need documentation. More interesting, developmentally speaking, is the evidence that this phenomenon emerges during early childhood.

COOPERATION AND FRIENDSHIP

Cooperation and sharing appear to be both antecedents and outcomes of children's friendships. That is, coordinated interaction in the service of superordinate objectives attracts children to one another. At the same time, children are disposed to cooperate with their friends more readily than with neutral associates. In fact, the evidence suggests that children are inclined to seek out cooperative opportunities to a greater extent with friends than with other associates.

COOPERATION AS A DETERMINANT OF FRIENDSHIP.   Although everyone recognizes that social reciprocities are important in "becoming friends," the nature of these events varies with age. To investigate children's ideas about the events that bring about friendships, Smollar and Youniss (1982) asked three questions of children ranging from 6 through 13 years of age: "What do you think might happen to make X and Y become friends? Not become friends? To become best friends?" Younger children indicated that strangers would become friends if they did something together or did something special for one another. Sharing and helping one another were mentioned with greatest frequency by 9- and 10-year-olds. In contrast, older children emphasized getting to know one another and the discovery of common interests and tastes. Conversely, *not* becoming friends was associated among the younger children with negative interaction ("We fight") and among the older children with the discovery that two individuals have different personalities.

Individual differences in social reciprocation are actually evident among infants and toddlers. Lee (1973) observed five babies ranging between 8 and 10 months who were enrolled in a day-care center. During the ensuing 6 months, differentiation based on both attraction and rejection occurred. One baby was approached more consistently than the others, and one was more consistently avoided. The most sought-after infant was a responsive social partner who both initiated and reacted contingently to the other babies and who was generally not very assertive. The least sought-after baby was relatively asocial: Both the number and intensity of his social interactions depended on whether or not he had initiated them. One cannot argue strongly that these characteristics were causally related to the differences in attraction observed, but personal styles clearly distinguished these two babies from the others.

Reciprocity and complementarity in play interactions also differ from dyad to dyad among toddlers and young children. These differences have some stability over time, as well as a special significance. In one investigation (Howes, 1983), dyads were distinguished from one another according to whether (a) social initiations resulted in interaction at least half the time, (b) complementarities occurred in play, and (c) affective exchanges were evident (e.g., smiling and laughing). The amount of social interaction was not considered among these criteria, although dyads showing the aforementioned characteristics were more interactive than those not showing them. Especially interesting is the observation that 97% of the dyads manifesting these complimentarities were identified by teachers as either best or second-best friends. Conversely, 100% of the dyads identified as friends by the teachers were shown to interact in the specified manner.

In this investigation, the proportion of dyads that could be considered friends was greater among toddlers and preschool children than among infants, but the number of children observed was so small that this difference is unreliable. The behavioral basis for maintaining these relationships over time, however, clearly varied with age. Babies remaining friendly over the school year exchanged objects more frequently than did toddlers or preschoolers who remained friends; on the other hand, older children who maintained their relationships spent more time in complementary and reciprocal play and vocalized more to each other than did the younger children. Finally, the greatest increases in the complexity of the children's interaction over time occurred in those dyads that maintained friendly relations for the longest times. At the end of the year, social overtures between stable friends were successful in eliciting interaction nearly all the time. Success rates between nonfriends, however, continued to be very low. Functionally speaking, then, friendships among these young children appeared to have made them freer to elaborate and extend their play together; nonfriends, on the other hand, seemed to have spent their energies on negotiations to determine whether interaction would take place at all. The evidence thus indicates that social relationships among young children are behaviorally differentiated—both quantitatively and qualitatively. Moreover, these differentiations may be functionally and developmentally significant.

Older children who are strangers to one another use their first social exchanges to determine the extent to which mutually rewarding coordinations exist between them. Furman and Childs (1981) observed 40 pairs of third-grade children while they became acquainted in a single laboratory session. The children usually began by asking questions to determine commonalities in background and attitudes. These "coorientations" were followed by mutually rewarding activities that served, in turn, as the content of the emerging relationship. Indeed, the observations suggested that these mutualities constituted norms by which the children distinguished these new relationships from others in their experience. In other interviews, conducted during a week-long summer camp, these investigators found that children also differentiated liked from not liked companions in terms of companionship and similarity, as well as in the extent to which they provided one another with prosocial support, intimacy, and affection. These differences were evident after only one day of camp experience and these relationships were stable across the week that the camp was in session. Thus, children are extraordinarily quick to form impressions of one another in terms of social reciprocity and to use these impressions to determine the course of friendship development.

Classroom experiments have yielded similar results: Among fifth- and sixth-grade students working cooperatively on arithmetic assignments for several months, perceptions of personal worth were greater than among students working individualistically and, at the same time, the children were more attracted to one another (Johnson, Johnson, & Scott, 1978). In a similar investigation (Johnson, Johnson, Johnson, & Anderson, 1976), children working in cooperative classrooms believed that the other children liked them better than did children working in individualized classrooms—an attributional difference with far-reaching implications.

So-called open classrooms are also known to produce more diffuse social organizations than traditional classrooms, with unreciprocated choices occurring less commonly and persisting over shorter times (Hallinan, 1976). Investigators (e.g., Epstein, 1983) have reported that more students are selected and fewer are neglected as best friends in open than in traditional situations, and sociometric choices are more commonly reciprocal. Because one of the hallmarks of open education is cooperative work opportunities, these results also support the notion that cooperative experience contributes to "becoming friends."

Working cooperatively toward superordinate objectives also affects friendship choices in intergroup relations. The best-known documentation is contained in the Robbers Cave Experiment (Sherif, Harvey, White, Hood, & Sherif, 1961). The two groups of 11-year-old boys assembled for this experiment behaved differently toward one another when cooperative effort was directed toward an important goal from when competition occurred: Not only did less conflict, aggression, and stereotyping occur, but friendship choices across groups were more frequent.

COOPERATION AS A CONCOMITANT OF FRIENDSHIP. Are qualitative differences observable when the interaction between friends is compared with the interaction between nonfriends? First, among preschool children, positively reinforcing exchanges, as well as neutral contacts, are significantly more frequent between friends (determined by means of picture sociometric interviews) than between unselected partners or between children who dislike one another (Masters & Furman, 1981; Hymel et al., 1982). Second, in situations in which access to resources is limited, young children who are friends interact differently from those who are not. In one study (Charlesworth & LaFreniere, 1983), children worked in four-child groups with a movie viewer that required some children to crank the apparatus and keep the lights on in order that one other child could see the movie. These resources were utilized more effectively (i.e., average individual viewing time was greater) when the children were friends, as measured sociometrically, than when they were not. Turn-taking was more common and social interaction was generally more harmonious.

Similar results were obtained in a simplified version of the prisoner's dilemma (Matsumoto, Haan, Yabrove, Theodorou, & Carney, 1986). In this instance, degree of friendship existing within 19 pairs of children was rated by the teacher using a five-point scale: "1" = "not friends"; "5" = "best friends." These ratings were significantly correlated with a measure of group orientation as well as with equalizations in their task negotiations. Friendship was thus related to a mutual orientation in this situation as well as to cooperation. Other relevant results were obtained with a small group of kindergarten children whose performance in a marble-dropping task was compared with partners who were either "preferred peers" or strangers (Philp, 1940). The children were more interactive with preferred partners, dropped more marbles, and were more helpful to one another; in addition, they told the experimenter afterward that they liked the cooperative version of the task better than the competitive one. Of course, contrasts between friends and strangers confound the familiarity of the children with the closeness of the relationship. Nevertheless, the results indicate that children may actually seek cooperative conditions to a greater extent as settings for engagement with their friends than they do for engagements with nonfriends.

Various arrangements have been used to compare cooperation among schoolchildren with friends and nonfriends. One experiment (Newcomb, Brady, & Hartup, 1979) demonstrated that success in a block-building task did not vary according to friendship status although clear differences were evident in the nature of the interaction: Friends were more interactive, smiled and laughed with each other more, paid closer attention to equity rules, and directed their conversations toward mutual ends rather than toward each other as individuals. Similar differences were obtained in a subsequent study (Newcomb & Brady, 1982) which also revealed that friends explored the apparatus more extensively than nonfriends and remembered more about it when the experiment was over. Other studies showed that social responsiveness while they watched humorous cartoons was greater between friends than between nonfriends, and response matching (a measure of behavioral concordance between children) was also greater (Foot, Chapman, & Smith, 1977; Smith, Foot, & Chapman, 1977).

Are friends more responsive than nonfriends to cooperative cues? The evidence is scarce. The effects of variations in goal structures have been compared between friends and nonfriends in only one instance: Newcomb et al. (1979) studied first- and third-grade partners performing a tower-building task under both "shared rewards" and "winner take all" conditions.

Although the friends evidenced greater mutuality in their interaction than the nonfriends, as previously noted, and the goal structures clearly affected the children's behavior, the friends were *not* more responsive to cooperative cues than the nonfriends were. Task constraints were heavy, in this instance, so that more work is needed—in other situations and with other tasks—to determine whether cooperative goal structures have different effects on friends and nonfriends.

Among adolescents, recent studies (Berndt, 1985) suggest that, when faced with an inequity between themselves and their friends, individuals are more likely to help one another (presumably in an effort to restore equity) than acquaintances are. In this study, fourth, sixth, and eighth graders were observed either with a close friend or a neutral acquaintance. On one task, the children were allowed to help their partners get rewards when the partner had been placed at a disadvantage. The eighth graders were more generous and helpful with their friends than with the acquaintances, reporting afterward that friends are more likely than other classmates to try for equality in the distribution of rewards and less likely to compete with one another. The fourth and sixth graders in this situation did not help their friends more than nonfriends, suggesting the emergence of a special sensitivity to the needs and wants of friends in early adolescence. Other interview studies also suggest an increased concern with cooperation between early adolescent friends (Furman & Bierman, 1984; Berndt & Perry, 1986). But the weight of the evidence suggests that cooperation more readily occurs between friends than between nonfriends throughout childhood—even in situations where resources are limited.

COMMENT.   The dynamics relating friendship and cooperation are undoubtedly complicated. Interviews with children tell us that equitable exchanges and cooperative problem-solving are *conditions* of friendship; children behave cooperatively with one another in order to become friends and to remain so (e.g., Bigelow, 1977; Selman, 1980; Furman & Bierman, 1984; Berndt & Perry, 1986). But these same studies (Selman; Youniss, 1980) also reveal that children consider their friendships to be important for reasons that go beyond equity in the distribution of rewards. With increasing regularity during middle childhood, these relationships are believed to be important because people need companionship and support. We come again to the observation that cooperation is both a condition that contributes to the maintenance of children's friendships and an outcome of them.

COMPETITION AND FRIENDSHIP

Competition refers to an interdependency between two individuals such that the attainment of rewarding outcomes by one constrains the attainment of rewards by the other. According to equity theory, competition between two acquaintances should work against their becoming friends, and competitive interaction should threaten the survival of existing relationships. The issue, however, is more complicated than this: Setting conditions may greatly modify the role of competition in interpersonal relations. Sex-role norms, for example, may support intense competition between two boys (friends) in some situations as long as they cooperate in obtaining superordinate goals in other important situations—for example, winning a soccer match or smoking dope. Moreover, the competitiveness between friends may differ from the competitiveness between nonfriends, according to who the nonfriends are: Interaction, for example, may not be the same with strangers and acquaintances. It is important to sort out these matters and to know more about the contextual constraints that affect the synergism involving competition and friendship relations among children. At the moment, however, the relevant literature is extremely thin.

COMPETITION AS A DETERMINANT OF FRIENDSHIP. Most commonly, the effects of competition on social attraction have been assessed in comparison with the effects of cooperation. As mentioned above, these studies indicate that cooperation encourages attraction to a greater extent than competition. Experiments with children have not been conducted, however, to demonstrate that competition *reduces* social attraction relative to "no treatment" conditions. This oversight is unfortunate because it leaves us without a clear understanding of competition and its role in friendship formation. Numerous studies demonstrate that working under winner-take-all conditions is associated with greater hostility and self-interest than occur when children work for shared rewards (see Hartup, 1983). One can reasonably conclude, then, that competition is not likely to be a setting that favors the attraction of children for each other. But one cannot be certain about this.

Interviews with children do not establish, either, that competition prevents one from becoming friends with someone else. Conflicts are frequently mentioned as barriers to friendship (e.g., fighting, divulging secrets, taking one's possessions, or calling one another names; Smollar & Youniss, 1982). Conflict and competition, however, are not the same (see following sections). Only in adolescence does competition seem to be an inhibitor of social attraction and, then, mainly among girls (Berndt, 1985).

It may be most accurate, then, to conclude that the effects of competition on social attraction are variable. At least one investigation supports this conclusion: Phillips and D'Amico (1956) discovered that competitive conditions increased cohesiveness in some small groups of children, decreased cohesiveness in others, and did not seem to affect group solidarity in the remainder. Increasing cohesiveness under the competitive conditions in this experiment occurred when the children spontaneously discovered how to exchange rewards equitably. Thus, a cooperative adjustment to a competitive situation made by the children themselves was the means whereby the effects of competition on social attraction were minimized. Cooperative conditions within groups are also known to promote solidarity when the groups themselves are in competition (Sherif et al., 1961).

COMPETITION AS A CONCOMITANT OF FRIENDSHIP. There are few behavioral studies relating to the hypothesis that, in the long term, friendships attenuate competitiveness between children. Moreover, different investigators have studied competition between friends and nonfriends in different contexts; results sometimes vary according to the sex and ages of the children. Considering that adolescents believe that friends should not compete with one another (Berndt, 1985), the lack of research attention to these dialer ˙cs is unfortunate.

One investigation with nursery school children suggests that in bargaining situations nonfriends behave more competitively than friends (Matsumoto et al., 1986). The situation in which these children were observed allowed either for solutions that guaranteed equal and moderate payoffs to both children or for solutions in which one or both children tried to score heavily (equalizations and defaults, respectively). As mentioned earlier, children who were friends (according to the teacher) evidenced more frequent equalizations than those who weren't. At the same time, friends engaged in fewer defaults. Although this small-scale study needs extension, the results suggest that, even among young children, friendship is accompanied by expectations of noncompetitiveness (or sharing) whereas competition is a more salient norm among neutral associates.

Bargaining among schoolchildren and their friends has been studied only with boys (Morgan & Sawyer, 1967). Equal outcomes (indicating a relatively high degree of self-interest) were demanded both by boys who liked and who disliked one another. Knowing what one's companion expected in this situation, however, produced different outcomes in the bargaining among friends and nonfriends. Friends would sometimes consent to an unequal division of rewards even though they evidenced some discomfort with this outcome; children who disliked one another, however, insisted on strict equality in outcome regardless of what they knew about their companion's expectations. In the words of the authors: "Information lets *friends* approach more closely the equality they *prefer;* it lets *nonfriends* approach more rapidly the equality they *require*" (p. 148).

Other observational studies show results that vary according to context. Newcomb et al. (1979) found that individualistic commands varied inversely with friendship status at the same time that mutual exchanges varied directly with this condition (see p. 879). Under winner-take-all conditions, nonfriends issued more individualistic commands than friends did and continued to do so even after cooperative conditions were established. These results did not vary according to the sex of the child, but other evidence suggests that boys may be especially competitive with their friends—that is, when the competition does not violate the terms of their relationships. Berndt (1981a) observed the behavior of schoolchildren while they worked with a friend or a nonfriend on a task in which they could either share the use of a crayon, at a cost to themselves, or not share, at a cost to their companions. Friend/ friend differences were not significant to girls, but boys were more competitive with their friends than with nonfriends: They tried to monopolize the crayon and refused more requests to share it with their friends than with nonfriends. It can be argued that, in this situation, friends felt freer to compete with one another than nonfriends and were more willing to risk an unequal outcome than were nonfriends (similar to the circumstances prevailing in bargaining situations). No one suggests that friends are more motivated to be competitive with one another than nonfriends in every situation, especially since older children generally recognize that competition poses a threat to the continuation of these relationships (Berndt, 1985).

Situations that are especially likely to induce competition with friends are those which are highly relevant to the child's definition of self (Tesser, Campbell, & Smith, 1984. In situations that are irrelevant to the maintenance of positive self-images, children are likely to be noncompetitive and to compare their own performance unfavorably to the performance of their friends (apparently preferring to bask in the reflected glory of their friends' superior performance). According to these notions, then, children who are heavily invested in school achievement are likely to make biased comparisons with their friends, favoring their own academic performance. Should musical skill (for example) not be relevant to a child's definition of self, comparisons between the musical performance of self and friends are likely to favor the latter. Thus, self-evaluative processes appear to play key roles in determining the relation between friendship and competition.

COMMENT.   Sex differences in the relation between competition and friendship should not be dismissed lightly. Male and female "cultures" differ in many ways during childhood. Social relationships among boys, for example, are more extensive than the relationships manifested among girls; that is, social networks are larger among boys than among girls and relationships are less exclusive (Eder & Hallinan, 1978). The character of social interaction differs. From an early age, rough-and-tumble play occurs more commonly among males than among females; more frequent fighting and agonistic encounters occur among boys than among girls. Moreover, the evidence shows that the social interactions among boys are more likely to involve fighting than interactions among girls; and it is not merely the case that aggressive boys are more numerous than aggressive girls. In addition, the social encounters observed among boys are more likely to be centered on issues of dominance and status than the interactions among girls. Even styles in exerting social influence differ: Boys use commands relatively more frequently than do girls, who use suggestions and the "convention of turn-taking" (Maccoby, 1986). Finally, evidence from various studies suggests that, among schoolchildren and adolescents, boys are actually more competitive than girls. But the circumstances need to be carefully specified. For example, the overwhelmingly greater likelihood for boys to engage in competitive sports activities than for girls to do so often involves groups competing with other groups—that is, situations involving within-group cooperation as well as between-groups competition. And, in laboratory situations, including the prisoner's dilemma and its variants, significant sex differences have been observed in only about 50% of the studies, but greater competition has been shown by boys in those cases (Maccoby & Jacklin, 1974).

One can argue, then, that heightened competition among male friends, as compared to the situation between male acquaintances, may be *normative:* that is, boys' friendships may entail giving one another room to express self-interest and individualism in certain situations. Existing studies, however, do not tell us where the limits to this generalization are: In what situations may friendship dampen competitive striving between individuals? Does between-groups competition always have this effect? Based on the Robbers Cave Experiment, the answer may be affirmative. When "friendly competitions" were arranged between the groups constituted for this experiment (baseball games, tugs-of-war), there was an initial decrement in cohesiveness within each group: complaining, blaming one another, and scapegoating were common. Within a short time, however, the internal disharmony decreased and cohesiveness within the two groups rose to higher levels than ever before.

To understand the dialectics of competition and friendship, then, requires attention both to the dependencies existing between the two individuals in reward distribution and also to the relation between the friends, as a unit, and to the social situation in which they are functioning. Social interaction between friends may differ according to whether the two individuals are cooperating or competing with two other friends. Interaction between friends may also vary according to whether they are members of a larger social network and whether that network is drawn into cooperation or into competition with other networks.

Other interesting questions await investigation. Is rivalry completely expunged by friendships among girls? Or, is it the case that competition is relevant to these relationships in some situations? How does the social context in which a dyad functions alter the interaction between friendship and competition among girls? To suggest that these questions are uninteresting because girls are not as competitive as boys seems simplistic, to say the least.

And still other issues need attention. Recall that, in the bargaining studies, friends were found to accept unequal outcomes when they knew something about one another's expectations. At the same time, *they were uncomfortable about these inequalities* (see also Berndt & Perry, 1986). Thus, when two boys are friends and there is a general commitment to reciprocity between them, the individual who is less favored in the bargaining may be inclined sometimes to let the other have the reward. At the same time, we know that schoolboys have a strong preference for strict equality in bargaining. In this way, the necessity to bargain with one's friends elicits conflicting motives and cognitive dissonance. Such dissonance has been experienced by almost everyone when confronted with the necessity for competing with a friend in the classroom or on the playing field. Being beaten by one's best friend in an important competition leaves one with a special pain. Victory over a friend is always bittersweet. These dynamics, however, are confirmed more by anecdote than by systematic investigation.

CONFLICT AND FRIENDSHIP

Although children expect their interactions with friends to be cooperative and equitable, conflicts inevitably arise. A conflict consists of an opposition between two individuals: "When one person does something to which a second person objects" (Hay, 1984, p. 2). In sociolinguistics, words like "refusing, denying, objecting, prohibiting, and disagreeing" (Garvey, 1984, p. 129) are used to anchor the construct. In fact, the word that most closely approximates the event as we use it, is "disagreement." Conflicts have sometimes been specified more particularly, to include only influence attempts that continue after being met once by resistance (D. Shantz, 1986; C. Shantz, 1987). In any event, conflict and competition are not the same, and conflict means something quite different from aggression, even though most aggression arises within episodes of conflict.

When asked why children do not become friends, youngsters between the ages of 6 and 10 more frequently mention disagreements than any other reason; personality differences are mentioned by 12- and 13-year-olds (Smollar & Youniss, 1982). Thus, a "climate of disagreement" is believed by children to discourage friendship formation. The reasons that disagreements discourage these attachments, however, may go beyond the constraints on equity that conflicts imply. In fact, disagreements do not lead inevitably to inequitable outcomes. Conflicts are also aversive emotionally, as suggested by the way children describe the events associated with "not becoming friends": "We fight," "We call each other names."

What are the consequences of the conflicts that inevitably occur during the time that children are becoming friends? Rizzo (1987) argues that these disputes play an important and necessary role in friendship formation—that is, children initiate them in an effort to change their companions so that they will better conform to friendship expectations. Along the way, disputes also allow children the opportunity to work out the terms of new relationships and to gain a better understanding of themselves as potential friends. Without these oppositions, children may not obtain the experience that enables them to negotiate subsequent challenges.

Conflicts and their role in ongoing relationships have been explored in interviews with children (Selman, 1980). When asked, young children state that the causes of conflict are unilateral; that is, one person acts in a way that causes a problem for the other. Somewhat older children more clearly understand that conflict exists between parties and that acceptable resolutions must satisfy both participants. And, still older children view conflicts more abstractly, understanding them to be inherent in close relationships and, when worked out, to strengthen them. Older children and adolescents also differentiate between conflicts that are relatively minor (and that the relationship itself may serve to ameliorate) from those that threaten the very existence of the relationship (usually violations of trust). Older adolescents also understand that when a friend is having trouble (within-individual conflict), there may be trouble between oneself and the friend; the necessity to resolve conflicts mutually through insight and self-reflection is also understood. Other developmental studies reveal that the differentiation between the supportive and conflict dimensions in friendship and acquaintanceship is clearer among older children than among younger ones (Berndt & Perry, 1986) but do not show, overall, increasing concern with conflicts as children grow older.

The synergism, then, between conflict and children's friendships seems to be complex. Overall, the frequency of conflict between friends may be lower than the baseline established between nonfriends, but this is not certain. Clearly, conflict and the necessity to manage it are not absent from well-functioning relationships. Rather, friends may work out especially effective ways to manage disputes with one another; the issues about which friends disagree may differ from those about which nonfriends disagree; and friends may choose resolution strategies that favor equitable rather than inequitable outcomes. Now, what behavioral evidence supports these suppositions?

CONFLICT AS A DETERMINANT OF FRIENDSHIP. Children's conversations suggest that those who are becoming friends use softer modes of conflict management than those who are not. Gottman (1983) recruited 18 pairs of children between the ages of 3 and 9, initially strangers, who were brought together on three occasions in one of the children's homes. The children were confined to a playroom, and a tape recorder monitored their conversations for up to 90 minutes during each biweekly session. Two months after the children were observed, their mothers completed a questionnaire to determine the extent to which the children had moved toward "becoming friends": how often they spoke positively about the other child, asked to see one another, telephoned, visited, and so on. Correlations indicated that those children who "hit it off" were especially likely to give reasons for disagreements, to issue weak demands (rather than strong ones) that were complied with, and to avoid extended "disagreement chains" in their conversations.

Across the three sessions, the number of agreements (e.g., "Right") by either host or guest was consistently correlated with friendship outcome (between .38 and .59) while the number of disagreements (e.g., "It is not") was less consistently related to this variable (between .09 and − .43). Only one measure of conflict resolution (weak host demands followed by the guest's agreement in the third session) significantly entered into the multiple regression predicting the mothers' evaluations of the children's relationships. Thus, the presence or absence of agreements rather than the presence or absence of disagreements was consistently related to friendship progress; that is, a "climate of agreement" supported budding friendships whereas a "climate of disagreement" did not necessarily damage them (see also Gottman, 1986). Whether conflict and its management would be negatively related to hitting it off in observations that were not restricted to conversations or that did not involve such highly selected children is unknown.

CONFLICT AND FRIENDSHIP MAINTENANCE.   When the interaction between longer-term friends is contrasted with the interaction between nonfriends, conflict and its management rather clearly differentiate between the two. Green (1933) compared 10 pairs of preschool children who were best friends (they spent substantially more of their time with each other than with other children) and 10 pairs who were not (children who did not differentiate among their playmates). Not only did the two groups differ in the amount of friendly interaction occurring between individuals but the friends also evidenced more quarreling with each other than did the nonfriends. More recently, observations of nursery school children showed that "strong associates" displayed both more active hostility (e.g., assaults or threats) and reactive hostility (e.g., refusals and resistance) toward one another than nonassociates did (Hinde et al., 1985).

Gottman (1983) compared the incidence of agreements and disagreements occurring in the conversations of preschool friends and those occurring between strangers (a companion experiment to the one described above). Neither agreements nor disagreements among the "hosts" varied according to friendship status, but "guests" both agreed and disagreed more with their friends than with strangers. Because these differences involved *proportions* of agreements and disagreements manifested in the interaction between the children, one may conclude that they represent qualitative differences in the social interaction and not a general tendency for friends to interact more vigorously with one another than with nonfriends.

Other studies show that the social conflicts between friends and nonfriends vary on several dimensions. For example, nursery school children were observed to engage in more conflicts, overall, with their friends than with neutral associates (Hartup et al., 1988). For individual children, though, slightly higher rates of conflict occurred between nonfriends than between friends. The relation between friendship and the occurrence of conflict is thus complex: The child's total experience with conflict may be greater with friends than with nonfriends, but only because more time is spent with them.

The conflicts occurring between friends differ qualitatively as well as quantitatively from those that occur between nonfriends. Spontaneous conflicts arising among preschool children were examined, and those occurring between friends were compared to those involving neutral classmates (Hartup et al., 1988). In this instance, friends consisted of children who each conducted at least 25% of their socializing with the other (Hinde et al., 1985). Observations, focused on 4-year-olds in three nursery school classes, were tape-recorded over 10 weeks and used to identify 146 conflicts (influence attempts by one child that were resisted by another). Conflicts between friends were then contrasted with those occurring between neutral associates. First, friends' conflicts did not arise in different contexts or during different activities from nonfriends' conflicts. Nor did friends' disagreements differ from nonfriends' disagreements in what they were about (i.e., possession of objects versus behavioral issues). Resolution strategies, however, were different: Friends made more use of negotiation and disengagement, relative to standing firm, than neutral associates did. Conflict outcomes also varied: Equal or nearly equal resolutions, relative to the occurrence of winners and losers, were more common between friends than between nonfriends. Conflicts involving friends were also rated as significantly less intense, overall, than those involving neutral associates, although it should be noted that aggression did not occur more frequently in nonfriends' conflicts than in disagreements between friends. Finally, conflicts and their management had different implications for friends and nonfriends in terms of subsequent events. Following conflict resolution, friends were more likely to stay in physical proximity and to engage in social interaction with one another than neutral associates were. No significant sex differences were observed in these results. Overall, this material substantially extends the results obtained in laboratory situations with the prisoner's dilemma (Matsumoto et al., 1986) in which the incidence of defaults (clear winners and losers in conflict resolution) was negatively correlated with the extent to which friendship exists between young children.

Close relationships are known to have a strong basis in the exchange of rewards or rewarding outcomes (Berscheid & Walster, 1978). The avoidance of heavy competitive tactics and the use of negotiation in conflict resolution between children and their friends would seem to confirm children's expectations about these "exchange relationships" but may also serve to maintain them. Two studies with preschool children actually demonstrate that, when conflict resolution involves conciliatory exchanges rather than dominance/submission, social interaction is more likely to continue than to be broken off (Sackin & Thelen, 1984; Hartup et al., 1988). Given that friends use conciliation more commonly than nonfriends, one can conclude that friends selectively manage conflicts in ways that keep their interaction going—an outcome that is not assured by the resolution strategies favored by nonfriends.

Scattered evidence suggests that school-aged friends also resolve conflicts in ways that differ from the tactics chosen by neutral associates. For example, when cognitive conflict is involved (i.e., when two children differ in their ideas about social rules), friends, as compared to nonfriends, more frequently explain themselves and criticize one another (Nelson & Aboud, 1985). Conflict resolution between friends seems to involve both underscoring differences and using explanations to negotiate a coordination of views to a greater extent than occurs between nonfriends. In this instance, friends also moved toward more mature solutions under pressure of disagreement than nonfriends did, although the frequency with which they changed their views did not differ. We gain an inkling, then, that the strategies for conflict resolution adopted by schoolchildren and their friends are also geared to the promotion of coordinated conflict outcomes.

Other studies dealing with conflict management between school-aged friends are scarce. As mentioned earlier, the expressive and reciprocal components of social interaction have been found to be more evident between friends than between nonfriends in both cooperative and competitive situations (Newcomb et al., 1979). In addition, the results show that friends complied with mutual commands more readily than nonfriends did; friends issued fewer individualistic commands than nonfriends did; and responses to individualistic commands were less negative among friends than among nonfriends. These results generally agree with what we know about social interaction among "friends-in-the-making" (Gottman, 1983) and support the thesis that friends are motivated to achieve more integrative solutions to conflict than nonfriends are. The literature tells us little beyond this.

Do friends become more effective in managing their conflicts as children grow older? Gottman (1983) reported, among children between 3 and 6, correlations of $-.52$ between age and dyadic disagreements during their conversations with their friends and $+.53$ between age and concessions by "hosts" to weak demands issued by "guests." Negative correlations were also obtained between age and dyadic disagreements during the friendship formation experiment conducted by that investigator. Otherwise, the interaction between friendship and chronological age has not been studied in relation to conflict management, even though the interview evidence strongly suggests that it should be (Selman, 1980; Furman & Bierman, 1984; Berndt & Perry, 1986).

COMMENT. Overall, then, we do not know a great deal about the relation between friendship and conflict. And yet the structure of childhood social relations cannot be fully understood without this information. Troubled children commonly have fewer and less stable friends than other children do (Hartup & Sancilio, 1986). Conflict management may also be a factor in social acceptance and rejection, as suggested by observations of ad hoc groups of boys and girls studied after school (D. Shantz, 1986). The frequency with which the children engaged in conflict (i.e., interfering with the actions of someone who then resists) was positively correlated with social rejection when frequency of aggression was held constant ($r = .58$ for boys, .52 for girls). At the same time, physical aggression and social rejection were not correlated significantly when the frequency of conflicts was held constant ($r = .04$ for boys, $-.20$ for girls). These results agree with other studies showing chronically rejected children to be disruptive, uncooperative, and likely to start arguments (e.g., Coie & Kupersmidt, 1983). But they also suggest that conflict management, rather than aggression, may be central to social acceptance and rejection.

We do not know whether rejected children instigate conflict under different circumstances from their nonrejected classmates in everyday situations, nor do we know whether conflict resolution differs among these children in everyday experience. The instability that is known to characterize the friendships of emotionally disturbed children, however, may derive from their failure to understand that these relationships necessitate reciprocity in conflict resolution. Indeed, Selman (1980) discovered that "referred" children understood the bilaterality involved in friendship relations less well than a matched sample of nonreferred children. One can argue, then, that a failure to discriminate among their close relationships in terms of necessities in conflict management may generally characterize disturbed, less mature, and less intelligent children. Clearly, the conflicts occurring between children and their friends (and how these are understood and managed) ought to figure more centrally in the psychological evaluation of children.

The relation between conflict and friendship has been studied mainly by comparing the interaction between friends with the interaction between nonfriends, based on the assumption that friendships are pretty much alike. This assumption is undoubtedly incorrect. Every close relationship may be based in equity, but the manifestations of equity may differ vastly from relationship to relationship. Ordinarily, we differentiate children from one another simply in terms of the number and identity of their "best friends." But common activities may attract some children to one another; intimacy gratifications may sustain other relationships. Similarly, conflict and its management may figure more importantly in some relationships than in others, and it may even be possible to classify friendships in terms of the "styles," or "modes," with which conflicts are resolved. We do not know, however, the importance of these differences in the social lives of children.

CONCLUSION

Beginning in early childhood, children's relations with other children are differentiated in terms of the time spent with them and the characteristics of their interaction. Cooperation and reciprocity emerge rather early as manifestations of what children come to know as "being friends," and these interactions are relevant to "becoming friends" as well as to maintaining these relationships. Competition does not seem to be a universal inhibitor of friendly relations, especially in early childhood. Even in middle childhood, friendship may support intense competition in certain situations—especially among boys. Conflict, too, seems to instigate different interactions among friends than among nonfriends, although relatively little is known about this matter. Whether conflicts among friends are less intense than conflicts among nonfriends is only suggested by the results of one or two studies, and we do not know definitely whether friends resolve conflicts in ways that differ from the ways that nonfriends resolve theirs. Moreover, we do not know whether socially rejected children have special difficulties with conflict and conflict resolution. Even so, the existing evidence shows that (a) children's friendships encompass a considerable amount of conflict and (b) these relationships are governed by different strategies for conflict management than are relationships with acquaintances.

DEVELOPMENTAL ISSUES.   Developmental issues have been stressed more heavily in studies of what children know about friendship or what they expect their friends to be like, than in studies of behavioral manifestations. Longitudinal studies are rare, except for several instances in which investigators have been concerned with the stability of children's friendships (e.g., Howes, 1983; Hinde et al., 1985; Berndt, Hawkins, & Hoyle, 1986). Even then, the interval between Time 1 and Time 2 has never been more than a school year, a relatively short time for charting changes in the organization and functioning of these relationships. Cross-sectional studies are more numerous, but the results have been disappointing in the extent to which we have learned about developmental changes in the behavioral manifestations of children's friendships.

The cross-sectional search for developmental changes, however, has often been perfunctory. An investigator begins (for example) with the knowledge that mutuality and reciprocity are common expectations of children about their friends and that young children identify friendship with more concrete, moment-to-moment reciprocities than older children do (Selman, 1980). On this basis, a search is then undertaken for age differences in the frequency (or proportion) of mutual support, sharing, and coordinated activity on tasks such as building towers out of blocks (Newcomb et al., 1979) or completing tasks with limited available resources (Berndt, 1981a). The design of the experiment may be elegant, but the situations may not call forth the manifestations of cooperation with their friends that children themselves say are changing.

In addition, centering our attention on the differences between friends and nonfriends may not reveal the most interesting and relevant developmental changes. For example, in one longitudinal investigation, greater selectivity in children's associations with one another was evidenced at 50 months than at 42 months (Hinde et al., 1985); twice as many children showed an increase in the range of times spent with different associates between Time 1 and Time 2 as showed decreases. This increased differentiation in partner choice is at least as important as the increases, with age, in stability of friendship choice that have been noted many times (see Hartup, 1983).

And yet we do not know whether this differentiation continues into middle childhood or whether it doesn't, nor what ramifications it may have.

Our assessment strategies may also not take into account the possibility that children's friendships are more differentiated psychologically among older children than among younger ones. Maximizing cooperation and minimizing conflict may not be equally relevant to every relationship, especially as children grow older. Berndt and Perry (1986) found an undifferentiated factor structure, including both cooperation and conflict issues, in the way children between the ages of 7 and 11 talk about their friends. On the other hand, these issues constituted different clusters of concern among young adolescents. We don't know whether this differentiation is evident behaviorally in the development of these relationships. Nevertheless, the possibility should be taken seriously: Relationships in which conflict is salient may have vastly different histories from those in which cooperation and sharing are central concerns. Cooperation and conflict may be behavioral covariates in their relation to friendship during childhood but orthogonal factors with the onset of adolescence. Considerable change in strategy will be needed, however, in order to puruse this notion. For starters, multivariate behavioral assessments of children's relations with their friends are required.

INDIVIDUAL DIFFERENCES.   Some children have fewer friends than others; some seem to have less stable friendships than others; and sometimes a child's friendships can be identified as "strong" or "weak." But one can imagine other differences among children and their friends that ought to be recognized—differences in the intensity, exclusivity, and security of these relationships, differences in the normative activities that govern them, the commitment of the children to one another, and the extent to which reciprocity and complementarily are salient issues.

Pair-to-pair variations in children's friendships have very seldom been studied. Mutual friends have sometimes been compared to unilateral friends, and various differences have been reported. For example, mutual friendships are more stable over time (Berndt et al., 1986; Hartup et al., 1988) and mutual friends know more about one another and perceive themselves as more similar to one another than unilateral friends do (Ladd & Emerson, 1984). These differences may have important implications.

Another example: The instability that characterizes the friendships of troubled children may trace to difficulties in their understanding and instantiation of social reciprocities. As mentioned, Selman (1980) found that clinically referred children understood the bilaterality involved in friendship relations less well than nonreferred children, and this difference was stubbornly resistant to therapeutic intervention.

Mostly, however, friendship variations have been overlooked along with the individual differences among children that affect the quality of these same relationships. We know that disturbed children are likely to be unpopular and to be ineffective in initiating and maintaining good social relations. But what amount of the variation in these measures is attributable to individual variation in social abilities and what amount to the relationships in which these children participate? These are difficult questions to which easy answers are not likely to be found. But it may be far more revealing to study the ways that children's friendships differ from one another than to search for commonalities among them.

Other issues deserve attention: Earlier sections of this chapter make clear that we know far too little about the interaction between friendship status and the situational context as determinants of cooperation and competition among children. At the same time, we do not know whether friends who are especially cooperative in some situations will be more or less likely to compete in other situations. Sex differences need more extensive exploration in relation to these issues, too. And especially urgent is the need to explore situational constraints that affect the synergy between friendship and conflict management. Only when such information is available will it be possible to design effective interventions on behalf of children without friends or children whose friendships are marked by ambivalence and instability.

REFERENCES

Attili, G., Hold, B., & Schleidt, M. (1986). Relationships among peers in kindergarten: A cross-cultural study. In M. Taub & F. A. King (Eds.), *Current perspectives in primate social dynamics* (pp. 13–30). New York: Van Nostrand, Reinhold.

Barker, R. G., & Wright, H. F. (1951). *One boy's day.* New York: Harper Brothers.

Becker, J. M. T. (1977). A learning analysis of the development of peer-oriented behavior in nine-month-old infants. *Developmental Psychology, 13,* 481–491.

Berndt, T. J. (1981a). Effects of friendship on prosocial intentions and behavior. *Child Development, 52,* 636–643.

Berndt, T. J. (1981b). Relations between social cognition, nonsocial cognition, and social behavior: The case of friendship. In J. H. Flavell & L. Ross (Eds.), *Social cognitive development* (pp. 176–199). Cambridge, UK: Cambridge University Press.

Berndt, T. J. (1985). Prosocial behavior between friends in middle childhood and early adolescence. *Journal of Early Adolescence, 5,* 307–318.

Berndt, T. J., Hawkins, J. A., & Hoyle, S. G. (1986). Changes in friendship during a school year: Effects on children's and adolescent's impressions of friendship and sharing with friends. *Child Development, 57,* 1284–1297.

Berndt, T. J., & Perry, T. B. (1986). Children's perceptions of friendships as supportive relationships. *Developmental Psychology, 22,* 640–648.

Berscheid, E., & Walster, E. H. (1978). *Interpersonal attraction* (2nd ed.). Reading, MA: Addison-Wesley.

Biehler, R. F. (1954). Companion choice behavior in the kindergarten. *Child Development, 25,* 45–50.

Bigelow, B. J. (1977). Children's friendship expectations: A cognitive developmental study. *Child Development, 48,* 246–253.

Bigelow, B. J., & LaGaipa, J. J. (1975). Children's written descriptions of friendship: A multidimensional analysis. *Developmental Psychology, 11,* 857–858.

Chapman, A. J., Smith, J. R., Foot, H. C., & Pritchard, E. (1979). Behavioural and sociometric indices of friendship in children. In M. Cook & G. D. Wilson (Eds.), *Love and attraction.* (p. 127–130). Oxford, UK: Pergamon.

Charlesworth, W. R., & LaFreniere, P. (1983). Dominance, friendship, and resource utilization in preschool children's groups. *Ethology and Sociobiology, 4,* 175–186.

Coie, J. D., & Kupersmidt, J. (1983). A behavioral analysis of emerging social status in boys' groups. *Child Development, 54,* 1400–1416.

Doyle, A., Connolly, J., & Rivest, L. (1980). The effects of playmate familiarity on the social interactions of young children. *Child Development, 51,* 217–223.

Eder, D., & Hallinan, M. T. (1978). Sex differences in children's friendships. *American Sociological Review, 43,* 237–250.

Epstein, J. L. (1983). Selection of friends in differently organized schools and classrooms. In J. L. Epstein & N. Kareweit (Eds.), *Friends in school: Patterns of selection and influence in secondary schools* (pp. 73–92). New York: Academic Press.

Foot, H. C., Chapman, A. J., & Smith, J. R. (1977). Friendship and social responsiveness in boys and girls. *Journal of Personality and Social Psychology, 35,* 401–411.

Furman, W., & Bierman, K. L. (1984). Children's conceptions of friendship: A multimethod study of developmental changes. *Developmental Psychology, 20,* 925–931.

Furman, W., & Childs, M. K. (1981, April). *A temporal perspective on children's friendships.* Paper presented at the biennial meeting of the Society for Research in Child Development, Boston.

Garvey, C. (1984). *Children's talk.* Cambridge, MA: Harvard Univerity Press.

Gottman, J. M. (1983). How children become friends. *Monographs of the Society for Research in Child Development, 48*(3, Serial No. 201).

Gottman, J. M. (1986). The world of coordinated play: same- and cross-sex friendship in young children. In J. M. Gottman & J. G. Parker (Eds.), *Conversations of friends* (pp. 139–191). Cambridge, UK: Cambridge University Press.

Green, E. H. (1933). Friendships and quarrels among preschool children. *Child Development, 4,* 237–252.

Hagman, E. P. (1933). The companionships of preschool children. *University of Iowa Studies in Child Welfare, 4,* 1–69.

Hallinan, M. T. (1976). Friendship patterns in open and traditional classrooms. *Sociology of Education, 49,* 254–265.

Hartup, W. W. (1983). Peer relations. In E. M. Hetherington (Ed.) & P. H. Mussen (Series Ed.), *Handbook of child psychology: Vol. 4. Socialization, personality, and social development* (pp. 103–196). New York: Wiley.

Hartup, W. W., Laursen, B., Stewart, M. A., & Eastenson, A. (1988). Conflict and the friendship relations of young children. *Child Development,* in press.

Hartup, W. W., & Sancilio, M. F. (1986). Children's friendships. In E. Schopler & G. B. Mesibov (Eds.), *Social behavior in autism* (pp. 61–80). New York: Plenum.

Hay, D. F. (1984). Social conflict in early childhood. In G. Whitehurst (Ed.), *Annals of child development* (Vol. 1, pp. 1–44). Greenwich, CT: JAI Press.

Hinde, R. A., Titmus, G., Easton, D., & Tamplin, A. (1985). Incidence of "friendship" and behavior with strong associates versus non-associates in preschoolers. *Child Development, 56,* 234–245.

Howes, C. (1983). Patterns of friendship. *Child Development, 54,* 1041–1053.

Hymel, S., Hayruen, M., & Lollis, S. (1982, May). *Social behavior and sociometric preferences: Do children really play with peers they like?* Paper presented at the annual meeting of the Canadian Psychological Association, Montreal.

Johnson, D. W., Johnson, R. T., Johnson, J., & Anderson, D. (1976). Effects of cooperative versus individualized instruction on student prosocial behavior, attitudes toward learning, and achievement. *Journal of Educational Psychology, 68,* 446–452.

Johnson, D. W., Johnson, R. T., & Scott, L. (1978). The effects of cooperative vs. individualized instruction on student attitudes and achievement. *Journal of Social Psychology, 104,* 207–216.

Ladd, G. W., & Emerson, E. S. (1984). Shared knowledge in children's friendships. *Developmental Psychology, 20,* 932–940.

Lee, L. C. (1973, July). *Social encounters of infants: The beginnings of popularity.* Paper presented at the biennial meeting of the International Society for the Study of Behavioral Development, Ann Arbor, MI.

Maccoby, E. E. (1986). Social groupings in childhood: Their relationship to prosocial and antisocial behavior in boys and girls. In D. Olweus, J. Block, & M. Radke-Yarrow (Eds.), *Development of antisocial and prosocial behavior* (pp. 263–284). New York: Academic Press.

Maccoby, E. E., & Jacklin, C. N. (1974). *The psychology of sex differences.* Stanford, CA: Stanford University Press.

Marshall, H. R., & McCandless, B. R. (1957). A study in prediction of social behavior of preschool children. *Child Development, 28,* 149–159.

Masters, J. C., & Furman, W. (1981). Popularity, individual friendship selections, and specific peer interaction among children. *Developmental Psychology, 17,* 344–350.

Matsumoto, D., Haan, N., Yabrove, G., Theodorou, P., & Carney, C. C. (1986). Preschoolers' moral actions and emotions in prisoner's dilemma. *Developmental Psychology, 22,* 663–670.

Medrich, E. A., Rosen, J., Rubin, V., & Buckley, S. (1982). *The serious business of growing up.* Berkeley, CA: University of California Press.

Morgan, W. R., & Sawyer, J. (1967). Bargaining, expectations, and the preference for equality over equity. *Journal of Personality and Social Psychology, 6,* 139–149.

Nelson, J., & Aboud, F. E. (1985). The resolution of social conflict between friends. *Child Development, 56,* 1009–1017.

Newcomb, A. F., & Brady, J. E. (1982). Mutuality in boys' friendship relations. *Child Development, 53,* 392–395.

Newcomb, A. F., Brady, J. E., & Hartup, W. W. (1979). Friendship and incentive condition as determinants of children's task-oriented social behavior. *Child Development, 50,* 878–881.

Philp, A. J. (1940). Strangers and friends as competitors and co-operators. *Journal of Genetic Psychology, 57,* 249–258.

Phillips, B. N., & D'Amico, L. H. (1956). Effects of cooperation and competition on the cohesiveness of small face-to-face groups. *Journal of Educational Psychology, 47,* 65–70.

Rizzo, T. A. (1987). *Disputes among friends.* Unpublished manuscript, Northwestern University, Evanston, IL.

Sackin, S., & Thelen, E. (1984). An ethological study of peaceful associative outcomes to conflict in preschool children. *Child Development, 55,* 1098–1102.

Selman, R. L. (1980). *The growth of interpersonal understanding: Developmental and clinical analyses.* New York: Academic Press.

Shantz, C. U. (1987). Conflict between children. *Child Development, 58,* 283–305.

Shantz, D. W. (1986). Conflict, aggression, and peer status: An observational study. *Child Development, 57,* 1322–1332.

Sherif, M., Harvey, O. J., White, B. J., Hood, W. R., & Sherif, C. W. (1961). *Inter-group conflict and cooperation: The Robbers Cave experiment.* Norman: University of Oklahoma Press.

Smith, J. R., Foot, H. C., & Chapman, A. J. (1977). Non-verbal communication among friends and strangers sharing humor. In A. J. Chapman & H. C. Foot (Eds.), *It's a funny thing, humor* (pp. 417–420). Oxford, UK: Pergamon.

Smollar, J., & Youniss, J. (1982). Social development through friendship. In K. H. Rubin & H. S. Ross (Eds.), *Peer relationships and social skills in childhood* (pp. 279–298). New York: Springer-Verlag.

Tesser, A., Campbell, J., & Smith, M. (1984). Friendship choice and performance: Self-evaluation maintenance in children. *Journal of Personality and Social Psychology, 46*(3), 561–574.

Vespo, J. E. (1987). *Best friends and associates: The core elements of social organization in preschool classes.* Unpublished manuscript, State University of New York, Stony Brook.

Youniss, J. (1980). *Parents and peers in social development: A Piaget-Sullivan perspective.* Chicago: University of Chicago Press.

CHAPTER 3

Social Conflict and Development
Peers and Siblings

CAROLYN U. SHANTZ AND CATHY J. HOBART
Wayne State University

In the ebb and flow of interactions among children—at school, at home, on the playground, or in the neighborhood—problems between them inevitably arise. Disagreements, quarrels, and fights develop about what is to be done, how things are to be done, who "owns" what, who broke what rule, and who is a member of the group and who isn't—and the list goes on. It goes on precisely because, in the course of children's interactions, virtually any action or statement by one child may be protested by another. Frequently, parents and teachers lament such episodes, feeling that the children involved "can't get along with each other" and responding as if conflict is always a sign (if not a symptom) of failed socialization. In this chapter, we take a different stance toward conflict. We propose that conflict is a process that contributes to social development. Further, we believe that the study of conflict holds substantial promise for understanding the dynamics of the development of individuals and their social relationships.

Conflict Metaphors

To suggest that conflict is a significant process in social development—and in human relations in general—may seem rather puzzling because conflict is so widely viewed as a totally negative phenomenon (Hocker & Wilmot, 1985). The assumptions underlying this negative conception of conflict are that harmony is the ideal state of affairs and that conflict is aberrant and should be reduced or avoided at all costs. The root metaphors of these assumptions, Hocker and Wilmot suggest, are that "conflict is war" or that "conflict is a mess."

Preparation of this chapter was supported in part by a Wayne State University grant awarded to the first author and an NIMH predoctoral training grant awarded to the second author.

But there is a sharply contrasting view of conflict, in which it is seen as representing social problems that are amenable to solution by reasoning and negotiation. The metaphoric image here, Hocker and Wilmot (1985) suggest, is "the bargaining table," that is, the process of coming together to reason together. It is an easily recognized image when one considers the fields of diplomacy, labor-management relations, and governmental structures such as congresses. These institutionalized mechanisms for confronting and resolving conflict have been of long-standing interest, of course, to social scientists. Conflict has been portrayed, however, in most social sciences as a symptom of discordant, destructive forces.

Only during the past few decades (with rare exceptions) have some potentially positive functions of conflict for individuals and groups been suggested (e.g., Coser, 1967). Deutsch (1973), in particular, elaborated on this proposal by distinguishing two types of conflict: destructive and constructive. He characterized destructive conflict as an interpersonal process in which there is an expansion and escalation beyond the initial issue and a reliance on threats and coercion as strategies. Constructive conflict, on the other hand, he described as issue-focused and negotiated by mutual problem-solving. In short, rather than assuming all conflict is harmful to social relationships, Deutsch distinguished between conflicts that enhance and those that impede ongoing relationships. We concur with Deutsch that conflict can have beneficial functions. To anticipate the position explicated in the last section of this chapter, we believe conflict can serve social development—fostering both the self's individuation and social connectedness.

Historical Context

Although conflicts are easily recognized as occasions for negotiation between large social units such as nations or industrial organizations, they are much less easily recognized as negotiable social problems in the everyday interactions of children with one another and children with their parents. Instead, within developmental psychology the major social "problems" of children were often identified as aggressive behavior with peers and noncompliance with adults' rules. It is not surprising—on several counts—that aggression and noncompliance, and not conflict per se, were two primary concerns. First, the traditional aims of the discipline of psychology have been to describe and explain the *individual's* behavior. With that focus, interest centered on whether, how often, and in what form the individual behaved aggressively or not and complied or not. The dyadic relation of conflict, which is often the context of aggression and noncompliance, was largely ignored.

Second, the two theoretical views that prevailed for many years in social development—psychoanalytic theory and social learning theory—shared to some extent the view that the nature of the young child is essentially passive and asocial (if not antisocial). Given that premise, it is reasonable that a major concern was how parents, as bearers of the values of the larger social system, teach children to regulate themselves and to learn and internalize society's rules in order to become socially acceptable members. Indeed, the classic socialization paradigm was focused on parental behavior and child "outcome" variables (e.g., compliance, cessation of aggressive behavior, expressed guilt, and moral behavior). Seldom was the process itself—the give-and-take, the mutual influence of parent on child and child on parent—given attention.

But, in a variety of fields, episodes of conflict in ongoing interactions have become of focal interest. This shift appears to be largely due to a number of changes in the field of child development and allied disciplines. First, as it became increasingly accepted that children make a unique contribution to each others' development (Hartup, 1983), social developmentalists and ethologists sought basic descriptions of children's social behavior in their natural settings. These observations revealed the ubiquitous phenomenon of conflict as children argued about such things as the ownership and use of toys and school materials, the inclusion or exclusion of others into play groups, matters of truth and fact, and the violation of rules. About the same time, some researchers in the fields of linguistics and communication also focused on natural conflicts in order to study the development of discourse and argumentation skills (Eisenberg & Garvey, 1981; O'Keefe & Benoit, 1982). In addition, sociologists who wished to understand the roots of social organization and processes began to study children's conflicts directly to determine how they function to establish group cohesiveness (e.g., Maynard, 1985). Finally, the applied field of clinical psychology contributed theory and research on both intrapsychic and interpersonal conflict. As the treatment of disturbed children increasingly became the treatment of the family as a whole and its subsystems (Minuchin, 1985), researchers began intensive study of the ways both clinic-referred and "normal" families, particularly those with adolescents, communicate during conflict (e.g., Grotevant & Cooper, 1983; Hakim-Larson & Hobart, 1987; Robin & Foster, 1984). In sum, the corpus of basic research on children's conflict appears to have emerged independently from the fields of social developmental and clinical psychology, ethology, linguistics, communication, and sociology.

From these diverse fields of research, we examine in this chapter what is currently known about children's social conflicts. Then we propose some ways in which conflict may function in the development of social relationships and in the development of the self. However, first we consider the more basic question of what constitutes social conflict and the assumptions underlying our presentation.

Definitions and Methods

Two primary approaches are used in studying children's conflicts: observations of naturally occurring disputes and interviews of children (and/or their parents) about conflict. For observational studies, conflict is most often defined as a state in which two or more individuals overtly oppose one another.[1] Opposition is indexed by one child protesting, denying, or in some way resisting another child's actions or statements. In contrast, when researchers use interviews, questionnaires, or rating scales, the respondent is generally asked to describe conflict episodes. Conflict is often defined in these studies by providing words that are presumed synonyms for it (e.g., "Tell me about the fights and quarrels you've had, the times you got mad at X"). The research to be reviewed here, then, falls within a range of conflict definitions.

Aggressive behavior is often confused with conflict and thus deserves a brief comment. It is most often defined (Parke & Slaby, 1983) as behavior intended to harm another person, verbally or physically. Although aggressive behavior may trigger a conflict or may be used during a conflict, it is not the same phenomenon as conflict. During adversative episodes, aggression may be entirely absent (and, in fact, often is absent, as we shall see). Likewise, one child may aggress against another and the second child may not protest, perhaps ignoring the aggression or immediately yielding to it, so no conflict state occurs. Thus, aggression is neither necessary nor sufficient to define a conflict state.

Assumptions

Several assumptions underlie the significance conflict has for development. First, conflicts represent potent episodes for changing the behavior of individuals and their relationships. This premise is held, in fact, by many major theorists of human development (e.g., Erikson, 1959; Freud, 1930/1961; Piaget, 1932; and Riegel, 1976). Central to each of these researcher's theories is the proposition that moments of conflict foster change, and this change may represent either growth or regression. Thus, the second assumption is that the outcome of conflict is indeterminate, that is, it is a turning point for better or worse.

The third assumption is that the matter causing a conflict between two individuals is of personal significance to them and to their relationship. It takes effort to oppose another, to persist in one's goals in the face of another's oppositions, and the conflict may put the continuation of the relationship at

---

[1]A significant distinction can be made between two types of oppositional states, those that are mutual versus those that are unilateral. In mutual opposition conflicts Child A does or says something that Child B protests, and then Child A reacts to B with counteropposition. In unilateral disputes Child A does or says something that Child B protests, but Child A does *not* persist or counteroppose. We believe the mutual definition is preferable in research because it represents a clear dyadic state of opposition and excludes simple common routines of ask → deny → accept; or demand → refuse → drop demand (e.g., A: Give me your pencil; B: No, I'm using it; A: OK). At the very least the social meaning and significance of unilateral versus mutual conflict deserves empirical study (C. Shantz, 1987a, 1987b).

risk. Therefore, conflicts represent matters of importance to the adversaries (at least at the moment they are occurring), especially if they are frequently recurring thematic conflicts.

The fourth assumption is that interpersonal (public, overt) conflict tends to engender intrapsychic conflict (private, covert). There are both theoretical reasons (e.g., Piaget, 1926/1955) and empirical reasons (e.g., Berkowitz, 1985) to assume so. But the exact relationship of conflict between individuals and conflict within individuals is a critical issue in its own right and goes far beyond the focus of this chapter. Here the discussion is limited to children's social conflict and excludes cognitive conflict.

Child-Child Relations

Social conflict in child-child relations is our fundamental focus in this chapter. Such relations include not only those between peers ("agemates," Hartup, 1983) but also those between siblings. We include sibling research in this review for several reasons. First, most children have at least one sibling (David & Baldwin, 1979; Dunn, 1985), and they are quite often closely spaced (Bank & Kahn, 1982), thus providing the first "peer group" that many children experience. In addition, children typically spend a great deal of time with their sibling(s) (Barker & Wright, 1954; Csikszentmihalyi & Larson, 1984; Koch, 1960). For example, Bank and Kahn (1975) reported that siblings (ages 4 to 6) spent more than twice as much time alone with each other as with their parents. Further, sibling relationships are among the longest lasting ones that people experience (Cicirelli, 1982). In a national sample, Harris (1975) found that of those adults with living siblings, 62% between ages 18 and 64 and 44% over age 64 had seen a sibling within the past two weeks.

An additional reason for including sibling research is that sibling relationships are quite distinct in some respects from other social relations. In adult-child relations, for example, children have much less social, physical, financial, and cognitive power than adults. The relations are largely asymmetrically structured, which induces complementary roles. In contrast, child-child relations are marked by more equal power among the children thereby encouraging bilaterality and mutuality in interaction (e.g., Piaget, 1932; Sullivan, 1953). Thus sibling relations are similar to peer relationships in that they are formed among children who are similar in status and power relative to adults. Sibling relations are distinct from peer relations on two accounts, however. First, except for twins, one sibling is always older than the other, and this age difference adds an asymmetrical component to the sibling relationship that is not present in relationships among agemates. Because of this, sibling relationships represent a mixture of both complementary and reciprocal roles (Dunn, 1983). Second, the daily lives of siblings, unlike the lives of other peers, are intertwined—by living together and by having to share space, objects, and most importantly parents.

Finally, large individual differences have been documented between siblings in personality, intellectual development, and psychopathology (Dunn, 1983). These differences occur in part, Dunn suggests, because siblings are creating different contexts for each other's development, both directly through their interactions and indirectly through their parents. Thus, because siblings are embedded within the family, their relationship is of particular, and probably unique, significance.

RESEARCH ON CHILDREN'S CONFLICTS

The empirical studies of child-child conflicts are reviewed here under the following topics: Issues (the points of contention between children); Strategies and Outcomes (the prosocial and antisocial behavior engaged in during adversative episodes; the usual ways conflicts end); and Individual and Dyadic Differences (particularly in relation to gender and age). These topics are first addressed using the research on unrelated peers, and then the research on siblings.

The inclusion of both data sets—peers and siblings—provides a broad picture of child-child conflicts. However, there are few instances in which the literature allows for direct comparison of peer and sibling disputes because the research differs in methods, settings, and ages of children. For example, the research on unrelated peers is based predominantly on observations of preschool children in school environments or laboratory playrooms; in contrast, siblings' conflicts are more often studied by interviews, questionnaires, rating scales, or natural observations in the home, with the mother present. In addition, a good deal of the sibling research is on children in elementary school and on adolescents. Finally, conflicts between children have not been studied extensively, especially in the case of siblings, and thus on several topics the data are insufficient to make direct, reliable comparisons.

Conflicts of Unrelated Peers

Children's conflicts with one another have been studied most often during group activity in nursery schools and during dyadic interactions in laboratory playrooms. Typically, observations are made during free play, with toys, school materials, and other equipment available. Two observational methods have usually been employed: (a) focal individual time sampling, repeated several times, in which each child is randomly selected for observation of his or her conflicts for a predetermined period of time; or (b) event sampling in which all incidents of conflict are recorded by multiple scans of the entire group.

ISSUES.   The manifest issues of the majority of conflicts between toddlers and young preschoolers are (a) object control and (b) social control. A typical object control conflict between two unrelated preschoolers is:

A.   I'm gonna play with the camper.
B.   *I'm* gonna play with the camper.
A.   I said I'm gonna play with that.
B.   We'll share it. (Eisenberg & Garvey, 1981, p. 161).

Social control issues are such matters as a child refusing to adopt a particular fantasy role in play (Houseman, 1972) or not enacting the role correctly (Genishi & DiPaolo, 1982) or refusing to play with another child. The following is an example of a social control conflict between two unrelated preschoolers:

MATT: Scott, don't bother me any more.
SCOTT: I didn't bother you.
MATT: You did too. Over at the blocks.
SCOTT: Oooh [*disagreeing*].
MATT: And you hurt me too. (O'Keefe & Benoit, 1982, p. 178).

Around the age of 4 or 5, there is a slight shift in the proportions of conflict issues from a majority of object control quarrels to about equal proportions of object control and social control quarrels (see C. Shantz, 1987a, for a review). These equal proportions continue up to at least the age of 6 or 7 (Shantz & Shantz, 1985), but there are no observational data at older ages to know if they continue as equally frequent issues throughout the elementary school years. Although object and social control issues predominate in children's conflicts, they also quarrel about factual matters (fact/belief disputes) and rules.

Issues of control, facts, and rules are called "manifest" issues in the sense that what the children do and say in their quarrels defines at the public level the issue of the conflict. Yet such categories as "object control," "social control," and "fact/belief disputes" are somewhat arbitrary in that any behavior can be conceptualized in different ways and may have latent, symbolic meaning as well. For example, the apparently transparent meaning of one child trying to take another's toy as an "object possession" issue may also represent a behavioral control issue. Hay and Ross (1982), for example, found that a toddler sometimes abandoned a toy to try to take an *identical* toy from a peer, suggesting that it is not solely the object that is at issue. Likewise, the violation of rules about objects may be what is at issue rather than the object per se. A toy that is "communal" (to the preschool) elicits more conflict over refusals to share than one which is "individually owned'' (Eisenberg-Berg, Haake, & Bartlett, 1981). Further, issues of ''face'' may be involved in object disputes. For example, a child may defend his or her rights by refusing to relinquish a toy or may seek to assert her or his identity by attempting to take another child's toy. Finally, unconscious motivations may underlie children's conflicts. This is clearly recognized in research on siblings in which rivalry for parental attention and approval is virtually assumed to be the primary and unconscious issue of most conflicts, as we will see. The point is simply that researchers need to be sensitive to the multiple meanings of behavior, and thus the many ways conflict issues can be coded.

STRATEGIES AND OUTCOMES. Moves during conflict can be conceptualized as strategies that either consciously serve as means to a particular goal or have the unintended effect of doing so. The most frequent strategy Eisenberg and Garvey (1981) found in their study of verbal conflicts of dyads of children (ages about 3 to 5½) was sheer insistence on one's desire (strings of ''noes'' and ''yeses'' from the two children), a strategy which often kept a conflict going. The second most frequent strategy when opposing was to give a reason or justification. Other strategies were to suggest an alternative, to compromise, and to make conditional statements. These strategies were more likely to end the conflict than insistence or ignoring the other's opposition.

What is particularly notable in the conflict literature is that aggressive tactics (physical and verbal) occur much less frequently than is commonly assumed. For example, among toddlers in two studies, aggression appeared in less than 25% of conflicts (Hay & Ross, 1982; Maudry & Nekula, 1939). Among preschoolers, Eisenberg and Garvey (1981) found that of 835 strategy uses, only 10 were physical force. And Shantz and Shantz (1982) found, in 72 hours of videotapes of 6- and 7-year-olds playing in groups, that 5% of all strategies used during conflict were physical attacks and 4% were verbal attacks (insults, etc.).

There is evidence that one child's strategies are related to the other child's strategies, that is, they are not random events (Eisenberg & Garvey, 1981; Walton & Sedlak, 1982). Likewise, some sequences of strategies are related in reliable ways to the outcome of the conflict. For example, Corsaro (1979) and Dodge, Schlundt, Shocken and Delugach (1983, Study 2) studied children as they tried to enter groups of peers at play, some of whom met with initial resistance from the group. One sequence of moves was quite successful: to silently approach a group and hover, and then copy group members' behavior. For preschoolers, Corsaro found that such a two-step sequence led to successful entry 88.5% of the time; for 7- and 8-year-old boys, 69% successfully entered the group (Dodge et al.). It is notable that if children *only* waited and hovered at the edge of a group, they were not very likely to be successful in entering, being ignored 80–90% of the time (Corsaro; Dodge et al.). Yet the same strategy was useful as the first move in a sequence of moves. Such data suggest that strategies should be studied as sequences rather than as isolated acts in order to provide a more complete picture of the negotiation process at work between children.

We turn, finally, to some general outcomes of conflicts. First, it is notable that most conflicts are settled by the children themselves without adults intervening (Bakeman & Brownlee, 1982; Dawe, 1934; Genishi & DiPaolo, 1982; Hay & Ross, 1982; Houseman, 1972). This may reflect that adults are not aware of many of children's conflicts, or that the conflicts are settled so rapidly that an adult does not have time to intervene, or that adults believe that children should learn to settle their own disputes.

It appears that in the majority of conflicts there are clear win/loss outcomes. That is, one child yields or complies with the other's wishes (Dawe, 1934; Shantz & Shantz, 1982), or one child "wins" in a tacitly defined index of winning—such as who can endure the longest in bouts of "yes"/"no," can argue the loudest, or can hurl the worst insult (O'Keefe & Benoit, 1982).

At the conclusion of conflicts, most preschoolers show little negative affect (Dawe, 1934; Houseman, 1972). However, this may not be the case for older children who have longer memories and who are beginning to conceptualize peers more in terms of personality traits than transient behavior (Livesley & Bromley, 1973). Unfortunately, there has been no study, to our knowledge, of affective reactions at the conclusion of conflicts between older children and adolescents.

The strategies and outcomes of conflicts may also be influenced by the settings in which they occur. For example, in group and home settings children may have simple, short conflicts, which often end in simple withdrawal or third party intervention. In contrast, lone dyads in laboratory playrooms may have more complex arguments, which more often eventually end in compromise because they cannot withdraw or appeal to another (Genishi & DiPaolo, 1982).

INDIVIDUAL AND DYADIC DIFFERENCES.   Some evidence exists of individual differences and dyadic differences in conflictual behavior of children. First, the frequency with which children are involved in conflict with others differs greatly, although such data are not often presented by researchers. Dawe (1934) observed 200 conflicts between 40 children, aged 2 to 5, in a preschool and noted that the range was anchored at one extreme by one child who quarreled once with one other child and at the other extreme by a child who quarreled 42 times with 29 different children. Houseman (1972) also reported a wide range in 62 hours of videotaped interaction among 37 preschoolers who produced 847 conflicts: The number per child ranged from 8 to 47. In a dyadic setting in a laboratory playroom, Hay and Ross (1982) observed each of 24 dyads of toddlers for an hour over 4 days and noted that 8 of the 48 children were not involved in any conflicts. The meaning of these individual differences is not clear at this point. They could reflect in part the rates of interaction of children in general, that is, the child who rarely interacts with other children may have fewer opportunities to be in conflict compared to the child who interacts with others frequently. Low conflict rates also could reflect a child who immediately yields to others or who, on the other hand, is very skillful in getting his or her way and avoiding others' resistance.

Gender appears to have some relation to conflict rates, boys tending to have higher rates than girls (Dawe, 1934; Miller, Danaher, & Forbes, 1986; Shantz & Shantz, 1985), although not in all cases (e.g., Houseman, 1972). One potential problem in studying sex differences is that when event sampling is used, the observers' attention may be drawn more often to physical fights and loud fights, whereas quieter verbal conflicts may go undetected. Similarly, with event sampling, observers may also be more vigilant of boys than girls, expecting to see more conflicts between boys in accord with stereotypes. On the other hand, when focal individual sampling is used, one is likely to pick up quieter, verbal disputes, which may be more characteristic of girls (Miller et al.). It is notable that the one major study of conflicts in which focal individual sampling was used (Houseman) revealed that girls engaged in more conflicts than boys.

The gender composition of dyads also influences rates. Both Dawe (1934) and Houseman (1972) found that more conflicts occur between same-sex dyads than different-sex dyads: 56% same-sex versus 44% different-sex in Dawe's sample and 59% versus 41% in Houseman's. Again, these percentages may reflect the fact that children interact more with other children of the same sex. Clearly, the issue of gender effects is far from settled.

Conflicts of Siblings

Although sibling relations have not been frequently studied, when they have been, it is often because they are assumed to be inherently conflictual. Freud (1920/1935) gave this emphasis when he wrote, "There is probably no nursery without violent conflicts between the inhabitants, actuated by rivalry for the love of the parents, competition for possessions shared by them all, even for the actual space in the room they occupy" (p. 182). Rivalry for the love and attention of the parents has been the major issue of sibling relationships for most psychoanalysts (e.g., Levy, 1937), and other potential areas of conflict have been largely ignored.

Not only are sibling relations regarded as conflictual, but the family in general may promote more conflict than other social groups. Gelles and Straus (1979) listed characteristics unique to the family that may operate to promote conflict: the substantial amount of time together, a broad range of activities and interests, intense emotional involvement among members, mutually exclusive family choices (e.g., "If we go to the deli, we can't eat pizza"), an implicit understanding that family members have the right to influence each other, age and sex discrepancies, involuntary membership, and social norms that both ensure privacy of the family and allow for overt conflict "behind closed doors." As a system, they note, the family is under opposing constraints to both remain intact and to break up, which inevitably leads to conflict.

Some empirical work supports the assertion that sibling relations are conflictual but certainly not exclusively so. Furman and Buhrmester (1985) developed a sibling relationship questionnaire that they administered to fifth and sixth graders. Factor analysis of the 17 scales revealed four dimensions: (a) warmth/closeness, (b) relative status/power (which included both dominance and nurturance items), (c) conflict, and (d) rivalry (parent partiality). Thus conflict seems to be an important dimension, but not the only one, of sibling relationships. The conflict and rivalry dimensions were factorially distinct, indicating that competition for parent love and attention is not the only issue leading to conflict between siblings.

Although overt conflict and arguments probably tend to diminish as the children grow into adulthood (Cicirelli, 1982), the feelings of competition and rivalry may continue, especially if the siblings use each other as "measuring sticks" by which to gauge their own success (Troll, Miller, & Atchley, 1979). Overt conflicts may resurface if the siblings move into the same home (Laverty, 1962) or are faced with important joint decisions, such as how to best care for elderly parents (Berezin, 1977, cited in Cicirelli).

Most accounts of sibling relationships imply that siblings are more often in conflict than are unrelated peers. Unfortunately, few data are available one way or the other on the matter. Further, those existing meager data do not support the assumption. Specifically, only one observational study could be located in which frequency of sibling conflicts was reported (Dunn & Munn, 1985). In this study, families with two children were observed repeatedly when the younger child was between 14 and 24 months and the firstborn child was from 12 to 57 months older. The average number of conflicts between these siblings ranged between 8 and 12 per hour. These rates are quite similar to those observational studies of dyads of peers: for toddlers, 9 per hour (Hay & Ross, 1982) and 10 to 15 per hour (Russell, 1981, cited in Hay, 1984); and for preschoolers, 10 per hour (Eisenberg & Garvey, 1981) and 19 per hour (O'Keefe & Benoit, 1982). Indeed, the sibling rates appear lower than most peer dyadic rates. However, most of the peer dyads were observed during initial encounters, and, to the extent that conflict occurs more frequently during early periods of interaction, the peer rates may not be directly comparable.

ISSUES.   In the sibling literature the latent issue of rivalry is often considered along with the manifest issues, and in fact may be seen to be the root cause of all sibling conflicts. For example, Neisser (1951, cited in Ames & Haber, 1982) holds that each squabble between siblings has three layers of meaning: (a) the immediate issue; (b) the struggle for status; and (c) the underlying core of resentment accumulated from years of rivalry for possession of the parent. Acus (1981) describes a conflict between two sisters over how their toothbrushes were to be arranged in the bathroom—a seemingly trivial issue until one realizes that the underlying issue had to do with each child being "next to" one of their parents and neither child monopolizing them both.

Issues other than rivalry also have been suggested as deeper causes of conflict. Reit (1985), for example, claims that, in addition to rivalry, the emerging sense of self, which is partially dependent upon the objects the child "owns" and "controls," is another source of conflict between siblings.

Despite the theoretical importance placed on latent issues in sibling conflict, actual research studies, by observation and interview, have focused on overt, manifest issues. Phinney (1986) examined verbal disputes between 5-year-olds and their siblings or peers (51% with peers, 26% with younger siblings, 23% with older siblings). Of these conflicts, 44% concerned procedures (what is going on, how something is to be done, who will do something in the immediate situation), 30% concerned facts and opinions, 11% dealt with possession, 11% dealt with intended future action, and 5% concerned attributions (usually name calling). Unfortunately, peer and sibling conflicts were not distinguished for this particular analysis, making it impossible to know whether certain categories were more characteristic of siblings than of other peers. This study has a unique category called *procedures,* which may account for the lower percentage of object possession disputes compared to the percentage in unrelated peer research.

In a study of 10th graders' conflicts with their siblings, Montemayor and Hanson (1985) found that the conflicts the teenagers described during telephone interviews could be coded into three categories: interpersonal conflicts (72%); family rule conflicts (9%); and other (19%). Interpersonal conflicts, which clearly predominated these sibling conflicts, were the result of differences in behavioral style, teasing, failure to extend courtesies, annoying behaviors, and disagreements about turn-taking.

Steinmetz (1977) asked a sample of 57 Delaware families with more than one child aged 3 to 18 living at home to keep a diary of family conflicts for a period of 1 week. Although she did not provide data regarding relative frequencies, issues of sibling conflict recorded in the diaries included problems in sharing toys, games, and the attention of adults (alleged to be characteristic of families with young children); infringements on personal space such as "making faces," "looking funny at me," touching, and teasing (characteristic of families with preadolescents); and responsibility, obligation, and social grace (characteristic of teenage siblings).

Thus, as is the case with nonsibling peers, almost anything can become an issue for conflict, although these issues may change with age. The varying ways in which issues are coded by researchers and the few available studies prevent direct comparisons between issues of sibling conflict and those of nonsiblings.

STRATEGIES AND OUTCOMES.   Once a conflict has been identified and the issue has been determined, the next logical step is to examine the strategies children use to deal with or resolve the conflict. Few studies to date have focused on the process by which the siblings themselves resolve their conflicts. Often, due either to the explicit focus of the research or the methodology employed (e.g., maternal reports), parental strategies for dealing with their children's conflicts are reported instead (e.g., Dunn & Munn, 1985; Newson & Newson, 1976; Steinmetz, 1977). To the extent that children imitate their parents' strategies, these data may have some indirect relevance for children's own strategies. Unfortunately, none of the studies located analyzed this relation, and therefore studies of parental strategies are not discussed.

In Phinney's (1986) examination of verbal disputes between 5-year-olds and their siblings and peers, she identified two verbal strategies: simple (unelaborated) and elaborated (reasons, explanations, or justifications provided; or counterassertion queried). About two thirds of both sibling and peer conflicts began with simple counterassertions, which tended to be followed by strings of simple counterassertions (e.g., "You did!" "Didn't!" "Did!" etc.). The third that began with elaborated counterassertions, in contrast, were more likely to lead to discussion.

In the only other study in which strategies were examined, Montemayor and Hanson (1985) found that conflicts between 10th graders and their siblings were resolved either by withdrawal (50%), authoritarian tactics (33%), negotiation (11%), or some other method (6%). Thus, in this sample the most frequent "resolution" tactic was simply to withdraw from the conflict without resolution.

INDIVIDUAL AND DYADIC DIFFERENCES. Although it is likely that all siblings engage in conflict at one time or another, the frequency, issues, and strategies of conflict are by no means uniform across sibling pairs. For example, Buhler (1940), as a participant observer of six middle-class Viennese families with two or more siblings, reported much disparity across families in the type and tone of interaction. In one family, the tendency of an 11-year-old girl to constantly berate her 7-year-old, smaller, and therefore (in the older sister's eyes) less capable sister resulted in frequent conflict and almost no friendly interaction, despite the sisters spending most of their time together. An example of one of their disputes is:

> Mother is telling the observer that Kathe would not enjoy being at the lake because she cannot swim. Kathe claims that she knows how, but Erna says: "Go on, you can't at all, and you haven't even begun to learn. You've only been in once." Kathe: "No, three times." Erna: "Well, anyway, you don't know how, and you can't sew, either." (p. 161)

In another family of sisters aged 7 and 3 years, antagonism on the part of either sibling was very rare; when conflict did occur it usually involved the younger sister protesting that her older sister was doing too much for her. In yet a third family with a sister aged 11 and a brother aged 9, interaction was more variable. Although the children frequently played together, had a genuine affection for each other, and were known to confide in each other, angry outbursts and less intense conflicts were also noted. Thus both dyadic and individual differences were clearly documented.

In a recent study by Welz (cited in Grossman, 1986) differences in sibling dyads were also striking. The data were narrative reports of observations of interactions of 13 families during the second-born child's first year, supplemented by interviews with the mothers. Four types of sibling relationships were described: (a) hostile and rivalrous; (b) ambivalent; (c) cooperative; and (d) emotionally supportive. Each pattern seemed to be associated in part with how the mother interacted with the siblings. For example, with the two hostile dyads the mothers were unreliable in regulating either sibling's behavior and often ignored the elder child completely. In contrast, mothers of the four cooperative pairs coordinated the play of the children, interacted positively with both of them, and encouraged the older child to contribute to the care of the younger. Some of the recent work by Kendrick and Dunn (e.g., 1983) indicates that mothers influence sibling quarrels but do so differently depending upon the gender of the older child.

The one general statement that can be made from the available research is that one of the siblings is likely to be consistently more influential in the interaction than the other (Ambramovitch, Corter, Pepler, & Stanhope, 1986; Brody, Stoneman, & MacKinnon, 1982; Buhler, 1940). Generally, the older, more mature sibling tends to have an advantage in terms of deciding what is to be done and by whom. The dominance of one sibling over the other can take the form of bossiness, friendly and polite direction of activity, or substitute mothering.

Older siblings are not only likely to be more influential in sibling interactions, they may also initiate more conflicts by being bossy and demanding, which is then protested by their younger siblings. At least this pattern is suggested by a longitudinal study of sibling interaction during the infancy of the second-born child. Kendrick and Dunn (1983) found that conflicts initiated by the younger siblings were so infrequent that they did not warrant analysis (or even reporting their frequency). Given that the younger siblings were only 8 and 14 months at the times of observation, however, this does not seem surprising. More data are needed to determine whether this trend continues as the children get older.

One point that does seem relatively clear is that this power differential affects the strategies used in the course of conflict. Phinney (1986) found that although simple moves made up the majority of the 5-year-olds' and their younger siblings' assertions and 47% of the older siblings' assertions, elaborated moves tended to increase with both the age of the speaker and the age of the partner. In addition, simple counterassertions were more likely to be ignored if they came from a younger sibling whereas elaborated counterassertions were more likely to be ignored if they came from an older sibling. Thus, older siblings may be more in control of the course of the dispute both by ignoring unelaborated arguments made by younger siblings and by making elaborate counterassertions which the younger siblings are unable to refute. This power differential seemed to be based more on relative age than on absolute age as the 5-year-olds took on either the more powerful or the less powerful role depending upon whether they were interacting with a younger or an older sibling.

As any older sibling knows, however, younger siblings are not totally without efficacy and often use what influence they have to their own advantage. Sutton-Smith and Rosenberg (1968) asked fifth and sixth graders: "How do you get your sibling to do what you want him or her to do?" and "How does your sibling get you to do what he or she wants you to do?" Both older and younger siblings agreed that older siblings were bossy and often used force (including tickling) or the threat of force to get their own way. Younger siblings, on the other hand, cried, pouted, and sulked, asked parents or other children for help, and threatened to tell or actually told parents. The only subgroup of younger siblings who did not recruit parents' help were brothers of older sisters, who tried to get their way by blackmail, wrestling and chasing, breaking and taking things, and making their sisters feel guilty.

As early as 14 months of age younger siblings may realize when it is advantageous to appeal to a parent for support during conflict. Dunn and Munn (1985, Study 1) reported that younger children appealed to their mothers in 36% of sibling conflicts. Whether or not an appeal was made, however, depended on who was behaving hostilely. Appeals were made in 66% of the conflicts in which the older child was hostile but in only 3% in which the younger child was hostile. By the end of the second year these appeals were accompanied by explicit statements of the older child's responsibility in initiating or escalating the conflict. Parents, it seems, may encourage this behavior on the part of the younger sibling by assuming that the older child is "to blame" in most conflicts and responding accordingly (Bossard & Boll, 1956; Dunn, 1985). If this is true, it may explain in part why rivalry is greatest for children reporting their relationship with a younger sibling, especially if the family is large (four or more children) and the younger child is more than 4 years younger (Furman & Buhrmester, 1985).

Another issue is whether the gender of the individuals or the gender composition of the dyad affects conflict behavior. It could be argued, on the one hand, that same-sex siblings will engage in more conflict because they spend more time together or, on the other hand, that mixed-sex dyads will be more conflictual because of incompatible goals and interests. It is also expected that brothers may engage in more conflict than will sisters. To date, none of these possibilities can be supported or refuted by the literature. Kendrick and Dunn (1983) reported that the frequency of physical quarrels did not differ between families with firstborn boys or firstborn girls, although firstborn girls were more likely to initate protest quarrels than were firstborn boys. Koch (1960) found that firstborn children were more likely to report "little" fighting if their sibling was a girl. In a longitudinal study of 7-year-olds in Nottingham, England, Newson and Newson (1976) reported that (based on interviews with the mother) 68% of the boys and 59% of the girls fought physically with their siblings "sometimes" or "often." Whether there was a difference in verbal disputes was not examined. As is the case with nonsibling peers, boys may appear to be more conflictual than girls because their conflicts may be more noticeable.

ROLE OF CONFLICT IN SOCIAL DEVELOPMENT

At the outset of this chapter we stated that the study of interpersonal conflict has potential for revealing some dynamics of social development. In this concluding section, we articulate our general view of social development and then specify what role conflict might have in that development.

Social development may be conceptualized as involving two primary life-long goals: becoming individuated from others, a distinct and unique self; while, simultaneously, becoming connected to others, an accepted and valued group member. According to many psychological theorists, separateness and connectedness relations are a core issue throughout human experience. The relations constitute a central theme of existence which theorists have expressed in various terms: Rank's (1936/1968) notion of tension between individuation and fusion; Erikson's (1959) psychosocial crises; Bakan's (1966) concepts of agency and communion; Angyl's (1965) concepts of autonomy and heteronomy; and Hess and Handel's (1959) concepts of individuality and mutuality in family life. The duality of human experience, however, has not been a dominant or even articulated view in traditional child development approaches. Although connectedness and separateness have each been extensively studied, they are often viewed as different "topics" of development, and therefore their relationship to one another is seldom explicated. To provide a context for the proposals being made here, the theories and major research on each aspect of development are briefly noted.

The developing individuated self—a separate, distinct person with unique characteristics and experiences—received a great deal of theoretical attention at the turn of the century (e.g., James, 1890/1963; Baldwin, 1897; Cooley, 1902). Although these and more contemporary theorists differ in their emphasis on self-concept, self-esteem, and self-regulation, the dominant position appears to be that a primary developmental task is to overcome an initial profound fusion of the young self with other people and objects. Harter (1983), in her review of the empirical literature on the self-system, documents with substantial evidence that the individuation process shows marked developmental change. In infancy individuation is shown by recognition that one is a separate physical being and an independent causal being. With further development characteristics are attributed to the self, the privacy of one's thoughts is recognized, and a coherent and distinctive self-system evolves throughout childhood and adolescence.

The other side of the duality, connectedness, encompasses establishing and maintaining satisfactory relationships with other people, that is, to be and to feel accepted and loved by others, to be a competent member of the group (be it play group, school class, family, or society in general). Connectedness has received a great deal of study throughout the history of child development: parent-child relations, mother-infant attachment, children's friendships, and acceptance or rejection of children by peer groups. More indirect studies of connectedness have been conducted in such areas as play behavior, communication, and prosocial and antisocial behavior. Whereas adult-child relatedness was emphasized by Freud and social learning theorists, child-child relatedness was emphasied by Sullivan (1953) and Piaget (1932). These later theorists thought that each type of relation serves significant but distinct functions in children's social development. Specifically, Sullivan and Piaget proposed that it is through children's interactions with one another, in contrast to interactions with adults, that they are most likely to develop mutual understanding, interpersonal sensitivity, and intimacy.

The view of individuation and connectedness as lifelong goals provides a useful and simple conceptual framework for analyzing social development. These goals should not be construed, however, as completely distinct and dichotomous. They overlap at a psychological level in important ways. For example, how one individuates and defines oneself presumably is highly related to experiences in close relationships with others, and the types of connected relations one has with others is influenced by one's degree of individuation and self-definition. However, to the extent that individuation and connectedness are distinct goals of development, their relation may be conceptualized as either antagonistic or complementary. That is, to establish individuality may require one to oppose others, to take a stand contrary to others' wishes, and to follow one's own way, all of which may threaten acceptance and approval by others. Similarly, to be connected to others may require foregoing personal wishes and needs in deference to others, which may threaten the sense of self and individuality. Such antagonistic tension between self and society is the relation assumed in most psychoanalytic theory, as explicated by Freud in *Civilization and Its Discontents* (1930/1961). Yet, individual and social needs are complementary in many respects, rather than antagonistic. Individual and social interests go hand-in-hand in establishing common ground and shared rules for interacting, in order to develop mutual trust and respect between self and others. For example, establishing a secure positive relationship with a caregiver (connectedness) allows the infant to confidently separate from that caregiver. The infant can then explore and become an increasingly unique self with unique experiences. Such development of the self further enriches the on-going attachment with the caregiver. It is a dynamic, creative relation between self and other that promotes the development of both, whether the "other" is considered as another child, sibling, parent, or, in plurality, as one's family or group.[2]

But what role might conflict have in establishing and maintaining individuation and connectedness? First, we propose that *both* goals are evidenced by the very fact that conflict occurs between parties. When children are at odds, they are tacitly affirming that one another's behavior is of significance. To be indifferent to one another is the epitome of asocial relations. To be in conflict indicates at a minimum that they are interdependent parties, agreeing to disagree and pursue the matter. What one child says and does, influences the other in an ongoing, interdependent cycle (Eisenberg & Garvey, 1981; Walton & Sedlak, 1982). These are the common grounds and mutual interests involved in conflict episodes.

Next, we consider the role conflict may serve in individuation itself. Conflict with others, we propose, enhances the individuation of the self because conflicts mark occasions when one takes a stand in opposition to others and others take a stand in opposition to the self. Even though the conflict may be brief, the self is aware (or is made aware by others) of self's differences. In the flow of agreeable, coordinated interactions with others, one's behavior is suddenly protested and the self either continues the behavior or responds directly to the protest with a counterprotest. At that point of opposition, the self is most aware of its difference from the other.

What, exactly, conflicts contribute to self's individuation is heavily dependent, no doubt, on the developmental state of the self. For example, infant protests and parental resistance to such protests may be the events by which, at least in part, the infant begins to understand that she or he is a separate physical and causal agent. But during the toddler and preschool years, conflicts may contribute toward differentiation of the self as a separate psychological being with wishes or abilities different from those of parents or siblings and may help foster, therefore, autonomy and self-reliance. For the child and adolescent, to challenge and be challenged by others would likely set in sharp relief differences in preferences, goals, capabilities, and

---

[2]The social relationship itself is of central concern, not each individual in isolation. Conflict is a dyadic relation (at a minimum) and needs to be studied from that viewpoint in order to reveal conflict as a process in social interaction. Future research on conflict may be in some peril, however, of being focused on the individual and not the dyad because of a tendency to study dyadic states as if they are an individual's attributes. One example is attachment research. Rutter and Garmezy (1983) state, "Attachment . . . rather than an infant characteristic . . . is a variable describing a dyadic relationship. . . . It cannot any longer be regarded as something within the child or part of the child's makeup" (p. 780). The need for a dyadic focus is echoed by Maccoby and Martin (1983), in their review of some research on self-regulation and compliance: Many "such studies may present a somewhat distorted picture, underrepresenting the degree of *mutual* compliance that actually prevails within parent–child pairs" (p. 65, Maccoby & Martin's italics). Of course these criticisms apply not only to the neglect of the dyad but of triads and larger groups as well.

personality traits, and thus would encourage direct comparisons with others as well as compelling awareness of the privacy of one's own thoughts and feelings (Bannister & Agnew, 1977; Damon & Hart, 1982; Kegan, Noam & Rogers, 1982).

That there are clear developmental changes in self-understanding is well documented (see Harter, 1983, for a review). Most of the research, however, is a *description* of developmental changes. Harter notes that there is "very little evidence (that) bears on . . . how knowledge of the self is dependent on one's social interactions with others" (p. 300). In short, the processes by which the self is constructed are virtually unknown. Theoretical views on the matter tend to emphasize imitation or incorporating others' labels and views of the self or perspective taking. Although these may be significant processes of self-evolution, we suggest that the everyday give-and-take, the minor and major conflicts with parents, siblings, and peers also contribute to individuation—precisely because such conflicts highlight, at the moment they occur, one's differences from others.

An illustration of a conflict among several first graders may illustrate more clearly the relation of opposition to self-definition.

> One dispute . . . started when Tanya was bumped by Craig, who was sitting next to her, whereupon she elbowed him and said, "You don't have to go like that. Gosh." Donald, sitting across from Tanya, and Craig, collaborated on opposition to her expletive. . . . Donald: "You said god." Craig: "That was a naughty word." . . . Tanya: "Gosh is not." . . . For a series of utterances, the parties continued to dispute whether she said "god" or "gosh." Subsequently Craig accused Tanya of being a liar, whereupon Tanya suggested that the two "guys," Donald and Craig, didn't "know" their words. . . . Karen entered the conversation: "God is not a word—a naughty word. It isn't, Tanya." Tanya: "I said gosh." . . . However, after Karen later repeats that "God is not a naughty word," which utterance Craig then contradicts, Tanya abandons the tactic of arguing about pronunciation: "Well sometimes my mom says goddamn it. Sometimes she does." Craig: "You said it now." Tanya: "Yeah cause she lets me. I can say any words I want. Cause I'm gonna be a swearin' lady when I grow up" (Maynard, 1986, p. 271 and p. 283).

All the children here are asserting themselves in several ways—what the reality was (what word was said), whether they approved or not, whether they will change their views or not. Finally, Tanya asserts her difference in being allowed to say any words she wishes and further escalates this to a future difference. It is such exchanges, such give-and-take over different issues with different people, that contribute, we propose, to the self's individuation.

The other fundamental goal of development—being accepted, connected, attached to others—would seem initially not to be served by conflict. Indeed, conflict may seem antithetical to connectedness relations. We submit, however, that this is not the case. First, as noted earlier, conflict itself is a demonstration of interdependence and recognition of the significance of one another's behavior. Second, the issues, strategies, and outcomes of conflict are embedded in connectedness relations. The issues, for example, often deal directly or indirectly with matters of connectedness, such as entrance into an ongoing group of peers at play (Corsaro, 1979, 1981) or friendship, as in the following example of two preschoolers.

PETER: Graham—if you play over here where I am, I'll be your friend.
GRAHAM: I wanna play over here.
PETER: Then I'm not gonna be your friend.
GRAHAM: I'm not—I'm not gonna let—I'm gonna tell my mom to not let you—
PETER: All *right*. I'll come over here (Corsaro, 1981, p. 232).

Sometimes the issue is the violation of rules that bind the group together, and, the notion goes, to be a competent, accepted member of the group one must abide by the rules—be they conventional or moral. The prior example involving Tanya can be viewed also as being based on her (apparent) violation of the rule, "No swearing is allowed." In the process, collaborations evolve—between Craig and Donald and between Karen and Tanya—that also contribute to feelings of connectedness.

Further, how one goes about trying to influence the other, that is, the strategies used, reveals the tacit perceptions one has of the other. For example, one who recognizes the similarities between the self and other is more likely to listen to the other's objections, try to persuade the other, and/or compromise so that the other's needs are partially met as well as one's own needs. If one perceives no similarities and tends to treat the other as an object rather than as a person, it is more likely that coercive tactics, insults, and threats will be used. In addition, the immediate and long-term outcomes of conflicts may vary widely in their impact on belongingness relations. There are few behavioral data on this point. It appears, however, that highly contentious children (those who start disputes frequently, argue with many different peers) tend to be disliked by other children (D. Shantz, 1986). But occasional conflicts between children play an important role in friendship (Gottman, 1983). Older children sometimes can articulate this view: "I think fights are an important part of a close friendship. Nobody is perfect . . . sometimes if you have a real fight and find out you're still friends, then you've got something that is stronger" (Selman, 1980, p. 89).

Sullivan (1953) and Piaget (1932) both posited that "true cooperation" between children emerges, in part, out of interpersonal conflicts. As Youniss (1980) describes these theorists' positions, "Children learn how to deal with differences of opinion. Specifically they construct procedures of *discussion, debate, argument, negotiation,* and *compromise*" (p. 32, Youniss's emphasis) that engender (through reciprocity) a true cooperation. That is, the use of such procedures enhances cooperative social relations and social order because they are based on mutual consent, not on submission to external authority.

The thesis being presented here is that conflictual episodes with peers and with siblings, as they naturally occur in the everyday social life of children, are particular kinds of social problems that contribute to both individuation of the self and connectedness to others. If this thesis is true, then the direct study of social conflict may well offer a particularly revealing view of the dynamics of development. Piaget, long ago, stated, "The study of arguing is . . . of great importance for the psychology of reflection" (1926/1955, p. 83). We propose that the study of conflict is equally important for the psychology of children's social relationships and their self-concepts. To examine such interchanges in detail, over time, and with many individuals should help reveal how conflicts function—for better and for worse—in the long-term development of individuals.

REFERENCES

Acus, L. K. (1981). *Quarreling kids.* Englewood Cliffs, NJ: Prentice-Hall.

Ambramovitch, R., Corter, C., Pepler, D. J., & Stanhope, L. (1986). Sibling and peer interaction: A final follow-up and a comparison. *Child Development, 57,* 217–229.

Ames, L. B., & Haber, C. C. (1982). *He hit me first.* New York: Dembner Brothers.

Angyl, A. (1965). *Neurosis and treatment: A wholistic theory.* New York: Wiley.

Bakan, D. (1966). *The duality of human existence.* Boston: Beacon Press.

Bakeman, R., & Brownlee, J. R. (1982). Social rules governing object conflicts in toddlers and preschoolers. In K. H. Rubin & H. S. Ross (Eds.), *Peer relationships and social skills in childhood* (pp. 99–111). New York: Springer-Verlag.

Baldwin, J. M. (1897). *Social and ethical interpretations in mental development.* New York: Macmillan.

Bank, S. P., & Kahn, M. D. (1975). Sisterhood-brotherhood is powerful: Sibling sub-systems and family therapy. *Family Processes, 14,* 311–337.

Bank, S. P., & Kahn, M. D. (1982). *The sibling bond.* New York: Basic Books.

Bannister, D., & Agnew, J. (1977). The child's construing of self. In A. W. Landfield (Ed.), *Nebraska symposium on motivation: 1976* (pp. 99–125). Lincoln: University of Nebraska Press.

Barker, R. G., & Wright, H. F. (1954). *Midwest and its children.* Evanston, IL: Row, Peterson.

Berkowitz, M. W. (Ed.). (1985). *Peer conflict and psychological growth: New directions for child development.* San Francisco: Jossey-Bass.

Bossard, J. H., & Boll, E. S. (1956). *The large family system.* Westport, CN: Greenwood.

Brody, G. H., Stoneman, Z., & MacKinnon, C. E. (1982). Role asymmetries in interactions among school-aged children, their younger siblings, and their friends. *Child Development, 53,* 1364–1370.

Buhler, C. (1940). *The child and his family.* London: Kegan Paul, Trench, Trubner.

Cicirelli, V. G. (1982). Sibling influence throughout the lifespan. In M. E. Lamb & B. Sutton-Smith (Eds.), *Sibling relationships: Their nature and significance across the lifespan* (pp. 267–284). Hillsdale, NJ: Lawrence Erlbaum.

Cooley, C. H. (1902). *Human nature and the social order.* New York: Scribner's.

Corsaro, W. A. (1979). "We're friends, right?": Children's use of access rituals in a nursery school. *Language in Society, 8,* 315–336.

Corsaro, W. A. (1981). Friendship in the nursery school: Social organization in a peer environment. In S. R. Asher & J. M. Gottman (Eds.), *The development of children's friendships* (pp. 207–241). Cambridge: Cambridge University Press.

Coser, L. A. (1967). *Continuities in the study of social conflict.* New York: Free Press.

Csikszentmihalyi, M., & Larson, R. (1984). *Being adolescent: Conflict and growth in the teenage years.* New York: Basic Books.

Damon, W., & Hart, D. (1982). The development of self-understanding from infancy through adolescence. *Child Development, 53,* 841–864.

David, H. P., & Baldwin, W. P. (1979). Childbearing and child development: Demographic and psychosocial trends. *American Psychologist, 34,* 866–871.

Dawe, H. C. (1934). An analysis of two hundred quarrels of preschool children. *Child Development, 5,* 139–157.

Deutsch, M. (1973). *The resolution of conflict.* New Haven: Yale University Press.

Dodge, K. A., Schlundt, D. C., Shocken, I., & Delugach, J. D. (1983). Social competence and children's sociometric status: The role of peer group entry strategies. *Merrill-Palmer Quarterly, 29,* 309–336.

Dunn, J. (1983). Sibling relationships in early childhood. *Child Development, 54,* 787–811.

Dunn, J. (1985). *Sisters and brothers.* Cambridge, MA: Harvard University Press.

Dunn, J., & Munn, P. (1985). Becoming a family member: Family conflict and the development of social understanding. *Child Development, 56,* 480–492.

Eisenberg, A. R., & Garvey, C. (1981). Children's use of verbal strategies in resolving conflicts. *Discourse Processes, 4,* 149–170.

Eisenberg-Berg, N., Haake, R. J., & Bartlett, K. (1981). The effects of possession and ownership on the sharing and proprietary behaviors of preschool children. *Merrill-Palmer Quarterly, 27,* 61–67.

Erikson, E. H. (1959). Identity and the life cycle. *Psychological Issues,* Monograph 1. New York: International Universities Press.

Freud, S. (1935). *A general introduction to psychoanalysis.* New York: Liveright. (Original work published 1920).

Freud, S. (1961). *Civilization and its discontents.* New York: Norton. (Original work published 1930).

Furman, W., & Buhrmester, D. (1985). Children's perceptions of the qualities of sibling relationships. *Child Development, 56,* 448–461.

Gelles, R. J., & Straus, M. A. (1979). Determinants of violence in the family: Toward a theoretical integration. In W. R. Burr, R. Hill, F. I. Nye, & I. R. Reiss (Eds.), *Contemporary theories about the family: Vol. 1. Research-based theories* (pp. 549–581). New York: Free Press.

Genishi, C., & DiPaolo, M. (1982). Learning through argument in a preschool. In L. C. Wilkinson (Ed.), *Communicating in the classroom* (pp. 49–68). New York: Academic Press.

Gottman, J. M. (1983). How children become friends. *Monographs of the Society for Research in Child Development, 48*(3, Serial No. 201).

Grossman, K. E. (1986). From idiographic approaches to nomothethic hypotheses: Stern, Allport, and the biology of knowledge exemplified by an exploration of sibling relationships. In J. Valsiner (Ed.), *The individual subject and scientific psychology* (pp. 37–69). New York: Plenum.

Grotevant, H. D., & Cooper, C. R. (Eds.). (1983). *Adolescent development in the family: New directions for child development.* San Francisco: Jossey-Bass.

Hakim-Larson, J., & Hobart, C. J. (1987). Intergenerational communication: Mother-daughter resolution of story conflicts. *Journal of Youth and Adolescence, 16,* 153–166.

Harris, Louis and Associates. (1975). *The myth and reality of aging in America.* Washington, DC: National Council on Aging.

Harter, S. (1983). Developmental perspective on the self system. In E. M. Hetherington (Ed.) & P. H. Mussen (Series Ed.), *Handbook of child psychology: Vol. 4. Socialization, personality, and social development* (pp. 275–385). New York: Wiley.

Hartup, W. W. (1983). Peer relations. In E. M. Hetherington (Ed.) & P. H. Mussen (Series Ed.), *Handbook of child psychology: Vol. 4. Socialization, personality, and social development* (pp. 103–196). New York: Wiley.

Hay, D. (1984). Social conflict in early childhood. *Annals of Child Development, 1,* 1–44.

Hay, D. F., & Ross, H. S. (1982). The social nature of early conflict. *Child Development, 53,* 105–113.

Hess, R. D., & Handel, G. (1959). *Family worlds: A psychosocial approach to family life.* Chicago: University of Chicago Press.

Hocker, J. L., & Wilmot, W. W. (1985). *Interpersonal conflict* (2nd ed.). Dubuque, IA: Wm. C. Brown.

Houseman, J. (1972). *An ecological study of interpersonal conflicts among preschool children.* Unpublished doctoral dissertation, Wayne State University, Detroit, MI. (University Microfilms No. 73-12533).

James, W. (1963). *Psychology.* New York: Fawcett. (Original work published 1890).

Kegan, R., Noam, G. G., & Rogers, L. (1982). The psychologic of emotion: A neo-Piagetian view. In D. Cicchetti & P. Hesse (Eds.), *Emotional development: New directions in child development* (pp. 105–128). San Francisco: Jossey-Bass.

Kendrick, C., & Dunn, J. (1983). Sibling quarrels and maternal responses. *Developmental Psychology, 19,* 62–70.

Koch, H. L. (1960). The relation of certain formal attributes of siblings to attitudes held toward each other and toward their parents. *The Monographs of the Society for Research in Child Development, 25*(4, Serial No. 78).

Laverty, R. (1962). Reactivation of sibling rivalry in older people. *Social Work, 7,* 23–30.

Levy, D. M. (1937). Studies in sibling rivalry. *American Orthopsychiatric Association Monograpsh, 2.*

Livesley, W. J., & Bromley, D. B. (1973). *Person perception in childhood and adolescence.* London, England: Wiley.

Maccoby, E. E., & Martin, J. A. (1983). Socialization in the context of the family: Parent-child interaction. In E. M. Hetherington (Ed.) & P. H. Mussen (Series Ed.), *Handbook of child psychology: Vol. 4. Socialization, personality, and social development* (pp. 1–100). New York: Wiley.

Maynard, D. W. (1985). On the functions of social conflict among children. *American Sociological Review, 50,* 207–223.

Maynard, D. W. (1986). Offering and soliciting collaboration in multiparty disputes among children (and other humans). *Human Studies, 9,* 261–285.

Maudry, M., & Nekula, M. (1939). Social relations between children of the same age during the first two years of life. *Journal of Genetic Psychology, 54,* 193–215.

Miller, P. M., Danaher, D. L., & Forbes, D. (1986). Sex-related strategies for coping with interpersonal conflict in children aged five and seven. *Developmental Psychology, 22,* 543–548.

Minuchin, P. (1985). Families and individual development: Provocations from the field of family therapy. *Child Development, 56,* 289–302.

Montemayor, R., & Hanson, E. (1985). A naturalistic view of conflict between adolescents and their parents and siblings. *Journal of Early Adolescence, 5,* 23–30.

Newson, J., & Newson, E. (1976). *Seven years old in the home environment*. New York: Wiley.

O'Keefe, B. J., & Benoit, P. J. (1982). Children's arguments. In J. R. Cox & C. A. Willard (Eds.), *Advances in argumentation theory and research* (pp. 154–183). Carbondale: Southern Illinois University Press.

Parke, R. D., & Slaby, R. G. (1983). The development of aggression. In E. M. Hetheringon (Ed.) & P. H. Mussen (Series Ed.), *Handbook of child psychology: Vol. 4. Socialization, personality and social development* (pp. 547–641). New York: Wiley.

Phinney, J. (1986). The structure of 5-year-olds' verbal quarrels with peers and siblings. *Journal of Genetic Psychology, 147,* 47–60.

Piaget, J. (1955). *The language and thought of the child*. Cleveland: World Publishing. (Original work published 1926).

Piaget, J. (1932). *The moral judgement of the child*. London: Routledge & Kegan Paul.

Rank, O. (1936/1968). *Will therapy and truth and reality*. New York: Knopf.

Reit, S. V. (1985). *Sibling rivalry*. New York: Ballantine Books.

Riegel, K. (1976). The dialectics of human development. *American Psychologist, 31,* 689–700.

Robin, A. R., & Foster, S. L. (1984). Problem-solving communication training: A behavioral-family systems approach to parent-adolescent conflict. In P. Karoly & J. J. Steffen (Eds.), *Adolescent behavior disorders: Foundations and contemporary concerns* (pp. 195–240). Lexington, MA: D. C. Heath.

Rutter, M., & Garmezy, N. (1983). Developmental psychopathology. In E. M. Hetherington (Ed.) & P. H. Mussen (Series Ed.), *Handbook of child psychology: Vol. 4. Socialization, personality, and social development* (pp. 775–911). New York: Wiley.

Selman, R. L. (1980). *The growth of interpersonal understanding: Clinical and developmental analyses*. New York: Academic Press.

Shantz, C. U. (1987a). Conflicts between children. *Child Development, 58,* 283–305.

Shantz, C. U. (1987b, April). *The promises and perils of social conflict*. Discussion paper presented at the meeting of the Society for Research in Child Development, Baltimore, MD.

Shantz, C. U., & Shantz, D. W. (1985). Conflict between children: Social-cognitive and sociometric correlates. In M. W. Berkowitz (Ed.), *Peer conflict and psychological growth* (pp. 3–21). San Francisco: Jossey-Bass.

Shantz, D. W. (1986). Conflict, aggression, and peer status: An observational study. *Child Development, 57,* 1322–1332.

Shantz, D. W., & Shantz, C. U. (1982, August). *Conflicts between children and social cognitive development*. Paper presented at the annual meeting of the American Psychological Association, Washington, DC.

Steinmetz, S. K. (1977). *The cycle of violence: Assertive, aggressive, and abusive family interaction*. New York: Praeger.

Sullivan, H. S. (1953). *The interpersonal theory of psychiatry*. New York: Norton.

Sutton-Smith, B., & Rosenberg, B. G. (1968). Sibling consensus on power tactics. *Journal of Genetic Psychology, 114,* 63–72.

Troll, L. E., Miller, S., & Atchley, R. C. (1979). *Families in later life*. Belmont, CA: Wadsworth.

Walton, M. D., & Sedlak, A. J. (1982). Making amends: A grammar-based analysis of children's social interaction. *Merrill-Palmer Quarterly, 28,* 389–412.

Youniss, J. (1980). *Parents and peers in social development: A Sullivan-Piaget perspective*. Chicago: University of Chicago Press.

CHAPTER 4

Social and Emotional Development in a Relational Context

Friendship Interaction from Early Childhood to Adolescence

JEFFREY G. PARKER AND JOHN M. GOTTMAN

University of Illinois

University of Washington

Consider the following excerpt from the conversation of two 4-year-old best friends at play:

ERIC: [*shouting*] Hold on there everyone! I am the skeleton! I'm the skeleton! Oh! Hee! Hugh, ha, ha! You're hiding.

NAOMI: Hey, in the top drawer, there's the, there's the feet! [*makes clattering noise of "feet"*]

ERIC: I'm the skeleton! Whoa! [*screams*] A skeleton, everyone! A skeleton!

NAOMI: I'm your friend, the dinosaur.

ERIC: Oh, hi Dinosaur. [*subdued*] You know, no one likes me.

NAOMI: [*reassuringly*] But I like you. I'm your friend.

ERIC: But none of my other friends like me. They don't like my new suit. They don't like my skeleton suit. It's really just me. They think I'm a dumb-dumb.

NAOMI: I know what. He's a good skeleton.

ERIC: [*yelling*] I am not a dumb-dumb!

NAOMI: I'm not calling you a dumb-dumb. I'm calling you a friendly skeleton.

This manuscript was supported in part by a NICHHD Traineeship (HD07205) to the first author and by a NIMH grant (MH 35447) to the second author. We are grateful to S. R. Asher, T.J. Berndt, J. J. Campos, G. W. Ladd, and the members of the "Thursday night research group" for their valuable comments on earlier versions.

With a simple, straightforward proclamation ("I am the skeleton"), Eric successfully launches the dyad into the high adventure fantasy world of ghosts and dinosaurs; there is none of the hesitancy, the explicit framing, the endless negotiation that often characterizes the initiation of fantasy play among nonfriends. The drama begun, Naomi is quick to join in and elaborate—spotting skeleton feet in her top drawer and fashioning a role for herself as the skeleton's friend, the dinosaur. Later, when Eric, as the skeleton, expresses concern that others do not like him, Naomi-the-dinosaur is reassuring ("I'm your friend"). And when Eric confesses that it is he—and not the skeleton—that children think is dumb, Naomi deftly alters the fantasy roles to allow Eric to feel competent ("He's a good skeleton").

Eric and Naomi's short exchange illustrates the involved, intimate, and supportive world that is formed by children's friendships. In this chapter, we consider this world, as it is revealed in the conversations of the participants. Although we provide a description of friendship conversation at different ages, our goal is more than just to describe what children do with friends. We also hope to show what friendships do for children—to specify their function as well as their form. Therefore, we go beyond description, to speculate on the links between friendship interaction at different ages and broader issues of social and emotional development.

We are not the first authors to speculate on the functions of friendships in childhood; efforts date at least as far back as Sullivan (1953). He argued, on the basis of clinical experience, that children did not form true friendships until preadolescence, at about age 9 or 10. After that age, he suggested, friendships serve several related functions: They offer consensual validation of interests, hopes and fears; bolster feelings of self-worth; and provide affection and opportunities for intimate disclosure. In addition, they promote the growth of interpersonal sensitivity and serve as prototypes for later romantic, marital, and parental relationships.

Authors since Sullivan have also offered itemized lists of the various benefits of close friendships in childhood and adolescence. For example, Furman and colleagues (Furman, & Buhrmester, 1985; Furman & Robbins, 1985) suggest friendships in childhood function to (1) enhance self-worth, (2) provide opportunities for intimacy and affection, (3) provide instrumental aid, (4) provide opportunities for nurturing behavior, (5) promote a sense of reliable alliance, and (6) provide companionship. Alternatively, Fine (1981) proposes that friendships serve (1) as a staging arena for behavior, (2) as a cultural institution for the transmission of social norms and knowledge, and (3) as a context for the display of appropriate self-images. Similarly, Hartup and Sancilio (1986) list three friendship functions: (1) providing emotional security and support, (2) serving as a context for growth in social competence, and (3) acting as prototypes for later relationships.

As evident, later taxonomic efforts generally highlight some of the same functions originally noticed by Sullivan (1953). In addition, the more recent efforts also sometimes suggest functions that did not appear in Sullivan's original compendium. From the standpoint of this chapter, however, what is more significant than the specific accuracy of any or all of these taxonomic formulations is the similarity in their origins: By and large, these itemizations, like Sullivan's, have been generated on a deductive basis, through intuition and experience or through downward extensions of adult friendship taxonomies which are themselves derived from intuition and experience. As will be seen, our approach to the issue of the functions of friendships departs radically from this "top-down" tradition. In the tradition of ethology, anthropology, and some natural sciences, such as astronomy, we began with a base of detailed observational data and worked forward to a set of generalizations and hypotheses. Thus, our approach is inductive, rather than deductive.

This chapter draws heavily upon a programmatic set of studies done in our laboratory. These studies, based almost entirely on observational methods, provide descriptions of friendship interaction from preschool age to adolescence (see Gottman & Parker, 1986). Observational studies of friendship interaction are rare (numbering perhaps no more than 10), and with few exceptions (e.g., Green, 1933), most of this work is very recent. This fact is sometimes surprising to scholars familiar with the large and venerable literature directed to describing the behavioral correlates of peer acceptance status (see Asher & Coie, in press). This is because studies of the behavioral processes involved in getting along successfully in the peer group are sometimes mistakenly thought to describe the skills involved in initiating and maintaining friendships (Masters & Furman, 1981). There is a distinction between friendship, on the one hand, and group acceptance or popularity, on the other (see Asher & Renshaw, 1981; Berndt, 1984; Feltham, Doyle, Schwartzman, Serbin, & Ledingham, 1985; Furman & Robbins, 1985; Gresham, 1981; Hartup, 1978). Acceptance is a group metric. It measures the consensus in a group with respect to an individual's attractiveness. Friendship, in contrast, indicates the existence of a dyadic relationship with certain properties and a history. Although a child's status in a group is enhanced by the existence of many friendships with members of the group, the two constructs are nonetheless conceptually and empirically distinct and are probably based on partly nonoverlapping sets of social skills.

The dearth of observational research on friendships means that much of what is known about friendship interaction is known through interviews and questionnaires (e.g., Crockett, Losoff, & Petersen, 1984; Douvan & Adelson, 1966; Hayes, Gershman, & Bolin, 1980; Richey & Richey, 1980). This is especially true of middle childhood and adolescent friendships. Asking children about their friendship interaction can be a valuable method of obtaining data on children's expectancies for friendships and their beliefs about their friendship interactions. But interviews and questionnaires cannot substitute for observation if one's aim is to describe actual friendship interaction (see Berndt, 1984; Furman, 1984). There are two particular difficulties with the interview/questionnaire approach. First, self-report measures are dependent on such factors as verbal fluency and cognitive capacity, which can place some children, especially young children, at a distinct disadvantage when they are asked to describe what they do with friends. It often happens that what they can actually do is far more sophisticated than what one would predict on the basis of their self-reports. For example, on the basis of children's responses in structured and semistructured interviews, it has been common to conclude that friendships in young children are little more than momentary, unilateral liaisons that grow out of specific situational exigencies (see Selman, 1980). However, some authors (e.g., Gottman, 1983) have anecdotally noted friendships lasting several years among young children. Moreover, data on friendship choices suggest that more than one half of all preschool children have reciprocated friendships, and fully two thirds of these friendships are stable over a 6-month period (Gershman & Hayes, 1983). Clearly, it does young children's friendships a disservice to base conclusions about mutuality and stability solely on self-report data.

Second, even if children have the requisite verbal and cognitive skills to accurately articulate their actions, children, like adults, are not always aware of their actions (Langer, 1978), nor do they always behave as they believe. There is little correspondence, for example, between children's reports of the intimacy of their friendships and actual rates of self-disclosure in friendship interaction (Hobart, 1987) or between friends' expectations for prosocial behavior and their actual prosocial behavior in interaction (Berndt, 1986b). This, of course, is not surprising. As Furman (1984) reminds us, knowledge and expectations are related in complex ways to behavioral performance. Whether expectations and knowledge are manifested in behavior depends on a whole host of mediating factors, including motivation, feedback, and social perceptions.

Within the observational tradition, most research on friendship interaction has focused on nonverbal or paralinguistic aspects of interaction (e.g., Foot, Chapman, & Smith, 1977) or has incorporated verbal categories of behavior into broader behavioral indices that include nonverbal acts as well (e.g., Rotherham & Phinney, 1981). This is unfortunate, because there is evidence that much of what friends do together, especially as they get older, is talk, both face-to-face and over the phone (Crockett et al., 1984; Johnson & Aries, 1983; Mettetal, 1982). It may be unwise to underestimate the potential importance of this verbal communication content. Our research therefore has given particular attention to what children converse about.

The remainder of the chapter is divided into five major sections. In the following section, we overview the program of observational research that serves as the basis for our descriptions of friendship interaction at different ages. We also describe the evolution of our understanding of the links between friendship interaction and children's social and affective development, highlighting the observations that led to four basic tenets that now make up the propositional framework of our model of the functions of friendship. In the three subsequent sections we describe the nature of friendship conversation at different points in development and offer our speculations as to the role of friendships in children's lives. The final section is devoted to some concluding comments, caveats, and suggestions for future research.

TOWARD A MODEL OF FRIENDSHIP AND SOCIAL AND EMOTIONAL DEVELOPMENT

The Data Base

Our speculations are based on a series of observational studies of friendship interaction and friendship formation begun in 1975 (see Gottman & Parker, 1986). The goal of this work has been to discover the processes by which children form and maintain friendships. This work rests on the belief that a careful account of these processes is essential to the design of interventions for children and adolescents who lack friends. Because this body of observational research plays such a central role in our inferences, and because the accounts of friendship interaction that follow will be brief sketches rather than formal data presentations, it seems appropriate to offer at least a general overview of this data base. For a more detailed presentation of the data base, the observational procedure, the coding systems, and a more formal presentation of the findings, see Gottman (1983), Gottman and Parker (1986), and Gottman and Parkhurst (1980).

Two conversation coding systems and their variations have been employed throughout our work. The first coding system, which we now call the MICRO system, took approximately 5 years to develop. The MICRO system uses 42 molecular content codes and 6 double codes to derive 20 mutually exclusive and exhaustive larger codes, called summary codes. The summary codes assess individual speech acts such as issuing demands, getting another's attention, asking questions, making comments about one's self, making comments about others, squabbling and disagreeing, and being humorous. By examining the temporal structure of the summary codes of an interacting dyad, the MICRO system can be used to index dyadic interpersonal processes such as play, self-disclosure, gossip, or conflict and its resolution.

Work with the MICRO system first appeared in published form in 1980 (Gottman & Parkhurst, 1980). Gottman and Parkhurst obtained audiotape recordings of 13 children, aged 3 to 6 years, interacting in their homes on separate occasions with a stranger and a best friend. They also obtained audiotaped data over an 8-month period on one 4-year-old best friend dyad. Six conversational processes were indexed using the summary codes in this preliminary study: (1) interaction connectedness, (2) communication clarity, (3) social comparison, (4) control, (5) conflict and its resolution, (6) fantasy.

In a subsequent, more thorough analysis, Gottman (1983) used the MICRO system to index seven conversational processes: (1) communication clarity and connectedness, (2) information exchange, (3) exploration of similarities and differences, (4) establishment of common ground play, (5) resolution of conflict, (6) positive reciprocity, and (7) self-disclosure. Gottman's (1983) sample included the audiotapes collected in the original (Gottman & Parkhurst, 1980) sample, as well as audiotapes of 18 dyads of previously unacquainted children, aged 3 to 9 years.

Modifications and extensions of MICRO were introduced even before its publication. Parker and Gottman (1985) operationalized six of the seven social processes of MICRO at the individual rather than the dyadic level and examined their role in friendship formation experimentally in two studies with large samples of 4- and 5-year-old children. Parkhurst and Gottman (1986) modified MICRO to study preschool children's request strategies with friends and nonfriends. The MICRO system was modified again to study friendship in late adolescence (Ginsberg & Gottman, 1986); among other things, detail was added to the self-disclosure category. Specifically, a distinction was drawn between high- and low-intimate self-disclosure. The extended MICRO system examined eight social processes: (1) self-disclosure, (2) gossip, (3) mindreading (comments about the other person, such as psychological attributions), (4) exploration of similarity, (5) exploration of differences, (6) the amount and type of affect in the interaction, (7) extended conflict, and (8) extended humor.

The second coding system, dubbed MACRO, was developed concurrently with the development of the MICRO system (Gottman, 1983). This system employed a larger interactional unit than the MICRO system did. Specifically, unlike MICRO, which *indexed* dyadic social processes with sequences of molecular codes, the MACRO system coded specific dyadic social processes *directly*. The MACRO system was initially designed for friendship interaction between 3 and 9 years (Gottman, 1983). Mettetal (1982) and Gottman and Mettetal (1986), however, have adapted the MACRO to code the interaction of children from 3 to 17 years of age. The social process codes of the MACRO system are as follows: (1) gossip, (2) common ground play, (3) common ground play escalation and de-escalation, (4) message clarification, (5) mindreading, (6) amity (humor), (7) self-disclosure (high- and low-intimate), (8) information exchange, (9) conflict, and (10) relationship talk. Within the gossip category a distinction is drawn between gossip that is about an actual person and gossip about stereotypes of persons (i.e., gym teachers), and between gossip that is disparaging and gossip that is complimentary. In addition the MACRO evaluates each occurrence of a code in terms of its interactional outcome (i.e., its success or failure).

Basic Tenets

As noted, our understanding of the functions of friendship grew out of our attempts to make sense of observational data we had before us. The data comprised a corpus of detailed observations at different ages of the conversations of best friends and of children becoming best friends. In considering these conversations, it was apparent to us that some conversational processes were more central to friendship interaction than others. We first noted this anecdotally, but these impressions were soon confirmed in other ways. For example, in statistical comparisons some processes were better than others at discriminating friends from pairs of strangers, or strangers who eventually became friends from strangers who never became friends. Similarly, when we compared the effects of the presence or absence of adults on friendship interaction, some conversational processes seemed adversely affected by the presence of adults whereas others did not. Processes that were easily disrupted by the intrusive presence of an adult were assumed to be more salient to the friendship dyads than robust processes.

It was further apparent that the processes that were salient to friendship changed developmentally, and in predictable ways. This was clear in the frequencies of specific processes among friends; for example, fantasy play among friends declined dramatically from preschool to middle childhood, whereas self-disclosure was relatively infrequent until adolescence. This developmental change was also clear in the power of specific processes to discriminate friendship dyads from other types of dyads at differing ages. Disparaging gossip, for example, discriminated friends from acquaintances in middle childhood, but not in early childhood or adolescence. But the most intriguing evidence of changes in salience with development emerged from our analyses of the effects of the presence or absence of adults. The point at which friendship interaction was disrupted by this contextual change differed for different social processes. Social comparison processes (discussing similarities and differences), for example, were robust to the intrusive presence of an adult in early childhood, but deteriorated under the same conditions among friends who were entering middle childhood (see Gottman, 1986). The fact that some social processes such as social comparison could be robust early on but fragile later, suggested that we were not simply dealing with a maturational issue. It seemed instead that at certain points in development specific processes came to be salient in friendship. We suspected that the salient period for a specific friendship conversational process corresponded to that period in which the process helped children negotiate broader social and emotional developmental tasks.

In general, peering into friendship conversations at different ages was reminiscent of looking through a kaleidoscope: Periodically the conversational processes would change with respect to one another—some processes would become more central, and some more peripheral, some processes would drop out completely and sometimes new ones would appear. In particular, friendship conversational processes seemed to get reorganized at least twice with development, once at the transition from early childhood to middle childhood and again at the transition from middle childhood to adolescence. In between these times, friendship interaction was relatively stable in the salience of differing social processes. On such evidence, two initial generalizations seemed warranted: First, *as a result of periodic up-heavals and reorganization, development is parsed into three major periods: early childhood, middle childhood, and adolescence.* These periods correspond roughly to the ages of 3 through 7 years, 8 through 12 years, and 13 through 17 or 18 years, respectively. Second, *friendship interaction during any given period has a characteristic organization and content with respect to conversational processes, giving each period a distinct signature or theme.*

In thinking more deeply about the various friendship interaction themes and their developmental progression, we began to see links between these patterns and broader issues of social and affective development. First, the periodic reorganizations of friendship interaction and the resulting friendship themes seemed to reflect changes in the demands afforded by the social "niche" or "subculture" (Higgins & Parsons, 1983) in which the children operated. With development, children participate in a variety of socioecological transitions that pose new challenges to adaptation (Bronfenbrenner, 1979). Each transition brings a shift in role definition and expected behaviors, a shift in the composition of social networks, a need to reorganize personal and social support resources, and a restructuring of ways of looking at one's world (Felner, Farber, & Primavera, 1983; Higgins & Parsons, 1983). Consider what is involved in the transition from early to middle childhood: In comparison to younger children, children in middle childhood spend more time in peer group activities, away from the watchful eyes of parents and other adults (Hartup, 1984). Whereas in early childhood children tend to interact in dyads rather than in larger sets, in middle childhood three-child and larger enclaves become more common (Hartup). And there are other changes. The peer group becomes more homogeneous with respect to gender. Friendships and friendship cliques stabilize. Play becomes more organized and more focused on games with formal rules, such as chess or baseball. These changes bring about a realignment of children's concerns, including an unprecedented need for group belonging (see Fine, 1980).

Our emerging view was that friendship interaction in a given period such as middle childhood played an important role in helping children to consolidate and adjust to concerns raised by such changes. Thus, our third generalization was that *the themes of each period and their developmental progression are normative insofar as they reflect children's attempts to adapt to demands of the social-ecological niche in which children in our society operate, and these demands change with development.*

Second, each reorganization seemed to unveil a new characteristic way in which children dealt with emotions and emotional issues. It has been recognized for some time that relationships with other people are the single most important source of an individual's experience of emotions throughout the life cycle (Berscheid, 1986). Still very little is known of the mechanism for the socialization of affective competence (see Campos, Barrett, Lamb, Goldsmith, & Stenberg, 1983; Saarni, 1980). The task is a formidable one: Emotions are governed by both display rules—rules dictating when individuals should or should not express emotions; and feeling rules—rules dictating what a person should feel under particular circumstances (see Campos et al.). In one author's words (Strayer, 1986; p. 43), affective development involves, among other things, learning "how and when to express emotions that are, or are not, experienced, how to regulate emotions in ways that are age and socially appropriate, and how to understand such affect management in others." Our observations suggested that friendship was shouldering perhaps a significant part of the burden of the socialization of emotional competence. In particular, our final generalization was that *through interaction with their friends, children were acquiring unique information about their own affective experiences and the probable responses of others to their overt displays of these experiences.*

These observations should become clearer over the next three sections of this chapter. Collectively, the next three sections represent a developmental model of friendship interaction and functioning—the model that emerged from our efforts to interpret the patterns we were discovering among the conversations of friends. Because the model is offered in the spirit of hypothesis generation and with the hope that it may inspire further research, we present the model in bold, conclusive terms and without the constraints of a formal data presentation. Indeed, supportive data simply does not exist for many of our conclusions, because we are dealing with hypotheses that *grew out of* rather than *guided* our data collection and analyses efforts to date.

Each section is concerned with friendship interaction and functional significance at a different developmental period—early childhood, middle childhood, and adolescence, respectively. The sections have parallel structures: First, we outline the implicit social concerns that are presumed to be driving friendship interaction during the periods. Next, we sketch the salient conversational process or processes of the period and describe how those processes are related to other conversational processes observed at each age. Finally, we discuss the kinds of skill acquisition and social learning that are presumed to be taking place in the affective domain during the period. It will become apparent, as one looks across sections, that we see the underlying concerns of friendship as evolving from a concern for coordinating play as means for maximizing mutual enjoyment and entertainment, to a concern for understanding and gaining peer group acceptance, and finally to a concern for self-understanding. We also see the salient processes of friendship as evolving developmentally from processes concerned with coordination of play to the process of gossip to the process of self-disclosure. Finally, we see an evolution in the affective developments of each period from behavioral organization in the face of high arousal, to concern for appropriate emotional displays in social contexts, to an integration of logic and emotion into a coherent understanding of how emotions function in social discourse and relationships. An overview of the model is presented in Table 4.1.

TABLE 4.1.   Characteristics of the Hypothesized Developmental Periods

	Developmental Period		
Characteristic	Early Childhood	Middle Childhood	Adolescence
Underlying theme or concern	Maximization of excitement, entertainment, and affect levels in play	Inclusion by peers, avoidance of rejection; self-presentation	Self-exploration; self-definition
Salient conversational processes in friendship	Processes of play coordination: activity talk, play escalation, play deescalation, conflict resolution	Negative evaluation gossip	Self-disclosure; problem-solving
Affective developments	Management of arousal in interaction	Acquisition of affect display and feeling rules; rejection of sentiment	Fusion of logic and emotion; understanding of implications of affect for relationships

Note. Adapted from Gottman & Mettetal (1986).

FRIENDSHIPS IN EARLY CHILDHOOD: THE WORLD OF COORDINATED PLAY

Underlying Theme or Concern

We have suggested that friendship interaction belies different social concerns at different points in development. Our observations indicate that what concerns children in early childhood is maximizing the level of enjoyment, entertainment, and satisfaction experienced in their play. It has been recognized for some time that young children place a premium on a child's potential as a playmate, both in their descriptions of actual friendships (Austin & Thompson, 1948: Berndt, 1986a; Berndt & Perry, 1986; Furman & Buhrmester, 1985; Hayes et al., 1980) and in their beliefs about friendships in general (Bigelow, 1977; Bigelow & La Gaipa, 1975; Douvan & Adelson, 1966; Furman & Bierman, 1984; La Gaipa, 1981; Reisman & Shorr, 1978; Smoller & Youniss, 1982). What has not been clear from these reports is what this implies for friendship interaction and what kinds of attendant considerations this expectation generates. Our observations indicate that this concern has a number of both diffuse and specific consequences for friendship interaction.

The level of enjoyment, entertainment, and satisfaction children experience in play depends almost completely on the level of coordination achieved. By level of coordination we mean the depth of interdependence among the interactive temporal sequences of behavior within the dyad—the extent to which the children fit together their separate lines of action into jointly produced, jointly understood discussions or activities. Two friends having a casual conversation while coloring side by side are participating in coordinated play, albeit at a minimal level. If the two friends are coloring a joint picture, then their play is further coordinated; and if the friends are drawing dinosaurs while letting out dinosaur "roars" in unison, their play is even further coordinated. The level of coordination is defined by the amount of social involvement and attention required of the participants. At the lowest level of involvement, play is coordinated but parallel. It involves conversation that is activity based, conflict free, and not intense. Play at this level is peaceful companionship. At a slightly higher level is joint activity. The attentional demands of this level are slightly higher than those of parallel play, as is the potential for conflict and disagreement. However, joint activity offers much more potential for solidarity, humor, and entertainment than does parallel play. To coordinate play at this and higher levels, children must be adept at managing conflict and excitement, which at a minimum requires children to regulate emotions and to inhibit some actions.

The highest level of coordinated play is fantasy play, as when two friends transform their crayons into "daggers" and their coloring paper into "dragon skin" and begin an adventure. Fantasy play requires continued, fluid negotiation of the roles, acts, props, and settings of the drama (see Corsaro, 1985; Forbes, Katz, & Paul, 1986). It has an unmistakable "flow" (Csikszentmihalyi, 1975), a quality of un-self-conscious involvement in ongoing activities. The children immerse themselves in the activity, ignoring all distractions. Two friends do not simply *act* like tigers or dragons or ghosts— they *become* tigers or dragons or ghosts. Two friends pretending to drive their sick child to the hospital, simultaneously *pretend* to be frightened in this life-or-death situation and *are* frightened. If they were not frightened to some degree, it would hardly be an adventure.[1] The following is an excerpt from the fantasy play of two friends. Bob is fixing their getaway car with a device called a "trouble shooter." Joe is the lookout:

B: Yeah. Let's get back to work. I'll work on the trouble shooter.

J: And I'll watch out for monsters

B: Yes. And in case I see a ghost, I'll use my specter detector.

J: I'm the one who that watches out for, for monsters.

B: And I'm the one who watches out for ghosts.

J: I'm a soldier.

B: Yes. And my name is Ted. I'm from *Ghost Chasers' Magazine.*

---

[1]This is not to say that preschool friends lose sight of the distinction between fantasy and reality. We know from work on metacommunication during fantasy play that this is not the case (see Bateson, 1956; Garvey, 1975; Griffin, 1985; Forbes, Katz, & Paul, 1986). Our claim is only that friends in early childhood are willing to fully immerse themselves in the adventure.

J: . . . Uh, oh, I see a ghost! A ghost don't even need a vest, a suit.

B: Well, I saw a monster.

J: Uh oh, there's a coat, a ghost!

B: And you can't shoot him. 'Cause I'm from *Ghost Chasers' Magazine*.

J: I can just put some stuff in a magazine, ghost. Hey! I got a picture if this come out right. A picture of a ghost's hand. The hand, it's a ghost. We'll put that in our magazine.

Fantasy play has the highest reward potential as well as the highest potential for conflict. When children are comfortable with one another, when they are capable of anticipating each other's upcoming moves, and when they share similar concerns, fantasy play proceeds relatively smoothly. When children are unable to second-guess one another or when their concerns are dissimilar, fantasy play rapidly deteriorates under the weight of disagreement after disagreement. This is why the incidence of fantasy play increases with increasing familiarity (Matthews, 1978), and why many forms of fantasy play are more common among friends than among acquaintances or strangers (Gottman & Parkhurst, 1980; Labinger & Holmberg, 1983; Roopnarine & Field, 1984).

Fantasy play has special significance for children's social and emotional development. It is a laboratory for the rehearsal of adult roles and relationships. It also provides the vehicle for working through major concerns and fears (see Breger, 1974; Corsaro, 1985; Gottman, 1986; Rubin, Fein, & Vandenberg, 1983). Although young children do self-disclose and discuss their fears directly with friends, this is uncommon. Instead they work through their fears with their friends in the context of fantasy. The fantasy context provides children with a safe context in which to distance themselves from intense emotions and the freedom to frame and reframe events in accordance with their wishes. Repetition seems essential to this process. Typically, children create a drama that deals in some form or fashion with a feared object or concept, ensure that the drama ends in some satisfactory, nonthreatening way, and then endlessly rehearse the drama, with only slight variations, in successive play episodes with a friend. For example, Gottman (1986) provides the following account of two best friends' interaction over time:

During the time that Eric and Naomi's conversations were recorded, Naomi was afraid of the dark and slept with a night light. The theme of their pretend play often involved dolls being afraid of the dark. They would turn the lights off and Naomi pretending to be the doll, would scream, and then, as the mommy, comfort the doll. After a few months, Naomi announced to her parents that she no longer needed the night light. Also the theme of being afraid of the dark disappeared from their fantasy play. (p. 160)

Although it has been recognized for some time that fantasy play is part of the child's arsenal for dealing with emotinal and interpersonal concerns (see Rubin et al., 1983), the kinds of concerns that children tackle through fantasy play with friends are not well documented. Naturally, the variability is nearly infinite, because the concerns of any particular pair of friends are the product the unique interests of the individual children. Nonetheless, it does seem to be possible to look across dyads and identify some common themes to fantasy play at this developmental period. In our data, for example, there were several recurrent themes, including: parental abandonment, growing up, power and powerlessness, life and death, and transformations of the self (see Gottman, 1986). The following is an example of a fantasy centering on the theme of parental abandonment. The two friends are playing house:

N   Huh, this is nice. Wow, where are you going? We're going back to our house.

E: This is my house, remember?

N: Where are your parents, remember?

E: My parents? I don't have any parents. My mommy and daddy went; they didn't like me anymore.

N: So they went someplace else?

E: I live here all alone. Hey, you can live with me.

Our listing of friendship fantasy themes would seem to be in partial agreement with that of Griffiths (1935), whose list of recurrent fantasy themes included: smallness and power relations with parents; jealousy and rivalry with siblings; abandonment, separation, and loss; and, birth. It also has much in common with the itemization provided more recently by Corsaro (1985). Corsaro identified three recurrent behavioral routines in the fantasy play of preschoolers: (1) a "lost-found" theme, in which children pretend to be lost in some fantasy world and invite and receive rescue; (2) a "danger-rescue" theme, in which children announce and subsequently avert some impending disaster or threat; and (3) a "death-rebirth" theme, which starts with a sudden pronouncement of death, followed by mourning, and rebirth. Corsaro's argument, like ours, is that each theme reflects an underlying, age-appropriate concern of children. He speculates, for example, that the lost-found theme is:

> a manifestation of and an attempt to cope with an underlying fear. This is the young child's fear of being lost and alone. Many preschool children have directly experienced, even if only briefly, the amorphous and almost overwhelming anxiety that accompanies being lost. If they have not experienced this anxiety first hand, most preschool children have been warned by parents of the danger of getting lost, or have shared the experience vicariously as a result of being told stories or fairy tales (p. 198).

He further argues that:

> by enacting lost-found themes in spontaneous fantasy play, the children are able *to share* both the anxiety of being lost and the relief and joy of being found. In this sense the children are able to directly confront and to cope with their anxiety in peer play without experiencing the actual risks and dangers of being lost in the real world. (p. 199)

Interaction

Friendship interaction in early childhood reveals children's concern for attaining the highest possible level of excitement and stimulation in their play. The salient social processes at this age are the processes involved in coordinating play: activity talk including fantasy role playing, conflict management, and play escalation and deescalation. One might assume that, given the desire, joint activity play is easily achieved by pairs of children. Certainly it sometimes appears that way to the casual adult observer, who may be surprised to find his or her child engrossed in sandbox play with another child only moments after arriving at the preschool in the morning. In fact, however, highly coordinated play is achieved only through doggedly persistent effort on the part of the participants. And this is true even among children who are friends. The finding that preschool children join the play of friends more successfully and more directly than that of nonfriends (Gottman & Parkhurst, 1980; Labinger & Holmberg, 1983; Rotherham & Phinney, 1981) in no way implies that the tasks facing friends are not formidable: A great deal of goundwork must be laid, and interactional success and failure must be closely monitored and adjusted to. To achieve even reasonably high levels of coordination in their play, friends must maintain clear communication, manage conflicts that arise, agree more than they disagree, and take the perspectives of one another. To maintain fantasy play, in particular, they must do all these things plus negotiate and renegotiate themes, props, roles, acts, and settings (Bateson, 1956; Forbes et al., 1986; Griffin, 1985).

Attaining highly coordinated play with friends is not a smooth, gradual process. Rather, it is achieved as a result of a number of tentative steps, which we call play escalations in our coding systems. An extended example from Gottman (1986) serves to illustrate this process. Two young friends are playing in parallel:

J: I got a fruit cutter plate.
D: Mine's white.
J: You got white playdough and this color and that color.
D: Every color. That's the colors we got.

They continue playing, escalating the responsiveness demand directly to one another:

D: I'm putting pink in the blue.

J: Mix pink.

D: Pass the blue.

J: I think I'll pass the blue.

They next move toward doing the same thing together (true collaborative activity):

D: And you make those for after we get it together, OK?

J: 'Kay.

D: Have to make these.

J: Pretend like those little roll cookies, too, OK?

D: And make, um, make a, um, pancake, too.

J: Oh rats. This is a little pancake.

D: OK. Make, make me, um, make two flat cookies. 'Cause I'm, I'm cutting any, I'm cutting this. My snake.

The next escalation includes offers:

J: You want all my blue?

D: Yes. To make cookies. Just to make cookies, but we can't mess the cookies all up.

J: Nope.

They then introduce a joint activity and begin using "we" terms in describing the activity:

D: Put this the right way, OK? *We're* making supper, huh?

J: *We're* making supper. Maybe *we* could use, if you get white, *we* could use that too maybe.

D: I don't have any white. Yes, *we*, yes, I do.

J: If you got some white, *we* could have some, y'know.

As they continue to play, they employ occasional contextual reminders that this is a joint activity:

D: Oh, we've got to have our dinner. Try to make some.

Escalation is not always successful, however, and when it is not, children often return to lower levels of coordinated play—a process we call deescalation in our coding systems. In a continuation of the preceding example, D tries to introduce some fantasy. This is not successful. J is first allocated a low-status role (baby), then a higher status role (sister), then a higher status (but still not an equal-status) role (big sister):

D:　I'm the mommy.
J:　Who am I?
D:　Um, the baby.
J:　Daddy.
D:　Sister.
J:　I wanna be the daddy.
D:　You're the sister.
J:　Daddy.
D:　You're the *big* sister.
J:　Don't wanna play house. I don't want to play house.

The level of play is deescalated (for the time being):

J:　Just play eat-eat. We can play eat-eat. We have to play that way.

The complexity of establishing highly coordinated play is apparent.

Preschool children seem to at least implicitly recognize the difficulty with which coordinated play is achieved. Corsaro (1985) notes that third parties trying to enter ongoing dyadic play very often meet rebuff or rejection. Corsaro proposes that preschoolers reject entering children to protect "interactive space"; young children have trouble maintaining complex dyadic interaction structures, and so they exclude others to maintain high-quality interaction.

A climate of interpersonal agreement and solidarity is essential for successful coordinated play, and several other conversational processes in early childhood seem directed toward this end. For example, a good deal of young children's friendship conversation involves social comparison processes (exploration of similarities and differences). But it is not so much the nature of their similarities, as the *presence* of commonalities that interests these children. Indeed, children destined to become friends sometimes give the appearance of going to almost any length to find commonality, regardless of how frivolous (A: "We both have chalk on our hands"; B: "Right!"). Social comparison comprises a good deal of older friends' conversation as well; but in older children, social comparison is more directed toward helping the friends understand themselves (see pp. 120–123) than toward establishing esprit de corps.

Gossip—that is, conversation about nonpresent third parties—also functions toward a similar end in young friends' conversations. Gossip is a very large part of middle childhood friendship (see pp. 113–116). In early childhood, however, gossip is less frequent, very brief, and usually occurs in the context of play. More importantly, gossip in early childhood has a "we against others" quality that seems to function as an end in itself:

B: Danny and Jeff did that. They did. They're dumb, aren't they?
S: Yeah.
B: Aren't they?
S: Yeah!

Gossip at this age may even contain direct references to we-ness. For example:

S: Go! We want her to go away. [*hammering*]
B: We don't want Alison here to bother us again.
S: We're very mad at her.
B: We are very mad.

Like social comparison processes at this age, gossip seems directed toward the establishment of a climate of agreement and solidarity, which makes high levels of coordinated play possible.

Friendship conversation at this age has another quality that reveals the centrality of sustained coordinated play during this period. Young children have greater difficulty than older children managing conflict and preventing small disagreements from escalating into long squabbles (Gottman & Parkhurst, 1980). On this basis, we might expect the friendship interaction of young children to be more conflicted than that of older children, as the young friends may be less able to keep disagreements in check. In fact, just the opposite is true: Young friends more successfully avoid negative affect and other dangerous social processes such as disagreement sequences than do older friends (Gottman & Parkhurst). This finding seems less paradoxical if one considers that squabbles have their most serious impact on children's ability to sustain complex forms of play, as we saw in the fantasy play of D and J. As coordinated play declines in importance as the central goal of friendship, so too does the need to avoid negative affect and conflict at almost any cost. Older friends are less obliged to mask their disappointments and disagreements in polite compliance or compromise.

Affective Developments

We noted earlier that friendship is one context in which children learn how to regulate their emotions and emotional displays to others. There is evidence that even infants are able to regulate their emotions and emotional displays to others to some extent (Campos et al., 1983). Nonetheless, even by early childhood, children are still a long way from being able to behave competently in the context of emotion-eliciting social transactions. The preschooler's understanding of emotions is still very concrete and undifferentiated, and children of this age have difficulty comprehending that a person can experience more than one emotion at a time (Harter, 1982). Moreover, preschoolers have a very limited mastery of display and feeling rules (Saarni, 1979); they are less likely than older children to know that the overt emotional displays of others may not match their covert emotional experience, or to strategically use their own facial expressions to pretend to like or dislike some pleasant or unpleasant event or object (Saarni, 1980). Indeed the preschooler is grappling with an even more fundamental task, that of modulating affect. Young children are emotionally labile (Maccoby, 1980). They can become flooded by emotional states—both positive and negative—that dominate their attention and disorganize their behavior. With development, children learn to control their emotions and to organize their behavior in the face of arousal. And they learn to cope with circumstances that interfere with immediate satisfaction of their needs and wishes. Maccoby pointed out that inhibition of action is a key to organized behavior. Actions must be delayed until the consequences are more appropriate. When goal-directed activity is blocked, ineffectual behavioral responses must be abandoned in favor of more adaptive responses. Frustration must be tolerated, and gratification delayed.

If one thinks of the requirements of coordinated play with friends, it is obvious that friendship is an extremely important context for learning how to manage one's emotions. If play is to be coordinated, it is simply not always possible to get one's own way. In service of the overall adventure, children must inhibit some actions; accept influence at times; and maintain organized behavior and attention in the face of anger, fear, joy, and excitement. Friendships in early childhood are clearly integral to affective growth.

FRIENDSHIPS IN MIDDLE CHILDHOOD: "DID YOU HEAR WHAT KATIE DID?"

Underlying Theme or Concern

As children move from early to middle childhood their social world undergoes important transformations (Higgins & Parsons, 1983). Social contacts increase dramatically with entry into elementary school. Moreover, children are not just exposed to far greater numbers of other children—the makeup of the peer group becomes more complex as well. There is increased exposure to representatives of various ascribed statuses (e.g., race, sex, ethnicity) and children encounter variability in peer personalities that was heretofore unimagined. Peer groups begin to become segregated on the basis of sex and, to a lesser extent, race and to become stratified into popularity and power hierarchies (Hartup, 1984). In addition, small, voluntary, informal cliques and coalitions begin to form among children with mutual friends or common interests.

These structural changes in social networks are accompanied by important attitudinal and motivational changes. By middle childhood, the attitudes and reactions of peers have come to rival those of parents in terms of importance to children's self-definition and self-esteem (Markus & Nurius, 1984). The basis for self-evaluation has also changed. Whereas the younger child is likely to evaluate his or her behavioral performance against a set of absolute standards, the middle childhood child is much more likely to base self-evaluation on a comparison of personal behavior with that of others (Markus & Nurius; Ruble, 1983). In addition, children in middle childhood are much more knowledgeable of the social forces on behavior and of the benefits of behaving in accordance with such forces (Markus & Nurius). Skills for self-presentation (Jones & Pittman, 1982) and impression management (Fine, 1980) develop, allowing children to shape their behaviors to create desired social impressions of themselves in specific persons within the social environment.

These and other factors conspire to create in chidren of this age a strong desire for belonging and social acceptance. Children recognize that classmates have different statuses and that their play groups are hierarchically arranged (e.g., Crockett et al., 1984). They also are aware of the many advantages of membership in small friendship cliques and are well informed with respect to the individuals who are inside and outside of these various primary reference groups. Just as importantly, they know, or soon come to learn, that in-group and out-group membership is a volatile, occasionally capricious affair. In the words of one author reflecting on his experience with children's descriptions of friendship at this age:

> what appears over and over again is the concern of children over their potential to be "hurt" and a vulnerability to rejection, to ridicule, and to exploitation. Instead of the order and rationality of the market-place implied by the notion of reciprocity, we find instead much emotion and anxiety; indeed there is an almost "jungle-like" quality to the way some children describe their social environment. (La Gaipa, 1981, p. 180)

As a consequence, children are often in a state of some insecurity about their social position and acceptability and devote considerable energy to trying to buttress their social status and guard against rejection. It is this broad concern for the understanding of and the gaining of social acceptance that underpins friendship interaction at this age.

Interaction

Gossip is far and away the most salient social process in friendship interaction at this age. Not only does gossip, primarily disparaging gossip, make up the great bulk of the content of conversation among middle childhood friends, but other social processes, such as information exchange, exploration of similarities, humor, and self-disclosure, occur almost exclusively in the context of gossip. Thus, gossip is the mortar as well as much of the brick of friendship conversation in middle childhood.

Gossip is so central to friendship interaction at this age because it serves at once to reaffirm membership in important same-sex peer social groups and to reveal the core attitudes, beliefs, and behaviors that constitute the basis for inclusion in or exclusion from these groups. As children gossip, they reaffirm the norms and values of their particular network (Fine, 1981; Cluckman, 1968; Rysman, 1977). For example, consider the conversation of two middle childhood friends, Erica and Mikaila, discussing a third classmate, Katie. In a lighthearted conversation that lasted for almost 45 minutes, the girls enumerated a whole set of norms and indicated their contempt for Katie's violations of these norms. Here are five of them:

1. *Not sharing*

E: Oh, see, um, you know that tub she gave us for the spider?
M: Yeah.
E: She acts like she owns the whole thing.
M: The whole spider.
E: I know.

2. *Being a crybaby*

M: Yeah, and she always cries about little things. Right, Erica?
E: Right, Mikaila?

3. *Being bossy or aggressive*

M: She's mean. She beat me up once [*laughs*]. I could hardly breathe, she hit me in the stomach so hard.
E: She acts like . . .
M: she's the boss.
E: "Now you do this." [*mimicking Katie*]
M: "And I'll . . ."
E: "And Erica, you do this. And you substitute for people who aren't here, Erica."
M: "And you do this, Mikaila. And you shouldn't do that, you shouldn't, you have to talk like this. You understand? Here. I'm the teacher here."
E: I know. She always acts like she's the boss.

4. *Telling lies*

M: Katie said that her father child-abuses her, and that she burned herself, that he burned her finger. This, this finger? This one right there? And, um, uh, about a week later after I looked at her finger, this one? And it, and, and there wasn't a burn. It was gone.

E: And remember she said that her father took a . . .

M: hot . . .

E: . . . burning hot iron and put it on her . . .

M: back.

E: And she said it was still there.

M: Yeah. And when she was wearing a one-piece bathing suit and she had to take it off you, you looked on her back and there was nothing there.

E: No, it was just a plain back.

5. *Being a tattletale*

E: Katie's just a . . .

M: tattletale.

E: Yeah, she tells on everything.

M: Yeah.

Where clear norms do not already exist, gossip provides children with a low-risk means for sampling peer attitudes, one that does not require making one's own views explicit first. Armed with knowledge of friends' reactions to the attitudes or behaviors of others, the child can tailor his or her behavior to preempt awkward, alienating, or embarrassing exchanges. Perhaps this is one reason why the objects of friends' gossip are frequently movie, sport, and rock stars, and in particular the sexual and drug exploits of these individuals (Fine, 1987; Gottman & Mettetal, 1987). Because sex and drug use are still relatively uncommon practices in preadolescents, children of this age are unlikely to have much opportunity to sample peer attitudes toward these practices through gossip about classmates.

As noted, gossip appears to be the backdrop for most other social processes in friendship at this age. As one example, humor in friendship frequently involves finding witty ways to disparage others:

A: [*drawing*] This is the way I draw Gale, as a fish 'cause I don't like Gale, So, do you?

B: I guess not.

A: And I think Gale is one of those ugly fish that go to the bottom of the sea and that's where they should stay.

Likewise, self-disclosure typically occurs as a reaction to something that emerges in gossip. For example, in the following excerpt from two 12-year-olds, discussion of classmates leads to one friend's (B) discovery that an acquaintance likes the same boy she likes. This prompts some solidarity self-disclosure:

A: She likes him?
B: Yeah. Oh, I wasn't supposed to tell you that. So just forget it. [*laughs*]
A: [*nonchalantly*] I wouldn't get mad. He likes Lucy.
B: He does? If he breaks up with you because of Lucy I will be so mad.

Affective Developments

Children in middle childhood are continuing to grapple with the complex task they begun in early childhood, that of managing emotions in a relational context. The task is no less difficult at this age:

> Anecdotal evidence suggests that during middle childhood children have some of their most intense emotional experiences. They can be devastated when they are rejected by a desired peer group, club, or team, and they can be enormously proud of themselves when they get a perfect score on a test or win an athletic event. (Markus & Nurius, 1984; p. 156)

But it has changed somewhat in nature. Whereas the child in early childhood is struggling to maintain behavioral organization in the face of intense emotion, the older child is directing greater energy toward abstracting display and feeling rules from friends' and other peers' reactions to emotional displays. Later in development, in adolescence, these display and feeling rules will be complex and subtle. For the moment, however, they are relatively crude: The rule of thumb is that open sentimentality is almost always to be avoided, even with one's friends. Rank sentimentality can lead to peer group rejection (or at least that is what children believe) at a time when concerns about acceptance are great. Instead, children reject emotionality in favor of reason and rationality, or at least try to project such an impression in their friendship interaction. The impression to be maintained is one of being "cool"— calm, unruffled, and always under emotional control.

An aversion to sentimentality has often been attributed to boys of this age, who are sometimes portrayed as preferring to sooner die than to admit affection (e.g., Fine, 1987; Stone & Church, 1957). But it applies to girls of this age as well. Indeed, one of us had the experience of interviewing two female 12-year-old best friends about their friendship. The mothers of these two girls were also friends, and after a while the discussion came to center on the ways in which their own friendship differed from that of their mothers. The girls insisted that their own friendship was superior to that of their mothers because it contained none of the overt sentimentality that evidently plagued their mothers' friendship. The girls described with some consternation and considerable embarrassment occasions when their mothers had exchanged "Hallmarky" notes—notes of appreciation that read like sentimental greeting cards.

The concerns during middle childhood for appearing unemotional find their clearest expression in conversation about embarrassment. Occasions of embarrassment are a common topic of self-disclosure at this age, and discussion of others' embarrassing *faux pas* are also a common form of gossip. Embarrassing situations involve being noticed and exposed. A critical component involves being "uncool" and stared at. Almost anything has the potential to become an embarrassing social event, including such seemingly innocuous events as spilling a soft drink or sitting at the wrong desk. But there are two areas in particular that are fraught with danger of embarrassment: sexuality and cross-sex relations. Some children begin to experience biological changes associated with puberty toward the end of the middle childhood period. This can lead to situations of embarrassment, as it did for these two female best friends:

J: You know what Mom did? Every time I go shopping with my mom and we're looking for a bra [*laughs*] she takes the bra rack and picks one of them. "Would this look good on you, Julie?" And everyone's staring at you. [*laughs*]. So embarrassing.

B: My mom always pulls the rack and holds them up to me!

Similarly, although cross-sex relations during this period are still highly ritualized, friends in middle childhood regularly and routinely "accuse" one another of romantic involvement with others, which occasions embarrassment and emphatic denial:

A: How's Lance? [*giggles*] Has he taken you to the movie yet?

B: No! Saw him today but I don't care.

A: Didn't he say anything to you?

B: Oh . . .

A: Lovers! [*tauntingly*]

B: Shut up!

A: Lovers at first sight! [*giggles*]

B: [*giggles*] Quit it!

Although part of the motivation to deny sentiment is based on the desire to avoid peer group criticism and taunting, undoubtedly other factors also come into play. In particular, it is likely that the motive for rejecting emotionality in favor of reason and rationality is at least in part due to the children's desire to flex their newfound cognitive muscle. Operational thought develops in middle childhood, heralding increasingly sophisticated skills for integrating ideas and plans (see Fischer & Bullock, 1984), and raising children's epistemological consciousness. In particular, children of this age develop a fascination with rules, and with the philosophical and the logical. Gurian and Formanek (1983) provide a delightful illustration of how this fascination can be played out in the context of friendship. Jonathon, a 10-year-old, recounts an argument he had with his best friend, Aaron:

> I said: Nothing is impossible, if you get technical.
> He said: It's impossible that at this very second you could fly.
> I said: Wait a minute, it's possible that a strong wind could come along and pick me off the ground.
> He said: It's impossible to relive yesterday.
> I said: If you went faster than the speed of light out of this earth's atmosphere, you could go into a time warp. (p. 66)

It is not hard to see how such a love affair with logic is incongruous with the decidedly nonlogical world of hot emotions.

FRIENDSHIPS IN ADOLESCENCE: "WHO AM I? WHO WILL I BECOME?"

Underlying Theme or Concern

Higgins and Parsons (1983) wrote of the social motives and concerns of adolescents:

> Adolescents . . . are expected to acquire and practice the social skills of adults, to experiment with what they are in relation to others, and to "try on" new behaviors and experiences. In other words, they are expected to begin the process of attaining a somewhat coherent, permanent answer to the questions "Who am I?" and "What will I become?" (p. 29)

Our observations make it clear that this process of defining who one is and who one will become is the underlying theme of friendship at this age. Adolescents and their friends discuss themselves and their futures outright and abstractly:

A: I don't know. Gosh, I have no idea what I want to do. And it really doesn't bother me that much that I don't have my future planned. [*laughs*]

B: [*laughs*]

A: [*laughs*] Like it bothers my Dad a lot, but it doesn't bother me.

B: Just tell your dad what I always tell my Dad: "Dad, I *am*."

A: [laughs] Exactly!

B: "And whatever happens tomorrow, I *still* will be!"

And they discuss themselves in relation to particular peer subgroups, as in the following comment of one adolescent girl to her best friend:

A: I don't have the qualities that general Calvin Kleiners [children who wear jeans designed by Calvin Klein] do and I don't get any security from the label. I just wear them as a pair of pants that keep me warm, and it's very obscene to go nude!

A peer subgroup, such as the trendy Calvin Kleiners in the above example, presents the adolescent with a set of expectations, practices, and ambitions that he or she may either accept or reject. The task of accepting or rejecting the norms of particular peer subgroups is part of the larger task of differentiating what is "me" from what is "not me," of developing what Goffman (1959) calls the "territories of the self." Whether through abstract, philosophical discussion or through gossip about others, what our observations make clear is that the territories of the self are in part worked out through discussion with friends.

The adolescent's task of self-exploration is made more complex by changes that have taken place since middle childhood in the fabric of the social niche. Most importantly, adolescent friendship groups are increasingly heterogeneous with respect to sex (Dunphy, 1966; Montemayor & Van Komen, 1985), and dating begins in earnest at this age. Thus, the adolescent operates in the mixed-gender as well as the same-gender peer culture. This circumstance and the biological changes that accompany puberty present the adolescent with entirely novel self-referent issues, most notably sexuality:

A: [*joking*] I think you should take Randy to court for statutory rape.

B: I don't. I'm to the point of wondering what "that kind of girl" is . . . I don't know about the whole scene.

A: The thing is . . .

B: It depends on the reasoning. And how long you've been going out with somebody.

A: Yeah. I'm satisfied with my morals.

At the same time, from the standpoint of cognitive maturity, the adolescent has probably never been better prepared to handle such thorny issues. Adolescence is the age of formal operational thought. Adolescents are capable of truly "thinking beyond old limits," of contemplating abstract possibilities and ideals, and of deliberate self-accusatory introspection (see, for example, Keating, 1980). These skills were only just emerging in middle childhood. Perspective-taking now matures (Selman, 1980), allowing adolescents to view themselves and their relationships, if they wish, with more objectivity than has ever been possible in the past. They can consider many viewpoints at a time, see alternatives, appreciate difficult decisions, and state hypotheses about problems and test them out. Adolescents are in a unique position to offer compassion and aid to their friends and to see their friends, themselves, and their problems in a longer perspective (Reisman, 1985). Indeed, adolescents see this as an obligation of friendship (Smoller & Youniss, 1982).

Interaction

The salient social process at this age is honest, intimate self-disclosure. Other social processes—notably humor, gossip, problem-solving, social comparison, and mindreading—operate to prompt and promulgate self-disclosure. Self-disclosure enjoys something of a privileged status in the literature on friendship. Psychologists generally view the amount of reciprocal intimate self-disclosure in a particular relationship as a measure of the closeness of that relationship. Conversely, they are reluctant to label a particular relationship a close friendship in the absence of a demonstrated willingness to share personal or private thoughts and feelings with each other (Mannarino, 1976; Oden, Herzberger, Mangione, & Wheeler, 1984; Serafica, 1982; Sullivan, 1953). Studies using interviews and questionnaires rather consistently indicate that adolescents emphasize self-disclosure, openness, and affection as components of friendship to a greater extent than younger children do, both in their general beliefs about friendships (Bigelow, 1977; Bigelow & La Gaipa, 1975; Douvan & Adelson, 1966; Furman & Bierman, 1984; Hunter & Youniss, 1982; Kon & Losenkov, 1978; Reisman & Shorr, 1978; Selman, 1980; Smoller & Youniss, 1982) and in their descriptions of their actual friendships (Berndt, 1986a; Berndt & Perry, 1986; Buhrmester & Furman, 1987; Crockett et al. 1984; Rivenbark, 1971; Sharabany, Gershoni, & Hofman, 1981). Thus, our conclusion about the importance of self-disclosure at this age is a familiar one. Observational studies of self-disclosure in adolescence friendship—or in friendship at any age—are exceedingly rare, however, leaving much to be learned about how self-disclosure is initiated and responded to in adolescent friendship.

Our observational data indicate that self-disclosure at this age is a different type of social event from self-disclosure at younger ages. To begin with, disclosures are responded to differently in adolescent friendships. At younger ages, a self-disclosure prompts a statement of solidarity ("Oh, I know! Me too"), but little else. In adolescence, self-disclosures occasion psychological attributions and lengthy discussions about the nature of the problem and possible avenues to its resolution. Consider this following representative excerpt:

L: But the thing is, if my parents go to Mexico in the middle of July, I won't; then I'll be missing the last two weeks of summer school. If I have to go.

R: Then, then, then you can't go.

L: I know. That's the thing, that's what I've been trying to. God, it's a hard decision. I don't know which would be better, going to Mexico, I mean, 'cause I don't know when I'll get a chance to go to Mexico again. Or just to stay here and get away from my parents for a while because I really need to.

R: If you went to Mexico would you be, would you be around your parents more or less?

L: Oh, constantly.

R: When you go on vacations with them do you get along with them very well?

L: I do, yeah. It's really amazing whenever we go on vacation.

R: It might be good for you.

L: That's what I was thinking, you know. I don't know.

In addition, adolescents are much more confrontational in their exchanges around self-disclosure than younger children:

A: You missed two weeks of school.

B: I know. That's what Dad said. He said, "I guess London didn't help your grades," and I said . . .

A: No, and then you came back and were depressed and that didn't help school too much either. I mean, not wanting to be there doesn't help things at all.

B: I've got to get my grades up.

A: You're only allowed one B this quarter.

B: Yep.

A: You work your tail off in English.

B: Yeah. I'll get an A in English now.

A: OK. [That bad grade] was your fault.

B: [*giggle*]

A: Because you were a stubborn little twit. [*jokingly*]

Such confrontation and honesty are signs of intimacy.

Finally, adolescents will self-disclose about the friendship itself. The intimacy of the friendship becomes a *topic* of conversation for the first time at this age. Younger friends will occasionally comment on their friendship with one another, either as a means to resolving disputes and facilitating coordinated play or as a show of solidarity and in-group membership. But adolescents will express their satisfaction or dissatisfaction with the *quality* of the intimacy of the relationship and discuss possible directions for the relationship:

Jane: I feel kind of icky about the past two weeks.

Suzie: What? What in the past two weeks do you feel icky about?

Jane: It was like "Hi, Jane," "Hi, Suzie," [*giggle*] you know. [*giggle*]

Suzie: Yeah.

Jane: "Hi, Jane," "Hi, Suzie."

Suzie: We didn't communicate. I haven't been communicating much with anybody.

Jane: I understand that. But I felt like, you know, Janet was . . .

Suzie: Janet had taken your place?

Jane: Yeah. That's what I felt like.

Suzie: Janet's not gonna take your place, kiddo. [*sigh*] How many times do I have to tell you that?

Jane: I'm insecure, you know.

Another change since middle childhood is the emergence of positive gossip. This change is partly due to a newfound willingness to admit attraction to the opposite sex, as in this example:

A: I can't handle any more [boyfriends].

B: Yes, you can!

A: [*laughs*] OK, I'll try.

B: Five more. [*pause*] I want that blondie.

A: He's cute, but he could be a real jerk. You never know.

Gossip involving negative evaluations continues to play a role in the lives and conversations of friends of this age, but it has a different form and function. The purpose of middle childhood gossip is discovering the norms of same-sex peer groups. It also promotes in-group solidarity. Although adolescent friendship gossip has this purpose, it serves the additional purpose of self-exploration, as in the following example from two female friends:

A: I can't stand the way she plays games so bad with all her boyfriends.

B: And they take it.

A: Uh, they play right back. That's the thing. "I wanna see other people." "Oh, no, please don't see other people. I love you, I love you."

B: [*laughs*]

A: And then the other one does it next week.

The girls' disparagement of the dating practices of others is as much an attempt to come to a comfortable understanding of their own position on these important issues as it is an attempt to promote solidarity between themselves.

Affective Developments

Many of the challenges of emotional development are behind adolescents. Most adolescents can maintain organized behavior in the face of high positive or negative arousal, and most can cope adaptively with circumstances that interfere with immediate satisfaction of their needs and wishes. Adolescents have relatively mature conceptions of emotions; they understand, for example, that people can experience ambivalent emotions, and they are able to integrate emotionally laden social constructs, such as nice and mean, into general abstract categories (Fischer & Bullock, 1984). Further, adolescents have a very sophisticated understanding of emotion display and feeling rules (Strayer, 1986), even if that understanding is only implicit. They no longer feel compelled to deny emotions outright in most circumstances or to insist to friends and others that their actions are motivated by nothing more than logic and reason. Instead, they appreciate that their own actions and those of others are often motivated by emotions (guilt, jealousy, anger, attraction, etc.) and that behavioral choices made under such circumstances can be illogical. But for all their progress, adolescents are still only part way to mature emotional competence. In the vista ahead they will integrate reason and emotion into a complex, versatile understanding of the role of emotions in the development and evolution of relationships.

Adolescent friends expend great amounts of energy analyzing the affective implications of interpersonal events and relationships. Sometimes this takes the form of discussions of interpersonal situations that cause themselves or people they know to overreact, lose control, cry, or get angry. At other times, it takes the form of affect-laden discussions of relationships and relationship changes (e.g., the breakup of friendships, the departure of a sibling to college, or the separation from a parent through death or divorce). In the following example, two adolescent girl friends compare their experiences with parents. Note the repeated reference to feelings:

R: 'Cause, see, when I go on vacation with my parents, I do *not* get along with them.

L: Really?

R: 'Cause I feel stuck with them and I just feel more imprisoned than I ever do. And I just sit there. [*laughs*]

L: It's so funny. You know, whenever my parents are away from everything it's like we really have compatible personalities. It's really nice when we go on trips, you know, 'cause I always feel so close to 'em. But like whenever, whenever I'm just at home, just because they just resent it a lot that I do lots of things outside the house and you know they just want me to stay home and I don't, and I'm not going to either. You know, and it's not, it's not. The thing is, they they take it personally, you know. They think that I'm getting away from them. And I'm not. And that's like the basis of like why we've been getting along so horribly lately. Just because they think I'm trying to get away from them.

The sphere of cross-gender romantic relations provides especially fertile ground for the integration of logic and emotion at this age. Whereas the preadolescent will deny attraction to the opposite sex, adolescents frankly acknowledge such emotions to friends. Further, an adolescent will turn to a best friend for help in interpreting emotions at the breakup of an intimate relationship:

J: [I want to] Throw the phone down and run back to John. I don't know about that. I've been wandering around sort of feeling kinda lost.

B: [*giggle*] Yeah.

J: People look at me, "What's the matter, Judy?" "Oh, I don't know." [*resignedly*]

B: You are coping with things much better than I did, though, [*giggle*] I must say.

The changes that have occurred since middle childhood are dramatic indeed.

Comments, Caveats, and Future Directions

In the preceding pages we presented the outline of a developmental model of the functions of friendships. As we noted at the outset, we are not the first (or last!) authors to wrestle with the same issue of the functions of friendships in childhood. Over the years, a number of other authors have undertaken this task, with the result that there now exist several alternative itemized lists of the various ways children benefit from their friendships. Without disparaging these earlier efforts, it is important to recognize that our model differs in several significant ways from the taxonomies of the past.

To begin with, past efforts are to certain extent developmentally static—

they emphasize the provisions of friendships that are invariant across development. Certainly, some authors (e.g., Furman & Robbins, 1985; Sullivan, 1953) have recognized that some friendship provisions, such as intimacy, are particularly salient at specific points in development. But it is one thing to describe how specific friendship provisions wax and wane with age and quite another to locate friendship in the broad context of child development. If we have been successful, we have conveyed the viewpoint that friendship operates as the nexus of developmental growth in social and emotional competence, and therefore has different functions at different points in development. In early childhood, friendship functions are closely tied to the social contextual demands of maximizing the excitement and amusement levels in play and to the challenges of organizing behavior in the face of such arousal. In middle childhood, when anxiety about peer relations develops, friendships serve children's needs for knowledge of behavioral norms and help them learn skills for self-presentation and impression management, especially with respect to emotional displays. In adolescence, friendships help children to explore themselves and to integrate logic and emotions.

In addition, with the notable exception of Fine (1980; 1981; 1987), past formulations for the most part have been generated without clear and systematic efforts to account for the actual behavior of friends across development. We would agree with Hartup (1986), who cautions that, as in any relationship, unless we have a clear description of friendship interaction, we cannot hope to understand friendship functions. Indeed, discouragingly little observational work on friendship exists, despite periodic calls for such data (e.g., Berndt, 1986b; Fine, 1980; Gottman & Parkhurst, 1980; Montemayor & Van Komen, 1985; Roopnarine & Field, 1984; Rubenstein, 1984; Tesch, 1983). Perhaps the reason for this is the pernicious assumption that once someone has told you about a friendship there are no surprises to be had in watching the friends together. Our experience is that the opposite is true. Observation leads to many surprises, phenomena, and mysteries about the nature of that relationship.

An interesting methodological point arises from the juxtaposition of the two points above: Although observational coding systems can be devised that will reliably code specific social processes in friends of ages 4 to 16, the interpretation of developmental changes in code frequencies or usage is difficult because the function of the same social process is different at different ages. Disparaging gossip in early childhood, for example, serves to establish a climate of agreement and solidarity as a prerequisite of coordinated play. In middle childhood, however, disparaging gossip serves to reaffirm membership in important same-gender peer groups and to reveal the core attitudes, beliefs, and behaviors that constitute the basis for inclusion in and exclusion from these groups. Still later, in adolescence, disparaging gossip is part of the process by which the child delimits behaviors that are or are not self-relevant. The researcher bent on coding changes in gossip from early childhood to adolescence must recognize not only changes in its form, but also in its function.

Our model of the functions of friendships is meant to be provocative. It is unabashedly speculative, based on inferences drawn from the coding and analysis of friendship conversations. Historically, friendship researchers have shown a strong tendency to favor experimental hypothesis-testing methods over hypothesis-generating methods (Hinde, 1979). As we have written elsewhere (Parker, 1987), a comprehensive account of friendship demands an iterative process of description, speculation, and experimentation. Our model, then, should be taken in the spirit of a research agenda and not a factual description. There is more than a pressing need for research that directly links developmental changes in the ways friends relate to one another to normative changes in children's social networks (size, heterogeneity, composition), expected roles, self-perceptions, and concerns.[2] Likewise, it is essential that researchers begin to examine the developmental link between properties of friendship interactions and (1) children's knowledge and use of emotional display and feeling rules and (2) children's "meta"-understanding of affect in relationships.

A concluding comment on generalizability is also warranted. Inductive inferences depend heavily for their accuracy on the representativeness of their data base. We wish to acknowledge two features of our data base that may bear on the generalizability of our conclusions. First, it is possible that our portrayal of friendships is more true for white, middle-class children than for children of other ethnic and socioeconomic groups because our studies have been largely limited to such groups. More descriptive work on the nature of friendships among minority children and children of low income is needed, even as work continues on white, middle-class samples. Similarly, because the bulk of our work is based on observations of girls, it is possible that our model is a more accurate representation of the functions of girls' friendships than of boys'. Girls' friendships and boys' friendships are known to differ in some important ways, especially with respect to intimacy and self-disclosure (see, for example, Berndt, 1986a; Berndt & Perry, 1986; Buhrmester & Furman, 1987; Crockett et al., 1984; Douvan & Adelson, 1966; Furman & Buhrmester, 1985; Hobart, 1987, Hunter & Youniss, 1982; Sharabany et al., 1981). Although many of these differences may be more stylistic than substantive (see Ginsberg & Gottman, 1987), male and female friendships may have at least somewhat disparate sets of functions.

---

[2]It bears mentioning that, although we have treated them as such, these factors are not really normative in the sense that they are constant across all children. The networks, self-perceptions, and concerns of popular and unpopular children are distinctive in many important respects (see Hymel & Franke, 1985; Ladd, 1983). These differences must be taken into account. Indeed, almost nothing is known of the differences between popular and unpopular children in terms of friendship quality and friendship interaction. The functions of friendships are undoubtedly very different in these two groups.

It is our hope that this chapter serves to prompt others to undertake the research necessary to address these and the other issues we have raised.

REFERENCES

Asher, S. R., & Coie, J. D. (Eds.). (in press) *Peer rejection in childhood*. New York: Cambridge University Press.

Asher, S. R., & Renshaw, P. D. (1981). Children without friends: Social knowledge and social skill training. In S. R. Asher & J. M. Gottman (Eds.), *The development of children's friendships* (pp. 273–298). New York: Cambridge University Press.

Austin, M. C., & Thompson, G. G. (1948). Children's friendships: A study of the bases on which children select and reject their best friends. *Journal of Educational Psychology, 39,* 101–116.

Bateson, G. (1956). The message "this is play." In O. Schaffner (Ed.), *Group processes: Transactions of the second conference*. New York: Macy Foundation.

Berndt, T. J. (1984). Sociometric, social-cognitive, and behavioral measures for the study of friendship and popularity. In T. Field. J. L. Roopnarine, & M. Segal (Eds.), *Friendships in normal and handicapped children* (pp. 31–52). Norwood, NJ: Ablex.

Berndt, T. J. (1986a). Children's comments about their friendships. In M. Perlmutter (Ed.), *Minnesota symposia on child psychology: Vol. 18. Cognitive perspectives on children's social and behavioral development* (pp. 189–212) Hinsdale, NJ: Lawrence Erlbaum.

Berndt, T. J., (1986b). Sharing between friends: Contexts and consequences. In E. C. Mueller & C. R. Cooper (Eds.), *Process and outcome in peer relationships* (pp. 105–127). New York: Academic Press.

Berndt, T. J., & Perry, T. B., (1986). Children's perceptions of friendships as supportive relationships. *Developmental Psychology, 22,* 640–648.

Berscheid, E. (1986). Emotional experience in close relationships: Some implications for child development. In W. W. Hartup & Z. Rubin (Eds.), *Relationships and development* (pp. 135–166). Hinsdale, NJ: Lawrence Erlbaum.

Bigelow, B. J. (1977). Children's friendship expectations: A cognitive developmental study. *Child Development, 48,* 246–253.

Bigelow, B. J., & La Gaipa, J. J. (1975). Children's written descriptions of friendships: A multidimensional study. *Developmental Psychology, 11,* 857–858.

Breger, L. (1974). *From instinct to identity: The development of personality*. Englewood Cliffs, NJ: Prentice-Hall.

Bronfenbrenner, U. (1979). *The ecology of human development*. Cambridge, MA: Harvard University Press.

Buhrmester, D., & Furman. W. (1987). The development of companionship and intimacy. *Child Development, 58,* 1101–1113.

Campos, J. J., Barrett, K. C., Lamb, M. E., Goldsmith, H. H., & Stenberg, C. (1983). Socioemotional development. In M. M. Haith & J. J. Campos (Eds.), *Handbook of child psychology: Vol. 2. Infancy and developmental psychobiology* (pp. 783–916). New York: Wiley.

Corsaro, W. A. (1985). *Friendship and peer culture in the early years*. Norwood, NJ: Ablex.

Crockett, L., Losoff, M., & Petersen, A. C. (1984). Perceptions of the peer group and friendship in early adolescence. *Journal of Early Adolescence, 4,* 155–181.

Csikszentmihalyi, M. (1975). *Beyond boredom and anxiety*. San Francisco: Jossey-Bass.

Douvan, E., & Adelson, J. (1966). *The adolescent experience*. New York: Wiley.

Dunphy, D. (1969). *Cliques, crowds, and gangs*. Melbourne, Australia: Cheshire.

Felner, R. D., Farber, S., & Primavera, J. (1983). Transitions and stressful life events: A model for primary prevention. In R. Felner, L. Jason, J. Moritsugu, & S. Farber (Eds.), *Preventative psychology: Theory, research, & practice* (pp. 199–220). Elmsford, NY: Pergamon.

Feltham, R. F., Doyle, A. B., Schwartzman, A. E., Serbin, L. A., & Ledingham, J. E. (1985). Friendship in normal and socially deviant children. *Journal of Early Adolescence, 5,* 371–382.

Fine, G. A. (1980). The natural history of preadolescent male friendship groups. In H. C. Foot, J. Chapman, & J. R. Smith (Eds.), *Friendship and social relations in children* (pp. 293–320). New York: Wiley.

Fine, G. A. (1981). Friends, impression mangement, and preadolescent behavior. In S. R. Asher & J. M. Gottman (Eds.), *The development of children's friendships* (pp. 29–52). New York: Cambridge University Press.

Fine, G. A. (1987). *With the boys: Little league baseball and preadolescent culture.* Chicago: University of Chicago Press.

Fischer, K. W., & Bullock, D. (1984). Cognitive development in school-aged children: Conclusions and new directions. In W. A. Collins (Ed.), *Development during middle childhood: The years from six to twelve* (pp. 70–147). Washington, DC: National Academy Press.

Foot, H. C., Chapman, A. J., & Smith, J. R. (1977). Friendship and social responsiveness in boys and girls. *Journal of Personality and Social Psychology, 35,* 401–411.

Forbes, D., Katz, M. M., & Paul, B. (1986). "Frame talk": A dramatistic analysis of children's fantasy play. In E. C. Mueller and C. R. Cooper (Eds.), *Process and outcome in peer relationships* (pp. 249–265). New York: Academic Press.

Furman, W. (1984). Some observations on the study of personal relationships. In J. C. Masters & K. Yarkin-Levin (Eds.), *Boundary areas in social and developmental psychology* (pp. 16–42). New York: Academic Press.

Furman, W., & Bierman, K. L. (1984). Children's conceptions of friendships: A multimethod study of developmental changes. *Developmental Psychology, 20,* 925–931.

Furman, W., & Buhrmester, D. (1985). Children's perceptions of the personal relationships in their social networks. *Developmental Psychology, 21,* 1016–1024.

Furman, W., & Robbins, P. (1985). What's the point: Selection of treatment objectives. In B. Schneider, K. H. Rubin, & J. E. Ledingham (Eds.), *Children's peer relations: Issues in assessment and intervention* (pp. 41–54). New York: Springer-Verlag.

Garvey, C. (1975). Requests and responses in children's speech. *Journal of Child Language, 2,* 41–63.

Gershman, E. S., & Hayes, D. S. (1983). Differential stability of reciprocal friendships and unilateral relationships among preschool children. *Merrill-Palmer Quarterly, 29,* 169–177.

Ginsberg, D., & Gottman, J. M. (1986). Conversations of college roommates: Similarities and differences in male and female friendships. In J. M. Gottman & J. G. Parker (Eds.), *Conversations of friends: Speculations on affective development* (pp. 241–291). New York: Cambridge University Press.

Gluckman, M. (1968). Psychological, sociological, and anthropological explanations of witchcraft and gossip. *Man, 3,* 20–34.

Goffman, E. (1959). *Presentation of self in everyday life.* New York: Doubleday.

Gottman, J. M. (1983). How children become friends. *Monographs of the Society for Research in Child Development, 48* (3, Serial No. 201).

Gottman, J. M. (1986). The observation of social process. In J. M. Gottman & J. G. Parker (Eds.), *Conversations of friends: Speculations on affective development* (pp. 51–102). New York: Cambridge University Press.

Gottman, J. M., & Mettetal, G. (1986). Speculations about social and affective development: Friendship and acquaintanceship through adolescence. In J. M. Gottman & J. G. Parker (Eds.), *Conversations of friends: Speculations on affective development* (pp. 192–240). New York: Cambridge University Press.

Gottman, J. M., & Parker, J. G. (1986). (Eds.). *Conversations of friends: Speculations on affective development*. New York: Cambridge University Press.

Gottman, J. M., & Parkhurst, J. T. (1980). A developmental theory of friendship and acquaintanceship processes. In W. A. Collins (Ed.), *Minnesota symposia on child development: Vol. 13: Development of cognition, affect, and social relations* (pp. 197–253). Hinsdale, NJ: Lawerence Erlbaum.

Green, E. H. (1933). Friendships and quarrels among preschool children. *Child Development, 4,* 237–252.

Gresham, F. M. (1981). Validity of social skills measures for assessing social competence in low-status children: A multivariate investigation. *Developmental Psychology, 17,* 390–398.

Griffin, H. (1985). The coordination of meaning in the creation of a shared make-believe reality. In I. Bretherington (Ed.), *Symbolic play: The representation of social understanding* (pp. 73–100). New York: Academic Press.

Griffiths, R. A. (1935). *A study of imagination in early childhood.* London: Kegan Paul.

Gurian, A., & Formanek, R. (1983). *The socially competent child: A parent's guide to social development from infancy to early adolescence.* Boston: Houghton Mifflin.

Harter, S. (1982). A cognitive-developmental approach to children's use of affect and trait labels. In F. C. Serafica (Ed.), *Social-cognitive development in context* (pp. 27–61). New York: Guilford.

Hartup, W. W. (1978). Children and their friends. In H. McGurk (Ed.), *Issues in childhood social development* (pp. 130–170). London: Methuen.

Hartup, W. W. (1984). The peer context in middle childhood. In W. A. Collins (Ed.), *Development during middle childhood: The years from six to twelve* (pp. 240–282). Washington, DC: National Academy Press.

Hartup, W. W. (1986). On relationships and development. In W. W. Hartup & Z. Rubin (Eds.), *Relationships and development* (pp. 1–26). Hinsdale, NJ: Lawrence Erlbaum.

Hartup, W. W., & Sancilio, M. F. (1986). Children's friendships. In E. Schopler & G. B. Mesibov (Eds.), *Social behavior in autism* (pp. 61–80). New York: Plenum.

Hayes, D. S., Gershman, E., & Bolin, L. J. (1980). Friends and enemies: Cognitive bases for preschool children's unilateral and reciprocal relationships. *Child Development, 51,* 1276–1279.

Higgins, E. T., & Parsons, J. (1983). In E. T. Higgins, D. Ruble, & W. W. Hartup (Eds.), *Social cognition and social behavior: Developmental perspectives* (pp. 15–62). New York: Cambridge University Press.

Hinde, R. A. (1979). *Towards understanding relationships.* New York: Academic Press.

Hobart, C. J. (1987, April) *Behavioral interactions of friends and acquaintances in childhood and adolescence.* Paper presented at the biennial meeting of the Society for Research in Child Development, Baltimore.

Hunter, F. T., & Youniss, J. (1982). Changes in functions of three relations during adolescence. *Developmental Psychology, 18,* 806–811.

Hymel, S., & Franke, S. (1985). Children's peer relations: Assessing self-perceptions. In B. Schneider, K. H. Rubin, & J. E. Ledingham (Eds.), *Children's peer relations: Issues in assessment and intervention* (pp. 75–92). New York: Springer-Verlag.

Johnson, F. L., & Aries, E. J. (1983). Conversational patterns among same-sex pairs of late adolescent close friends. *Journal of Genetic Psychology, 142,* 225–238.

Jones, E. E., & Pittman, T. S. (1982). Toward a general theory of strategic self-presentation. In J. Suls (Ed.), *Psychological perspectives on the self* (Vol. 1, pp. 231–262). Hinsdale, NJ: Lawrence Erlbaum.

Keating, D. P. (1980). Thinking processes in adolescence. In J. Adelson (Ed.), *Handbook of adolescent psychology* (pp. 211–246). New York: Wiley.

Kon, I. S., & Losenkov, V. A.. (1978). Friendship in adolescence: Values and behavior. *Journal of Marriage and Family, 40,* 143–155.

Labinger, M. R., & Holmberg, M. C. (1983, April). *Dimensions of sharing and helping in preschool children with friends and acquaintances.* Paper presented at the biennial meeting of the Society for Research in Child Development, Detroit.

Ladd, G. W. (1983). Social networks of popular, average, and rejected children in school settings. *Merrill-Palmer Quarterly, 29,* 283–307.

La Gaipa, J. J. (1981). Children's friendships. In S. Duck & R. Gilmore (Eds.), *Personal relationships: Vol. 3. Developing personal relationships* (pp. 161–185). New York: Academic Press.

Langer, E. J. (1978). Rethinking the role of thought in social interaction. In J. H. Harvey, W. J. Ickes, & R. F. Kidd (Eds.), *New directions in attribution research* (Vol. 2). Hinsdale, NJ: Lawrence Erlbaum.

Maccoby, E. E. (1980). *Social development: Psychological development and the parent-child relationship.* New York: Harcourt Brace Jovanovich.

Mannarino, A. P. (1976). Friendship patterns and altruistic behavior in preadolescent males. *Developmental Psychology, 12,* 555–556.

Markus, H. J., & Nurius, P. S. (1984). Self-understanding and self-regulation in middle childhood. In W. A. Collins (Ed.), *Development during middle childhood: The years from six to twelve* (pp. 147–183). Washington, DC: National Academy Press.

Masters, J. C., & Furman, W. (1981). Popularity, individual friendship selection, and specific peer interaction among children. *Developmental Psychology, 17,* 344–350.

Matthews, W. S. (1978). Sex and familiarity effects upon the proportion of time young children spend in spontaneous fantasy play. *Journal of Genetic Psychology, 133,* 9–12.

Mettetal, G. (1982). *The conversations of friends at three ages: The importance of fantasy, gossip, and self-disclosure.* Unpublished doctoral dissertation, University of Illinois, Champaign.

Montemayor, R., & Van Komen, R. (1985). The development of sex differences in friendship patterns and peer group structure during adolescence. *Journal of Early Adolescence, 5,* 285–294.

Oden, S., Herzberger, S. D., Mangione, P. L., & Wheeler, V. A. (1984). Children's peer relationships: An examination of social processes. In J. C. Masters & K. Yarkin-Levin (Eds.), *Boundary areas in social and developmental psychology* (pp. 131–160). New York: Academic Press.

Parker, J. G. (1986). Becoming friends: Conversational skills for friendship formation in young children. In J. M. Gottman & J. G. Parker (Eds.), *Conversations of friends: Speculations on affective development* (pp. 103–138). New York: Cambridge University Press.

Parker, J. G., & Gottman, J. M. (1985, April). *Making friends with an "extra-terrestrial": Conversational skills for friendship formation in young children.* Paper presented at the biennial meeting of the Society for Research in Child Development, Toronto.

Parkhurst, J. T., & Gottman, J. M. (1986). How young children get what they want. In J. M. Gottman & J. G. Parker (Eds.), *Conversations of friends: Speculations on affective development* (pp. 315–345). New York: Cambridge University Press.

Reisman, J. M. (1985). Friendship and its implications for mental health or social competence. *Journal of Early Adolescence, 5,* 383–391.

Reisman, J. M., & Shorr, S. E. (1978). Friendship claims and expectations among children and adults. *Child Development, 49*, 913–916.

Richey, M. H., & Richey, H. W. (1980). The significance of best-friend relationships in adolescence. *Psychology in the Schools, 17*, 535–540.

Rivenbark, W. H. (1971). Self-disclosure patterns among adolescents. *Psychological Reports, 28*, 35–42.

Roopnarine, J. L., & Field, T. M. (1984). Play interactions of friends and acquaintances in nursery school. In T. Field, J. L. Roopnarine, & M. Segal (Eds.), *Friendships in normal and handicapped children* (pp 89–98). Norwood, NJ: Ablex.

Rotherham, M. J., & Phinney, J. S. (1981, April). *Patterns of social overtures among preschool friends and non-friends.* Paper presented at the biennial meeting of the Society for Research in Child Development, Detroit.

Rubenstein, J. (1984). Friendship development in normal children: A commentary. In T. Field, J. L. Roopnarine, & M. Segal (Eds.), *Friendships in normal and handicapped children* (pp. 125–135). Norwood, NJ: Ablex.

Rubin, K. H., Fein, G., & Vandenberg, B. (1983). Play. In E. M. Hetherington (Ed.) & P. H. Mussen (Series Ed.), *Handbook of child psychology: Vol. 4. Socialization, personality, and social development* (pp 693–774). New York: Wiley.

Ruble, D. (1983). The development of social comparison processes and their role in achievement-related self-socialization. In E. T. Higgins, D. Ruble, & W. W. Hartup (Eds.), *Social cognition and social behavior: Developmental perspectives* (pp. 134–157). New York: Cambridge University Press.

Rysman, A. (1977). How the gossip became a woman. *Journal of Communication, 27*, 176–180.

Saarni, C. (1979). Children's understanding of display rules for expressive behaviors. *Developmental Psychology, 15*, 424–429.

Saarni, C. (1980, August). *Observing children's use of display rules: Age and sex differences.* Paper presented at annual meeting of the American Psychological Association, Montreal.

Selman, R. L. (1980). *The growth of interpersonal understanding: Developmental and clinical analysis.* New York: Academic Press.

Serafica, F. C. (1982). Conceptions of friendship and interaction between friends: An organismic-developmental perspective. In F. Serafica (Ed.), *Social-cognitive development in context* (pp. 100–132). New York: Guilford.

Sharabany, R., Gershoni, R., & Hofman, J. (1981), Girlfriend, boyfriend: Age and sex differences in intimate friendship. *Developmental Psychology, 17*, 800–808.

Smoller, J., & Youniss, J. (1982). Social development through friendship. In K. H. Rubin & H. S. Ross (Eds.), *Peer relationships and social skills in childhood* (pp. 277–298). Springer-Verlag: New York.

Stone, L. J., & Church, J. (1957) *Childhood and adolescence.* New York: Random House.

Strayer, J. (1986). Current research in affective development. In N. Curry (Ed.), *The feeling child: Affective development reconsidered* (pp. 37–55). New York: Haworth Press.

Sullivan, H. S. (1953). *The interpersonal theory of psychiatry.* New York: Norton.

Tesch, S. A. (1983). Review of friendship development across the lifespan. *Human Development, 26*, 266–276.

PART TWO

Peer Relationships in the School Context

From kindergarten on, the school is the arena in which most relationships with peers are formed, consolidated, and changed. To a large degree, schools create peer relationships by putting large groups of children of the same age in regular contact with each other. Naturally, these children form most of their closest friendships with other children in the same school, the same grade, and usually in the same classes. Moreover, popularity with peers could hardly be assessed and would probably have little significance if schools did not exist or did not group large numbers of peers together.

Despite the ubiquity and frequency of peer interactions at school, most educational planning ignores this facet of the school experience. William Damon and Erin Phelps point out that most schools still operate as if the only interactions of importance occurred between teachers and students, not between students themselves. Damon and Phelps argue that this blind spot in current systems of schooling may be costly, because classmates could contribute in major ways to their mutual education. In particular, programs in which some students tutor other students, programs of cooperative learning, and programs that foster collaboration between peers have all shown positive effects on academic learning. Damon and Phelps especially emphasize the value of peer collaboration, and they report data from their own 2-year study of the effects of peer collaboration on students' ability to solve mathematical and spatial problems.

Joyce Epstein places less emphasis on how schools might be changed and more emphasis on how they affect the formation and maintenance of friendships between children and adolescents. Indeed, she casts an even wider net, discussing developmental changes in the selection of close friends and the influences of school characteristics and other aspects of children's environments on their selection of friends. Epstein focuses on the importance of proximity, similarity in age, and similarity in personality or other characteristics for friendship selection. She concludes by describing the influence of selected friends on children's own attitudes, behavior, and achievement. More specifically, she points out that similarity between friends partly reflects children's selection of friends who were already like themselves and partly reflects processes of influence that lead students to grow more similar to their friends over time.

In the chapter by B. Bradford Brown, the focus is not on specific friendships but on the influence of the larger peer group. Brown reviews research showing that cliques and crowds with distinctive characteristics emerge in most schools between childhood and adolescence. He describes the variety of crowd types present in secondary schools and some factors that affect their size and characteristics. He then addresses questions about the influence of peer groups on adolescents. He points out, for example, that adolescents often perceive their friends as pressuring them to act in socially desirable rather than in undesirable ways. He comments, however, that peer influence is rarely due to coercion. On the contrary, adolescents often conform willingly to peers because they identify with the high-status members of their own crowd. In other words, they view their crowd as a reference group that helps them define their own values and formulate guidelines for their own behavior.

CHAPTER 5

Strategic Uses of Peer Learning in Children's Education

WILLIAM DAMON AND ERIN PHELPS

Clark University

Radcliffe College

Despite popular suspicions about the dangers that "peer pressure" poses for youth, scientific studies have left little doubt that peer relations can greatly benefit children's social and intellectual development. The case for children's peer relations has been made repeatedly and conclusively in developmental theory and research (Cooper, Marquis, & Edward, 1986; Damon, 1984; Hartup, 1983; Youniss, 1980). Repeated studies have shown that peer interaction is conducive, perhaps even essential, to a host of important early achievements: children's understanding of fairness, their self-esteem, their proclivities toward sharing and kindness, their mastery of symbolic expression, their acquisition of role-taking and communication skills, and their development of creative and critical thinking. In some cases peer relations support such achievements, whereas in other cases they play a unique and irreplaceable role.

Although this favorable view of children's peer relations is widely accepted in social science, it has had a limited impact on educational practice. Granted, in the past decade or so there have been some experimental attempts to introduce peer learning to the classroom. We shall discuss these later in this chapter. But despite the promise of such early attempts and despite the impressive body of literature documenting the developmental

The research reported in this chapter was supported, in part, by a grant to the first author from The Spencer Foundation. Preparation of the manuscript was supported, in part, by a grant from The Van Leer Fund of The New York Community Trust. The authors gratefully acknowledge both sources of support but stress that all statements made herein reflect solely the opinions of the authors and not necessarily those of the funding agencies. We also gratefully acknowledge the assistance of Wendy Yang, Karl Staven, Jill Hopfenbeck, Robert Mitchell, and Wendy Praisner on our research project.

benefits of peer interaction, standard models of education have changed hardly at all.

Virtually all schooling, in this country and elsewhere, is structured around the traditional belief that knowledge is best transmitted from adult to child in linear fashion. Educational challenges to this belief have been few and short-lived. In most schools, child-to-child communication during classroom hours is either discouraged, confined to recreational activities, or limited to experimental programs and other special projects that are segregated from the school's core curriculum. Historically there have been a few alternative educational models endorsing collaborative learning among students. Dewey's "progressive education" and the "open classrooms" of the 1960s were two such alternative models. But most experimental implementations of such models have been inadequately planned, incompletely executed, poorly (if at all) evaluated, and quickly aborted.

To what may we attribute the near hegemony of linear adult-child teaching models in our schools? Certainly there are doubts about the wisdom of harnessing children's peer relations for "serious" learning goals. These doubts may arise from lingering suspicions about the potentially antisocial nature of "peer pressure" (suspicions which have some legitimacy in certain contexts (see Brown, this volume; Rowe, this volume). There is also a valid concern that frequent peer exchanges may distract children from the real business of the classroom; as well as a deeply held conviction that adults know more than children and thus need to remain in sole control of the teacher's authoritative role. These are all beliefs that have some truth to them and that need to be addressed by advocates of peer learning.

In fact, however, answers to these concerns do not readily spring from the literature as it now stands. Beyond presenting its overall case for the value of peer interaction, developmental theory does not offer a prescription for how and under what conditions peer learning can contribute most to a child's education. Nor does it resolve the converse concerns about the limitations and potential negative effects of peer interaction in the classroom. Sympathetic educators interested in combining a peer-based approach with the traditional adult-child model in order to arrive at the optimal pedagogical mix have little to go on. We do not yet know enough about the relative strengths and shortfalls of the two; nor do we have a model for their effective integration.

It is this problem that we shall examine in the present chapter. We shall first need to take a closer look at the global "peer learning" construct itself, breaking it apart into its distinguishable components. This will help us arrive at guidelines for the most effective educational use of each distinct type of peer learning. We shall then consider the adult teacher's new role in a peer learning approach. Then we will be in a position to propose a model for integrating peer learning strategies with traditional instructional approaches. In examining these issues, we shall draw on recent research by ourselves and others, which is too new to provide definitive answers but which suggests directions in which answers may be found and takes important beginning steps in these directions. We focus in this chapter on the elementary school years, where the evidence is strongest and our knowledge clearest. In principle, we believe that processes of peer education are as valuable before and after the elementary school years, but we would not argue that the guidelines for optimal application remain the same across all ages.

THREE TYPES OF PEER LEARNING

There are three main types of peer learning, known as *peer tutoring, cooperative learning,* and *peer collaboration.* These three types can be distinguished from one another by comparing the extent to which they embody two central dimensions of peer discourse: (1) *equality* and (2) *mutuality of engagement.*

"Peer" by definition means equal. Equality, therefore, is one unquestionable marker of a peer relation. Mutuality has been shown by psychological research to be another such marker (Berndt, 1987). Berndt defines mutuality in a relationship as extensive, intimate, and "connected" engagement ("the degree to which children are involved in a conversation and 'in tune' with one another," p. 283).

Although equality and mutuality are basic dimensions for all peer relations, the three types of peer learning noted above reflect these dimensions quite differently. *Peer tutoring* is relatively *low* on *equality* and *high* on *mutuality;* cooperative learning is *high* on *equality* and *low* on *mutuality;* and peer collaboration is *high* on *both.*

Peer Tutoring

In this approach, one child instructs and drills another child in material on which the first child is an expert and the second child is a novice. Because the first child has greater information or competence than the second child, the two do not begin the relationship with equal status. Further, the unequal knowledge status of the two children is usually compounded by other factors as well. Most attempts at peer tutoring pair an older child with a younger child, or a bright child with an educationally disadvantaged one. In fact, peer tutoring is often called "cross-age" tutoring, because the tutor is usually two or more years older than the tutee. In a strict sense, the phrase "peer tutoring" is something of an oxymoron.

Peer tutoring, therefore, replicates the traditional teacher-student relationship in which a teacher transmits expertise to a student. Of course in peer tutoring the teacher is a fellow child rather than an adult, and this makes a difference even when the tutor and tutee are two or three years apart in age. For one thing, another child, even an older one, never possesses the same degree of authority over a child as does an adult teacher. Second, there is far less of an "informational gap" between two children than between a child and an adult. Third, the peer tutor possesses none of the adult teacher's acquired skill in transmitting knowledge to the unlearned.

For these reasons, peer tutoring occupies a relational ground somewhere between adult-child instruction and peer discourse. Like adult-child instruction, peer tutoring is based upon a transmission-of-knowledge model. This model assumes that one party knows the answers and must communicate them to the other party. Knowledge is "passed down" from person to person in linear fashion rather than coconstructed by persons who are both seeking answers.

Unlike adult-child instruction, however, in peer tutoring the expert party is not very far removed from the novice party in authority or knowledge; nor has the expert party any special claims to instructional competence. Such differences affect the nature of discourse between tutor and tutee, because they place the tutee in a less passive role than does the adult/child instructional relation. Being closer in knowledge and status, the tutee in a peer relation feels freer to express opinions, ask questions, and risk untested solutions. The interaction between instructor and pupil is more balanced and more lively. This is why conversations between peer tutors and their tutees are high in mutuality even though the relationship is not exactly equal in status.

A theoretical grounding for peer tutoring can be found in Vygotsky's writings about the "zone of proximal development" (Vygotsky, 1978, p. 114). Vygotsky wrote that "problem solving in collaboration with more capable peers" could enable children to enter into new areas of potential.

These new areas, which Vygotsky called the "leading edge" of children's intellectual growth, constitute the zone of proximal development. The zone is created when a child interacts with a more experienced mentor. Because the mentor guides the interaction's direction in intellectually productive ways, the child's intellectual performance during the interaction surpasses anything that the child has been able to do outside of the interaction.

In the course of such experiences, the child retains the ability to reproduce these jointly produced intellectual performances on his or her own. When this happens, the achievement becomes part of the child's actual capabilities rather than merely a potential skill that can be realized only through interaction. In this sense, the insights and competencies become internalized, belonging now to the child's own repertoire of intellectual skills.

The acquisition of information through tutoring can, of course, be explained by any internalization model of development, including imitation and social learning theory. But Vygotsky's theory (1978) adds a component that is particularly helpful in the case of peer learning. From Vygotskian theory it is possible to explain why *both* children, tutor as well as tutee, can profit from peer tutoring interactions. This would be difficult from a strictly imitation or social learning perspective, since these "copy" models account only for a one-way transmission of information from socializer to socializee. Yet data from peer tutoring experiments (see Allen, 1976) clearly show both children learning from the encounter.

Vygotsky argues that it is not only information that is internalized from interactions in the zone, but also fundamental cognitive processes that are implicit in the communications. Accordingly, both parties in the communication stand to benefit. The tutee profits from the very acts of questioning, challenging, and providing feedback to the tutor. The tutor profits from the act of reformulating knowledge for transmittal to the tutee, from answering the tutee's questions, and from responding to the tutee's challenges. This is what is meant by the old saying, "You never really know a subject until you try to teach it."

When two children enter into a peer tutoring relationship, they become exposed to new patterns of thought. This is because any peer dialogue is a (relatively) cooperative, consensual, and nonauthoritarian exchange of ideas. As such, it relies on rationality for its maintenance and emulates several key features of critical thinking.

In particular, beliefs must be justified and verified rather than merely asserted by force of mandate. This requires significant intellectual effort for both parties. It calls for skill in symbolically representing ideas as well as the ability to notice and resolve logical contradictions. These are central areas of cognitive competence, areas in which children at all levels and ages have room for improvement.

The Vygotskian perspective is well suited for showing how repeated exposure to social interactions that embody key characteristics of rational thought can lead to permanent improvements in a child's cognitive functioning. In a sense, the child takes on, or internalizes, the very communicative procedures experienced during the peer encounter. For both children, this represents at least as important a developmental acquisition as the specific knowledge that the expert child is teaching the novice.

Of the three types of peer learning, it was peer tutoring that first made inroads into actual school settings. In the 1970s, a number of educators experimented with peer tutoring as an alternative form of instruction. Generally they found it to be effective in spurring educational progress of both tutor and tutee (Allen, 1976; Bloom, 1976; Gartner, Kohler & Riessman, 1971).

From these and subsequent research programs, the following picture has emerged. Peer tutoring, when carried out over a substantial period of time with carefully trained and supervised tutors, is educationally valuable for its participants (Hartup, 1983). It is also surprisingly cost-effective when compared with other instructional techniques. When done well, it can aid children's acquisition of both verbal and quantitative skills as well as substantive curriculum topics like history, physics, and social studies (East, 1976). Finally, peer tutoring can also yield personal benefits for both tutor and tutee. Children's self-esteem, educational motivation, school adjustment, and altruistic inclinations all improve in the course of peer tutoring engagement (Allen, 1976; Staub, 1975).

Cooperative Learning

In the 1980s, a new paradigm of peer-based education has found its way into the American classroom. This approach, called cooperative or "small group" learning, differs conceptually as well as methodologically from peer tutoring. Cooperative learning advocates emphasize the distinction between the two, although there is practically no empirical research contrasting their educational outcomes.

Cooperative learning has been introduced to many schools because educational researchers have devised practical programs that are relatively easy for teachers to adopt. These programs can be integrated into the normal school day and neither disrupt nor challenge the teacher's usual way of doing business. Although many teachers enthusiastically adopt cooperative learning exercises when they are made available, they may confine these exercises to as little as an hour a week of classroom time.

There are a variety of cooperative learning techniques now in use, but they all have certain features in common. All cooperative learning exercises begin by dividing the classroom into small "teams," or groups, of no more than four or five children. These groups are generally heterogeneous with respect to students' abilities. The teacher presents a problem or a task to the team, and the team sets out to master it. All cooperative learning methods rely on team solidarity and the motivation that it engenders. The assumption is that students will want to perform well for their team and that they will work for the success of their fellow team members and the team as a whole.

Some widely adopted versions of cooperative learning are Aronson's "jigsaw teaching," Sharan's "group investigation," and Slavin's "student teams-achievement divisions" (Aronson, Stephan, Lides, Blaney, & Snapp, 1978; Sharan, 1980; Slavin, 1983). In jigsaw teaching each member of a student team becomes an expert on one aspect of a larger topic. After studying that aspect in depth, the expert reports back to the team on what he or she has found. The team as a whole is taught by each "specialist" member in turn. In Sharan's method, team members plan and assign themselves specialized roles and prepare detailed reports for each other's edification. Group discussion of the reports is encouraged. Slavin's method sets up competition between opposing teams. It encourages team members to share work and information with one another so that they will individually perform better than members of other teams on quizzes derived from the learning exercises.

Outcome studies of cooperative learning have shown a pattern of consistent gains in areas ranging from reading and language to social studies and math (Slavin, 1983). In addition to improved academic achievement, benefits have been demonstrated on social dimensions like mutual concern and race relations (Slavin, 1980, 1983; Sharan, 1984). Not surprisingly, effects are greatest in long-term, intensive programs that cover broad curriculum areas.

Cooperative learning approaches vary in the extent to which they encourage individual versus collective activity in the learning groups. In Aronson's version (Aronson et al., 1978), team members assume different roles while they are learning about the task. Only when they have finished individual work, do the team members share the results with the rest of the team. In Slavin's version (Slavin, 1983), the team works together to prepare for individual tests or performances that will be given later. At least two versions (Johnson, Johnson, & Skon, 1979; Sharan, 1984) encourage joint planning and discussion throughout the exercise.

In addition, cooperative learning approaches vary in the extent to which they rely on competition between teams as a motivator. Many techniques extrinsically reward strong team performances in order to spur children's interest in the tasks. Rewards are usually allocated on the basis of scores on tests given after the exercise. The explicit message to the team is that they will jointly benefit by beating other teams only if they see to it that all team members master the task. Other cooperative learning approaches spurn this competitive component and rely on intrinsic motivation to engage the learning groups in the exercise (Johnson, Johnson, & Skon, 1979; Sharan, 1980).

Such variations make it difficult to generalize about the quality of children's interaction, or its effects, in the cooperative learning approach as a whole. No doubt there is a range in the intensity and mutuality of student's group discourse across the various cooperative learning paradigms. Approaches that place children in specialized learning roles clearly would be on the low end of this range. Approaches that encourage collective planning and discussion throughout the task likely foster greater interactional mutuality.

Intergroup competition may or may not have a further effect on the mutuality of student discourse; but if so, we do not even know the direction of the effect. Intergroup competition could increase team solidarity, thus enhancing intragroup exchange; or it could distract children from the real group of learning, thus distorting the substance of the intragroup discourse. Since researchers have not yet directly observed and analyzed the quality of children's interactions across cooperative learning approaches, we can only speculate about such matters.[1]

Overall, however, it is reasonable to conclude that most cooperative learning paradigms rely more heavily on students' individual initiative and per-

---

[1]The few studies comparing outcomes of the various cooperative learning approaches rarely link such outcomes to group interaction patterns and when they do touch on such patterns they have not analyzed the contrast in sufficient depth to establish clear or consistent results (Sharan, 1984; Webb, 1982).

formances than do other peer learning paradigms. This is particularly true in learning exercises where students take on specialized roles and do all their information seeking on their own. Specialization of this sort leaves little room for joint discovery, reciprocal feedback, or collective shaping of ideas.

This is also likely to be true in cooperative learning approaches where the exercise's explicit goal is to enable individual students to perform well on a test. The group activity still centers on reporting information already learned, as well as on encouraging one another to work hard and do well. The group does not formulate or negotiate task solutions, but rather exchanges and practices them for the purpose of mastering (rather than constructing) them. Accordingly, in this as in most of its other forms, cooperative learning is relatively low on the mutuality of participant engagement, while at the same time relatively high on the equality of status.

Peer Collaboration

In peer collaboration, a pair of novices work together to solve tasks that neither could do previously. Unlike peer tutoring, the children begin at roughly the same levels of competence. Unlike cooperative learning, the children work jointly on the same problem rather than individually on separate components of the problem. These differences, however, are ideal-type contrasts. In actual practice peer collaboration bears some resemblance to both other types of peer learning, since often the collaborators will draw apart for independent work, with one child assuming a lead role in solving the task.

Peer collaboration forces children to communicate about task-solving strategies and solutions. It simulates the challenges of discovery learning but places these challenges in a context of peer assistance and support. Like discovery learning, its promise lies in provoking deep conceptual insights and basic developmental shifts on the part of its participants. This is because it encourages experimentation with new and untested ideas and demands a critical reexamination of one's old assumptions. But unlike individual discovery learning, where the child may feel like an isolated incompetent, peer collaboration provides a sympathetic forum for this sort of creative risk taking. As the child works with a fellow novice, the insufficiencies in his or her own knowledge become less discouraging and the challenge of discovery becomes less forbidding.

Despite its promise, peer collaboration has been used far less frequently in educational programs than have the other two forms of peer learning. Likely this is because peer collaboration as a technique has its roots in experimental developmental psychology rather than in educational research. As yet there are no systematic curricula designed around principles of peer collaboration. Only recently have some initial attempts been made to apply some techniques from the developmental research to actual educational settings.

Peer collaboration as a systematic learning strategy emerged from Piagetian intervention studies in this country and abroad. These studies generally focus on the acquisition of conservation, a notion that has been resistant (though not impervious) to training through standard instructional techniques. Among the experimental methods that developmentalists explored as a means of facilitating children's acquisition of conservation was asking children to work jointly with peers. The strategy of placing novices together on a difficult task and expecting them to come up with a productive approach seems on the face of it so odd that data reports have had titles like "When two wrongs make a right" (Ames & Murray, 1982). Still, peer collaboration has proven to be the most consistently effective means of helping children acquire conservation and the basic reasoning skills underlying it (Bearison, Magzamen, & Filardo, 1986; Botvin & Murray, 1975; Damon, 1984; Doise & Mugny, 1979, 1984; Miller & Brownell, 1975; Murray, 1968, 1972, 1974; Perret-Clermont, 1980; Silverman & Geiringer, 1973; Silverman & Stone, 1972).

The dominant rationale for this seemingly odd strategy of teaming novices together has been the Genevan construct of "socio-cognitive conflict" (Doise, Mugny, & Perret-Clermont, 1976). The idea is that social interactions between peers will inevitably lead to disagreements that present the participants with both a social and a cognitive conflict. This unsettling experience in turn leads children to a number of important realizations. First, they become aware that there are points of view other than their own. This is the Piagetian process of "decentering." Second, they reexamine their own points of view and reassess their validity. Third, they learn that they must justify their own opinions and communicate them thoroughly if others are to accept them as valid.

In this way, children can benefit both cognitively and socially from peer collaboration. The social benefits are their improved communication skills and their sharper sense of other persons' perspectives. The cognitive benefits derive from their forced reexamination of their own conceptions under the guidance of a peer's feedback. Piaget believed that these social and cognitive benefits were directly related, in that improved social communication instigates progressive change. When people need to explain and justify their beliefs to others, they realize that these beliefs must be rationalized as fully as possible. This sense of "social responsibility" in communication ultimately leads to improvements in the logical quality of reasoning.

The Genevan explanation of peer collaboration, therefore, posits a clash of ideas that triggers a need to reexamine, rework, and justify one's understanding of the world. This triggering process, it should be noted, does not provide the substance, or "stuff," of change. Although in Piagetian theory the perturbing, conflictual feedback provided by peer interaction initiates a process of intellectual reconstruction, it does not do the main work of formulating new knowledge. This is done by the individual, in solitary reflection, through symbolic manipulations of the world and inferences based on these manipulations. The ideas themselves, in other words, remain the product of the child's internal reasoning processes.

Despite this theoretical support behind sociocognitive conflict as an explanatory construct, some questions have been raised about its sufficiency as a process model for peer collaborative learning. An alternative but still somewhat complementary perspective emphasizes more the constructive, or "coconstructive" aspects of peer collaboration. In this view, introduced by Sullivan and elaborated by Youniss, children learn through peer interaction because it introduces children to the possibilities of cooperative activity (Youniss, 1980).

In a truly cooperative effort, children devise plans together, share ideas, and mutually validate one another's initiatives. Not only is this a powerful procedure for generating new insights, it also yields solutions that are superior to those arrived at by an individual in isolation.

Unfortunately there have been very few studies that have attempted to identify the peer interaction processes leading to progressive change. This requires lengthy and complex videotape analyses of the sort not always available in experimental studies. But the few empirical hints that we do have from such research place in question the sociocognitive model of learning through peer collaboration.

In a training study of distributive justice concepts, children who disagreed with one another the most were the least likely to progress, whereas children who accepted one another's views and worked positively with them were the most likely to change (Damon & Killen, 1982). Constructive rather than conflictual interaction was clearly the key facilitator. A study of spatial concepts found that large degrees of conflict in peer dyads were inversely related to change (Bearison et al., 1986). This study also reported that moderate conflict was associated with change but assessed moderate conflict in a way that made it indistinguishable from coconstructive activity. Finally, a recent analysis of peer interaction processes during task engagement found such interactions to be heavily loaded with "transactive" activity (Kruger & Tomasello, 1986). Transactions constitute a constructively compromising form of social discourse especially suited for joint exploration into unknown areas of thought.

Peer collaboration, therefore, is a promising method of spurring basic conceptual development in children. But it is little used in actual educational practice and virtually untested in educational research. Researchers experimenting with peer-based instruction have focused primarily on the peer tutoring and cooperative learning approaches. Only within basic developmental theory and research has peer collaboration been systematically examined. And developmental research thus far has left many unanswered questions concerning peer collaboration's advantages, limitations, and optimal uses.

For example, we need to know more about the interactional conditions under which peer collaboration leads to lasting learning gains. To what extent does sociocognitive conflict describe these conditions, or to what extent do other notions like "coconstruction" or "transaction" provide a better account? What are the limits of peer collaboration in relation to other forms of peer learning, and what are its special strengths? How may peer collaboration be integrated with the other peer learning paradigms, and with other instructional models in general?

These are some of the questions that we are asking in our own research program. We present in the next section our initial research efforts to address some of these questions. In the final section we shall discuss these as well as some more general peer learning issues that we have not yet had a chance to study empirically.

RESEARCH FINDINGS ON STRENGTHS AND LIMITATIONS OF PEER COLLABORATION

Our findings are intended to address the following questions about the educational potential of peer collaboration:

1. Are some types of cognitive tasks more amenable to learning through peer collaboration than other types?
2. Does peer learning on one type of task generalize to other types?
3. Does progress made during one year carry over to a subsequent year; and, if so, does it provide children with an advantage in learning further concepts?
4. Assuming that some children show learning gains through peer collaboration while others do not: Are there differences in children's social interaction patterns that may explain how the "gainers" are able to profit from peer engagement?

The following research was not designed to answer all questions concerning the efficacy of peer collaboration. For example, we did not pit peer collaboration against other adult or peer-based instructional techniques in order to see which had the greatest effect. Although this comparison is of potential interest, it was not a high priority of our research. Therefore we did not choose to expend our limited resources on control groups in which students were exposed to other learning opportunities.

Instead, we ran only control groups unexposed to any learning intervention. Our purpose was to establish that peer collaboration produces significant learning gains when compared with the mere passage of time and normal school experience. Our primary agenda then was to understand the nature of these learning gains and the group-interaction conditions under which they occurred. For the present, we are content with the possibility that equal or greater learning gains on our tasks may be available through other instructional techniques and leave it to future studies to challenge this possibility. Our main interest in this current research program was to understand the dynamics of peer collaboration and not to test its relative power vis-à-vis other techniques.

STUDY DESIGN.   The research group consisted of 164 fourth and fifth graders, with equal numbers of boys and girls, who participated in a 2-year longitudinal study. The children were of approximately average ability from public schools in eastern and central Massachusetts.

In Year 1, there were two experimental groups and one control group. Experimental Group 1 (the "Math Group") was comprised of 40 fourth graders who worked in pairs to solve math problems. Experimental Group 2 (the "Spatial Group") was comprised of 40 children working on spatial problems. There were 6 weekly training sessions, during which the children were given increasingly difficult math or spatial problems. The control group (Control Group 1) was made up of 42 children who received only the same pretests and posttests as the two experimental groups.

In Year 2, all the Year 1 children, including those in the Year 1 control group, were given a problem in physical equilibrium (Siegler's "balance beam") to work on (Siegler, 1976). Again they worked in dyads over a 6-week period, and the dyads remained intact so that all children had the same partners for Year 2. A new control group (Control Group 2) of 42 fifth graders who did not participate in the balance beam learning sessions was added.

In all experimental groups, boys and girls worked in same-sex pairs and received absolutely no help from adults. The children were initially instructed to work together on trying to find the right answers to the problems. The children fed their answers into a programmed lap-sized computer, and the computer gave them feedback (through preprogrammed musical signals) about whether their answers were right or wrong. Otherwise the only interactions to which experimental subjects were exposed were their own peer discussions.

The purpose of the multitask, 2-year study design was to test for transfer of learning across different types of cognitive tasks and to see whether learning gains in Year 1 would persist in Year 2. The transfer issue was also under investigation in the Year 1/Year 2 comparisons, since math learning of the type to be fostered in Year 1 (proportionality) is a specific prerequisite for balance beam reasoning. Spatial reasoning is not a prerequisite for reasoning about the operation of a balance beam, so we were interested in seeing whether the Math Group had an advantage over the Spatial Group during balance beam training. We also were interested in seeing whether the

Spatial Group had an advantage over Control Group 2, since it could be expected that prior peer collaboration on any task would at least help children develop the communication procedures that facilitate collaborative learning.

INTERVENTION RESULTS.   In general the intervention had a salutary effect on subjects' performance. Children in the experimental peer collaboration groups showed significantly greater learning gains than did control group children. Nevertheless, certain tasks were more likely than others to show change due to peer collaboration. Children who collaborated with a partner on math problems changed significantly more between Testing Times 1 and 2 on tasks involving ratios and proportionality than did children in the Spatial Group and Control Group 1 (Figure 5.1). Peer collaboration did not

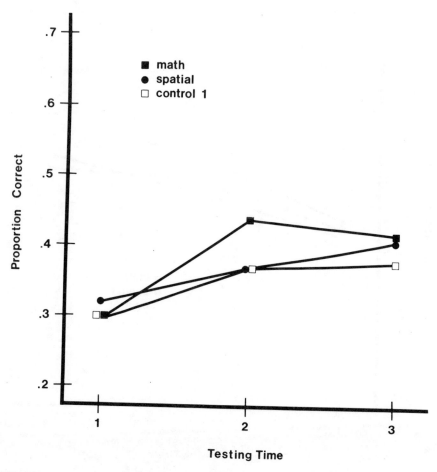

Figure 5.1. Ratio and proportion tasks: Proportion correct at Testing Times 1 (Year 1 pretest), 2 (Year 1 posttest), and 3 (delayed posttest in Year 2).

affect performance on arithmetic problems, however. Children who collaborated with a partner on spatial problems showed significant gains on the perspective-taking tasks, especially at Time 3 (Figure 5.2). Collaboration on the spatial problems did not affect performance on tasks of model building, however.

This pattern of findings reveals a great deal about the educational potential of peer collaboration. As expected, the method facilitates learning of deep, basic concepts that often resist direct instruction. Proportionality is an example of such a concept. It is central for the child's mastery of fractions as well as many other mathematical and logical operations. Educators and experimental psychologists frequently have reported difficulty teaching the concept of proportionality to elementary schoolchildren (Case, 1980; In-

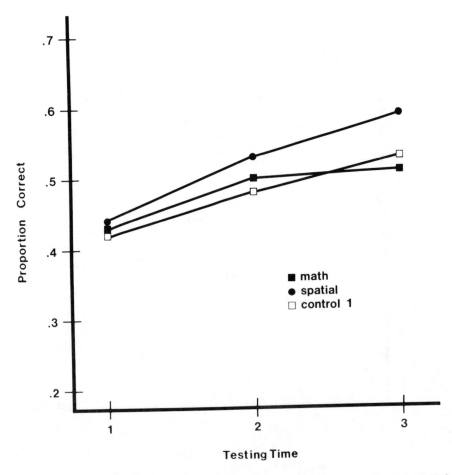

Figure 5.2. Perspective-taking tasks: Proportion correct at Testing Times 1 (Year 1 pretest), 2 (Year 1 posttest), and 3 (delayed posttest in Year 2).

helder & Piaget, 1958; Vergnaud, 1983). This is also true for spatial perspectives, another core conceptual area in higher order thinking (Piaget, Inhelder, 1956; Snyder & Feldman, 1977).

The tasks that proved less successful in instilling change during our experiment rely less on deep conceptual insights and more on formulas and procedures that can be imparted through direct tutelage. These included addition and subtraction word problems and model-copying tasks.

Peer collaboration may not be the best medium for showing children how to "carry" numbers, for reminding them about their multiplication tables, or for increasing the accuracy of their copying skills. This is because it orients children toward discovery and reflection rather than practice and implementation. Both types of learning activity certainly are essential for educational achievement.

Because of our longitudinal study design, we could determine the extent to which our Year 1 intervention effects lasted into Year 2 as well as the extent to which they contributed to further progress. We had two indicators of such longitudinal effects. First, our Year 2 pretest included a range of items representing all of the Year 1 intervention areas. Second, our Year 2 intervention problem, the balance beam, relied on conceptual skills closely related to the proportionality tasks that we used in our Year 1 math intervention. Thus we expected that the children who took part in the Year 1 math sessions would be best prepared for learning about the balance beam. The children who took part in the Year 1 spatial sessions, we believed, would do better than Control Group 1, because the Spatial Group had the benefits of prior peer communicative experience; but they would not do as well as the Year 1 Math Group because they did not learn concepts of mathematical proportionality in Year 1. We expected Control Group 1 to do better than Control Group 2, however, because pairs of children in the former group did work collaboratively on the balance beam task and the children in the latter group did not.

Our longitudinal results by and large confirmed our expectations, although more clearly in some areas than in others. As shown in Figure 1, the Year 1 training effects in math were maintained fairly well in Year 2, but the Spatial Group and Control Group 1 improved so that the differences between these three conditions were nonsignificant at Time 3. As shown in Figure 2, spatial training effects persisted and even increased to a significant degree by Year 2. Such accelerating "post-posttest" effects generally mean that important and permanent learning gains have been made.

On the balance beam problem, trends were in line with our hypotheses concerning differential carry-over effects from the respective Year 1 experiences of the Math, Spatial, and Control Groups (Figure 5.3). At the Year 2 posttest (Time 4), children in the Math Group scored highest on the balance beam task, followed by children in the Spatial Group and Control Group 1. The children in Control Group 2 showed no progress whatsoever. When Year 1 pretest scores were used as covariates, in order to control for pre-

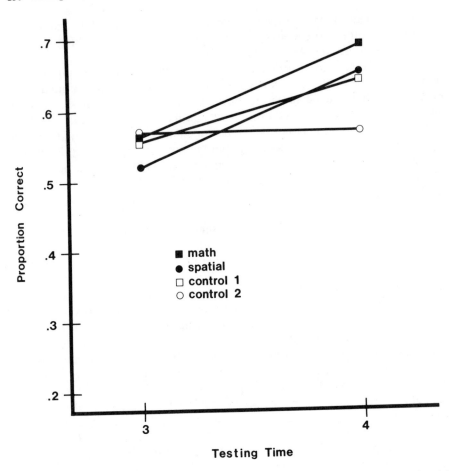

Figure 5.3. Balance beam task: Proportion correct at Testing Times 3 (Year 2 pretest) and 4 (Year 2 posttest).

existing differences between groups, the children in the Math Group scored significantly higher than did children in the Spatial Group and Control Group 1. The balance beam results were clearest for the males and were only marginally significant in many instances. But the overall pattern of results was strong enough and clear enough for us to conclude that our peer collaboration intervention had lasting effects, significantly improving children's future capacities to learn about related math and science problems.

We take these data as confirmation of our belief that peer collaboration can have lasting effects on children's understanding of difficult conceptual material like proportionality. Further, such effects can transfer to other closely related problem areas in the following predictable manner: the closer the area, the greater the transfer.

Social Interactional Patterns of Peer-Collaborative Learning

The special educational potential of peer collaboration has been demonstrated by the experimental findings we have reported in this chapter. We must now ask again our original question: Does peer collaboration engage children in social interactions that are qualitatively distinct from those in other kinds of instructional interchange; and, if so, are these patterns responsible for deep conceptual insights of the type fostered by our experimental intervention?

We are currently analyzing our videotapes of the peer collaboration sessions in order to link subjects' social discourse patterns with their progress on the math, spatial, and balance beam tasks. Even in the experimental groups, of course, some children learned more than others, and still others learned not at all. We are looking to the tapes for social interaction clues that might explain our experimental subjects' differential degrees of success.

At this point we have some initial results that look promising. One clear finding is that children who changed were particularly likely to share ideas about the logic of the task with one another. These children's communications focused on solutions to the problem, strategies for solving the problem, and information directly related to the problem. In contrast, children who talked mostly about each other's roles and behavior rather than about the task itself were not likely to change. Especially adverse to progress was having a partner who expressed frequent role-and-behavior statements, such as commands concerning who should do what or how each other should act.

It seems that, in a peer collaboration setting, social interactions that draw children into the logic of the problem facilitate intellectual progress. Interactions that distract children from the problem and toward the social activities of the participants impede such progress.

In addition, a very high proportion of the learning engagements that we observed were positive and agreeable in quality, rather than negative and conflictual.

Conclusions from Our Research on Peer Collaboration

Peer collaboration is an effective educational technique. In our study, children of approximately equal capabilities, working in dyads, made learning gains in every area that we presented to them. The areas included challenging math, spatial, and physical-equilibrium problems that were at least a year ahead of our subjects' fourth- and fifth-grade curricula. On most of these problems our subjects' learning gains were significant in magnitude relative to those made by control groups not exposed to any learning experiences. Our subjects' gains were made with virtually no help or instruction from adults other than the initial instructions to work together toward correct solutions. Feedback on right and wrong answers was given strictly by a programmed computer. The children managed their own interactions, invented their own problem-solving procedures, and discovered their own solutions.

As we expected, peer collaboration is particularly appropriate for enhancing children's basic conceptual abilities. Our subjects made the greatest progress relative to the control group on problems requiring new conceptual insights. Specifically, tasks requiring an understanding of ratios and proportions, spatial proportions, or physical equilibrium were the ones that fostered progress through peer-collaborative learning. In contrast, tasks that required computational skills and accurate model-copying abilities did not induce significant learning through peer collaboration.

This finding is compatible with previous educational research on the value of various forms of peer learning. Although previous comparisons have not tested peer collaboration directly, they have compared cooperative types of peer learning with peer tutoring (where an "expert" child instructs a usually younger "novice" child). Generally the previous findings are that in equal and cooperative peer interactions, children's "higher order" reasoning skills become engaged, leading to developmental shifts in conceptual insight. Unequal tutoring interactions, in contrast, are more suited to the practice and consolidation of insights already attained.

Our peer collaboration procedure established a more equal and cooperative context of learning interactions than anything previously attempted in educational research. As noted previously, our results demonstrate that this kind of equal and cooperative work can lead to improvements in children's reasoning skills. In particular, it can promote deep conceptual change in challenging areas like math and science. We believe that this is because peer collaboration provides an ideal atmosphere for discovery learning. In this atmosphere, children become motivated to attack challenging problems. They also feel secure enough to risk expressing the new and untested ideas needed to solve such problems.

Further, in order to work productively with their partners, children must publicly recapitulate their own emerging understanding of the task. This, we believe, is a process that strongly facilitates intellectual growth, because it forces subjects to bring to consciousness the ideas that they are just beginning to grasp intuitively. The responsibility that children feel for communicating well with their peer partners induces them to gain greater conceptual clarity for themselves. In this way, the social demands of the peer encounter combine with its other motivational and affective benefits to spur cognitive growth.

Most striking of our initial social interaction findings was that the children who showed learning gains were the ones most likely to share information about the task with their partners. These were the children who were most engaged in solving the problem while at the same time most dedicated to communicating their ideas about the problem to their partners.

In addition, as noted, most of the learning engagements that we observed were positive and agreeable in quality, rather than negative and conflictual. This account stands in contrast to previous characterizations of peer learning experiences in much of the developmental literature (as, for example, the emphasis on "socio-cognitive conflict" by Piaget's followers). We would point out, however, that most of the previous literature is based on informal observation and theoretical speculation, whereas we have videotaped and coded children's actual collaborative interactions.

Our emerging picture shows peer collaboration creating an atmosphere of social stimulation and support. In this atmosphere, children can become increasingly motivated to solve and discuss challenging tasks. They also can feel comfortable expressing new ideas, even when this involves the risk of being wrong or looking foolish. Engagements that do not work this way, but that instead focus children's attention on the participants and their conduct, lead to self-consciousness rather than improved cognitive performance and learning gains. Similarly, engagements that are highly conflictual and prone to disagreement may foster a critical and self-deprecating attitude on the part of participants, with adverse consequences for learning. The strength of peer collaboration lies in its potential for mutually constructive discourse. In the course of development, as social interaction theory predicts and as our research has shown, such discourse can lead directly to an individual construction of new conceptual insight.

GENERAL CONCLUSIONS ABOUT INTEGRATING PEER LEARNING TECHNIQUES INTO A SYSTEMATIC EDUCATIONAL STRATEGY

In this concluding section we return to the more general issues raised at the beginning of the chapter. Where we can, we draw on the findings of our study; but many of our conclusions go far beyond our own data—or, for that matter, beyond the evidence provided by any research program that we know of. Until, therefore, we and others have opportunities for further empirical examinations of comprehensive peer-based educational strategies, many of the convictions expressed in this section will remain speculative.

Our first conviction is that the three peer learning techniques discussed at the outset—peer tutoring, cooperative learning, and peer collaboration—all have valuable and unique contributions to make toward children's education. They all deserve a place in the school curriculum. None of them, of course, can replace the necessary instructional and classroom management functions of the adult teacher. But they all can be used to supplement these functions and to add further opportunities for cognitive and personality growth. In fact, some of the growth opportunities offered by productive peer exchanges may be currently unavailable in most traditional classrooms. Given the disappointing state of public education today, this makes the introduction of promising peer-based techniques a matter of some urgency.

If we could create a demonstration school to comprehensively test our visions of an ideal educational atmosphere, it would integrate peer and adult instructional techniques in the following manner. The teacher would set the program and priorities of instruction; and the teacher would introduce, as teachers do now, new topics, procedures for learning, and critical elements of knowledge. But large parts of the school day would be set aside for students to discover and master new ideas in peer settings.

The adult teacher would arrange and monitor the peer learning groups and would work individually with children who required additional attention. The peer learning groups would be structured according to the functions required of them: Discovery learning would be accomplished through groups organized for peer collaboration and cooperative learning, whereas skill mastery would be accomplished through peer tutoring arrangements. Social, emotional, and motivational considerations could be addressed both through cooperative learning and peer tutoring.

Because the three types of peer learning have distinct sets of advantages, they should be administered differently from one another. The manner in which each is coordinated with adult instruction, the instructions given to the pupils, even the time of school day during which each is offered, all have important consequences for the effectiveness of the educational experience. Therefore we propose some theoretical and practical guidelines for administering the three types of peer instruction in coordination with adult-directed instruction.

Peer tutoring should be used as a means of consolidating skills and mastering information to which children have already been exposed. It is an ideal end-of-the-day activity. At the close of each school day, teachers could direct tutorial pairs to practice areas of math, reading, and other instructional subjects that may have proven difficult for some children to grasp. The teacher should regularly supervise the tutorial pairs, to insure both that the tutee is making progress and that the tutor is passing along no misinformation. To this end, the teacher should give the tutor guidance about communication techniques and, where necessary, about the subject matter being conveyed. All peer tutoring should be done on a one-to-one basis.

Because peer tutoring offers both tutor and tutee valuable opportunities for cognitive and personal growth, a systematic school approach would expose children to both roles. Every child has some area of competence that can be imparted to another child less skilled in that particular area. Conversely, all children can benefit from tutoring in areas where they are relative novices. In assuming both tutor and tutee roles during the course of the school year, children would have a chance to gain the self-esteem, motivation, and instructional benefits of the tutor's role as well as the competence-improving benefits of the tutee's role. In addition, they would learn the important social-cognitive lessons of role reversal: switching from expert to novice and back again would impart to children a deeper and more sympathetic understanding of other people, themselves, and the enduring human challenge of learning.

Cooperative learning's greatest contribution is in spurring students' motivation. Every school topic has its "essential drudgery," such as multiplication tables, spelling, incidental names and facts, and so on. Cooperative learning can turn such drudgery into enjoyable competitive or cooperative games. In the process, a variety of cognitive skills can be acquired. Cooperative learning is best done in groups of four or five. Its ideal use would be at times during the school day when things start to drag. The teacher could arrange cooperative learning groups on short notice in order to educe from students sustained concentration on important but laborious learning tasks.

Peer collaboration's appeal lies in its potential to foster the acquisition of basic concepts. It is a relatively new technique that has emerged from developmental research and that is almost unknown in the current educational world. Yet it offers a promising means of helping children discover and master those elusive ideas that are at the heart of long-term cognitive growth. This is why our own research interests have been directed at the collaborative forms of peer exchange.

When peer collaboration is used, children should be of approximately equal ages and abilities. The collaboration group may vary in size from two to four children and should be kept intact for the length of time, and the number of sessions, necessary to master the challenging concept under study. The teacher should direct collaboration groups to concepts that are new to them but that are not far beyond their cognitive reach. For example, we found the concept of ratios to be appropriate peer collaboration tasks for fourth- and fifth-grade children.

The teacher should monitor the groups in order to determine whether productive dialogues are taking place; and, if not, the teacher should intervene with guiding comments and suggestions. But the teacher should not go so far as to give the group the right answer or even the best strategy for attaining the right answer. The role of the adult supervisor should be first to keep the children focused on the task at hand and second to review with the children the ideas that they have discovered during their peer discussions.

In collaboration groups, all children should be encouraged to offer solutions and express opinions. No child should be allowed to assume a permanent leadership role: If this seems inevitable, the group should be rearranged or new task material assigned. Intellectual conflict between the children should be kept to a moderate degree, and, where disagreement exists, children should be encouraged to provide verbal explanations to one another concerning the ground of their disagreements. Because children wrestle, largely unaided, with difficult new ideas during peer collaboration sessions, collaboration groups should be arranged in the morning hours of the school day, when children are still fresh and maximally attentive.

Introducing systematic peer-based education to the schools would not mean weakening the roles of adult teachers. Traditional adult-based teaching must still remain the school's major component: Nothing can replace the trained teacher's ability to impart knowledge to pupils. In addition, adult teachers would be essential in training, guiding, and monitoring peer tutors, as well as in selecting material, arranging groups, and facilitating discussions in cooperative learning and peer collaboration sessions. All of the critical arrangements and moment-by-moment decisions about how and when to use peer learning techniques would still rest in the hands of the teacher. As a consequence, peer-based education would enhance the goals and directions that teachers already hold for themselves. But it would offer teachers a new chance to implement these goals by tapping a natural source of children's personal, motivational, and cognitive growth: the peer discourse.

REFERENCES

Allen, V. L. (Ed.). (1976). *Children as teachers: Theory and research on tutoring*. New York: Academic Press.

Ames, G., & Murray, F. B. (1982). When two wrongs make a right: Promoting cognitive change through social conflict. *Developmental Psychology, 18,* 894–897.

Aronson, E., Stephan, C., Lides, J., Blaney, N., & Snapp, M. (1978). *The jigsaw classroom*. Beverly Hills, CA: Sage.

Bearison, D., Magzamen, S., & Filardo, E. (1986). Socio-cognitive conflict and cognitive growth in young children. *Merrill-Palmer Quarterly, 32,* 236–245.

Berndt, T. J. (1987). Conversations between friends: An appraisal of processes and theories. In J. Gewirtz & W. Kurtines (Eds.), *Social interaction and moral development* (pp. 281–300). New York: Wiley.

Bloom, S. (1976). *Peer and cross-age tutoring in the schools*. N.I.E. monograph, U. S. Department of Health, Education, and Welfare, Washington DC.

Botvin, G. J., & Murray, F. B. (1975). The efficacy of peer modeling and social conflict on the acquisition of conservation. *Child Development, 46,* 796–799.

Case, R. (1980). The underlying mechanism of intellectual development. In J. R. Kirby & J. B. Biggs (Eds.), *Cognition, development, and instruction* (pp. 161–186). New York: Academic Press.

Cooper, C. R., Marquis, A., and Edward, D. (1986). Four perspectives on peer learning among elementary school children. In E. C. Mueller & C. R. Cooper (Eds.), *Process and outcome in peer relationships* (pp. 269–300). New York: Academic Press.

Damon, W. (1984). Peer education: The untapped potential. *Journal of Applied Developmental Psychology, 5,* 331–343.

Damon, W., & Killen, M. (1982). Peer interaction and the process of change in children's moral reasoning. *Merrill-Palmer Quarterly, 28,* 347–367.

Doise, W., & Mugny, G. (1979). Individual and collective conflicts of centrations in cognitive development. *European Journal of Psychology, 9,* 105–108.

Doise, W., & Mugny, G. (1984). *The social development of the intellect*. N.Y.: Pergamon.

Doise, W., Mugny, G., & Perret-Clermont, A. (1976). Social interaction and cognitive development. *European Journal of Social Psychology, 6,* 245–247.

East, B. A. (1976). Cross-age tutoring in the elementary school. *Graduate Research in Education and Related Disciplines. 8,* 88–100.

Gartner, A., Kohler, M. C., & Riessman, F. (1971). *Children teach children*. New York: Harper & Row.

Hartup, W. W. (1983). The peer system. In E. M. Hetherington (Ed.) & P. H. Mussen (Series Ed.), *Handbook of child psychology: Vol. 4. Social development* (pp. 103–196). New York: Wiley.

Inhelder, B., & Piaget, J. (1958). *The growth of logical thinking from childhood to adolescence.* New York: Basic Books.

Johnson, D., Johnson, R., & Skon, L. (1979). Student achievement on different types of tasks under cooperative, competitive, and individualistic conditions. *Contemporary Educational Psychology, 4,* 99–106.

Kruger, A. C., & Tomasello, M. (1986). Transactive discussions with peers and adults. *Developmental Psychology, 22,* 681–685.

Miller, S. A., & Brownell, C. A. (1975). Peers, persuasion, and Piaget: Dyadic interaction between conservers and non-conservers. *Child Development, 46,* 992–997.

Murray, F. B. (1968). Cognitive conflict and reversibility training in the acquisition of length conservation. *Journal of Educational Psychology, 60,* 82–87.

Murray, F. B. (1972). Acquisition of conservation through social interaction. *Developmental Psychology, 6,* 1–6.

Murray, J. F. (1974). Social learning and cognitive development: Modelling effects on children's understanding of conservation. *British Journal of Psychology, 65,* 154–160.

Perret-Clermont, A-N. (1980). *Social interaction and cognitive development in children.* New York: Academic Press.

Piaget, J. & Inhelder, B. (1956). *The child's conception of space.* London: Routledge & Kegan Paul.

Sharan, S. (1980). Cooperative learning in small groups: Recent methods and effects on achievement, attitudes, and ethnic relations. *Review of Educational Research, 50,* 241–271.

Sharan, S. (1984). *Cooperative learning.* Hillsdale, NJ: Lawrence Erlbaum.

Siegler, R. S. (1976). Three aspects of cognitive development. *Cognitive Psychology, 8,* 481–520.

Silverman, I. W., & Geiringer, E. (1973). Dyadic interaction and conservation induction: A test of Piaget's equilibration model. *Child Development, 44,* 815–820.

Silverman, I. W., & Stone, J. M. (1972). Modifying cognitive functioning through participation in a problem-solving group. *Journal of Educational Psychology, 63,* 603–608.

Slavin, R. (1980). Cooperative learning. *Review of Educational Research, 50,* 315–342.

Slavin, R. E. (1983). *Cooperative learning.* New York: Longman.

Snyder, S. S., & Feldman, D. H. (1977). Internal and external influences on cognitive developmental change. *Child Development, 48,* 937–943.

Staub, E. (1975). To rear a pro-social child: Reasoning, learning by doing, and learning by teaching others. In D. DePalma & J. Foley (Eds.), *Moral development: Current theory and research* (pp. 113–136). Hillsdale, N.J.: Lawrence Erlbaum.

Vergnaud, G. (1983). Multiplicative structures. In R. Lesh & M. Landau (Eds.), *Acquisition of mathematics concepts and processes* (pp. 127–174). New York: Academic Press.

Vygotsky, L. S. (1978). *Mind in society.* Cambridge, MA: Harvard University Press.

Webb, N. M. (1982). Student interaction and learning in small groups. *Review of Educational Research, 52,* 421–445.

Youniss, J. (1980). *Parents and peers in child development.* Chicago: University of Chicago Press.

CHAPTER 6

The Selection of Friends

Changes Across the Grades and in Different School Environments

JOYCE L. EPSTEIN

The Johns Hopkins University

The process of selecting friends changes with age and in differently organized environments. In an earlier paper I identified three aspects of selection: *the facts of selection, the surface of selection,* and *the depth of selection.* The facts of selection referred to the number of friends chosen and the number of isolates. The surface of selection included the influence of visible features of sex and race on the selection of friends. The review of research on the depth of selection concentrated on patterns of reciprocity and stability in friendships. In each case, I called attention to how the process of selection changes from early childhood through adulthood and described how differently designed school, neighborhood, and work environments affect patterns of interaction, selection, isolation, the proportion of cross-sex and cross-race friends, and the reciprocity and stability of choices (Epstein, 1986). This chapter is an examination of three added features of selection that change over the life course and in differently organized settings. *Proximity* is the most basic fact of selection. As a condition of location, it requires little or no awareness of the attributes or characteristics of others. The next level of selection involves attention to the surface features or visible cues of others. The discussion considers *age* as one surface characteristic that influences the selection of friends. The third, more advanced, level of selection is based on the deep features, personalities, or characters of others. The important issue at this level is how *similarity* and dissimilarity give depth to the selection of friends.

In this review, development refers to the years from early childhood through adolescence, including children from preschool through high school. Environment refers mainly to school and classroom settings, with brief consideration of the other environments in which children interact before and after school in homes and neighborhoods. The studies of proximity, age, and similarity in the literature differ widely in their clarity and rigor of methods, data, and analyses. Few studies include more than one age group, making developmental patterns difficult to document. Few studies of children's friendships include information about the school, classroom, or other environments in which friends are chosen. Despite these problems, the patterns of results across studies show how students of different ages and in different settings select friends based on proximity, age, and similarity. But, because of these problems, the patterns, projections, and conclusions must be considered hypotheses for confirmation or refutation in new research.

A FACT OF SELECTION—PROXIMITY

Proximity places students in context and defines the boundaries within which friends are chosen. As a fact of selection, proximity does not require attention to the characteristics of others. It requires primarily the recognition and use of shared space.

Developmental Patterns

Proximity provides opportunities for eye contact, gestures, other nonverbal communications, physical contact, and verbal communication. These positive, neutral, or negative signals (or "proxemics") may or may not be received, interpreted, or returned by those to whom they are directed. Among 3–5-year-olds, 59% of affiliative actions were ignored or, if received, were not returned (Strayer, 1980). Youngsters become increasingly adept at sending and receiving communications and interpreting them, but even older students and adults overlook, misinterpret, ignore, or reject signals from others who seek a friend. In laboratory and preschool settings, toddlers 18–24 months old—much younger than researchers once believed—began to use proximity to select friends for play and not just for coexistence (Gottman & Parkhurst 1980; Lewis & Rosenblum, 1975; Stambak & Verba, 1986; Vandell & Mueller, 1980).

Three major settings establish the boundaries that place children in proximity—home, community, and school. In each setting, differences in the organization of space and activities affect how and with whom children are permitted to interact. In each setting, the definition of "close proximity" changes with age. At home, close proximity refers expandingly to one's own backyard, block, neighborhood, other neighborhoods, and community. In school, students also are given increasingly wider space for interactions with other students, ranging from one classroom to several classrooms, the library, cafeteria, playground, gym, and other areas in and out of the school building.

Infants depend on their parents, siblings, or caretakers to put them in contact with other children in homes, play groups, or playgrounds. Early social contacts occur because of *naturally occurring proximities* with siblings, relatives, and neighbors; *accidental proximities* created by chance meetings with other children and adults; and *planned proximities* arranged by parents. Vandell and Mueller (1980) studied mothers' efforts to create social experiences for their infants. Up to 60% of the babies in their sample met with other babies at least once a week. These planned proximities for some infants may be important for understanding the development of social skills in school-aged youngsters.

Families may move to particular neighborhoods to place their children in proximity with potential friends (Rubin, 1980). Although we tend to consider neighborhoods separate and different from school environments, the two settings are closely related in the selection of friends. Children bring to school different histories of friendships and patterns of choosing friends from their experiences at home and in their communities (Newson & Newson, 1978). These histories are likely to affect the social skills children use at school and the selections they make and receive there. If schools ignore these histories, youngsters who were isolated at home may remain ignored or rejected at school. If researchers ignore these histories, their measures of choice and rejection at school may overstate or misrepresent the social adjustment and acceptance of popular children at school.

Neighborhoods continue to define the boundaries for students' choices of friends in school. Seagoe's (1933) early studies of students in Grades 3 to 8 showed that students and their friends lived an average of .26 miles apart, whereas students and other classmates lived .92 miles apart. Furfey (1929) reported that 89% of elementary school students' friends were from the same neighborhood, and half a century later, Fine (1980) found similar patterns of selection by 9- to 12-year-olds. Proximity is correlated with the quality of relations. Coates' (1985) data suggest that compared to other classmates, high school friends who live near each other interact more frequently, have known each other longer, and are closer psychologically in their feelings of friendship.

Studies have not specified developmental changes in the geographic distance between friends' homes, but it is likely that older students and their friends live further apart than younger students, on average. Epstein (1983b) reported clear trends of increasingly wider boundaries of selection within school settings from Grade 6 through Grade 12. In the upper grades, students selected more friends from beyond their own teachers' classrooms. Also, although about equal numbers of male and females were present at all grade levels, the number of cross-sex choices of best friends increased with age (Epstein, 1983a). Older students reassessed their friendships with those in proximity and changed at least some same-sex to other-sex choices to meet new social needs and demands. There is, then, some evidence that the meaning of being "in proximity" changes with age.

Environmental Conditions

The opportunities and demands in home, community, and school environments can alter the typical or expected patterns of proximity at every age level. For example, some neighborhoods are designed to give young children broader boundaries for play and exploration. In these neighborhoods youngsters roam further earlier than would typically be the case. Some schools design educational programs that give even young children wide latitude in finding space in which they can work and interact with other students.

The importance of proximity for social contact and play is affected by cultural traditions. For example, Pitts (1968) described how, in France, preschool children in close proximity did *not* play together until they obtained permission to do so from their parents. French parents granted permission mainly on the basis of the known or assumed socioeconomic status of the nearby child. New social arrangements can change cultural patterns. Preschoolers in French "crèches" (day-care settings) are affected by school programs and school rules about playing together and not by traditional parental gatekeeping (Stambak & Verba, 1986).

Neighborhood arrangements and social interactions are affected by cultural patterns of housing and work (Whiting, 1986). And, within cultures, different housing patterns create natural variations in population distributions that affect young children's associations (Kon, 1981). For example, youngsters who live in urban apartment houses, a neighborhood of row houses, a suburban sprawl of single-family houses, or a rural community of widely spaced farms will have different patterns of contact with different numbers of potential acquaintances and friends. Proximity and contact depend on the configuration of residential areas, as well as the number of children per housing unit and the socially structured opportunities to meet other children.

Five major conditions in schools (and, one could argue, in other settings) affect the proximity of students: *architectural features* of the school building, play yards, and other spaces that encourage or discourage small or large groups to work or play together; *equipment and supplies* that permit individual activities, require sharing, or, if insufficient in number, create crowding; *demographic factors* such as the sex, race, age, or social-class compositions in the school and their distributions in classrooms; *instructional methods* that discourage or encourage students to contact, help, and interact with other students during the school day; and *the organization of nonacademic activities* such as the number of extracurricular activities before, during, and after school that encourage or limit participation based on interests or talents. Each of these environmental conditions puts particular students in close proximity or separates them. Each factor encourages or limits movement and social exchange among students.

For example, *instructional methods* encourage, restrict, or prohibit peer interaction in classrooms as teachers organize learning tasks, shared-authority or decision-making opportunities, rewards and recognitions, grouping practices, evaluation techniques, and time allocations. I call these manipulable structures the Task (T), Authority (A), Reward (R), Grouping (G), Evaluation (E), and Time (T) (or TARGET) structures of classroom organization (Epstein, 1988; in press). Each of the TARGET structures is linked to different motivational forces and to different measures of student success. These structures determine where, when, how, and why some students are placed in proximity and interact with others in learning and social activities.

The *task* structure determines whether assignments at appropriate levels of difficulty are designed to be completed alone or with others, whether students use books, filmstrips, computer terminals or other media independently or in groups, and whether there are other social arrangements for learning. The *authority* structure defines whether few or many students participate in classroom lessons and activities, in decisions that affect school life and learning, and in positions of responsibility and leadership. Teachers may make all decisions, or students may share authority in creating proximities by choosing their own work partners, seat partners, committee members, dance partners, and so on for different school activities. The *reward* structure determines whether students are officially recognized and rewarded for working together and helping each other in pairs, teams, or groups. The *grouping* structure arranges student proximities for the delivery of instruction. Research has documented the impact on children's choices of friends of being in the same reading groups within classes (Bossert, 1979; Hallinan & Sorenson, 1985), in the same curricular tracks (Hansell & Karweit, 1983), and in the same extracurricular activities (Karweit, 1983). These proximities create similarities in location, status, and interests among students and directly affect the selection of friends. The *evaluation* structure determines whether teachers judge classwork and behavior fairly, publicly, and privately. Public and private assessments affect children's perceptions of each other and their selection of friends. Teachers also use the evaluation structure to arrange or ignore opportunities for peer evaluation, as in peer coaching in the writing process, peer tutoring, or peer checking and correcting of tests. And, teachers may structure *time* in ways that permit or prohibit the exchange of ideas among students in proximity. The organization of the TARGET structures creates proximities that encourage or discourage friendly behavior among students, communication about learning activities, and opportunities for meeting and selecting new friends.

Among the ubiquitous grouping practices in school, *seating* has received some attention in the literature on students and their friends. Several studies show that seating proximity affects the selection of friends in the elementary and secondary grades (Bossert, 1979, Cooper, Marquis, & Edwards, 1986; Hallinan, 1980) and in college (Byrne, 1961). Teachers' seating practices put some students in contact for instruction and for other classroom activities. Seats may be in rows, circles, sections, or other arrangements and may be selected by the teachers or the students, with fixed or open assignment for a school year. Students in adjacent seats, more than other students, exchange information about schoolwork, ask and answer questions of each other, check each other's papers, and share ideas. Seating arrangements can be positive or negative factors for teaching and learning. Seating is used to *restrict student interaction*, thereby reducing distractions. Teachers change students' seats when problems arise from too much friendly behavior (Grant & Sleeter, 1986; Hrybyk & Farnham-Diggory, 1981). This may become a periodic procedure if new seatmates become friends and become annoying to teachers. Seating can also be used to *increase student interaction,* enabling students to work together and help each other (Cooper, Marquis, & Edwards, 1986).

Eder (1985) observed a developmental pattern of change and stability in seating arrangements in a middle school lunchroom where seating was open, not assigned. Sixth-grade students changed seats from day to day more often than did seventh- or eighth-grade students. The sixth graders who were new to the middle school were in a period of creating and seeking proximities to consider new friends and to reevaluate old friends. Their changing proximities reflected their explorations, choices, rejections, and new selections. Older students who had already spent at least one year pursuing viable friendships were more stable in their seating arrangements. Their proximities more often reflected acceptance and maintenance of selections.

Some schools organize open-education, high-participatory, child-centered, or project-oriented programs, or use other instructional methods to redesign the TARGET structures. Minuchin (1976) reported more interactions and Hallinan and Tuma (1978) reported more selections of friends by children in open-education elementary schools compared to traditional schools. Epstein (1983b) showed that students in more participatory middle and junior high schools chose a greater number of friends and selected them from wider boundaries than did students in less participatory schools. Downing and Bothwell (1979) demonstrated in an experimental setting that students with experience in open-space schools chose seats in expectation of doing more cooperative work with those who sat nearby. Research is needed at all grade levels to explain how different designs of the TARGET structures, separately and in combination, affect the proximities of students, their interaction, learning, and the selection of friends.

Summary and Suggestions

Physical distance remains an important fact for the selection of friends all across the life span, although its definitions and uses change. There is complete reliance by infants and very young children on close, physical proximity for the selection and definition of friends and increasingly less reliance thereafter on close proximity to define or maintain friendships. The meanings and functions of proximity change with age and with the development of cognitive and social skills. Proximity means "security" and "familiarity" to infants and toddlers but begins to have the added meaning of "play and shared activity" to preschool children (Maccoby & Jacklin, 1974; Selman, 1976). The definition of proximity broadens as students expand their social spheres. Older students make friends in wider circles and keep friends longer who are at greater distances or who move away. Research is needed on developmental patterns of neighborhood proximity and on the effects of the histories of students' selections on new choices of school friends.

There are several environmental issues that deserve attention. Studies show that there are social consequences from architecturally and programmatically diverse home, neighborhood, school, and classroom environments that support different patterns of student proximity. Some environments encourage active learning and assign tasks that require talking, planning, sharing, leading, helping, tutoring, evaluating, recognizing, appreciating, and communicating in other ways. Students in proximity in these settings have many reasons to interact on academic and social activities, discover each other's strengths and weaknesses, and enter friendships. By contrast, some environments emphasize passive learning and assign tasks that require silence, the following of directions and rules set only by others, and individual competition for few rewards. Students in these settings have infrequent reasons to interact on academic matters, despite their close proximity.

There is only limited information across the grades about how student proximities that result from differently organized schools and classrooms affect students' social skills. And even less is known about whether school and classroom attention to patterns of proximity enhances or reduces student academic success or personal growth in other desired outcomes of schooling. These factors may be especially important for helping youngsters learn to appreciate students from different racial or ethnic cultures, as suggested by several studies that have observed or measured patterns of social contact and the selection of friends (Epstein, 1983a; Grant & Sleeter, 1986; Lipsitz, 1984).

There are other patterns that should be studied. School factors that affect proximity probably have stronger influences on patterns of selection among elementary, middle, and junior high school students than among high school students because younger students form and change friends more frequently and have access to fewer settings from which to choose friends (Epstein, 1983b). Environmental conditions that affect proximity should have stronger influence on selection during times of transitions or upheavals, as when students enter new and larger middle, junior high, or high schools, or when they move to new communities and enter new schools. Research is scarce on differently organized middle or junior high schools where patterns of friendship of early adolescents may be especially influenced by school and classroom environments.

Three additional issues could energize research on proximity as a fact of selection—patterns and effects of seeking proximity, the increasing importance of multiple proximities, and the problems created by proximity in measuring selection.

SEEKING PROXIMITY. Students may seek proximity by taking the initiative to contact another individual or to join a group. Or, students may "hover" near a potential friend or at the edges of group activities waiting to be asked to join (Putallaz & Gottman, 1981). Students at all ages and in all settings demonstrate proximity-seeking. For example, middle school students may "hang around" a popular person, hoping to be recognized and accepted (Eder, 1985). In part, proximity-seeking by hovering or asserting oneself reflects the students' personalities, the other students' attitudes, and the environmental opportunities, encouragement, or punishment for seeking new social contacts. Research is needed on this intriguing process across age groups and in differently organized school environments.

MULTIPLE PROXIMITIES. The importance of any single type of proximity changes as students increase the number of different locations in which they work and play with others. For example, children in Grades 1–6 spend about 35% of their time with classmates, peers, or friends in relatively few school, home, and community settings (Institute for Social Research, 1981). High school students spend 50% or more of their time in activities with classmates or friends (Csikszentmihalyi & Larson, 1984). In an average week, older students come in contact with friends and potential friends in a dozen or more different school, classroom, and community locations. Multiple and accumulated proximities within and across environments contribute to the changing nature of selection. Students increasingly have more opportunities to make friends in different settings, increasing the strength of some friendships with those who share activities in many locations, decreasing the strength of other friendships by diluting time for interaction, or creating site-specific friendships. Small and large, cross-sectional and longitudinal, ethnographic and empirical studies are needed on the influence over time of multiple proximities on the choice of friends. This complex characteristic of proximity is a key topic for advancing research on friendship selection and influence.

PROXIMITY AS A MEASUREMENT PROBLEM. Proximity itself is thought to affect the measurement of selection. Foot, Chapman, and Smith (1980) suggested that children's reports about their friends could be affected by seeing nearby students as they look around the room when they are completing sociometric forms. Children who are close in proximity may be named or checked more often than others who are across the room, in another class, or absent from school, even if those students are equally or more important friends. To determine if and how proximity creates errors in the measurement of choices of friends, studies are needed that supplement written names or checklists of friends with individual interviews, observations, diaries of social contacts, or other behavioral measures. Multiple measures of selection would help document more accurately the number, identity, and location of friends in school and out.

Proximity is a necessary but increasingly insufficient condition for the selection of friends. In most instances, if students are not physically near each other, they will not meet, interact, or become friends. But many students who are in close and frequent proximity do not become friends, and very few become close friends. The next sections review and discuss other factors that affect the selection of friends from among those children in proximity.

THE SURFACE OF SELECTION—SAME- AND MIXED-AGE CHOICES

The surface of selection refers to the visible characteristics that people notice in each other and use to choose among equally proximate potential friends. One surface feature—age—has been a topic of interest in research on students' selection of friends. I examine patterns of same-age, near-age, and mixed-age choices of friends across the grades and in differently designed environments.

Developmental Patterns

Many researchers have reported that students select their friends in school almost exclusively from same-age peers, usually because of the age-graded character of most classrooms. The predominance of same-age choices of friends is also the result of the measurement instruments used in most research on schoolchildren's selections. Students in age-graded schools may be asked to limit their choices of friends to students in their classroom or grade, or they may be asked to check the names of their friends or best friends only from lists of students in their class or grade. The age-graded organization of schools and the restrictive measures used in many studies combine to distort understanding of same- versus mixed-age choices.

Some researchers have used innovative methods of data collection to improve knowledge about age as a surface feature of selection. In one study, Ellis, Rogoff, and Cromer (1981) systematically observed 2,000 children under the age of 18 in a neighborhood and recorded the number, ages, and sexes of the children and their friends. By telephone they also asked parents to report the ages and characteristics of the friends playing with their children at home at the time of the phone call. Of course, infants and very young children were most often in mixed-age groups, in the company of caretaking adults or older children. But for all ages, Ellis and associates found more near- and mixed-age interaction than they expected. Fewer than 15% of 11–12-year-olds played with only same-age peers at home. Similar patterns were found whether or not siblings were included as playmates.

Csikszentmihalyi and Larson (1984) obtained comprehensive accounts by asking high school students to record their contacts with friends in school, at home, and in the neighborhood or community whenever a randomly scheduled beeper directed them to do so. Although they did not record the actual ages of the students' friends, they did record the percentage of time spent with parents, relatives, and "others," including other adults. They found that 9th graders spent more time with their families than did 12th graders. And 12th graders interacted in many different environments, giving them more opportunities than 9th graders had for multiage contacts and friends. Their unusual method of data collection could be useful for improving research on the developmental patterns of selection of same- and mixed-age friends.

Whiting (1986) reported that same-age friends are not the rule in most developing countries; instead mixed-age groups predominate. Recent studies support Barker and Wright's (1955) earlier finding that about 65% of the children's interactions in and out of school were among friends who differed 12 months or more in age.

The metric that defines same-age friends differs in the literature for young children, older children, and adults. Schoolchildren's friendships are considered "same age" if the youngsters are within 12 months of each other's ages (Hartup, 1976). Adult friendships are considered "same age" if the parties differ 4 to 5 years (Feld, 1984) or even 10 years or more in age (Verbrugge, 1979). The different definitions of "same age" reflect, in part, the different spans of time of childhood (18 years) and adulthood (50 to 70 years) and the more dramatic developmental changes over short periods in childhood. Through adolescence, students' physical, emotional, social, moral, and intellectual growth and development assure dynamic, fluctuating qualities to students' social awareness, social and cognitive skills, and choices of friends. The definition and metric of "same age" seem largely arbitrary. Research is needed to explain if or how youngsters think about the ages of their friends in and out of school, and whether and when age differences of 1 year, 4 years, or 10 years and more become important in the selection process.

Maas (1968) suggested that students who select older and younger friends have different personalities. In a study of a small sample of "warm" and "aloof" 8- to 12-year-olds, he found that males and females with warm, sociable personalities more often selected older friends, whereas aloof males more often selected younger friends. Ladd (1983) showed that on school playgrounds where children were free to create their own proximities, there was considerable grade-level mixing. All children played predominantly with others in the same grade, but popular children interacted more with older, upper grade friends. Rejected children spent more time with younger children and less time in multigrade groups. These patterns carried over to the out-of-school friends of popular and rejected children. In another small study, Hansell (1981) found that high school students with high ego levels (i.e., high independence of others) made proportionately more mixed-age choices of friends than students with low ego levels (i.e., high dependence on others, conforming). Despite the lack of dramatic differences between groups of students, these three studies suggest intriguing links between personality and the structure of same-age versus mixed-age choices. These connections deserve attention in research across the age span.

Certain behaviors may be more common in the friendships of students of particular age combinations. Hartup's (1983) review suggests that children who differ in age have fewer other similarities and more complementaries in social behaviors. For example, older children may be more nurturing and younger children more dependent in mixed-age dyads or groups. Rubin (1980) found that among 3- and 4-year-old mixed-age pairs, the older friend more often took the role of the teacher or comforter. Aggressive behavior may be more common between same-age friends (Hartup, 1978, 1983; Brody, Stoneman, MacKinnon, & MacKinnon, 1985; Whiting, 1986; Maccoby & Jacklin, 1974). Friends who differ in age may be selected to fulfill needs for dominance or dependence, care giving or care receiving (French, 1984; Graziano, French, Brownell, & Hartup, 1976). Or, mixed-age friendships may carry expectations that help students to develop certain qualities. For example, older students, feeling that they are expected to be helpful or show leadership in activities with younger friends, may develop those behaviors. On the other hand, equal chronological age is not a requirement for friendship (Rubin, 1980; Hartup, 1983). Mixed-age friends may be chosen as equals on the basis of similarities other than age (Lewis & Rosenblum, 1975; Reisman & Shor, 1978). An older or younger friend selected as an equal need not take on special or different social roles in a friendship.

The importance or influence of same- or mixed-age friends for students' social development is not clear in extant research. Mixed-age friends are alternatively assumed to be beneficial or detrimental. In one study, same-age friends made more reciprocated choices than mixed-age friends as early as the preschool years (Drewry & Clark, 1983). This suggests that same-age selections may yield stronger and better friendships. But there are counterclaims. Lever (1976) found that males who played mixed-age, large-group games naturally chose more mixed-age friends than did females who had different patterns of play. Ladd's (1983) study also found that similarity of interests in games, levels of skill, and social status were more important than similarity of age in activities on the open playground.

Those who consider mixed-age patterns as deviant from regular or expected choices are especially concerned about the selection of younger friends by older students. These choices may signify social problems of unpopular children. Alternatively, these choices may be useful, healthy solutions for establishing and maintaining social contacts by students who are physically smaller, psychologically shyer, socially less experienced, or cognitively slower than their same-age peers. Schunk (1987) suggests that same-age interactions may be especially important for influencing age-appropriate behaviors and skills. He points out, however, that the dynamics of same- and mixed-age influence are uncertain, because previous studies have been severely restricted in their coverage of different combinations of age pairs. Most studies compare the influence of same-age peers to child-adult pairs, rather than to mixed-age dyads or groups of students.

The early adolescent years hold great potential for mixed-age interactions. Students between the ages of 10 and 15 develop at very different rates. Younger students may be taller and more mature than older students, because they enter puberty at different times. Some students move to "the fast crowd." Billy, Rodgers, and Udry (1984) show that younger teens who engage in early sexual activity or who are involved in deviant or delinquent activity may interact more with older teens and select more mixed-age, older friends. In a study conducted in the Soviet Union, Kon and Losenkov (1978), found that adolescents more readily chose older than younger friends. Another study found that adolescent females chose older male friends more often than males chose females (Dunphy, 1963). The latter two studies describe mainly normal, not deviant, patterns. But the contrasting patterns and interpretations show the need for clearer studies of the benefits and disadvantages of same- or mixed-age friendships in social adjustment and academic development for students of different ages.

Environmental Conditions

When environments permit and encourage mixed-age interaction, students' selections of friends reflect their opportunities and experiences. For example, Allen and Devin-Sheehan (1976) reported that in a mixed-age, one-room school, children regularly named friends older and younger than themselves.

Grades	% with at Least One Mixed-age Friend
1–3	82
4–6	67
7–8	60

The youngest children's choices were least bound by age considerations. From Grade 4 on, students increasingly selected friends of their same age and grade. Nevertheless, even among the older students in this school, there were about three times as many mixed-age choices as might be expected in age-graded schools. In the one-room school, 76% of the children said it was "easy" to be friends with children of other ages.

School practices increase the interactions of students of different ages. Minuchin (1976) reported more mixed-age contacts in open-space elementary schools where activities often occurred across teaching areas or grade levels. In some schools, mixed-age tutoring is organized so that older students tutor younger children in nearby schools or in the same school. Friendship choices can be affected by the interactions of tutors and tutees of different ages (Allen, 1976), although there is little research on the extent of mixed-age, stable friendships that result from tutoring. Other organizational forms such as ungraded classes, mixed-grade classrooms, multigrade regrouping by level of competence, and activities such as whole-school clubs or activity periods based on interests and talents may include mixed-age populations and encourage the selection of friends of different ages (Lipsitz, 1984).

Although most schools are age-graded, there has been little attention to the natural variation of ages in classrooms. In Grade 1, students are usually 6 or 7 years old—a range of about a year. By Grade 8, because of patterns of retention, skipping, and school transfers, students may be 2, 3, or more years apart. High school seniors may range from 16 to 19 years old. In postsecondary schools and colleges, the age range will be even greater, from 16 to 65, or older. There is, then, greater correspondence in friends' grade levels than ages, with one study of high schools reporting that about 80% of students' friends were in the same grade (Kandel, 1978). New studies are needed of the effects of retention on social interaction and the selection of friends across the grades. This area of study is especially important in settings where school improvement programs set higher standards for promotion and change the typical variation of ages of students in classrooms.

After age 12, there may be an increase in cross-age friendships as students enter middle and junior high schools where school programs, sports, teams, and other extracurricular activities bring students from all grades together. One middle school in Baltimore is organized so that students in Grades 6, 7, and 8 are assigned to mixed-grade classes and academic teams. The curriculum is presented in topical sequences to cover required subjects over the three years in middle school. Because of the school and classroom organizations, these preadolescents interact with students across grade levels in class, conversations, activities at school, phone calls about homework, and activities out of school.

Variations in school environments have not been well researched for new knowledge on same- or mixed-age friends. It is important to ask these questions: What benefits or disadvantages are associated with younger or older friends in schools that encourage or discourage such interactions? How might the research results on this topic improve the effectiveness of school programs?

Summary and Suggestions

Age is a physical, visible cue—like sex or race—of a basic similarity to or difference from others who are potential friends. The meaning of "same age" changes over the school years. The importance of age as a criterion for selection differs in response to opportunities for mixed-age interactions in school and in other environments. Differently organized schools and classrooms alter the emphasis on same- or mixed-age contacts and friendships. Studies of friends in one-room schools or in mixed-age classrooms suggest that mixed-age friends are natural and positive choices. Almost all out-of-school patterns of selection include mixed-age friends.

Research needs to incorporate innovative methods for collecting data on all friends in school and out to improve understanding of the actual numbers of same-age, near-age, and mixed-age choices of friends at different grade levels. Even more important, studies are needed that focus on these choices and their effects in differently organized schools and other settings.

Proximity is basically similarity of place. Age is a simple form of similarity of person or characteristic. Both location and chronology can affect the selection of friends. Proximity is a crude indicator of similar goals and purposes for being in a particular place. Age may be a proxy for measures of social and academic development. The next section examines the deeper qualities of personality, character, or behavior that may influence the choice of friends.

THE DEPTH OF SELECTION—SIMILARITY OF FRIENDS

One of the continuing debates about patterns of selection is whether, when, and why friends are chosen for their similarities, complementarities, or differences of attitudes, behaviors, goals, or personalities. Do similarities lead to choice, reciprocity, and stability in friendships, or to boredom or competition in relationships? Do differences lead to conflict and rejection, or to excitement and enrichment in relationships? And, in terms of the key questions in this chapter: How do age and differently organized schools, classrooms, or other social environments affect the importance of particular similarities or differences in the selection of friends?

Developmental Patterns

Students select ever more similar friends. Very young children select friends without much thought about the characteristics or characters of others. From kindergarten to high school, children become increasingly aware of, interested in, and articulate about their similarities (Peevers & Secord, 1973). The trend is highly linear, although there is some evidence that even young children can make judgments and deep commitments to their friends (Gottman, 1983). Research shows that children choose friends more similar to themselves on more traits over the years from preschool to Grade 3 to Grade 6 (Drewry & Clark, 1984). Similarity of friends from age 12 to age 16 was greater than the similarity of random pairs of students (Duck, 1973).

Stronger, deeper friends tend to be more similar. For example, first-named friends and best friends were more similar than later-named friends and were more apt to be reciprocated and stable choices (Epstein, 1983a; Kandel,

1978). Among adolescents, best friends were more similar than other friends on attitudes and behaviors concerning drug use (Kandel, 1978). Friends became more similar, too, in other deviant behaviors (Jessor & Jessor, 1975).

Ironically, similarity becomes more salient in friendships as the potential for differences increases. Young students' personalities and goals are in the process of formation, and development proceeds at different rates. This assures a dynamic, volatile quality to questions of "similarities" that may, at any time, change to "differences." One friend may crystallize personal goals sooner than another. The resulting discrepancies (e.g., one friend decides to study harder, get good grades, take an art or science course, while the other does not) may lead friends to accept their differences, to attempt to influence each other so they become similar again, or to dissolve the friendships and select new friends who are more similar or more easily influenced. As the students' social boundaries broaden to include new contacts in multiple settings, their earlier friends selected for close proximity, similar age, similar sex, or other characteristics may not be similar enough. This process may be especially complex in early adolescence as students enter new and larger middle or junior high schools.

In one study, children in Grades 6 to 12 made increasingly discriminating interpretations of their own and others' characteristics, preferences, values, and goals (Epstein, 1983a). Changing perceptions of self and others may help to explain why older students' choices are more selective and their similarities to or differences from friends are more clear. Smollar and Youniss (1982) studied concepts of friendship of students aged 6–24. They reported important developmental patterns in beliefs about friendships such as the increasing importance of shared talk about personal problems and feelings. Changing concepts of friendship—a favorite topic of developmental psychologists (Selman, 1976; Selman and Jaquette, 1978)—are reflected in the changing patterns of selection discussed in this chapter. More advanced articulation and understanding of what friendship means can lead to increased attention to the deep qualities of individuals in the selection process. Similarity in students' ideas about friends, similar abilities to discuss friendship as an abstract concept, and similar abilities to translate abstractions into practice are examples of the complex forms of similarity that may influence the selection process.

In a series of studies on hypothetical choices of friends by middle grade children in Scottish schools, Bigelow and La Gaipa (1980) showed that older children selected hypothetical friends who were at higher levels of social development than themselves. More 8- to 10-year-olds picked friends at their own developmental level than did children 10 to 12 years old. The older children may have viewed themselves as more mature than the researchers had categorized them or may have been aspiring to new behaviors. This study suggests that students may actively seek differences and challenges in relationships. By contrast, Byrne and Griffitt (1966) reported that students in Grades 4 to 12 preferred hypothetical friends who liked the same things the students liked. The seemingly contradictory results of the two studies suggest that it may be unwise to draw conclusions about choices of real friends from studies of hypothetical selections.

There are subjective and objective similarities in friends. Children (Davitz, 1955), adolescents (Billy, Rodgers, & Udry, 1984), and adults (Fiedler, 1954) perceive or report greater similarity between themselves and their friends than is in fact true. The *perception* of similarity may be as important as its reality (Byrne & Griffitt, 1966), at least in the initial selection of friends. Because respondents tend to overreport similarity with their friends, researchers must measure the characteristics, attitudes, and goals of friends directly and not rely only on the respondents' reports.

Brown and Lohr (1987) and Clasen and Brown (1986) look at similarity in clique and crowd membership. Students who are members of a crowd have higher self-esteem than those who seek but are refused crowd membership. Students who do not care about crowd membership are not affected by their lack of affiliation. Self-esteem, then, may be enhanced and maintained when students find either a compatible crowd or other types of friendships, but self-esteem is negatively influenced by rejection. This process may be especially dramatic in middle schools or junior high schools when self-esteem is in an important phase of development and when students' elementary school friendship groups are shaken by exposure in larger schools to new students and to the formation of new groups and cliques.

Although students are generally positive about the importance of friends, older adolescents are less responsive than early adolescents to demands for conformity in crowds and groups. Late adolescents move toward finding and building similarities with a few close friends. As they search for independence and individuality, groups of friends remain important, but similarity-for-similarity's sake decreases in appeal and importance (Brown, Eicher, & Petrie, 1986). Two provocative hypotheses for new studies are that conformity guides the selection of early adolescent friends more than of later adolescent friends, and that older students actively work toward individuality, even if it means the loss of some friends in a group.

SIMILARITY: AN IMPORTANT LINK BETWEEN SELECTION AND INFLUENCE. In a national sample of students from families with low socioeconomic status (SES), Ginsburg and Hanson (1986) used cross-sectional data to show the potential importance of choices of friends for creating or maintaining similarities. Among low-SES white students, 75% of those in the top 20% in grade point average (GPA) had at least one close friend who planned to attend college, compared to 34% of those in the bottom 20% in GPA. About 50% of students whose friends respected high report card grades achieved good grades themselves, compared to 22% of students whose friends did not think highly of good grades. Similar dramatic patterns were found for black students and their friends. The implication is that students who have friends who are positive about school in skills, goals, or attitudes are more likely to be influenced to become or remain positive themselves.

Studies using longitudinal data are even more convincing. Kandel (1978) reported several important patterns: Students were more similar to new friends than to friends they dropped; new friends were already similar to the chooser prior to selection; and friends became more similar from the fall to the spring of the school year. Similarity increased most among friends who made stable and reciprocated choices.

Cohen (1977) studied selection and socialization patterns in high school students' cliques of four members or more. He found that clique members were more similar to each other than to other students on 18 attitudes and behaviors, with several of the differences significant. New members in cliques became increasingly similar to original members in their attitudes and behaviors.

Epstein (1983c) reported that students' current friends were more similar on several academic and nonacademic measures than friends selected one year earlier. This was especially true for students in Grades 6, 7, and 9. By the time they were in Grade 12, students' current friends were not much different from their earlier friends in a specific aspect of personality (self-reliance) or in school success (report card grades). Even in Grade 12, however, current friends continued to be more similar than earlier friends on college plans, achievement test scores, and attitudes toward school.

In all three longitudinal studies, the increase in similarity from fall to spring or from one school year to the next was due partly to the selection of new and more similar friends, and partly to friends' influence on particular outcomes so that they became more similar as they continued their friendship. The three studies measured similarity on multiple educational and social outcomes of importance to students—academic success, drug use, attitudes, and personality variables. They illustrate the importance of asking, "Similarity on what?" in new research.

Although *unselected classmates* and other acquaintances can influence attitudes and behavior by example, by modeling, or by group norms (Schunk, 1987), research shows convincingly that *selected* friends are likely to have stronger positive or negative influences on attitudes and behaviors. Friends either *anchor* and maintain already similar attitudes and behaviors or *change* important differing attitudes and behaviors to make themselves more similar (Cohen, 1983). Epstein (1983c) documented patterns of maintenance and change of friends' attitudes and behaviors. Longitudinal data from one school year to the next indicated that similar friends changed least over time. Their attitudes and behaviors were anchored by their similarities. For example, on several measures of attitudes and achievements similarly high-scoring students and their friends remained high, and similarly low-scoring friends remained low over 1 year. Low-scoring students were especially disadvantaged by the selection of similar friends. By anchoring their behaviors with similar friends, they reduced their potential for change toward positive school attitudes and accomplishments. Dissimilar friends changed most over time. Initially low-scoring students with initially high-scoring friends changed in a more positive direction than other low-scoring students. Initially high-scoring students with initially low-scoring friends changed in a more negative direction than other high-scoring students. Dissimilar students influenced each other in both positive and negative directions and became more similar over the year in attitudes toward school and school achievements.

There are times in the life course that certain similarities are more salient and when influence is more important. For example, sometime before high school graduation, students face important decisions about attending college. Cohen (1985) found that influence on a friend's college plans was stronger in the sophomore year than in the senior year. Epstein (1983c) used data from Grade 8 to Grade 9 and from Grade 11 to Grade 12 to compare influence on college plans and other outcomes. Over 45% of the students who had *no definite plans* to attend college in Grade 11 made definite plans by Grade 12 *if* some or all of their best friends had college plans. Epstein's data indicate that influence occurs over 1 year in Grades 6, 7, 9, and 12, but especially dramatic patterns are clear between the fall of Grade 11 and the fall of Grade 12. By the spring of the senior year, most decisions about attending college have been made, and so measures from fall to spring of Grade 12 should not reveal as much active influence as measures taken at earlier, critical decision points. Research is needed on how friends influence critical-time decisions, such as college plans, choice of jobs, dating styles, and other behaviors at particular times in the life course.

Environmental Conditions

Schools and classrooms are organized in ways that emphasize similarities or differences among students. The different emphases can affect the importance that students place on certain characteristics as criteria for selecting friends. For example, many schools separate students into groups that are similar in achievement (tracking or ability grouping); sex (same-sex schools or activities); race (racially homogeneous schools, resegregated classrooms or instructional groups); age (grade levels); and other interests or abilities (sports and activity programs). Other schools purposely create heterogeneous, multiability, racially integrated, mainstreamed, or mixed-age groups that emphasize interaction, tolerance, and the positive use of students' differences. These divisions and assignments influence the choice of friends by creating proximities and by establishing attitudes in students about the importance of similarities and differences in surface characteristics or deep qualities of personalities.

School organizations place different emphases on particular status criteria. High socioeconomic status (SES) or high achievement may or may not be indicators of high peer status depending on the school's grouping practices, course offerings, extracurricular activities, teachers' attitudes, and other policies and practices. Epstein (1983a) found that in high-participatory schools, students selected friends from more diverse socioeconomic and achievement groups than did students in other schools. Low-SES students in high-participatory schools selected more high-SES friends, and students with no plans for college selected more friends with college plans than did similar students in low-participatory schools. Schools that offer many opportunities for interaction and group work may promote the selection of friends on the basis of their interests, goals, ideas, helpfulness, or other qualities of personality, rather than on traditionally defined status characteristics. Studies are needed to identify how different school and classroom environments alter the importance of particular surface characteristics (such as age, sex, race) or deeper qualities (such as college plans or academic ability, positive or negative attitudes toward school or particular subjects, or personal standards of tolerance, etc.) as criteria for selecting friends.

Bossert (1979) looked closely at within-class instructional groups in elementary classrooms. He described how some teachers rewarded students from the same reading group for working together in class and playing together during recess and for not interacting with students from different reading groups. Other teachers encouraged students to make broad contacts and arranged curricular and extracurricular activities so that students interacted with others they might not meet in their reading groups. When they changed teachers, students appeared to alter their friendship choices to match their new teachers' philosophies. The teachers' different practices of grouping and their attitudes about interaction and integration restricted or expanded the students' choices of friends to those with the same or different reading abilities.

Similarity of friends is often equated with high support, low conflict, mutual rewards, self-confirmation, and positive social development. However, some quarreling, tension, aggression, competition, and dissimilarity may be important experiences in friendships, even if these qualities do not sound desirable (Berndt, 1986; Hartup, 1978; La Gaipa, 1981). These dissensions give students opportunities to deal with difficult social situations, solve social problems, and learn what qualities are most important in the friends they keep or in new friends they choose. Teachers can design or select classroom management and instructional strategies (as suggested by the TARGET structures outlined earlier) that encourage or discourage discussion, debate, negotiation, and resolution of conflict among students in classrooms or other school settings. Schools can officially recognize and support many or few groups of students by the way they spotlight and reward students' projects, clubs, actions, and group efforts, and by the way they establish lines of communication and respect among groups of students. Determination of which students are popular, important, recognized as leaders, and worthy of selection as friends is, in part, influenced by the evaluation and reward structures of the school. When communication skills and social interactions are encouraged, students may become more aware of each others' similarities, strengths, or weaknesses in ways that encourage new alliances and friendships, especially among those students who might otherwise be overlooked or ignored.

Being in the same teacher's classroom and in the same reading and math groups each day fostered friendships and stability of friends among elementary school students (Hallinan & Sorensen, 1985; Hallinan & Tuma, 1978). Of course all students in a reading group do not become friends or best friends. Friends may be made across groups, in part because of *accumulated similarities* that are more powerful than any one similarity. For example, friends who are *not* in the same reading group may walk to school together from the same neighborhood, be players for the same ball team, scouts in the same troup, campers in the same summer camp, and so on. Many similarities—academic skills, class projects, homework assignments, sports activities, and other talents and interests—can encourage students to work together on similar projects and become friends. Students' interests in school lead to the selection of friends who share those interests out of school. Keeves (1972) found that students who liked math and science in school tended to select friends with similar attitudes and that they spent time together on math and science activities at home. This kind of selection can, in turn, maintain or strengthen math and science skills and learning in school. Berndt's (1982) conclusion is still true—research is not very informative about the particular similarities that are important in children's friendships. Research is greatly needed on the difficult questions of multiple and accumulated similarities to determine how selections based on many or different combinations of similarities may affect learning, interests, and other important outcomes.

In other ways, *accumulated differences* reduce or eliminate interactions. School rules and grouping policies that limit student mobility encourage in-group, in-class friendships and discourage broader contacts. When schools set rules that limit interaction in classrooms (e.g., when reading ability determines class membership in all subjects through the day), on playgrounds (e.g., classes must play together), or in lunchrooms (e.g., classes must eat together), differences between students accumulate and may discourage the selection of certain students as friends. When students are separated from other students, differences are exaggerated in ways that decrease chances for positive interaction, shared goals, or mutual regard. School rules and practices make students similar to some and different from other students *before* information on important personal qualities of an individual can be determined or explored.

At the high school level, curricular tracking organizes the separation of large segments of the school. "Honors" students may seldom interact with "regular" college-bound students or other students. Students in vocational tracks may be in separate wings, or separate buildings, or may leave the school building each day for work-related training. Studies of high school students in the United States and West Germany showed that at least 75% of students' friends were chosen from their own curricular track, and most friends were located in the same extracurricular activities (Hansell & Karweit, 1983; K. Hurrelmann, personal communication, April 17, 1987; Karweit, 1983). It seems clear that accumulated similarities and accumulated differences due to school regulations and teachers' practices combine to influence students' choices of friends. There are obvious connections between multiple proximities (i.e., similar locations) and accumulated similarities or differences on deep qualities of personality or goals that need to be investigated in new research on the selection process.

Summary and Suggestions

When children see peers as "similar," they are more likely to become friends. This mechanism guides selection across the grades, first in terms of similarity of place or proximity, then in terms of age or other surface features, and increasingly in terms of the deeper qualities in potential friends. This relatively clear progression is neither simple or static. Friends may be encumbered by too-great similarity; they may find themselves in competition with each other, or their friendship may be too predictable and uninteresting. They may dissolve their relationships and seek and select more interesting, less similar, complementary friends. Alternatively, friends may be distressed by too-great dissimilarity, finding that they have little in common and that they need to compromise too often and too much to maintain their individual preferences and goals. They may dissolve their friendship and seek less stressful relationships with new friends who are more similar on characteristics that are especially important to them. Friends who are dissimilar in some ways can be important influences on each other. But, to reciprocate selections and stabilize their friendships, friends may need to be similar enough on at least a few important characteristics.

Research is at an early stage of understanding the complex process of influence that results from choices of similar and dissimilar friends. Little is known of developmental patterns and less is known of environmental conditions that affect the identification of important similarities. Research has not pushed questions about similarity to interesting extremes. A new generation of studies could enliven peer research with more pointed questions about how students define and perceive similarity and about the tensions and trade-offs created when friends are selected for similarities or differences at different ages and in differently organized environments. To obtain multiple measures that will reveal credible patterns of maintenance or influence on attitudes and behavior over time, longitudinal research is needed over more than 1 school year. New longitudinal studies need not be based on huge samples to make clear contributions on the ways similarities and differences in friendships influence behavior.

There are benefits and disadvantages to selecting similar friends. Similarities may facilitate positive social ties and reinforce self-esteem as similar individuals reaffirm their shared qualities and goals. But similarities can also restrict and stratify friendships, reducing the richness of relations that can assist social and academic development. Schools play an important role at each grade level in creating opportunities for students to discover similarities in each other, to interact widely with others, and to recognize, appreciate, and benefit from differences in the talents and goals of others. It may be that students are best served by school programs that organize goal-oriented activities requiring the interaction of students who are similar *and* students who are different on a number of important characteristics. The TARGET structures described in an earlier section can assist teachers to think about and organize the ways they use tasks, authority (decision-making activities), rewards, groups, evaluations, and time periods to help students recognize, appreciate, and benefit from the commonalities and diversities in their ranks. Indeed, the potential for positive influence of dissimilar friends stands as a challenge to school organizations and teachers' classroom practices. Educators need to consider how their grouping strategies, rewards, and other teaching practices can use peer power to boost positive school attitudes, achievements, and goals. Research on alternative organizational arrangements in schools and classrooms would extend and improve the depth of research on the meanings of similarities and differences for children's selections of friends.

SUMMARY AND CONCLUSIONS

Three aspects of selection were examined: proximity as a basic fact of selection, age as a surface feature of selection, and similarity as a deep characteristic of selection. Information on proximity tells whether and where students have opportunities for selection. Surface or ascriptive characteristics such as age tell whether students are attracted by others' visible attributes. Deep qualities such as similarities and differences in personality, values, attitudes, and goals tell whether students base their selections on the characters of potential friends. There are three basic conclusions from these diverse studies of proximity, age, and similarity that may guide new research and assist educators to understand their roles in students' social contacts and friendship choices.

1. There are important developmental patterns in the selection of friends.

The patterns of selection of friends by older students are different from those by younger students. Figure 6.1 suggests how chronological age affects the three aspects of selection.

> Proximity—Curve I: From early childhood to adolescence there is a gradual decrease and then a leveling off of the importance of close proximity for selecting friends. The definition of "close proximity" changes across the years. Older students define proximity more broadly and make their choices from wider boundaries and from multiple locations.

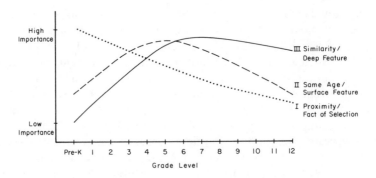

Figure 6.1. Curves estimating the importance of proximity (I), same age (II), and similarity (III) for the selection of friends across the grades, based on research reviewed.

Same Age—Curve II: There is a curvilinear pattern of same-age versus mixed-age choices. Very young children are more often in the company of elders, though not necessarily by choice. Elementary and middle grade students are more often with same-age friends, especially in school settings. Older students increase their choices across age groups as they enter more situations where age is not a criterion for participation.

Similarity—Curve III: There is an initial linear (perhaps deceptively linear) increase and then a leveling off of students' choices of friends based on similarities. Young children select friends more on the basis of similarity of location or surface features. They pick friends who are similarly willing to play a game or spend time on an activity. Older students become increasingly aware of the deeper characteristics of potential friends, and begin to look for similarities in character or personality. Conformity— one type of similarity—may peak in the middle grades when students build self-confidence from group support. Selections of similar friends reflect students' increasing abilities to make more accurate estimates of their own and others' personalities and their similarities and differences. Older students who are better able to deal with stresses and conflicts in friendship can create or restore similarities or compatabilities in their relationships and seek and learn from differences.

The different, hypothesized developmental patterns of these three aspects of selection are due, in part, to the advancement and accumulation of students' cognitive and social skills and experiences. The patterns are also affected by the opportunities designed and encouraged in schools and other settings—which leads to a second conclusion.

2. There are important environmental effects on the selection of friends.

Typical characteristics of environments affect the selection of friends. Neighborhood configurations, age-graded classrooms, and school tracking or grouping policies create predictable patterns of contact and affect the selection of friends.

Natural changes in environments also affect friendship choices. Junior high or middle schools are typically larger than elementary schools, and high schools are larger than middle schools. With each school change, students come into contact with more students from different schools and neighborhoods to consider as friends. Compared to elementary and middle schools, high schools require more self-direction and permit more self-selection of courses, classes, and extracurricular activities. When students make these choices, they join other students who are similar in achievements, goals, or interests, which increases the likelihood of selecting friends who are similar on important characteristics. More than elementary schools, middle schools, junior high, and high schools organize extracurricular activities, dances, sports, and other activities that arrange new proximities and encourage mixed-age interactions for the selection of friends.

Purposeful changes in environments can be made that affect the selection of friends. Typical characteristics of schools and classrooms can be changed and natural conditions can be revised in ways that purposely limit or extend boundaries and opportunities for social contact, increase or decrease mixed-age contacts, and emphasize or deemphasize particular similarities of students. For example, to increase interaction of younger and older students, age-graded schools can be revised to support mixed-age academic classes. Or, grouping practices can be altered to create new patterns of student interactions.

The hypothesized developmental curves in Figure 6.1 are based on studies conducted in typical school and social environments that occur across the grades. But the estimated curves are not constant. Each one can be affected by purposeful changes in schools, classrooms, neighborhoods, and other settings in which children meet and interact. There are, then, unspecified upper and lower bounds of each curve that reflect the influence of more or less restrictive or differently designed environments.

The shape of *Curve 1—Proximity* could swing widely depending on the design of school and classroom environments at different grade levels. For example, across the grades in highly structured schools that restrict movement and interaction there should be more choices made of friends in "close" proximity. By contrast, there is less dependence on close proximity in the selection of friends in schools that organize activities so that students meet and work with others outside their own instructional groups, classrooms, and grade levels. Some schools extend the boundaries of the school with service or work activities in the community and in businesses. These opportunities for learning place students in multiple locations, with different groups in proximity as potential friends.

The shape of *Curve II—Same Age* can be dramatically altered by different environmental designs. There will be more same-age choices in age-graded schools that also limit student contacts in work and play groups. There are more mixed-age choices in one-room schools, multiage classrooms, open playground activities, or other settings where age is not the criterion for attendance. Differently organized schools and classrooms may reward, ignore, ridicule, or punish mixed-age choices. These decisions will create the upper and lower bounds of Curve II.

Curve III—Similarity will change its form in schools, classrooms, and other settings that encourage or discourage the interaction of students with different skills, talents, beliefs, and backgrounds. Schools create groups of similar or diverse students, place them in proximity, create opportunities and rewards for interaction, and affect the selection of friends. More students will select more friends who are similar in ability where schools group students homogeneously for all subjects, every year. Fewer friends will be similar in ability where schools use heterogeneous groups, mixed-ability projects, and other arrangements that enable different students to interact.

Developmental patterns have been described for increasingly abstract concepts of friendship (Bigelow and La Gaipa, 1980), increasingly complex stages of friendship (Selman, 1981), and increasingly diverse social processes in the acquaintance process (Gottman, 1983). Unlike the generally linear patterns of increasing cognitive capacities, the developmental patterns of selection are curvilinear, different from each other, and affected by the opportunity and demand structures of important social and educational environments.

3. Social and historical events can affect patterns of social exchange and selection of friends.

This review revealed two examples of changing patterns of selection caused by important social and educational changes. First, the increase in day-care facilities in the 1970s and 1980s changed the environments in which preschool children meet and interact. More young children have been put in proximity with other young children in small and large day-care and nursery settings. Studies of infants' and preschoolers' social behavior in day-care centers will be quite different from research conducted in laboratory settings where mothers and children or pairs of toddlers or preschoolers interacted in contrived ways. Increased day care will change many young children's opportunities to select friends and will change our understanding of young children's friendships. It will be important to study differently designed day-care settings and preschool programs for their influence on early and later peer relations, social skills, and patterns of selection.

Second, the construction of open schools and the introduction of open education in the 1960s and 1970s changed the environments in which some elementary and secondary students interacted. Open-school architecture and high-participatory programs changed the physical boundaries where students were permitted or required to work and measurably affected social exchange among students in classrooms. Many open-space buildings and other types of high-participatory, active-learning educational programs are still operating. Schools at all grade levels vary in the ways that they permit students to participate in school and classroom decisions and activities. Research in contrasting elementary, middle, and high school settings can stretch our awareness of the effects of specific environmental conditions on friendship choice.

The conclusions about major influences on the selection process have basic implications for research and for educational practice. Dickens and Perlman (1981) suggest that changes in friendships across the grades may be caused by a third factor that is linked to chronological age and social development. A crucial hidden factor may be the design of the educating and socializing environments in which students make friends. It is no longer feasible to study or explain the selection of friends with attention only to psychological constructs and child development terms. It is also necessary to give attention to the designs of the school, classroom, family, and other environments in which peer relations and the selection and influence of friends take place. Research across age groups and in contrasting school and classroom organizations is needed to test the patterns extrapolated from the disparate studies. Studies will invigorate the field by giving attention to patterns of selection and their implications in new school environments for young children, alternative schools for older children, and other environments that purposely revise patterns of social and academic exchange.

Students choose their own friends. Teachers and parents have been hesitant to interfere in children's friendships (Rubin, 1980). But tacit acceptance of typical environmental conditions is, in fact, "passive interference" in students' opportunities for social and educational experiences that lead to the choice of friends. This discussion suggests that educators have an obligation to understand the impact of organizational and instructional decisions on students' selections of friends.

REFERENCES

Allen, V. L. (1976). *Children as teachers*. New York: Academic Press.

Allen, V. L., & Devin-Sheehan, L. (1976). *Cross-age interactions in one-teacher schools* (Working paper 161). Madison, WI: University of Wisconsin Research and Development Center for Cognitive Learning.

Barker, R. G., & Wright, H. F. (1955). *Midwest and its children*. New York: Harper & Row.

Berndt, T. J. (1982). The features and effects of friendship in early adolescence. *Child Development, 53,* 1447–1460.

Berndt, T. J. (1986). Sharing between friends: Contexts and consequences. In E. Mueller and C. Cooper (Eds.), *Process and outcome in peer relationships* (pp. 105–129). New York: Academic Press.

Bigelow, B., & La Gaipa, J. (1980). The development of friendship values and choice. In H. C. Foot, A. J. Chapman, & J. Smith (Eds.), *Friendship and social relations in children* (pp. 15–44). New York: Wiley.

Billy, J. O. G., Rodgers, J. L., & Udry, J. R. (1984). Adolescent sexual behavior and friendship choice. *Social Forces, 62,* 653–678.

Bossert, S. T. (1979). *Tasks and social relationships in classrooms.* New York: Cambridge University Press.

Brody, G. H., Stoneman, Z., MacKinnon, C. E., & MacKinnon, R. (1985). Role relationships and behavior between preschool-aged and school-aged sibling pairs. *Developmental Psychology, 21,* 124–129.

Brown, B. B., Eicher, S. A., & Petrie, S. (1986). The importance of peer group affiliation in adolescence. *Journal of Adolescence, 9,* 73–96.

Brown, B. B., & Lohr, M. J. (1987). Peer group affiliation and adolescent self esteem: An interpretation of ego identity and symbolic interaction theories. *Journal of Personality and Social Psychology, 52,* 47–55.

Byrne, D. (1961). The influence of propinquity and opportunities for interaction and classroom relationships. *Human Relations, 14,* 63–69.

Byrne, D., & Griffitt, W. B. (1966). A developmental investigation of the law of attraction. *Journal of Personality and Social Psychology, 4,* 699–702.

Clasen, D. R., & Brown, B. B. (1986). *The relationship between adolescent peer groups and school performance.* Paper presented at the annual meeting of the American Educational Research Association, San Francisco.

Coates, D. L. (1985). Relationships between self concept measures and social network characteristics for black adolescents. *Journal of Early Adolescence, 5,* 319–338.

Cohen, J. (1977). Sources of peer homogeneity. *Sociology of Education, 50,* 227–241.

Cohen, J. (1983). Commentary: The relationship between friendship selection and peer influence. In J. Epstein & N. Karweit (Eds.), *Friends in school: Patterns of selection and influence in secondary schools* (pp. 163–174). New York: Academic Press.

Cohen, J. (1985). *Adolescent peer influence on college aspirations: Some differentials.* University of Maryland, Baltimore County. (mimeo)

Cooper, C. R., Marquis, A., & Edward, D. (1986). Four perspectives on peer learning among elementary school children. In E. C. Mueller & C. R. Cooper (Eds.), *Process and outcome in peer relationships* (pp. 269–300). New York: Academic Press.

Csikszentmihalyi, M., & Larson, R. (1984). *Being adolescent: Conflict and growth in the teenage years.* New York: Basic Books.

Davitz, J. R. (1955). Social perception and sociometric choice of children. *Journal of Abnormal and Social Psychology, 50,* 173–176.

Dickens, W. J., & Perlman, D. (1981). Friendship over the life cycle. In S. Duck & R. Gilmour (Eds.), *Personal relationships: Vol. 2. Developing personal relationships* (pp. 91–122). New York: Academic Press.

Downing, L. L., & Bothwell, K. H. (1979). Open space schools: Anticipation of peer interaction and development of cooperative independence. *Journal of Educational Psychology, 71,* 478–484.

Drewry, D. L., & Clark, M. L. (1983, March). *Factors important in the formation of preschoolers' friendships.* Paper presented at the Southwestern Psychological Association, Atlanta.

Drewry, D. L., & Clark, M. L. (1984, April). *Similarity effects and age differences on children's friendships.* Paper presented at the annual meeting of the American Educational Research Association, New Orleans.

Duck, S. (1973). Personality, similarity and friendship choices by adolescents. *Journal of Personality, 41,* 543–558.

Dunphy, D. C. (1963). The social structure of urban adolescent peer groups. *Sociometry, 26,* 230–246.

Eder, D. (1985). The cycle of popularity: Interpersonal relations among female adolescents. *Sociology of Education, 58,* 154–165.

Ellis, S., Rogoff, B., & Cromer, C. C. (1981). Age segregation in children's social interactions. *Developmental Psychology, 17,* 349–401.

Epstein, J. L. (1983a). Examining theories of adolescent friendships. In J. L. Epstein & N. Karweit (Eds.), *Friends in school: Patterns of selection and influence in secondary schools* (pp. 39–61). New York: Academic Press.

Epstein, J. L. (1983b). Selection of friends in differently organized schools and classrooms. In J. L. Epstein & N. Karweit (Eds.), *Friends in school: Patterns of selection and influence in secondary schools* (pp. 73–92). New York: Academic Press.

Epstein, J. L. (1983c). The influence of friends on achievement and affective outcomes. In J. L. Epstein & N. Karweit (Eds.), *Friends in school: Patterns of selection and influence in secondary schools* (pp. 177–200). New York: Academic Press.

Epstein, J. L. (1986). Friendship selection: Developmental and environmental influences. In E. Mueller & C. Cooper (Eds.), *Process and outcome in peer relationships* (pp. 129–160). New York: Academic Press.

Epstein, J. L. (1988). Effective schools or effective students? Dealing with diversity. In R. Haskins & D. MacRae (Eds.), *Policies for America's public schools: Teachers, equity, and indicators* (pp. 89–126). Norwood, NJ: Ablex.

Epstein, J. L. (in press). Family structures and student motivation: A developmental perspective. In C. Ames & R. Ames (Eds.), *Research on motivation in education* (Vol. 3). New York: Academic Press.

Feld, S. L. (1982). Social structural determinants of similarity among adolescents. *American Sociological Review, 47,* 797–801.

Feld, S. L. (1984). The structured use of personal associates. *Social Forces, 62,* 640–652.

Fiedler, F. E. (1954). Assumed similarity measures as predictors of team effectiveness. *Journal of Abnormal and Social Psychology, 49,* 381–388.

Fine, G. A. (1980). The natural history of preadolescent male friendship groups. In H. C. Foot, A. J. Chapman, & J. R. Smith (Eds.), *Friendship and social relations in children* (pp. 293–320). New York: Wiley.

Foot, H. C., Chapman, A. J., & Smith J. (Eds.). (1980). *Friendship and social relations in children.* New York: Wiley.

French, D. C. (1984). Children's knowledge of the social functions of younger, older, and same age peers. *Child Development, 55,* 1429–1433.

Furfey, P. H. (1929). Some factors influencing the selection of boys' chums. *Journal of Applied Psychology, 11,* 47–51.

Ginsburg, A. L., & Hanson, S. L. (1986). *Values and educational sources among disadvantaged students.* Washington, DC: U.S. Department of Education. (mimeo)

Gottman, J. M. (1983). How children become friends. *Monographs of the Society for Research in Child Development, 48*(3, Serial No. 201).

Gottman, J. M., & Parkhurst, J. (1980). A developmental theory of friendship and acquaintanceship processes. In W. A. Collins (Ed.), *Minnesota Symposia on Child Psychology* (Vol. 13). Hillsdale, NJ: Lawrence Erlbaum.

Grant, C. A., & Sleeter, C. E. (1986). *After the school bell rings.* Philadelphia: The Falmer Press.

Graziano, W., French, D., Brownell, C. A., & Hartup, W. W. (1976). Peer interaction in same- and mixed-age triads in relation to chronological age and incentive condition. *Child Development, 47,* 707–714.

Hallinan, M. T. (1980). Patterns of cliquing among youth. In H. C. Foot, A. J. Chapman, & J. R. Smith (Eds.), *Friendship and social relations in children* (pp. 321–342). New York: Wiley.

Hallinan, M. T., & Sorensen, A. B. (1985). Ability grouping and student friendships. *American Educational Research Journal, 22,* 485–499.

Hallinan, M. T., & Tuma, N. B. (1978). Classroom effects on changes in children's friendships. *Sociology of Education, 51,* 270–282.

Hansell, S. (1981). Ego development and peer friendship networks. *Sociology of Education, 54,* 98–106.

Hansell, S., & Karweit, N. (1983). Curricular placement, friendship networks, and status attainment. In J. L. Epstein & N. Karweit (Eds.), *Friends in school: Patterns of selection and influence in secondary schools* (pp. 141–161). New York: Academic Press.

Hartup, W. W. (1976). Cross-age vs. same-age peer interaction. Ethnological and cross cultural perspectives. In V. Allen (Ed.), *Children's teachers: Theory and research on tutoring.* New York: Academic Press.

Hartup, W. W. (1978). Children and their friends. In H. McGurk (Ed.), *Issues in childhood social development* (pp. 130–170). London: Methuen.

Hartup, W. W. (1983). Peer relations. In E. M. Hetherington (Ed.) & P. H. Mussen (Series Ed.), *Handbook of child psychology: Vol. 4. Socialization, personality, and social development* (pp. 103–196). New York: Wiley.

Hrybyk, M., & Farnham-Diggory, S. (1981). *Children's groups in school: A developmental case study.* Unpublished manuscript.

Institute for Social Research (ISR). (1981). *Panel study of time use in American households.* Ann Arbor: University of Michigan.

Jessor, S. L., & Jessor, R. (1975). Transition from virginity to non virginity during youth. A social psychological study over time. *Developmental Psychology, 11,* 473–484.

Kandel, D. B. (1978). Similarity in real-life adolescent friendship pairs. *Journal of Personality and Social Psychology, 36,* 306–312.

Karweit, N. (1983). Extracurricular activities and friendship selection. In J. L. Epstein & N. Karweit (Eds.), *Friends in school: Patterns of selection and influence in secondary schools* (pp. 131–139). New York: Academic Press.

Keeves, J. P. (1972). *Educational environment and student achievement.* Stockholm: Almqvist and Wiksell.

Kon, I. S. (1981). Adolescent friendship: Some unanswered questions for future research. In S. Duck & R. Gilmour (Eds.), *Personal relationships: Vol. 2. Developing personal relationships* (pp. 187–204). New York: Academic Press.

Kon, I. S., & Losenkov, V. A. (1978). Friendship in adolescence: Values and behavior. *Journal of Marriage and the Family, 40,* 143–155.

Ladd, G. W. (1983). Social networks of popular, average, and rejected children in school settings. *Merrill-Palmer Quarterly, 29,* 283–307.

La Gaipa, J. L. (1981). Children's friendship. In S. Duck & R. Gilmour (Eds.), *Personal relationships: Vol. 2. Developing personal relationships* (pp. 161–185). New York: Academic Press.

Lewis, M., & Rosenblum, L. (1975). *Friendship and peer relations.* New York: Wiley.

Lever, J. (1976). Sex differences in the games children play. *Social Problems, 23,* 478–487.

Lipsitz, J. (1984). *Successful schools for young adolescents.* New Brunswick, NJ: Transaction Books.

Maas, H. S. (1968). Preadolescent peer relations and adult intimacy. *Psychiatry, 3,* 161–172.

Maccoby, E., & Jacklin, C. (1974). *The psychology of sex differences.* Stanford, CA: Stanford University Press.

Minuchin, P. P. (1976). *Differential use of the open classroom: A study of exploratory and cautious children* (Final Report). Washington, DC: National Institute of Education.

Newson, J., & Newson, E. (1978). *Seven-year-olds in the home environment*. London: Penguin.

Peevers, B. H., & Secord, P. (1973). Developmental change in attribution of descriptive concepts to persons. *Journal of Personality and Social Psychology, 27,* 120–128.

Pitts, J. (1968). The family and the peer group. In N. W. Bell & E. F. Vogel (Eds.), *A modern introduction to the family* (pp. 290–310). New York: Free Press.

Putallaz, M., & Gottman, J. M. (1981). Social skills and group acceptance. In S. R. Asher and J. M. Gottman (Eds.), *The development of children's friendship*. New York: Cambridge University Press.

Reisman, J., & Shorr, H. (1978). Friendship claims and expectations among children and adults. *Child Development, 49,* 913–916.

Rubin, Z. (1980). *Children's friendships*. Cambridge: Harvard University Press.

Schunk, D. H. (1987). Peer models and children's behavioral change. *Review of Educational Research, 57,* 149–174.

Seagoe, M. V. (1933). Factors influencing the selection of associates. *Journal of Educational Research, 27,* 32–40.

Selman, R. (1976). Toward a structural analysis of developing interpersonal relations concepts: Research with normal and disturbed preadolescent boys. In A. Pick (Ed.), *Minnesota Symposia on Child Psychology* (Vol. 10). Minneapolis: University of Minnesota Press.

Selman, R. (1981). The child as a friendship philosopher. In S. R. Asher & J. M. Gottman (Eds.), *The development of children's friendships* (pp. 242–272). New York: Cambridge University Press.

Selman, R. L., & Jaquette, D. (1978). Stability and oscillation in interpersonal awareness: A clinical developmental analysis. In C. B. Keasey (Ed.), *Nebraska Symposium on Motivation* (Vol. 25, pp. 261–304). Lincoln: University of Nebraska Press.

Smollar, J., & Youniss, J. (1982). Social development through friendship. In K. H. Rubin & H. S. Ross (Eds.), *Peer relations and social skills in childhood* (pp. 279–298). New York: Springer-Verlag.

Stambak, M., & Verba, M. (1986). Organization of social play among toddlers: An ecological approach. In E. Mueller & C. Cooper (Eds.), *Process and outcome in peer relationships* (pp. 229–247). New York: Academic Press.

Strayer, F. F. (1980). Child ethology and the study of preschool social relations. In H. C. Foot, A. J. Chapman, & J. R. Smith (Eds.), *Friendship and social relations in children* (pp. 235–265). New York: Wiley.

Vandell, D. L., & Mueller, E. C. (1980). Peer play and friendships during the first two years. In H. C. Foot, A. J. Chapman, & J. R. Smith (Eds.), *Friendship and social relations in children* (pp. 181–208). New York: Wiley.

Verbrugge, L. M. (1979). Multiplexity in adult friendships. *Social Forces, 57*(4) 1286–1309.

Whiting, B. (1986). The effect of experience on peer relationships. In E. Mueller and C. Cooper (Eds.), *Process and outcome in peer relationships* (pp. 77–99). New York: Academic Press.

CHAPTER 7

The Role of Peer Groups in Adolescents' Adjustment to Secondary School

B. BRADFORD BROWN

University of Wisconsin at Madison

Ask a group of young adults what they liked *least* about high school and, amidst their array of responses, one is likely to find a recurrent theme: "The cliques," "social stereotypes," "being prejudged by who you hang around with," they will say with a bemused groan or a tinge of anxiety. According to many scholars (Erikson, 1968; Hartup, 1984), peer group relations are a major factor in the developmental agenda of adolescence, so it is not surprising that they figure heavily in the lives of high school students. Because, however, adolescent peer groups bring to mind a host of undesirable images or memories for many people—conformity, clannishness, stereotyping, peer pressure, delinquent gangs, and so on—peer group influences often are portrayed in unduly harsh and simplistic terms.

There is little question that peer group forces have a substantial impact on the academic interests and social development of many, if not most, high school students (J. C. Coleman, 1980; J. S. Coleman, 1961; Hartup, 1984). But there is some controversy and considerable confusion about the ways in which and the degrees to which peer groups exert their influence. Part of this stems from simple confusion about what constitutes a "peer group" or a "peer group influence." Thus, to fully appreciate the peer group's role in adolescents' adjustment to school, it seems sensible to begin with more basic issues: How should adolescent peer groups be defined or conceptualized? Why and how do they emerge during this stage of life, and how do they change over the course of the secondary school years? Once these issues are settled, it will be easier to examine the weightier issues of how peer groups exert influence, when and why adolescents are receptive to such influence, and what the consequences are for adolescents' attitudes and behaviors in school.

Attempts to address these questions, however, quickly confront a modest dilemma: Although most studies of adolescent peer groups have concentrated on high school populations, it is increasingly clear that the formative stages of peer groups occur in the middle school (or junior high school) years (Brown & Clasen, 1986; Crockett, Losoff, & Petersen, 1984; Eder, 1985). Questions about the emergence of peer groups and growth of peer group influences cannot be answered fully unless both middle school and high school students are included in studies, or at least in reviews of studies such as this chapter. Accordingly, in this chapter, "secondary school" will be conceived as including both middle school and high school students.

These questions and insights serve to frame the scope and central mission of this chapter. I shall begin by attempting to clarify the conceptualization of adolescent peer groups and then discuss their emergence and metamorphosis across adolescence. With this background, I will then focus on current knowledge of peer group influences in the area of central importance to secondary schools: students' academic aspirations and achievement levels. Finally, from this review, several recommendations will be drawn to guide future research in this area.

CONCEPTUALIZING PEER GROUPS

Much of the confusion about peer group influences in adolescence stems from inconsistent usage of the term "peer group." Some regard information on an adolescent's association with a single agemate as evidence of peer group influence (e.g., Ide, Parkerson, Haertel, & Walberg, 1981). Others concentrate on an individual's circle of close friends as the locus of peer group influences (e.g., Berndt, 1979; Brown, Clasen, & Eicher, 1986; Cusick, 1973), and still others refer to the entire population of agemates (or all students in the same grade or same school) as a teenager's peer group (e.g., Faunce, 1984). Many researchers identify peer groups strictly on the basis of interaction patterns (Dunphy, 1963; Hallinan, 1979), whereas others insist that factors such as status, reputation, and prominent activities or personality traits figure heavily in defining peer groups (Crockett et al., 1984; Hartup, 1984; Larkin, 1979; Poveda, 1975).

For the sake of clarity, I believe it is best to group peer interactions in adolescence into three levels: dyads, cliques, and crowds. Dyads refer to pairs of friends or lovers; they are not peer *groups* and will not be dealt with in this chapter (instead, see Epstein, Chapter 6, this volume). Cliques are *interaction-based* peer groups, describing a small number of adolescents who "hang around" together and develop close relationships. Cliques can vary in size and density (the degree to which each person regards all other clique members as regular friends). They may be tight-knit and closed to outsiders, or they may include a central core of members and a set of marginal associates who join in clique interactions less frequently. Such variations force researchers to make some arbitrary decisions in defining or operationalizing cliques. Generally, however, adolescent cliques number from five to ten individuals, who all understand and appreciate each other better than do people outside the clique and who regard the clique as their primary base of interaction with groups of agemates.

By contrast, crowds are *reputation-based* peer groups—larger collectives of similarly stereotyped individuals who may or may not spend much time together. An adolescent's crowd affiliation denotes the primary attitudes or activities with which one is associated by peers. It can also be a commentary on one's status among peers or one's level of social skills. Crowd labels common among secondary school students reflect these characteristics: jocks, brains, druggies, populars, loners, unsociables, nerds, rogues, and so forth. Whereas clique norms develop from within, according to principles of small-group interaction (Moreland & Levine, 1982), crowd norms are imposed from outside the group, reflecting the stereotypic image that peers have of crowd members. This difference has important implications for the process of peer group influence at clique versus crowd levels.

Because, theoretically at least, crowd labels group together individuals with similar characteristics, clique members often may share the same crowd affiliation. Yet, the distinction between clique and crowd being drawn here is quite different from Dunphy's (1963), in which crowds were simply amalgams of several cliques. I suggest, instead, that cliques and crowds have different structural bases. One might conceive of cliques as the adolescent's friendship group (based on social interaction patterns) and crowds as her/his reference group (based on personal attitudes, interests, or abilities). Differentiating between dyads, cliques, and crowds helps considerably in clarifying peer group influences in adolescence.

DEVELOPMENTAL CHANGES IN PEER GROUPS' STRUCTURE AND FUNCTION

Peer groups exist and exert influence in students' lives well before adolescence. The common wisdom, however, is that both the importance and the power of influence of peer groups are far greater in adolescence than childhood (J. C. Coleman, 1980; Hartup, 1984). Undoubtedly, the intensification of peer influence is related to major structural transformations in peer groups that occur with the onset of adolescence. Subsequent changes in cliques and crowds across the secondary school years may alter the nature and extent of peer group influences. Thus, to understand peer group influences on secondary school students, it is advisable to begin with an overview of developmental changes in cliques and crowds across adolescence. Following this, I will comment on the causes of these changes and speculate on their consequences for the process of peer group influence.

Structural Transformations of Adolescent Cliques

Dunphy's (1963) classic ethnography remains the most comprehensive effort to describe structural transformations in peer groups across adolescence.

From observations of several groups of Australian teenagers, supplemented with interview and diary data, Dunphy identified five stages of peer group structure. In Dunphy's model the isolated, monosexual cliques that characterized early adolescent peer interactions begin to be drawn together as a result of the budding heterosexual interests of each clique's leaders. Opposite-gender cliques begin to meld in the third stage as members engage in "dating" relationships. Once heterosexual activities become the norm for members, the cliques seek associations with other cliques in order to form a "crowd," a loose association of cliques brought together for major social functions. This fourth stage of "fully developed crowds" continues until, toward the end of adolescence, crowds disintegrate into relatively isolated cliques reminiscent of early adolescence, except that the groups now are heterosexual.

Dunphy's (1963) study has never been formally replicated, and one may wonder whether or not the metamorphosis he described is still applicable 30 years later or in a society such as the United States where, unlike Australia in the late 1950s, most individuals remain in school through their late teens. In the early years of sociometric studies, researchers pointed out the complexity of clique structure in American high schools (J. S. Coleman, 1961; Gordon, 1957). The more sophisticated sociometric techniques for mapping cliques that grew out of these early studies limited the sample size to about 30 students. This was quite functional for studies of self-contained classrooms of elementary students (Lewis & Rosenblum, 1975) but not for secondary school students, who are less likely to draw their social network from one classroom of peers (Cusick, 1973). Some have been trapped by this methodological shortcoming (e.g., Hallinan, 1979), but others have provided more useful commentary on Dunphy's (1963) model.

Crockett et al. (1984) found that the percentage of middle school students who claimed to be part of a clique increased from 6th to 8th grade, suggesting that "cliquing" intensifies across early adolescence. Quite a different picture emerges from a recent sociometric study of Shrum and Cheek (1987), who mapped out the clique structure from students' listing of their closest friends in the entire school. They found a sharp decline from 6th to 12th grade in the percentage of students who were definitely clique members, and a modest increase across the same grades in the percentage who were isolates. Equally interesting was the steady increase across grades in the percentage of students whom they labeled "liaisons." These were students whose primary social ties were to peers in a variety of cliques or for whom most close associates were fellow liaisons (marginal members of a clique but with definite ties to people outside the clique).

In other words, rather than there being an increasing division of students into tight-knit cliques, the clique structure actually dissipated across the secondary school grades into a melange of more loose-knit ties. Shrum and Cheek (1987) labeled this the "degrouping" process, but it might better be regarded as evidence of an individual's emergence, in Dunphy's (1963) terms, from isolated cliques of early adolescence to middle adolescent, fully developed crowds. Dunphy's crowds represent a loose association of cliques who socialize together. Although close associates may still be drawn primarily from one's own clique, members of neighboring cliques in the crowd may become part of one's larger circle of friends. A key question is whether or not "crowdlike" boundaries can be drawn around the network of clique and liaison relationships that emerge in Shrum and Cheek's (1987) data.

The general trend toward a loosening of clique ties across adolescence need not hold true across all types of crowds, however (returning to the conceptualization of crowds as reputation-based entities). Ethnographers have found that the popular or elite crowds, for example, seem to maintain tight-knit relationships, earning members a reputation for being "cliquish" or snobbish (Eder, 1985; Larkin, 1979).

Developmental Transformations of Adolescent Crowds

It is more difficult to ascertain developmental transformations in crowds. Because these are reputation-based rather than interaction-based entities, they are difficult to observe. In some sense, they have a greater reality in adolescents' minds than in the day-to-day interaction patterns of students. At this cognitive level, there is mounting evidence of developmental shifts in adolescents' conceptions of crowds and the crowd structure. O'Brien and Bierman (1987) examined adolescents' open-ended descriptions of the identifying features and characteristic attitudes and behaviors of crowds they perceived in their school. Across the three grade levels in their sample (5th, 8th, 11th grade), conceptions of crowds became broader and focused more on dispositional characteristics and less on behavior patterns. Abstract and relative comparisons among crowds (such as arranging the crowds into a status hierarchy) were quite common among 11th graders, but rare among 5th graders.

With a more sophisticated cognitive map of the peer group system, it is not surprising that older adolescents seem better able to identify their position within the system. Brown, Clasen, and Niess (1987), for example, reported that the percentage of students who correctly identified the crowd with which they were associated most often by peers increased significantly with age. Interestingly, however, the percentage varied substantially across crowds: About 75% of jocks and druggies correctly guessed their peer-rated crowd affiliation, compared to less than 15% of those classified by peers as loners, nobodies or unpopulars. It remains to be seen in future studies whether unpopulars lack the cognitive sophistication of students in other crowds or simply prefer to ignore the undesirable label placed on them by peers.

Not all developmental patterns in adolescents' conceptions of crowds are linear changes. Using a snowball sampling technique in a study of three, overwhelmingly white, midwestern communities, Brown and Clasen (1986) identified a sample of students regarded by peers both as exemplars of the range of crowds in the school and as especially aware of the school's social structure. In individual interviews, respondents were asked to name the major crowds they perceived in their school. Responses were coded into nine major "crowd type" categories (brains, druggies, jocks, loners, nobodies, normals, populars, toughs, or special interest groups) that had been identified in previous studies, or into a "hybrid" (a mixture of two major crowd types) or "uncodeable" category. The average number of crowds named increased across grade levels, from just under 8 among 6th graders to over 10 among 12th graders. The average number of major crowd types represented in respondents' lists also increased modestly across this grade range. More interesting, however, was that the percentage of crowds named that fit into the major crowd types (that is, that weren't coded as hybrids or uncodeable) climbed from 80% in 6th grade to 95% in 9th grade, then fell steadily through 12th grade. In addition, respondents' awareness of specific crowd types did not all follow the same grade-related trajectory. Druggie and brain crowd types, as well as hybrids, appeared more often on the lists of high school respondents than middle school respondents; toughs, noted by nearly all of the 6th and 7th graders, were rarely mentioned by high school respondents.

One possible explanation of these findings is that the range of provisional identities open to adolescents does not remain constant across adolescence. The more constricted range of crowd types (the concentration on major crowd types) visible to students in the middle of the secondary school years is noteworthy because this is the age of greatest susceptibility to peer pressure (Berndt, 1979; Costanzo & Shaw, 1966). It is subtle evidence that efforts to cut across crowds or to forge a self-concept somewhat apart from standard identity prototypes puts a student at odds with the peer group structure in the early high school years. Because, theoretically (Newman & Newman, 1976), fitting into a crowd is a major preoccupation at this age, students may decide to forgo efforts to forge a less stereotyped identity until the later high school years, when the peer group structure seems to make more room for hybrid or less orthodox crowds.

Forces Fostering the Emergence of Peer Groups

We should wonder what propels adolescents from the rather simple network of classroom-based cliques in elementary school into the complex arrangement of cliques and crowds that emerge in secondary school. Shrum and Cheek (1987) point out there has been little systematic study of the restructuring of cliques in early adolescence. The same may be said about the emergence of crowds. Nevertheless, one can hazard guesses about what triggers these changes. For example, with the transition into middle school or junior high school, students generally move from a school structure based on self-contained classrooms (in which most time is spent with the same small number of agemates) to one in which they confront a much larger, constantly shifting array of peers, many of whom they have never seen before. Typically, the new environment is more age homogeneous, bringing together students from only two or three grades as opposed to the six or seven of elementary school. Supervision by adults is looser, as teachers and administrators move to encourage some sense of autonomy and personal responsibility among students (Eichhorn, 1980; Ianni, 1983; Rutter, 1983). Because of these factors, it is no longer easy for students to know personally all the peers with whom they interact regularly. To complicate matters further, one's familiar circle of associates from grade school may be dispersed among different classes and different activities, undermining the survival of these friendships (Eder, 1985). At the same time, peer interactions become a more central preoccupation of daily life in school (Rosenberg & Simmons, 1975).

Moving into this environment, early adolescents seek new strategies for negotiating the rush of new peer relationships. Securing one's place in a clique prevents students from having to confront this sea of new faces alone. Employing crowd labels to stereotype strangers and acquaintances provides a useful strategy for responding to peers outside one's own clique: Who might I befriend? Who should I avoid in order to keep in good standing with current friends? In other words, the stabilization of cliques and the classification of peers into crowds are adaptive responses to the emergence of a larger peer network.

Both of these responses, however, also reflect other developmental milestones of early adolescence. High on the agenda of this stage of life is achieving greater emotional and behavioral autonomy from parents (Steinberg and Silverberg, 1986). At approximately the same age, researchers report a developmental change in friendship expectations—the shift from a primary interest in friends as activity partners to insistence on loyalty and trust in friendship ties (Bigelow, 1977; Selman, 1980). It is as if early adolescents counter their psychological distancing from parents with an insistence on more stable and intimate relationships with peers.

From an Eriksonian (1968) perspective, this is quite appropriate because of the early adolescent's nascent preoccupation with developing a sense of identity. Newman and Newman (1976) conceive the "identity crisis" as a two-stage process. In the first stage, during early adolescence, the normative crisis involves struggles to achieve group identity versus alienation. That is, the central concern is becoming attached to a group of peers who can provide friendship, support, and reassurance of one's self-worth. Belonging to a clique that is not closely supervised by adults helps to wean early adolescents from psychological dependence on parents (increasing their sense of individual autonomy). Cliques that are stable, tight-knit, and fairly rigid in membership boundaries can nurture the loyal and trusting relationships (among cliques members) that foster identity testing. The obvious, sometimes rigidly enforced behavioral norms of the clique provide a provisional sense of identity, a temporary source of self-definition while members fashion a more autonomous sense of identity. Furthermore, having a set of crowds with sharply different norms or provisional identities helps each student locate a group that fits well with her or his own dispositions and abilities. In Newman and Newman's (1976, p. 266) words, "Peer group membership involves the development of close friendship bonds among age mates and the process of personal assessment about which peers will make satisfying companions."

Of course, this system works only when students have sufficient social-cognitive sophistication to sort out the different provisional identities of crowds. Understanding the concept of a "crowd" requires an ability to deal with abstract concepts, to realize, for example, that there is more to being a "jock" than just playing sports. The jock crowd stereotype also embraces certain attitudes toward school, ways of relating to adults or members of the opposite sex, self-conceptions (a friendly sort of cockiness or egotism), and so on (Larkin, 1979; Sherif & Sherif, 1964). The fact that such conceptualizations of crowds appear initially in early adolescence (O'Brien & Bierman, 1987) certainly helps explain why crowds themselves emerge at this stage of life.

In other words, it is probably no accident that cliques become more autonomous or that a well-articulated image of crowds emerges in the minds of most young people at the beginning of adolescence. These seem to be adaptive responses to features of the social system that stem from the structure of secondary schools. Moreover, such responses appear to facilitate the psychosocial agenda of adolescence and, in turn, are facilitated by social-cognitive developments that occur at about this age.

Forces Shaping the Peer Groups That Emerge

How cliques come to incorporate structural features necessary to meet adolescents' psychological and social needs is an important and intriguing topic for future research. To date, however, investigators have been more interested in how the emerging system of adolescent peer groups is related to the adult world. Some argue that each crowd represents a different subculture that has its counterpart in adult society. This theme, appearing initially in Clark's (1962) description of the "academic," "fun," and "delinquent" teenage subcultures and continuing in later studies (Buff, 1970; Cohen, 1979), regards adolescent peer groups merely as points of entry into prototypic adult lifestyles. Others regard the adolescent peer system as wholly separate from the adult world (J. S. Coleman, 1961). Different peer groups represent different patterns of activities or value orientations within that self-contained system.

A more careful reading of information on peer groups in secondary school compels a less extreme position. Adolescent crowds do not merely mimic alternative adult life styles, nor are they impervious to influences outside the adolescent culture. Instead, a number of forces seem to influence the types of groups that emerge in secondary school, as well as the relationships among groups. First among these is the student's socioeconomic status.

Some accounts of the British school system suggest that cliques and crowds develop strictly along social class lines (Willis, 1977), partly, no doubt, because British adolescents' peer relationships spring more from neighborhood associates than school associates. Hollingshead (1949) argued that American peer groups also tend to separate the social classes, but more recent studies suggest that crowds are not so socioeconomically homogeneous (Clasen & Brown, 1985; Larkin, 1979). Crowds such as the populars or elites often are portrayed as drawing rather exclusively from students in high socioeconomic strata (Buff, 1970; Larkin, 1979); when asked what it takes to be part of these crowds, students often will say, "being from the right family" or simply, "money helps" (J. S. Coleman, 1961). Groups such as normals, loners, brains, or "special interest" (e.g., performers) crowds, however, seem to draw from more diverse socioeconomic backgrounds (Clasen & Brown).

A second influential force is the ethnic or racial composition of the school. In schools with a variety of ethnic groups or a substantial minority population, race or ethnicity itself may be the defining variable for crowds. For example, Larkin (1979) found that along with jocks, greasers, freaks, and intellectuals, blacks were an identifiable crowd in the suburban community high school he studied. In another study that compared peer and family influences among students in rural, suburban, and urban areas, Ianni (1983) discovered the standard fare of personality/activity-based crowds in the suburban school (jocks, freaks, etc.), whereas crowds in the more racially mixed urban school were endowed with ethnic labels. These two studies stand as exceptions to the predominant focus on white, middle-class populations in research on school-based peer groups in adolescence. Thus, questions about how ethnically mixed adolescent peer groups are, or under what conditions race supersedes personality/activity stereotypes as the basis for defining crowds must await further research on racially and ethnically diverse populations of secondary school students.

A community's predominant value system can influence not only the types of crowds that emerge among the community's adolescents but also the values within each crowd. J. S. Coleman (1961), for example, demonstrated that the importance of good grades in gaining membership in the elite crowd in different high schools varied in rough equivalence with the intellectual climate of each community. From my own conversations with teenagers, it appears that groups such as jocks or "bandies" enjoy more status and larger membership in schools in which athletic competitions or band concerts are community-wide events, rather than being attended primarily by friends and parents of participants.

The menagerie of adolescent peer groups also seems to shift in response to historical events. Crowd labels (e.g., the "beatniks" of the 1950s or "freaks" of the 1960s) may capture the ephemeral markings of one generation of teenagers. In other cases, the crowd may persist but undergo a metamorphosis in response to historical events. From interviews with students and faculty, Larkin (1979) traced the transformation of one crowd, the "politicos," from a small group of radicals at the fringe of the school's peer group structure in the 1960s to a firmly rooted, high status crowd by the late 1970s. Ironically, this group, born in a rebellious spirit of seeking greater freedom of expression for fellow students, had become a conservative force, censoring students' behaviors that might invite the school administration to rescind hard-won liberties that represented the politicos' power base among students.

Finally, adults can influence the structure of peer groups through more direct and intentional behaviors. In a classic study of peer group dynamics Sherif and Sherif (1953) created a highly competitive environment in which to place groups of preadolescent boys at summer camp. As expected, the environment created strong intragroup loyalty and fierce antagonism between groups. When conditions were changed, however, so that desirable goals could be accomplished only by the groups working together, the Sherifs witnessed a sudden end to the antagonism as the groups combined to work in a remarkable spirit of cooperation. Of course, it may not be possible for adults to have such powerful influences over older adolescents or in less controllable environments. Yet, in a less conscious fashion, such behind-the-scenes manipulation of the social environment by adults may be quite routine in secondary schools. Newman and Newman (1976), for example, point out that teachers rely upon certain peer groups to accomplish particular tasks in a school. Thus, teachers have a vested interest in maintaining certain structures and patterns of association among crowds.

In sum, the growth of autonomous cliques and the emergence of crowds seem to be part of the developmental timetable of secondary school students. But the specific contours of the peer group system are much less universal. They bend to the influence of such factors as the community's size, value systems, and socioeconomic and ethnic composition. They also reflect historical forces and, to some extent, adults' efforts to mold the adolescent peer group system to meet their own needs. All of these factors undercut the autonomy or isolation from the adult world that characterizes the image of adolescent peer groups in the minds of many teenagers and adults. The subtle operation of these forces, however, allows this image to remain and, perhaps, to encourage misguided assumptions among researchers about the nature and degree of influence that peer groups exert over secondary school students.

Changes in Peer Group Membership Across Adolescence

As clique boundaries loosen and the range of crowds shifts across adolescence, it is reasonable to expect that membership in cliques and crowds also will undergo changes. Erikson (1968) implies that forging a self-concept is facilitated by "trying on" a variety of identities. This would require shifting one's crowd membership several times in order to sample a range of provisional identities. Unfortunately, there is virtually no research on the stability of peer group membership in adolescence. Investigators have reported on the relatively short-term (Skorepa, Horrocks, & Thompson, 1963) and long-term stability (Epstein, 1983; Kandel, 1978) of adolescent friendship dyads. Sociometric (Hallinan, 1979) and ethnographic studies (Eder, 1985) have reported on the stability of early adolescent cliques, but only among an arbitrarily fixed range of youngsters.

Studies of the stability of peer group membership in adolescence are sorely needed. For several reasons, however, I would suspect that shifts in crowd allegiance are not common. First, it must be understood that adolescents do not choose to be part of a crowd so much as they are "selected in" by their personality or behavior. The preadolescent absorbed with computers and Dungeons and Dragons is destined, in some sense, to become part of the brain crowd, just as the outgoing athlete with a fastidious eye for the latest fashion is destined for membership in the jock or popular crowd. Early adolescents do not select a crowd but are classified into one by peers, based on attitudes and interests. Even cliques do not routinely open their arms to any student who wishes to join them (Eder, 1985). Because initial clique and crowd membership is not simply a matter of free choice, subsequent group affiliation is unlikely to be a matter of free choice either.

A second constraint on shifting groups is that because crowd affiliations are reputation-based, they reflect relatively enduring personality traits or behaviors that must change *both* in the individual and in the eyes of peers before a student can consummate a shift in peer groups. Druggies who have gone through a rehabilitation program, for example, may not win easy acceptance by other crowds despite apparent changes in attitudes and behavior. They must live down their reputation and suffer the skepticism of peers in other groups—as well as their own crowd—that their conversion is only temporary.

Related to this is a third constraint: Although teenagers often are averse to discuss it, there is evidence from ethnographic (Eder, 1985; Larkin, 1979) as well as interview and survey data (Brown & Lohr, 1987; J. S. Coleman, 1961; Crockett et al., 1984) that crowds in most schools are arranged in an informal status hierarchy. In order to protect their own status ranking, crowds typically resist opening their ranks to expatriots of groups lower in status (J. S. Coleman; Eder). Crowd members also may be highly skeptical of overtures from students in higher status groups for fear that their friendliness is some kind of mockery or subterfuge. These dynamics are rich fodder for screenwriters, who delight in recounting the whimsical or tragic difficulties of relationships between friends or lovers from widely distant crowds in the adolescent hierarchy (for example, such movies as *Grease, Lucas,* or *Pretty in Pink*). Shifts in membership seem most probable between crowds with adjacent positions in the status hierarchy.

A final constraint, alluded to earlier, is that the range of crowds may not remain stable across adolescence (Brown et al., 1987). A member of the normals in middle school who wishes to achieve recognition as a brain in high school may learn, much to her or his dismay, that the "brains" are not a recognized crowd in the high school. This can also work in the opposite direction, as when a student who has achieved recognition as a performer in one school transfers to a school in which performers are not a widely acknowledged group.

These constraints on shifting crowd affiliations across adolescence cast an image of adolescent peer groups as a relatively rigid system in which students find their place early in secondary school and tend to remain "locked in" to it. Certainly, for most students, this would constrict the process that Erikson (1968) described of "trying on" several provisional identities—fitting into several crowds—before settling on a more stable sense of identity. Again, however, because students' membership in crowds is more a matter of cognitive perceptions than concrete reality, the system may not be as rigid as it appears. Researchers who have attempted to classify students into crowds (Brown & Clasen, 1986; Schwendinger & Schwendinger, 1985) have found that only a fraction of students are associated exclusively with one crowd. Many are perceived as partially in one crowd, partially in another, or in a distinguishable crowd that represents a hybrid of two larger groups (e.g., the "party jocks" or the "preppie brains"). Still others are portrayed as floaters, drifting easily in and out of several crowds and seemingly accepted by each group. Stereotypic portrayals of crowds belie the somewhat fluid character of crowd membership (Varenne, 1982).

Although evidence about the stability of clique and crowd membership is lacking, two related factors may provide a good starting point for research in this area. First, using quite different methodologies (self-report versus projective responses) on samples of adolescents in different nations and decades, both Brown, Eicher, and Petrie (1986) and J. C. Coleman (1974) found that the importance attached to belonging to a peer group peaked in early adolescence and then diminished steadily through the end of secondary school. This waning concern with fitting into a group, which is consistent with Newman and Newman's (1976) conjectures, should have an impact on students' interest in changing groups or defending the boundaries of crowds against unwelcome outsiders. In fact, it may be one explanation for a second factor: the "senior year" phenomenon noted by many ethnographers (Cusick, 1973; Larkin, 1979; Varenne, 1982). Students report that in their last year of high school there is a curious dissipation of crowd boundaries and a new sense of cohesiveness among class members. Reminiscent of the Sherifs' (1953) work on integrating crowds through creating superordinate goals, it is as if the class draws together to confront their shared challenge of adjusting to the demands and opportunities of life beyond high school. Here, at the other end of secondary school, the early adolescent preoccupations with joining a clique, fitting into a crowd, and protecting one's social turf against others no longer have much significance in the shadow of the new developmental tasks of young adulthood. As late adolescents join forces to face these new challenges, the peer group system they carefully crafted to negotiate now-completed tasks seems to disintegrate.

THE LOCUS OF PEER GROUP INFLUENCES

The numerous gaps in our understanding of how peer groups and group membership evolve across adolescence limit our understanding of just how peer groups influence teenagers' school and social behavior. Nevertheless, researchers have drawn at least a partial portrait of the process of peer group influence. Cliques exert influence through peer pressure, by offering desirable rewards to those who conform to group norms and/or undesirable sanctions to those who resist them. Newman and Newman (1976) emphasize the role of peer pressure in maintaining group cohesivenses and according some meaning to group membership, but they stop short of spelling out the specific processes by which peer pressure is exerted. Ethnographic accounts of adolescent peer group interaction imply that pressure or influence is sometimes direct and overt, as members exhort the person to do something or *not* do something, and other times much more subtle—the sudden, unspoken ostracization of a member who does not conform to group norms, for example (Cusick, 1973; Eder, 1985; Varenne, 1982). Regardless of its form, peer pressure is influential only if adolescents are willing to respond to it. Researchers have paid more attention to adolescents' general susceptibility to peer pressure than to their tendency to attend to one source of pressure over another. But to understand the locus of peer group influences among adolescents, three issues must be addressed: teenagers' susceptibility to peer influence, their perceptions of actual peer pressures, and their attentiveness to a particular source of peer influence.

Susceptibility to Peer Pressure

Adolescents are "developmentally primed" to attend to both direct and subtle pressures because their willingness to conform to peer pressures, generally, exceeds that of both children and young adults. Susceptibility to peer pressure is not a constant force across adolescence, however. It seems to reach its height in early adolescence, then steadily diminish to levels more characteristic of early childhood (Berndt, 1979; Bixenstine, DeCorte, & Bixenstine, 1976; Costanzo & Shaw, 1966). Even at the peak of susceptibility, however, adolescents seem less receptive to antisocial peer pressures than to those pressures involving more innocuous social behaviors (Berndt, 1979; Brown, Clasen, & Eicher, 1986).

The power of peer pressure in adolescence stems not only from individuals' heightened receptiveness to peers' suggestions but also from the waning influence of parental pressures or expectations (Steinberg & Silverberg, 1986). Susceptibility to parental pressures diminishes steadily from childhood through adolescence (Berndt, 1979) so that, even though middle adolescents' willingness to follow peers' directives returns to the level observed in middle childhood, the impact of peer pressure on individuals' behavior does not dissipate so quickly.

Perceptions of Peer Pressure

Studies of adolescents' susceptibility to peer pressure have dealt with hypothetical or contrived pressure situations. They do not indicate just how secondary school students perceive peer pressusre. A more recent set of studies has given us a better sense of students' perceptions. Brown and his colleagues (Brown, 1982; Brown, Clasen, & Eicher, 1986; Clasen & Brown, 1985) derived a list of common adolescent peer pressures and asked samples of middle and high school students to rate the degree and direction of pressure they perceived from their friends. In their findings they emphasized four points. First, peer pressure is multidimensional: Adolescents reported notable pressures from peers in a variety of areas of their life, not just in relation to the antisocial behaviors that are often of greatest interest to adults. Second, peer pressure is multidirectional. That is, whereas some students reported that they felt pressure to use drugs, to study hard, or whatever, others reported that their friends generally discouraged such activities. A related, third point is that adolescents often report feeling peer pressure toward positive, adaptive behaviors. For example, in all schools in which these investigators used their peer pressure instrument, the item receiving the highest average rating was pressure to finish high school. Pressure to "excel, to do something better than anyone else" also received a surprisingly high score, considering the common image of peer pressure as a force compelling conformity. Such findings are consistent with Newman and Newman's (1976, p. 269) argument that peer group expectations ". . . may be perceived by the adolescent as a force drawing him to be more than he thinks he is, to be braver, more confident, more outgoing, etc."

A final point emerging from these studies is that perceived peer pressures are not uniform across adolescents, but vary by such factors as age and crowd affiliation. Older adolescents reported significantly less pressure toward family involvement, slightly more school involvement pressures, and substantially more pressures in the misconduct area (particularly regarding sex and drinking). These age differences point out the possible role of peer pressure in moving adolescents along the developmental pathway to adulthood (relinquishing parental dependencies and practicing more adultlike behaviors).

Of course, the importance of peer pressure is not simply that it exists but that it has some influence over adolescents' attitudes or behaviors. In addition to ethnographic evidence, there is limited support for such a connection in self-report studies. Brown, Clasen, and Eicher (1986) found significant but modest associations between the strength of pressures secondary students perceived from friends and the extent of self-reported involvement in related activities. Associations remained significant after controlling for respondents' susceptibility to peer pressure. Perceived pressures explained more of the variance in self-reported misconduct (9%) than peer involvement (frequency and importance of socializing with peers) (3%). More interesting was that the association between perceived pressures and self-reported behaviors was stronger for students who were relatively more susceptible to peer pressure.

Three limitations of these studies should be addressed in future work on peer pressure. First, there was no validation of the respondents' perceptions, no indication that students' reports of the pressures they received from friends corresponded to a more objective evaluation of such pressures. Second, self-reports are likely to yield underestimates of peer pressure because teenagers may be unaware of the subtle nature of some peer pressures, or unwilling to admit their friends would generate such pressures. Perceived pressures were stronger in the retrospective accounts of college students that Brown (1982) surveyed than among his teenage samples. Finally, and most importantly, there is little in this body of studies to indicate the specific processes by which peer pressure is expressed. How direct or indirect, how persistent and consistent are the pressures that students sense from friends? What sanctions are applied to those who violate group norms? What forms of pressure are most effective in constraining and directing adolescents' behavior? These are important issues about which we know very little.

Several strategies can help address these limitations. One way to validate perceived peer pressures is to compare an adolescent's description of pressure received from friends in a given area with his/her friends' assessment of the pressure they have exerted in that area. Such an approach requires the investigator to identify and work within well-defined friendship groups (cliques). Also, asking about peer pressure in concrete, behavioral terms (e.g., how often have your friends encouraged you to study for a class, versus how much pressure do you feel to do well in school) would help to minimize underreporting of pressure and specify processes of peer influence.

Sources of Peer Influence

The common image of peer pressure is one of a monolithic force, imposing a relatively standard set of values and behaviors with relatively equal intensity on all students in secondary schools. This notion, inspired by J. S. Coleman's (1961) classic study of the adolescent peer culture, has been disputed in a number of studies. Smith (1987) pointed out that the concept of a monolithic youth culture, especially popular in the early 1960s, was quickly modified to suggest that adolescents occupied multiple youth cultures. In a reanalysis of some of Coleman's data, Cohen (1979) concluded that there was not one (as Coleman had maintained) but three distinct value orientations among the sample's students.

J. S. Coleman's (1961) contention that students were influenced most by the school's social elite, whether or not they were members of the elite, has been questioned in another reanalysis of his data by Cohen (1983). In this study, the evidence suggested that students were influenced by the value systems of peers whom they selected as friends, but not by the values of students who were not considered friends. Therefore, contrary to Coleman's assertions, the only students to be influenced heavily by the norms and value system of the elite crowd were the students who comprised this group. An ethnographic corollary comes from Cusick (1973), who was particularly struck by the tendency of the cliques he observed to simply ignore outsiders. When a nonmember attempted to enter an ongoing interaction of group members—joining a conversation between Cusick and the clique, for example, or being with the clique as part of a work group for a class assignment—the clique responded by acting as if the outsider literally was not present and did not exist. In most cases, neither the clique nor the outsider seemed to be particularly surprised or bothered by this arrangement. The tendency of cliques to ignore outsiders should seriously undermine the ability of one individual or one crowd to influence another group.

Researchers have been more attentive to—and more successful at—sketching the dynamics of influence patterns within cliques. Studies of the coalescence of cliques in summer camp settings demonstrate the tendency for dominance positions to emerge quickly and, especially at either end of the dominance hierarchy, to remain quite stable through the natural history of the group (Savin-Williams, 1987; Sherif, White, & Harvey, 1955). The power of the most dominant member to influence group opinion is readily apparent in such studies. Yet, members beyond the most dominant person also wield influence, albeit more constricted.

In some cliques the leadership role seems to be divided or to shift according to group tasks. Dunphy (1963), for example, discovered that most of the consolidated cliques in his sample had two leaders, serving very different functions. One, the gregarious sociocenter, modeled appropriate heterosexual behavior for group members while the task leader, working quietly behind the scenes, made more general decisions about group activities, membership, and enforcement of group norms. Sherif and Sherif (1964) reported on one clique in which the most dominant member temporarily relinquished his leadership role when the group played basketball. Consciously or unconsciously, the leader recognized the superior talents of another member in directing the clique's activity during this task.

With the exception of Cusick (1973), all of these studies focused on clique interactions in quite circumscribed settings. Cliques that are based on interactions in secondary school must cope with the demands of a more complex social setting, which rewards a broader range of skills. It is likely that different abilities are needed to function effectively in academic tasks, in structured extracurricular activities, in informal interactions under the loose supervision of adults (lunchroom conversation or attendance at athletic contests), and in social situations without adult supervision. It may well be that leadership or dominance in cliques shifts noticeably as members move from one school task to the next. Or it may be that separate cliques emerge for each activity, so that a student is part of one clique in academic settings and another clique (probably with partial overlap in membership) in extracurricular or less structured socializing settings. This would help account for the loose-knit structuring of cliques that Shrum and Cheek (1987) found in secondary schools. At any rate, the tendency for leadership or influence to pass from one member to another may be more characteristic of adolescent cliques than we realize from existing research.

There is also evidence that attempts by clique leaders to exert influence in areas beyond their own competence can have disastrous effects for the clique. Cusick (1973) describes a fascinating case in which a male clique decided to work on a major project for Humanities Class. Jim, the most dominant member, encouraged the group's natural inclination to turn class work time into socializing time and to postpone serious work on the assignment. As the deadline drew near, other clique members began working to salvage the project, but all members ultimately received low grades on the project, and Jim's grade was the lowest. When the teacher commented to the group on their mediocre work—and Jim's poor leadership—group members voiced their resentment toward Jim with a barrage of sarcastic comments. Ultimately, Jim was displaced not only from his position of dominance but from the group altogether. Cusick lamented the teacher's ability to upset peer group relationships, but perhaps the greater lesson is that without an ability to adjust influence patterns to the multiple demands of secondary school, cliques have little opportunity to survive.

Identifying Adolescents' Reference Group

If there is some fluidity in dominance or leadership within cliques, then the pattern of peer influence within adolescent crowds also may not be as straightforward or rigid as we normally conceive it to be. J. S. Coleman's (1961) expectation that all adolescents are influenced primarily by the "leading crowd" in school may not be so much inaccurate as it is an oversimplification. Students who are content with their current clique and crowd affiliations are likely to be influenced most by the norms and pressures of these groups. But a substantial number of adolescents are only loosely associated with a peer group or aspire to membership in a group other than the one to which they belong. For these people, the peers with whom they would like to associate may be a more influential reference group than the peers with whom they really do associate. Indirect support for this possibility comes from studies of the association between peer group affiliation and adolescents' self-esteem. J. S. Coleman found that, among students who were not part of the school's elite crowd, the proportion desiring to be someone else if they could—an indication of low self-esteem—was much higher among those who wished to be part of the elites than among those without such a desire. In a more elaborate study, Brown and Lohr (1987) compared the self-perceived and peer-rated crowd affiliations of students in one high school. Some students emerged as "outsiders," not classified by peers into any major crowd and not even recognized by most of the members of any crowd. Within this group, those who recognized they were outsiders but wished to be part of a crowd had significantly lower self-esteem than those who acknowledged their position but seemed content not to be in a group.

It is, of course, a leap of faith to presume that such differences in self-esteem are highly correlated with differences in students' reference group orientation. But the research strategies typically employed by investigators seem to work against identifying this phenomenon. Ethnographies tend to concentrate on one or two cohesive cliques whose members are quite satisfied with their group affiliation (e.g., Cusick, 1973; Eder, 1985). Survey researchers often determine peer group membership by measuring students' value systems: Adolescents whose values match the values of a particular crowd are presumed to be members of that peer group (e.g., Cohen, 1979). Because, however, crowd affiliation is determined by *peer* assignment, it should be measured independently of self-perceived or ideally desired crowd affiliation.

In fact, a clear understanding of sources of peer influence requires the coordination of several pieces of information from adolescents. Peer ratings can reveal how consistently a student is associated (by reputation) with one or more crowds. Sociometric data can indicate whether the student is a central or peripheral member of a given clique or crowd. Self-report responses can reveal the importance of belonging to a group, along with the student's sense of actual and desired crowd membership. This information, coupled with an understanding of the norms and pressures characteristic of each crowd, can help us understand whether or not and when students are influenced most by their membership group or their reference group. It can also shed light on the influence process among "floaters"—those students who seem to fit into several crowds and who move easily among them—as well as the large mass of students who do not seem to fit clearly into any clique or crowd (Larkin, 1979).

CONSEQUENCES OF PEER GROUP INFLUENCES

The ultimate concern of research on adolescent peer groups, of course, is the consequences that group membership or group influences have on adolescents' attitudes, behavior, or psychological well-being. One area of great interest has been how peer groups shape adolescents' academic aspirations and achievement. One could expect considerable peer influence in school-related behaviors because, as Cusick (1973) pointed out, it is rare to find a teenager not interacting with friends during the school day. Even during classes, Cusick found that students carry on conversations with friends concurrently with their work on class assignments. On the other hand, because academically related matters rarely enter the conversation (Cusick), peer influence in this area may be minimal. Unfortunately, the debate is difficult to settle because studies in this area bear the marks of the deficits in conceptualizing peer groups or measuring group influences that I have pointed out.

Shortcomings of Existing Research

Ide et al. (1981) reviewed 10 major studies of peer influences on academic achievement. The method employed by most researchers was either to correlate a student's perceptions of a best friend's achievement or aspirations with self-reported standing on the same variable or to use sociometric techniques to identify friendship dyads and then correlate the two students' self-reports on the achievement variable of interest. There are three major problems with such approaches. First, the unit of analysis, conceptually and empirically, is a dyad, even though the author purports to measure peer *group* influence. Occasionally, students are asked to give a generalized response for their group of friends—what I would call a clique—but these data are virtually always respondents' perceptions of clique members' behavior, rather than more objective measures (see Ide et al., 1981). Reliance on such self-perceptions is a second common shortcoming with existing studies because, as Davies and Kandel (1981), among others, have shown, self-perceived measures artificially inflate the degree of similarity between self and other in studies of achievement variables.

The most serious shortcoming, however, is that whereas researchers express an interest in measuring peer group influence, they actually measure peer similarity—the simple correlation between self and other's attitudes or behavior. There is considerable evidence that the similarity between pairs of friends or acquaintances is more likely to have been a prerequisite to rather than a consequence of their relationship. Cohen (1977), for example, demonstrated that the homogeneity within peer groups is primarily a result of homophilic selection of friends, rather than a result of group conformity pressures or the departure of members whose attitudes deviate from group norms. In a later, longitudinal study that controlled for initial similarity of friendship pairs, Cohen (1983) found that peer influence was only weakly associated with students' college aspirations.

Efforts to measure peer group influences more precisely in this area are confounded by the reciprocal nature of peer influences. In examining friendship dyads, both Kandel (1978) and Epstein (1983) found that similarity is both a cause and consequence of friendship. Furthermore, both studies reported that stable, reciprocated dyads had more influence over each other's academic orientations than unreciprocated relationships or those that seemed to dissipate over the course of a school year. Extending the logic of these findings to clique-level interactions, one would expect to find that, by dint of shared personal characteristics, like-minded students will coalesce into cliques that vary in stability and closeness and that those in more stable and closely knit cliques will show greater evidence of peer influence.

The inverse association observed between academic achievement and deviance also may be traced, in part, to a sort of reciprocal pattern of peer influence. Smith (1987) cited several British studies that indicated that poor achievement patterns propel adolescents into peer groups with a more delinquent orientation. Once there, individuals respond to group pressures to engage in delinquent activities, and participation in such activities further undermines their chances of improving academic standing. Galambos and Silbereisen (1987) also found that poor school performance predicted subsequent involvement with delinquent peers, although, in their longitudinal study, they did not see the reciprocal effect of this peer group association further diminishing the student's achievement level.

Davies and Kandel (1981) reported that girls were more likely than boys to adjust their academic aspirations in line with peer norms. This is an interesting contrast to studies showing that adolescent boys are more susceptible than girls to antisocial peer pressures (Berndt, 1979; Brown, Clasen, & Eicher, 1986). More importantly, however, it points up the probability that peer groups are not necessarily equally successful in influencing achievement patterns of adolescents who differ on such factors as age, race, or crowd affiliation.

The Influence of Peer Group Norms

Ironically, the most compelling evidence of peer group influence on academic achievement concerns one of the most subtle influence processes—the crowd's implicit messages about what it takes to be popular. J. S. Coleman (1961) found that most students regarded "getting good grades" as well down the list of prerequisites for being part of the "leading crowd" in high school, although the salience of good grades did vary in accordance with the academic orientation of the community. To validate students' opinions, Coleman derived several sociometric ratings of students' popularity among peers (average number of nominations by classmates as someone who is popular with girls, as a friend of the respondent, or as someone with whom the respondent would like to be friends) and then compared the popularity of students regarded by peers as the best athletes to that of students regarded as the best scholars. Generally, across schools, those regarded as both outstanding scholars and athletes enjoyed the highest popularity. Students recognized only as good athletes had lower ratings on popularity but considerably higher than those recognized only as good scholars, whose ratings were only marginally higher than those of the average student. Thus, the reality of sociometric ratings matched students' perceptions that concentrating energies on academic achievement was not a successful strategy for achieving peer status.

Other studies, however, have not necessarily confirmed J. S. Coleman's (1961) reading of the link between peer popularity and academic achievement. In a sample of Nigerian adolescents, Eyo (1984) reported only a weak inverse association ($r = -.20$) between the need for achievement and the need to appear socially desirable among peers. Ishiyama and Chabassol (1985) found that fear of the social consequences of academic success was greater among girls than boys, and greater among middle school than high school students. This fear was due not only to the negative sanctions high achievement would engender from peers, but also because getting good grades would make one stand out among peers or would create an expectation for high achievement that would be difficult to maintain. Finally, Faunce (1984) reported a strong, *positive* correlation ($r = .73$) between grade point average and sociometrically determined status among peers in a sample of high school seniors. In sum, academic achievement is consistently significantly associated with peer popularity among adolescents, but not always in the same direction or to the same degree for both genders or different age groups.

Race also may be a mediating factor. Investigators have expressed concern that black students, especially in urban, lower class secondary schools, encounter strong pressure from black peers not to do too well in school. High achievement is associated with "acting white," renouncing one's cultural roots, and trying to appear better than fellow blacks. Fordham and Ogbu (1986) use this argument to explain the diligent efforts of bright students in one all-black high school to avoid being labeled a "brainiac." Students are confronted with the choice of either masking their abilities by earning less than outstanding grades or masking their achievements by being a comic or a "cut-up" in class in front of peers. Fuller (1984) reported the same phenomenon among black girls in a British school.

Fordham and Ogbu's (1986) study points up another interesting facet of peer pressure ignored by most researchers, namely, that pressures emanate from both within and beyond one's circle of friends. The tendency has been to focus on peer pressure from friends (theoretically, clique mates), appealing to principles of small-group socialization (Moreland & Levine, 1982). Yet, the norms of one's crowd also can be a source of peer pressure, in that students exerting pressure are not confined to friends. If brains are expected to be intellectual, or populars snobbish, or loners shy and socially unsophisticated, they will be approached and treated that way by members outside their crowd. These interaction styles, adopted by acquaintances outside one's clique or crowd, represent a source of peer pressure. Students who step outside the social stereotype of their crowd often are greeted with hostile responses from members of other groups—forcing them to get "back in line" with the crowd's norms (Cusick, 1973; Eder, 1985).

Placing Peer Influences in Proper Context

In examining how academic achievement relates to adolescents' actual or anticipated popularity among peers, researchers consistently have treated the peer group system as a monolithic entity—assuming that there is only one set of criteria for peer status or one status hierarchy. This approach probably obfuscates the association between achievement and group pressures concerning popularity because the peer system actually is a complex network of crowds and cliques, each having somewhat different norms (and, therefore, status criteria). Fordham and Ogbu (1986) noticed, for example, that when blacks with exceptional abilities were placed in an environment of exclusively high achievers, their anxiety about peer sanctions for doing well in school seemed to diminish dramatically.

To achieve an accurate reading of peer group influences on students' achievement patterns, researchers must be more sensitive to a student's place in the peer group system—to the membership groups and reference groups that matter to the student. At the same time, it is important to place peer group influences in the larger context of adolescents' lives. Studies have reported quite consistently that, with regard to academic aspirations or achievement, parents appear to wield more influence over adolescents than do peers (Brittain, 1963; Davies & Kandel, 1981). Similarly, adolescents' susceptibility to antisocial peer pressures is related to family structure and the dynamics of relationships with parents (Steinberg, 1987). Ianni (1983, p. 11) cautions, "The development of an ego-syntonic value system is a dynamic interplay between modeling parents, sensitivity to peer influences, and the individual's own striving for independence." The multiple sources of influence that teenagers confront, which are probably more often mutually reinforcing than contradictory, make it unlikely that any single source of influence will dominate as a determinant of students' attitudes or behaviors.

MOVING FORWARD: CONSIDERATIONS FOR FUTURE RESEARCH

The groans or whimsy that adults—and even teenagers—display in discussing adolescent peer groups should not be taken lightly. They are signs of the significance of cliques and crowds in adolescents' success or failure in the academic and social tasks of secondary school. As researchers continue to probe the social world of secondary school, they uncover more of the complexities of peer group influences. In pressing forward with this agenda, six factors seem helpful for researchers to keep in mind.

1. Peer groups and group affiliations are dynamic phenomena. The temptation to regard cliques and crowds as stable entities must be eschewed in respect for the many changing features of peer groups in adolescence. The peer group structure itself goes through a notable metamorphosis, evolving from isolated cliques into a complex array of interlocking cliques and crowds, whose diversity seems to expand through the high school years. Membership in peer groups also seems to change, if not from one clique or crowd to the next, then at least in the devotion that members display to their group and its norms. The individual's susceptibility to peer pressure and, apparently, the uniformity of peer pressures emanating from the group seem to rise and fall across the course of the secondary school years. Each of these dynamic forces contributes to the flexible and fluctuating nature of peer group influences. The task for researchers becomes chartering peer group influences within the framework of these several developmental patterns.

   2.   *Peer groups exert influences at multiple levels.* Dyads, cliques, and crowds do not describe equivalent patterns of peer interaction, nor do they display equivalent patterns of peer influence. Pairs of friends can exert influence on each other in direct and individualistic terms. Influences stemming from one's crowd affiliation are more difficult to observe because they involve pressures from students outside as well as within the group. Students' motivations to respond to peer influences also may differ among these forms of peer relations. The concern in responding to pressures from a single friend may be primarily to maintain the dyadic relationship, whereas efforts to conform to crowd norms reveal an interest in maintaining one's image or "identity" among peers as a whole. Measuring influence at one level, as has been the tendency of researchers (the friendship dyad), does not provide a comprehensive portrait of peer influences. More attention must be directed at clique- and crowd-level influences, as well as to the ways in which patterns of influence at each level tend to complement and reinforce each other.

   3.   *Not all peer group influences emanate from the membership group.* Peer group affiliation is not always a matter of personal choice. Some students happily stay with the same group of friends and the same crowd affiliation throughout high school. Others transfer groups naturally as their personality and interests grow in new directions. Still others express a discontentment strong enough to prompt them to reach out to other crowds for acceptance. The common assumption that teenagers are influenced exclusively by their own friends or their own crowd is a tenuous one. The fluid nature of peer group ties compels researchers to consider the possibility that adolescents' primary reference group is not necessarily their membership group. In more concrete terms, efforts to measure crowd influences must consider the student's subjective and desired crowd affiliation as well as objective (peer-rated) crowd affiliation. In cases where objective, subjective, and desired crowd affiliations coincide, crowd-related influences should be relatively clear-cut. In cases where the affiliations differ, crowd influences should vary with the strength of the student's ties to the different reference groups and the "social distance" or degree of normative discrepancies among them.

4. *Peer group influences are not strictly a matter of coercion.* Researchers now recognize that charting the similarity between self and peers is not an adequate measure of peer influence. As the search for more meaningful measurement strategies continues, it is important not to limit conceptions of peer group influence to acts of pressure or coercion. A substantial proportion of peer group influences may be by example of group members, such as the efforts Dunphy (1963) noted of crowd leaders to model appropriate heterosexual behavior for less socially advanced group members. The more cooperative effort of group members to establish group norms also can engender shifts in members' beliefs or activities. Even the efforts of group members to offer assistance to an individual can become a significant source of influence. When group members routinely offer a student help with homework or with sharpening some sports skills, or when such offers are *never* made, the actions serve as a subtle message about what is important and what is not. Although no pressure is involved, such actions as modeling, offering assistance, or inviting cooperation for defining group norms, may comprise a powerful source of influence. This influence may be especially strong because more unilateral and coercive tactics violate the spirit of friendship that supposedly forms the basis of adolescent peer associations (Davies & Kandel, 1981).

5. *Studies should employ multiple methods to examine peer group influences.* The more subtle, indirect, noncoercive strategies that comprise a healthy proportion of peer influences are difficult to ascertain through reliance on adolescents' perceptions of peer group influences. Yet, the ethnographic techniques that reveal such strategies more clearly are costly and time-consuming. The solution, I think, is to integrate multiple methodologies into future studies of the structure and influence processes of adolescent peer groups. Self-report surveys are efficient means of discerning the importance students attach to peer group affiliations, their willingness to attend to peer pressure in general, and which crowds serve as their primary reference groups. Interviews help tap the social-cognitive dynamics of peer groups: students' understanding of the peer group system and the rules that govern an individual's placement and movement within it. Ethnographic observations reveal specific processes by which groups try to shape and maintain members' behavior. Traditionally, each of these avenues of investigation has been pursued independently. It is time to begin combining them in more elaborate studies that can tease out the range of peer influences to which adolescents are submitted.

6. *Peer groups should be evaluated in the larger context of the adolescents' social world.* In the past, researchers have been absorbed with the relation between peer groups and parents, or adults in general, in the lives of adolescents. Are parents or peers a stronger source of influence (Brittain, 1963)? Do adolescent peer groups exist independently of adults or simply mimic the range of life styles available to students as they move into the

adult world (Cohen, 1979; J. S. Coleman, 1961)? These questions are too basic to continue pursuing, but they do point up the need to place peer groups in the larger context of the social world of secondary students. This world consists not only of peer groups, but also of parents and families, teachers and school personnel, and the rules of social interaction in the larger society. Each of these entities exerts some influence over adolescents, and the challenge to researchers is to identify the processes by which these separate forces reinforce, complement, or supplant each other.

The probable conclusion to emerge from studies following these guidelines—that peer group influences are conditional and modest—may disappoint many individuals. Our memories of peer pressure and clannishness and social stereotyping may be more vivid and vicious than the realities we experienced in secondary school. Yet, this does not diminish the integral role that peer groups play in adolescents' adjustment to secondary school. It simply humbles us to be fascinated with the subtle complexities of peer relations amidst the broad range of psychological and social forces that shape individual lives during adolescence.

REFERENCES

Berndt, T. (1979). Developmental changes in conformity to peers and parents. *Developmental Psychology, 15,* 606–616.

Bigelow, B. J. (1977). Children's friendship expectations: A cognitive developmental study. *Child Development, 48,* 246–253.

Bixenstine, V. E., DeCorte, M. S., & Bixenstine, B. A. (1976). Conformity to peer-sponsored misconduct at four grade levels. *Developmental Psychology, 12,* 226–236.

Brittain, C. V. (1963). Adolescent choices and parent-peer cross-pressures. *American Sociological Review, 28,* 385–391.

Brown, B. B. (1982). The extent and effects of peer pressure among high school students: A retrospective analysis. *Journal of Youth and Adolescence, 11,* 121–133.

Brown, B. B., & Clasen, D. R. (1986, March). *Developmental changes in adolescents' conceptions of peer groups.* Paper presented at the biennial meeting of the Society for Research in Adolescence, Madison, WI.

Brown, B. B., Clasen, D. R., & Eicher, S. A. (1986). Perceptions of peer pressure, peer conformity dispositions, and self-reported behavior among adolescents. *Developmental Psychology, 22,* 521–530.

Brown, B. B., Clasen, D. R., & Niess, J. D. (1987, April). *Smoke in the looking glass: Adolescents' perceptions of their peer group status.* Paper presented at the biennial meeting of the Society for Research in Child Development, Baltimore.

Brown, B. B., Eicher, S. A., & Petrie, S. (1986). The importance of peer group ("crowd") affiliation in adolescence. *Journal of Adolescence, 9,* 73–96.

Brown, B. B., & Lohr, M. J. (1987). Peer group affiliation and adolescent self-esteem: An integration of ego-identity and symbolic interaction theories. *Journal of Personality and Social Psychology, 52,* 47–55.

Buff, S. A. (1970). Greasers, dupers, and hippies: Three responses to the adult world. In L. Howe (Ed.), *The white majority* (pp. 60–77). New York: Random House.

Clark, B. R. (1962). *Educating the expert society*. San Francisco: Chandler.

Clasen, D. R., & Brown, B. B. (1985). The multidimensionality of peer pressure in adolescence. *Journal of Youth and Adolescence, 14*, 451–468.

Cohen, J. (1977). Sources of peer homogeneity. *Sociology of Education, 50*, 227–241.

Cohen, J. (1979). High school cultures and the adult world. *Adolescence, 14*, 491–502.

Cohen, J. (1983). Commentary: The relationship between friendship selection and peer influence. In J. L. Epstein & N. Karweit (Eds.), *Friends in school* (pp. 163–174). New York: Academic Press.

Coleman, J. C. (1974). *Relationships in adolescence*. Boston: Routledge & Kegan Paul.

Coleman, J. C. (1980). Friendship and the peer group in adolescence. In J. Adelson (Ed.), *Handbook of Adolescent Psychology* (pp. 408–431). New York: Wiley.

Coleman, J. S. (1961). *The adolescent society*. New York: Free Press.

Costanzo, P. R., & Shaw, M. E. (1966). Conformity as a function of age level. *Child Development, 37*, 967–975.

Crockett, L., Losoff, M., & Petersen, A. C. (1984). Perceptions of the peer group and friendship in early adolescence. *Journal of Early Adolescence, 4*, 155–181.

Cusick, P. A. (1973). *Inside high school*. New York: Holt, Rinehart, & Winston.

Davies, M. & Kandel, D. B. (1981). Parental and peer influences on adolescents' educational plans: Some further evidence. *American Journal of Sociology, 87*, 363–387.

Dunphy, D. (1963). The social structure of urban adolescent peer groups. *Sociometry, 26*, 230–246.

Eder, D. (1985). The cycle of popularity: Interpersonal relations among female adolescents. *Sociology of Education, 58*, 154–165.

Eichhorn, D. H. (1975). The school. In M. Johnson (Ed.), *Toward adolescence: The middle school years* (pp. 56–73). Chicago: National Society for the Study of Education (University of Chicago Press).

Epstein, J. L. (1983). The influence of friends on achievement and affective outcomes. In J. L. Epstein & N. Karweit (Eds.), *Friends in school: Patterns of selection and influence in secondary schools* (pp. 177–200). New York: Academic Press.

Erikson, E. H. (1968). *Identity, youth, and crisis*. New York: Norton.

Eyo, I. (1984). Relationships between the need to appear socially desirable, achievement motivation, and attribution of academic outcomes in secondary school students. *Psychological Reports, 55*, 247–252.

Faunce, W. (1984). School achievement, social status, and self-esteem. *Social Psychology Quarterly, 47*, 3–14.

Fordham, S., & Ogbu, J. U. (1986). Black students' school success: Coping with the burden of "acting white." *Urban Review, 18*, 176–206.

Fuller, M. (1984). Black girls in a London comprehensive school. In M. Hammersley & P. Woods (Eds.), *Life in school: The sociology of pupil culture* (pp. 77–88). New York: Open University Press.

Galambos, N. L., & Silbereisen, R. K. (1987, April). *Troubles with family, school, and peers: Effects on adolescent substance use*. Paper presented at the biennial meeting of the Society for Research on Child Development Baltimore.

Gordon, C. W. (1957). *The social system of the high school*. Glencoe, IL: Free Press.

Hallinan, M. T. (1979). Structural effects on children's friendships and cliques. *Social Psychology Quarterly, 42*, 43–54.

Hartup, W. W. (1984). The peer system. In E. M. Heatherington (Ed.) & P. H. Mussen (Series Ed.), *Handbook of child psychology: Vol. 4. Socialization, personality, and social development* (pp. 103–196). New York: Wiley.

Hollingshead, A. B. (1949). *Elmtown's youth.* New York: Wiley.

Ianni, F. A. J. (1983). *Home, school, and community in adolescent education.* New York: Clearinghouse on Urban Education.

Ide, J. K., Parkerson, J., Haertel, G. D., & Walberg, H. J. (1981). Peer group influence on educational outcomes: A quantitative synthesis. *Journal of Educational Psychology, 73,* 472–484.

Ishiyama, F. I., & Chabassol, D. J. (1985). Adolescents' fear of the social consequences of academic success as a function of age and sex. *Journal of Youth and Adolescence, 14,* 37–46.

Kandel, D. B. (1978). Homophily, selection and socialization. *American Journal of Sociology, 84,* 427–438.

Larkin, R. W. (1979). *Suburban youth in cultural crisis.* New York: Oxford.

Lewis, M., & Rosenblum, L. A. (Eds.). (1975). *Friendship and peer relations.* New York: Wiley.

Moreland, R. L., & Levine, J. M. (1982). Socialization in small groups: Temporal changes in individual-group relations. In L. Berkowitz (Ed.), *Advances in experimental social psychology,* (Vol. 15, pp. 137–183). New York: Academic Press.

Newman, P. R., & Newman, B. M. (1976). Early adolescence and its conflict: Group identity versus alienation. *Adolescence, 11,* 261–274.

O'Brien, S. F., & Bierman, K. L. (1987, April). *Conceptions and perceived influence of peer groups: Interviews with preadolescents and adolescents.* Paper presented at the biennial meeting of the Society for Research in Child Development, Baltimore.

Poveda, T. G. (1975). Reputation and the adolescent girl: An analysis. *Adolescence, 37,* 127–136.

Rosenberg, F. R., & Simmons, R. G. (1975). Sex differences in the self-concept in adolescence. *Sex Roles, 1,* 147–159.

Rutter, M. (1983). School effects on pupil progress: Research findings and policy implications. *Child Development, 54,* 1–29.

Savin-Williams, R. C. (1987). *Adolescence: An ethological perspective.* New York: Springer-Verlag.

Selman, R. (1980). *The growth of interpersonal understanding: Clinical and Developmental Analyses.* New York: Academic Press.

Schwendinger, H., & Schwendinger, J. S. (1985). *Adolescent subcultures and delinquency.* New York: Praeger.

Sherif, M., & Sherif, C. W. (1953). *Groups in harmony and tension: An integration of studies on intergroup relations.* New York: Harper & Row.

Sherif, M., & Sherif, C. W. (1964). *Reference groups.* Chicago: Regnery.

Sherif, M., White, B. J. & Harvey, O. J. (1955). Status in experimentally produced groups. *American Journal of Sociology, 60,* 370–379.

Shrum, W., & Cheek, N. H. (1987). Social structure during the school years: Onset of the degrouping process. *American Sociological Review, 52,* 218–223.

Skorepa, C. A., Horrocks, J. E., & Thompson, G. G. (1963). A study of friendship fluctuations of college students. *Journal of Genetic Psychology, 102,* 151–157.

Smith, D. M. (1987). Peers, subcultures, and schools. In D. Marsland (Ed.), *Education and youth* (pp. 41–64). London: Falmer Press.

Steinberg, L. (1987). The impact of puberty on family relations: Effects of pubertal status and timing. *Developmental Psychology, 23,* 451–460.

Steinberg, L., & Silverberg, S. B. (1986). The vicissitudes of autonomy in early adolescence. *Child Development, 57,* 841–851.

Varenne, H. (1982). Jocks and freaks: The symbolic structure of the expression of social interaction among American senior high school students. In G. Spindler (Ed.), *Doing the ethnography of schooling* (pp. 213–235). New York: Holt, Rinehart, & Winston.

Willis, P. (1977). *Learning to labor.* New York: Columbia University Press.

PART THREE

Family Relationships and Peer Relationships

In the prototypical pattern of human development, relationships with parents are the first and for a long time the most significant of children's relationships. Relationships with peers only begin to acquire significance as children move out of the family context into playgroups or preschools. In part because family relationships come first in development, they have often been assumed to set the pattern for later relationships with peers. This common assumption is critically evaluated by all of the authors in this section.

Michael Lamb and Alison Nash argue that the evidence taken as support for the hypothesis that parent-child relationships have a causal influence on developing relationships with peers is incomplete and equivocal. More specifically, they argue that research often described as demonstrating the importance of secure infant-mother attachments for later competence in the peer group was not designed in a way that would rule out several plausible alternative hypotheses. One alternative hypothesis consistent with most of the research is that a third factor, such as a general disposition to behave sociably or unsociably, accounts for the relations of attachment security to observed success with peers. Lamb and Nash also review findings consistent with the hypothesis that infant-mother and infant-peer relationships have distinctive properties and develop fairly independently. They conclude, however, that the existing data are too scanty to draw more than tentative conclusions about the presence or absence of connections between parent-child and peer relationships in infancy and early childhood.

Michael Lewis and Candice Feiring approach the same question from the perspective of a longitudinal study of parent-child relationships and friendships. They mention the hypothesis that parent-infant attachment may influence the formation of friendships during childhood, but they also suggest the possibility of genetic influences on friendship formation. Their own data, however, indicate only limited predictability of friendship measures in middle childhood from measures of attachment and measures of one constitutional factor, namely, temperament. Their data are most easily assimilated to the hypothesis that family and peer relationships do not strongly influence each other.

David Rowe explicitly argues for the importance of genetic influences on peer relationships. Indeed, he adopts the role of an advocate for greater consideration of genetic contributions to all aspects of family and peer relationships. For this reason, he devotes part of his chapter to an exposition of behavior genetic designs and methods. As an illustration of the potential value of the behavior-genetic approach, he marshals empirical data consistent with the hypothesis that there are significant genetic determinants of one commonly used measure of peer relationships, popularity, or sociometric status.

Finally, James Youniss and Jacqueline Smollar argue persuasively that neither family relationships nor peer relationships can be understood without a recognition of their social and historical context. These authors focus on adolescents' relationships with parents and peers. They suggest that conflicts between parents and peers may be inevitable but may, perhaps, be desirable in societies that are rapidly changing. In these societies, parents and peers may jointly share the responsibility of preparing adolescents for adult roles. Youniss and Smollar conclude that an awareness of the social context is necessary for a full understanding of the psychological issues that affect relationships between adolescents, their parents, and their peers.

CHAPTER 8

Infant-Mother Attachment, Sociability, and Peer Competence

MICHAEL E. LAMB AND ALISON NASH

National Institute of Child Health and Human Development

State University of New York at New Paltz

I. INTRODUCTION

It is widely believed today that peer social skills are to a large extent determined by variations in the quality or security of infant-mother attachment. This belief is, of course, a successor to psychoanalytically inspired hypotheses concerning the formative role of infant-mother interactions in the first year, but its resurgent popularity rests most heavily on widely cited evidence purporting to show a causal relationship between attachment security and subsequent social skills with peers (e.g., Sroufe, 1978, 1983). The putative causal pathway is completed by evidence suggesting that attachment security is itself determined by individual differences in the quality of mothering during the early months of life. In this chapter we pose two questions: (1) How well established are the causal links between attachment security and peer competence? and (2) Is there an alternative formulation that could better explain the association between mother-child and peer relationships? Questions about the origins and developmental course of peer relationships are of increasing relevance today in light of the number of children enrolled in extrafamilial child care facilities, which ensure extensive exposure to other young children.

In fact, there are four ways to conceptualize the association between infant-mother and peer relationships. First, there is the popular notion that sociability with mother serves as a precursor of sociability with peers. In terms of the "maternal precursor" hypothesis, it is widely presumed that infants are biologically prepared to form social relationships with their pri-

The authors are grateful to Drs. Thomas Berndt, Gary Ladd, and Ross Thompson for helpful comments on an earlier draft of this chapter.

mary care providers and that later relationships are based on earlier infant-parent relationships, even though the biological assumption is not an essential component of the maternal precursor hypothesis. Two strategies have been used to explore this hypothesis: an individual difference approach, like that involving correlates of "attachment security," and a nomothetic approach, in which it is determined whether skills that are first used and honed in interaction with mothers are later used in interaction with peers. This approach implies that (1) new social skills emerge first in interaction with mothers and only later with peers and (2) infants use particular (although not necessarily all) social skills more with mothers than with peers.

Second, Vandell (1985) notes that there may be bidirectional influences with characteristics of peer relationships affecting infant-mother interaction and vice versa. In such a model, the infant-mother relationship is not considered unique; rather the model suggests as a general principle that a person's relationships with one person may affect his or her relationships with other social partners.

This view is compatible with a third alternative, in which it is proposed that capacities for relationships with peers and mothers develop concurrently from the beginning of life within the context of generalized developing sociability (Hay, 1985; Lewis & Rosenblum, 1975; Vandell, 1985). Again, both individual difference and nomothetic approaches have been taken to explore this issue. Vandell, outlining an individual difference hypothesis, proposed that sociability with mothers and peers stems from underlying temperamental factors, such that inherently sociable infants are sociable with a variety of social partners (including mothers and peers) and that individual differences in sociability are stable over time. Alternatively, Hay and Lewis and Rosenblum have suggested parallel developmental trajectories, in which social skills with mothers and peers develop concurrently from the beginning of life. This view implies that the processes of relationship formation are the same, regardless of partner, and that particular skills will be used, at least initially, with mothers and peers alike. Of course, characteristic interactions may emerge as a result of social learning processes involving particular partners or classes of partners.

Fourth, Mueller (1979) has proposed that toddlers come to master peer relationships by discovering skills that are effective in controlling peer behavior and that the skills needed to interact with peers are ontogenetically distinct from the skills developed in interaction with mothers. As described below, primatologists such as Harlow (Harlow & Harlow, 1965; Suomi & Harlow, 1978) have further suggested that infant-mother and infant-peer relationships may be distinct not only in terms of their *ontogeny* but also in terms of their *function*.

In this chapter, we first review the evidence relevant to the first—and currently most popular—hypothesis and then examine evidence relevant to the three competing hypotheses. In Section II we examine the available evidence closely in order to determine whether there are indeed reliable associations between attachment security and social competence with peers. Thereafter (Section III), we describe other research on the development of social interaction with peers and mothers and use it to examine alternatives to the maternal preeminence hypothesis. Finally, in Section IV we summarize the available evidence and briefly outline some research needed to determine more conclusively which hypotheses best describe the origins of individual differences in peer social skills.

References to a number of interpretive problems pervade the chapter. These include difficulties in determining whether differences in infantile behavior are at least in part derivatives of differences in the partners' behavior, and/or age, and/or familiarity. Researchers also face difficulties in reaching conclusions about developmental pathways using designs in which crucial pieces of information are lacking. These problems are discussed more fully below.

II. MATERNAL PRECURSOR HYPOTHESIS

Attachment and Social Competence with Peers

Research on the association between infant-mother attachment and peer competence is part of a broader concern with the correlates of behavior in the "Strange Situation." This procedure (see Table 8.1) was developed by Ainsworth and Wittig (1969) as a means of observing how children organize their behavior around attachment figures when mildly distressed by the unfamiliar environment, the entrance of an unfamiliar adult, and brief separations from the parent. Ainsworth, Bleher, Waters, and Wall (1978) have described three major patterns of behavior in the Strange Situation, as well as 8 subgroups. B-group infants, who are deemed secure, use the parent as

TABLE 8.1. Strange Situation

Episode	Persons Present	Change
1	Parent, Infant	Parent and infant enter room
2	Parent, Infant, Stranger	Unfamiliar adult joins dyad
3	Infant, Stranger	Parent leaves
4	Parent, Infant	Parent returns Stranger leaves
5	Infant	Parent leaves
6	Infant, Stranger	Stranger returns
7	Parent, Infant	Parent returns Stranger leaves

Note. After Ainsworth and Wittig (1969).
Episodes are usually 3 minutes long, but episodes 3, 5, and 6 can be curtailed if the infant becomes too distressed, and episodes 4 and 7 are sometimes extended.

a secure base from which to explore or socialize, and they attempt to reengage the parent (either distally or by seeking proximity and/ or contact) upon reunion before returning to exploration. A-group infants are labeled insecureavoidant because they avoid rather than seek to engage the parent, especially in the reunion episodes. C-group infants are labeled insecure-resistant because they both seek contact comfort and angrily reject it when offered, or else because they are passive and helpless. They seem unable to gain security from proximity to or contact with the parent.

Research using the Strange Situation to categorize the security of infantmother attachments became popular in light of claims that Strange Situation behavior was both determined by individual differences in the quality of infant-parent interaction in earlier months of life and itself predicted how the child would behave subsequently in a variety of situations (Ainsworth et al., 1978). As Lamb and his colleagues (Lamb, Thompson, Gardner, & Charnov, 1985; Lamb, Thompson, Gardner, Charnov, & Estes, 1984) concluded in two recent reviews, however, the available evidence only provides limited support for the sweeping claims that have been made. For example, mothers of B-group infants appear to behave in more nurturant, nonrestrictive, and socially desirable ways than the mothers of insecure infants, but researchers have not identified which specific aspects of interaction are formatively important and have not been able to identify the distinctive origins of A- and C-group behavior. Similarly, research on the predictive validity of Strange Situation behavior has been quite inconclusive. Unfortunately, the literature is widely misrepresented, leading to popular misconceptions of its conclusiveness. For this reason, the studies are scrutinized very closely here, following the pattern established by Lamb et al. (1985) in their earlier and more comprehensive review. In this chapter, we focus on one aspect of predictive validity, the association between Strange Situation behavior and concurrent or subsequent patterns of interaction with peers. Readers are referred to Lamb et al.'s (1985) book for a fuller discussion of the Strange Situation literature.

One problem with the literature on predictive validity is the generality and vagueness of the predictions tested. Researchers have typically explored only the prediction that B-type behavior in the Strange Situation will be associated with better skills or more socially desirable behavior in other contexts. Despite behavioral differences between A- and C-group infants in the Strange Situation and different hypotheses concerning the origins of these behavioral patterns, differential outcomes are seldom studied, although they would be expected (Lamb et al., 1985; Sroufe, 1983). In the case of associations between Strange Situation behavior and peer interaction, the prediction has simply been that "securely attached" (i.e., B-type infants) will subsequently behave in a more socially desirable and competent fashion with peers.

Several researchers have studied the association between Strange Situation behavior and later interactive skills with peers. In the first such study, Lieberman (1977) attempted to relate the quality of the child-mother relationship to preschoolers' social competence with peers in an independent setting. Instead of the A/B/C classifications, several composite measures of attachment security were derived by principal components analysis of variables from both home and Strange Situation observations. The first factor comprised behaviors indicating absence of anxiety on the part of the child and a relaxed maternal demeanor during the home observation. The second factor comprised "anxious mother-oriented versus toy-oriented behavior in the strange situation. The third component [sociability] represented expansive sociability versus social withdrawal in the strange situation" (p. 1283). Ratings of maternal attitudes and scores on a composite measure based on the first factor were related to the peer competence measures drawn from a 15-minute free-play session. None of the composite measures based on Strange Situation behavior was similarly related. Since both 3-year Strange Situation ratings and the home-based measure of attachment security are of unknown validity, these data provide equivocal evidence concerning the association between Strange Situation behavior and peer competence. In addition, associations between concurrent measures of mother-child and child-peer relationships do not demonstrate that individual differences in child-mother relationships *produced* differences in peer competence. Such a conclusion would require assessments of both relationships at two points in time. As they stand, Lieberman's findings are also consistent with the general sociability hypothesis described earlier in this chapter.

More impressive findings concerning the association between Strange Situation behavior and peer competence were reported by Waters, Wippman, and Sroufe (1979), who used films of thirty-two 15-month-old infants interacting with their mothers in a novel situation involving 5 to 10 minutes of free play, the entrance of a stranger, a 1-minute separation, and then a mother-infant reunion. To rate security of attachment, information about reunion behavior was supplemented by measures of separation and preseparation behavior, with the avoidant and resistant infants placed together in a single "anxious" group for purposes of analysis.

When the children were 3½ years old, naive observers performed Q-sort assessments on the basis of a 5-week observation in a preschool setting. The means of the scores assigned by two independent raters were summed to yield composite scores on two highly correlated 12-item scales (peer competence; ego strength/effectance). Eleven of the 12 peer competence items, as well as the composite scores, distinguished the two attachment groups. In addition, 5 of the 12 ego strength/effectance items distinguished the two groups, as did the summary score. Thus there was evidence of group differences, especially in peer competence, two years after assessment of attachment status. It is important to note, however, that families were specifically selected for study on the grounds that their circumstances were likely to remain stable throughout the duration of the study (Bronson, 1981). As noted by Lamb et al. (1984, 1985), this consistency in caretaking circumstances is likely to heighten predictive associations with measures of earlier attachment status, because the quality of contemporaneous care may influence the quality of peer relationships. In addition, in the absence of earlier measures of peer competence and later measures of mother-child relationships, the data do not demonstrate that individual differences in infant-mother attachment *cause* later individual differences in peer competence. Like Lieberman's, Waters et al.'s findings are also consistent with the general sociability model described earlier.

The most widely cited studies concerned with the predictive validity of Strange Situation classifications were conducted in Minneapolis by Sroufe and his colleagues. Extensive attempts have been made to assess predictive validity in a sample of disadvantaged families (Egeland & Farber, 1982, 1984). In the first attempted follow-up, Pastor (1980, 1981) observed 62 of the children at 20 to 23 months of age in a study of dyadic peer interaction. Subjects were included only when the child obtained the same attachment classification at both 12 and 18 months (Pastor, 1980). Twelve A-, 13 B-, and 12 C-group infants were selected as target infants. Each was paired with another child (always a B-group toddler) who was considered the control member of the dyad. Four of the six ratings revealed significant group differences, with the B-group children scoring higher on overall sociability, orientation to peer, orientation to mother, and mother supportiveness than the A- and C-group infants, between whom no differences were found. (Note, however, that only one of these ratings explicitly measured peer sociability). Three of the 12 discrete measures of peer-directed behavior revealed differences, with A- and B-group children making more social bids and ignoring fewer offers by peers than those in group C, whereas B-group children redirected their own activities after an object struggle more than A-group children did. Six of the 16 discrete measures of mother-child interaction revealed significant differences, but in only two cases (proportion of the time that mother rejected a bid; proportion of the time that child complied) were the B-group children distinguished from both of the "insecure" groups. Once again, even if the associations had been statistically impressive, the absence of earlier measures of peer competence and later measures of infant-mother attachment would preclude inferences about the formative role of early infant-mother attachment because differences in peer competence could have antedated the assessed differences in attachment behavior.

A later follow-up of subjects in the same sample occurred when 40 of the children, then around 4 to 5 years of age, were invited to participate in a special nursery school program (La Freniere & Sroufe, 1985; Sroufe, 1983; Sroufe, Fox, & Pancake, 1983). The children were divided into two groups. One contained 25 children, with equal numbers classified in the A, B, and C groups when seen in the Strange Situation at 18 months. Twenty-one of the 25 were selected because they had the same classification at both 12 and 18 months, and there was consistency between the 18-month Strange Situation and 24-month tool use assessments in three of the remaining four cases, thus reflecting stability in their socioemotional functioning as well. Nine of the 15 children in group 1 had the same classification at 12 and 18 months

(7 Bs, 2 As), 2 children shifted from one non-B classification to the other during the time period and the remaining 4 received a non-B classification in one assessment and a B-group classification in the other. Three of the latter were placed in the C group for certain analyses (Sroufe et al., 1983, p. 1620). One other child was deemed "mixed," and because no final decision could be made about his classification status, he was excluded from certain analyses. Some of these decisions regarding which classification to use in the analysis appeared to have been changed by the time of La Freniere and Sroufe's (1985) report, so their results are presented separately. Overall, however, the subsample was a highly stable subset of Egeland's sample (Sroufe, 1983, p. 53). The groups were equated on IQ, age, race, and (for group 2) sex.

An enormous amount of data was gathered using a variety of procedures, and only findings concerning peer competence are discussed here. According to Sroufe (1983) the B-group infants ranked higher in social competence, number of friends, popularity (on sociometric instruments), and, on ratings of social skills, compliance and empathy. None of these measures yielded differences between the A and C groups. In a later report, La Freniere and Sroufe (1985) considered many measures of peer interaction: amount of attention received, 19 discrete social behaviors, the accompanying affect and the affective quality of the response (excluding neutral, mild, or unclear responses), dominance (assessed using seven verbal and nonverbal indices), social participation (assessed using a modification of Parten's, 1932, scale), rank orderings of social competence made by the teachers (whose independent evaluations were later combined), and a picture peer-sociometric interview. Data from the two classes were combined for analyses involving 5 "broad band" assessments of peer competence (social competence, sociometric status, social participation, attention structure, and social dominance) as well as "rates of social behavior" and rates of positive and negative expressions. B-group versus A- plus C-group differences emerged on two measures: teacher ratings of social competence and sociometric status. B-group children displayed fewer negative expressions than A-group children, while C-group children were lower than the B- plus A-group children on social dominance and social participation. Post hoc analyses of the 5 broad band measures yielded significant sex by attachment (B vs. A/C) differences on sociometric status and social competence with effects stronger for girls than boys; indeed the main effects for attachment classification were probably not significant for boys, judging from the data reported. This gender effect—apparently showing boys less vulnerable than girls to variations in their experiential histories—is the reverse of that which would have been expected on the basis of other research (Zaslow & Hayes, 1986).

Overall, this study appeared to yield strong evidence of differences between the B- and non-B-group children—differences evident on a number of measures. On several crucial measures, however, there were substantial sex differences that undercut confident assertions about the association between attachment history and peer competence. Furthermore, as in the studies discussed earlier, the absence of earlier measures of peer competence and later measures of child-mother attachment preclude inferences about the causal or formative importance of attachment history. In addition, the specific subsample was carefully selected from the larger sample to ensure stability of attachment classifications. This means that there was probably substantial continuity in the quality of care, whether good or bad. It is thus impossible to tell whether the differences among preschoolers are due to differences in earlier rather than contemporaneous patterns of parent-child relationships, since continuity in parent-child interaction may extend to the preschool years also. This issue is extremely important, given the tendency to attribute later differences in child behavior to *earlier* patterns of maternal behavior and mother-child interaction. This interpretation could be sustained only if there were associations between 12- and 18-month classifications and later behavior in samples in which marked discontinuity in quality of care was evident, or which were unselected in this respect, and when longitudinal associations remained significant after taking autocorrelations and synchronous correlations into account. Since Vaughn, Egeland, Sroufe, and Waters (1979) reported that stable attachments were related in this sample to the frequency and severity of life stresses in the family, it is reasonable to conclude that prediction of later infant behavior was improved by studying only those infants whose attachments were stable and whose families thus experienced more consistent circumstances. Indeed, Sroufe (1983) himself acknowledged, "Selection [for stable attachments] was deliberate . . . to increase the likelihood of continuity across this substantial age span" (p. 53).

Researchers other than members of the Minnesota group have also studied the association between Strange Situation behavior and subsequent peer competence. In their study, Easterbrooks and Lamb (1979) focused on differences between infants in the B1 or B2, B3, and B4 subgroups within the "secure" B-group in order to test the validity of these subgroup distinctions as predictors of peer interactional skills. No A- or C-group infants were studied. All observations took place when the infants were 18 months old; "focal" infants from three groups (B1/B2, B3, B4) were observed in an unfamiliar playroom for 30 minutes with an unfamiliar "foil" playmate who was always drawn from either the B1 or B2 subgroup to ensure comparable playmates for all subjects. Of 21 discrete behavior measures and 3 composite measures of peer interaction, there were significant overall group differences on 2 of the discrete measures and 2 of the composite measures, with the focal B1/B2 infants spending more time interacting with and being close to their peers than focal B3 and B4 infants. Pairwise contrasts revealed significant B1/B2 versus B3 differences on 7 measures (including all 4 measures showing overall differences) and B1/B2 versus B4 differences on 5 measures (including 2 of the 4 showing overall differences). The B1/B2 infants also spent less time in the peer session touching and being near their mothers, indicating that there was some transsituational consistency in their responses to mothers. This response was expected because B1/B2 infants are also noted for distal interaction in the Strange Situation. These differences in mother-directed behavior, however, make it difficult to interpret the group differences on peer interaction measures. The groups may not actually have differed in social competence; rather, different reactions to the unfamiliar situation may have produced differences in peer interaction. It would be important to know whether group differences on the peer interaction measures remained when variance attributable to differences in mother-directed behavior was partialed out. And even if such differences remained, it would not be clear that the intended differences in infant-mother attachments *caused* the differences in peer sociability. Such interpretational problems attend all studies of this genre; Easterbrooks and Lamb's findings simply underscore the issue.

Jacobson, Wille, Tianen, and Aytch (1983) observed 107 infants in the Strange Situation at 18 months and then observed 15 As, 15 Bs, and 15 Cs interacting for 25 minutes with an unfamiliar same-sex B infant at 23½ months. Group differences were found on 5 of 11 measures of child behavior. The B- and A-group infants engaged in more onlooker behavior than did the C-group infants. Surprisingly, however, the C-group infants engaged in *more* solitary play and more positive interaction with peers than either B- or A-group infants; indeed, the B infants engaged in the *least* positive interaction with peers. The A infants engaged in the most positive interaction with their mothers. Clearly, the findings of Pastor (1980, 1981) and Waters et al. (1979) concerning the greater peer competence of B-group toddlers were not replicated.

Subsequently, Jacobson and Wille (1984, 1986) reported observing presumably overlapping subsamples of the children (*N*s = 19 and 24 respectively) as focal partners in 25-minute peer play sessions at 24 and 35 months, always with a B-group same-sex unfamiliar playmate. Six measures of each child's behavior in the dyadic context were then analyzed. There were no significant group differences among focal children in either assessment, but on one measure (number of positive responses), playmates paired with B-group focal children scored higher than C-group or A-group children when data from both observations were pooled. There were also some significant Age by Attachment group interactions in behavior directed to focal children that were unpredicted and difficult to interpret. Given the small sample size, the inconsistency of the results at 2 and 3 years, the small number of significant effects, and the absence of clear group differences in the behavior of target or focal children, it is difficult to interpret these findings. Even if they were stronger, we would again be unable to infer that the differences in infant-mother attachment caused later differences in peer competence because later assessments of attachment and earlier measures of peer competence were missing.

Pierrehumbert, Iannotti, Cummings, and Zahn-Waxler (1986) assessed attachment security on the basis of reactions to 1-minute departures by and subsequent reunions with the mothers of 49 two-year-old subjects. Children were accompanied by peers during the separation, but unfortunately the report does not make clear whether the peers' mothers were also present, or whether both children were separated from their mothers simultaneously. Security of attachment in such situations was rated twice, on the basis of behavior in two sessions, 1 month apart, involving different peers. Only 65% of the children obtained the same classification on both occasions, with fewer children classified in the B group on the second occasion. For the purpose of analysis, reunion behavior in the first session defined the independent variable, although reportedly the same results were obtained "when children were classified based on both sessions" (p. 13). Peer social skills were assessed in these sessions at age 2 and in another session at 5 years of age. At both ages, A- and C-group children showed less dense interactions and tended ($p < .10$) to be less responsive to both peers and mothers than B-group children. Interestingly, "insecure" attachment predicted reduced social interactions with age: Exploratory analyses revealed that the peer's attachment status did not influence the interaction style of target children. In the peer session, mothers of A- and C-group children were less interactive but tended to be more responsive ($p < .10$) than the mothers of B-group infants.

In another recent study, Vandell, Wilson, Owen, and Henderson (1986) studied the association between Strange Situation behavior and peer competence in a study of 33 pairs of same-sex twins (16 monozygotic pairs) from upper and upper middle class families. One considerable strength of this study was its inclusion of data from peer interaction sequences before (6 and 9 months), at the same time as, and after (18 and 24 months) the Strange Situation assessments at 12 months. In their analyses, Vandell and her colleagues compared dyads in which both twins were "securely attached" with dyads in which at least one was "insecurely attached" and found that dyads composed of B-group twins had more interaction exchanges and spent more time in interaction exchanges than did dyads that included an infant classified in the A or C groups. A post hoc analysis revealed that the effect on the number of exchanges was moderated by age, such that the difference was most pronounced at 18 months of age. Strange Situation behavior had the same association for interaction with cotwins and other peers. There were no significant effects on four other measures (frequencies of isolated socially directed behaviors (SDBs), simple SDBs, coordinated SDBs, or total social acts). The results were thus consistent with the tenor of those reported by some of the other researchers whose work we have just described. Note, however, that the differences in peer competence were evident even before attachments are presumed to consolidate, calling into question the notion that attachment security per se is formatively significant. Rather, the more harmonious patterns of infant-mother interaction that appear to antedate B-type Strange Situation behavior (see Lamb et al., 1985) may be associated with greater peer competence. Without observation of mother-infant and peer interaction at all ages, however, we cannot tell whether patterns of interaction with mothers are formatively significant, or whether babies who are sociable with their mothers simply have more harmonious interactions with *all* social partners.

Overall, therefore, associations between prior Strange Situation classifications and later indices of social competence or engagement with peers are equivocal. Few investigators have identified clear, reliable associations between attachment status and peer competence in studies of either contemporaneous or predictive associations. Furthermore, the methodology typically used to see if the differences in infant-mother attachment produce individual differences in peer competence cannot, in fact, distinguish between findings supportive of the maternal precursor and general sociability models. By taking early measures of attachment and later measures of peer competence, researchers give the impression that the precursor model is being supported, but the infants may also have interacted well with peers at the time that attachment was earlier assessed. Both peer competence and infant-mother attachment differences may thus have been produced by some third factor, such as general sociability.

Other Measures of Infant-Mother Relationships

A small number of researchers, using procedures other than separation-reunion responses to classify infant-mother relationships, have also explored the possibility that the quality of infant-mother interaction has an important impact on subsequent sociability with peers. Instead of viewing infant-mother interaction indirectly, Vandell and Wilson (1982, 1983, 1987) compared infant-mother interaction at 6 months with the same infants' interaction with peers 3 months later. In addition, unlike researchers who have used the Strange Situation to explore the maternal precursor hypothesis, Vandell and Wilson (1982, 1983, 1987) have been careful to take into account concurrent and bidirectional associations between infant-mother and infant-peer relationships. Using cross-lagged panel correlations, they infer causal links between infant-mother interaction at Time 1 and peer interaction at Time 2 only when cross-lagged correlations remain significant even after autocorrelations and synchronous correlations have been taken into account. Although this technique does not permit researchers to infer that causal associations have been demonstrated conclusively (e.g., Rogosa, 1978), it permits stronger inferences than the typical procedure (assessment of mother-infant attachment only at Time 1, assessment of peer interaction only at Time 2).

Vandell and Wilson (1983, 1987), for example, found that infants who spent more time interacting with their mothers at 6 months interacted more with peers 3 months later, even when the autocorrelations and synchronous correlations were taken into account. However, although Vandell and Wilson (1983) found that *infants'* behavior with mothers predicted infants' later behavior with peers, *mothers'* behaviors at 6 months did not influence their infants' later behavior. No significant cross-lagged correlations were found for any aspect of maternal behavior at 6 months and infantile behavior at 9 months. Likewise, Clarke-Stewart, Vander Stoep, and Killian (1979) found no association between aspects of mother-child interaction at 24 months and the children's play with peers between 24 and 30 months of age. On the other hand, infants whose mothers shared toys with them more at 16 months shared toys with peers more often at 22 months, whereas infants whose mothers used imperatives and took toys at 16 months were more aggressive at 22 months (Mueller, 1979; Vandell, 1977). There is thus some evidence that the behavioral style mothers use with their infants may influence infants' later styles of interaction with peers.

Developmental Sequences in the Acquisition of Social Skills

One implication of the hypothesis that peer skills are in some sense derivatives of social relationships with mothers is that new skills should first appear in interaction with mothers and only later emerge in interactions with peers. Unfortunately, several problems arise when researchers attempt to compare the social skills used with mothers and with peers. First, social skills have been investigated in a variety of ways. Some investigators have compared the frequencies with which particular behaviors—such as looking, touching, and approaching—are used in interaction with mothers and peers (e.g, Eckerman, Whatley, & Kutz, 1975; Vandell, 1980). Others have examined the structure of interaction (Nash, 1986; Vandell & Wilson, 1982, 1987), and still others have closely studied specific patterns of interaction, such as conflicts and compliance (Nash, 1986), the coordination of affect and attention (Adamson & Bakeman, 1985), and the use of conventionalized gestures (Bakeman & Adamson, 1986). The varying focus of researchers makes it difficult to determine whether social skills *in general* first appear with mothers and only later with peers. Hay, Pedersen, and Nash (1982) have suggested that when infants perform conventional acts (i.e., acts considered social by adult standards, such as smiling, vocalizing, and touching), they indicate that they recognize another as a human being, and in this sense, they can be said to be socializing. Consistent with this, we review here all studies in which social skills with mothers and peers were compared, recognizing nonetheless the need in certain cases for an explicit justification for the choice of dependent measures.

A second difficulty arises from the attempt to assess *individual* competencies from *dyadic* encounters. Infants may appear to be more skilled with mothers than with peers because mothers are more skillful, and thus, by timing their speech or behavior to fit into their infants' pauses or by interpreting their infants' nonsocial behavior in a social manner, can make infants appear more socially competent (Ratner & Bruner, 1978; Schaffer, 1984). Some investigators have avoided (but not resolved) this problem by making dyads their unit of analysis instead of emphasizing individual competencies

(Bakeman & Adamson, 1986; Nash, 1986; Vandell, 1980; Vandell & Wilson, 1982) but although this issue has been addressed theoretically (see Appelbaum & McCall, 1983), it has not been resolved empirically.

A related problem is raised by marked individual differences in the competencies of peer partners. For example, Vandell and Wilson (1982) found that the frequency of social acts infants directed toward peers ranged from 1 to 115 per 15-minute session. Similarly, Nash (1985) found that the number of times 24 different infants initiated interaction with a standard peer partner ranged from 1 to 28 during a 20-minute session.

Another series of problems can be traced to issues of methodology and procedure. In some studies, infant-peer dyads were observed with mothers present, and infant-mother dyads were observed alone (Vandell & Wilson, 1982), providing infants' with more opportunity to interact with mothers (as there were no other distractions) than with peers. In other cases, mothers and peers were observed in the same situation, but mothers were instructed not to initiate interactions with their children (Eckerman et al., 1975; Eckerman & Whatley, 1977; Lewis, Young, Brooks, & Michalson, 1975; Vandell, 1980), again depriving infants of equivalent opportunities to interact with both partners.

A final problem in making infant-mother and infant-peer comparisons is that mothers differ from peers with respect to both age and familiarity. Both factors may account for differences between infant behavior in interaction with mothers and peers. The issue might be addressed by comparing infant-unfamiliar adult and infant-peer interaction. For some comparisons, furthermore, the confound between age and familiarity is not an issue, as for example, when examining whether infants first use new social skills with mothers and only later use them with peers. In this case the uniqueness of mother-infant interaction might best be determined by comparing interactions with mothers and those individuals with whom infants are least likely to interact in a similar manner—relatively unfamiliar, unskilled agemates.

However, the confound between age and familiarity would be of critical importance in comparing infants' capacities to form attachments with mothers and peers. Familiarity is important in determining whether infants form only one primary attachment (as specified by Bowlby's (1969) notion of monotropy), whereas age is important in determining whether infants can only form attachments with individuals "older and wiser" than they are, as Bowlby also suggested. Thus, the only way to compare infants' abilities to form attachments to both mothers and peers is to have both mother and peer be equally familiar, as happens only in the case of twins.

Given these problems, it is perhaps not surprising that there is currently little support for the belief that peer skills are ontogenetic derivatives of infant-mother skills. Vandell (1980) examined social behaviors found in the repertoires of 6-, 9-, and 12-month old infants, including looking, smiling, vocalizing, and touching, whereas Vandell and Wilson (1982) examined these behaviors as well as the frequency and structure of interactions. Cross-lagged correlations provided no evidence that social skills emerged first in interaction with mothers and later with peers. However, 6-month-olds who spent more time interacting with their mothers spent more time interacting with their peers 3 months later (Vandell & Wilson, 1987). Although the finding is consistent with the maternal precursor hypothesis, no association was found between mother-infant and peer-infant interaction at 6 and 9 months of age respectively on the other three measures employed.

Other researchers have found no evidence that skills emerge first with mothers and only later with peers. Bakeman and Adamson (1984, 1986; Adamson & Bakeman, 1985) examined the ability to coordinate attention to both people and objects, the expression of affect, the coordination of affect and attention to others, and the use of conventionalized acts (gestures and words) in a sample of infants observed with their mothers and with peers every 3 months between 6 and 18 months of age. For the majority of infants, skills first appeared with both mothers and peers at the same age. In addition, Nash (1986) found that infants who could take turns with one another, protest another's actions, and comply with another did so to the same extent with both mothers and peers when 13 to 15 months old, the age at which these skills are believed to emerge (Carpenter, Mastergeorge, & Coggins, 1983; Goldman & Ross, 1978; Hay, Nash, & Pedersen, 1983; Hay & Ross, 1982; Ratner & Bruner, 1978; Schaffer & Crook, 1980).

A second implication of the maternal precursor hypothesis—that infants hone and refine skills with mothers and subsequently use these skills with peers—is that infants should use social skills with mothers more than with peers. The data do not support this prediction. Eckerman and colleagues (Eckerman et al., 1975; Eckerman & Whatley, 1977) found that infants interacted more with peers than with their mothers when both were present, but unfortunately the procedure may have biased these results: The mothers were instructed not to initiate interactions with their infants, whereas the peers could freely interact with one another. Even when mothers are instructed to interact "normally" with their infants, however, infants play with, imitate, and offer objects significantly more often to peers than to their mothers when both are present at home (Rubenstein & Howes, 1976), and 13- to 15-month-olds interact more with peers than with mothers in a laboratory playroom (Nash, 1986). This is not because mothers ignore instructions and are inhibited by the laboratory setting: In Nash's (1986) study, mothers initiated more interactions with their infants than their infants initiated with them. Furthermore, she found that on Bronson's (1981) indices of incompetence (i.e., passive responses and unsuccessful attempts at interaction) infants appeared to interact as competently with peers as with mothers. Infants had as many "passive interactions" (interactions in which infant subjects did no more than merely look at their partners in response to the partners' active attempts to interact) with their mothers as with peers and made fewer unsuccessful attempts at interaction with peers than with mothers. Pierrehumbert et al. (1986) found that 2-year-olds were not more responsive and did not engage in more complex interactions with mothers than with peers. Likewise, Vandell and Wilson (1982, 1983) found that strictly social interchanges—"those exchanges that required social involvement from both partners throughout" (1982, p. 200)—occurred more commonly in interaction with peers. Their findings underscore the extent of peer competence because mothers were present during the peer interactions whereas infant-mother dyads were observed alone, thus providing infants with more opportunity to interact with mothers (as there were no other distractions) than with peers. Bakeman and Adamson (1984) found that 6- to 18-month-old infants did not spend more time in "person engagement"—mutual social engagement with another without using toys—with their mothers than with peers. Overall, the findings reported by Bakeman and Adamson (1984, 1986; Adamson & Bakeman, 1985), Eckerman et al. (1975; Eckerman & Whatley, 1977), Nash (1986), Rubenstein and Howes (1976), Pierrehumbert et al. (1986), and Vandell and Wilson (1982, 1983) tend to support the general sociability model rather than the maternal precursor hypothesis.

Infants may in fact use some skills more with mothers than with peers, although the findings are inconsistent. Vandell and Wilson (1983) reported that vocalizations, motor acts, smiles, and object-related social acts were more frequent when infants were with mothers than with peers, whereas Vandell and Wilson (1982) reported that infants did *not* vocalize and perform motor acts more with mothers than with peers and that they performed object-related social acts more with peers than with mothers. Only with respect to social smiles were the same results obtained in both studies. It is difficult to interpret these findings, however, because the procedure allowed more opportunity for interaction with mothers than with peers.

Other kinds of interaction may also occur more frequently in mother-infant than in peer-infant interaction. Vandell and Wilson (1982, 1983, 1987) reported that infants had more frequent interactions with mothers than with peers. In addition, the sequences of interaction with mothers were longer and more likely to contain some non-SDBs than the sequences with peers. Similarly, Bakeman and Adamson (1984; Adamson & Bakeman, 1985; Bakeman & Adamson, 1986) reported that infants attended to their partners and objects at the same time, expressed affect throughout such episodes of joint attention, engaged in action formats, and used some conventional gestures and words more often with mothers than with peers. As Vandell and Wilson (1982) observed, however, many of these differences may reflect maternal rather than infantile skills because adults take major responsibility for dialogues and games (Ratner & Bruner, 1978) and respond to nonsocial behaviors as though they are socially directed, thus extending interchanges, as described earlier in this chapter. Furthermore, Bakeman and Adamson (1986) found that conventionalized acts occurred most often during "action formats," which occurred more frequently when infants were interacting with mothers. It is important, therefore, to distinguish between putative measures of social skill which reflect infant competence and measures which reflect maternal skills. Infants may appear more competent with mothers than with peers because of their mothers' skills, rather than because of their own competencies. Infants seem to use whatever skills they have to the same extent with both their mothers and peers. There is thus some evidence supporting the maternal precursor hypothesis, although researchers have had problems distinguishing *infant* skills or characteristics from maternal skills because of the dyadic measures and contexts involved and have failed to articulate clear developmental hypotheses.

Summary

Overall, the findings reviewed in this section provide ambiguous support for the hypothesis that styles of sociability with peers are causal derivatives of the infant-mother relationship. Most of the research has involved associations between attachment security and subsequent measures of interaction with peers, but the resulting literature is riddled with ambiguous findings and failures to replicate, despite attempts to stack the hypothesis-testing deck by restricting analysis to samples in which there is likely to be continuity in the quality of child-mother interaction. Such strategies would preclude inferences about the causal importance of *earlier* infant-mother attachment, even if the reported findings were more persuasive, however, and are also consistent with the general sociability model. Vandell's cross-lagged panel procedure allows stronger (but not conclusive) tests of these models, and her somewhat inconsistent results have not supported the precursor hypothesis. Perhaps the problem lies in her reliance on molecular rather than molar measures, on which evidence of continuity and causal associations are more likely to be found. Associations between contemporaneous assessments of peer competence and infant-mother attachment are consistent with the precursor hypothesis, but the support they provide is ambiguous. Such associations are also consistent with the general sociability hypothesis that developmental sequences and individual differences in the acquisition of social skills follow the same general pattern in interactions with both mothers and peers. In the next section we review additional evidence relevant to the general sociability hypothesis.

III.   ALTERNATIVE HYPOTHESES

Bidirectional Influences

Demonstrating that infant-mother relationships influence later infant-peer sociability provides some nonconclusive support for the maternal precursor hypothesis. To prove that the first relationship influences later relationships, bidirectional influences must be ruled out. Otherwise, the infants' relationships with *any* partner may simply influence relationships with other partners. In this case, mothers might influence their infants' relationships with peers while peers influenced interactions with mothers.

There is some evidence that infant-peer relations do influence infant-mother relations. The immediate effect of peer interactions on infant-mother interactions was examined by Rubenstein and her colleagues (Rubenstein & Howes, 1976; Rubenstein, Howes, & Pedersen, 1982) who compared the behavior of 19-month-olds observed with their mothers and with both peers and mothers. In both studies, the presence of peers reduced the frequency of toddler-mother interaction: There were both more positive *and* more nonharmonious interchanges with mothers in the peer-absent condition than in the peer-present condition. By contrast, toddler-mother touching and proximity were unaffected by the presence or absence of peers. These findings, of course, do not indicate whether peer interaction had effects on infant-mother interaction outside the immediate context.

Such issues were explored by Vandell (1979), however, who found that infants' interactions with their parents changed after having experience with peers in a playgroup. Even after Vandell controlled for initial group differences in the children's and parents' behavior, playgroup children assumed more initiative in their interactions with parents and became more responsive to the social initiations of their parents than did a matched group of children who did not have playgroup experience. Furthermore, the parents of the children without playgroup experience used significantly more imperatives, negatives, questions, and rituals when interacting with their children. In at least this one study, therefore, there was evidence of peer influences on sociability with parents and on parental behavior.

The General Sociability Hypothesis

As mentioned in the introduction, the general sociability hypothesis actually has two incarnations. In one, the emphasis is on the parallel development of social skills with mothers and social skills with peers, whereas in the other the emphasis is on transinteractant individual differences in sociability. The former was discussed in the previous section as an alternative to the maternal precursor interpretation of some extant data, and we now turn attention to the latter version of the general sociability hypothesis. This version suggests that sociability is consistent across types of partners and over time, such that infants who are more sociable with their mothers are also more sociable with their peers, and infants who are more sociable early in infancy are also more sociable later in infancy. As we have mentioned repeatedly, much of the evidence gathered in support of the maternal precursor hypothesis is also consistent with the general sociability hypothesis, although the studies were not designed to be conclusive in this regard and the evidence itself is rather inconsistent.

Vandell (1980) found significant correlations between the frequency of infants' vocalizations to their mothers and to peers, as well as between the frequencies of smiles to mothers and peers. Significant correlations have been found for other social behaviors as well: Nash (1986) found consistency across partners (mother or peer) in the number of interactions in which infants took turns with a partner, the length of the longest reciprocal interaction, and the percentage of partners' provocations that elicited protests. Similarly, Vandell and Wilson (1983) found that infants who were sociable with one partner were sociable with the other, and that sociability appeared to be stable over time.

Not only do infants behave similarly with mothers and peers: Vandell and her colleagues (1986) reported that, during the first year of life, twins behaved similarly with their cotwins and with unfamiliar agemates. Infants who frequently directed social acts to their own cotwins also did so to an unfamiliar peer at 6, 9, and 12 months of age. Such stability across partners was not found at 18 and 24 months of age, however. By contrast, temporal stability in sociability was more apparent in the 2nd year than in the 1st year. Those twins who spent more time interacting with one another at 18 months were also more likely to interact more at 24 months, and the same pattern held for interactions with unfamiliar peers.

Such stability over time has been found in other studies as well. Vandell and Wilson (1982) found significant positive correlations between several frequency measures of infants' behaviors with the same peers at 6 and 9 months of age: Included were the frequencies of social interactions, initiations, vocalizations, and simple SDBs. There was similar temporal stability with respect to several measures of infant-mother interaction, including frequencies of social initiations, SDBs, social motor acts, and object-related social acts. Thus it appears that infants who are sociable with mothers are also sociable with peers and that infants who are sociable at 6 months are also sociable at 9 months. Temporal stability in sociability was also reported by Lamb, Hwang, Bookstein, Broberg, Hult, and Frodi (1988) in a study of Swedish toddlers. Infants' sociability with familiar peers and unfamiliar adults was assessed at 16 months (on average) and then again 12 months later. Between the two assessments, some of the children were admitted to family day-care and center day-care facilities. Effects on later peer competence of the type and quality of care received in and out of the home, socioeconomic status, social support, and child temperament were examined. The best predictor of peer competence in the second assessment was a latent variable measuring prior sociability with peers and strange adults. These findings suggest both stability in peer competence and, more generally, of sociability with multiple interactive partners.

However, interpartner stability was not found when sociability with different peer partners was examined in a study of 2-year-olds by Pierrehumbert et al. (1986), who reported that the complexity of interaction and the responsivity of toddlers were uncorrelated in observations with two different peers at about 24 months of age. Similarly, Hay and Ross (1982) observed 21-month-olds with two different peer partners and found that the likelihood of winning conflicts with one peer partner was unrelated to the likelihood of winning with another peer partner. Finally, Nash (1985) charted the social behaviors of one infant with 24 different peer partners over a 2-month period (13 to 15 months of age) and found that the infant's behaviors varied more in relation to partner than in relation to age or state (irritable or content).

These studies underscore the difficulty of assessing sociability or competence with peers. Most attempts to study the association between the infant-mother relationship and competence or sociability with peers involve observations with only one peer. In such circumstances, the observed competence or sociability of the subject may be constrained by the characteristics of the peer rather than by the subjects' social skills. Vandell's (1980; Vandell et al., 1986; Vandell & Wilson, 1982), Lamb's (Lamb et al. 1988), and Nash (1986) studies yield support for the general sociability hypothesis, at least for some behaviors. Studies which do not yield evidence consistent with the hypothesis are ones in which researchers have examined consistency across peer partners. It may be difficult to assess such stability because of the wide variability in the social behavior of particular peer partners (e.g., Nash, 1986; Vandell & Wilson, 1982). It is noteworthy that Vandell's studies involved the most intensive observations (which may have increased the reliability with which the phenomena were observed) but also involved small or selected samples (which may limit the generalizability of the findings). Clearly, more research on this promising hypothesis is needed.

Are Skills with Peers Unrelated to Relations with Mothers?

The third alternative hypothesis implies that the development of sociability with mothers and peers proceeds independently. There is in fact some evidence that infants use some behaviors predominantly with peers and others predominantly with their mothers. Both Lewis et al. (1975) and Vandell (1980) found that infants use some skills with mothers and others with peers: When both mothers and peers were available, infants were more likely to look and to vocalize to peers and more likely to touch their mothers.

Differential responsiveness to mothers and peers is consistent with Harlow and Harlow's (1965) notion that there are discrete affectional systems. Based on their research with rhesus monkeys, Harlow and Harlow proposed that "five affectional systems may be described for most primate forms" (p. 287). Among these five systems are the infant-mother and infant-peer systems, each believed to develop through its own maturational stages. The functions of the two systems were explored by depriving infant rhesus monkeys of either mothers or peers and examining the effects on their subsequent functioning (see review by Suomi & Harlow, 1978). Monkeys reared with mothers but not peers for the first 8 months of life developed relatively normal relationships with their mothers, but when later exposed to peers, they were hyperaggressive and antisocial. They were unable to develop normal relationships with other monkeys, and sometimes this inability persisted into adulthood. As a result, Suomi and Harlow concluded that the presence of peers is essential for normal social development in rhesus monkeys, with peer interactions being crucial for the appropriate socialization of aggression. Without experience with peers, they argue, rhesus monkeys cannot modulate their aggression and thus cannot interact or form relationships with others.

Infants raised with peers but without mothers also developed behavioral problems. Because they could not nurse, they developed behavioral stereotypes which involved sucking on their own fingers and toes, and because they could not cling to their mothers, they clasped one another as intensely as they would cling to their mothers and continued to do so later in the life course. Suomi and Harlow suggested that prolonged and obsessive clinging to peers may delay the appearance of play, because clinging peers do not make effective playmates. Furthermore, infant peers reduce fear less effectively than mothers do, so monkeys raised with peers but without mothers tend to become timid adults. Unlike infants raised only with mothers, however, peer-raised monkeys do not have difficulty in socializing aggression and develop relationships with other monkeys similar to the ones formed by monkeys raised in normal environments.

These studies support the view that infant-mother and infant-peer relationships serve different functions, at least among rhesus monkeys. The existence of distinct behavioral systems in humans is suggested by studies concerning the relation between infant-sibling and infant-parent interactional systems (Lamb, 1978a, 1978b, 1979, 1985–1986). The presence of the other parent greatly affects interactions with either parent but has little influence on interactions with a sibling, whereas the presence of a sibling has little effect on infants' interactions with mothers or fathers but the presence of the other parent has a large effect. Similarly, the presence of additional children affected the levels of interaction with siblings but not the amount of interaction with parents (Lamb, 1986). According to Lamb, the presence of both parents establishes competition within the adult interactional system, so that the infant divides social attention between the two parents. The presence of a parent does not affect the level of interaction with a sibling, however, because the adult and child interactional systems are at least partially independent.

Although interactions with children and with adults or parents may serve different functions for infants, different processes need not be involved in the development of interactional skills or relationships with each class of partners. Infants may behave differently with peers and adults simply because peers and adults themselves behave differently. When developing relationships, infants respond to the distinctive behaviors of particular individuals, as illustrated by studies showing that infants adjust their own behavior to that of their peer partners (Hay, Nash, & Pedersen, 1981, 1983) and parents (Lamb, 1976, 1977). In this way, the same processes (e.g., matching behaviors to those of a partner) may underlie the development of relationships that differ in other respects. In addition, differential responding to mothers and peers may be consequences of differential familiarity with each.

Vandell (1980), too, cautioned against concluding from evidence of differential responsiveness that the infant-peer and infant-mother systems are independent. Rather, other results led her to conclude that the infant-peer and infant-mother systems are linked by an underlying dimension of generalized sociability. In addition, Suomi and Harlow's (1978) deprivation studies do not clearly identify the distinctive functions of mothers and peers because infants raised only with their mothers are deprived not only of peers but of everyone else as well. Perhaps it is the experience of interacting with a variety of individuals, not simply peers, that influences later relationships. Infants raised with peers and without mothers, on the other hand, seem better adjusted in general than those raised by mothers alone (Harlow & Harlow, 1965). In the former situation, peers seem able to function (to some extent) as mothers do in a normal rearing environment.

We have thus far examined two sources of evidence that infant-mother and infant-peer interactions comprise distinct systems: (1) infants use different behaviors with mothers and peers, and (2) peers and mothers serve different functions for infants. Neither of these approaches, however, directly examines the development of infant-mother and infant-peer interactional skills.

Another way to determine whether sociability with peers and mothers develops independently is to seek support for Mueller's (1979) developmental hypothesis that experience with peers increases competence with peers. In fact, the evidence concerning this hypothesis is inconsistent. Vandell, Wilson, and Whalen (1981) found that 9-month-olds who had more prior experience with toddlers interacted with peers *less* than infants who had less prior experience, whereas among 6-month-olds, prior experience *improved* interaction with new peers. Adamson and Bakeman (1985) found that the amount of prior contact with the peer used in the test session did not affect scores in any systematic way. On the other hand, Becker (1977) found that both experience with peers and the degree of familiarity with the partner affected the behavior of 9-month-olds. Pairs of infants who had met for 10 sessions interacted more on the 10th time than in the 1st session, whereas infants who only met for the 1st and 10th sessions did not. Furthermore, when the infants who had completed 10 sessions met new peer partners, they interacted with them less frequently than they had with their regular partners in the 10th session (revealing the effects of familiarity) but more frequently than they had in the first session with the regular partner (indicating that peer experience had a generalized effect). Similarly, Harper and Huie (1985) found that both familiarity and prior experience with peers affected 3- and 4-year-olds' social play with one another in a preschool. The children who had more prior experience with peers engaged in more social play in the preschool than those who did not, and social play, regardless of prior experience, increased over time. In both these studies, however, no attempt was made to see whether peer experience affected infant-mother interaction, and so crucial information relevant to the independence hypothesis was lacking.

Summary

The evidence in support of the maternal primacy hypothesis was inconsistent, and we have seen in this section similar inconsistencies in the results of studies designed to address the other hypotheses. Much of the evidence, however, is consistent with the general sociability hypothesis, and there is also some support for the independence hypotheses. The availability of support for two apparently incompatible hypotheses underscores the imprecision with which the hypotheses have been formulated. It seems that sociable infants tend to have harmonious relationships with all social partners but that different types of relationships develop with different classes of partners, presumably as a result of social learning about the propensities, tendencies, and utility of different social partners (Lewis et al., 1975). Even if there are distinct parent-child and peer interactional systems, therefore, the independence is clearly not absolute: temperamental variations and formative experiences may have generalized cross-system effects, although the within-system effects of experience may be manifest sooner and more dramatically.

IV.   CONCLUSION

Despite repeated assertions that the quality of social competence with peers is determined by the prior quality of infant-mother attachment relationships, there is actually little empirical support for this hypothesis. If the Strange Situation is a good index of prior maternal influences, one would have to conclude that maternal-infant interaction is only a weak correlate of developing peer competence. There is also little evidence using other measures that skills learned with mothers are later generalized to peers; indeed, skills tend to emerge simultaneously in interaction with all social partners. And even if there were a clear association between infant-mother interaction and peer competence, the *formative* importance of *earlier* maternal influences would not be demonstrated because of the substantial stability in caretaking patterns in the families studied. More generally, without assessments of both infant-mother and infant-peer interactions at Time 1 and Time 2 so that one can partial out autocorrelations and synchronous correlations, one cannot conclude that the association between prior infant-mother and subsequent infant-peer interactions reveal a causal, maternal-precursor link. Such findings are also consistent with the general sociability hypothesis.

Unfortunately, the other hypotheses are also ambiguously supported. Even if peer and adult-child interactions represent different interactional systems, the independence appears to be, at best, relative; cross-system continuities are evident even in the face of the independent systems. There is some evidence that peer experiences influence patterns of parent-child interaction, suggesting bidirectional influences, and there is more impressive evidence that sociability may be a generalized disposition or developmental dimension—a hypothesis that has the advantage of being both parsimonious and consistent with the bulk of the extant literature. The evidence is ambiguous, however, and there is a clear need for further longitudinal research involving larger samples of subjects and lengthy detailed observations. The inconsistency among findings reported in this chapter may in large part be due to the unreliability of measures based on small samples of observed behavior.

The inconsistency may also reflect another problem—the failure to specify more precisely what aspects of infant-mother relationships should be related to aspects of infant-peer interactions and relationships, and *why* these associations are to be expected. Likewise, what aspects of social style should be affected by a general sociability dimension, and what aspects would be expected to diverge as a result, perhaps, of distinctive experiences with particular individuals or classes of people? Which social skills should be typical of either infant-mother or infant-peer interaction, and which might be similar in interactions with the two? We can tentatively conclude that friendly, sociable babies tend to have harmonious interactions with parents as well as with peers, but that the qualities of infant-mother and infant-peer interaction diverge somewhat as infants learn about the distinctive propensities of different classes of partners. Confident assertion of this tentative conclusion, however, must await further research.

REFERENCES

Adamson, L. B., & Bakeman, R. (1985). Affect and attention: Infants observed with mothers and peers. *Child Development, 56,* 582–593.

Ainsworth, M. D. S., Blehar, M. C., Waters, E., & Wall, S. (1978). *Patterns of attachment.* Hillsdale, NJ: Lawrence Erlbaum.

Ainsworth, M. D. S., & Wittig, B. A. (1969). Attachment and exploratory behavior of one year olds in a strange situation. In B. M. Foss (Ed.), *Determinants of infant behavior* (Vol. 4, pp. 111–136). London: Methuen.

Applebaum, M. I., & McCall, R. B. (1983). Design and analysis in developmental psychology. In P. H. Mussen (Series Ed.), W. Kessen (Vol. Ed.), *Handbook of child psychology. Vol. 1: History, theory, and methods* (pp. 415–476). New York: Wiley.

Bakeman, R., & Adamson, L. B. (1984). Coordinating attention to people and objects in mother-infant and peer-infant interaction. *Child Development, 55,* 1278–1289.

Bakeman, R., & Adamson, L. B. (1986). Infants' conventionalized acts: Gesture and words with mothers and peers. *Infant Behavior and Development, 9,* 215–230.

Becker, J. N. T. (1977). A learning analysis of the development of peer-oriented behavior in nine-month-old infants. *Developmental Psychology, 13,* 481–491.

Bowlby, J. (1969). *Attachment*. New York: Basic Books.

Bronson, W. C. (1981). *Toddlers' behaviors with agemates: Issues of interaction, cognition, and affect*. Norwood, NJ: Ablex.

Carpenter, R. L., Mastergeorge, A. M., & Coggins, T. E. (1983). The acquisition of communicative intentions in infants eight to fifteen months of age. *Language and Speech, 216*, 101–116.

Clarke-Stewart, K. A., Vander Stoep, L. P., & Killian, G. A. (1979). Analysis and replication of mother-child relations at two years of age. *Child Development, 50*, 777–793.

Easterbrooks, M. A., & Lamb, M. E. (1979). The relationship between quality of infant-mother attachment and infant competence in initial encounters with peers. *Child Development, 50*, 380–387.

Eckerman, C. O., & Whatley, J. L. (1977). Toys and social interaction between infant peers. *Child Development, 48*, 1645–1656.

Eckerman, C. O., Whatley, J. L., & Kutz, S. L. (1975). Growth of social play with peers during the second year of life. *Developmental Psychology, 11*, 42–49.

Egeland, B., & Farber, E. A. (1982). *Antecedents of infant-mother attachment relationships in economically disadvantaged families*. Unpublished manuscript, University of Minnesota, Minneapolis, MN.

Egeland, B., & Farber, E. A. (1984). Infant-mother attachment: Factors related to its development and changes over time. *Child Development, 55*, 753–771.

Goldman, B. D., & Ross, H. S. (1978). Social skills in action: An analysis of early peer games. In J. Glick & K. A. Clarke-Stewart (Eds.), *The development of social understanding* (pp. 177–212). New York: Gardner.

Harlow, H. F., & Harlow, M. K. (1965). The affectional systems. In A. M. Schrier, H. F. Harlow, & F. Stollnitz (Eds.), *Behavior of nonhuman primates*, (Vol. 2, pp. 287–334). New York: Academic Press.

Harper, L. V., & Huie, K. S. (1985). The effects of prior group experience, age, and familiarity of the quality and organization of preschoolers' social relationships. *Child Development, 56*, 704–717.

Hay, D. F. (1985). Learning to form relationships in infancy: Parallel attainments with parents and peers. *Developmental Review, 5*, 122–161.

Hay, D. F., Nash, A., & Pedersen, J. (1981). Responses of six-month-olds to the distress of their peers. *Child Development, 52*, 1071–1075.

Hay, D. F., Nash, A., & Pedersen, J. (1983). Interaction between six-month-old peers. *Child Development, 54*, 557–562.

Hay, D. F., Pedersen, J., & Nash, A. (1982). Dyadic interaction in the first year of life. In K. H. Rubin & H. S. Ross (Eds.), *Peer relationships and social skills in childhood* (pp. 11–39). New York: Springer-Verlag.

Hay, D. F., & Ross, H. S. (1982). The social nature of early conflict. *Child Development, 53*, 105–113.

Jacobson, J. L., & Wille, D. E. (1984, April). *The influence of attachment patterns on peer interaction at 2 and 3 years*. Paper presented at the International Conference on Infant Studies, New York.

Jacobson, J. L., & Wille, D. E. (1986). The influence of attachment pattern on developmental changes in peer interaction from the toddler to the preschool period. *Child Development, 57*, 338–347.

Jacobson, J. L., Wille, D. E., Tianen, R. L., & Aytch, D. M. (1983, April). *The influence of infant-mother attachment on toddler sociability with peers*. Paper presented at the biennial meeting of the Society for Research in Child Development, Detroit.

La Freniere, P. J., & Sroufe, L. A. (1985). Profiles of peer competence in the preschool:

Interrelations between measures, influence of social ecology, and relation to attachment history. *Developmental Psychology, 21,* 56–69.

Lamb, M. E. (1976). Effects of stress and cohort on mother- and father-infant interaction. *Developmental Psychology, 12,* 435–443.

Lamb, M. E. (1977). The development of mother-infant and father-infant attachments in the second year of life. *Developmental Psychology, 13,* 637–648.

Lamb, M. E. (1978a). The development of sibling relationships in infancy: A short-term longitudinal study. *Child Development, 49,* 1189–1196.

Lamb, M. E. (1978b). Interactions between 18-month-olds and their preschool-aged siblings. *Child Development, 49,* 51–59.

Lamb, M. E. (1979). The effects of the social context on dyadic social interaction. In M. E. Lamb, S. J. Suomi, & G. R. Stephenson (Eds.), *Social interaction analysis* (pp. 253–268). Madison, WI: University of Wisconsin Press.

Lamb, M. E. (1984–1985). A comparison of "second order effects" involving parents and siblings. *Annual Report: Research and Clinical Center for Child Development* (pp. 1–8). Faculty of Education, University of Hokkaido, Sapporo, Japan.

Lamb, M. E. (1986). Toddler social choice among siblings, peers, and preschool-aged strangers. Unpublished manuscript, University of Utah, Salt Lake City.

Lamb, M. E., Hwang, C.-P., Bookstein, F. L., Broberg, A., Hult, G., & Frodi, A. (1988). Determinants of social competence in Swedish preschoolers. *Developmental Psychology, 24,* 58–70.

Lamb, M. E., Thompson, R. A., Gardner, W., & Charnov, E. L. (1985). *Infant-mother attachment.* Hillsdale, NJ: Lawrence Erlbaum.

Lamb, M. E., Thompson, R. A., Gardner, W. P., Charnov, E. L., & Estes, D. (1984). Security of infantile attachment as assessed in the Strange Situation: Its study and biological interpretation. *Behavioral and Brain Sciences, 7,* 127–147.

Lewis, M., & Rosenblum, L. (1975). Introduction. In M. Lewis & L. Rosenblum (Eds.), *Friendship and peer relations* (pp. 1–9). New York: Wiley.

Lewis, M., Young, G., Brooks, J., & Michalson, L. (1975). The beginning of friendship. In M. Lewis & L. Rosenblum (Eds.), *Friendship and peer relations* (pp. 27–66). New York: Wiley.

Lieberman, A. F. (1977). Preschoolers' competence with a peer: Relations with attachment and peer experience. *Child Development, 48,* 1277–1287.

Matas, L., Arend, R. A., & Sroufe, L. A. (1978). Continuity of adaptation in the second year: The relationship between quality of attachment and later competence. *Child Development, 49,* 547–556.

Mueller, E. (1979). (Toddler + toys) = (an autonomous social system). In M. Lewis & L. A. Rosenblum (Eds.), *The child and its family* (pp. 169–194). New York: Plenum.

Nash, A. (1985). *Infants' social competence with their mothers and a peer.* Unpublished doctoral dissertation, State University of New York at Stony Brook.

Nash, A. (1986, August). *A comparison of infants' social competence with mother and peer.* Paper presented at the meeting of the American Psychological Association, Washington, DC.

Parten, M. S. (1932). Social participation among preschool children. *Journal of Abnormal and Social Psychology, 27,* 243–269.

Pastor, D. L. (1980, April). *The quality of mother-infant attachment and its relationship to toddlers' initial sociability with peers.* Paper presented at the International Conference on Infant Studies, New Haven, CT.

Pastor, D. L. (1981). The quality of mother-infant attachment and its relationship to toddlers' initial sociability with peers. *Developmental Psychology, 17,* 326–335.

Pierrehumbert, B., Iannotti, R. J., Cummings, E. M., & Zahn-Waxler, C. (1986). *Social functioning with mother and peer at 2 and 5 years of age: The influence of attachment.* Unpublished manuscript. Laboratory of Developmental Psychology, National Institute of Mental Health, Bethesda, MD.

Ratner, N., & Bruner, J. S. (1978). Games, social exchange, and the acquisition of language. *Journal of Child Language, 5,* 391–401.

Rogosa, D. (1978). A critique of cross-lagged correlation. *Psychological Bulletin, 88,* 245–258.

Rubenstein, J., & Howes, C. (1976). The effects of peers on toddler interaction with mothers and toys. *Child Development, 47,* 597–605.

Rubenstein, J., Howes, C., & Pedersen, F. A. (1982). Second order effects of peers on mother-toddler interaction. *Infant Behavior and Development, 5,* 185–194.

Schaffer, H. R. (1984). *The child's entry into a social world.* Orlando, FL: Academic Press.

Schaffer, H. R., & Crook, C. K. (1980). Child compliance and maternal control techniques. *Developmental Psychology, 16,* 54–61.

Sroufe, L. A. (1978). Attachment and the roots of competence. *Human Nature, 1*(10), 50–57.

Sroufe, L. A. (1979). The coherence of individual development. *American Psychologist, 34,* 834–841.

Sroufe, L. A. (1983). Individual patterns of adaptation from infancy to preschool. In M. Perlmutter (Ed.), *Development and policy concerning children with special needs. Minnesota symposium on child psychology* (Vol. 16, pp. 41–81). Hillsdale, NJ: Lawrence Erlbaum.

Sroufe, L. A., Fox, N. E., & Pancake, V. R. (1983). Attachment and dependency in developmental perspective. *Child Development, 54,* 1615–1627.

Suomi, S. J., & Harlow, H. F. (1978). Early experience and social development in rhesus monkeys. In M. E. Lamb (Ed.), *Social and personality development* (pp. 252–271). New York: Holt, Rinehart & Winston.

Vandell, D. L. (1977). Boy toddlers' social interactions with mothers, fathers, and peers (Doctoral dissertation, Boston University). *Dissertation Abstracts International, 37,* 6309B–6310B. University Microfilms No. 77-11, 428.

Vandell, D. L. (1979). Effects of a playgroup experience on mother-son and father-son interaction. *Developmental Psychology, 15,* 379–385.

Vandell, D. L. (1980). Sociability with peer and mother during the first year. *Developmental Psychology, 16,* 335–361.

Vandell, D. L. (1985, April). *Relations between infant-peer and infant-mother interactions: What we have learned.* Paper presented at the biennial meeting of the Society for Research in Child Development, Toronto.

Vandell, D. L., & Wilson, K. S. (1982). Social interaction in the first year: Infants' social skills with peers versus mother. In K. H. Rubin & H. S. Ross (Eds.), *Peer relationships and social skills in childhood* (pp. 187–208). New York: Springer-Verlag.

Vandell, D. L., & Wilson, K. S. (1983, April). *Infants' interactions with mother, sibling, and peer: Contrasts and relations between interaction systems.* Paper presented at the biennial meeting of the Society for Research in Child Development, Detroit.

Vandell, D. L., & Wilson, K. S. (1987). Infants' interactions with mother, sibling, and peer: Contrasts and relations between interaction systems. *Child Development, 58,* 176–186.

Vandell, D. L., Wilson, K. S., Owen, M. T., & Henderson, V. K. (1986). *Social development in infant twins: Patterns of attachment and peer interaction.* Unpublished manuscript, University of Texas at Dallas.

Vandell, D. L., Wilson, K. S., & Whalen, W. T. (1981). Birth order and social experience differences in infant-peer interaction. *Developmental Psychology, 17,* 438–445.

Vaughn, B., Egeland, B., Sroufe, L. A., & Waters, E. (1979). Individual differences in infant-mother attachment at twelve and eighteen months: Stability and change in families under stress. *Child Development, 50,* 971–975.

Waters, E., Wippman, J., & Sroufe, L. A. (1979). Attachment, positive affect, and competence in the peer group: Two studies in construct validation. *Child Development, 50,* 821–829.

Zaslow, M., & Hayes, C. (1986). Sex differences in children's responses to psychosocial stress: Toward a cross-context analysis. In M. E. Lamb, A. L. Brown, & B. Rogoff (Eds.), *Advances in developmental psychology* (Vol. 4, pp. 235–337). Hillsdale, NJ: Lawrence Erlbaum.

CHAPTER 9

Early Predictors of Childhood Friendship

MICHAEL LEWIS AND CANDICE FEIRING

Institute for the Study of Child Development, University of Medicine and Dentistry of New Jersey

Robert Wood Johnson Medical School, University of Medicine and Dentistry of New Jersey

FRIENDSHIP AS ONE TYPE OF RELATIONSHIP

Before exploring the origin of friendship, it might be valuable to embed the concept of friend within a broader perspective, taking into account the possible range of relationships that may exist in human experience. Both children and adults, during their lives, have *love* relationships, *friend* relationships and *acquaintance* relationships, each with a set of rules governing actions and goals and each associated with different feeling states. Within these categories, relationships vary and are quite complex.

While each of these relationships can be viewed as separate, we recognize that the boundaries between them are flexible. For example, friendship encompasses a broad set of people and activities and as such is difficult to distinguish from love or acquaintance relationships. In fact, friendship may be the most varied and complex class of relationships that people possess. Before focusing on friends, let us mention briefly the others.

First, consider *love relationships*. These take place both within the family as well as outside of it. Love relationships may be of two kinds: attachment relationships, which provide a secure base, and nonattachment relationships, which do not. It is clear that a secure base is not necessarily a part of all love relationships. For example, parents love their children, but children do not offer a secure base for parents.

Love relationships also are divided by sexuality. In some love relationships, such as between spouses, sexuality plays a significant role, but in others, such as with mothers, fathers, and children, sexuality is absent. Thus, the dimensions of secure base or attachment and sexuality form a complex

Preparation of this chapter was made possible by funding from William T. Grant Foundation. The assistance of John Jaskir in data analyses is considerably appreciated.

structure for a variety of different love relationships that exist in our experience.

Friendship relationships will be discussed in detail below. These relationships appear to be different from love, and although difficult to describe, the difference is indicated by language usage itself. Friendship relationships also vary along different dimensions and at times may merge with love relationships. To some extent, friendship is associated with terms such as "affection" and "liking" rather than "loving," although best friends may be loved. Like love relationships, friendship may involve sexual behavior. Friendship relationships tend to vary with the age of the participants; thus they may involve same-age peers, or they may exist between older and younger persons, such as between a teacher and student. Like love, friendship relationships can be enduring and can exist even without extended interactions, as in the case of friends separated by long distances.

Acquaintance relationships tend to be the least enduring and the most specific to the particular interactions that bring them into existence. They usually occur as a consequence of a particular and highly structured social exchange such as with a storekeeper or bank clerk. These relationships vary along a dimension of familiarity, from ones in which members recognize one another, know each other's names, and exchange information (employers and employees; a shop owner and a customer), to less familiar interactions with the ticket collector on a train or with people whom we greet casually as we pass them in the street. These casual contacts lead to more familiarity and thus may lead to friendship relationships (Berscheid & Walster, 1978). There is reason to believe that repeated exposure to people, even casually, can promote mutual liking (Zajonc, 1968). Thus acquaintances can become friends through familiarization.

Across the life-span, there is evidence that suggests a strong proclivity for making acquaintances with unfamiliar people. Lewis, Young, Brooks and Michalson (1975), for example, found that infants and toddlers who were exposed to each other in short play sessions over a week or so showed increased friendship patterns. Repeated exposure increases the quality, complexity and reciprocated interaction among toddlers (Becker, 1977). In preschool children, exposure to others relates to increased positive interactions as well as more mature social play (Doyle, Connolly, & Rivest, 1980). It is regrettable that the work on acquaintances in middle childhood is meager (Hartup 1983), because the formation of friendships is likely to start with exposure to others.

Although people do not have relationships with *strangers,* this discussion requires that the category of nonrelationships be included, especially because so much attention has been paid to children's social interactions with strangers. Strangers are, by our definition, those people with whom we have no relationship and who are unfamiliar to us. Yet even in this category of nonrelationship there are variations which may be of some importance to our analysis. For example, strangers who possess particular characteristics may elicit different interactions than strangers without those characteristics and may be more likely to become acquaintances or friends. Thus, strangers who are the same sex or ethnic background as the child are likely to evoke interactions that are different from interactions with strangers of the opposite sex or of another ethnic background (Lewis, 1980).

In the study of the child's social development, the full array of possible relationships has not been explored or even considered. The development of friendships, its causes and outcomes, has received some study in middle childhood and adolescence but has not been the subject of much work in the preschool period (Hartup, 1983). In fact, the studies of preschoolers usually refer to peers, since the general assumption has been that friendship in the very young is not possible. Friendship has not been thought to be possible until the age of 3 or 4 years at the earliest, although now there is little doubt that friendships are probably formed earlier (Lewis & Rosenblum, 1975). Because of these biases, early friendship formation has not been carefully studied.

In the following discussion we explore the origins of friendship by examining models and data that are designed to relate early individual differences and experiences to later differences in friendship patterns. Because there is so little work on this issue, much of what follows is an attempt to articulate the potential usable models. In some cases, we will use data from our longitudinal study of 130 children seen from infancy (3, 12, 24 months) until childhood years (3, 6, 9 years) to provide some support for the models being discussed. Having considered the possible models and supportive evidence for predicting friendship patterns, we will turn to a discussion of the meaning and functions of friendship. Finally, we suggest directions for future conceptualization and research in the development of friendship.

MODELS FOR THE DEVELOPMENT OF FRIENDSHIP

Many models for the development of friends are possible, including (1) epigenetic or attachment, (2) social network, (3) genetic or temperament, and (4) demographic characteristics models. Each model will be described in turn.

Epigenetic or Attachment Model

The epigenetic model is the most widely held view about the origins of friendship patterns. This model has as its central thesis the assumption that there is a direct relationship from one set of earlier social experiences to the next. More specifically, the epigenetic model is a linear model in which the infant first adapts to one relationship, and from this primary relationship, subsequent ones follow. The attachment theories of both Bowlby (1969) and Ainsworth (1972; Ainsworth, Blehar, Waters & Wall, 1978) have this feature as one of their basic propositions. Simply stated, this view holds that sub-sequent social relationships are dependent upon the attachment relationship between mother and infant. In particular, friendships should be affected by mother-child attachment in the 1st year of life. Infants who are securely attached to their mothers in the 1st year should be more competent in sub-sequent childhood peer interactions than are insecurely attached infants.

A small number of studies following this hypothesis yielded mixed results. Pastor (1980, 1981) examined 12 secure (B) and 24 insecure (A + C) children in peer interaction when they were 2 years old. Infants who had been rated secure as compared to insecure showed more orientation to peer and soci-ability. In particular, the secure children made more social bids and ignored fewer peer bids compared to the insecure children. In addition, the secure children were better at redirecting their behavior after a conflict over a toy. Additional support for the relationship between early infant-mother attach-ment and later peer competence comes from a study by Waters, Wippman, and Sroufe (1979). At 15 months, 32 infants were rated as securely or in-securely attached; these same infants were observed and Q-sort ratings were completed on their preschool behavior when they were 3½ years old. On 11 out of 12 Q-sort items which indexed peer competence, the securely attached group rated higher than the insecurely attached group.

Other research has failed, however, to replicate these results. Fifteen securely and 30 insecurely attached children were examined in same sex peer interaction at 24 months and the results revealed that the secure group did not differentiate from the insecure group (Jacobsen, Wille, Tianen & Aytch, 1983). Another study examined the relationship between attachment and changes in interaction for toddler and preschool children (Jacobsen & Wille, 1986). Twenty-four children who were rated for attachment quality at 18 months were observed at 2 and 3 years in interaction with a playmate. No differences by attachment classification were found in the subjects' peer interaction toward the playmate at 2 or 3 years.

In our own longitudinal study of friendship patterns, we were able to observe whether early attachment to the mother was related to a few mea-sures of children's friendship patterns. In particular, data were available on 125 subjects' one year attachment classification, and these data were used to predict the same children's report of their friendship patterns at 9 years of age. In interviews with these children at 9 years, we obtained information on (1) their total number of friends; (2) total number of best friends (we left the definition of "best" up to the child); (3) total number of male friends; and (4) total number of female friends.

Regression analyses using secure versus insecure attachment to predict the four friendship outcome measures were conducted. Overall subjects' attachment classifications were unrelated to the number of friends and the total number of best friends at 9 years. While for girl subjects there was no relationship between attachment and total number of male or female friends, boys' attachment was related to the number of male, but not to the number of female, friends. Securely attached boys were more likely to have more male friends than were insecurely attached boys. In general then, our data indicate that the attachment classification for girls is unrelated to subsequent friendship patterns, and for boys it appears only related to the number of male friends but not to the total number of friends, best friends, or female friends. Overall, our data provide only limited support for a relationship between friendship patterns at 9 years and children's early attachment relationships.

In general, the theoretical belief that early infant-mother security of attachment relates to later friendship patterns is not well supported by the empirical findings. Neither contemporaneous nor predictive relationships have been consistently demonstrated. One problem with the epigenetic hypothesis of security of attachment to mother as the cause of good peer relations is that it does not take into account other relationships which might have an impact on peer behavior, for example, the child's relationship to siblings or others in its social network. The assumption that only the mother-infant attachment relationship is primary for all other relationships has yet to be confirmed. Given the prevalence of the attachment theory and the belief that early mother-infant relations provide the working model for all other relations, it is surprising how few studies explore this issue either theoretically or by collecting data relevant to the theory.

The Social Network Model

In the social network model, the mother-child relationship is not the primary determinant of every type of relationship. The infant experiences and learns different things from the various people in its network. Mother-child, father-child, sibling-child, grandparent-child, are examples of early relationships that may influence the child's developing social competence and subsequent friendship patterns. Multiple social objects are viewed simultaneously, rather than sequentially, since they satisfy multiple and differential social needs (Harlow & Harlow, 1965; Hartup, 1983; Lewis, 1979; Lewis & Feiring, 1978, 1979; Lewis et al., 1975). The articulation of the matrix formed by social objects and needs is an important task in the study of social development (Edwards & Lewis, 1979; Lewis & Feiring, 1979) and suggests that the child's social relationships center around the child's needs and the culturally determined methods of meeting these needs. For example, some cultures promote the use of multiple caregiving in the form of both mother and older female sibling or friend (Whiting & Whiting, 1975); others support day-care settings with multiple adults; still others support the more traditional mother-infant relationship. The particular goals and values of a culture will determine the nature of the social network, the number and nature of the people, and the tasks they perform. For example, in a culture where only the mother interacts with the infant for the first 2 or 3 years, the mother is assigned both a caregiving and playmate function. Such a culture will differ from ones in which the mother is the caregiver but early peer experience is available and will differ still more from ones where the mother is not the only caregiver but shares the function with the infant's older female sibling.

In American culture, the articulation of the relationship between function and people in young children clearly indicates a separation of function and person, with adults assigned the role of caretaking, older peers that of teaching, and similar-age peers that of play (Edwards & Lewis, 1979). Thus, the social network model argues that children have multiple needs, which are satisfied by both parents and friends. Moreover, although one system will affect another, the development of social relationships is not necessarily sequential. Thus, mother-infant attachment may affect the child's friendship formation, but these friendships are not determined directly by the attachment relationship.

Two ways in which the maternal-infant attachment relationships may affect friendships, although not determine them in the epigenetic sense, are through peer availability and generalized fear. For example, mothers who are unable to facilitate an attachment relationship (for whatever reasons) may at the same time prevent the infant from having peer experience. Given that, in American culture, it is usually the mother who must facilitate and maintain early exposure to others, her failure to do so will result in the absence of contact. Absence of contact will likely prevent the child from learning how to interact with peers. In this case, poor attachment and poor friendships are related, although the inadequate attachment relationship is not the immediate cause of the poor friendships. The cause is lack of exposure to and experience with peers. In addition, inappropriate maternal behaviors, resulting in a poor attachment relationship, also may produce general fearfulness in the child, which might have the effect of inhibiting contact with peers. It is the lack of contact and interaction, caused by fear, that affects subsequent friendship patterns. This fact may explain why younger rather than same-age or older peer therapists are better able to help depressed children. These children may be less fearful of younger peers because skills of younger peers are less advanced (Suomi & Harlow, 1972). Note that, in both cases, it is not the poor interpersonal relationship with the mother that leads directly to poor subsequent friendship patterns.

The epigenetic and social network models can be compared by examining the relationship between mother-infant attachment and friendships. The epigenetic model predicts that poor attachments will lead to poor friendship patterns; the social network model allows for the independence of these two relationships provided that the mutual interactions (as discussed earlier) can be controlled. Work with nonhuman primates provides some support for the social network model. Harlow (1969) studied infants raised by mothers without peers present and another group raised with peers present but without mothers. The general findings that peer behavior was facilitated by early exclusive peer contact and not by exclusive maternal contact suggest that maternal attachment is not necessary for peer relations even though earlier work indicates that being raised without a mother does affect peer relationships. Unfortunately the infant monkeys raised without mothers were raised in isolation and therefore the effect of maternal attachment was confounded with social isolation. Additional support for the importance of peer relationships has been supplied by Suomi and Harlow (1972), as well as Novak and Harlow (1975), all of whom found that interaction with peers can overcome depression caused by the absence of the infant's mother. Moreover, the work of Furman, Rahe, and Hartup (1979) also bears on this issue. Socially withdrawn preschool children were assigned to two peer-therapy and one control condition. The therapy conditions were effective, and the children's peer behavior appeared normal. Even though this study provides no direct information on the attachment relationship, the results would appear to support the idea that friendship is independent from the mother-infant system, because the peer system can be altered without altering the attachment relationship. These results, taken together (Furman et al.; Harlow; Novak & Harlow; Suomi & Harlow) indicate that there is little reason to suppose that infant-maternal attachment will lead to successful friendships without peer experience, although early peer experience can overcome poor maternal interaction and its negative effects on subsequent peer behavior.

A more direct approach would be to locate a group of children who had inadequate attachment relationships and who at the same time had adequate peer experience. If it could be demonstrated that inadequate maternal-infant relationships did not affect friendships when friends were available, there would be more support for the social network than the epigenetic model. Morever, the demonstration that concurrent peer experience in the presence of a poor mother-infant relationship can foster adequate subsequent friendships would provide support for relevant intervention programs. The investigation of a sample of maltreated infants attending a day-care program allowed consideration of these issues.

Lewis and Schaeffer (1981) examined young children who had been maltreated with a matched controlled group. Observation of children interacting with their mothers and peers were made at the day-care center the children were attending. The results indicated that there were significant differences in maternal behavior toward children in the maltreated group compared to children in the control group—mothers in the maltreated group scolded more, were less positive, maintained and initiated less proximity, and spoke less to their children. The maltreated children interacted less with and stayed away from their mothers more than the control children did. In contrast to parent-child interactions, there were no significant differences in the maltreated and control children in peer interactions. For example, sociability and play variables showed no group differences. The results of this study of maltreated children suggests that poor infant-maternal relationships do not of necessity lead to poor peer relationships. These and the other findings we have presented raise serious questions about the epigenetic view of social development and friendship.

Given the findings that early peer availability may influence subsequent friendships patterns, we explored this possibility by observing our longitudinal data. As before, the four measures of friendship at 9 years of age were used as outcomes. To explore the effect of early peer availability we obtained information on the total number of peers and adults in the children's social networks when they were 3 and 6 years old. Contrary to our expectation, the number of peers that the children were exposed to when younger did not predict the four measures of friendship when they were 9 years old. When the total size of the social network was considered, including adults, relatives, and peers, we did find that for girls, but not boys, larger network size at 6 years was associated with having more same sex friends at 9 years. In general then, network variables show very limited relationship to friendship patterns, and only for girls. The failure to find any association between early peer exposure and later friendship patterns is difficult to explain, especially given the data that support such a model. It may well be the case that both attachment relationship and peer exposure, in some complex fashion, impact subsequent friendship patterns.

Like the attachment theory, the social network theory has important implications for development. It is, therefore, surprising that so little exploration of early social behavior and of its effect on later social behavior has been undertaken. The failure to explore the development of friendship patterns can be viewed as part of the general failure to explore most of social development.

The Genetic or Temperament Model

Theory and research suggest that friendship patterns may be related to individual biological and genetic differences. The tendency to approach people, the desire to be around other people, extroversion, inhibition, and sociability are all terms that have been used to imply that social contact is affected by individual biological differences (Buss & Plomin, 1984; Chess & Thomas, 1982; Eysenck, 1956; Kagan, 1982; Lewis & Rosenblum, 1974). Certain specific aspects of temperament seem to impact the formation of friendships as well as the extensiveness of the friendship network. Thomas, Chess, and Birch's (1968) characterization of the easy child (e.g., immediate approach, adaptive, positive in mood) suggest the profile of a child who would have a predisposition to make social contacts readily. This would be in contrast to general inhibition shown by some children in social situations (Kagan). The sociability or asociability in children may be related to individual preference for social as compared to nonsocial stimulation. We have found individual differences in 3-month-old infants, indicating that some children prefer to play with objects and interact less with people. We have considered such children to be asocial in nature (Lewis & Feiring, in press). This individual difference in sociability shows some consistency across the 1st year of life. These types of findings suggest that some children may prefer less extensive social contact with peers and may form fewer friendships as a consequence of their dispositions (Eysenck, 1956).

In general, a dispositional or temperament model holds that friendship patterns have their foundation in definite predispositions to seek out and feel comfortable with social contacts. This is not to say that an underlying biological sociability could not be modified by environmental influences such as family relations or other social contacts (e.g., Goldsmith & Campos, 1982; Lerner & Lerner, 1983; Rothbart & Derryberry, 1981; Thomas et al., 1968), but all other variables being equal, temperament differences might definitely impact friendship. There is some research which supports this view. Several studies show that individual differences in the tendency to approach others in social interaction is related to positive sociometric nomination in nursery school (Abramovitch, 1979; Hartup, Glazer, & Charlesworth, 1967; Marshall & McCandless, 1957). Moreover, extroverted behavior has been reported to be positively related to peer acceptance in grade school (Bonney & Powell, 1953), and in knowing how to make friends (Gottman, Gonzo, & Rasmussen, 1975). Temperament factors also have been related to adolescent social behavior (Lerner & Lerner).

Although these data suggest some role of temperament, little work has examined its role in friendship patterns and development. Using the longitudinal data, early temperament variables were examined as they predicted friendship outcomes. The temperament variables of sociability at 3 months and temperament ratings obtained at 6 years (easy, intermediate, difficult, McDevitt & Carey, 1978) were used to predict friendship patterns at 9 years. These temperament variables did not significantly explain the variance in total number of peers or best friends; however, for boys there was a significant relationship between temperament and the number of male, but not the number of female, friends. The easier a boy's temperament, the more male friends he had in his network. For the girls, the temperament variables did not predict the numbers of male or female friends in their network. Overall, these findings only weakly support a dispositional model for explaining a significant component in the formation of childhood friendship patterns. However, as was true for attachment, there is some indication that for boys, temperament may have some relationship to the number of same sex friendships. Boys who are characterized as low in intensity, positive in mood and approach and adaptive, appear to have more male friends than do boys who are more difficult in temperament. Why a more easygoing temperament should influence friendship patterns for boys but not for girls is unclear.

Although there are relatively little data for a dispositional model of friendship development, the idea that temperamentally difficult or asocial children might have friendship pattern deficiencies is appealing and consistent with the clinical data for some children (Thomas et al., 1968). It may be the case that except for a few extreme subjects, temperament variables may not impact children's friendships. Given that temperament might affect only 10%

of the subjects in any study of normal children, such differences might not be obvious. In order to observe the effects of temperament differences it may be necessary to examine extreme populations much the same way we study extreme groups in developmental psychopathology. Until we have such studies, it will be difficult to demonstrate the possible effects of these dispositional factors.

Perhaps most important temperament factors may only be relevant as they interact with specific characteristics of the environment. Thus, asocial and social children may show little difference if both are raised in the presence of many friends but may show large differences if raised in the presence of a few friends. That is, as exposure becomes more difficult, individual differences in temperament may exert their impact. Such interactive processes need careful study.

Demographic Model

Whereas the first three models focus on developmental processes, the demographic model is more descriptive of the children's "social address" than it is of any dynamic mechanism (Bronfenbrenner 1986). Three demographic variables have been shown to affect or to be related to many different social outcomes; birth order, sex, and socioeconomic status. These factors may be related to the development of friendship patterns.

In regard to birth order and friendship patterns the evidence is mixed. Some studies indicate that firstborns and onlies may be more affiliative and assertive in peer relations than later-borns (Hoyt & Raven, 1973; Snow, Jacklin, & Maccoby, 1981). Firstborns may also have more extensive peer networks than onlies or later-borns (Feiring & Lewis, 1984). In contrast, later-borns have been found to be more popular than firstborns (Miller & Maruyama, 1976: Schachter, 1964; Sells & Rolf, 1963).

A child's sex has been shown to have a large influence on preference for same-sex friends from preschool throughout the life-span (see Hartup, 1983 for a review). It appears that many processes contribute to this phenomenon including direct reinforcement for same-sex interaction by parents and other socialization agents (Fagot, 1977; Lewis et al., 1975; Lewis & Weinraub, 1979), the child's preference (Serbin, Tonick, & Sternglanz, 1977), peer reinforcement, (Lamb, Easterbrooks, & Holden, 1980; Lamb & Roopnarine, 1979), and the social structure of the network, which facilitates same-sex affiliations and activities (Cochran & Riley, 1988; Feiring & Lewis, 1987a, 1988). The relationship between socioeconomic status (SES) and friendship patterns has not been well explored (Hartup, 1983); however, we do know that there are differences in what activities or values are seen as important for peer acceptance or popularity as a function of SES (Feinberg, Smith, & Schmidt, 1958).

Our longitudinal data allowed us to explore friendship outcomes as a function of the SES, sex, and birth order of the subjects. While there was no relationship between the demographic variables and total number of friends there was a trend for these variables to predict the number of best friends. In particular, firstborns are more likely to have a greater number of best friends than are later-borns. The most potent variable in predicting the number of same-sex friends is the sex of the child; boys have more male than female friends and girls have more female than male friends. In addition to sex, birth order also is related to the number of friends such that firstborns tend to have the greatest number of same-sex friends compared to all other groups.

In general, the best predictor of the number of male and female friends is the sex of the child. Boys are oriented toward male friends, girls toward females. This sex differentiation appears early, at least by 2 to 3 years of age, and continues throughout the life-span with an increase in the number of opposite sex friends at adolescence (Hartup, 1983). Nevertheless, the ratio of same- to opposite-sex friends remains heavily weighted toward same-sex friends. The demographic data alone rather than the data for the other models seem best predictive of subsequent friendship patterns. In part, this is due to the powerful effects of sex on friendship patterns.

Multiple Factors as a Model of Friendship Patterns

As mentioned before, it is necessary to consider the interaction of these various models and their combined effect on subsequent patterns of friendship. It is clear from the literature review and from a survey of our longitudinal data that any single model of the development of friendship patterns is inadequate. The potential factors which influence development of any capacity including friendship are many and models need to capture this complexity. For example, in the literature on developmental psychopathology it has been found that combinations of factors are necessary to follow any developmental path (Elder, 1974). Consider the concept of vulnerability (Garmezy, 1971). Here individuals, either through early social experience and/or genetic factors, are placed at risk for some outcomes. A negative outcome may not occur unless another set of factors occur; for example, family stress (e.g., Werner & Smith, 1982). Neither early nor later factors themselves are sufficient to predict the outcome. The same is likely to be the case for the prediction of friendship patterns. There are few studies to support this possibility so we again turn to the longitudinal data as a means for exploring multiple factor models. While each of the variables representing the constructs of the models has limited predictability, it might be the case that their combination is more predictive of friendship outcomes.

In order to explore how the early predictors of later friendship patterns operated in combination, multiple regression analyses were conducted using attachment, sex of child, birth order, temperament ratings, and network size at 6 years. These variables were chosen because they were found to be predictive in the previous analyses and we felt this approach would give us some idea concerning the relative importance of the potential predictors. The regression analyses used to predict total number of friends and total number of best friends were not significant; however the regression analyses used to predict same-sex friends were significant.

The results suggest the overwhelming importance of sex in understanding patterns. In addition, the findings suggest that predictors of same sex friendships are different for boys and girls. For boys, temperament plays a role in how many male friends are in the network, more so than attachment, birth order, or network size. For girls, network size at 6 years plays a role in how many female friends are in the network, more so than attachment, birth order, or temperament.

These regression analyses allow us to consider the effect of multiple predictors on a particular outcome and support the view that no single set of variables alone is likely to predict friendship pattern development. Interactive models are necessary to understand development. Lewis, Feiring, McGuffog, and Jaskir (1984), for example, showed that the psychopathology at 6 years was best predicted by a combination of variables including attachment, demographic and stress factors. The same appears so for friendship development. Moreover, our developmental models are made even more complicated by the apparent differences in predictors as a function of sex.

Not only may the developmental patterns from prediction to outcome differ for females and males (Kagan & Moss, 1962; Lewis et al., 1984; Macfarlane, 1963), the meaning of the predictor factors or antecedent conditions may differ by sex as well. For example, secure attachment between mother and son and mother and daughter may have different meanings. For boys it may be related to the development of intimacy and behavior problems; for girls it may be related to school behavior (Feiring & Lewis, 1987b; Lewis et al., 1984). Such findings alert us to the difficulties of exploring developmental changes in social behavior.

Models relating early differences to later friendship patterns have been considered in our discussion and have been classified as (1) attachment, (2) network, (3) temperament/genetic, and (4) demographic. Little discussion or research has been conducted on the longitudinal question of early predictors of friendship patterns. With the exception of attachment theory, no clear model relating earlier patterns of behavior to later friendship has been examined. The review of the attachment literature does suggest that the early maternal infant relationship has some association with later peer behavior, although the exact mechanisms remain unclear and very narrow in focus. Our longitudinal study provides the opportunity to explore the possible antecedents of subsequent friendship patterns. We do not view our findings as confirmatory, rather, they represent our first attempt to study this issue and to generate hypotheses that can be better tested in new studies focusing on friendship patterns. However, in studying friendships developmentally one problem is the determination of outcome measures.

Our attempt to capture the antecedents of friendship behavior was limited by the outcome measures we had available to use. However, it is not clear what measures ought to be used. Friendship is a complex construct, including types of people, functions, and the settings in which friends interact, an issue we will return to in the following section. Friendship varies as a function of intimacy so that a friend compared to a best friend is qualitatively different. To capture the complex construct of friendship requires more than a few measures. Which measures to use remains a question for further debate. What is clear is that study is required to observe what friendship variables are predicted by what antecedent conditions. It is not likely that all friendship pattern outcomes will be predicted from the same antecedent condition. For example, in our study we observed the relationship of multiple measures of each model on the outcome variables we were able to study.

The limited findings of the study support the notion that outcome and predictors have unique paths and that developmental paths have to be considered for each of the outcome measures. No single set of variables predicts the total number of children's friends. The factors which account for number of friends in the child's network do not appear related to the models proposed. Rather, number of friends might be predicted by where a child lives or the type of housing. A child who lives on a farm is going to have fewer total number of friends than a child who lives in a city. Similarly, a child who lives in a private house may have fewer friends than one who lives in a large apartment complex with many families and children. In other words, accessibility and density of children available rather than psychological, dynamic factors may be responsible for size of friendship network (Parke & Bhavnagri, in press).

Number of best friends makes reference to the interpersonal quality of friendship patterns. Even in the case of this outcome, there was a paucity of significant predictor variables. This is surprising since the quality of friendship should be related to the quality of the child's early relationships (Erickson, Sroufe, & Egeland, 1986; Lewis et al., 1984; Waters et al., 1979). Nevertheless, there was a trend which indicated that the firstborns had more best friends than later borns. Neither attachment nor sociability was related to the best friend outcome. Perhaps the number of best friends does not tap the intimacy dimension of friendship. Having one or two best friends may be as good as having three or four. Indeed having many best friends might be argued to be a less adaptive outcome than having a few best friends. For our sample of 9-year-old children, the mean number of best friends was four. This number suggests that more than a couple of best friends may be the rule at 9 years. On the other hand, intimacy may not be captured by inquiring about a "best" friend. Descriptive detail about shared feelings and activities may be a better index of intimacy. Nevertheless, it is striking that there is a lack of relationship between predictors and the best friend outcome.

The number of male friends and the number of female friends were considered separate outcomes, because the data show that same- and opposite-sex friendship patterns differ by 3 years (Feiring & Lewis, 1987a; Lewis, Feiring, & Kotsonis, 1984; Maccoby & Jacklin, 1978). The predominance of same-sex compared to opposite-sex friendship in childhood is a phenomenon structured by society. By 9 years of age this division of friends by sex is a set feature of children's networks (Feiring & Lewis, 1988; Tietjen, 1982; Hartup, 1983). Sex-related friendship patterns are the most predictable of the outcomes considered here. Overall, the sex of the child informs us about the number of male and female friends in the child's network. However, other variables come into play and account for additional variance. For both sexes, being firstborn and having an easy temperament are related to having more male friends. Why this might be the case is difficult to explain. Firstborns differ from later-borns in a number of ways. Firstborns are more achievement oriented, and there is some suggestion that they may be more interactive with their fathers (Lewis & Feiring, 1981). If these differences exist, they may orient the firstborn more toward males than toward females and thus explain the effect of birth order in addition to the effect of the child's sex. Children with difficult temperaments may get into more interpersonal conflict with others, especially with boys. It may also be the case that such children have a harder time making friends and in particular male friends, who prefer more rough and tumble play. Difficult-temperament children may shy away from such contact.

For both sexes, having a larger social network, in addition to the sex of the child, predicts the number of female friends. Given that there are more females, it may be that being exposed to and interacting with more females as a consequence of a larger network, predisposes the child to have more female friends. Whatever the reasons for these differences, the prediction of friendship patterns appears more illusive than our theories would lend us to believe. Measurement issues are clearly important to consider and require more study.

Another issue may be related to stability. Friendship patterns during preadolescence may not be stable since the nature of children's friendships may undergo elaborate change (Berndt, Hawkins, & Hoyle 1986). Prediction might be better if we restricted our study to childhood patterns or if we explored friendship patterns past adolescence. Even so the continuity of friendship patterns may be limited since a host of environmental factors may play a role in our social behavior. Density of peers available, type of housing, school structure and size, and family mobility may all play important roles in friendship patterns, in addition to individual characteristics and histories (Moore & Young, 1978).

THE MEANING AND FUNCTIONS OF FRIENDS

Having considered the possible models related to the development of friendship we now turn our attention to the issue of the meaning and functions of friends. Here, we need to consider both how others have treated the concept of friend and what we feel is necessary in order to understand the nature of friendships and how they develop.

Research and theory suggest that throughout the life-span, friends are persons who make us feel good about ourselves, enhancing self-esteem, self-worth, and pride (Berndt & Perry, 1986; Cohen, Mermelstein, Karmarck & Hoberman, 1985; Sullivan, 1953). In fact, ego enhancement may be one of the earliest characteristics to emerge from friendship (Bigelow & La Gaipa, 1975). Friends can also be sources of information for solving emotional and other kinds of problems. For example, they can help with homework assignments, they can be a source of information on where to find objects, people or activities of interest, or they can help fix broken toys and objects (Berndt & Perry; Cohen et al.). In a large-scale study of children in first through eighth grade it was found that children use multiple characteristics to describe friends (Bigelow, 1977; Bigelow & LaGaipa, 1975). In order of their emergence, these characteristics included: common activities, helpmate, proximity, evaluation, acceptance, admiration, loyalty, intimacy, genuineness, and common interest.

The various meanings of friendship have been explored from childhood to adulthood (Berndt, 1981; Bigelow, 1977; Damon, 1977; Selman, 1981; Youniss, 1980), and a review will not be attempted here (see Hartup, Chap. 2; Parker & Gottman, Chap. 4, this vol.). Rather we wish to present a framework in which to consider the full range of types of friends, the functions friends fulfill, and the types of people who are potential friends.

Friendship Matrix

In an analysis of friendship patterns, there are two major dimensions that should be considered: the people who can become friends and the functions that friends fulfill. Figure 9.1A presents this simple matrix. Notice that there are at least five functions friends can perform—play, teaching, nurturance/intimacy, protection, and caregiving. Certainly these functions can be performed by people who are not friends, such as parents and teachers, but friends do satisfy some, if not all, of them.

The people dimension can cover a broad range of individuals. This possible range is restricted by social rules and conventions as well as by time and space. Consequently, we need to consider a finer differentiation of individuals. The age of the person is an important attribute as is the person's sex and kinship status (see Feiring & Lewis, 1987a, 1987b; Lewis & Feiring, 1979). Friendship patterns are affected by setting; in fact, setting may influence functions. Figure 9.1B presents friendship patterns divided into a three-dimensional space that includes people, settings, and functions. This matrix provides a convenient way of categorizing individuals and should be helpful in understanding the development of friendship patterns. Let us consider each of these dimensions separately.

Functions

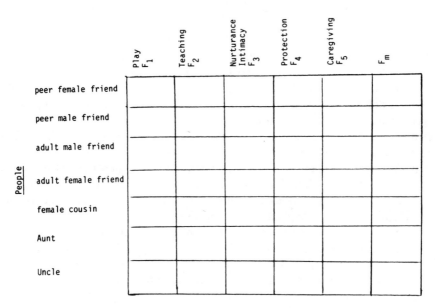

Figure 9.1A. The social network matrix of people and functions.

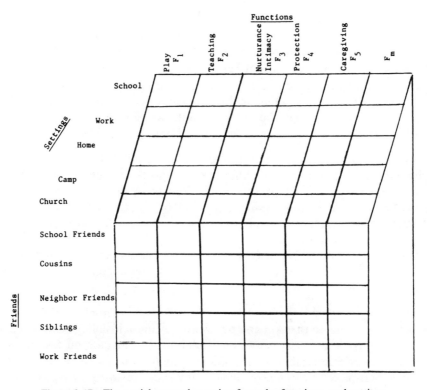

Figure 9.1B. The social network matrix of people, functions, and settings.

Setting

Friendships are formed as a function of setting. For children, some friendships are established by proximity in school; for example, the child at the next desk or a laboratory partner. Other friendships can be established by living next door to a child or by going to the same playground or overnight camp. Each of these settings may restrict the nature of the friendship or may be related to specific functions, an issue we will address later. The settings we have specified in these examples include school and home but could include church or synagogue and the soccer field or shopping mall as well. Although such a classification is useful, we could describe setting along other dimensions such as large nonrestrictive areas versus small controlled settings, distance from home, or the distribution of adults and peers. The specification of the exact nature of settings is a general theme in need of more elaboration; nevertheless, however described, setting is an important dimension (Whiting, 1980; Bryant, 1985). For example, although children choose same-sex peers for friends at school, they are somewhat more likely to have mixed friendship groups in their neighborhood (Ellis, Rogoff, & Cromer, 1981).

People

AGE.   The age of friends can vary markedly. Although our society tends to age-stratify most activities, friends need not be limited by age (Kandel, 1978). Agemates may be close friends or not friends at all; for example, girls mature earlier than same-age boys and therefore tend to prefer older boys as friends. Children with older siblings also may be more likely to have older friends (i.e., met through the older sibling). Socially isolated children may prefer younger friends to same-age peers (Ladd et al., 1988).

SEX.   Although we often consider friends to be of the same sex, it is obvious that friends can be of either sex. It appears that infants and toddlers have mixed friends, but preschool children have more same-sex friends (Charlesworth & Hartup, 1967; Clark, Wyon & Richards, 1969; Serbin, Tonick, & Sternglanz, 1977). Same-sex friends also are the rule during middle childhood but this arrangement becomes somewhat more flexible in later adolescence (Hartup, 1983). However, for the status of best friends, it appears that in adolescence, at least, gender concordance is extremely high (Kandel, 1978).

KINSHIP STATUS.   We tend to think of friends as nonkin, but there is evidence to indicate that kin can be friends. Although siblings can serve as friends, cousins also may serve this function. In our data on 6-year-olds' friendships, we note that some children invite cousins to their birthday parties (Feiring & Lewis, 1987a). That many states restrict marriage between first cousins suggests that friendship (and indeed love) is likely between such kin. The selection of friends from kin is probably easier for those children who do have a large extended kin network and who do not have many nonkin peers available for interaction.

Functions

In describing the social functions that friends fulfill, we begin with the range of activities we have previously studied; in particular, protection, caregiving, nurturance, play, and teaching (Lewis & Feiring, 1978; 1979). The functions friends fulfill are quite varied, and it is important to focus on these functions so that we can appreciate the complexity of the term friendship (see Figure 9.1A & B).

PLAY.   Play is a complex activity including groups of others, couples, or even one's self. Play also includes formal activities like games with rules or informal "playing around." Although play has been thought of as an important aspect of learning cognitive skills (for example, Piaget, 1952), it also has been conceptualized in terms of its opportunity for rehearsal of already learned skills and its social interactive quality (Sutton-Smith, 1976; Watson & Fischer, 1980). Both aspects need to be considered in terms of friendship. In play, the child can learn about social rules, actions, and feelings; there is evidence that peer learning is an important feature in young children's educational experience. However, it is more likely that play allows for the forming and maintenance of friendship. Play provides the basis of friendship by offering opportunities for peer interaction as well as the material for the interaction.

TEACHING.   Friends serve as teachers. Although we tend to think of teachers as adults, children also instruct other children, and children often learn more readily from other children than from adults (Allen, 1976). Edwards and Lewis (1979), for example, found that 3- to 5-year-old children preferred that older children rather than adults teach them. Peer learning and teaching are well documented (Allen). Adult teachers can be friends too, although this is less likely to occur until students become older. What is important is that teaching as a function involves friends as well as others usually assigned that function.

NURTURANCE.   One very important function of friends is nurturance. As children move from a home-centered existence, they come to rely on others besides their parents/siblings for a sense of belonging and a sense of worth. These needs are satisfied by friends and constitute the function of nurturance or intimacy. While nurturance includes affection, we have chosen to exclude sexuality, preferring instead to consider this as a separate function.

SEXUALITY.   This function needs little explanation except to suggest that in early adolescence it need not be fulfilled only by the opposite sex. The issue of early same sexuality is relatively unexplored, although we know that the incidence of same-sex contact does occur. Sexuality is a function which matures at adolescence although there is some early sexual interaction; e.g., playing "doctor" or "mommy and daddy."

PROTECTION.   In early childhood, protection is a function performed mainly by adults or sometimes by older siblings. Once the child is less often in adult company, friends and peers are more likely to fulfill this function. Situations which require protection include aggression from other children (bullies) and external circumstances likely to cause harm. Protection from a friend also can include speaking up for the child in his/her absence. Although not normally considered a necessary function between friends, the need for protection probably occurs more frequently than imagined, especially in groups who fight more on playgrounds.

CAREGIVING.   While caregiving is more characteristic of a parent-child relationship, there is no reason to think that this function does not occur between friends. Consider children's sharing of dessert or giving of money to one another. This type of function has a strong prosocial aspect because it refers to helping others in need of assistance. Research supports the idea that for children, caregiving between friends may involve sharing and helping activities as well as prosocial behavior (Berndt & Perry, 1986; Bigelow & La Gaipa, 1980; Furman & Bierman, 1983). Some investigators have referred to the instrumental support nature of these caregiving functions (Berndt, in press).

Other functions and ways of conceptualizing social functions exist and our list should not be considered exhaustive (Murray, 1938; Berndt, in press; Shumaker & Brownell, 1984; Youniss, 1980). Furman (1982) and Furman and Buhrmester (1987) have explored another set of functions, some of which are ones already mentioned here; others are new. These are enhancement of worth, reliable alliance, instrumental help, companionship, affection, intimacy, and nurturance. In middle childhood and adolescence, research based on this framework of functions has examined a matrix of people—in particular, parents, siblings, grandparents, teachers, same and opposite sex friends—and how such people provide these functions.

The discussion of friendship is usually limited to the social objects of nonkin peers and the functions of play and nurturance (e.g., intimacy and support), but friendship can be specified from a broader perspective. Although different social objects may be characterized by particular social functions, social objects (friends), functions, and situations may be only partially related (Lewis & Weinraub, 1976).

Figure 9.2 represents a matrix of possible friends and possible social functions for a 9-year-old child. In this figure the vertical axis, P_1-P_n is the set of friends in the child's life at a given point in time. Notice that for this

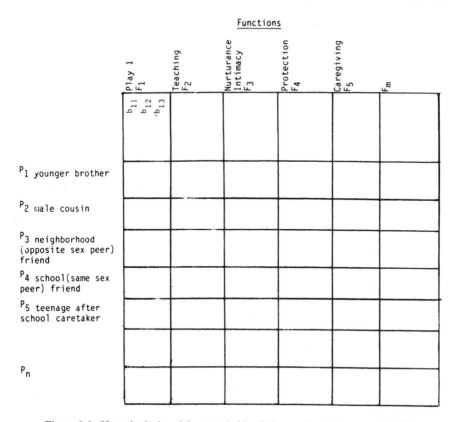

Figure 9.2. Hypothetical social network friendship matrix of a 9-year-old child.

9-year-old child, the vertical dimension lists different types of friends. On the horizontal axis, the possible social functions, F_{1-m}, are represented and within each function, particular activities or behaviors can be specified. For example, for play, F_1, there are the possible behaviors of team sports (b_{11}), games (b_{12}), and fantasy play (b_{13}).

The matrix given in Figure 9.2 offers the possibility of representing the variety of friends and social functions in a child's friendship network at a given point in time. By examining the vertical axis of the matrix, one obtains information concerning the extent to which a particular function characterizes a child's friendship network. In exploring friendship in a 9-year-old, we might focus on the functions of play and nurturance as contrasted with the functions of teaching and caregiving. We can ask to what extent play characterizes the child's activities across social objects. By examining the horizontal axis of the matrix, we may explore the functions and specific activities that characterize particular friends. Best friends, for example, might show higher levels of nurturance as compared to other friends.

EXPLORING EARLY PREDICTORS OF FRIENDSHIP
DEVELOPMENT IN CHILDREN: FUTURE DIRECTIONS

How might the model of types of friends and functions aid our interest in explicating models of development and in predicting subsequent friendship behavior? When we attempt to model build we need to be concerned with outcome. The question we need raise is that of nature of outcomes. In our longitudinal study as well as in the few studies that have explored this problem, outcome measures are limited. Although we can look at number of best friends or even whether one has a peer for intimate disclosure, there are a limited set of measures. We need to *broaden the possible number of different outcomes,* and this matrix provides the opportunity to consider possible ways to generate them.

Even more important is that *different types of friends may be a function of different antecedents.* Thus, number of male friends for a girl may be related to the number of past male friend experiences while total number of friends may be related to the child's relationship with her mother. Number of close friends or depth of the friendship may be related to early mother-child relationship, whereas number or variety of friends may be related to the father-child relationship. Specified models are needed, in which particular outcomes are related to specific and unique antecedents. Attachment theory suffers from this lack of specificity both in terms of the likely outcome and differences as a function of the type of attachment. Moreover, by considering only early attachment to mother, the child's early relationships to others—fathers, siblings, friends—are not considered as possible antecedents for the variety of friendship outcomes. We have some reason to believe that children learn different types of skills from mothers, fathers, or siblings (Power & Parke, 1983; Weinraub & Frankel, 1977). Early attachment relationships with mother or older sister may be particularly significant for a boy's tendency to share feelings with best friends of the opposite and same sex. For girls, the attachment relationship with mother may be somewhat less related to the intimacy aspect of friendship, because there appears to be a strong social press for females to be skilled in intimacy (Blyth & Foster-Clark, 1987). For girls, early attachment to a father or brothers may be predictive of later close relationships with friends.

From our longitudinal data we have some idea that different antecedents are related to different friendship outcomes. For example, for girls, network size is important for same-sex friends, but for boys temperament plays more of a role. The model we have formed is considerably more complex in terms of outcomes and is beyond our ability to test. Nevertheless, unless we are prepared to consider the complexity of friends, their nature and function, we are likely to have limited understanding about the development of friendship.

This realization brings us to the issue of functions and the variety of exchanges that can typify friendships. Friends who serve the function of play may have antecedents that are different from the ones of friends who serve the function of teaching. To make the issue of specificity even more complex, it is possible that for some children, friends have multiple functions while for others, friends fulfill a limited number of functions. The antecedents for multiple versus single function friendships may differ. Thus, the friend who is only fun to go to the movies with may have different antecedents than the friend with whom it is fun to do many things, such as going to the movies, studying, and talking about problems.

Constraints in person × function interactions also may affect friendship development. Consider the constraints of family composition or culture. One child may use an older sister for the friendship function of intimacy and another might use a nonkin peer friend. The former is related to birth order, that is, you have to have an older sibling to have this person × function pattern. The constraint of culture means that friend or best friends have different meanings and involve different types of exchanges.

In examining models of friendship antecedents, it is necessary to consider that *friendship patterns are not static.* Thus, what predicts friendship outcomes in childhood may be different from what predicts friendship patterns in adolescence or adulthood. For example, there is some reason to believe that the functions of intimacy undergo several shifts as the distributions of friends and parents change. Some research has considered developmental changes in friendship relationships. Of particular interest have been the shifts in the distribution of support and intimacy for family members as compared to friends. Although this work is almost entirely cross-sectional it does reveal some interesting insights into the possible development of friendship patterns. Furman and his colleagues (Buhrmester & Furman, 1987; Furman, in press) have examined developmental changes in schoolchildren and adolescents' relationships with friends and family. In middle childhood parents are seen as somewhat more supportive than friends, but by adolescence friends are rated as slightly more supportive. While conflict between friends decreases, it increases between adolescents and their parents. Blyth and Foster-Clark (1987) have also found an increase in intimacy with friends from early to late adolescence. However, they find that girls report more intimacy sooner and maintain a higher level than boys, who show more gradual changes in increased intimacy.

In a study of children and adolescents, Hunter and Youniss (1982) examined changes in friendship and parent relationships. Nurturance between friends increased with age and remained at a relatively high level for parents. Intimacy with mother remained high across ages while increasing for friends. Intimacy with fathers may fall below intimacy with mother and friends, although less so for boys than for girls (Blyth & Foster-Clark, 1987). Research also suggests that the kinds of topics children discuss with friends broaden with age (Hunter, 1985). For example, peer problems are discussed with friends, but academic/career and social/ethical issues are discussed more with parents in early adolescence. However, when adolescents get older they also begin to talk about social/ethical and academic/career issues with friends as well as with parents.

SUMMARY

In this chapter, we have attempted to consider various models that can be used to predict friendship patterns. Although there are many theories that suggest a relationship between early differences and later friendship patterns, there is a paucity of data on this subject. While our own longitudinal study is useful in exploring these models, the reported findings should only be used as suggested ways to go about investigating the possible antecedent conditions. Unfortunately, the problem of conducting longitudinal studies over long periods of time makes this area of investigation difficult.

Of particular concern is the design of longitudinal studies that would explore multiple antecedents as they are related to multiple outcomes. As we discussed earlier, cross-sectional work has examined the different meanings of friendship in childhood, adolescence, and adulthood. Work is needed that specifies and examines how specific antecedents may bring about specific aspects of friendship. For example, sharing common activities and interests or sharing personal problems might be two different aspects of friendship with different antecedents. The rates of these types of friendship activities, as well as their possible antecedents, might differ for males and females. Sharing problems might show a higher incidence for girls than for boys and might be predicted by early exposure to settings where dyadic interaction is the rule. For boys, sharing common activities might show a higher incidence as a friendship activity and might be related to early exposure to experience in nonkin group activities.

From our analysis of people, setting, and functions, it is clear that the definition of friendship is multifaceted and related to multiple processes. Is friendship to be defined by the subject, or is it useful to look at the number of types of friends generated by the matrix of peers and functions? Will different outcomes have different antecedents? Will developmental factors differ for males and females? Clearly we have raised more questions than we have answered. Nevertheless, friendship patterns constitute an important aspect of social life and development, and although we have not answered these difficult questions, we have provided a beginning by suggesting a framework for further study.

REFERENCES

Abramovitch, R. (1979). *Proximity, prosocial and agonistic behaviors of preschool children: An observational study.* Unpublished manuscript, University of Toronto.

Ainsworth, M. D. S. (1972). Attachment and dependency: A comparison. In J. L. Gewirtz (Ed.), *Attachment and dependency.* New York: Wiley.

Ainsworth, M. D. S., Blehar, M. E., Waters, E., & Wall, S. (1978). *Patterns of attachment: A psychological study of the strange situation.* Hillsdale, NJ: Lawrence Erlbaum.

Allen, V. L. (1976). *Children as teachers: Theory and research on tutoring.* New York: Academic Press.

Becker, J. M. T. (1977). A learning analysis of the development of peer-oriented behavior in nine-month old infants. *Developmental Psychology, 13,* 481–491.

Belle, D. (In press). Gender differences in the social mediator of stress. In D. Belle (Ed.), *Children's social network and social supports.* New York: Wiley.

Berndt, T. J. (1981). Age changes and changes over time in prosocial intentions and behavior between friends. *Developmental Psychology, 17,* 408–416.

Berndt, T. J. (in press). Obtaining support from friends during childhood and adolescence. In D. Belle (Ed.), *Children's social networks and social supports.* New York: Wiley.

Berndt, T. J., Hawkins, J. A., & Hoyle, S. G. (1986). Changes in friendship during a school year: Effects on children's and adolescent's impressions of friendship and sharing with friends. *Child Development, 57,* 1284–1297.

Berndt, T. J., & Perry, T. B. (1986). Children's perceptions of friendships as supportive relationships. *Developmental Psychology, 22,* 640–648.

Berscheid, E., & Walster, E. H. (1978). *Interpersonal attraction* (2nd ed.). Reading, MA: Addison-Wesley.

Bigelow, B. J. (1977). Children's friendship expectations: A cognitive developmental study. *Child Development, 48,* 246–253.

Bigelow, B. J. & La Gaipa, J. J. (1975). Children's written descriptions of friendship: A multidimensional analysis. *Developmental Psychology, 11,* 857–858.

Bigelow, B. J. & La Gaipa, J. J. (1980). The development of friendship values and choice. In H. C. Foot, A. J. Chapman, & J. R. Smith (Eds.), *Friendship and social relations in children* (pp. 15–24). New York: Wiley.

Blyth, D. & Foster-Clark, F. S. (1987). Gender differences in perceived intimacy with different members of adolescents' social networks. In C. Feiring & D. L. Coates (Issue Eds.) [Special issue: Social networks and gender differences in the life space of opportunity]. *Sex Roles: A Journal of Research, 17*(11/12), 689–718.

Bonney, M. E., & Powell, J. (1953). Differences in social behavior between sociometrically high and sociometrically low children. *Journal of Educational Research, 46,* 481–495.

Bowlby, J. (1969). *Attachment and loss: Vol. 2. Attachment.* New York: Basic Books.

Bronfenbrenner, U. (1986). Ecology of the family as a context for human development: Research perspectives. *Developmental Psychology, 22,* 723–742.

Bryant, B. K. (1985). The neighborhood walk: Sources of support in middle childhood. *Monographs of the Society for Research in Child Development, 50*(3 Serial No. 210).

Buhrmester, D., & Furman W. (1987). The development of companionship and intimacy. *Child Development, 58,* 1101–1113.

Buss, A. H., & Plomin, R. (1984). *Temperament: Early developing personality traits.* Hillsdale, NJ: Lawrence Erlbaum.

Charlesworth, R., & Hartup, W. W. (1967). Positive social reinforcement in the nursery school peer group. *Child Development, 38,* 993–1002.

Chess, S., & Thomas, A. (1982). Infant bonding: Mystique and reality. *American Journal of Orthopsychiatry, 52,* 213–222.

Clark, A. H., Wyon, S. M., & Richards, M. P. M. (1969). Free play in nursery school children. *Journal of Child Psychology and Psychiatry, 10,* 205–216.

Cochran, M., & Riley, D. (1988). Mother reports of children's personal networks: Antecedents, concomitants and consequences. In S. Salzinger, J. Antrobus, & M. Hammer (Eds.), *Social networks of children, adolescents, and college students* (113–147). Hillsdale, NJ: Lawrence Erlbaum.

Cohen, S., Mermelstein, R. J., Karmarck, T., & Hoberman, H. M. (1985). Measuring the functional components of social support. In I. G. Sarason & B. R. Sarason (Eds.), *Social support: Theory, research and applications* (pp. 73–94). The Hague, Holland: Martinus Nijhoff.

Damon, W. (1977). *The social world of the child*. San Francisco: Jossey-Bass.

Doyle, A., Connolly, J., & Rivest, L. (1980). The effects of playmate familiarity on the social interactions of young children. *Child Development, 51*, 217–223.

Edwards, C. P., & Lewis, M. (1979). Young children's concept of social relations: Social functions on social objects. In M. Lewis & L. Rosenblum, (Eds.), *The child and its family: The genesis of behavior* (Vol. 2, 245–266). New York: Plenum.

Elder, G. H., Jr. (1974). *Children of the Great Depression*. Chicago: University of Chicago Press.

Ellis, S., Rogoff, B., & Cromer, C. C. (1981). Age segregation in children's social interactions. *Development Psychology, 17*, 399–407.

Erickson, M. F., Sroufe, L. A., & Egeland, B. R. (1986). The relationship between quality of attachment and behavior problems in preschool in a high risk sample. In I. Bretherton & E. Waters (Eds.), *Growing points of attachment theory and research*. Monograph for the Society for Research in Child Development, *50*, (209), pp. 147–166.

Eysenck, H. J. (1956). The questionnaire measurement of neuroticism and extraversion. *Riv. Psicol., 50*, 113–140.

Fagot, B. I. (1977). Consequences of moderate cross-gender behavior in preschool children. *Child Development, 48*, 902–907.

Feinberg, M. R., Smith, M., & Schmidt, R. (1958). An analysis of expressions used by adolescents of varying economic levels to describe accepted and rejected peers. *Journal of Genetic Psychology, 93*, 133–148.

Feiring, C., & Lewis, M. (1984). Only and first-born children: Differences in social behavior and development. In T. Falbo (Ed.), *The single child family* (pp. 25–62). New York: Guilford.

Feiring, C,. & Lewis, M. (1987a). The child's social network: Sex differences from three to six years. In C. Feiring & D. L. Coates (Issue Eds.) [Special issue: Social networks and gender differences in the life space of opportunity]. *Sex Roles: A Journal of Research, 17*(11/12), 621–636.

Feiring, C., & Lewis, M. (1987b, April). *Equibility and multifixability. Diversity in development from infancy into childhood*. Paper presented at the biennial meeting of the Society for Research in Child Development, Baltimore.

Feiring, C. & Lewis, M. (in press). Children's social networks from early- to middle-childhood. In D. Belle (Ed.), *Children's social networks and social supports*. New York: Wiley.

Furman, W. (1982). Children's friendships. In T. Field, A. Huston, H. Quay, L. Troll, & G. Finley (Eds.), *Review of human development* (pp. 327–339). New York: Wiley.

Furman, W. (in press). The development of children's social networks. In D. Belle (Ed.), *Children's Social Networks and Social Supports*. New York: Wiley.

Furman, W., & Bierman, K. (1983). Developmental changes in young child's conception of friendship. *Child Development, 54*, 549–556.

Furman, W., & Buhrmester, D. (1987). *Developmental changes in children and adolescents' perceptions of their social network*. Unpublished paper, University of Denver.

Furman, W., Rahe, D. F., & Hartup, W. W. (1979). Rehabilitation of socially withdrawn preschool children through mixed-age and same-age socialization. *Child Development, 50*, 915–922.

Garmezy, N. (1971). Vulnerability research and the issue of privacy prevention. *American Journal of Orthopsychiatry, 41*, 101–116.

Goldsmith, H. H., & Campos, J. J., (1982). Toward a theory of infant temperament. In R. N.

Emde & R. J. Harmon (Eds.), *The development of attachment and affiliative systems* (pp. 161–193). New York: Plenum.

Gottman, J., Gonzo, J., & Rasmussen, B. (1975). Social interaction, social competence, and friendship in children. *Child Development, 45,* 709–718.

Harlow, H. F. (1969). Age-mate or peer affectional system. In D. S. Lehrman, R. A. Hende, & E. Shaw (Eds.), *Advances in the study of behavior* (Vol. 2, pp. 333–383) New York: Academic Press.

Harlow, H. F., & Harlow, M. D. (1965). The affectional systems. In A. M. Schrier, H. F. Harlow, & F. Stollnitz (Eds.), *Behavior of nonhuman primates* (Vol. 2, pp. 287–334). New York: Academic Press.

Hartup, W. W. (1983). Peer relations. In E. M. Hetherington (Ed.), & P. H. Mussen (Series Ed.), *Handbook of child psychology: Vol. 4. Socialization, personality, and social development* (pp. 103–196). New York: Wiley.

Hartup, W. W., Glazer, J. A., & Charlesworth, R. (1967). Peer reinforcement and sociometric status. *Child Development, 38,* 1017–1024.

Hoyt, M. P., & Raven, B. H. (1973). Birth order and the 1971 Los Angeles earthquake. *Journal of Personality and Social Psychology, 28,* 123–128.

Hunter, F. T. (1985). Adolescents' perceptions of discussions with parents and friends. *Developmental Psychology, 21,* 433–440.

Hunter, F. T. & Youniss, J. (1982). Changes in functions of three relationships during adolescence. *Developmental Psychology, 18,* 806–811.

Jacobsen, J. L. & Wille, D. E. (1986). The influence of attachment patterns on developmental changes in peer interaction from the toddler to the preschool period. *Child Development, 57,* 338–347.

Jacobsen, J. L., Wille, D. E., Tianen, R. L., & Aytch, D. M. (1983, March). *The influence of infant-mother attachment on toddler sociability with peers.* Paper presented at the biennial meeting of the Society for Research in Child Development, Detroit.

Kagen, J. (1982). *Psychological Research on the Human Infant: An Evaluative Summary.* New York: William T. Grant Foundation.

Kagen, J., & Moss, H. A. (1962). *Birth to maturity.* New York: Wiley.

Kandel, D. (1978). Homophily, selection and socialization in adolescent friendships. *American Journal of Sociology, 84,* 427–436.

Ladd, G. W., Hart, C. H., Wadsworth, E. M., & Golter, B. S. (1988). Preschoolers' peer networks in nonschool settings: Relationship to family characteristics and school adjustment. In S. Salzinger, J. Antropes, & M. Hammer (Eds.), *Social network of children, adolescents and college students* (pp. 61–92). Hillsdale, NJ: Lawrence Erlbaum.

Lamb, M. E., Easterbrooks, M. A., & Holden, G. W. (1980). Reinforcement and punishment among preschoolers: Characteristics, effects, and correlates. *Child Development, 51,* 1230–1236.

Lamb, M. E., & Roopnarine, J. L. (1979). Peer influences on sex-role development in preschoolers. *Child Development, 50,* 1219–1222.

Lerner, J. V., & Lerner, R. M. (1983). Temperament and adaptation across life: Theoretical and empirical issues. In P. B. Baltes & O. G. Brim, Jr. (Eds.), *Life-span development and behaviors* (Vol. 5). New York: Academic Press.

Lewis, M. (1979, October). *Developmental principles and educational practice.* Paper presented at the invited 1979 Pickering Lecture sponsored by the Department of Psychology, Carleton University, Ottawa, Canada.

Lewis, M. (1980). Self-knowledge: A social cognitive perspective on gender identity and sex role-development. In M. E. Lamb & L. R. Sherrod (Eds.), *Infant social cognition: Empirical and theoretical considerations* (pp. 395–414). Hillsdale, NJ: Lawrence Erlbaum.

Lewis, M., & Feiring, C. (1978). The child's social world. In R. M. Lerner & G. B. Spanier

(Eds.), *Child influences on marital and family interaction: A life-span perspective* (pp. 47–69). New York: Academic Press.

Lewis, M., & Feiring, C. (1979). The child's social network: Social object, social functions and their relationship. In M. Lewis & L. Rosenblum (Eds.), *The genesis of behavior. Vol. 2: The child and its family* (pp. 9–28). New York: Plenum.

Lewis, M., & Feiring, C. (1981). Direct and indirect interactions in social relationships. In L. Lipsitt (Ed.), *Advances in infancy research* (Vol. 1, pp. 131–161). New York: Ablex.

Lewis, M., & Feiring, C. (1987). Some American families at dinner. In L. Laosa & I. Sigel (Eds.), *Families as learning environments for children* (pp. 115–145). New York: Plenum.

Lewis, M., & Feiring, C. (in press). Maternal, infant and mother-infant interaction behavior and subsequent attachment. *Child Development*.

Lewis, M., Feiring, C., & Kotsonis, M. (1984). The social networks of the young child. In M. Lewis (Ed.), *Beyond the dyad* (pp. 129–160). New York: Plenum.

Lewis, M., Feiring, C., McGuffog, C., & Jaskir, J. (1984). Predicting psychopathology in six year olds from early social relations. *Child Development, 55,* 123–136.

Lewis, M., & Rosenblum, L. (1974). Introduction in M. Lewis & L. Rosenblum (Eds.), *The effect of the infant on its caregiver: The origins of behavior* (Vol. 1, pp. xv–xxiv). New York: Wiley.

Lewis, M., & Rosenblum, L. (1975). Introduction in M. Lewis & L. Rosenblum (Eds.), *Friendship and peer relations: The origins of behavior,* (Vol. 4, pp. 1–9). New York: Wiley.

Lewis, M., & Schaeffer, S. (1981). Peer behavior and mother-infant interaction in maltreated children. In M. Lewis and L. A. Rosenblum (Eds.), *Genesis of behavior: Vol. 3. The uncommon child* (pp. 193–224). New York: Plenum.

Lewis, M., & Weinraub, M. (1976). The father's role in the child's social network. In M. Lamb (Ed.), *The role of the father in child development* (pp. 157–184). New York: Wiley.

Lewis, M., & Weinraub, M. (1979). Origins of early sex role development. *Sex Roles, 5* (2) 135–153.

Lewis, M., Young, G., Brooks, J., & Michalson, L. (1975). The beginning of friendship. In M. Lewis & L. Rosenblum (Eds.), *Friendship and peer relations: The origins of behavior,* (Vol. 4, pp. 27–66). New York: Wiley.

Maccoby, E. E., & Jacklin, C. N. (1978). *The psychology of sex differences*. Stanford, CA: Stanford University Press.

Marshall, H. R., & McCandless, B. R. (1957). Relationships between dependence on adults and social acceptance by peers. *Child Development, 28,* 413–419.

Macfarlane, J. W. (1963). From infancy to adulthood. *Childhood Education, 39,* 336–342.

McDevitt, S. C., & Carey, W. B. (1978). The measurement of temperament in 3–7 year old children. *Journal of Child Psychology and Psychiatry, 19,* 245–253.

Miller, N., & Maruyama, G. (1976). Ordinal position and peer popularity. *Journal of Personality and Social Psychology, 33,* 123–131.

Moore, R., & Young, D. (1978). Child outdoors: Toward a social ecology of the landscape. In I. Altman & J. F. Wohlwill (Eds.), *Children and the environment* (pp. 83–130). New York: Plenum.

Murray, H. A. (1938). *Explorations in personalities*. New York: Oxford University Press.

Novak, M. A., & Harlow, H. F. (1975). Social recovery of monkeys isolated for the first year of life: Rehabilitation and therapy. *Developmental Psychology, 11,* 453–465.

Parke, R. D., & Bhavnagri, N. P. (in press). Parents as manager of children's social relationships. In D. Belle (Ed.), *Children's social networks and social supports*. New York: Wiley.

Pastor, D. L. (1980, April). *The quality of mother-infant attachment and its relationship to toddlers' initial society*. Paper presented at the International Conference of Infant Studies, New Haven.

Pastor, D. L. (1981). The quality of mother-infant attachment and its relationship to toddlers' initial sociability with peers. *Developmental Psychology, 17,* 326–335.

Piaget, J. (1952). *The origins of intelligence in children.* New York: International Universities Press.

Power, T. G., & Parke, R. D. (1983). Patterns of mother and father play with their 8 month old infant: A multiple analyses approach. *Infant Behavior and Development 6,* 453–459.

Rothbart, M. K., & Derryberry, D. (1981). Development of individual differences in temperament. In M. Lamb & A. Brown (Eds.), *Advances in Developmental Psychology* (Vol. 1, pp. 37–77). Hillsdale, NJ: Lawrence Erlbaum.

Schachter, S. (1964). Birth order and sociometric choice. *Journal of Abnormal and Social Psychology, 68,* 453–456.

Sells, B., & Roff, M. (1963). Peer acceptance—rejection and birth order. *American Psychologist, 18,* 355.

Selman, R. L. (1981). The child as a friendship philosopher: A case study in the growth of interpersonal understanding. In S. R. Asher & J. M. Gottman (Eds.), *The Development of Children's Friendships* (pp. 242–272). Cambridge, UK: Cambridge University Press.

Serbin, L. A., Tonick, I. J., & Sternglanz, S. H. (1977). Shaping cooperative cross-sex play. *Child Development, 48,* 924–929.

Shumaker, S. A., & Brownell, A. (1984). Toward a theory of social support: Closing conceptual gaps. *Journal of Social Issues, 40,* 11–36.

Snow, M. E., Jacklin, C. N., & Maccoby, E. E. (1981). Birth-order difference in peer sociability at thirty-three months. *Child Development, 52*(2), 589–595.

Sullivan, H. S. (1953). *The interpersonal theory of psychiatry.* New York: Norton.

Suomi, S. J., & Harlow, F. (1972). Social rehabilitation of isolate-reared monkeys. *Developmental Psychology, 6,* 487–496.

Sutton-Smith, B. (1976). Current research and theory in play, games and sports. In T. Craig (Ed.), *The humanistic and mental health aspects of sports, exercise and recreation.* Chicago, IL: American Medical Assoc.

Thomas, A., Chess, S., & Birch, H. G. (1968). *Temperament and behavior disorders in children.* New York: New York University Press.

Tietjen, A. M. (1982). The social networks of preadolescent children in Sweden. *International Journal of Behavioral Development, 5,* 111–130.

Waters, E., Wippman, J., & Sroufe, L. A. (1979). Attachment, positive affect, and competence in the peer group: Two studies in construct validation. *Child Development, 50,* 821–829.

Watson, M. W., & Fischer, K. W. (1980). Development of social roles in elicited and spontaneous behavior during the preschool years. *Developmental Psychology, 16,* 483–494.

Weinraub, M., & Frankel, J. (1977). Sex differences in parent-infant interaction during free play, departure and separation. *Child Development, 48,* 1240–1249.

Werner, E. Z., & Smith, R. S. (1982). *Vulnerable but invincible.* New York: McGraw-Hill.

Whiting, B. B., & Whiting, J. (1975). *Children of six cultures: A psychocultural analysis.* Cambridge, MA: Harvard University Press.

Whiting, D. B. (1980). Culture and social behavior: A model for the development of social behavior. *Ethos, 2,* 95–116.

Youniss, J. (1980). *Parents and peers in social development: A Sullivan-Piaget perspective.* Chicago, IL: The University of Chicago Press.

Zajonc, R. B. (1968). Attitudinal effects of mere exposure. *Journal of Personality and Social Psychology Monographs, 9,* 1–27.

CHAPTER 10

Families and Peers

Another Look at the Nature-Nurture Question

DAVID C. ROWE

University of Arizona

Children display a tremendous variation in their peer relations, from children who are virtually friendless to peer leaders who have many friends. The popular child often possesses an array of traits, in areas such as sociability and group entry skills, that is quite distinct from the array possessed by the unpopular child. The origin of these individual differences is an important topic for research, both as a theoretical issue in understanding social development and as a basis for implementing social interventions to help unpopular children. Most research on childhood peer relations has been descriptive, uncovering behavioral differences without evaluating theories about their development. When theories of origin are advanced, they usually emphasize environmental factors—such as social learning models. Fewer theories explicitly recognize genetic factors as contributing to individual differences in peer relations.

In this chapter, I advocate considering genetic factors in our theories of the development of peer relations. The chapter has two disparate purposes. First, I have in view educating peer relations researchers about behavior genetic goals and methods. Because these goals and methods are novel to many researchers, the initial sections briefly summarize them. The sections are intended only to whet the appetite for tasting some offerings of behavior genetics—not to cover the full range of possibilities (for more extended reviews, see Ehrman & Parsons, 1981; Hay, 1985; Plomin, DeFries, & McClearn, 1980). In the next section, I will outline two environmental views of the origin of peer relations: socialization in the family or in the peer group. Following this section, I will discuss how genetic factors might produce confounds in the typical study of peer relations.

Nancy Mergler's helpful comments for improvement of this chapter are gratefully acknowledged. The twin research on physical attractiveness was supported by a grant from the Research Council of the University of Oklahoma.

My second purpose is to review, from a behavior genetic perspective, studies of sociometric status. Topics covered include between- and within-family variation in sociometric status and a survey of the inheritance of statuses' trait correlates. The final section will review implications of the behavior genetic approach for designing effective social interventions.

GOALS OF BEHAVIORAL GENETICS

As a field, behavior genetics has roots reaching back into the 19th century, when Sir Francis Galton invented the twin study method and first argued for the genetic causes of traits leading to great intellectual and social accomplishment. Since Galton's founding contributions, one goal of behavior genetics has been studying the genetic architecture of behavior—the degree to which it is heritable, the particular type of genetic variation underlying behavioral variation (for example, the number of genes, the degree of genetic dominance), and the structure of genetic and environmental relations among traits. Less appreciated, though, is that behavior geneticists are also concerned with environmental influences that may be responsible for familial resemblances. A most recent advance in behavior genetics is adding to the analysis of potential genetic influences an analysis of potential environmental influences shared by family members and environmental influences not shared by them, as I will discuss shortly.

Behavior geneticists have done little work on the familial determinants of sociometric status. Instead, most work has been directed toward dissecting the factors influencing personality traits and IQ. It is conceptually clearer to analyze the inheritance of traits, rather than of social statuses, because the former are properties of individuals that are measurable without observing the individual in a particular social context. In contrast, from the start, peer relations researchers have been interested in studying the sociometric statuses of individuals embedded in their social context. The goals are also disparate. Peer relations researchers have had an interest, as well, in designing social interventions for unpopular and rejected children. Behavior genetics does not share this same applied orientation of making changes in social relations. Workers in the latter field seek the causes of natural variation in behavior. Hence, the behavior genetic approach will appeal most to those researchers interested in theoretical questions of developmental origin and causation and will appeal less to the scientists and practitioners with social intervention goals in mind.

What can behavior genetics contribute to peer relations research? First, there is the issue of whether peer relations originate in family environmental influences, especially in the environmental variance that exists between families differing in social class and in child-rearing styles. Methodologies from behavior genetics can help supply an answer. Second, sociometric statuses appear to arise partly from preexisting behavioral differences among children, some of which can be summarized in terms of trait labels. Hence, behavior genetic work on traits bears on the origin of sociometric status types (e.g, popular, rejected), because children may acquire a status partly because of their trait dispositions. To draw these lines of thought together, the demonstrated presence of genetic influence on many behaviors means that it should never be ignored. It therefore seems reasonable to consider heredity in studies of peer relations or in studies of other social contextual behaviors that may not be obviously viewed as heritable traits.

BEHAVIORAL GENETIC METHODS

One point that is often confusing is that behavior genetic studies analyze individual differences (Plomin, DeFries, & McClearn, 1980). Hence, traits that almost everyone exhibits—like language acquisition or reflexes—can be genetic in origin without serving as a place of departure for a behavior genetic study. The genes that determine such traits are possessed by virtually everyone; indeed, many genes can occur in only one form—though people will possess two of the nonvarying genes—one inherited from their fathers and the other from their mothers. Without genetic variation, the only individual differences, of course, are the ones that are environmentally induced. On the other hand, some genes exist in multiple forms and so can produce different traits depending on which combination of form(s) has been inherited.

The individual difference perspective also allows for some separation of environmental and genetic influences. Although it is undeniable that both factors must be present for any trait to develop, variation among individuals can come about predominately because of one or the other influence, or by some additive or nonadditive interactive processes between the two. Most physical appearance traits, such as height and skin color, have a high *heritability,* meaning that the individual differences in them owe primarily to genetic differences among individuals and not to family environments or to other environmental factors that vary in a population. A hypothetical contrasting example is that dress styles may depend more on environmental influence, both familial, such as discretionary income to purchase expensive or inexpensive clothing, and nonfamilial, such as cohort-specific clothing fads.

In behavior genetics, we analyze trait variation into theoretical components that can account, in mathematical models of observed individual differences, for all variations of a particular type. Measured environmental factors might be a stronger or weaker contributory cause to one theoretical component but not another.

One theoretical component, the *shared* environment, represents the total environmental influence that operates to make family members similar to one another. The idea of shared environmental influences has a natural linkage with many of the variables studied in child development. Economic level, father-absence, child-rearing styles, divorce, and other environmental differences between families have received the attention of thousands of studies. Between-family variation for such shared environmental influences is usually large, whereas children within a family may receive approximately equal exposure to them. Therefore, these shared environmental factors can be conceptualized as exerting effects that will increase sibling (or parent-child) resemblance.

The *nonshared* environment refers to environmental influences operating on each family member independently. Nonshared and shared factors are defined as uncorrelated. The variation is within families and is not the same from one sibling to another. Rowe and Plomin (1981) gave a convenient listing of examples of nonshared environmental influences. These examples are presented in Table 10.1, along with examples of shared influences. The apportionment, as just described, demonstrates the power of behavior genetics methodology to delineate "how" environmental influences act on behavioral development, instead of only "how much" trait variation is environmental or genetic.

The hereditary component of variation refers to the additive and non-additive effects of particular gene combinations on a trait. Except for identical twins, heredity will cause resemblance and difference among relatives.

TABLE 10.1.   Shared and Nonshared Environmental Influences

Shared	Nonshared
Divorce	Accidental factors
Absence of father	Teratogenic agents
Religion	Physical illness
Social class	Perinatal trauma
Child-rearing styles	Separation
Maternal employment	Family structure
Family size	Birth order
Parental age	Sibling spacing
Parental mental illness	Sibling differential
	Interaction
	Sibling identification
	Sibling deidentification
	Parental treatments
	Unequal treatments
	Interactions of parent-child traits
	Extrafamilial influences
	Peer groups; relatives; teachers; television

Note. Examples show anticipated predominate effect of different measured variables in terms of nonshared and shared theoretical components of variation.

Shared heredity is the 50% of genes siblings have in common. They explain resemblance. *Nonshared* heredity is the 50% of noncommon genes, creating differences in behavioral traits. Genetic theory makes quantitative predictions of trait correlations for different degrees of biological kinship.

To demonstrate the applicability of this methodology, I first consider, in general terms, how variance components can be estimated using research designs involving siblings. Table 10.2 shows methods that might be used in peer relations research.

Shared environmental influences (Table 10.2, III) can be investigated using the twin method, or more directly, using adoptive siblings. The latter children have different biological parents so that their genotypes are unrelated except for selective placements (a matching of the traits of the adoptive and biological parents). Methods of handling selective placement, which is sometimes a problem for IQ but rarely for other traits, are discussed elsewhere (Plomin et al., 1980). Because genetic resemblance is absent, phenotypic (i.e., measured trait) resemblance must arise from the shared environment in adoptive families. Hence, if we had sociometric status scores for adoptive siblings, then the sibling correlation would be the percent of status variation due to shared-family environment. No squaring of the correlation is done because the latent causes—shared factors—are a theoretical variable explaining the observed variation (see Ozer, 1985).

Nonshared environment can be assessed by differences within pairs of related or unrelated individuals. For example, suppose within-pair differences in sociometric statuses were compared for the two types of twins. Equal within-pair variances might be found—implying environmental causation (see Table 10.2 IV). However, if genetic effects are also present, then

TABLE 10.2.   Univariate Behavioral Genetic Research Designs

Type of Influence	Type of Component	
	Shared (pair correlation)	Nonshared (within-pair variance)
Heredity	Identical twins > Fraternal twins	Fraternal twins > Identical twins
	I	II
	Nonadoptive siblings > Adoptive siblings	Adoptive siblings > Nonadoptive siblings
Environment	Identical twins = Fraternal twins	Identical twins = Fraternal twins
	III	IV
	Adoptive siblings > Zero	Nonadoptive siblings = Adoptive siblings

Note. In a twin study, heritability, $h^2 = 2(r_{MZ} - r_{DZ})$. In a twin study, shared environment = $r_{MZ} - h^2$. h^2, heritability; r, correlation coefficient. MZ, identical twins, DZ, fraternal twins.

the within-pair fraternal twin differences should be somewhat greater than within-pair identical twin differences (see Table 10.2, II).

In Quadrant I, genetic influences are estimable from comparing kinships differing in biological relatedness. For example, identical twins should be more alike than fraternal twins because the former have twice the genetic resemblance of the latter. This comparison is often criticized on the grounds that identical twins receive more similar treatment than fraternal twins. However, there is now empirical research that suggests that those identical twins who receive more twin-unique treatments (identical clothing, same teachers in school, effort on part of parent to treat alike) were not made more alike in personality or IQ scores (Loehlin & Nichols, 1976). Other supportive evidence was summarized by Rowe (1984).

Other assumptions of twin and adoptive studies are discussed in behavior genetic textbooks. In general, small departures from them will not greatly distort the standard interpretations of behavior genetic studies (see Plomin et al., 1980).

More sophisticated behavior genetic methods rely on fitting equations to statistics (correlations, mean squares) from different kinship relationships using maximum likelihood procedures (Eaves, Last, Young, & Martin, 1978; Fulker, 1981). These fits can be evaluated using a chi-square statistic of goodness-of-fit. Although the details are beyond this scope of this chapter, some understanding of behavior genetic modeling procedures can be gleaned from the two equations that follow. They express twin correlations in terms of the sum of independent *shared* environment (c^2) and heredity (h^2) components:

$$\text{Identical twins:} \quad ri = h^2 + c^2$$

$$\text{Fraternal twins:} \quad rf = 1/2h^2 + c^2$$

Using these equations, the classical twin method is to solve for h^2 (heritability) and c^2 (shared environment). For example, if, for sociometric status, the identical twin correlation was .65 and the fraternal twin correlation, .55, then inheritance would explain 20% of the variation in status ($h^2 = .20$) and shared family environment, 45% ($c^2 = .45$). *Nonshared* environment can account for the remainder (35%; $1 - ri = .35$). In this example, the solution was exact because the number of equations and unknown parameters were the same. In general, when certain other statistics are used (that is, mean squares), the number of equations will exceed the number of parameters to be estimated, leaving degree of freedom for evaluating the goodness-of-fit.

Although such model fitting is an excellent way to analyze behavior genetic data, the basic information is implicit in the raw correlations obtained in a study. Shared environmental effects imply an identical twin correlation that is *less* than double the fraternal twin one; the inference of genetic inheritance requires a significant difference between them. The logic of adoptive/nonadoptive comparisons is shown in Table 10.2.

The Analysis of Bivariate Relationships

Another direction in behavior genetic research is decomposing the relationship between two traits into genetic and environmental components. For instance, shyness and emotionality are positively correlated (Buss & Plomin, 1984). This phenotypic relationship might be so decomposed. Some subset of genes might influence developmentally both traits—a genetic component of trait correlation. Specific experiences, or developmental accidents, may affect both traits. They can be classified as belonging to the nonshared environmental component.

As shown in Figure 10.1, a path diagram can be employed to conceputalize the relationship between two traits. It is possible to correlate x and y through a genetic pathway containing genetic regression weights (h_x, h_y) and the genetic correlation of the traits (r_g). This would be 1.0 if the genes influencing one trait were exactly the same as those influencing the other; it would be zero if none of the genes was common to the two traits. Notice that in this latter example, both traits could be heritable, but their correlation could be entirely an environmental one. The other pathway is through nonshared environmental regression weights (e_x, e_y) and the correlation of these environments (r_e). Although shared environmental factors are not shown in Figure 10.1, they could be added as another source of correlation between x and y. More technical discussions of the analysis of multivariate relation-

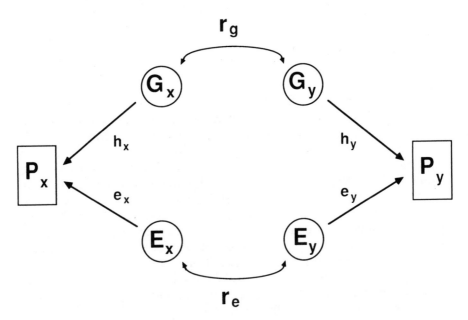

Figure 10.1. Phenotypic correlation between traits x and y decomposed into environmental (E) and genetic (G) pathways.

ships appear in DeFries and Fulker (1986), Plomin and DeFries (1979), and Rowe (1986).

Mechanisms of Genetic Influence

Behavioral genetic studies suggest that about 50% of the variation in personality test scores is due to genetic variation (Goldsmith, 1983; Rowe & Plomin, 1981). We do not know, however, for most heritable traits the mechanisms by which different genotypes produce different behavior outcomes. Jencks (1987) cautioned that even genetic variation could have a strongly environmental interpretation if the behavioral differences among people came about by a process of social response to the direct effect of genes on physical appearance traits. His example of the X and Y sex-determining chromosomes explaining variation in hair length exaggerates the point that in some situations genetic variation is not a cause but is merely a correlate of behavioral (hair length) variation. As Jencks remarked, ". . . if some social scientist read a study showing that genes explained 60 percent of the variation in hair length, he would be an even greater fool to conclude, as many do now, that environmental influence explained only 40 percent" (p. 34).

Although Jencks' example may be applicable to some traits, for most behavioral traits, the mechanism of influence is probably through genetic control over the structure and physiology of the brain, which is identified as the anatomical origin of behavior. Multiple, widely disparate lines of research exist that clearly link variance in neurophysiology with variance in behavior. Certainly, we can find a host of neurophysiological differences among animal lines selected by breeding programs for behavioral differences (Fuller & Thompson, 1978). In their chapter in the *Annual Review of Psychology,* Wimer and Wimer (1985) concluded that genetically controlled morphological characteristics of the mouse brain were responsible for inherited differences in learning rates. Among inbred mouse lines, learning score means correlated .97 with the density of mossy fiber synapses in a particular brain region. In humans, nonmedicated schizophrenics appear to have an excess number of neurotransmitter receptors in certain brain areas (Wong et al., 1986). In the research of Kagan and his colleagues (Kagan, Reznick, Clarke, Snidman, & Garcia-Coll, 1984), high and stable heart rates in cognitively demanding situations have differentiated socially inhibited and uninhibited children. The explosion of new techniques in the neurosciences will undoubtedly increase our knowledge of the specific biological mechanisms by which genotypes lead to differences in behavior.

In this regard, multivariate genetic analyses are useful. Instead of correlating two behavioral traits, a behavioral trait can be correlated with some physiological marker (e.g., evoked potentials, hormone levels, CAT scans). The genetic correlation between them can establish whether the marker has weak or strong genetic effects on the trait. Using this procedure, marker traits could be screened in a search for the biological underpinnings of behavior.

MODELS OF THE ORIGIN OF PEER RELATIONS

Family Socialization

Peer relation qualities may depend on the kind of interaction style children have learned through previous interactions with their parents. The idea that familial socialization determines the quality of peer relations has been given different names. Berndt (1983) called it the continuity position, referring to the relationship that would be anticipated between the style or quality of parent-child relations and those of child-peer relations. Lamb and Nash (this vol., Chap. 8) called it the "maternal precursor" view, which captures the idea that later peer relationships are based on earliest parent-infant ones that may have taught a child different modes of social interaction.

What empirical support do we have for these hypotheses, which can be jointly labeled the familial hypothesis? One common idea among peer relations researchers is that different patterns of child rearing can give rise to different behavioral traits in children which, in turn, can affect their peer relations (Furman & Buhrmester, 1982; Hartup, 1983; Putallaz & Heflin, 1987). Child-rearing styles can be classified into a two-dimensional framework of social power (undemanding versus demanding styles) and social warmth (accepting versus rejecting styles; Maccoby & Martin, 1983). Associations among these styles and children's personality traits could be interpreted as effects of the family on peer relations as well (see examples in Table 10.3). In one study (Putallaz, 1987), observations of mother-child and child-peer social interactions also confirmed a linkage between the two contexts for social behavior.

Statements of this position also appear in reviews of the peer relations literature. Rubin and Sloman (1984) offered a modeling explanation for shyness in family and in peer relations:

> We suspect that modeling (of parent-adult friend) relationships often contribute to such (child-peer) resemblances, as children observe their parents' modes of interacting with others and adopt some of those modes in their own interactions. (p. 243)

According to Rubin and Sloman, conceivable ways in which parents might influence their children's peer relations include (a) providing a "secure base," (b) teaching or coaching them about peer relations directly (i.e., telling a child not to choose someone as a friend), (c) acting as role models, (d) "setting the stage" by creating a context for peer interactions (e.g., purchasing a house in a middle-class neighborhood), and (e) arranging for activities with the children's peers. In their model of potential parental con-

TABLE 10.3. Child-Rearing Styles and Personality Traits Classified by Social Warmth and Social Power

Social Power	Social Warmth	
	Accepting Responsive Child centered	Rejecting Unresponsive Parent centered
Demanding	AUTHORITATIVE Social competence with peers (leadership, approach and initiation, friendliness, social maturity)	AUTHORITARIAN Lack of social competence with peers (aggressiveness, withdrawal, low initiation)
Undemanding	INDULGENT Lack of social competence with peers (low impulse control, social immaturity, dependence, aggressiveness)	NEGLECTING Lack of social competence with peers (low ego control, hedonism, antisocial peer groups, early sexual development)

Note. Descriptions drawn from Maccoby and Martin's (1983) account of the correlates of each child-rearing type. The table refers to average differences among children belonging to the different classifications of parenting types. These relationships are only probabilistic and do not imply that socially mature and well-adjusted children could not be found for each classification.

tributions to peer relations, Putallaz and Heflin (1987) distinguished between four mechanisms of "direct" influence, namely, modeling, operant conditioning, classical conditioning, and coaching; and mechanisms of "indirect" influence in which parents create a setting for child-peer interactions without controlling the specific behaviors in which their children engage.

Capturing the spirit of all the family-based theories of child-peer relations, Hartup, in his review in the *Handbook of Child Development,* concluded:

> Considerable support thus exists for the theory that the child's relations with its parents provide emotional and instrumental bases for success in peer relations. (1983, p.168)

Peer Socialization

Other theories emphasize the independent contribution peer groups can make to a child's socialization. Most frequently, the peer group is seen as an influence opposing the family, the primary example being the adolescent gang that rewards violence and immediate gratification rather than the adult values of nonviolence and delayed gratification. Most peer researchers now agree that this picture is an overstatement (Hartup, 1983). The delinquent, in particular, seems to be alienated from his family (Hirschi, 1969) so that the family has lost influence before the delinquent group takes over. Nevertheless, peer relations researchers defend the idea that the peer group is determining the development of a child's enduring traits: "It is difficult to believe, however, that trouble with contemporaries does not contribute its own variance to the etiology of psychopathology" (Hartup, 1983, p. 167).

Theories of peer socialization often cite the different structure or function of peer relations as opposed to parent-child relations. In comparison with parent-child relations, peer relations imply less initial difference in power and authority, which can lead to the acquisitions of reciprocity norms, equality norms, and cognitive role-taking skills (Piaget, 1932/1965; Youniss, 1980). Acquisition of such skills is necessary for maintaining equalitarian friendships and perhaps also for maintaining more general social relations in the peer group.

Another type of peer group socialization occurs when peers compensate for deficiences in family relations. Sullivan (1953) thought that emotional security and support unique to peer relations could replace emotional support that was absent from the family. In a way, this theory is a direct challenge to the "family socialization" view expressed earlier because it implies that damage to social development presumably inflicted in the family need not carry over into peer relations. As Berndt (1983) noted:

> Can friendships be a corrective for difficulties created by inadequate parenting? The question is important because an affirmative answer would be contradictory to theories that emphasize continuities in the development of interpersonal relationships. (p. 27)

We have seen here that conceptions of connections of parent-child and child-peer relations can grow more complex. The possibility of peer compensation for deficits of familial socialization describes an independence of peer and family influence most unlike that of the "opposing contexts" view initially proposed. At the same time, the two contexts may be interdependent, with the tendencies induced by family socialization reinforced or augmented by further learning in the peer context. Most peer relations researchers recognize to some extent this potential for complexity, a situation in which it is difficult indeed to derive clear hypotheses concerning the direction of peer group effects.

Genetic Confounds

Today, neither extreme environmentalism, such as "radical behaviorism," nor extreme genetic determinism is accepted widely in the scientific community. Most scholars would be willing to concede behavior as a joint function of genetic and environmental influences.

But what does granting even a partial genetic component mean for studies of peer relations? As mentioned previously, family relations might carry over to some degree into peer relations. Any such bivariate relationship may be partly explained by a "third variable" originally ignored—in this case, inherited behavioral dispositions. For example, a child might be sociable with his parents and also sociable with peers because of the inheritance of genes predisposing toward sociability (see Buss & Plomin, 1984). The same traits might have developed even if the child was given up for adoption and thus not exposed to the same kind of family experience. Overlapping heredity can also account for the greater sociability of the parents with their own adult peers. Phenotypes can be matched simply because genotypes are incidentally matched. Lamb and Nash's (this vol., Chap. 8) general sociability hypothesis for individual differences in infant attachment could be given this kind of inherited-disposition interpretation. Buss and Plomin (1984) argued that the temperaments of sociability and emotionality could be the origin of secure, resistant, and avoidant attachment types (but see Sroufe, 1985, for a rejoinder to theories reducing attachment to temperament).

Adoption studies suggest this kind of genetic confounding is a profound problem. In the Colorado Adoption Project (Plomin, Loehlin, & DeFries, 1985), associations were found among family environment and infant behavior measures. In nonadoptive families, the mean of 10 such environment-child "behavior problem" correlations was .23. In a matched group of adoptive families, however, the mean for the same set of relationships was statistically nonsignificant ($r = .07$). For several temperamental traits, the corresponding correlations were .20 and .06 in nonadoptive and adoptive families, respectively. One of the family environment measures—the Family Environments Scale's Personal Growth Factor—assessed aspects of typical interaction styles among family members. About three fourths (.36) of its relationship with temperamental traits, the authors concluded, was mediated genetically and only one fourth (.13) was mediated environmentally. Thus, children's behavior seems to correlate with family relations in large part because genes produce such associations incidentally. For IQ, about half the relationship between family environment and children's IQs was mediated genetically. Conceptualizations of the "family environment" refer, in reality, to characteristics of parental behavior—which can depend on genetic differences among parents as much as any other behavioral trait.

In the same vein, I found that adolescents' perceptions of parental acceptance-rejection were heritable (Rowe, 1983). Correlations of identical twins' reports of acceptance-rejection were greater than those of fraternal twins, which were about equal to those of nontwin siblings. This study could not determine whether genetic influence on these perceptions was the result of siblings reacting differently to similar parental treatments or of siblings eliciting from their parents different treatments depending on their genotypes. However, one lesson that can be drawn is that for environmental effects on many behaviors to be easily understood, genetic variation must be first partialed from them.

Genetic variation also can confound the analysis of peer socialization. The socializing functions of the peer group may operate either without regard to children's genotypes, or they may depend to some extent on genotypic differences.

In the latter case, genotypes will to some degree be associated with differences in children's peer relations and peer relations will show some degree of familial transmission. It is noteworthy that peer relationships could be unrelated to parent-child ones but still show a degree of inheritance. This outcome could occur if the genes that influence peer relations were different from those influencing parent-child ones. In this circumstance, siblings alone would show similarities in their peer relations due to shared heredity. In summary, genetic inheritance can potentially affect the continuity of family relations to peer relations (the "third variable" hypothesis) and also the discontinuities in family relations to peer relations (genetic systems subserving aggressive or sexual development, as expressed only in the peer group).

BETWEEN FAMILY VARIATION AND SOCIOMETRIC STATUS

Are sociometric statuses transmitted in families by genetic or shared environmental mechanisms? To address this question, we need data on the sociometric statuses of biological relatives. Such data were collected in a multisite study of sociometric status (Roff, Sells, & Golden, 1972). These researchers found that opposite- and same-sex siblings, in Grades 3–6, were significantly correlated for classroom-based popularity scores ($r = .24$, $r = .31$, sample sizes about 2,000 pairs). The slightly lower value of the opposite-sex correlation suggests that some factors affecting status were different in the two sexes, or that method artifacts existed (peer nominations were within-sex). Given these data alone, we can conclude that about 30% of the variation of boys' or girls' sociometric statuses can be explained by either genetic or environmental *shared* family factors.

Fortunately for resolving shared variance into genetic and environmental effects, there were also data on twins. In agreement with the correlation of opposite-sex siblings, unlike-sex twins correlated .27. This finding means that there was nothing unusual about twinship insofar as opposite-sex pairs were concerned. The same-sex fraternals, however, presented a striking discrepancy. They were about 40% more alike than siblings ($r = .52$, $N = 78$).

The greater fraternal twin resemblances in status can be interpreted in several ways. As peer nominators were used, a halo effect might have exaggerated the twins' resemblance because they were known to some of the same raters. Identical twins in the same classrooms were rated "somewhat" more alike than identical twins in different classrooms—but the authors did not seem to think this was a major source of bias. Age itself could be a source of their greater resemblance in sociometric status. Siblings can be different because of age-paced developmental changes; if assessed at the same age (but in different years), they might have resembled each other as much as did the fraternal twins. Most likely, both explanations hold some truth.

Under assumptions of the twin method, sociometric status was heritable. Doubling the correlational difference between identical and fraternal twins (.70–.52) yields a heritability estimate of about 36%; taking this value from the identical twin correlation gives 34% of variation as shared environmental. This shared component was unusually large for a twin study (see Rowe & Plomin, 1981). Hence, a replication would be desirable. It should examine if shared method variance had inflated either the fraternal or identical twin correlations. Another test of shared environment would be a replication using adoptive siblings. As mentioned previously, the adoption study is an excellent way to assess shared family environment using adoptive siblings with small age separations.

WITHIN FAMILY VARIATION AND SOCIOMETRIC STATUS

If peer groups actively socialize children so that they develop different traits, we might expect nonshared environmental factors to appear in the analysis of sibling differences. For example, Bill, despite relatively warm and loving parents, may have antisocial friends and be influenced by them. His brother, John, may associate with a different set of friends, who have weak antisocial inclinations. The influence of these two peer groups would serve to increase the difference between Bill and John, acting in behavior genetics terminology as a "nonshared" environmental factor. On the other hand, given the many ways genotypes could also contribute to sibling differences, nonshared genetic factors might also be involved in producing these sibling differences. For example, genetically based IQ differences could be one reason for the two brothers choosing such different peer groups.

The idea that peer groups are potentially different worlds for siblings receives some empirical support. In a survey study of teenage pregnancy risk, I asked college students and their siblings whether they joined in the activities of friends together. Table 10.4 presents responses to this question. As the table shows, a majority of brothers (52%), sisters (66%), and opposite-sex siblings (75%) reported having never or infrequently (<25% of the time) joined siblings in activities with friends. In another study, 37% of adolescent siblings reported having peer groups that were "similar," 42% reported "a bit of difference," and 20% reported "much difference" (Daniels & Plomin, 1985). By way of contrast, their perceptions of parental treatments suggested greater equality of treatment in the home than in the peer group: 57% rated parental treatment as "similar," 35% rated it as "a bit of difference," and 9% rated it as "much difference."

TABLE 10.4.   Frequency of Siblings Joining Together in Activities with Friends

Response	Brothers (%)	Sisters (%)	Opposite Sex (%)
Almost always	13	5	3
75% of time	15	9	5
50% of time	19	21	17
25% of time	31	35	40
Almost never	21	31	35
N	105	182	168

Note. The subjects were white, unmarried college students and their siblings, 15–29 years of age.

Two studies have looked at within-family differences in peer relations using the innovative approach of correlating sibling differences in peer relations with their differences in personality and behavior (Daniels, 1986; Daniels, Dunn, Furstenberg, & Plomin, 1985). Although their dependent variable was not sociometric status, I included them here because of their relevance to familial effects on statuses—for example, a dependent variable of belonging to an antisocial peer group might be related to lower social status in regard to all peers. Another general point about the two studies is that they offer an example of multivariate behavior genetic analysis, with a focus on within-family differences.

In the Daniels et al. (1985) study, 384 families with adolescent (11–17 years) children were surveyed to be representative of the United States population. Short behavioral scales completed by parents and teachers were used to assess adjustment (e.g., emotional distress, delinquency, disobedience). To look for unshared effects, differences within the sibling pairs, that is, the signed difference scores taken on two variables, were intercorrelated. Sibling differences in friendliness to peers were associated with adjustment differences, namely, with parental ratings of delinquency, emotional distress, and disobedience. The less friendly sibling scored more unfavorably (relative to the brother or sister) on these adjustment ratings. Siblings' self-reports of sociability predicted their adjustment in much the same way. Despite these positive results, the direction of cause and effect among the characteristics measured was unclear. In addition, nonshared heredity could be a common factor determining lack of friendliness to peers and the adjustment traits.

Daniels (1986) has made a pioneering effort to resolve the genetic and environmental components of sibling differences. Her sample consisted of 50 biological and 98 adoptive sibling pairs, mostly late adolescent and young adult. The outcome variables were six temperamental traits (anger, fear, distress, activity, sociability, shyness), expected education, and expected occupation. The siblings answered SIDE (Sibling Differential Experience

Inventory) scales about the relative similarity of their peer groups. *Relative similarity* refers to the procedure of making a judgment that was a comparison to the sibling, not to people in general. For example, both siblings might belong to antisocial peer groups—in comparison to the average—but they still could perceive a large relative difference between their friends. In turn, peer group similarity was correlated against signed within-pair differences on the outcome variables.

Sibling pairs who said they belonged to more different types of peer groups had greater differences in personality scores. These differences were also directional, for instance, the sibling in the less delinquent peer group (relative to the brother or sister) was more fearful. The following relationships were found: anger negatively with peer college orientation; fear negatively with peer delinquency; sociability positively with peer popularity; and expected education and occupation positively with peer college orientation. Because the relationships were about the same size for adoptive and biological sibling pairs (r^2 = .06–.26), Daniels concluded that the SIDE ". . . goes beyond the genetic makeup of individual family members to assess nonshared environmental influences" (p. 345).

In spite of the confidence voiced in this conclusion, Daniels's study leaves some important questions unanswered. Was the lack of greater biological than adoptive sibling resemblance partly the result of the use of a relative scale of sibling difference? The measures also dealt with siblings' perceptions of their peer relations. A next step would be to obtain data on the siblings' actual peer relations. It is important to pursue peer group norms and pressures as a particular nonshared environment determining behavioral differences among siblings (and, therefore, among individuals in general).

TRAITS AND SOCIOMETRIC STATUS

In an earlier section, I presented evidence of genetic influences on a peer-nomination measure of sociometric status. A reasonable inference is that the traits that influence sociometric outcomes are themselves genetically influenced. According to Hartup (1983), "No single trait is of over-riding importance in determining children's popularity with peers" (p. 126). Hence, variation in sociometric status must represent some kind of averaging of shared environmental and nonshared environmental genetic components in the related traits. For convenience, it is useful to distinguish two kinds of trait correlates (McConnell & Odom, 1986). One set consists of stable features of the child that are relatively unchangeable: sex, race, names, physical attractiveness, and mental retardation. Also belonging in this category are body type and rate of physical maturation. The other set consists of behavioral traits that are more open to situational influences and more malleable.

Evocative Genotype-Environment Effects

Several stable features can be conceptualized as influencing sociometric status through an evocative genotype-environment effect because ". . . the child receives from others responses that are influenced by his genotype" (Scarr & McCartney, 1983, p. 427). In other words, these stable features are highly heritable; they elicit from peers predictable favorable or unfavorable social reactions, which, in turn, help to establish sociometric status. I believe that several stable features which are individual difference factors are appropriately viewed in these terms: body type, physical attractiveness, and mental retardation. The same analysis could be made for rates of pubertal maturation. Age of menarche, the development of secondary sexual characteristics, and growth spurts are all heritable (Fischbein, 1977a; 1977b). According to Petersen and Taylor (1980, p. 143), however, "There is substantial inconsistency between the results of various studies . . . regarding the relationship of pubertal maturation and peer acceptance." Given this inconsistency, I do not regard pubertal stage as an important determinant of sociometric status.

Shaffer (1979) reviewed the small literature on body-build and peer status. The studies all used Sheldon's (1940) classification of body types into muscular (mesomorphic), lanky and thin (ectomorphic), and overweight (endomorphic). In elementary school children, mesomorphs were higher in status and also received more positive trait attributions than either ectomorphs or endomorphs. Ironically, in adolescence, the correlates of a mesomorphic build are no longer so favorable; muscular builds are overrepresented in groups of delinquents (Wilson & Herrnstein, 1985).

An unanswered issue is whether body-build effects reside largely in social reactions to the builds themselves or to behavioral differences associated with the build (athletic ability, dominance, assertiveness). If temperamental differences induce body-build effects, then this might account for the changing correlates of body-build from the preteen to the teenage years, assuming dominant and assertive preteens sometimes become delinquent teenagers. For example, Ellis (1986) hypothesized that the mesomorphy-antisocial behavior association is a result of sex hormones, because male hormones can alter both target nerve and target muscle cells. The former could affect temperament; the latter, body build. On the side of genetic determination, both height and weight are highly heritable. Although genetic studies of Sheldon's classifications have not been undertaken, we can be fairly sure that genotypic differences account for a considerable portion of the variation in body types in the American population (body building may transform the 90-pound weakling into a stronger person, but does not necessarily change the way fat and muscle tissue are distributed throughout the body). In sum, body-builds seem to produce evocative effects, but how this happens is by no means clear.

In elementary school, facially attractive children receive more peer acceptance than others (Hartup, 1983; McConnell & Odom, 1986). Hartup noted that this effect was stronger for peers' reports of their friends' attractiveness than for adult judgments, a difference he attributed to a halo effect, whereby friends attribute an excess of positive traits to one another. The attractiveness-status relationship may be somewhat stronger and more consistent in females than in males (McConnell & Odom). In addition, according to Hartup's review, attractiveness biases trait attributions so that more attractive children are seen as more sociable and as better prospects for friends. More than any other trait possessed by individuals, facial attractiveness is a coin that can be exchanged for social status.

Although perceptions of beauty are partly in the "eye of the beholder," beauty also resides in facial features representative of middle-class American culture. In a study of female faces, Cunningham (1986) presented data that a set of discrete facial features were associated with perceptions of attractiveness; namely, more attractive faces had higher and wider eyes, greater distance between eyes, a smaller nose area and more prominent cheekbones. These associations accounted for more than half the variance in attractiveness. The facial features satisfied the hypothesis that female beauty is greatest in faces retaining immature, infantlike features and containing other, mature features. Given these results, it is unsurprising that facial attractiveness scores are temporally stable during childhood and adulthood (Adams, 1977; Sussman, Mueser, Grau, & Yarnold, 1983), possibly cross-culturally universal (Cunningham, 1986), and heritable.

In one twin study, a panel of college students rated 25 pairs of identical twins' facial attractiveness from photographs (raters saw just one of the twins and did not know they were rating twins; Rowe, Clapp, & Wallis, 1987). Identical twins' attractiveness scores correlated .54, and corrected for unreliability, .94. These figures are especially impressive because 68% of the twins were judged to have dissimilar dress and 24% dissimilar hair styles. As it turns out, heritable facial features make a major contribution to perceived attractiveness and thus to sociometric status.

Another interpretation of the physical attractiveness-status relationship is possible. It may be that more attractive individuals possess better social skills than other individuals, so that it is their skills rather than their appearance which accounts for their higher social status. The literature addressing this hypothesis is rather small, because most studies look at traits *attributed* to the attractive instead of at their actual traits. Some modest correlations do exist, however, between greater emotional instability and unattractiveness (Rowe et al. 1987). In addition, one study (Dodge, 1983), taking children at sociometric extremes, found that social behavioral differences could account statistically for status differences between those children who were physically attractive and unattractive.

What mechanisms could produce a cross-association of attractiveness and behavioral traits? One possibility is that unattractive children fail to learn proper social skills because they are shunned or harassed by other children.

Another possibility is that the association is the result of a *genetic* correlation imposed by nonrandom mating in parental generations. Briefly, if attractive individuals are able to marry spouses with positive personality traits—causing a spouse correlation among traits and facial appearances—then the genes for physical feature traits will become correlated with those determining personality traits. Hence, in individuals, both set of characteristics also will become phenotypically correlated. A similar mate-selection process could explain, for instance, why a taller height is weakly associated with higher IQs. A sibling study design can be used for evaluating a mate-selection hypothesis (Rowe et al., 1987). The genetic consequences of mate selection can be used to illustrate the subtlety with which heredity can potentially affect behavior—and our conclusions from research studies.

Mental handicaps are also a source of lowered peer status. Handicapped children are less often named as friends than other children and their poor status remains stable even as peer group membership changes (McConnell & Odom, 1986). In the two-group theory of mental retardation (Nichols, 1984), one genetic source of mental handicap is simply inheriting many genes unfavorable to high IQ—that is, positioning at the low end of the many genetic factors influencing intelligence. Another group of children is affected by a large number of specific genetic factors, such as chromosomal abnormalities (e.g., fragile X, Down's syndrome), that can create severe mental retardation. Retarded children are unable to acquire normal facility with the complexities of social interaction, and they are disliked by peers. These may be causal relationships. Hence, genetic factors produce retardation, which in turn, evokes low social status.

BEHAVIORAL TRAITS AND SOCIOMETRIC STATUS

Peer researchers have identified behavioral traits associated with sociometric status, whereas behavior geneticists have attempted to identify which traits are heritable. Any overlap between the two sets of classifications could be used to determine which status-relevant traits are genetically influenced and which are not. A lack of correspondence could point to new areas for investigation. Identifying points of correspondence, however, is made difficult by the use of different measures in the two fields. Concepts used in only one domain of research may be usefully employed within the other domain; the operationalization of any particular concepts within both domains should be made equivalent. In particular, the concepts of athletic, temperamental, and cognitive traits should be carefully measured. Each concept may contribute some genetic component to sociometric status and at least the two latter concepts have been found to be largely independent.

Considering athletic skills, it is apparent that athletic accomplishment and sociometric status are highly associated. Eitzen (1975) replicated parts of Coleman's (1961) famous survey of American high schools. He showed once again that the primary determinant of status in adolescent male groups was athletic success. At much younger ages, motor skills are also important (Hops & Finch, 1985). In a sample of 2½–6-year-olds, general motor co-ordination—based on a series of physical tests—explained 20% (for girls) and 14% (for boys) of the variance in teacher ratings of social competence and 12% (for girls) and 9% (for boys) of that in peers' ratings for popularity and friendships. Age was factored out of these analyses. A remarkable finding was that motor skills predicted social competence better than social skill scores based on classroom observations. Behavior geneticists have not in-vestigated the genetic components of physical coordination (Plomin, 1986). This neglect seems to be a result of lack of interest, because most people readily assume a partly genetic basis to physical skill differences. However, in light of its strong relationship with social status, it is imperative to include motor skills as a source of heritable variation.

Heritable traits can be aligned with sociometric differences. Hymel and Rubin (1986) are among a number of observers of peer research to notice regular behavioral correlates of children that are assigned to different status groupings. They describe the rejected child as aggressive and socially active, and as displaying behaviors that might foreshadow later externalizing dis-orders like delinquency. In contrast, the neglected child is portrayed as shy and socially hesitant; his or her future might be one of an internalizing disorder like depression. Popular children engage in cooperative play more than other children—they seem to have a strong interest in social interaction (Dodge, 1983).

Based on these profile sketches, it would seem that neglected children, beyond their mere overt behavior, probably have inherited a more neurotic disposition. Indeed, recent descriptions of neglected children emphasize their cognitive appraisal of social situations, as much as any overt behavior. Rubin (1985) wanted to learn about the fate of socially neglected children as they moved from preschool into elementary school. To this end, his Waterloo Longitudinal Study observed neglected children in kindergarten through third grade. A number of results were surprising. First, although neglected kindergarten children were deficient in social knowledge, by third grade they had acquired this knowledge to the same extent as others. Second, they were not actively disliked by peers. If these children possessed knowl-edge about social behavior and, at least at these ages, could have entered into the peer group without an automatic rebuff, what caused their hesitation? These children, according to Rubin ". . . *felt* that they were unpopular and socially incompetent" (italics in original, p. 133). Although Rubin speculated that these self-perception biases had resulted from some unknown factors in early socialization, the genetic data suggest otherwise. No specific family-socialization experiences are required for individual differences in neuroti-cism to be manifest (see for example, Shields, 1962, data on twins raised apart, as reanalyzed by Fulker, 1981).

The popular child may inherit high levels of extraversion and sociability.

Buss and Plomin (1984) defined as one component of sociability the re-wardingness of social exchanges with others; if this is strong, a powerful motivation exists to enter into cooperative play and to seek friends. Of course, many other factors must be present to assure popularity, such as appropriate social skills, athletic ability, and physical attractiveness, as was suggested previously.

There is difficulty finding proof for heritable components to the rejected status. Rejected children are usually characterized as more aggressive and antagonistic than other children. In a group entry study, aggressive children were 10 times more likely than other children to disrupt the group (Dodge, Schlundt, Schocken, & Delugach, 1983). On the playground, they engage in more rough-and-tumble play and get into more arguments (Ladd, 1983). The usefulness of prior behavior genetic data is not great, because few studies deal explicitly with aggressive behaviors, especially in childhood. Some suggestive evidence does exist, however. Delinquency may have a partly genetic basis (Rowe & Osgood, 1984). One study indicates that adult aggres-sion—as assessed by questionnaire—has a genetic basis and no shared en-vironmental basis (Rushton, Fulker, Neale, Nias, & Eysenck, 1986). In childhood, aggressive conduct disorder is associated with increased rates of psychopathology in biological but not adoptive parents (Jary & Stewart, 1985). Further genetic work on the rejected child, and on aggression in childhood, is sorely needed.

In the intellectual domain, IQ is a heritable trait that affects social status. Over a decade ago, Roff, Sells, and Golden (1972) found that IQ was a correlate of popularity—and that this relationship held, controlling for levels of socioeconomic status of children's parents. A number of recent studies have shown that popular and unpopular children differ in the knowledge of what is the correct response to make in social situations (Hymel & Rubin, 1986). To develop social knowledge requires extracting from the complex and ambiguous information of daily social encounters certain insights into motives and also requires adopting a nonegocentric frame of reference. Un-doubtedly, a higher IQ aids this kind of learning. Peer researchers in general, however, have not controlled for IQ in their studies of social knowledge. It would be desirable to have evidence of IQ-independent effects of social knowledge.

CHANGING SOCIOMETRIC STATUS

Many peer researchers are interested in the problem of improving the social statuses of unpopular or rejected children. Genetic interpretations of be-havior are often seen as an obstacle to such efforts at social change because they imply to many scholars a notion of a fixed genotype and a predetermined behavioral outcome.

A reasonable reply from behavior geneticists—who probably feel a bit on the defensive—is that a "reaction range" exists for any genotype. The relationship between genotype and behavioral outcome is always probabilistic, so that the notion of a fixed, immutable set of traits determined at conception is simply wrong. Although this statement is true, it is also something of a platitude. After all, in the abstract everyone can agree with it—the hard question is how much latitude will be seen for a specific trait over a range of environmental conditions. In other words, a debate solved in theory often resumes for real-life examples.

In regards to sociometric status, one way to evaluate the potential of a social intervention is to use the partition of environmental influences into shared and nonshared ones. Any time a behavior genetic study produces a large *shared* component of environmental variation, data on families can be used to identify the effective environmental factors. Families with poorer rearing outcomes can be advised to adopt the rearing methods, teaching methods, or daily routines of those families with the better outcomes. Hence, it is discouraging that most behavior genetic studies reveal small or no shared environmental components in nonintellectual trait variation—that is, (biologically unrelated) children raised together are no more alike than children raised in different families (Goldsmith, 1983; Rowe & Plomin, 1981). The manner of raising, within the range of family environmental variation from normal working class to professional class, will not assure a more negative or more positive outcome in children's behavior. This generalization also seems to apply to the lack of pathogenic *shared* family environmental effects on deviant conditions such as alcoholism and schizophrenia. On the other hand, it may be that sociometric status is an exception—Roff et al.'s twin study, discussed earlier, did reveal a shared environmental component of variation in sociometric status.

About 50% of the variation in personality traits is due to nonshared environmental influences. Because it is difficult to put one's finger on the exact factor producing the nonshared component of variation, the latter gives the social engineer less of a guide as to possible methods of intervention. In addition, efforts to find identifiable and regular genotype × environment interactions for IQ and personality have failed (Plomin, 1986), although attempts to find them will certainly continue. In part because of these problems, experimental methods will remain the most appropriate means of assessing the potential of social interventions, where the existence of genetic variation does not prove that a particular intervention will fail or succeed.

CONCLUSIONS

The prospects for joining behavior genetics and peer relations research are good if researchers adopt the approach of controlling for genetic influences while they seek the quarry of environmental ones. The sibling study can be used to apportion individual differences to family background effects and nonfamily effects; the adoption study to assess *shared* family environmental effects; and more complicated research designs to apportion variation into genetic, shared environmental, and nonshared environmental components. Multivariate behavior genetic analysis might reveal which traits contribute most to individual differences in peer statuses—and can further apportion a correlation into its genetic and environmental components. The sociometric status of peer researchers in the scientific community may itself increase in proportion to the insightful borrowing of the methods of behavior genetics for the exploration of issues of concern to peer relation researchers.

REFERENCES

Adams, G. R. (1977). Physical attractiveness research: Toward a developmental social psychology of beauty. *Human Development, 20*, 217–239.

Berndt, T. J. (1983). Peer relationships in children of working parents: A theoretical analysis and some conclusions. In C. D. Hayes & S. B. Kamerman (Eds.), *Children of working parents: Experiences and outcomes* (pp. 13–43). Washington, DC: National Academy Press.

Buss, A. H., & Plomin, R. (1984). *Temperament: Early developing personality traits*. Hillsdale, NJ: Lawrence Erlbaum.

Coleman, J. S. (1961). *The adolescent society: The social life of the teenager and its impact on education*. New York: Free Press.

Cunningham, M. R. (1986). Measuring the physical in physical attractiveness: Quasi-experiments on the sociobiology of female beauty. *Journal of Personality and Social Psychology, 50*, 925–935.

Daniels, D. (1986). Differential experiences of siblings in the same family as predictors of adolescent sibling personality differences. *Journal of Personality and Social Psychology, 51*, 339–346.

Daniels, D., Dunn, J., Furstenberg, F. F., Jr., & Plomin, R. (1985). Environmental differences within the family and adjustment differences within pairs of adolescent siblings. *Child Development, 56*, 764–774.

Daniels, D., & Plomin, R. (1985). Differential experience of siblings in the same family. *Developmental Psychology, 21*, 747–760.

DeFries, J. C., & Fulker, D. (1986). Multivariate behavioral genetics and development. *Behavioral Genetics, 16*, 1–10.

Dodge, K. A. (1983). Behavioral antecedents of peer social status. *Child Development, 54*, 1386–1399.

Dodge, K., Schlundt, D., Schocken, I., & Delugach, J. (1983). Social competence and children's sociometric status: The role of peer group entry strategies. *Merrill-Palmer Quarterly, 29*, 309–336.

Eaves, L. J., Last, K. A., Young, P. A., & Martin, N. G. (1978). Model-fitting approaches to the analysis of human behavior. *Heredity, 41*, 249–320.

Ehrman, L., & Parsons, P. A. (1981). *Behavior genetics and evolution*. New York: McGraw-Hill.

Eitzen, D. S. (1975). Athletics in the status system of male adolescents: A replication of Coleman's The Adoelscent Society. *Adolescence, 10*, 267–276.

Ellis, L. (1986). *Criminality as an evolved form of victimizing behavior: An evolutionary-neurohormonal theory*. Unpublished manuscript.

Fischbein, S. (1977a). Intra-pair similarity in physical growth of monozygotic and dizygotic twins during puberty. *Annals of Human Biology, 4,* 417–430.

Fischbein, S. (1977b). Onset of puberty in MZ and DZ twins. *Acta Geneticae et Med. Gemellol., 26,* 151–158.

Fulker, D. W. (1981). The genetic and environmental architecture of psychoticism, extraversion, and neuroticism. In H. J. Eysenck (Ed.), *A model of personality* (pp. 88–122). New York: Springer-Verlag.

Fuller, J. L., & Thompson, W. R. (1978). *Foundations of behavior genetics.* St. Louis: C. V. Mosby.

Furman, W., & Buhrmester, D. (1982). The contribution of peers to the parenting process. In M. J. Kostelnik, A. I. Rabin, L. A. Phenice, & A. K. Soderman (Eds.), *Child nurturance: Patterns of supplementary parenting* (Vol. 2, pp. 69–100). New York: Plenum.

Goldsmith, H. H. (1983). Genetic influences on personality from infancy to adulthood. *Child Development, 54,* 331–335.

Hartup, W. W. (1983). Peer relations. In E. M. Hetherington (Ed.) & P. H. Mussen (Series Ed.), *Handbook of child psychology: Vol. 4. Socialization, personality, and social development* (pp. 103–196). New York: Wiley.

Hay, D. (1985). *Essentials of behavior genetics.* Melbourne, Australia: Blackwell.

Hirschi, T. (1969). *Causes of delinquency.* Berkeley: University of California Press.

Hops, H., & Finch, M. (1985). Social competence and skill: A reassessment. In B. H. Schneider, K. H. Rubin, & J. E. Ledingham (Eds.), *Children's peer relations: Issues in assessment and intervention* (pp. 23–39). New York: Springer-Verlag.

Hymel, S., & Rubin, K. H. (1986). Children with peer relationships and social skills problems: Conceptual, methodological, and developmental issues. In G. J. Whitehurst (Ed.), *Annals of child development* (Vol. 3), Greenwich, CT: JAI Press.

Jary, M. L., & Stewart, M. H. (1985). Psychiatric disorder in the parents of adopted children with aggressive conduct disorder. *Neuropsychobiology, 13,* 7–11.

Jencks, C. (1987, February 12). Genes and crime. *New York Review of Books,* pp. 33–41.

Kagan, J., Reznick, J. S., Clarke, C., Snidman, N., & Garcia-Coll, C. (1984). Behavioral inhibition to the unfamiliar. *Child Development, 55,* 2212–2225.

Ladd, G. W. (1983). Social networks of popular, average, and rejected children in school settings. *Merrill-Palmer Quarterly, 29,* 283–307.

Loehlin, J. C., & Nichols, R. C. (1976). *Heredity, environment, and personality: A study of 850 sets of twins.* Austin: University of Texas Press.

Maccoby, E. E., & Martin, J. A. (1983). Socialization in the context of the family: Parent-child interaction. In E. M. Hetherington (Ed.) & P. H. Mussen (Series Ed.), *Handbook of child psychology: Vol 4. Socialization, personality, and social development* (pp. 1–101). New York: Wiley.

McConnell, S. R., & Odom, S. L. (1986). Sociometrics: Peer-referenced measures and the assessment of social competence. In P. S. Strain, M. J. Guralnick, & H. M. Walker (Eds.), *Children's social behavior: Development, assessment, and modification* (pp. 215–284). New York: Academic Press.

Nichols, P. L. (1984). Familial mental retardation. *Behavior Genetics, 14,* 161–170.

Ozer, D. J. (1985). Correlation and the coefficient of determination. *Psychological Bulletin, 97,* 307–315.

Petersen, A. C., & Taylor, B. (1980). The biological approach to adolescence. In J. Adelson (Ed.), *Handbook of adolescent psychology* (pp. 117–155). New York: Wiley.

Piaget, J. (1965). *The moral judgment of the child.* New York: Free Press. (Original work published 1932)

Plomin, R. (1986). *Development, genetics, and psychology.* Hillsdale, NJ: Lawrence Erlbaum.

Plomin, R., & DeFries, J. C. (1979). Multivariate behavior genetic analysis of twin data on scholastic abilities. *Behavior Genetics, 9,* 505–517.

Plomin, R., DeFries, J. C., & McClearn, G. E. (1980). *Behavioral genetics: A primer.* San Francisco: W. H. Freeman.

Plomin, R., Loehlin, J. C., & DeFries, J. C. (1985). Genetic and environmental components of "environmental" influences. *Developmental Psychology, 21,* 391–402.

Putallaz, M. (1987). Maternal behavior and children's sociometric status. *Child Development, 58,* 324–340.

Putallaz, M., & Heflin, A. H. (in press). Parent-child interaction. In S. R. Asher & J. D. Coie (Eds.), *Children's status in the peer group.* New York: Cambridge University Press.

Roff, M., Sells, S. B., & Golden, M. M. (1972). *Social adjustment and personality development in children.* Minneapolis: University of Minnesota Press.

Rowe, D. C. (1983). A biometrical analysis of perceptions of family environment: A study of twin and singleton sibling kinships. *Child Development, 54,* 361–368.

Rowe, D. C. (1984). Environmental and genetic influences on behavioral development. In N. S. Endler & J. McVicker Hunt (Eds.), *Personality and the behavior disorders* (Vol. 1, pp. 479–510). New York: Wiley.

Rowe, D. C. (1986). Genetic and environmental components of antisocial behavior: A study of 256 twin pairs. *Criminology, 24,* 513–532.

Rowe, D. C., Clapp, M., & Wallis, J. (1987). Physical attractiveness and the similarity of identical twins. *Behavior Genetics, 17,* 191–201.

Rowe, D. C., & Osgood, D. W. (1984). Heredity and sociological theories of delinquency: A reconsideration. *American Sociological Review, 19,* 526–540.

Rowe, D. C., & Plomin, R. (1981). The importance of nonshared (E_1) environmental influences in behavioral development. *Developmental Psychology, 17,* 517–531.

Rubin, K. H. (1985). Socially withdrawn children: An "at risk" population? In B. H. Schneider, K. H. Rubin, & J. E. Ledingham (Eds.), *Children's peer relations: Issues in assessment and intervention* (pp. 125–139). New York: Springer-Verlag.

Rubin, Z., & Sloman, J. (1984). How parents influence their children's friendships. In M. Lewis (Ed.), *Beyond the dyad* (pp. 223–250). New York: Plenum.

Rushton, J. P., Fulker, D. W., Neale, M. C., Nias, D. K. B., & Eysenck, H. J. (1986). Altruism and aggression: The heritability of individual differences. *Journal of Personality and Social Psychology, 50,* 1192–1198.

Scarr, S., & McCartney, K. (1983). How people make their own environments: A theory of genotype–environment effects. *Child Development, 54,* 424–435.

Shaffer, D. R. (1979). *Social and personality development.* Monterey, CA: Brooks/Cole.

Sheldon, W. H. (with collaboration of S. S. Stevens & W. B. Tucker). (1940). *The varieties of human physique.* New York: Harper.

Shields, J. (1962). *Monozygotic twins brought up apart and together.* London: Oxford University Press.

Sroufe, L. A. (1985). Attachment classification from the perspective of infant-caregiver relationships and infant temperament. *Child Devlopment, 56,* 1–14.

Sullivan, H. S. (1953). *The interpersonal theory of psychiatry.* New York: Norton.

Sussman, S., Mueser, K. T., Grau, B. W., & Yarnold, P. R. (1983). Stability of females' facial attractiveness during childhood. *Journal of Personality and Social Psychology, 44,* 1231–1233.

Wilson, J. Q., & Herrnstein, R. J. (1985). *Crime and human nature.* New York: Simon & Schuster.

Wimer, R. E., & Wimer, C. C. (1985). Animal behavior genetics: A search for the biological foundations of behavior. *Annual Review of Psychology, 36,* 171–218.

Wong, D. R., Wagner, H. N., Jr., Tune, L. E., Dannals, R. F., Pearlson, G. D., Links, J. M., Tamminga, C. A., Broussolle, E. P., Ravert, H. T., Wilson, A. A., Toung, T., Malat, J., Williams, J. A., O'Tuama, L. A., Snyder, S. H., Kuhar, M. J., & Gjedde, A. (1986). Positron emission tomography reveals elevated D_2 dopamine receptors in drug-naive schizophrenics. *Science, 234,* 1558–1563.

Youniss, J. (1980). *Parents and peers in social development.* Chicago: University of Chicago Press.

CHAPTER 11

Adolescents' Interpersonal Relationships in Social Context

JAMES YOUNISS AND JACQUELINE SMOLLAR
Catholic University of America

The aim of this chapter is to examine the question of the connections among adolescents' relationships with parents and peers from a perspective that incorporates the social context. Wertsch (1985), Ochs (1982), and others have argued that psychologists can gain from an understanding of the social context as governed by properties that become translated into psychological features. Such authors call for a close connection between psychological and sociological structures. In their view, the major question is not whether but how the sociological dimension is mediated. In this chapter we will examine what in fact might be gained by applying a consideration of sociological structures to an understanding of parent-adolescent and adolescent-peer relationships.

Psychologists have traditionally studied adolescents' relationships with parents and peers apart from the social context in which they occur. One approach has focused on the relative influence parents and peers have on the behaviors and attitudes of adolescents. In this approach, parents are assumed to be important in the socialization process insofar as they have knowledge of societally adaptive attitudes and actions. During adolescence, peers are seen as new sources of influence but with less awareness than adults of appropriate societal orientations. Research based on this perspective has examined the question of whether peers replace parents as major sources of influence during the adolescent era, and if so, at what point is peer influence the strongest (cf. Hartup, 1970; 1983).

Another, more recent, approach to this issue is based on the theoretical assumption that children are not passive participants in the influence process, but instead are active transformers of experiential events. Riegel (1976), Damon (1977), and others have pointed to the importance of dialogue and discussion through which concepts of reality are coconstructed. This viewpoint resulted in investigations of interpersonal interactions and the meaning given to these interactions by the participants.

In the late 1970s, the concept of relationship was added to this approach as a means for understanding sequences of interactions. Hinde (1979) defined "relationship" as recurrent forms of interacting that allow participants to make sense of the respective contributions. Among other things, this definition of relationship implies that persons usually enter into interactions with specific expectations and anticipations about one another's potential actions. In a relationship, then, persons come to interactions with a shared history which serves as a framework through which independent actions take on meaning (Cook-Gumperz & Corsaro, 1977; Garvey & Hogan, 1973).

The idea that relationships consist of recurrent forms of interacting suggests that they have a definite structure with an underlying dynamic (Furth, 1983; Youniss, 1980). It follows from this that relationships may be classifiable into particular types or forms, and that within particular types or forms, some interactions will have a higher likelihood of occurrence than others. The reason for this likelihood is not an incapacity for certain action potentials, but a structural limitation which is psychological in constitution.

What is missing from the work described above is an analysis of the social context in which adolescents' relationships with others exist. In the literature on influence, for example, although the main concern is with appropriate socialization for society, there is little consideration of the characteristics or features of society that the adolescent is being socialized into. Similarly, the research on interactions and relational conceptions has not considered the features of the social context that may mediate the forms that particular relationships take. In the remainder of this chapter, we will speculate on how a consideration of the social context may alter or enhance our understanding of parent-adolescent relationships in themselves, and how these relationships may be conjoined with adolescent peer relationships.

PARENT-ADOLESCENT RELATIONSHIPS

In our own studies, conducted over a period of 8 years, we examined adolescents' relationships with parents and friends using a variety of methodologies. Our particular concerns included the following: the interactions that characterized the relationships; the concept of self within the context of the relationships; the issues that caused conflicts in the relationships and how they were resolved; the topics of conversation that were taken up or avoided in the relationships; and the types of negotiation or cooperation strategies that characterized the relationships when differences of opinion arose.

The results of our studies are reported in detail elsewhere (Youniss & Smollar, 1985). One major finding, however, was that from the perspective of adolescents, their relationships with parents and peers were distinctly different in form. Not only did adolescents describe these relationships differently with respect to the kinds of characteristic interactions, but they also described themselves differently in the two relationship types. Similarly, the areas of conflict and the procedures for conflict resolution differentiated the two relationship forms, as did the common topics of conversation and the communication and negotiation styles.

In both parent-adolescent and friend relationships, adolescents' descriptions of all relational characteristics changed as a function of progression through the adolescent era. That is, preadolescents' (aged 11–12 years) descriptions differed from those provided by early and midadolescents (13–15 years), which, in turn, differed from those given by older adolescents (17–19 years) and young adults (20–24 years). However, in both relationship types, the developmental changes were always in the direction of increased awareness of self and other as individuals, and descriptions included interactions based on mutual respect concurrent with the recognition of individuality (Smollar & Youniss, 1982).

With respect to the parent-adolescent relationship, the differences among the age groups and the direction of change suggested that the parent-offspring relationship is not severed during the adolescent era, but is instead reconstructed from the form it had during the childhood years so that it becomes more appropriate for adolescence and impending adulthood. Support for this conclusion can be found in the work of several other researchers (cf. Waterman, 1981) and is consistent with the concept of individuation recently introduced as a means to understand development within parent-adolescent relationships (Cooper, Grotevant, & Condon, 1983; Grotevant & Cooper, 1986).

The process of individuation can be described as one in which both parents and adolescents work toward the separation of the adolescent as an individual while maintaining connections with one another based on mutual respect and consideration of individuality. The specific steps involved in this process include parental acceptance that adolescents may have independent ideas and opinions; adolescents' recognition that parents are fallible persons rather than paragons; joint movement toward mutuality in the sense of understanding as well as emotional concern; and evolvement of negotiation procedures that would enable much of the above to be accomplished (Hunter, 1984; White, Speisman, & Costos, 1983; see also Selman, Beardslee, Schultz, Krupa, & Podorefsky, 1986).

There is much support in the literature on adolescence for the idea that adolescents remain connected to their parents while seeking to separate themselves as individuals. From Brittain's (1963) work to the present, several investigators have reported that adolescents seek parents' advice on particular matters, for instance, choice of schooling or career (Wintre, Hicks, McVey, & Fox, 1988). Marcoen and Brumagne (1985) reported that parents were likely persons to whom adolescents would "go to speak" when depressed or unhappy. O'Donnell (1979) reported that black and white male and female adolescents felt "close" to their parents and as close to their mothers as to their close friends. Greenberg, Siegel, and Leitch (1983) reported an almost identical result with closeness being defined through items measuring attachment. Youniss and Ketterlinus (1987) found that male and female adolescents responded almost at the maximum in stating how close they felt to their mothers and their fathers. Hunter (1984) found that adolescents acknowledged that their mothers and fathers, as much as their friends, were sought out as persons who would verify questions and opinions.

These studies are not meant to imply that the parent-adolescent relationship is conflict free. In our studies, as well as in those of other researchers (cf. Fisher & Lisa-Johnson, 1987) adolescents at all age levels have had little difficulty generating descriptions of conflicts with their parents. However, these conflicts, rather than destroying the relationship, may instead serve as vehicles for change and reconstruction. In fact, a group of studies has helped to show more precisely the negotiation procedures that are used and developed through parent-adolescent verbal discussions. For example, observations of interactions suggest that when parents and adolescents express differing points of view, parents, while seeking conformity to the views they hold, encourage adolescents to assert their views. In addition, there appear to be numerous instances in which joint views are evolved through successive arguments (Bell & Bell, 1983; Cooper, Grotevant, & Condon, 1983; Powers, Hauser, Schwartz, Noam, & Jacobson, 1983; Zahaykevich, 1987).

In summary, we can conceptualize contemporary parent-adolescent relationships as involving both a movement toward separateness prior to adulthood and a simultaneous pull to remain connected to those persons one has come to love and on whom one has relied. This means that during adolescence there must be a considerable amount of parent-adolescent negotiation of a complex sort, such that adolescents can form views separate from those of their parents and yet, at the same time, make clear and justify these views to their parents. On the other side, parents need to permit adolescents freedom to separate themselves, while at the same time, communicating and reinforcing parental values and perspectives.

Parent-Adolescent Relationships in a Social Context

We would now like to add to this view of parent-adolescent relationships by speculating on the ways the interpersonal structure of the relationship may be conjoined with aspects of social structure. The basic assumption is not that social structure simply determines interpersonal relationships. Rather, we agree with Stinchcombe (1978) that the material structure is a grounding point from which persons then construct, at the psychological level, relationships with one another.

Gadlin (1978) has offered an insightful synthesis of a historical literature pertaining to the social-historical basis of changes in parent-child relationship styles. He tracked broad patterns of major groups, beginning in colonial New England with the Puritans, whose chief emphasis was on conformity to community standards. The Puritan context is understood to be that of a commonwealth (Demos, 1970) in which political and religious interests were synonymous and were given priority over individual interests. The apparent goal of socialization was to subjugate children to the will of God, who was represented by parents, in particular, the father. The line of authority from God to heads of families in the community was clearly stated in ideology as well as practice. Given this context, there is an inherent coherence in the demand that children obey their parents. Hence, practices such as those outlined by Greven (1977) may have fit a defunct social structure, but appear inappropriate for the present (for example, withholding food from a fifteen-month-old boy until he obeys his father, p. 39ff).

Skipping quickly to a more contemporary scene, Gadlin (1978) points out that for many present-day parents, establishing and maintaining a relationship with their adolescents—a relationship that has psychological force—has become a goal in itself, apart from economic or other pragmatic causes. He also notes that from a historical perspective such an approach to parenting is relatively new. There are a variety of complex reasons why contemporary parent-adolescent relationships may have this focus. The issues may be related to whether the family participates in a transcendent value system, how pluralistic a society is, and whether a family's orientation is conjoined with an economic reinforcement.

The economic realities of contemporary society as they pertain to parent-offspring relationships provide one source for a focus on the relationship as an end in itself. In the not-so-distant past, the parents' generation typically controlled resources that the children's generation needed to become economically independent. Today, it is more typical that the younger generation becomes self-sufficient while the older generation is able to sustain itself. Insofar as this is accurate, parents and offspring do not need each other for fundamental survival as may have been the case when the family's land was the only means for sons to begin their own economic functioning, and sons, in turn, incurred the responsibility to care for their surviving parents (Shorter, 1975).

Other aspects of contemporary society contribute to the focus that modern-day parents give to their relationships with their children. That mothers can now select the number and timing of births has important implications for their perceptions of the parenting role (Degler, 1980). In addition, the likelihood that many families have little in the way of tradition that they can pass on to offspring with the assurance that it will be of lasting value may shape the ways these relationships are viewed (Riesman, 1953). This is particularly important with respect to the passing on of parental occupation or the conveyance of economic assets (Sennett, 1974).

An additional factor is added by Degler's (1980) description of the demographic phenomenon of simultaneous adulthood in successive generations. In past generations, parents' relationships with their adult offspring were limited by the fact that the life expectancy was considerably shorter than it is today. Thus contemporary parents, unlike parents in the past, can expect many years of adult relationships with their offspring.

There are several implications of this analysis for the concept of individuation as a means to understand development within parent-adolescent relationships. We suggest that the steps through which parents and adolescents restructure their relationship are not arbitrary but are necessary for maintenance of the relationship in the present societal context. Once adolescents reach adulthood, they may not need the relation for survival purposes any more than parents need it. The act of sustaining it is voluntary to a degree and is a psychological prerequisite only if the parties view one another with mutual respect. For Gadlin (1978) social structure and relational structure come together through a long-term orientation, which is not necessarily conscious but tones the relationship throughout its history. During adolescence both parents and offspring seem to realize that the bond tendered for so many years may be severed soon and probably cannot be forced to continue. Lastingness must be consciously cultivated.

PARENT AND PEER RELATIONSHIPS

The question of how adolescents' relationships with parents are connected to their performances outside the home has been the subject of an extensive body of research (Cooper & Ayers-Lopez, 1985; Hartup, 1970; 1983). However, attempts to relate these performances have often had to face two major problems. One difficulty is that actions are often relationally specific, and therefore it is necessary to make adjustments in matching any type of action to any other (Hinde, Stevenson-Hinde, & Tamplin, 1985).

Another problem is that actions are given meaning depending upon the relationship in which they occur. For example, Eisenberg, Lundy, Shell, and Roth (1985) reported that even preschool children who met requests for help from other persons clearly distinguished reasons for helping adults from reasons for helping peers. The most common reason for helping adults was their authority, but for peers it was their "need." Similarly, in one of our studies adolescents frequently described themselves as "nice" or "considerate" when they were with both parents and friends. However, they added that they were nice when with their parents because it was expected of them or because they might get into trouble if they were not, but they were nice when with their friends because it made the friend feel better or because it strengthened their relationship.

These difficulties suggest that an understanding of how parent-adolescent relationships are conjoined to adolescent relations outside the home must be approached with caution. Perhaps this question may be most enhanced by considering the structures of the social context and how these structures have changed historically.

A HISTORICAL PERSPECTIVE.   Historical studies of European and North American life in the 18th and 19th centuries revealed patterns in which adolescents were almost always under the watchful eyes of adults (Gillis,

1981; Kett, 1977). For instance, most recreational time was spent with large groups comprised of mixed ages, singing, dancing, talking, and eating together. Even when youths were physically on their own, they were apparently acting within the adult framework, doing what their parents had done at the same age and having tacit approval from their parents (Shorter, 1975).

With the advent of the high school as we know it today—a place that gathered together youths by age rather than by social standing, religion, or interests—there was an increase in intergenerational spacing between adolescents and their parents. Lynd and Lynd's (1929) classic study of family life in *Middletown* in 1924 describes this phenomenon. The Lynds compared family life in Middletown of 1924 with that of Middletown of the later decades of the 19th century, focusing on the high school as the basis for change in the community.

In 1882, Middletown had 5 high school graduates, or one for each 1,110 persons. By 1924, there were 236 graduates, one for every 161 citizens. Still, in 1924 only 30% of all 16–17-year-olds were enrolled in school, with nonstudents usually employed and contributing to their own as well as their family's support (p. 185). While it was clear that parents in Middletown of 1924 understood schooling as a means by which their children were being prepared for the modern world, they were also aware that it created gaps between them and their children. As the Lynds stated it: "Nor can parental authority reassert itself as completely as formerly by the passing on of skills from father to son . . . nor do so many daughters learn cooking or sewing at their mothers' side; more than a few mothers interviewed said unhappily that their daughters fresh from domestic science in school, ridiculed the mothers' inherited rule of thumb practices as 'old-fashioned'" p. 133. Apparently, while schooling provided a bridge to the future, it simultaneously created a gap between youth and their parents by making parents seem out-of-date.

This same point is made in historical studies of Chicago during the last decades of the 19th century (Sennett, 1974) and of Hamilton, Ontario, for the same period (Katz, 1981). In all these cases, parents saw school as the medium that prepared their children for a world different from the one the parents had known. They accepted this circumstance, probably realizing that one consequence might be a generational split in interests and orientations.

School also contributed to intergenerational spacing by creating an environment in which youths interacted with one another independent of adult purview. The Lynds, for example, listed the clubs and teams that the high school era had spawned. They properly placed the listing under "social life" to emphasize that adolescents were beginning to experience socializing events outside the aegis of their parents. These clubs gave institutional legitimacy to peer association that was distinct from the kind of legitimization that would have been achieved had adults been part of the ongoing experiences.

The Lynds' report is similar to Hollingshead's study, *Elmtown's Youth*

(1949). One of his major points is that the high school is the principal institution the culture has developed for helping youth define themselves as adolescents in making the transition from children to adults (pp. 148–149). He notes further that youth groups, clubs, and other such institutions segregate adolescents from knowledge about the inner workings of adult society. Hollingshead attributes these facts to adolescents having lost their traditional roles in the economic sphere as wage earners, apprentices, and the like.

Although these studies support the notion that the advent of the high school contributed to intergenerational spacing between adolescents and their parents, this fact appears to have been generally accepted by parents as necessary for the preparation of their offspring for the type of society they were going to enter as adults. It also appears that the advent of the high school in the first half of the 20th century provided the opportunity for greater social-class mixing than could have occurred prior to development of this institution. However, it is less clear that social-class mixing actually occurred during this historical period.

Hollingshead (1949) looked carefully at the teenagers of Elmtown when they were in, as well as outside, school. One of his strongest findings was that youths were segregated from each other along sharp class lines. This was true in terms of youths who were students in contrast to those who had withdrawn from student status. It was also true for the kind of course curriculum taken by the students. It was true further for membership in cliques, whose structure almost all the youths could identify. And it was true again with respect to recreational choices. Finally, the ubiquitousness of class is illustrated by Hollingshead's finding regarding friendship. When asked to specify best friends, students nominated only others who were from the same class groupings.

Both in and out of school, then, the adolescents of Elmtown kept within their social-class grouping. Adolescents with the same or similar backgrounds associated primarily with one another and had little contact with peers from other class groups. One implication of this finding is that peers were operating with one another from a common base, which they shared with their parents. Parents did not need to be physically present to affect behavior and attitudes. The common outlook that class membership promotes may have been sufficient to guarantee that adolescents, when acting outside the purview of their parents, were likely to duplicate the values and attitudes of their parents because of implicitly shared class structure. Class in this sense refers not only to economic position in the community but also to commonality in education, religion, and the like.

Thus, in the first half of the 20th century, adolescents began to separate from their parents with respect to increased association with their peers and in terms of preparation for a world that was different than the one their parents had known. At the same time, youths maintained the values of their parents within their peer associations, and whatever the peers coconstructed in their relationships was, as a result, fairly consistent with their parental orientations. Parents generally accepted their offsprings' associations with peers with little concern for negative consequences.

PARENTS VERSUS PEERS.   In the 1950s, however, there was a dramatic change in this perspective. Gilbert (1986), a social historian, has recently recaptured the era of the 1950s when the role of peers and the peer culture became national issues. Gilbert argues that, with little evidence, peers were given responsibility for almost all adolescent problem behaviors. Authors of popular articles, policy makers in federal agencies such as the FBI, and social scientists began to generate the notion that the peer culture counteracts the positive effects cultivated during 12 or so years of rearing in the home. As he points out, the term "peers" suddenly took on a negative connotation.

Gilbert goes on to speculate why this happened at this particular time. He suggests that the 1950s began an era when the mass media allowed previously demarcated subcultures to meet and to interact. For instance, music that was previously heard only by black audiences became accessible to all teenagers. Further, youths began to dress and speak in ways that made them less distinguishable in terms of social class. In addition, by the 1950s, high school had become a more universal experience for teenagers. It should not be surprising then that some parents began to fear the blurring of values as their adolescent offspring went to the same schools as adolescents from a variety of backgrounds. Thus, in the 1950s it may have appeared to parents that previously sharp divisions were disappearing into a democratic mix and that such a mix might have a negative effect on their children's behaviors and attitudes.

As Gilbert notes, the negative connotation attributed to peers in the 1950s occurred with little evidence to support it. The notion that contemporary peers counteract the socializing influence of parents may now be considered from the perspective of data. Fortunately we can begin this review by returning to Middletown in 1977 (Bahr, 1980) to assess whether further opportunities for class mixing and exposure to mass media resulted in significant changes in parent-adolescent relationships from the ones characteristic of 1924.

In 1924, high school students in Middletown were still statistically elite. By 1977, however, the great majority of young people under age 18 were still in school. This suggests greater opportunities for social-class mixing and an increased potential for intergenerational spacing. Bahr's findings did not support this hypothesis. In his study Bahr compared student reports from 1924 and 1977 about the number of evenings they spent at home, the sources of their spending money and of their knowledge about sex, their perceptions of topics about which they and their parents disagreed, and the qualities they defined as most desirable in mothers and fathers.

Despite the more than 50-year time span and the enormous economic, social, and technological changes that occurred in that time span, relatively few differences were found between Middletown youth in 1977 and in 1924.

The most significant findings were that (1) females in 1977 spent more evenings away from home, making them more similar to the males of 1924; (2) males, but not females, in 1977 were more likely to have fixed allowances, and students of both sexes were more likely to earn their own money; (3) males and females in 1977 were much less likely to receive their sex information from their parents and, for females, friends played a much greater role in the transmission of sex knowledge, again making them more similar to males of 1924; (4) helping with household tasks, which was not a major source of family conflict in 1924, was a major source of family disagreement in 1977; (5) respect for homemaking skills as a desirable characteristic of mothers declined; and (6) the importance of parental respect for children's opinions increased markedly from 1924 to 1977.

Overall, Bahr notes, "There is no evidence in these data that the generation gap in 1977 is any wider than it was in 1924. Indeed the much higher value placed on parental respect for children's opinions and the continued affirmation that parents should spend time with their children suggest that the expressive/emotional function of the family is more important for Middletown students of 1977 than it was in 1924" (p. 51).

Other research findings pertaining to the question of whether peer associations negate parental influence and importance also have not provided support for this assumption. John Coleman (1980) has presented the fullest and strongest argument against the negative connotation of "peers" in his review of recent research. Coleman concludes that parents' and peers' values are usually found to overlap and that adolescents tend to choose friends whose values are similar to the values held by their parents. This was also reported by Kandel and Lesser (1972) who note that adolescent peers tend to reinforce adult influence rather than negate it. In addition, Montemayor (1982) found that time spent with peers is not correlated with level of conflict with parents.

A few studies, however, have noted that adolescents' susceptibility to peer pressure, particularly for deviant behaviors, does increase from pre-adolescence to around age 13 or 14 years but then decreases again at the onset of the high school years (cf. Berndt, 1979; Steinberg & Silverberg, 1986). These studies suggest that the onset of adolescence may be marked by a sudden shift away from parental values toward experimentation with deviant behaviors in the company of peers. This period, however, appears to be short-lived (see "maturational reform" in Hirschi & Goffredson, 1983), and may correspond to the onset of the realization of the fallibility of parents (Smollar & Youniss, 1988; Steinberg & Silverberg, 1986). The shift away from parents that occurs as children enter adolecence may also be the basis for the reconstruction of the parent-adolescent relationship.

Although the studies noted above are important in that they focus more or less directly on the ways parent and peer relationships are conjoined in adolescence, the strongest evidence against the widespread concern with peer influence as counteracting parent influence may be found in the literature on adolescents' conceptions of relationships with parents. Studies have reported that adolescents between roughly 13 and 19 years of age view parental authority as reasonable and appropriate (Coleman & Coleman, 1984; Harris & Howard, 1981) and perceive their parents as accepting of them as individuals (Schludermann & Schludermann, 1983). Indeed, from Douvan and Adelson (1966) through Kandel and Lesser (1972) to Offer, Ostrov, & Howard (1981) and Youniss and Smollar (1988) the evidence has been overwhelming that parent-adolescent relations are not necessarily marked by high tension, that adolescents respect and emulate their parents, and that adolescents do not view their friends as oppositional to their parents.

Again, this does not mean that conflict is not a part of parent-adolescent relationships or that adolescent peers do not engage in "acting-out" behaviors either with one another or at the encouragement of one or the other. Instead, we wish to demonstrate that when the larger picture of adolescent development is considered, parent-adolescent conflict and peer influence to deviant behavior may be seen as parts of the process of reconstruction in both types of relationships. Within this perspective, it is possible to turn from a presumption that parents and peers are counterinfluences and to try to understand how their psychological functioning and conjoining may be mediated sociologically.

Parents and Peers in the Social Context

Historians of family life in Western societies tend to agree that one cannot find a single definition for the parental role. As Hollingshead (1949) wisely noted, father-son relations may vary depending on whether the father's craft or trade is being passed on to his son or whether what the father does is independent from what the son will do for economic subsistence. Other modes of variation revolve around such matters as type of inheritance, contractual marriage, and joint life expectancies for parent and child generations (cf. Aries, 1962; Degler, 1980; Shorter, 1975). Thus, it is questionable whether it is plausible to propose a singular role for parents, namely that of replicating themselves through their children.

A valuable analysis of parenthood may be found in Riesman (1953), one of the first social scientists to tie parenting actions explicitly to the societal structure to which parents believed that their offspring were headed. Riesman differentiated parental duties in traditional eras from those in eras when values are undergoing change. The latter appears to apply to parents whom psychologists have studied from roughly 1920 to the present. This broad cohort has witnessed a host of alterations in such important dimensions as the role of government in the regulation of citizens' lives, on the one hand, and basic values regarding women's working after marriage and through motherhood, on the other hand. Were one to have interviewed parents at moments during these changes, the likely result might have been that positions held at one time were later altered in light of the factually altered sociological context. A slight indication of this is seen in Bronfenbrenner's (1958) classic review.

Although Riesman's (1953) analysis is not directly related to the ways adolescents' relationships with parents and peers are conjoined, it does have some implications for the issue. His depiction of this situation is centered on parents who had clear value positions and equally clear desires to successfully adapt their children to the society they would confront. Such parents, however, often did not know precisely what it was that they should have been passing on to their children. To handle this type of uncertainty, these parents utilized several means for socialization beyond themselves. One of these means was the school, but another was their adolescents' peer relationships. In this sense parents recognized that the younger generation was working toward the future in ways the older generation could not. Riesman, of course, is not endorsing the abdication of parental responsibility. He is, however, suggesting that effective modern parents are able to distinguish between themselves and society, including the past that was valid for them and the future as their children may face it. Insofar as the younger generation will face this future together, peer relationships during adolescence take on importance to parents as well as to the adolescents themselves.

Fasick (1984) has provided a recent updating of Riesman's analysis that distinguishes parental strategies according to socioeconomic status (SES) levels. He proposes that parents from the upper levels tend to co-opt their adolescents by sharing many of their interests and recreational pleasures with them. Adolescents from this level are grouped institutionally in select schools where the values of parents are virtually duplicated. For these youths, the peer group is of small consequence since it is not an independent source of ideas or values. Fasick adds also that neither identity nor autonomy are special problems here. Whatever exploration occurs, these youths can be fairly well assured of economic success. Autonomy is not a problem when adolescents believe that their parents' value systems are correct not only for them but also in principle.

Adolescents from the lower SES levels may also experience little sense of conflict with parents. This is probably because their parents tend to perceive them to be adultlike rather early and therefore grant them considerable freedom to act outside parental supervision. A factor here may be acceptance of roles in work and marriage without much discussion of alternatives. Fasick adds that for these youths, the peer group is usually not a major point of reference. Often these youths have adult-oriented recreational tastes and spend time at work where they earn money for their own use. Identity is almost given through acceptance of roles within a limited range. Autonomy from parents is typically granted as parents encourage these adolescents to finish school, get into the workplace, and grow up.

This leaves adolescents from the middle SES levels. Fasick (1984) suggests most social scientists have focused on this group. He notes that the influence of the full-force market economy dominated by large corporations means that most families at this level are unable to play a direct role in placing their children within an occupation. Therefore, in their efforts to help their children attain success, parents must rely on others. Peers come to play a role in this effort as adolescents form the basis for an independent social life. Fasick describes this independent social life as follows: "[the youth culture] is constructed for the most part of such transitory and trivial matters as those dealing with clothes, music, sports, and dating that have little carryover to adult life. Although constructed primarily of nonessentials, youth culture provides a foundation on which teenagers can build an important, meaningful and distinctive social life with their peers. For the most part, young people must make their own way in this social world, since parents can usually be of little help. Integration into the peer culture is the first major move most adolescents make toward a life independent of their families" (p. 155). Fasick goes on to note that involvement in the youth culture is done without rejecting fundamental parental values or undermining bonds of affection with parents.

The analyses provided by both Riesman (1953) and Fasick (1984) offer a perspective for assessing the ways parents treat adolescents in such matters as their demands, their expectations, and their priorities. Moreover, once social structure is made central to a psychological appraisal, functions such as socialization become clearly separable from matters of relationship. Of course, once the separation is made conceptually, researchers can more clearly study the interweaving of these functions.

IMPLICATIONS FOR FUTURE RESEARCH

This chapter has not solved the riddle of how learned behavior within the family controls, transfers, or otherwise affects social development outside the family or vice versa. This question is now several generations old and still some distance away from a satisfactory answer. We are suggesting that two changes may be necessary to attain an answer.

One change is to shift research focus from the model which presumes that influence flows from parents as one objective force, and subsequently, from peers as a contrasting objective force. The alternative approach would be to focus on the meaning of behaviors found in the structure of interpersonal relationships. Relationships differ from one another in terms of both the interactions that characterize them and the meaning that is attributed to these interactions. As such, they differ in structure and consequently in the acquisitions they engender (cf. Furman & Buhrmester, 1985; Smollar & Youniss, 1982).

Another change that we believe is essential is to view psychological relationship structures as stemming from and as coordinated with aspects of the social structure. The examples given in this chapter pertaining to historical variations in parental and peer relationships illustrate the importance of this focus. An argument can be made that contemporary parents do not provide total socialization for adolescents. They are probably unable to do so alone, and they willingly grant socializing powers to others, including teachers and peers. A consideration of social structure would also involve a focus on social class differences. Although we have not explained them in this chapter or made them explanatory of psychological effects, there is sufficient evidence to suggest that the coordination of SES with relationship structures should be a direction for future research.

These changes would serve as a basis for a new approach to the study of relationships, which, in turn, can provide insights into adolescence with its intense commitments and problems with parents and peers. For example, with Riesman's (1953) assumption that parents expend energies to advance the likelihood of success for their children, one can view parent-adolescent relationships from the perspective of strategies that parents direct toward offspring with a sense of their implications for adaptation to present society. This perspective is virtually absent at present from the psychological literature, which instead is oriented almost solely inward to intrafamilial struggles. It is not that conflict is unimportant, but that a critical focus is being ignored and, in the process, key aspects of parent-adolescent relationshps are overlooked.

Peers are an important case in point; parents may understand that peers provide the potential for support as well as serve as socializers in ways that parents cannot. An analogy from the therapeutic situation is appropriate here. In describing the valuable role which peers play in the therapeutic process, Grunebaum and Solomon (1982) cite the following example.

> Not all interaction by group members needs to occur in the presence of the leader. For instance, one of us had led a group that has endured for 15 years, with a continually changing membership. At several junctures the group members would routinely go out together after the group meeting. At first, the leader viewed the dining-out routine as a form of resistance, but when he realized that it was the only meal those people ate with anyone with whom they could share any intimate feelings during their entire week, his point of view changed. He concluded that the meal was a positive socializing experience and the informality could not have occurred with the leader present. (p. 303)

In addition, the work of Riesman (1953) and Fasick (1984) should help psychologists to see more clearly how parental and peer relations are sociologically conjoined. We are not arguing that a sociological program of research ought to replace the questions that psychologists raise. Rather our position is that questions should be informed by a clear perspective on the social context. Specifically, it is assumed that parents socialize with a definite view of the society that they believe their adolescents will enter. Irrespective of the particular position taken, the context will have an effect on parent-adolescent relationships because the social context has worked its way into the family via the methods parents have chosen for the outcomes that they desire.

As psychologists, we are not promoting one sociological view over any other. The goal is to encourage greater sensitivity to the social context beyond that of treating it as a variable that affects families. We suggest a more constitutional approach wherein the social context shapes the psychological structures created by persons living in that context. For the present, it is sufficient to suggest that by keeping social structure clearly in mind, one might see better the grounds for psychological issues that parents and adolescents are facing.

REFERENCES

Aries, P. (1962). *Centuries of childhood: A social history of family life*. New York: Knopf.

Bahr, H. M. (1980). Changes in family life in Middletown, 1924–77. *Public Opinion Quarterly, 44*, 35–52.

Bell, D. C., & Bell, L. G. (1983). Parental validation and support in the development of adolescent daughters. In H. D. Grotevant & C. R. Cooper (Eds.), *Adolescent development within the family* (pp. 27–42). San Francisco: Jossey-Bass.

Berndt, T. J. (1979). Developmental changes in conformity to parents and peers. *Developmental Psychology, 15*, 608–616.

Brittain, C. V. (1963). Adolescent choices and parent-peer cross-pressures. *American Sociological Review, 28*, 385–391.

Bronfenbrenner, U. (1958). Socialization and social class through time and space. In E. E. Maccoby, T. M. Newcomb, & E. L. Hartley (Eds.), *Readings in social psychology* (pp. 400–425). New York: Holt, Rinehart, & Winston.

Coleman, J. C. (1980). Friendship and the peer group in adolescence. In J. Adelson (Ed.), *The handbook of adolescent psychology* (pp. 408–431). New York: Wiley.

Coleman, J. C., & Coleman, E. Z. (1984). Adolescent attitudes toward authority. *Journal of Adolescence, 7*, 131–141.

Cook-Gumperz, J., & Corsaro, W. A. (1977). Social-ecological constraints on chlidren's communicative strategies. *Sociology, 11*, 411–434.

Cooper, C. R., & Ayers-Lopez, S. (1985). Family and peer systems in early adolescence: New models of relationships in development. *Journal of Early Adolescence, 5*, 9–21.

Cooper, C. R., Grotevant, H. D., & Condon, S. M. (1983). Individuality and connectedness in the family as a context for adolescent identity development and role-taking skill. In H. D. Grotevant & C. R. Cooper (Eds.), *Adolescent development in the family* (pp. 43–60). San Francisco: Jossey-Bass.

Damon, W. (1977). *The social world of the child*. San Francisco: Jossey-Bass.

Degler, C. (1980). *At odds: Women and family in America from the Revolution to the present*. New York: Oxford University Press.

Demos, J. (1970). *A little commonwealth: Family life in Plymouth Colony*. New York: Oxford University Press.

Douvan, E., & Adelson, J. (1966). *The adolescent experience*. New York: Wiley.

Eisenberg, N., Lundy, T., Shell, R., & Roth, K. (1985). Children's justifications for their adult and peer-directed compliant (prosocial and nonprosocial) behaviors. *Developmental Psychology, 21*, 325–331.

Fasick, F. A. (1984). Parents, peers, youth culture and autonomy in adolescence. *Adolescence, 19*, 143–157.

Fisher, C. B., & Lisa-Johnson, B. (1987, April). Getting mad at mom and dad: Children's changing views of family conflict. Paper presented at the biennial meeting of the Society for Research in Child Development, Baltimore.

Furman, W., & Buhrmester, D. (1985). Children's perceptions of the personal relationships in their social networks. *Developmental Psychology, 21,* 1016–1024.

Furth, H. G. (1983). Freud, Piaget, and Macmurray: A theory of knowledge from the standpoint of personal relations. *New Ideas in Psychology, 1,* 51–65.

Gadlin, H. (1978). Child discipline and the pursuit of the self: A historical perspective. In H. W. Reese & L. P. Lipsitt (Eds.), *Advances in child development and behavior* (pp. 231–265). New York: Academic Press.

Garvey, C., & Hogan, R. (1973). Social speech and social interaction. *Child Development, 44,* 562–568.

Gilbert, J. (1986). *A cycle of outrage: America's reaction to the juvenile delinquent in the 1950s.* New York: Oxford University Press.

Gillis, J. R. (1981). *Youth and history: Tradition and change in European age relations.* New York: Academic Press.

Greenberg, M. T., Siegel, J. M., & Leitch, C. J. (1983). The nature and importance of attachment relationships to parents and peers during adolescence. *Journal of Youth and Adolescence, 12,* 373–386.

Greven, P. (1977). *The Protestant temperament.* New York: New American Library.

Grotevant, H. D., & Cooper, C. R. (1986). Individuation in family relationships: A perspective on individual differences in the development of identity and role-taking skills in adolescence. *Human Development, 29,* 82–100.

Grunebaum, H., & Solomon, L. (1982). Toward a theory of peer relationships, II: On the stages of social development and their relationship to group psychotherapy. *International Journal of Group Psychotherapy, 32,* 283–307.

Harris, I. D., & Howard, K. I. (1981). Perceived parental authority: Reasonable and unreasonable. *Journal of Youth and Adolescence, 10,* 273–284.

Hartup, W. W. (1970). Peer interaction and social organization. in P. H. Mussen (Ed.), *Carmichael's manual of child psychology* (Vol. 2, pp. 361–456). New York: Wiley.

Hartup, W. W. (1983). Peer relations. In E. M. Hetherington (Ed.) & P. H. Mussen (Series Ed.), *Handbook of child psychology: Vol. 4. Socialization, personality, and social development* (pp. 103–196). New York: Wiley.

Hinde, R. A. (1979). *Towards understanding relationships.* London: Academic Press.

Hinde, R. S., Stevenson-Hinde, J., & Tamplin, A. (1985). Characteristics of 3- to 4-year-olds assessed at home and in their interactions in preschool. *Developmental Psychology, 21,* 130–140.

Hirschi, T., & Goffredson, M. (1983). Age and the explanation of crime. *American Journal of Sociology, 89,* 552–584.

Hollingshead, A. B. (1949). *Elmtown's youth.* New York: Wiley.

Hunter, F. T. (1984). Socializing procedures in parent-child and friendship relations during adolescence. *Developmental Psychology, 20,* 1092–1099.

Kandel, D. B., & Lesser, G. S. (1972). *Youth in two worlds: U.S. and Denmark.* San Francisco: Jossey-Bass.

Katz, M. B. (1981). Social class in North American urban history. *Journal of Interdisciplinary History, 11,* 579–605.

Kett, J. (1977). *Rites of passage.* New York: Basic Books.

Lynd, R. S., & Lynd, H. M. (1929). *Middletown: A study of American culture.* New York: Harcourt, Brace, & World.

Marcoen, A., & Brumagne, M. (1985). Loneliness among children and adolescents. *Developmental Psychology, 21,* 1025–1031.

Montemayor, R. (1982). The relationship between parent-adolescent conflict and the amount of time adolescents spend alone and with parents and peers. *Child Development, 53,* 1512–1519.

Ochs, E. (1982). Talking to children in Western Somoa. *Language Socialization, 11,* 77–104.

O'Donnell, W. J. (1979). Affectional patterns of adolescents. *Adolescence, 14,* 680–686.

Offer, D., Ostrov, E., & Howard, K. I. (1981). *The adolescent: A psychological self-portrait.* New York: Basic Books.

Powers, S. I., Hauser, S. T., Schwartz, J. M., Noam, G. G., & Jacobson, A. M. (1983). Adolescent ego development and family interaction: A structural-developmental perspective. In H. D. Grotevant & C. R. Cooper (Eds.), *Adolescent development in the family* (pp. 5–24). San Francisco: Jossey-Bass.

Riegel, K. F. (1976). The systemization of dialectical logic for the study of development and change. *Human Development, 19,* 321–324.

Riesman, D. (1953). *The lonely crowd.* Garden City, New York: Doubleday.

Schludermann, S., & Schludermann, E. (1983). Sociocultural change and adolescents' perceptions of parent behavior. *Developmental Psychology, 19,* 674–85.

Selman, R. L., Beardslee, W., Schultz, L. H., Krupa, M., & Podorefsky, D. (1986). Assessing adolescent interpersonal negotiation strategies: Toward the integration of structural and functional models. *Developmental Psychology, 22,* 450–59.

Sennett, R. (1974). *Families against the city.* New York: Vintage.

Shorter, E. (1975). *The making of the modern family.* New York: Basic Books.

Smollar, J., & Youniss, J. (1982). Social development through friendship. In K. H. Rubin & H. S. Ross (Eds.), *Peer relations and social skills in childhood* (pp. 279–98). New York: Springer-Verlag.

Smollar, J., & Youniss, J. (1988). Transformations in adolescents' perceptions of parents. *International Journal of Behavioral Development,* in press.

Steinberg, L., & Silverberg, S. B. (1986). The vicissitudes of autonomy in early adolescence. *Child Development, 57,* 841–851.

Stinchcombe, A. R. (1978). *Theoretical methods in social history.* New York: Academic Press.

Waterman, A. S. (1981). Individualism and interdependence. *American Psychologist, 36,* 762–773.

Wertsch, J. V. (1985). *Vygotsky and the social formation of mind.* Cambridge, MA: Harvard University Press.

White, K. M., Speisman, J. C., & Costos, D. (1983). Young adults and their parents: From individuation to mutuality. In H. D. Grotevant & C. R. Cooper (Eds.), *Adolescent development in the family* (pp. 61–76). San Francisco: Jossey-Bass.

Wintre, M. G., Hicks, R., McVey, G., & Fox, J. (1988). Age and sex differences in choice of consultant for various types of problems. *Child Develoment,* in press.

Youniss, J. (1980). *Parents and peers in social development.* Chicago: University of Chicago Press.

Youniss, J., & Ketterlinus, R. D. (1987). Communication and connectedness in mother- and father-adolescent relationships. *Journal of Youth and Adolescence, 16,* 265–280.

Youniss, J., & Smollar, J. (1985). *Adolescent relationships with mothers, fathers, and friends.* Chicago: University of Chicago Press.

Zahaykevich, M. (1987, April). An object relations view of adolescent gender formation in maternal discourse. Paper presented at the biennial meeting of the Society for Research in Child Development, Baltimore, MD.

PART FOUR

Intervention

Important information about the contributions of peers to children's development can also be obtained from research on disordered peer relationships. A commonly cited thesis in the peer relations literature is that disordered peer relationships place children at risk for later adjustment problems. Although the actual factors that enhance or reduce psychological risk are not yet well understood, some evidence suggests that characteristics of the child (e.g., aggressiveness, timidity), and/or the child's experiences in disordered relationships (e.g., rejection by peers, friendlessness), are responsible for later maladjustment.

Research on the dynamics of disordered peer relationships may provide important clues not only about the potential ways in which children foster their own social difficulties, but also about the potential contributions of peers. Perspectives in which children are seen as the architects of their own difficulties, which have dominated past research, may be misleading because they ignore or oversimplify the potential contributions of peers and the reciprocal or bidirectional nature of peer relationships. Moreover, the functions of peers in disordered relationships may vary; whereas peers may contribute to the development and maintenance of children's social difficulties, they may also play an important role in resolving them. Under some circumstances, and within certain types of relationships, peers may help children overcome debilitating social difficulties and possibly reduce the risk of later maladjustment.

In the first chapter of this section, Wyndol Furman and Leslie Gavin, by examining relevant evidence from the literature on peer-based intervention research, explore the hypothesis that peers contribute to children's development and adjustment. They review a broad spectrum of intervention programs, including those designed to foster children's academic achievement and social competence, and critically analyze their effects to determine whether gains in adjustment can be attributed to changes in peer relationships. The authors identify a number of conceptual and methodological limitations that constrain the interpretation of existing research findings and illustrate potential directions for further research.

Joseph Price and Kenneth Dodge offer a unique perspective on the potential contributions of peers to children's social difficulties. Within this chapter, Price and Dodge consider aspects of the peer system that may foster and perpetuate problems such as peer rejection. Their analysis is based on a model of reciprocal social exchange and focuses on the processes by which children and their peers construe and respond to each other during social interaction. Particular attention is devoted to the role that peers' perceptions and behaviors may play in perpetuating children's perceptual biases, maladaptive behaviors, and negative social reputations. Based on this framework, Price and Dodge also identify a number of potential intervention strategies for changing peers' perceptions and behaviors and illustrate how these methods may help rejected children to change their behavior and status in the peer group.

In the final chapter of this section, Robert Selman and Lynn Schultz describe a developmental approach for analyzing the dynamics of children's dyadic peer relationships. Their method, which combines traditional observational methods and interpretive analyses of behavior, is designed to isolate, evaluate, and interpret the strategies children use to negotiate social activities with a peer. These assessments are used to illuminate the processes through which children develop close interpersonal relationships with a peer and to guide children's progress toward successful relationships during "pair therapy" interventions. Of particular interest is the interface between the types of strategies that pairs of children employ to organize and regulate their interactions with each other and the effects of differing patterns of negotiation on relationshp formation and maintenance.

CHAPTER 12

Peers' Influence on Adjustment and Development

A View from the Intervention Literature

WYNDOL FURMAN AND LESLIE A. GAVIN

University of Denver

The fundamental thesis of this book is that interactions or relationships with peers influence development and adjustment. Many pieces of evidence can be cited to support this argument. Perhaps the largest body of research relevant to this thesis is the sociometric literature, which has shown that positive peer relations are associated with and predictive of adjustment. For example, sociometric status has been found to be related to self-esteem (Helper, 1958; Horowitz, 1962; Putallaz, White & Shipman, 1985), prosocial behavior (see Hartup, 1983), social cognitive skills (Asarnow & Callan, 1985, Jennings, 1975), and school achievement (Roff, Sells, & Golden, 1972). Inverse relations have been found with social anxiety and loneliness (Hymel & Franke, 1985). In addition, some classic studies have demonstrated that children who were rejected by peers at a young age were later more likely to suffer adjustment difficulties (Cowen, Pederson, Babigian, Izzo, & Trost, 1973; Roff, Sells, & Golden), suggesting that poor peer relationships may lead to unsatisfactory developmental outcomes.

Of course, these sociometric studies consist almost exclusively of correlational research. Ever since the beginning of our undergraduate training, we have all learned that "correlation does not show causation." The obvious problem with the correlational model is that the reverse models of causation seem just as plausible. For example, it seems very possible that positive self-esteem or prosocial behaviors could lead to peer acceptance. The existing longitudinal data are impressive but do not really shed light on the causal processes. For example, in Roff et al.'s (1972) study, the rejected children may have been poorly adjusted at an early age; if so, that poor

---

Preparation of this paper was supported by a W. T. Grant Faculty Scholars Award to the first author.

adjustment may have led to both early peer rejection and subsequent adjustment difficulties.

Given that correlational data can only be suggestive of peers' impact upon the course of development, we need to look elsewhere to bolster our thesis that peers affect development. Ethically, one cannot experimentally manipulate peer relations by assigning some children to the good peer relations condition and others to the poor peer relations condition. However, intervention research can be thought of as an experimental manipulation of sorts. Specifically, intervention programs can be used to improve peer interactions or relationships. If that improvement in turn fosters adjustment or development, then we would have some evidence that peer interactions can influence development or adjustment. Thus, the intervention literature can be used to support our argument that peer relations *affect* development.

In this chapter we will review the research on different interventions for peer relationship problems, with the goal of determining how that literature supports the thesis that peers have an impact on development and adjustment. Our review will consider a range of different interventions, including cooperative learning programs, modeling and reinforcement programs, peer contact programs, and social skills training programs. The programs that are reviewed have targeted children of all ages, although most focus on elementary school children.

One should keep in mind that the intervention research was not designed to demonstrate that peer relationships affect the course of development or adjustment. Therefore, studies do not necesarily include many of the measures that we would be interested in, nor do they necessarily isolate the treatment mechanisms that may be operative.

Moreover, one also needs to recognize that intervention studies simply demonstrate what *can* happen, not what *does* happen (Petrinovich, 1979). That is, because one can improve development by involvement with peers does not necessarily mean that peers ordinarily affect development. We need to ascertain whether the intervention manipulations normally occur in the natural environment. Our general impression is that the cooperative learning experiences, modeling, reinforcement, and social skills training processes that are used in intervention studies do occur in the natural environment, but not as frequently or systematically. On the other hand, these experiences occur continually throughout childhood. Whether the effects of short-term, intensive, systematic interventions are comparable to those of long-term, irregular, inconsistent interventions is difficult to determine. These caveats notwithstanding, our exploration of this literature may shed some light on the impact of peers on development and adjustment.

Finally, although it is beyond the scope of this paper to define formally the concepts of adjustment and development, a few words should be said about how these terms are used here. When we refer to effects on adjustment or development, we are referring to effects that are relatively sustained and broad in scope. That is, we are interested in how peer relations change children's adaptation to their environment, the course of growth, or the acquisition of competencies. We intend the concepts of adjustment and development to be quite broad, encompassing variables from many areas, including the academic, social, and intrapsychic domains. As we review the following intervention literature, we will focus on studies showing that variables from all of these different domains can be affected by peers.

This review will also cover studies of intervention techniques, such as modeling or reinforcement, that demonstrate that peers affect children's behavior or interactions. Sometimes, these techniques may have positive effects on adjustment (e.g. imitating prosocial behavior); in other cases, these techniques may have negative effects (e.g. imitating aggression) or no effect on adjustment or development per se. We will briefly review this literature, however, to illustrate the potential processes by which peers may affect children's adjustment and development.

COOPERATIVE LEARNING

One kind of intervention in which peer interactions play a central role is cooperative learning. These programs are classroom-based techniques that have small groups of students work together on academic material. Typically, the groups receive a group reward for good performance.

The theoretical basis for cooperative learning programs can be traced in part to Allport (1954). He theorized that superficial contact between individuals of different races or different status levels, particularly competitive contact, can damage relations. In contrast, positive results can come about through nonsuperficial contact, such as when individuals work together on common goals. Individuals can get to know one another on an equal status level, thereby fostering the development of relationships and reducing prejudice.

Classroom programs based on these principles have several goals. First, proponents believe that children can benefit from the opportunities to learn from each other and to teach one another. Second, they believe that children can profit from more opportunities to learn the cooperative skills that they will need as adults. Third, cooperative learning is believed to be a powerful way to break down race and status barriers and foster relationships among children from different backgrounds. Developers of these programs have attempted to show that a cooperative learning environment can enhance personal growth, interracial relations, general peer relations, classroom environment, and academic achievement.

In recent years, at least four major formal school programs have been developed and evaluated. The programs include (1) the Group Investigation method, developed by Sharan and Sharan (1976) in Israel; (2) Learning Together, developed by Johnson and Johnson (1975) at the University of Minnesota; (3) Jigsaw, originally developed by Aronson (1978); and (4) Student Team Learning, developed by Slavin and associates at the Johns Hopkins University (DeVries & Slavin, 1978; Slavin, 1980).

Although most of these programs are aimed at achieving the same goals, they are designed differently and include somewhat different treatment components. Specifically, the programs differ in terms of whether they make individual students accountable for what they have learned, what kind of reward structure they use, and how interdependent the students must become in order to achieve (Slavin, 1980).

The first program, the Group Investigation method (Sharan & Sharan, 1976), is perhaps the least structured of all the programs. Here a group of students work on an open-ended project. Each student takes responsibility for a different task, and they work together to present their material to the rest of the class. The students are graded as a group on their project.

The second approach, Learning Together (Johnson & Johnson, 1975), is similar to the Group Investigation method. Within this framework, students are assigned to a group and instructed to work together on an academic task. They hand in an assignment that they have done together and receive praise as a group, but no formal reward is given.

In the third approach, Jigsaw (Aronson, 1978), students are also divided into small groups of five or six students. Each group is given a particular topic to study, and each student in a group is responsible for becoming the expert on a particular aspect of that topic. Once the experts have researched their topics, the group members come together and teach one another the information that they uniquely have. The key to this program is that the group members will be tested on all areas of information, and they are thus dependent upon their other group members to provide them with the necessary information.

The fourth approach, Student Team Learning (DeVries & Slavin, 1978; Slavin, 1980), includes two different programs, Student Teams-Achievement Divisions (STAD) and Teams-Games-Tournaments (TGT). In STAD, teachers first present the instructional material to the entire class. Then students meet in their four- to five-member groups to work together on worksheets related to the material presented in class. Students are instructed to teach one another the material and to make sure that each member has mastered it. Students are then quizzed on the material individually. The scores that the students contribute to their teams are based on the degree to which they have improved over their individual past quiz performances. Thus, children at all ability levels can contribute to a team's success. The teams with the highest scores are recognized in a weekly class newsletter.

Teams-Games-Tournaments is similar to Student-Teams-Achievement Divisions in how the students learn the material (i.e., class instruction and group tutoring). However, instead of having individual quizzes, class tournaments are held in which students compete on a quiz against members of other teams. In the competitions, students compete against others of comparable ability so that all children have an equal chance to contribute to their teams' success. Slavin (1980) emphasizes that Student Team Learning programs are different from other cooperative learning techniques in their emphasis on individual accountability and group incentive motivation.

The evaluation research on cooperative learning has focused on the following outcome measures: self-esteem, cooperation and altruism, locus of control, peer and race relations, academic achievement, and classroom environment. Each is reviewed subsequently.

A few investigators have found that cooperative learning fosters self-esteem. For example, Blaney, Stephan, Rosenfield, Aronson, and Sikes (1977) had students in racially integrated classrooms participate in a series of Jigsaw activities. They found that students in the experimental cooperative groups showed higher self-esteem than students in the control groups. In a study of one classroom in which fifth- and sixth-grade children were divided into cooperative and individualistic learning conditions, Johnson, Johnson, and Scott (1978) found that the children in the cooperative group showed higher self-esteem than those in the individualistic learning condition.

Cooperative learning techniques also seem to affect the degree of interpersonal cooperation and altruism by students. Johnson, Johnson, Johnson, and Anderson (1976) found that fifth-grade students involved in a cooperative learning condition were more altruistic than those in an individualistic condition where they worked alone on their work. In another study, Hertz-Lazarowitz, Sharan, and Steinberg (1980) compared the degree of cooperative behavior shown by 243 third- through seventh-grade students from cooperative classrooms and that displayed by 150 children from regular classrooms. They found that the students from the cooperative classrooms were more altruistic and cooperative and less competitive and vengeful than children from regular classrooms.

Two investigators have explored the impact of cooperative learning on locus of control. Johnson, Johnson, and Scott (1978) found that fifth- and sixth-grade children in the cooperative learning condition reported having a stronger sense of an internal locus of control than those in the individualistic learning condition. Johnson, Johnson, and Scott (1978) found that students in the cooperative condition were less extrinsically motivated than control students, although they were not more intrinsically motivated.

Other socioemotional variables that have been investigated include perspective taking and tolerance of others. In a study with a 120 fifth-grade students using the Jigsaw technique, Bridgeman (1981) found that the experimental children demonstrated a significant enhancement of role-taking ability as compared to control children. Johnson et al. (1976) found that the students in the cooperative condition were more accurate in their recognition of feelings than those in the control group. Finally, Johnson, Johnson, and Scott (1978) found that children in cooperative versus individualistic learning conditions had greater tolerance of conflict and more positive attitudes toward heterogeneity among their peers.

The next outcome variable of interest is sociometric status. Johnson et al. (1978) found that students in a cooperative learning condition developed higher sociometric status than those in the individualistic learning condition. In a similar study in one classroom, Johnson et al. (1976) found that the students in the cooperative condition felt that teachers and fellow students liked and cared about them more and wanted to help them more than students in the control condition felt. In a combined study of STAD, TGT, and Jigsaw II, Slavin and Karweit (1981) found that students who had participated in cooperative learning programs named more students as their friends than did control students. However, there were no differences in how much they reported liking their classmates or in their feelings of being liked. In his summary of the evidence regarding changes in peer relations and likability, Slavin (1983b) found that of the 19 studies measuring interpersonal attraction among classmates, 14 showed significantly greater liking among those in cooperative classrooms, 2 showed marginally greater liking, and 3 showed lower liking. Thus, it appears that cooperative learning improves peer relations among students.

Similar changes have been found in interracial relations. In three studies of Teams-Games-Tournament in desegregated schools, DeVries, Edwards, and Slavin (1978) found that classes using TGT showed greater increases in cross-race friendship choices than control classes did. In a fourth study, no differences were found. Slavin (1983a) summarizes the literature on cooperative learning and intergroup relations. On the basis of results from a series of studies, using Student Team Learning and other programs such as Jigsaw, Slavin concluded that although not all of the results are completely consistent, the pattern of results indicates that cooperative learning generally improves interracial relations. Improvement in interracial relations can be considered an important analogue to the improvement of peer relations among children of different social status. If one is able to demonstrate improvement in relations among students of different ethnicity, these results may generalize to improvement of relations among children who differ in other dimensions, such as social status.

Another important outcome of cooperative learning programs is change in classroom climate. Classroom climate is typically evaluated on the basis of such variables as degree of competition, cooperation, student involvement, and friendliness. Some research has shown that children in TGT and STAD programs show higher proportions of on task behavior than control students (DeVries & Slavin, 1978). In a study using Jigsaw, Wright and Cowen (1985) found that students in the Jigsaw classroom liked their classroom more and found it more involved, orderly, organized than those who were in the control classroom. Interestingly, these investigators also found that the experimental classrooms were more competitive. The reason for this finding, which is inconsistent with other studies (Hertz-Lazarowitz et al., 1980), is unclear, but it may be a function of the way competitiveness was measured.

A great deal of attention has been focused on the effects of cooperative classroom programs on student achievement. In the past several years review articles and meta-analyses have appeared in this area (Johnson, Maruyama, Johnson, Nelson, & Skon, 1981; Sharan, 1980; Slavin, 1983b). In general, there is consensus that structured cooperative learning programs in the class-room setting are effective in improving or at least maintaining academic performance. Reviewers, however, tend to differ in their conclusions re-garding the most effective methods of cooperative learning.

In a meta-analysis conducted by Johnson et al. (1981), the investigators reviewed 122 studies and found that children in cooperative learning pro-grams showed greater improvement in achievement than children in either interpersonal competition or individualistic efforts. Interestingly, Johnson et al. found no differences between cooperative learning programs with and without intergroup competition. They concluded that intergroup competition is not a necessary component for effective group learning.

In contrast to the Johnson et al. meta-analysis, Slavin (1983b) conducted a review of only those studies that examined individual academic achieve-ment. That is, he did not review those studies in which only group achieve-ment or productivity was measured. Slavin suggested that if one is interested in using these programs in the classroom, individual achievement must be the variable of interest, not how the group as a whole performs. Of the 46 studies evaluating academic achievement, Slavin found that 29 (46%) dem-onstrated positive effects of cooperative learning on achievement, 15 (33%) showed no differences between cooperative and individual learning control groups, and 2 (4%) found significantly higher achievement in the control group. Furthermore, Slavin found that certain characteristics of programs were predictive of enhanced achievement. Of the 27 studies that used group study plus a *group* reward for *individual* learning, 24 (89%) showed higher achievement, whereas 3 (11%) found no differences between the experi-mental and control groups. On the other hand, none of the 5 group study programs that provided *individual* rewards for *individual* learning was suc-cessful. Similarly, the 4 group study programs that provided *group* rewards for *group* products did not yield positive effects on individual achievements. However, *group* rewards for *group* products were successful in 3 of the 4 studies in which the tasks were specialized and children had different re-sponsibilities. This pattern of results seems to indicate that the powerful mechanism of these group learning programs may not be students simply working together, but it instead may be students working together for a common reward. Moreover, it seems necessary to require the students to be accountable individually by either rewarding the group on the basis of individual achievement or by having specialized tasks so that the group's success depends on the adequacy of each member's contribution. It is un-clear if these same components are needed to effect the socioemotional changes described previously.

In summary, our review of the literature suggests that interacting with peers within a structured cooperative context can have an impact on de-velopment and adjustment in both the socioemotional and academic do-mains. Many of the studies have various methodological flaws, but as a whole, the literature seems to reflect relatively consistent positive outcomes.

There are, however, some important limits on how far we can generalize at this point. For example, studies have not yet looked at the relative influence of these programs on children experiencing peer problems and those having healthy peer relations. For that matter, many of them have not determined whether the programs are effective with children having academic difficulties. Additionally, socioemotional variables have been looked at to a limited degree. It would be particularly valuable to determine which kinds of programs have an effect on socioemotional adjustment and which do not. Further work needs to be done in order for us to have a clearer sense of the clinical implications of this work.

Do these findings support our thesis that peer interactions influence development and adjustment? Perhaps. In their papers on the dynamics of the cooperative learning group, Johnson and Johnson (1985) and Slavin (1985) described how the group situation creates a positive peer climate for growth and development. Within the cooperative group, peers have to pay attention to one other, reinforce each other, and apply social sanctions to one another if they are to succeed individually and as a group. They have a mutual incentive for a reward that depends upon their helping one another achieve to the best of their abilities. In this way peers become powerful agents of motivation and support, yet at the same time relationships are being fostered. Finally, the interaction of students from different ability levels helps them all master the material.

The Johnsons' and Slavin's descriptions nicely illustrate how peer interactions may be important processes in the cooperative learning programs, but we cannot decisively attribute the outcomes to the effects of positive peer interactions. The academic effects are more likely to have resulted from the intensive peer tutoring than from the hypothesized general changes in peer interactions. One could still say that peers were responsible for the effects, but it would be more difficult to generalize these experimental findings to the natural environment where peers are less likely to do such systematic tutoring. Moreover, some effects may not be due to peers at all, but instead may simply be due to the simple presence of a reward or increased enthusiasm for learning as a function of program novelty. Slavin's (1985) review provides us some clues about the processes important for fostering change in the academic domain, but a comparable review has not been conducted for the literature of socioemotional outcome. A related body of literature on programs designed to elicit cooperative interactions may, however, shed some light on the processes responsible for the effects of cooperative learning programs on socioemotional variables.

COOPERATIVE INTERACTIONS

In cooperative interaction programs children are involved in cooperative games or activities in which they have a shared goal. As with the cooperative learning programs reviewed in the prior section, the activities are designed to foster cooperation and interdependence; thus they can tell us whether cooperative peer interactions may influence adjustment and development. The primary difference between these programs and the preceding ones is the use of nonacademic, rather than academic, activities to reach those goals. Importantly, in both kinds of programs children are not simply placed together in a group without structure. In fact, studies examining the effectiveness of these programs have compared them to control groups in which children are involved in simple, unstructured contact with others.

A number of studies have looked at the efficacy of structured peer contact as an intervention for improving the social status of retarded children. Chennault (1967) placed 64 unaccepted mentally retarded adolescents in organized cooperative group activities with accepted mentally retarded peers. At the end of the 5-week program, the participants had improved in peer acceptance and perceived peer acceptance. In a replication study, Rucker and Vincenzo (1970) also found short-term gains, but they reported that these effects were not maintained a month later. McDaniel (1970) attempted to increase the social acceptance of retarded children through involvement in extracurricular activities. After participating in the program, the retarded children showed increases in peer acceptance, but long-term effects were not examined. Finally, Ballard, Corman, Gottlieb and Kaufman (1977) tried to change the low status of mainstreamed mentally retarded children by having them participate in cooperative activities with their nonretarded classmates. After an 8-week program, these students made significant gains in their sociometric status compared to control students, and these gains were maintained 2 to 4 weeks later.

Other investigations have examined the effects of structured cooperative peer contact on the sociometric status of nonretarded, socially isolated, or rejected children. In an early study, Kinney (1953) demonstrated that the number of social isolates was reduced in elementary school classrooms where children participated in small-group activities. In a later, more methodologically sophisticated study, Lilly (1971) placed unaccepted children in groups with higher status peers. The groups were assigned the cooperative task of making a movie to present to the class. In an attempt to isolate the possible treatment mechanisms, Lilly included five treatment groups to identify salient treatment factors. This included manipulations of degree of adult contact, whether or not the intervention was in or out of the classroom, and whether peer partners were of high or low status. Short-term gains in acceptance were found in all the treatment groups that included peer contact, and none of the groups were more powerful than others. Lilly found, however, that gains did not endure over a 6-week follow-up period.

Bierman and Furman (1984) intervened with socially unaccepted fifth- and sixth-graders using cooperative peer involvement alone or in combination with skills training. In the peer involvement condition, unaccepted children and their classmates worked in groups of three making a video film about friendships. These investigators found that peer involvement increased the frequency of peer interactions, improved sociometric status, and changed peer partner ratings of friendship, though at follow-up these increases were not maintained. However, when structured peer contact was combined with skills training, changes in peer partner ratings were maintained. Target children participating in cooperative group interactions also tended to report increases in their perceptions of social efficacy.

Cooperative interactions can also be elicited indirectly by structuring the situation properly. Furman, Rahe, & Hartup (1979) used such an approach in their study of the effects of mixed-age socialization. Socially withdrawn preschool children were assigned to either dyadic play sessions with a younger peer, similar sessions with an agemate, or a no-treatment control group. Although the children were usually withdrawn in their classroom, their play sessions were characterized by very high rates of reinforcing, prosocial interactions. After the treatment, the children in the two play conditions, particularly those in mixed-age condition, showed marked increases in the rate of interaction, specifically reinforcing interactions with their peers. When placed in the appropriate context, peers may be proven to be effective treatment agents.

Some investigators have looked at the effects of structured cooperative activities on the social behavior of nonproblem children. For example, Stendler, Damrin, and Haines (1951) assessed the effects of cooperative interactions on subsequent prosocial behavior. These investigators found that 7-year-olds who participated in cooperative group activities improved on several measures of prosocial behavior, including friendliness, sharing, and helping others. There was also some evidence that cooperative group members stayed on a task and took more responsibility for the task than children in a competitive condition. Orlick (1981) placed 5-year-old children in either an 18-week program of cooperative games or a program of similar length involving traditional competitive games. Children in the cooperative condition showed greater changes in sharing and feelings of happiness than children in the competitive condition. In both of these studies, the results may reflect either positive effects of cooperation or negative effects of competition.

Though not within the realm of intervention research per se, several studies with normal children have yielded results consistent with those of the intervention research on cooperative peer involvement. In an early study, Heber and Heber (1957) demonstrated that children who were placed together to cooperate on a task increased their liking of one another if they succeeded on the task. Sherif, Harvey, White, Hood, and Sherif (1961) conducted a novel study examining the effects of cooperative tasks on intergroup hostility in a camp setting. First, two sets of boys were brought to a summer camp, unaware of each other's presence. Over the course of the next few days, each set developed into a cohesive group. The two groups were introduced to each other and invited to compete in a series of team sports. The competitions resulted in marked hostility, which the investigators tried to reduce by bringing the groups together for a series of noncompetitive contacts (e.g., meals, movies). When this intervention only made conflict worse, Sherif et al. designed a series of experiences in which the groups had to work together cooperatively to meet common goals (e.g., fixing a broken water tank so they could each have water). As a result of these cooperative experiences, the hostility, negative stereotypes, and lack of acceptance that had developed between the two groups diminished.

In summary, both the intervention literature and these studies with normal children provide evidence that cooperative peer contact may have positive effects on peer acceptance and prosocial behavior, important measures of development and adjustment. Given the control groups for these studies typically involved some form of peer contact, it seems clear that children cannot simply be placed together in a group and be expected to automatically have a positive impact on each other. Instead, the contact must be designed to elicit positive, cooperative interactions among children. The children need to have rewarding experiences with each other—experiences that can foster positive perceptions of each other or alter the negative reputations some children may have (Hymel, Wagner, & Butler, in press).

As with the cooperative learning literature, however, it is still unclear whether such programs are effective because of the cooperative peer contact or because of the rewarding nature of the activity. Another problem with many studies is the lack of follow-up data, or follow-up data that indicate that the influence of these interventions is short-lived. It is important to identify the key components in those interventions that foster sustained changes in children's behavior.

When comparing the effects of cooperative interaction on children with problems (e.g., retarded and socially unaccepted children) and the effects on those without major problems, it appears that cooperative interventions with problem children may be less successful. In our own clinical efforts, we have observed that the desired cooperative interactions do not always occur. Although not commonly done, intervention studies should ascertain whether the desired interactions did in fact occur. Moreover, cooperative interactions simply provide *opportunities* for children to develop positive relationships with each other. When some children have social skills deficits or other problems, the interactions may not be rewarding for their peers, and the opportunities for change may not be realized. Our own work suggests that interventions providing both skills training and opportunities for cooperative interactions may have more sustained effects than interventions providing either alone (Bierman & Furman, 1984).

PEER-INITIATED CONTACT

In other intervention programs, peers have initiated contact with target children or reinforced target children for social interaction. For example, a series of studies performed by Strain and associates has demonstrated that peers can have an impact on the social behavior of withdrawn children. Strain, Shores, and Timm (1977) used normal children to engage withdrawn peers in play. As a result of this intervention, the withdrawn children demonstrated both an increase in social responding and an increase in social initiations toward other children. Other studies have shown that similar interventions can be used to increase the positive social behavior of autistic children (Strain, Kerr, & Ragland, 1979) and withdrawn retarded children (Lancioni, 1982). In general, these studies provide evidence that children can foster social behavior in one another. Unfortunately for our purposes, these studies have not examined the impact of this intervention on other aspects of adjustment and development. Until this is done, we do not know whether the experiences brought about by peer-initiated contact lead to general improvements in adjustment.

PEER REINFORCEMENT

In this section, we will review studies demonstrating that peers can be powerful dispensers of social rewards and punishments, thus providing further evidence that peers can change behavior and influence development in important ways. For example, Wahler (1967) had peers reinforce the social behavior of five withdrawn children and found increased rates of social behavior by all five. In a later study, Solomon and Wahler (1973) found that the selective use of peer rewards served to reduce the amount of disruptive activity in a sixth-grade classroom. Other studies have also demonstrated that children can be trained to elicit and reinforce appropriate behaviors in peers (Bailey, Timbers, Phillips & Wolf, 1971; Johnston & Johnston, 1972; Surratt, Ulrich, & Hawkins, 1969).

These studies illustrate that peer reinforcement *can* shape social behaviors, but do peers systematically reinforce behaviors in the natural environment? Children may not be professional behavior modifiers, but the evidence is clear that they naturally shape social behavior. For example, a number of investigators have investigated the role of peer reinforcement in the development of sex-typed behavior in young children. In a study of nursery school children, Fagot (1977) found that boys received more positive reinforcement than girls when engaging in "boy's play," whereas girls received more positive reinforcement than boys for engaging in "girl's play." Boys received greater criticism than girls for playing with dolls and dressing up. Lamb and Roopnarine (1979) and Lamb, Easterbrooks, and Holden (1980) also found that preschool peers positively reinforced behavior consistent with sex-role stereotypes and punished behavior inconsistent with the stereotypes. Moreover, they found that the reinforced behaviors continued longer than the punished behaviors.

A study by Patterson, Littman, and Bricker (1967) demonstrated that peers can also reinforce undesirable behavior. They observed preschoolers' interactions and found that approximately three fourths of the aggressive behaviors were reinforced by peers' compliance or submission. Unfortunately, such reinforcement had long-term effects. Children who displayed aggressive behavior and were reinforced by passivity on the part of the victim were more likely to continue the aggressive behavior in the future than those children whose aggression was responded to with counteraggression. Solomon and Wahler (1973) reported that peers tended to ignore prosocial behavior exhibited by problem children and to focus only on their negative behaviors. By selectively attending to and reinforcing negative behavior, peers may aggravate and perpetuate the behavior of children who are already in a socially rejected role. Thus, peers can have major effects on children's development by reinforcing or punishing various behaviors, although sometimes the behaviors that are fostered may not be the ones we desire.

PEER MODELING

Peers can also teach one another new behaviors by modeling. The behaviors children acquire through observational learning may affect their subsequent adjustment and development. For example, several treatment studies have used peer models to increase the rate of social interaction of withdrawn children. Using symbolic modeling procedures, O'Connor (1969) had an experimental group of withdrawn preschool children watch a film that portrayed positive peer interactions, whereas another group watched a film on dolphins. After viewing the modeling film, the children in the experimental group significantly increased their rate of social interaction, whereas those in the control group did not. O'Connor (1972) replicated these findings in a subsequent study and, in fact, found that the modeling effects lasted longer than when the children received contingent adult attention for peer interaction. Other investigators have also found modeling programs to be effective, although long-term effects are not necessarily obtained (Evers & Schwarz, 1973; Gresham & Nagle, 1980; Keller & Carlson, 1974). Peer models have also been found to affect problem-solving behavior (Debus, 1970; Miller & Dollard, 1941), performance on a memory task (Walters, Parke, & Cane, 1965), and sex-role behavior (Kobasigawa, 1968). Although most of the research on modeling has consisted of laboratory studies, observational studies have shown that peer modeling not only can affect children's behavior but also does affect it in the natural environment (Abramovitch & Grusec, 1978).

In relating these findings of the modeling literature to our thesis that peers affect adjustment and development, we see that children can and do have an impact on other children's behavior. This impact can be either positive or negative. Modeling studies do not include other measures of adjustment, however, such as self-esteem or interpersonal relationships. The inclusion of such measures would enhance our understanding of not only the influence of peers on others' behavior but also how this influence affects the child's self esteem and adjustment.

SOCIAL SKILLS INTERVENTION

Having reviewed the literature on how peers may affect development and adjustment through cooperative group interactions, peer contact, peer reinforcement and modeling, we will now review the literature on social skills interventions that have included peer contact as a central component. The basic premise of social skills interventions is that unaccepted children lack the requisite skills to develop and maintain peer relationships (Asher & Renshaw, 1981). By teaching the children these skills, one can improve peer relationships and ultimately foster overall development and adjustment. In the standard social skills program, a series of individual skills are taught one at a time. For example, Oden and Asher (1977) focused on four skills: (1) participation in play, (2) cooperation, (3) communication by listening and talking, and (4) validation support by looking, smiling, or offering encouragement. For each skill, children are typically first taught the general concept underlying it. Examples of skillful and unskillful behavior are provided, and children are asked to generate additional examples. Then the children practice applying the skill during an interaction with a peer or peers. Finally, the children receive feedback and reinforcement for their performance.

Social skills training programs have met with some success. Because these programs have as their goal the improvement of peer relationships, sociometric status is usually the primary outcome variable. Improvements in sociometric status have been reported in several studies (Bierman & Furman, 1984; Gresham & Nagle, 1980; Ladd, 1981; Oden & Asher, 1977; Siperstein & Gale, 1983), but not in all instances (Hymel & Asher, 1977; La Greca & Santogrossi, 1980). The reasons for such inconsistent findings have not been adequately explored as yet.

Changes in peer social behavior have also been reported. Specifically, changes have been reported in the rate of peer interaction (Christoff, Scott, Kelley, Schlundt, Baer, & Kelly, 1985; La Greca & Santagrossi, 1980), frequency of targeted prosocial behaviors (Bierman & Furman, 1984; Ladd, 1981), frequency of positive interaction (Gresham & Nagle, 1980), and proficiency in targeted prosocial skills (Bornstein, Bellack, & Hersen, 1977; Christoff et al, 1985; La Greca & Santagrossi, 1980). The preceding studies demonstrate that skills training affects peer interactions, although they do not really address the chapter's question of whether peer relations affect development and adjustment. Certainly, the quality of peer interactions is an index of development and adjustment, but the question of interest here is whether these changes in peer relations are associated with other changes.

A few investigators have examined the effects of social skills training on other domains such as school achievement, self-esteem, and perceived locus of control. Using a standard social skills training intervention with rejected, low-achieving children, Coie and Krehbiel (1984) demonstrated that skills training led to significant improvement in reading performance, though not in math. Intervening with adolescent male offenders, Long and Sherer (1985) were able to bring about an increased sense of internal locus of control, but no changes on perceived self-esteem were found. In another study with juvenile delinquents, Ollendick and Hersen (1979) reported increases in internal locus of control and decreases in state anxiety.

Several investigators have looked at change in self-esteem as a result of social skills intervention. Intervening with hyperactive adolescents, Waddell (1982) found an increase in self-esteem after participation in a social skills intervention.

Christoff et al. (1985) also found an increase in self-esteem when intervening with shy adolescents. Intervening with emotionally disordered adolescents, Plienis et al. (1987) demonstrated improvement in self-esteem, as well as depression and loneliness. In a social skills intervention with unaccepted preadolescents, Bierman and Furman (1984) found no changes in their measures of social self-efficacy and perceived social competence, although children who participated in cooperative group interaction tended to report increases in social self-efficacy.

In summary, there is evidence that interventions that utilize structured peer contact facilitate change on many adjustment variables. These include prosocial behavior, self-esteem, locus of control and school achievement. However, this literature provides us with limited evidence for our thesis that peer relations affect development. The literature has simply shown that changes in social skills are associated with changes in adjustment. In order to be able to better extrapolate from the intervention research, we would need to show that skill training leads to improved peer relations, which in turn affect adjustment.

Even if peer relations do play a role, we do not know what the precise role is. That is, it is unclear how peer relations are affected by the social skills interventions or any of the other interventions that we have reviewed here. These programs may improve children's peer relationships generally, perhaps resulting in children becoming socially accepted where they were once rejected. Alternatively, these interventions may foster the development of a few specific friendships. One might expect different effects depending upon which of these outcomes occur (Furman & Robbins, 1985). Sullivan (1953) in particular has stressed the major impact having a close friend or chum has on preadolescent adjustment, particularly self-esteem and prosocial behavior. Earlier in development, being accepted by the general peer group may be a more critical outcome, as the need for acceptance is particularly salient (Buhrmester & Furman, 1986). In future research, it would be interesting to investigate how the role of peers changes throughout the life cycle. One would expect that the processes by which peers influence one other would change with age, as well as the areas in which they would be expected to have influence and the potency of their influence. This topic has received surprisingly little attention, although it is a critical component in both designing effective treatment interventions and assessing their impact (Furman, 1980).

FUTURE DIRECTION

In our review of the programs using various intervention approaches, we have tried to point out limitations and future directions. A few general directions, however, warrant particular emphasis. First, in order to evaluate these models of the role of peers in development, it is important to understand what processes are at work in peer interventions. In the research that has been discussed thus far, the role of peers has been difficult to isolate and quantify precisely. For example, in interventions described as cooperative peer contact, it is likely that there are other treatment components at work, such as modeling, adult reinforcement, and skill acquisition. Similarly, the changes in adjustment brought about by social skills training may or may not be mediated by changes in peer interactions. In order to understand the role of peers above and beyond these other factors, it is crucial to isolate each of the potential components.

Ladd and Mize (1983) discussed the importance of identifying and quantifying process variables in social skills intervention research. They noted that the typical program contained several training variables, including skill instruction (focused on social goals, strategies, and skill contexts), rehearsal, and feedback. Moreover, programs had multiple objectives, including enhancing skill concepts, promoting skill performance, and fostering skill maintenance and generalization. As yet, it is unclear which training variables and objectives are responsible for the observed treatment effects.

Another important set of processes are nonspecific treatment factors. These would include the relationship between the therapist and the target child, the presence of a structured plan to effect change, and motivational components. For example, perhaps one reason peer intervention programs work is that we tell the children it is important for them to change their behavior and we encourage them to do so. Aside from the potential effect of simple contact with peers or an adult, such nonspecific factors have received little attention in the peer intervention literature. Such factors have, however, been shown to have major effects in adult psychotherapy (Kazdin, 1979; Shapiro, 1971; Shapiro & Morris, 1978).

In order to understand the process of change, we need more detailed descriptions of the nature of the interventions. Videotaped treatment sessions and treatment manuals would be invaluable. Until we fully know the content of the treatment process, we cannot begin to identify the change ingredients.

Data analytic techniques can also be used to enhance our understanding of the process of change. If a particular process is an important treatment component, one would expect that the degree of engagement or change in that process would be related to changes in the outcome variable of interest. For example, if a skills training model is correct, one would expect changes in social skills to be associated with changes in our different outcome measures. If improvement in peer relations fosters self-esteem, one would expect changes in sociometric status to be correlated with changes in peer relations.

Unfortunately, few investigators have included such analyses. When they have been included, they have typically consisted of correlations among various pre–post change measures (either gain scores or simple difference scores, the former being more appropriate). Although such analyses are valuable, they may not be the most sensitive measure of therapeutic change. Premeasures and postmeasures are often based on single assessments, which can be less reliable than desired, particularly when one derives difference or gain scores. The problem of reliability can be compounded by the fact that the measures often have a restricted range at the time of pretest. Additionally, there are serious limitations in the causal inferences one can draw from such analyses. For example, a correlation between changes in sociometric status and changes in self-esteem may mean that improvement in peer relations fosters self-esteem, but the reverse seems equally plausible.

It may be more fruitful to examine the relations between behavior in the treatment sessions and outcome than to examine pre–post changes. For example, Bierman (1986) examined taped excerpts of treatment sessions from a recent intervention study with unpopular preadolescents (Bierman & Furman, 1984). The skills training consisted of engaging in cooperative activities with socially accepted peers. In addition, half the subjects received skills training and half received nonspecific adult support. Bierman explored the changes that occurred during training sessions and found that the display of conversational skills and positive peer responses in the treatment sessions were associated with successful outcomes. Interestingly, Bierman was not as successful in demonstrating change when she used pre–post measures (Bierman, personal communication, May, 1981).

One important goal for the future should be to include a greater variety of outcome measures that relate to adjustment. Aside from the literature on cooperative interventions, only a few studies (e.g., Bierman & Furman, 1984; Coie & Krehbiel, 1984) have examined outcome variables other than sociometric status or social interactions with peers. To evaluate the impact of peers on adjustment and development, we need to include measures of self-esteem, school performance, and emotional functioning. Ladd and Mize (1983) suggested including measures of children's ability to self-monitor, attributions for success and failure, and affective variables such as anxiety level. In addition to these variables, it would seem important to include more measures of changes in the peer group. For example, we do not really know if individual intervention programs have generalized effects on other children who did not participate in the actual intervention. It is critical to examine these components, particularly when trying to understand the role of peers in adjustment and development.

We should also examine how other relationships are influenced by the interventions. For example, it seems possible that these programs could improve relations with other persons, such as siblings or parents, as well as with peers (Furman & Robbins, 1985). The social skills that are taught may be applicable in other relationships. Alternatively, generalized effects could be obtained through other mechanisms such as changes in self-esteem or changes in children's "working models" of relationships. One implication of this idea is that we should not just assess changes in social status, but we should assess changes in specific peer relationships, such as friendships. As we begin to analyze the process of change and broaden our battery of outcome measures, we should obtain a more complete picture of the effects of peers on development. Much can also be learned by studying the different treatment approaches described here. Investigators using different intervention techniques have remained relatively isolated from one another. Their target populations often differ, and the effects of the program are assessed differently. We believe, however, that an integrated approach will be most likely to yield effective intervention programs and to help us understand how peers affect development.

REFERENCES

Abramovitch, R., & Grusec, J. E. (1978). Peer imitation in a natural setting. *Child Development, 49*, 60–69.

Allport, G. (1954). *The nature of prejudice*. Cambridge, MA: Addison-Wesley.

Aronson, E. (1978). *The Jigsaw classroom*. Beverly Hills, CA.: Sage.

Asarnow, J. R., & Callan, J. W. (1985). Boys with peer adjustment problems: Social cognitive processes. *Journal of Consulting and Clinical Psychology, 53*(1), 80–87.

Asher, S. R., & Renshaw, P. D. (1981). Children without friends: Social knowledge and social skill training. In S. R. Asher & J. M. Gottman (Eds.), *The development of children's friendships*. (pp. 273–296) New York: Cambridge University Press.

Bailey, J. S., Timbers, G. D., Phillips, E. L., & Wolf, M. M. (1971). Modification of articulation errors of pre-delinquents by their peers. *Journal of Applied Behavior Analysis, 4*, 265–281.

Ballard, M., Corman, L., Gottlieb, J., & Kaufman, M. J. (1977). Improving the social status of mainstreamed retarded children. *Journal of Educational Psychology, 69*, 605–611.

Bierman, K. L. (1986). Process of change during social skills training with preadolescents and its relation to treatment outcomes. *Child Development, 57*, 230–240.

Bierman, K. L., & Furman, W. (1984). The effects of social skills training and peer involvement on the social adjustment of preadolescents. *Child Development, 55*, 151–162.

Blaney, N. T., Stephan, S., Rosenfield, D., Aronson, E., & Sikes, J. (1977). Interdependence in the classroom: A field study. *Journal of Educational Psychology, 69*, 121–128.

Bornstein, M. R., Bellack, A. S., & Hersen, M. (1977). Social skills training for unassertive children: A multiple baseline analysis. *Journal of Applied Behavior Analysis, 10*, 183–195.

Bridgeman, D. L. (1981). Enhanced role-taking through cooperative interdependence: A field study. *Child Development, 52*, 1231–1238.

Buhrmester, D., & Furman, W. (1986). The changing function of friends in childhood. A neo-Sullivanian perspective. In V. Derlega & B. Winstead (Eds.), *Friendship and social interaction* (pp. 41–62). New York: Springer-Verlag.

Chennault, M. (1967). Improving the social acceptance of unpopular educable mentally retarded pupils in special classes. *American Journal of Mental Deficiency, 72*, 455–458.

Christoff, K. A., Scott, W. O., Kelley, M. L., Schlundt, D., Baer, G., & Kelly, J. A. (1985). Social skills and social problem-solving training for shy young adolescents. *Behavior Therapy, 16*, 468–477.

Coie, J. D., & Krehbiel, G. (1984). Effects of academic tutoring on the social status of low-achieving, socially rejected children. *Child Development, 55*, 1465–1478.

Cowen, E. L., Pederson, A., Babigian, H., Izzo, L. D., & Trost, M. (1973). Long-term follow-up of early detected vulnerable children. *Journal of Consulting and Clinical Psychology, 41*, 438–446.

Debus, R. L. (1970). Effects of brief observation of model behavior on conceptual tempo of impulsive children. *Developmental Psychology, 2*, 22–32.

DeVries, D. L., Edwards, K. J., & Slavin, R. E. (1978). Biracial learning teams and race relations in the classroom: Four field experiments on Teams-Games-Tournaments. *Journal of Educational Psychology, 70*, 356–362.

DeVries, D. L., & Slavin, R. (1978). Teams-Games-Tournament: Review of ten classroom experiments. *Journal of Research and Development in Education, 12*, 28–38.

Evers, W. L., & Schwartz, J. S. (1973). Modifying social withdrawal in preschoolers: Filmed modeling and teacher praise. *Journal of Abnormal Child Psychology, 3*, 179–185.

Fagot, B. I. (1977). Consequences of moderate cross-gender behavior in preschool children. *Child Development, 48*, 902–907.

Furman, W. (1980). Promoting social development: Developmental implications for social learning approaches. In B. B. Lahey & A. E. Kazdin (Eds.), *Advances in clinical child psychology* (Vol. 3, pp. 1–40). New York: Plenum.

Furman, W., Rahe, D. F., & Hartup, W. W. (1979). The rehabilitation of socially withdrawn preschool children through mixed-age and same-age socialization. *Child Development, 50*, 915–922.

Furman, W., & Robbins, P. (1985). What's the point? Issues in the selection of treatment objectives. In B. H. Schneider, K. H. Rubin, & J. E. Ledingham (Eds.), *Children's peer relations: Issues in assessment and intervention* (pp. 175–192). New York: Springer-Verlag.

Gresham, F., & Nagle, R. (1980). Social skills training with children: Responsiveness to modeling and coaching as a function of peer orientation. *Journal of Consulting and Clinical Psychology, 48*, 718–729.

Hartup, W. W. (1983). The peer system. In P. H. Mussen (Editor-in-chief) & E. M. Hetherington (Ed.), *Carmichael's Manual of Child Psychology*, (Vol. 4, pp. 103–198). New York: Wiley.

Heber, R. F., & Heber, M. E. (1957). The effects of group failure and success on social status. *Journal of Educational Psychology, 48*, 129–134.

Helper, M. M. (1958). Parental evaluations of children and children's self-evaluations. *Journal of Abnormal and Social Psychology, 56*, 190–194.

Hertz-Lazarowitz, R., Sharan, S., & Steinberg, R. (1980). Classroom learning style and co-operative behavior of elementary school children. *Journal of Educational Psychology, 72*, 99–106.

Horowitz, F. D. (1962). Incentive value of social stimuli for preschool children. *Child Development, 33*, 111–116.

Hymel, S., & Asher, S. R. (1977). *Assessment and training of isolated children's social skills.* Paper presented at the biennial meeting of the Society for Research in Child Development, New Orleans.

Hymel, S., & Franke, S. (1985). Children's peer relations: Assessing self-perceptions. In B. H. Schneider, K. H. Rubin, & J. E. Ledingham (Eds.), *Children's peer relations: Issues in assessment and intervention* (pp. 78–92). New York: Springer-Verlag.

Hymel, S., Wagner, E., & Butler, L. J. (in press). Reputational bias: View from the peer group. In S. R. Asher and J. D. Coie (Eds.), *Peer rejection in children: Origins, consequences, and intervention.* New York: Cambridge University Press.

Jennings, K. D. (1975). People versus object orientation. Social behavior and intellectual abilities in preschool children. *Developmental Psychology, 11,* 511–519.

Johnson, D., & Johnson, R. (1985). The internal dynamics of cooperative learning groups. In R. Slavin, S. Sharan, S. Kagan, R. Hertz-Lazarowitz, C. Webb, & R. Schmuck (Eds.), *Learning to cooperate, cooperating to learn* (pp. 103–124). New York: Plenum.

Johnson, D. W., & Johnson, R. T. (1975). *Learning together and alone.* Englewood Cliffs, NJ: Prentice-Hall.

Johnson, D. W., Johnson, R. T., Johnson, J., & Anderson, D. (1976). The effects of cooperative and individualized instruction on student attitudes and achievement. *The Journal of Social Psychology, 104,* 207–216.

Johnson, D. W., Maruyana, G., Johnson, R., Nelson, D., & Skon, L. (1981). Effects of cooperative, competitive, and individualistic goal structures on achievement: A meta-analysis. *Psychological Bulletin, 89,* 47–62.

Johnson, R. T., Johnson, D. W., & Scott, L. (1978). The effects of cooperative and individualized instruction on student attitudes and achievement. *The Journal of Social Psychology, 104,* 207–216.

Johnston, J. M., & Johnston, G. T. (1972). Modification of consonant speech-sound articulation in young children. *Journal of Applied Behavior Analysis, 5,* 233–246.

Kazdin, A. E. (1979). Nonspecific treatment factors in psychotherapy outcome research. *Journal of Consulting and Clinical Psychology, 47,* 846–851.

Keller, M., & Carlson, P. (1974). The use of symbolic modeling to promote social skills in preschool children with low levels of social responsiveness. *Child Development, 45,* 912–919.

Kinney, E. E. (1953). A study of peer-group social acceptability at the fifth grade level in a public school. *Journal of Education Research, 47,* 57–64.

Kobasigawa, A. (1968). Inhibitory and disinhibitory effects of models on sex-inappropriate behavior in children. *Psychologia, 11,* 86–96.

Ladd, G. (1981). Effectiveness of a social learning method for enhancing children's social interaction and peer acceptance. *Child Development, 52,* 171–178.

Ladd, G. W., & Mize, J. (1983). A cognitive-social learning model of social-skill training. *Psychology Review, 90,* 127–157.

La Greca, A. M., & Santogrossi, D. (1980). Social skills training with elementary school students: A behavioral group approach. *Journal of Consulting and Clinical Psychology, 2,* 220–227.

Lamb, M. E., Easterbrooks, M. A., & Holden, G. W. (1980). Reinforcement and punishment among preschoolers: Characteristics, effects, and correlates. *Child Development, 50,* 1219–1222.

Lamb, M. E., & Roopnarine, J. L. (1979). Peer influences on sex-role development in preschoolers. *Child Development, 50,* 1219–1222.

Lancioni, G. E. (1982). Normal children as tutors to withdrawn mentally retarded schoolmates: Training, maintenance, and generalization. *Journal of Applied Behavior Analysis, 15,* 17–40.

Lilly, M. S. (1971). Improving social acceptance of low sociometric status, low achieving students. *Exceptional Children, 37,* 341–348.

Long, S. J., & Sherer, M. (1985). Social skills training with juvenile offenders. *Child and Family Behavior Therapy, 6,* 1–11.

McDaniel, C. O. (1970). Participation in extracurricular activities, social acceptance and social rejection among educable mentally retarded students. *Education and Training of the Mentally Retarded, 5,* 4–14.

Miller, N. E., & Dollard, J. (1941). *Social learning and imitation.* New Haven, CT: Yale University Press.

O'Connor, R. D. (1969). Modification of social withdrawal through symbolic modeling. *Journal of Applied Behavioral Analysis, 2,* 15–22.

O'Connor, R. D. (1972). Relative efficacy of modeling, shaping, and the combined procedures for the modification of social withdrawal. *Journal of Abnormal Psychology, 79,* 327–334.

Oden, S., & Asher, D. R. (1977). Coaching children in social skills for friendship making. *Child Development, 48,* 495–506.

Ollendick, T. H., & Hersen, M. (1979). Social skills training for juvenile delinquents. *Behavioral Research and Therapy, 17,* 1–8.

Orlick, T. (1981). Positive socialization via cooperative games. *Developmental Psychology, 17,* 426–429.

Patterson, G. R., Littman, R. A., & Bricker, W. (1967). Assertive behavior in children: A step toward a theory of aggression. *Monographs of the Society for Research in Child Development, 32* (6, Whole No. 113).

Petrinovich, L. (1979). Probabilistic functionalism: Conception of research method. *American Psychologist, 34,* 373–390.

Plienis, A. J., Hansen, D. J., Ford, F., Smith, S., Stark, L., & Kelly, J. A. (1987). Behavioral small group training to improve the social skills of emotionally-disordered adolescents. *Behavior Therapy, 18,* 17–32.

Putallaz, M., White, A., & Shipman, R. (1985, April). *Sociometric status and adjustment: A developmental perspective.* Paper presented at the biennial meeting of the Society for Research in Child Development, Toronto.

Roff, M., Sells, B., & Golden, M. (1972). *Social adjustment and personality development in children.* Minneapolis: University of Minnesota Press.

Rucker, C. N., & Vincenzo, F. M. (1970). Maintaining social acceptance gains made by mentally retarded children. *Exceptional Children, 36,* 679–680.

Shapiro, A. K. (1971). Placebo effects in medicine, psychotherapy, and psychoanalysis. In A. E. Bergin & S. L. Garfield (Eds.), *Handbook of psychotherapy and behavior change: An empirical analysis* (pp. 439–473). New York: Wiley.

Shapiro, A. K., & Morris, L. A. (1978). Placebo effects in medical and psychological therapies. In S. L. Garfield & A. E. Bergin (Eds.), *Handbook of psychotherapy and behavior change: An empirical analysis* (2nd Ed., pp. 369–410). New York: Wiley.

Sharan, S. (1980). Cooperative learning in small groups: Recent methods and effects on achievement, attitudes, and ethnic relations. *Review of Educational Research, 50,* 241–271.

Sharan, S., & Sharan, Y. (1976). *Small group teaching.* Englewood Cliffs, NJ: Educational Technologies Publications.

Sherif, M., Harvey, O. J., White, B. J., Hood, W. R., & Sherif, C. W. (1961). *Intergroup conflict and cooperation: The Robbers Cave experiment.* Norman: University of Oklahoma Press.

Siperstein, G., & Gale, M. (April, 1983). *Improving peer relationships of rejected children.* Paper presented at the annual meeting of the Society for Research on Child Development, Detroit.

Slavin, R. E. (1985). An introduction to cooperative learning research. In R. Slavin, S. Sharan, S. Kagan, R. Hertz-Lazarowitz, C. Webb, & R. Schmuck (Eds.), *Learning to cooperate, cooperating to learn* (pp. 5–16). New York: Plenum.

Slavin, R. E. (1983a). *Cooperative learning.* New York: Longman.

Slavin, R. E. (1983b). When does cooperative learning increase student achievement? *Psychological Bulletin, 94,* 429–445.

Slavin, R. E. (1980). *Using student learning.* The Johns Hopkins University, Center for Social Organization of Schools, Baltimore.

Slavin, R. E., & Karweit, N. (1981). Cognitive and affective outcomes of an intensive student team learning experience. *Journal of Experimental Education, 50,* 29–35.

Solomon, R. W., & Wahler, R. G. (1973). Peer reinforcement of classroom problem behavior. *Journal of Applied Behavior Analysis, 6,* 49–55.

Stendler, C. B., Damrin, P., & Haines, A. C. (1951). Studies in cooperation and competition: I. The effects of working for group and individual rewards on the social climate of children's groups. *Journal of Genetic Psychology, 79,* 173–193.

Strain, P. S., Kerr, M. A., & Ragland, E. U. (1979). Effects of peer-mediated social initiations and prompting/reinforcement procedures on the social behavior of autistic children. *Journal of Autism and Developmental Disabilities, 9,* 41–54.

Strain, P. S., Shores, R. E., & Timm, M. A. (1977). Effects of social initiations on the behavior of withdrawn preschool children. *Journal of Applied Behavior Analysis, 10,* 289–298.

Surratt, P. R., Ulrich, R. E., & Hawkins, R. P. (1969). An elementary student as a behavior engineer. *Journal of Applied Behavior Analysis, 2,* 85–92.

Waddell, K. J. (1982, September). *Teaching social skills to hyperactive adolescents.* Paper presented at the annual meeting of the American Psychological Association, Washington, DC.

Wahler, R. G. (1967). Child-child interactions in five field settings: Some experimental analyses. *Journal of Experimental Child Psychology, 5,* 278–293.

Walters, R. H., Parke R. D., & Cane, V. A. (1965). Timing of punishment and the observation of consequences to others as determinants of response inhibition. *Journal of Experimental Child Psychology, 2,* 10–30.

Wright, S., & Cowen, E. L. (1985). The effects of peer-teaching on student perceptions of class environment, adjustment, and academic performance. *American Journal of Community Psychology, 13,* 417–431.

CHAPTER 13

Peers' Contributions to Children's Social Maladjustment

Description and Intervention

JOSEPH M. PRICE AND KENNETH A. DODGE
Vanderbilt University

The study of children's peer relations has been a marvelous story of how multiple perspectives within psychology have converged to investigate an obviously important topic. The topic is the role that a child's friendships and peer status play in development. The importance of this topic has been demonstrated in numerous studies indicating that children who fail to get along with the members of their peer group, in particular children who are actively disliked by their peers (i.e., rejected), are often unable to break out of this negative status (Coie & Dodge, 1983). These children are lonely (Asher & Wheeler, 1986) and are at increased risk for a variety of difficulties in later life, including school maladjustment (Kupersmidt, 1983) and a number of conduct and psychiatric disorders (see Parker & Asher, 1987, for a review).

The multiple perspectives that have been brought to bear on this problem suggest that multiple processes are implicated in the establishment, maintenance, and exacerbation of the interpersonal difficulties of socially rejected children. These perspectives have included applied behavioral analysis of the patterns of social interaction that lead a child to become socially rejected by peers; examination of the social cognitive skills, biases, and deficits that may be responsible for a rejected child's behavioral incompetence; social psychological analysis of the cognitive processes that lead the peer group to ostracize, label, and stereotype a rejected child; and analysis of the behavioral processes through which the peer group inadvertently reinforces and perpetuates a rejected child's inappropriate behavior through their own prejudicial behavior toward the child. These four aspects of peer transactions

---

The writing of this chapter was supported by Grant BSN-8615434, awarded to the second author by the National Science Foundation.

are not independent; indeed, they may operate in reciprocally influential ways.

A general model of social functioning incorporating these aspects of peer transactions is presented in Figure 13.1. The model describes the reciprocal interactions among them. As is evident from the model, the processing of social cues and the social behavior of both the rejected child and the members of his or her peer group can contribute to the problem of social rejection.

Beginning with the child's own contribution to social rejection, there is considerable evidence to suggest that the behaviors children employ with peers play an important role in determining their social status in the peer

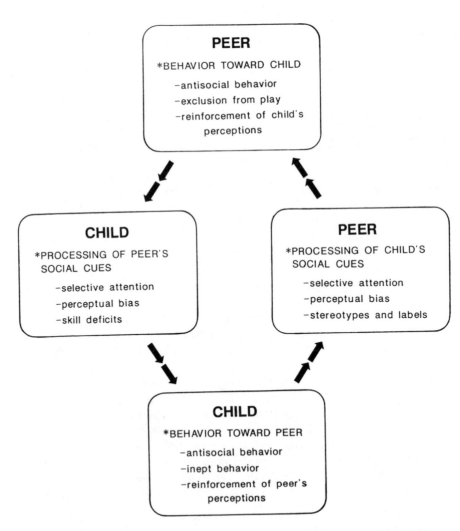

Figure 13.1 Reciprocal influences in peer transactions involving socially rejected children.

group. Some of the more convincing evidence comes from two short-term longitudinal studies of the emergence of social status in small play groups (Coie & Kupersmidt, 1983; Dodge, 1983). Coie and Kupersmidt (1983) selected boys from each of four sociometric status groups in their schools (i.e., popular, average, neglected, rejected). They examined the boys' social interactions and the development of their social status in play groups composed of either familiar or unfamiliar peers. Analysis of boys' behavior in both kinds of play groups indicated that rejected boys displayed higher levels of inappropriate and aggressive behaviors than did either popular or neglected peers. In contrast, popular boys in both contexts tended to employ prosocial behaviors and seldom engaged in aggressive behaviors. In a study employing a similar design, Dodge (1983) found that the boys who eventually became rejected within the peer group were those who displayed relatively high rates of rough play and unprovoked aggressive behaviors and were less likely to engage in positive or prosocial forms of behavior such as cooperative play and social conversation. The evidence from these studies supports the findings from correlational studies of behavior in classroom and playground settings in suggesting that individual behavior differences are at least partly responsible for the establishment and maintenance of children's social reputations (see Coie, Dodge, & Kupersmidt, in press, and Ladd & Asher, 1985, for reviews).

Just as strong is the literature indicating that a large proportion of the children who come to be socially rejected display inadequate and biased processing of social cues. Socially rejected children have been found to be relatively deficient in skills of intention-due detection (Dodge, Murphy, & Buchsbaum, 1984), social problem solving (Asarnow & Callan, 1985; Dodge, McClaskey, & Feldman, 1985; Rubin & Krasnor, 1986), social knowledge (Asher & Renshaw, 1981), and response evaluation (Crick & Ladd, 1987; Feldman & Dodge, 1987). Rejected children have also been found to be negatively biased in their attributions of peers' intentions (Dodge & Frame, 1982) and inappropriately optimistic in their expectations regarding outcomes of their aggresive behavior (Crick & Ladd). It seems quite clear that children who are developmentally lagging or unskilled in critical social-cognitive tasks are likely to become socially rejected by the peer group, even as young as the kindergarten age (Putallaz, 1983). In addition, social-cognitive processes undoubtedly act to perpetuate and exacerbate negative peer status of these children (Dodge & Richard, 1985).

Complementing these literatures relating to the child's contribution to social rejection is a growing body of evidence to suggest that once a child's social reputation is established in a particular peer group, the social cognitive processing and social behavior of the individual members of the peer group may play an important role in maintaining and perpetuating both the child's behavior reputation (Hymel, Wagner, & Butler, in press). With regard to peers' processing of social cues, Dodge (1980) examined children's attributions for the negative behavior of others and found that peers were five times more likely to attribute hostile intentions to a child that they knew was aggressive toward peers and rejected by peers than they were toward a nonaggressive, nonrejected child. Thus, a child's reputational status biased peers' perceptions of his or her subsequent behavior. More recently, Hymel (1986) extended this research by examining variations in children's interpretations for the behavior of known peers as a function of prior liking for the peers. In contrast with the behavior of liked children, the behavior of disliked children was more likely to be interpreted in a negative manner. More specifically, whereas positive behaviors were attributed to more stable causes for liked children than for disliked children, negative behaviors were attributed to more stable causes for disliked children than for liked children. Furthermore, disliked children were attributed greater responsibility for negative behaviors than were liked children. These findings suggest that the peer group displays stereotypic processing of a child's social cues in ways that perpetuate the child's negative reputation.

Not only does the peer group have stereotyped perceptions of a rejected child, the peer group is also known to display prejudicial behavior toward rejected children. Consider the findings of the Dodge (1980) study. Peers' attributions regarding a child's behavior were directly related to the peers' behavioral responses toward a child. Peers who attributed hostile intentions to a child were likely to retaliate aggressively toward a child, whereas peers who attributed benign intentions were likely to refrain from retaliation. Since peers attributed hostile intent to aggressive-rejected children more frequently than they did to nonrejected children, they were more likely to behave aggressively toward the rejected children. Direct observations by Dodge and Frame (1982) confirmed this tendency by peers to distribute disproportionately high rates of aggressive behavior toward aggressive children.

The evidence from these investigations carries important implications for intervention research aimed at improving the peer acceptance of rejected children. In spite of numerous efforts, the gains achieved through experimental interventions aimed directly at changing the skills and/or behavior of the rejected child have been modest (Dodge, in press; Ladd & Asher, 1985). Since the peer group appears to play a role in the maintenance of inappropriate behavior by disliked children and in their social reputations, it would appear that the peer group of a rejected child should be involved in any attempts at intervention. The results from a recent social skills intervention study by Bierman (1986) support this contention. She found that the greatest gains in a child's social skills and peer acceptance were evidenced for an intervention program that combined training in conversational skills with cooperatively structured experiences with classroom peers. This program led to greater gains than mere skills training alone. One possible interpretation of this finding is that the peer experience condition served as a better staging area of rehearsal context for learning and applying new skills. It is also feasible, as Bierman points out, that the peers' responses were somehow instrumental in changing the target children's behavior. For example, the peer partners may have provided modeling and reinforcement for the performance of skillful behavior by the target child. Additionally, in contrast with the classroom environment, the peer partners provided an environment more positively responsive to skillful behavior, thus reinforcing appropriate behavior by rejected children during training. Furthermore, the peer partners' increased positive responsivity toward the targeted rejected childen may have served as an attributional cue both to themselves and to their classmates which, in turn, may have led to improved evaluations of the rejected children. Thus, a receptive and facilitative peer environment may be necessary for lasting improvements in peer relations for rejected children.

In light of this evidence, the goals of this chapter are (1) to highlight the transactional nature of peer relations, involving processing of social cues and social behavior by both rejected children and the peer group; (2) to review evidence concerning the possible consequences of negative reputations; and (3) to present literature and concepts addressing the utilization of the peer group in the process of intervention. Toward these ends, the model of reciprocal influences in peer transactions presented earlier will be utilized as an organizing framework for examining the role of the peer group in maintaining and changing children's social behavior and reputations. More specifically, the aspects of the peer system to be considered in this paper include (1) the role of peers' perceptions and attitudes in maintaining and exacerbating a child's negative reputation; (2) the role of peers' behaviors toward a rejected child in maintaining inappropriate behavior by the rejected child as well as negative reputations of that child; (3) the role of peers in a child's development of social-cognitive skills and in the maintenance of a child's patterns of processing social information; and (4) the role played by peers in reinforcing and maintaining a child's social behavior. Within each of these dimensions of the model, relevant literature on peer processes and intervention will be reviewed. From these analyses, suggestions for intervention strategies utilizing the peer group will be proposed.

Peer Processing of Information about a Disliked Child

ANALYSIS OF PROCESSES.   As mentioned earlier, the degree to which the children are accepted or rejected by the members of their peer group depends, in part, on the quality of their behavior in interactions with those peers. Whereas the employment of prosocial behaviors such as cooperative play and social conversation is related to peer acceptance, agonistic displays such as verbal insults and physical aggression are linked to being disliked by peers (see Coie & Kupersmidt, 1983; Dodge, 1983). Furthermore, once children's perceptions of one another are established, they appear to remain somewhat stable over time (Coie et al., in press). One explanation for this stability is that the structure of children's social cognitive processes is conducive to the maintenance of the perceptions and impressions children develop for one another. In this section, we will examine several social cognitive processes that might be involved in the maintenance and perpetuation of a child's social reputation. A model of social information processing (Dodge, 1986) will serve as the conceptual framework that will guide this examination.

The model proposes that a child's social behaviors act as cues to a peer, leading to the peer's behavioral response to the child as well as the peer's evaluation of the child. The cues are processed by the peer in sequential stages, including early stages at which the cues are encoded (i.e., received through sensory processes guided by attention) and mentally represented (i.e., interpreted, understood, and evaluated). At later processing stages, the represented cues act as stimuli to the generation of possible behavioral responses (which are brought from long-term memory stores to working memory, as in a "calling-to-mind process"). These responses are evaluated (through representation of probable outcomes), and then a chosen response is enacted.

Biases and heuristics are proposed to guide processing at each stage, in ways that may lead to perpetuate a child's negative social reputation. First, at the encoding stage, peers may be perceptually ready to attend to certain types of behavior. The types of behavior to which peers attend depends on both their attitudes and perceptions of the child displaying the behavior (i.e., whether they like the child) and the valence of the behavior. Research with adults suggests that knowledge structures or schema such as stereotypes help to guide the allocation of a person's attention by directing attention to information that is relevant to these knowledge structures (Crocker & Park, 1986). "Relevant" information is that which is either consistent or inconsistent with the stereotype, rather than neutral or irrelevant to it.

It is possible that a similar process may be involved in children's processing of social information. Since children cannot attend to all the stimuli and cues in an interpersonal context, the perceptual knowledge or schema that they have of a child may help to guide attention by directing it toward relevant cues. Thus, when interacting with either a liked or disliked child, a peer would be likely to attend to behaviors that are relevant to his or her schema for the child (e.g., antisocial behaviors).

The implications of this work are quite clear. If a peer develops a schema for a child that involves the display of aggressive and inappropriate behavior, the peer may attend to the child's future aggressive behaviors. If the display of prosocial behaviors is not a part of this schema, the peer may ignore any future prosocial behaviors by the child (since they are not relevant to the schema).

In addition, qualities of the behaviors within the stimulus field for a peer may be involved in guiding the allocation of attention. For example, in their study of the reliability and validity of preschoolers' perceptions of child behavior, Ladd and Mars (1986) found differences in the stability of peers' perceptions of certain types of behaviors. Whereas preschoolers' perceptions of cooperative play and aggression were most stable, their perceptions of social conversation, solitary play, and teacher-oriented behavior were least stable. The authors suggested that one explanation for this finding may be that peers are more aware of aggression and cooperative play than they are of more neutral behaviors, possibly because the former are inherently more salient to peer interactions. For instance, the saliency of aggression may be attributable to the painful outcomes produced by this behavior. Cooperative play, on the other hand, may be salient to children because it provides social rewards. It is also the case that individuals are more likely to attend to the display of a behavior than to the absence of its display (that is, individuals attend to aggressive behaviors and do not attend to the absence of aggression).

Therefore, if a peer develops a schema for a child that involves the display of highly salient antisocial behavior, the peer will be likely to attend to future antisocial behavior and will be less likely to attend to the display of schema-irrelevant prosocial behaviors and less salient absence of antisocial behavior.

Given this perceptual readiness to attend to information that is relevant to a peer's knowledge structures of a child, how does a peer then interpret such information? The second stage of social information processing that might be involved in the maintenance of a child's social reputation is the peer's mental representation of the child's behaviors. With regard to peer relations, the most important heuristic at this stage of processing is the confirmation bias (Darley & Fazio, 1980; Gurwitz & Dodge, 1977). After experience with a child, a peer develops a set of expected or normative behaviors for the child. These normative behaviors lead the peer to entertain hypotheses regarding the future behavior of a child (such as a hypothesis about whether the child will act prosocially or aggressively). The peer tests these hypotheses by matching the encoded behavioral cues from the child to the hypothesis. Peers are in most respects data-based in evaluating their hypotheses, but they may be subject to the hypothesis-confirmation bias to which adults fall prey. Adults who hold conflicting hypotheses show a bias toward confirming rather than disconfirming them, even when the same information is available (Sherman, 1987). For example, consider that one peer has a hypothesis that a child is aggressive and another peer has a hypothesis that the same child is nonaggressive. If presented with the very same subsequent information, both peers may be likely to conclude that their hypotheses are correct.

Other biases may be evidenced in peers' interpretations as well. Recently, Hymel (1986) examined whether peers' interpretations of the behavior of familiar children varied as a function of prior liking for a child. Popular and unpopular second- and fifth-grade peers were asked to explain the behavior of either liked or disliked children in situations that had either a positive or negative outcome for the peers. The results indicated that peers' explanations of a child's behavior varied as a function of both affect toward the child and the valence of the behavior. Whereas positive behaviors were attributed to more stable causes (e.g., personality trait or ability) for liked children than for disliked children, negative behaviors were attributed to more stable causes for disliked children than for liked children.

These results suggest that when a child acts in a manner that is consistent with a peer's perceptual schema for the child (i.e., liked peers displaying positive behaviors), the behavior is attributed to a stable cause. Conversely, when a child displays a behavior that is inconsistent with a peer's perceptual schema, that behavior is attributed to an unstable cause (it is discounted, Darley & Fazio, 1980) and is therefore not expected to recur. These biased interpretations of another's behavior are likely to contribute to the maintenance of children's social reputations.

It is important to note that the subjects in Hymel's (1986) investigation were 7, 10, and 15 years old. Whether or not these patterns of interpretive bias would hold for younger children is not known. Rholes and Ruble (1984; 1986) have demonstrated that peers' understanding or dispositional characteristics of others, as evidenced by their ability to predict behavioral consistency on the bases of previously observed behavior, does not emerge until around age 7. Furthermore, research by Livesley and Bromley (1973) suggests that peers do not employ personality traits to describe others until 7 or 8 years of age. These data suggest that the limitations of younger children's social cognitive skills may actually lead them to be *less* prone to the type of interpretive bias described above. There is, however, some evidence that young children display yet another type of interpretive bias—a bias toward a persistently positive view of others (Rholes & Ruble, 1986).

Another important qualifying note about Hymel's (1986) investigation is that the subjects were presented with only a few instances in which the behavior of a disliked child led to a positive outcome. It remains to be determined whether a similar pattern of attributional biases would hold if peers were presented with numerous instances in which the behavior of a disliked child led to a positive outcome. A recent investigation by Rothbart and Park (1986) on the ease of confirming and disconfirming various trait concepts may provide some insights into a possible answer to this question. Undergraduates were asked to rate 150 trait adjectives on the following dimensions: (1) the frequency with which occasions arise that would allow for behavior that would confirm or disconfirm a given trait; (2) the number of instances of behavior that are required to confirm or disconfirm a trait once it has been established; (3) the ease of imagining specific observable behaviors that confirm or disconfirm a particular trait; (4) favorableness (i.e., how favorably or unfavorably an individual would be regarded if he or she possessed this trait); and (5) the frequency in the population. The results indicated that favorability was highly positively correlated with the number of behaviors required to confirm a trait and highly negatively correlated with the number of behaviors required to disconfirm a trait. Thus, perceived favorable traits appear to be hard to acquire and easy to disconfirm, whereas unfavorable traits appear to be easy to acquire and difficult to disconfirm.

Among the negative trait dimensions that were rated as requiring a large number of instances to disconfirm were aggression, argumentativeness, hostility, cruelty, quick temper, and rudeness. Therefore, if these same traits are difficult to disconfirm among children, a child who has acquired a reputation for displaying any of these types of behaviors might have a difficult time dispelling that reputation. In order to change a peer's perceptions of a disliked child, it might be necessary to present that peer with a relatively large number of disconfirming instances. A small or moderate number of disconfirming instances would possibly be discounted by peers.

APPROACHES TO INTERVENTION.   Based on the theoretical and empirical work just reviewed, it seems logical to suggest that the effectiveness of efforts to improve the social acceptance of a disliked child might be enhanced by attempts to modify directly peers' negative perceptions of that child. This contention is supported by evidence indicating that intervention programs that focus exclusively on teaching social skills to disliked children have not always been successful in improving the level of social acceptance, even when objective accounts indicate that the disliked children's behaviors have changed favorably. The findings from Hymel's (1986) study offer several possible explanations for this lack of change in social acceptance. Were a disliked child to begin to display more socially appropriate behavior, the members of the child's peer group might attribute those behaviors to unstable causes, such as the presence of a teacher. They might also believe that the child is not responsible for his or her behavioral changes. Furthermore, they might fail to attend to the changes or might prevent the disliked child from displaying newly acquired behavioral patterns by failing to offer opportunities for such displays. Therefore, newly acquired skills could be unlikely to alter the peers' negative perceptions of the child.

What types of intervention approaches might be effective in altering peers' negative perceptions of a disliked child? Based on the prior discussion of how the structures of children's social cognitive processes (i.e., encoding of social stimuli and the subsequent interpretation of this stimuli) might be involved in maintenance of social reputations, it seems plausible to suggest that effective intervention programs would involve two components: (1) opportunities for the members of a disliked child's peer group to observe the rejected child performing highly salient reputation disconfirming behaviors (e.g., prosocial behaviors); and (2) opportunities for the disliked child to perform a large number of these behaviors. In designing such intervention programs, one of two types of strategies could be employed. The first involves designing a seminatural or contrived setting in which the members of a rejected child's peer group are required by the nature of the activities to interact with him or her. A less direct strategy would be to have peers observe via videotape the rejected child displaying a high frequency of prosocial behaviors.

In support of the strategy utilizing child/peer interactions, there is evidence that a child's liking for a specific peer is based on that particular peer's behavior toward the child rather than on the peer's behavior toward others (Masters & Furman, 1981). Thus, creating a social context that provides the disliked child with numerous opportunities to act prosocially *toward individual peers who dislike him or her* may prove to be an effective strategy for directly altering the peers' perceptions of that child. One way in which this type of context might be created is through structured cooperative activities. The nature of cooperative activities would provide a rejected child with the opportunity to display a salient reputation-disconfirming behavior (i.e., cooperation). Furthermore, a rejected child who was allowed to continue in these activities would have numerous opportunities to display cooperative behavior, which in turn would help to disconfirm the negative reputation. In the following paragraphs, several sources of evidence indicating the potential effectiveness of cooperative activities as a means of changing attitudes toward members of a disliked group will be reviewed. For a more detailed review of the literature on cooperative activities, see Chapter 12 in this volume, by Wyndol Furman and Leslie Gavin.

The first source of evidence for the potential effectiveness of cooperative activities is derived from research with adults on the effect of personal contact with a disliked person. Briefly, this contact hypothesis is tested by creating a context in which an individual who holds a negative stereotype of the numbers of a particular group (e.g., blacks) participates in a cooperative activity with a member of that group. Cook and his colleagues (see Cook, 1985, for a review) have found that a favorable change in attitudes and interpersonal attraction will result when there is personal contact with members of a particular group, provided that the following five conditions are met: (1) the status of the members of the two groups must be equal in the situation in which the contact occurs; (2) the attributes of the disliked group that become visible during the contact must be such as to disconfirm the prevailing stereotypes about the group; (3) cooperation in the achievement of a joint goal must be encouraged; (4) the contact situation must provide the opportunity for the members of the disliked group to communicate personal information about themselves so that they are seen as individuals rather than as members of a stereotyped group; and (5) the social norms of the contact situation must favor group equality.

The relevant feature of a social context created by these five conditions is that the members of a stereotyped group are provided with numerous opportunities to display behaviors that disconfirm the stereotype, in front of the individuals holding the stereotype. On some occasions, disconfirming evidence is discounted, however, so it is essential to attend to the manner of presentation of the disconfirming evidence. Gurwitz and Dodge (1977) found that disconfirming evidence resulted in lower stereotype ratings only when it was presented in a concentrated form (that is, three behaviors displayed by one person were each completely inconsistent with the stereotype). In contrast, evidence presented in a dispersed form (that is, three members of a stereotyped group each displayed one behavior that discon-firmed the stereotype) had no effect on stereotyped evaluations. The authors suggest that individuals may evaluate their stereotypic hypotheses each time that they are presented with relevant data. If the data only mildly disconfirm the hypothesis, the data will be discounted and the hypothesis will be re-affirmed. If the data are so strong and so salient (in terms of frequency of occurrence) that they cannot be discounted, the result will be a decreased use of the stereotype subsequently in making inferences about group mem-bers. It is interesting that Gurwitz & Dodge found an opposite pattern for confirming data. That is, confirming evidence that was presented in dispersed form had a stronger effect on strengthening the stereotype than did the same evidence presented in a concentrated form. Presumably, the dispersed evi-dence provided three occasions for hypothesis confirmation (though the evidence was mild, a confirmation bias operated), whereas the concentrated evidence provided just one such opportunity. The implications of this study are that lasting disconfirmation of a stereotype may occur only when dis-confirming evidence is presented in a concentrated form that cannot be discounted.

A second line of evidence indicating the potential effectiveness of co-operative activities in changing peers' attitudes toward others is derived from Aronson, Blaney, Stephan, Sikes, & Snapp's (1978) research on the jigsaw method of instruction. Briefly, this method involves dividing a class-room into small groups, composed of six or seven children. Each child is responsible for learning some material. However, he or she is taught only one piece of the total material and must, in turn, teach that particular piece of information to the other group members. Thus, each member performs a behavior that directly benefits other members of the group. Aronson's (1976) research on this procedure reveals that children who participated in these groups grew to like their groupmates more than their other classmates, even though the students had liked their groupmates slightly less than their other classmates at the beginning of the study. It is important to note, however, that children were not placed in groups with either their best friends or enemies. Thus, it remains to be determined whether this procedure would be effective in changing children's attitudes toward those they especially dislike.

Yet another line of evidence indicating that cooperative activities are an effective means of changing attitudes toward members of a disliked group comes from research on intergroup conflict among children, most notably the work of Sherif and colleagues (Sherif, Harvey, White, Hood, & Sherif, 1961). Sherif explored procedures for reducing intergroup hostility between two groups of boys in a summer camp. One procedure was to introduce a common enemy, which appeared to reduce some tension between the groups. Another approach, involving noncompetitive personal contact between the groups (such as at dinnertime and when watching movies) actually increased intergroup hostility. Thus, mere contact was insufficient for stereotype reductions. Finally, Sherif confronted the groups with problematic situations that demanded mutual cooperation (e.g., repairing a vehicle bearing camp food). This procedure was successful in reducing intergroup hostility and even led to several intergroup friendships. It is possible that the cooperative behavior elicited by this contrived situation served to disconfirm children's negative perceptions of one another.

A final line of evidence for the utility of cooperative activities is derived from the results of two intervention studies. In one study, Oden and Asher (1977) designed a coaching procedure that incorporated cooperative activities. Even though the stated goal of that procedure was to enhance social skills in unaccepted children, the procedure included periods of "practice" with six different peers. The adult coach observed these periods to assure that positive interaction indeed took place. Thus, the target child was required by the task to display prosocial behaviors toward each of six peers. An alternative explanation for the gains in peer acceptance experienced by the target children (alternative to a skills enhancement explanation) is that the structured cooperative activities had a direct effect on perceptions by those six peers. Unfortunately, the authors did not examine whether the positive changes in acceptance occurred on the part of only the six peers or the rest of the peer group as well.

More recently, Bierman (1986) designed an intervention program directed toward unpopular children with clear skills deficits by combining social skills training with participation with peers in cooperative tasks. This combined intervention led to greater improvements in peer relations than did the skills training procedure alone. The author suggested that participating in cooperative activities and observing positive changes in the target child firsthand during treatment appeared to improve the peer partners' attitudes toward the target children. Unfortunately, the author did not examine whether the positive changes in perceptions occurred both in the peer partners of the intervention and in other peers.

It is important to note several distinctions between Bierman's investigation and the research on the contact hypothesis and intergroup conflict. First, unlike the latter research, it is not clear that the peer partners who participated in Bierman's (1986) combined skills training and peer involvement condition had initially disliked the target child. It remains to be determined whether this type of intervention would have improved the attitudes of peer partners who actually disliked the target child. Second, unlike the participants in the research on the contact hypothesis, the target subjects of Bierman's study were known to be deficient in specific social skills and received training to improve these skills. Without such training, the cooperative activities component of the intervention may not have contributed to changes in peers' attitudes toward target children.

In sum, evidence from four different lines of research suggests that a favorable change in attitudes and interpersonal attraction may occur when an individual participates in cooperative activities with a disliked person. Cooperative activities appear to create conditions that are conducive to a positive change in attitudes toward a disliked person. Perhaps the most important of these conditions is that the disliked person has the opportunity, and is even encouraged, to display behaviors that disconfirm the other's negative perceptions. Since cooperative activities involve achieving a common goal and, therefore, demand interdependence between group members, behaviors such as helping and sharing are elicited from the participants. Furthermore, a cooperative context elicits concentrated numbers of such behaviors. Of course, as indicated earlier, before such behaviors can be elicited from a child, that child must become skilled enough to perform those behaviors. Thus, some rejected children must be taught skills in addition to participating in cooperative ventures with peers, as Bierman and Furman (1984) have shown. For instance, by using an approach similar to Oden and Asher's (1977), a rejected child could receive some type of social skills training, followed by the opportunity to practice newly acquired skills during cooperative activities involving the peers by whom he or she is disliked. Yet another possible approach is to design an intervention similar to Bierman's (1986) where both the rejected child and the members of the peer group who dislike the child are involved in skills training that incorporates cooperative activities. The added advantage of this later approach is that peers have the opportunity to observe the positive changes in the rejected child's behavior during treatment. The possibility exists, however, that some rejected children may be capable of performing the reputational-disconfirming behaviors elicited by cooperative activities. These children may require only the opportunity to display positive behaviors in the presence of their peers. Such opportunities might be provided either through a structured cooperative intervention program or through incorporation of cooperative activities into normal learning activities using procedures similar to the jigsaw method of Aronson et al. (1978).

Although the use of cooperative activities is a promising approach to increasing a child's acceptance in the peer group, numerous questions remain. Research is needed on the types of behaviors that are elicited in a cooperative context and whether these behaviors are linked to attitude change in the peer participants. To date, Bierman (1986) is one of the few investigators to examine the link between specific behaviors displayed in a cooperative context and attitude change. Another line of research that may prove beneficial is to examine types of cooperative activities that are most effective in eliciting prosocial behaviors.

A less direct approach to modifying peers' perceptions of a disliked child would be to present to the members of the child's peer group videotaped vignettes of the disliked child performing a concentration of prosocial behaviors in a number of social situations. Some support for the effectiveness of this approach can be derived from research by Rholes & Ruble (1984;

1986) on the formation of children's impressions of others. Typically, children were asked to view videotapes in which a child actor is behaving in either a prosocial or selfish manner. They were then asked to give their impressions of the actor and to indicate how much they liked the actor. In general, children had more positive impressions of the benevolent actor than of the selfish actor.

It is important to note, however, that the child actors in the videotapes used by Rholes & Ruble were previously unknown to those children viewing the tapes. Thus, it remains to be determined whether this approach could be effective in changing attitudes of children who already dislike the actor that they are observing.

In designing this type of intervention, it is important to consider the results of Masters and Furman's (1981) research, which indicates that a child's liking for a specific peer is based on how that peer behaves toward him or her personally rather than how the peer behaves toward others. Videotaped situations could be designed so that the prosocial behavior displayed by the rejected child would in some way benefit the peer viewing the tape. Although in this type of intervention peers are unable to interact with the disliked child, it is an alternative strategy for providing disliked children the opportunity to display behaviors that aid in disconfirming their negative social reputations.

Peer Behavior Toward a Disliked Child

ANALYSIS OF PROCESSES. In addition to the role played by peers' perceptions in maintaining children's social reputations, there is evidence to suggest that peers' behavior toward a child may be involved in the maintenance of social reputations. In this section, we will review this evidence, as well as research on attempts to change a peer's behavior toward an unpopular child.

It is clear that a peer's perceptions of and attitudes toward a child are likely to influence the behavior displayed toward that child. For instance, Dodge (1980) manipulated the status of a child provocateur as either a known aggressive child or a known nonaggressive child. Subjects were five times more likly to attribute hostile intentions to a child that they knew to be aggressive than to a child known to be nonaggressive. Furthermore, they were also more likely to retaliate aggressively toward an aggressive child than toward a nonaggressive child. In this study, no labels of "aggressiveness" were stated to the peer subjects; the only manipulation was that real names of children in the classroom were associated with the hypothetical provocative behavior. Thus, these perceptual and behavioral biases occur at the level of active dyadic interchanges, and not just with regard to a hypothetical stereotyped group.

In another study, Feldman and Ruble (1986) manipulated whether a child actor was "generous" or "stingy" in allocating toys to a subject. In addition, the expectation for future interaction with this actor was manipulated. Subjects left significantly fewer toys for the "stingy" actor than for the "generous" actor. In addition, subjects expecting future interaction with the actor differentiated toy allocations more clearly than subjects not expecting future interactions. Clearly, children's perceptions of one another serve to guide their subsequent behavioral interactions. Furthermore, these behavioral exchanges are likely to contribute to the maintenance and perpetuation of negative social perceptions on the part of both participants in the interaction.

There appears to be a number of ways in which a peer's behavior toward a child might play a role in perpetuating the peer's perceptions of that child. First, the peer's behavior may set up a self-fulfilling prophecy. The theory of self-fulfilling prophecy predicts that (1) a person's behavior toward a target will be influenced by his or her other perceptions of that target and expectations for that target person; (2) this will set up a cycle in which the target comes to engage in behavior consistent with the person's perceptions and expectations; and (3) the target's behavior comes to reinforce and affirm the person's original perceptions and expectations. Support for the self-fulfilling prophecy hypothesis among adults can be found in a number of studies. For example, Snyder, Tanke, and Berscheid (1977) manipulated subjects' expectations of an individual as either friendly or unfriendly. When subjects expected the individual to be friendly, their behavior toward that person led to more friendly responses from that person. Conversely, when the subject expected the other to be unfriendly, the other became less friendly. Snyder and Swann (1978) found evidence for a similar process when expectations of hostility were elicited.

More recently, Dodge and his colleagues (1980; Dodge & Frame, 1982) found evidence for a self-fulfilling prophecy among aggressive children and their peers. The findings of this work suggest the following. Aggressive children often display antisocial behavior that is perceived by peers as unwarranted. These peers develop an expectation that the aggressive child will be capriciously aggressive. They come to dislike the child and to feel justified in treating him or her in antisocial ways. Their behavior serves to incite further antisocial behavior by the aggressive child, which is viewed by the peer group as confirming evidence of its negative expectations of this child. The peer group responds with further antisocial behavior, thus perpetuating a negative cycle.

Empirical support for this model of reciprocally influential peer interaction is provided by an observational study by Dodge and Frame (1982). These investigators observed boys in free interaction with previously unacquainted peers on 8 consecutive days and then examined aggressive interchanges within dyads. First, a positive correlation was found between the frequency of aggression displayed by a boy and the frequency with which he was the object of a peer's aggression, even after controlling for overall interpersonal activity level. Thus, aggression is distributed reciprocally. Next, a positive correlation was found between the frequency of displaying aggression in early interactions and the probability of being the object of a peer's aggression in later interactions, even when the level of aggression received in early interactions is controlled. Also, it was found that being the target of aggression by peers in early interactions increased the probability that a subject would aggress against peers in later interactions. Thus, the reciprocal cycles of aggression in boys' peer groups not only maintain levels of aggressive exchange, they exacerbate those levels.

In sum, once a peer has developed perceptions and attitudes of a particular child, those attitudes serve to influence his or her behavior toward that child. That peer's behavior serves to elicit behavioral patterns from the child which, in turn, reinforce the peer's original perceptions of that child.

Finally, antisocial behavior toward a rejected child may contribute to the maintenance of the child's social reputation when the peer performing the behavior uses it as a cue to justify perceptions of the negative attributes of the rejected child. Thus, it is as if the peer thinks, "If I treat him as a mean and disliked child, I must have reason to do so, and so he is mean and worthy of being disliked." Evidence by Bem (1965) suggests that individuals sometimes make inferences about their beliefs and attitudes from observing their own behavior. Thus, in the case of a peer acting negatively toward a rejected child, the negative behavior serves as a cue to the peer that he or she dislikes the child. Thus, perceptions of that child are reinforced.

APPROACHES TO INTERVENTION.   Intervention strategies might take one of two approaches. The first focuses on teaching the peer to respond differently to the social overtures of the disliked child. The second focuses on fostering positive social interactions between a disliked child and the members of the peer group.

To date, there have been several intervention programs that have focused on altering peers' responses to low-status children. For instance, Kirby and Toler (1970) reinforced, with candy, peers' positive responses to the social initiations of a noninteractive 5-year-old child. The noninteractive child's rate of social initiations increased. In another example, Strain, Shores, and Timm (1977) taught two 4-year-old peers how to engage others in play and how to persist when initially rebuffed. The two were then encouraged to get withdrawn children to play with them, and they received delayed praise for their efforts. The two children were able to get the withdrawn children to respond more to social overtures and to make more social initiations. Whether or not these interventions altered the social reputations of the withdrawn children was not evaluated, however.

Along these lines, a number of possibilities exist for the types of interventions that could be designed. For instance, the peers of the rejected child, especially those who actively dislike the child, could be taught new ways of responding to the rejected child's social overtures, including both positive and negative overtures. Peers might be taught to look for, and to be responsive to, any of the rejected child's positive approaches. In addition, peers might also be taught new strategies for responding to a rejected child's aggressive behaviors. For instance, peers might be taught to communicate their disapproval of the rejected child's use of aggression. They might also be taught how to offer the rejected child aternative ways of behaving.

A related intervention approach is to focus on getting members of a disliked child's peer group to initiate positive interactions with that child. Thus far, a number of behavioral approaches have been used to increase social interaction between an isolated child and members of his or her peer group. For instance, Walker and Hops (1973) showed a classroom of first-grade children a modeling film made by O'Connor (1969) and told them that the group would earn tokens on the basis of the number of social initiations made by a withdrawn child. The peers displayed an increase in their social initiations toward the child. Furthermore, the target child also displayed increases in her social initiations.

In similar studies, Greenwood et al. (1979) and Todd (1977) developed intervention programs for preschoolers in which reinforcement of both the subject and group members was contingent upon measured increases in the target subject's percentage of playground social behavior. Results from both studies indicated that in addition to changes in rate and duration of interaction, peers initiated more interactions with target children, and target children spent less time alone observing peers and less time alone at tasks.

It is possible that similar behavioral approaches might also be effective in getting the members of a peer group to initiate positive interactions with a rejected child. It is important, however, that the emphasis be placed on eliciting positive or prosocial behavior from peers, and not on increasing rates of social interaction between peers and a rejected child. An emphasis on simply increasing rates of interaction might result not only in more positive initiations, but in more negative initiations as well.

A hypothesized benefit of changing peers' behavioral responses to a rejected child's overtures and getting them to initiate social interactions with that child is that these changes may serve as attributional cues leading peers to develop more positive perceptions of the child. By no longer treating the child as disliked, they might reevaluate their negative evaluations. Also, changes in the target child's behavior might be hypothesized to alter peers' evaluations of the child. Unfortunately, effects of these interventions on peers' evaluations of the target child were not evaluated directly in these studies. Given the fact that peers control the child's behavior, however, the peers might attribute the child's behavior to external and unstable causes. They might not alter their evaluations of the target child at all. Thus, the efficacy of these procedures in changing a child's social status remains an open question. It is also important to note that the target children in these investigations were withdrawn rather than rejected. It is likely that they were not actively disliked by their peer group, as is the case with rejected children. Getting peers to initiate interactions with a disliked peer may prove a more difficult task than getting them to interact with a withdrawn child. Nevertheless, this body of research points to a direction that may prove useful in helping to change the negative reputation of a disliked child.

A Rejected Child's Processing of Information about Peers

ANALYSIS OF PROCESSES.   In the same way that peers attend to, interpret, and respond to information about the rejected child, the rejected child is also an active processor of social information about the peer group. This processing constitutes the mechanism through which the peer environment, as a stimulus, leads to characteristic behavioral responses by a rejected child. As shown in Figure 13.1, this processing also is a response to peers' behavior. Many researchers have established that rejected-aggressive children, relative to average children, are indeed biased and deficient in their processing patterns, even when standardized stimuli are used to elicit processing responses. For example, Dodge and Tomlin (1987) have recently shown that rejected, aggresive children are relatively unlikely to attend to relevant aspects of a social stimulus (such as a peer's cues indicating his or her intentions) and instead are likely to attend to inappropriate aspects of the stimulus (such as idiosyncratic expectations). This misplacement of attention is related to another processing pattern of rejected, aggressive children, namely, the tendency to misinterpret peers' intentions as being hostile (Dodge et al., 1984) and to attribute hostility to peers in ambiguous provocation circumstances (Dodge, 1980; Dodge & Frame, 1982). Rejected children also demonstrate a processing deficit in skills of social problem solving, in that they are likely to generate inadequate, incompetent, unusual, and aggressive solutions to interpersonal dilemmas (Asarnow & Callan, 1985; Ladd & Oden, 1979; Rubin & Krasnor, 1986). They also are biased and inaccurate in their evaluations of the probable outcomes that would accrue following various social behaviors. Specifically, they anticipate that positive outcomes will accrue if they act aggressively and less positive outcomes will accrue if they act nonaggressively (Crick & Ladd, 1987; Feldman & Dodge, 1987). The literature on processing patterns of rejected children is quite large and complicated, in that patterns of deficits and biases have not always been found among rejected children. Dodge and Feldman (in press), in reviewing this literature, have concluded that the patterns are robust when processing is assessed in situations that are highly relevant to the peer group (such as social play, provocation, and group entry situations).

It is intuitively obvious and has been empirically demonstrated that the processing patterns displayed by rejected children lead directly to deviant social behavior that is evaluated negatively by peers. When children misinterpret a peer's intention as being hostile, they are likely to retaliate aggressively toward the peer (Dodge et al., 1984), leading the peer, who views the retaliation as unjustified, to dislike the child (Dodge & Frame, 1982). Likewise, children who generate aggressive solutions to interpersonal dilemmas and who evaluate aggressive responses as having positive outcomes are likely to behave aggressively toward peers, again leading peers to dislike them (Richard & Dodge, 1982). The relation between a child's processing and that child's socially competent behavior has been found to be a strong one, when aggregated assessments of processing are conducted (Dodge, Pettit, McClaskey, & Brown, 1986).

The processing patterns of rejected children have been conceptualized as inappropriate, deficient responses, unrelated to actual social stimuli from peers. This conceptualization has received empirical support and has been the basis of social cognitive skill training programs aimed at improving the processing performance of rejected children (Bierman & Furman, 1984; Ladd, 1981; Lochman & Curry, 1986). Alternatively, these processing patterns have also been conceptualized as the normal result of continually biased and negative social treatment by peers (Hymel, Wagner, & Butler, in press). The empirical basis for the latter contention is indeed quite strong. Peers are known to dispense more positively reinforcing and fewer punishing behaviors toward popular children than unpopular children (Dodge & Frame, 1982; Gottman, Gonso, & Rasmussen, 1975; Hartup, Glazer, & Charlesworth, 1967). Likewise, peers are more socially responsive toward friends than nonfriends (Masters & Furman, 1981; Newcomb & Brady, 1982). Peers visually attend to popular children more than to rejected children (Vaughn & Waters, 1978; 1981), and they respond more favorably to an entry attempt of popular than of rejected children, even when the behavioral strategy used during the entry attempt is similar (Dodge, Schlundt, Schocken, & Delugach, 1983; Putallaz & Gottman, 1981a). Once a child's social reputation is established, it seems quite clear that peers become biased (either positively or negatively) in their behavior toward that child.

It would not be surprising to find that rejected children begin to anticipate negative and biased treatment from peers and to process subsequent information in ways that are consistent with this biased treatment. Expectations of future behavior and the interpretations of behavior are often made directly as a function of past experiences with the stimulus object (Darley & Fazio, 1980). Thus, children who are actively rejected and treated in antisocial ways are likely to expect further such treatment, to process future information in accord with these expectations, and to behave in antisocial ways that are reciprocal to the expectations. Also, being the object of antisocial treatment and social rejection may lead a child to become lonely (Asher & Wheeler, 1986). Negative mood states, in turn, are known to affect adversely the accuracy and efficiency of information processing (Masters, Felleman, & Barden, 1983).

APPROACHES TO INTERVENTION.   It is most likely the case that the processing patterns of rejected children are related *both* to inadequate skills and to antisocial treatment by peers. Independent of the etiology of these patterns, peers (and information about peers) may be employed in efforts to improve and alter the processing patterns of rejected children. Most interventions, however, have focused on enhancing skills directly rather than on using peers to alter a child's processing patterns. Peers might be employed in any of several ways.

Consider, for example, the rejected boy who expects that same-sex peers will act in antisocial ways toward him and is quick to interpret peers' behavior as hostile. Intervention might consist of training this child to read peers' cues more accurately (a skills training approach) or of altering this child's expectations about peers. Merely exhorting the boy to change his expectations may not be effective, of course. The ways in which this attitude change might occur are similar to the ways that were described in an earlier section on changing peers' attitudes toward a rejected child. Simply put, the child must be presented this new information in a way that cannot be discounted. The information might be presented in concentrated forms (Gurwitz & Dodge, 1977) and under the conditions outlined by Cook (1985), that is during a cooperative interaction between the child and a peer in which the children enjoy equal status and the child has an opportunity to experience the peer as an individual rather than as a representative of a particular group. These are the same conditions under which peers might be expected to change their expectations of rejected children. The cooperative games employed by Oden and Asher (1977) thus may change attitudes of both the peers and the rejected child.

Additional interventions, accomplished during these cooperative games as well as at other times, might be necessary to alter the rigid processing patterns of rejected children. These interventions might be directed toward the biased processing of rejected children. For example, when a conflict arises or a provocation occurs (as is inevitable) between the rejected child and a peer, the peer could make it clear to the child that he or she is not aiming to cause the child any harm. This communication might be mediated by an adult, who focuses the rejected child's attention on the nonhostile aspects of the peer's behavior. This adult might provide an alternative explanation for the peer's behavior (for example, the peer, by moving without looking around carefully, might have pushed the child accidentally). The adult might encourage the peer to communicate this explanation clearly. The peer's role in this process thus may be critical.

Similar interventions might be employed to alter other aspects of the rejected child's deviant processing. For example, following a provocation, the rejected child might be likely to generate aggressive responses and to evaluate these responses as being efficacious. An adult intervening with the child in the middle of a conflict might encourage the child to generate alternative responses and to evaluate the consequences of those responses. Peers could be employed to describe how they would likely respond to the various alternatives, thereby allowing the child to imagine actual outcomes in a safe environment. This dialogue between the child and the adult is a central component of most problem-solving interventions (Weissberg, 1986).

What is being suggested here is that since the rejected child's processing is based on experiences with peers (rather than with the adult intervener) the greatest improvements might occur when the peers are actively involved in the change process. Of course, coordinating peers' involvement may be a difficult task.

There may be more direct ways of changing a rejected child's expectations about peers, particularly in new peer group situations. A clever experiment by Rabiner and Coie (1987) illustrates these possibilities. Rejected child subjects were given the task of entering a room to initiate play with a group of previously unacquainted peers. Half the boys were led to believe that the peers liked them and wanted them to play with them. The other half were not given an expectation. Thus, the manipulation of the rejected child's expectations was direct, though artificially induced. Relative to the boys not given an expectation, the boys who expected to be liked came to be liked more by the peers, who were unaware of any manipulation. Presumably, a child's expectations of being liked led him to behave in particular ways that led peers to like him, although observers in that study were unable to detect which aspects of the child's behavior had been altered. Since the experimenters did not follow these children for longer than several minutes, it is not known how long the manipulation of expectations lasted. Whether or not a rejected child would eventually display behaviors that peers dislike is not clear.

A Rejected Child's Behavior Toward Peers

ANALYSES OF PROCESSES. This link in the circular chain of Figure 13.1 is so obvious that its importance is difficult to dispute. Nevertheless, it has been seldom demonstrated that aspects of a child's behavior are directly responsible for peers' liking and behavioral responses. Observational studies of children who are already accepted or rejected are unable to shed light on the antecedents of that acceptance or rejection. Observational studies of children's behavior during initial contact with peers (e.g., Coie & Kupersmidt, 1983; Dodge, 1983; Putallaz, 1983; Putallaz & Gottman, 1981a; 1981b) more convincingly demonstrate the direct relation between aspects of a child's behavior and peer rejection.

Modification of a child's behavior has been related to improvements in peer acceptance in some studies (e.g., Ladd, 1981), but behavioral changes have not led to sociometric improvements in other studies (e.g., Bierman & Furman, 1984; LaGreca & Santogrossi, 1980). Bierman (1986) has attributed these discrepancies to differences in design features. Her analyses of the process of change during social skills training have indicated that indeed when treated children begin to display skilled conversational behavior, peers begin to respond positively. Also, those rejected children who, as a result of skills training, begin to display skilled conversational behavior are most likely to demonstrate increases in peer acceptance as well.

Likewise, there is now evidence that a child's processing of social information is related to social behavior, as described in the previous section of this chapter. The role of peers' perceptions and peers' behavior in the rejected child's social behavior has also been examined. There are at least four ways in which peer variables are linked to the rejected child's behavior and (potentially) to changes in this child's behavior. First, it is known that the experience of being liked or disliked by a peer has an effect on one's behavior. The study by Rabiner and Coie (1987) and extensive laboratory studies of adult social interactions (Darley & Fazio, 1980; Snyder & Swann, 1978) support this conjecture. In an observational study, Dodge (1983) found that rejected children altered their behavioral approaches toward peers following the time when peers began to reject them overtly. These rejected children began to withdraw from the group, they reduced their rate of approaching the group, and they increased their rate of aggression. Presumably, being liked leads one's mood state to elevate, causing greater awareness of others' feelings and reciprocity in affective displays.

Another way in which peers affect a child's behavior is through positive reinforcement and punishment of the behavior. Bierman's (1986) sequential analyses of peer interactions during social skills training indicate that when peers positively support a child's conversational behavior, that child subsequently increases his or her display of that behavior. Likewise, when the peer group is trained to punish a child's aggressive behavior, the rate of that behavior decreases (Buckley, 1977).

Peers also act as behavioral models for children. O'Conner (1969; 1972) has demonstrated that presentation of appropriate behavioral models to withdrawn children leads to increases in their rate of displaying social initiations.

A fourth way in which peers affect a child's behavior is through their conditioned stimulus qualities. Peers are often a cue to a child to behave appropriately or inappropriately. It is commonly known that some children improve their social behavior dramatically once they are removed from a particular peer group. Teachers sometimes find improvements in a child's antisocial behavior merely through a change of classrooms. The value of peers of similar age as a stimulus for inappropriate behavior in low-status children led Furman, Rahe, and Hartup (1979) to expose these children to a younger age group. Not only did the younger group have stimulus value that led to improvements in socially competent behavior, it also allowed the children exposed to improve skills through practice in a more benign environment. Sociometrically neglected children in a study by Coie and Kupersmidt (1983) provide another example. In that study, children who had been neglected in their classrooms participated in a play group with novel peers. Their behavior changed from that observed in the classroom, and their status improved as well. Socially rejected children, on the other hand, repeated their antisocial behavior patterns and were again rejected in novel groups. For this latter sociometric group, the antisocial behavior was obviously not controlled by a single set of peers, but perhaps by the stimulus category of "peers" more generally.

APPROACHES TO INTERVENTION.   Peers might modify a child's behavior through any of the four ways described in the preceding section. The experimental manipulation of peers' liking for a rejected child (Rabiner & Coie, 1987) has already been described in the section on a rejected child's processing of information. Manipulation of liking might also be included as a part of treatment through a clinician's efforts to emphasize peers' affective responses to a child's behavior. Whenever a child displays a relevant behavior, the clinician might solicit peers' affective responses to it, in order to teach the child that liking and disliking may be under the child's control, rather than externally imposed.

Peers' value in reinforcing appropriate social behavior has been examined first by Wahler (1967) and subsequently by Strain and his colleagues in several intervention studies (Odom & Strain, 1984; Strain & Timm, 1974; Strain, Shores, & Timm, 1977). In general, these interventions have been more successful in increasing the rate of social initiations and other prosocial behaviors than they have been in reducing the rate of antisocial behaviors (Kazdin, 1985). Also, evidence for long-term maintenance and generalization from these interventions is weak (Greenwood & Hops, 1981). Part of the difficulty lies in teaching the peers how to reinforce and punish behaviors appropriately (at the right time, in the right manner, etc.). Rather than focusing on specific means of reinforcing an individual child's behavior, Walker and Hops (1973) employed group contingencies to enhance a withdrawn child's prosocial behavior. The peer group was reinforced each time that the withdrawn child displayed an appropriate behavior. The intervention was successful, indicating that the peers used their own means to reinforce, enhance, and encourage prosocial behavior in the withdrawn child. A similar approach, with comparable success, was employed by Weinrott, Corson, and Wilchesky (1979).

The use of peer models of appropriate behavior has been employed in numerous interventions, primarily in efforts to increase a withdrawn child's rate of interacting with peers. O'Connor's work (1969; 1972) has already been mentioned in this regard. In those studies, symbolic modeling or reinforced social interactions on a 25-minute videotape were found to increase a child's rate of social interactions immediately following presentation of the tape. Some investigators have replicated these effects with maintenance over at least 6 weeks (Evers & Schwartz, 1973; Evers-Pasquale & Sherman, 1975; Gresham & Nagle, 1980), whereas another investigation (Gottman, 1977) failed to find enhancement over 8 weeks. The value of a peer (in contrast with an adult) as a behavioral model has been demonstrated by Jakibchuk and Smeriglio (1976), who found that a modeling film led to greater gains in interaction rates when it was narrated by a child from a first-person perspective than by an adult from a third-person perspective.

These aspects of peers' influence on a child (liking, reinforcement, modeling, and stimulus value) are combined in interventions that involve guided exposure to peers in structured groups. Oden and Asher's (1977) coaching procedure, even though it was designed to emphasize skill training, involved guided interaction between the target child and each of six peers. Thus, the child experienced each of six peers who presumably reinforced and modeled appropriate behavior. A number of other interventions have employed the peer group structure to teach social skills (Bierman & Furman, 1984; Gresham & Nagle, 1980; Ladd, 1981; LaGreca & Santogrossi, 1980; Lochman, Burch, Curry, & Lampron, 1984; Lochman & Curry, 1986). Some of these interventions involved training rejected children in groups, a procedure that would be less likely to encourage peers' appropriate modeling and reinforcement than when the peer group includes some average and popular peers (as was the case in the intervention by Bierman & Furman, 1984).

Theoretical Implications and Unresolved Questions

The reciprocal influence model of child-peer transactions in Figure 13.1 seems to have some support from descriptive studies, experimental manipulations, and interventions. This model depicts children and their peers as active agents who construe their social environment and act on it. The model implies strong relations between processes of construal and processes of behavior. Also, the model suggests that reciprocity in social exchanges, at both the information processing and the behavioral levels, will be the norm in children's peer groups. This model is similar to other interactionist models of human personality (e.g., Carson, 1969; Heider, 1958; Kelly, 1955). It goes beyond those models in describing in greater detail the information processing components of the individual's construal process, in describing how a peer partner might influence a child's processing and behavior, and in describing its applications to peer dyadic exchanges.

Like other interactionist models, the reciprocal influence model presents itself as a framework for organizing and guiding research on social interactions. In particular, the model has the potential to serve as a framework for organizing the multiple perspectives brought to bear on the problem of social rejection and to guide future research on the development and maintenance of negative social reputations. One area in which further research is especially needed is on the contributions of peers' processing and behavior to social rejection. At this point, we know far more about the contribution of the child's processing and behavior than we do about peers' processing and behavior. We need to know much more about the process by which children form impressions of one another, the different factors that influence the development of these impressions, and the factors involved in the maintenance of person perceptions. For instance, what types of behaviors are salient to children, and under what conditions? In addition, what types of factors influence how children interpret and mentally represent the encoded behavior of others? As Hymel's research points out, one of those factors appears to be children's affect toward the person performing the behavior. Other biases might exist as well, such as confirmation bias. Children, like adults, might show a bias toward confirming a hypothesis they have for another person rather than toward disconfirming that hypothesis. In addition, if children do possess confirmation biases, at what age does this cognitive orientation emerge? Is confirmation bias related to when children begin to employ personality traits to describe others?

Similarly, we know less about the role of peers' behavior in the development and maintenance of children's social reputations than we do about the role of the child's behavior. With the exception of a handful of investigations (e.g., Dodge & Frame, 1982), little attention has been directed toward examining how peers' behavior toward a rejected or aggressive child contributes to the development and maintenance of negative social reputation. The proposed model highlights the importance of pursuing further research in this area.

In regard to intervention, one implication of this model is that change processes can be initiated at any point in the circle. Since each construct ultimately affects each other construct, intervention at any one point could, theoretically, influence all other points. This postulate is the basis for focusing on peer variables in an effort to change child behavior, and vice versa. It is also the basis for the host of untried interventions suggested in this chapter. Most interventions in the past have focused on changing the target child's cognitive skills and behavior, even though this model explicitly suggests that focusing on the peer group is also warranted.

Unfortunately, since all processes act to maintain homeostasis and are reciprocally influential, a change in a single process might not always lead to spreading of changes to other processes. If only one process is changed, the other processes may act to maintain existing patterns. Thus, interventions that focus on one aspect of the model exclusively (such as the target child's information processing) may not be successful. Successful change might require intervention at multiple points in the social exchange. This is the strategy that we are recommending, based on the points in this chapter. The interventions aimed at peers are not meant to replace interventions aimed at target children. On the contrary, they are suggested as supplementary features that are likely to enhance treatment efficacy. The strongest empirical evidence in support of this perspective is the study by Bierman and Furman (1984), in which treatment emphasizing *both* target child skills training and peer group involvement was found to be more effective than skills training alone. Many skills training interventions currently involve the peer group in the treatment process, but few of these interventions focus on changing the peers' behavior and processing. The peers are present mostly as "props" to aid in the change efforts with the target child. A more explicit focus on the group is warranted in both future intervention efforts and in descriptive studies of social exchange.

Finally, the discussion of interventions in this chapter raises the question of which aspect of a child's social ecology is responsible for long-term outcomes. Historically, the long-term predictability of school dropout, juvenile delinquency, and psychiatric impairment has been the basis for interventions directed toward a target child and aimed at improving a child's social standing among peers (Parker & Asher, 1987). Even though the four processes depicted in Figure 13.1 are often related and consistent with each other, it is not apparent that all four aspects are related to long-term outcomes. One aspect (such as peer status) might simply be a "marker variable" which has no potent role in long-term development (Putallaz & Gottman, 1982). The possibility of directing an intervention toward one aspect of this process over other aspects raises the question of differential predictability of long-term outcomes among these processes. This possibility is an unanswered empirical question.

REFERENCES

Aronson, E., Blaney, N., Stephan, C., Sikes, J., & Snapp, M. (1978). *The jigsaw classroom.* Beverly Hills: Sage.

Asher, S. R., & Renshaw, P. D. (1981). Children without friends: Social knowledge and social skill training. In S. R. Asher & J. M. Gottman (Eds.), *The development of children's friendships* (pp. 273–296). New York: Cambridge University Press.

Asher, S. R., & Wheeler, V. A. (1986). Children's loneliness: A comparison of rejected and neglected peer status. *Journal of Consulting and Clinical Psychology, 53,* 500–505.

Asarnow, J. R., & Callan, J. W. (1985). Boys with peer adjustment problems: Social cognitive processes. *Journal of Consulting and Clinical Psychology, 53,* 80–87.

Bem, D. L. (1965). An experimental analysis of self-persuasion. *Journal of Experimental Social Psychology, 1,* 199–218.

Bierman, K. L. (1986). Process of change during social skills training with preadolescents and its relation to treatment outcome. *Child Development, 57,* 230–240.

Bierman, K. L., & Furman, W. (1984). The effects of social skills training and peer involvement on the social adjustment of preadolescents. *Child Development, 55,* 151–162.

Buckley, H. (1977). *A peer-group intervention to reduce aggression in the elementary school classroom.* Unpublished manuscript, Duke University, Durham, NC.

Carson, R. C. (1969). *Interaction concepts of personality.* Chicago: Aldine.

Coie, J. D., & Dodge, K. A. (1983). Continuities and changes in children's social status: A five year longitudinal study. *Merrill-Palmer Quarterly, 29,* 261–282.

Coie, J. D., Dodge, K. A., & Kupersmidt, J. A. (in press). Group behavior and social status. In S. R. Asher & J. D. Coie (Eds.), *Peer rejection in childhood: Origins, consequences, and intervention.* New York: Cambridge University Press.

Coie, J. D., & Kupersmidt, J. A. (1983). A behavioral analysis of emerging social status in boys groups. *Child Development, 54,* 1400–1416.

Cook, S. W. (1985). Experimenting on social issues: The case of school desegregation. *American Psychologist, 40,* 452–460.

Crick, N. R., & Ladd, G. W. (1987, April). *Children's perceptions of the consequences of aggressive behavior: Do the ends justify being mean?* Paper presented at the biennial meeting of the Society for Research in Child Development, Baltimore.

Crocker, J., & Park, B. (1987). *The consequences of social stereotypes.* Unpublished manuscript.

Darley, J. M., & Fazio, R. H. (1980). Expectancy confirmation processes arising in the social interaction sequence. *American Psychologist, 35,* 867–881.

Dodge, K. A. (1980). Social cognition and children's aggressive behavior. *Child Development, 51,* 162–170.

Dodge, K. A. (1983). Behavioral antecedents of peer social status. *Child Development, 54,* 1386–1399.

Dodge, K. A. (1986). A social information processing model of social competence in children. In M. Perlmutter (Ed.), *Minnesota Symposium on Child Psychology* (Vol. 18, pp. 77–126). Hillsdale, NJ: Lawrence Erlbaum.

Dodge, K. A. (in press). Treatment of social skills deficits. In E. J. Mash & R. A. Barkley (Eds.), *Behavioral treatment of childhood disorders.* New York: Guilford.

Dodge, K. A., & Feldman, E. (in press). Issues in social cognition and sociometric status. In S. R. Asher & J. D. Coie (Eds.), *Peer rejection in childhood: Origins, consequences, and intervention.* New York: Cambridge University Press.

Dodge, K. A., & Frame, C. L. (1982). Social cognitive biases and deficits in aggressive boys. *Child Development, 53,* 620–635.

Dodge, K. A., McClaskey, C. L., & Feldman, E. (1985). A situational approach to the assessment of social competence in children. *Journal of Consulting and Clinical Psychology, 53,* 344–353.

Dodge, K. A., Murphy, R. R., & Buchsbaum, K. (1984). The assessment of intention-cue detection skills in children: Implications for developmental psychopathology. *Child Development, 55,* 163–173.

Dodge, K. A., Pettit, G. S., McClaskey, C. L., & Brown, M. M. (1986). Social competence in children. *Monographs of the Society for Research in Child Development, 51*(2, Serial No. 213).

Dodge, K. A., & Richard, B. A. (1985). Peers perceptions, aggression, and the development of peer relations. In J. B. Pryor & J. D. Day (Eds.), *Social and developmental perspectives of social cognition* (pp. 35–58). New York: Springer-Verlag.

Dodge, K. A., Schlundt, D. G., Schocken, I., & Delugach, J. D. (1983). Social competence and children's sociometric status: The role of peer group entry strategies. *Merrill-Palmer Quarterly, 29,* 309–336.

Dodge, K. A., & Tomlin, A. (1987). Utilization of self schemas as a mechanism of interpretational bias in agressive children. *Social Cognition, 5,* 280–300.

Evers, W., & Schwartz, S. A. (1973). Modifying social withdrawal in preschoolers: The effects of filmed modeling and teacher praise. *Journal of Abnormal Child Psychology, 1,* 248–256.

Evers-Pasquale, W., & Sherman, M. (1975). The reward value of peers: A variable influencing the efficacy of filmed modeling in modifying social isolation in preschoolers. *Journal of Abnormal Child Psychology, 3,* 179–189.

Feldman, E., & Dodge, K. A. (1987). Social information processing biases and deficits in rejected and neglected boys and girls. *Journal of Abnormal Child Psychology.*

Feldman, N. S., & Ruble, D. N. (1986). *The effect of personal relevance on dispositional inference: A developmental analysis.* Unpublished manuscript.

Furman, W., Rahe, D. F., & Hartup, W. W. (1979). Rehabilitation of socially withdrawn children through mixed-aged and same-aged socialization. *Child Development, 50,* 915–922.

Gottman, J. M. (1977). The effects of modeling film on social isolation in preschool children: A methodological investigation. *Journal of Abnormal Child Psychology, 5,* 69–78.

Gottman, J. M., Gonso, J., & Rasmussen, B. (1975). Social interaction, social competence, and friendship in children. *Child Development, 46,* 709–718.

Greenwood, C. R., & Hops, H. (1981). Group-oriented contingencies and peer behavior change. In P. Strain (Ed.), *The utilization of peers as behavior change agents* (pp. 189–259). New York: Plenum.

Greenwood, C. R., Hops, H., Walker, H. M., Guild, J., Stokes, J., Young, K. R., Keleman, K., & Willardson, M. (1979). Standardized classroom management program: Social validation and replication studies in Utah and Oregon. *Journal of Applied Behavior Analysis, 12,* 235–253.

Gresham, F. M., & Nagle, R. J. (1980). Social skills training with children: Responsiveness to modeling and coaching as a function of peer orientation. *Journal of Consulting and Clinical Psychology, 18,* 718–729.

Gurwitz, S. B., & Dodge, K. A. (1977). Effects of confirmations and disconfirmations on stereotype-based attributions. *Journal of Personality & Social Psychology, 35,* 495–500.

Hartup, W. W., Glazer, J. A., & Charlesworth, R., (1967). Peer reinforcement and sociometric status. *Child Development, 38,* 1017–1024.

Heider, F. (1958). *The psychology of interpersonal relations.* New York: Wiley.

Hymel, S. (1986). Interpretations of peer behavior: Affective bias in childhood and adolescence. *Child Development, 57,* 431–445.

Hymel, S., Wagner, E., & Butler, L. J. (in press). Reputational bias: View from the peer group. In S. R. Asher & J. D. Coie (Eds.), *Peer rejection in children: Origins, consequences, and intervention.* New York: Cambridge University Press.

Jakibchuk, Z., Smeriglio, V. L. (1976). The influence of symbolic modeling on social behavior of preschool children with low levels of social responsiveness. *Child Development, 47,* 838–841.

Kazdin, A. E. (1985). *Treatment of antisocial behavior in children and adolescents.* Homewood, IL: Dorsey Press.

Kelly, G. (1955). *The psychology of personal constructs* (2 vols.). New York: Norton.

Kirby, F. D., & Toler, H. C., Jr. (1970). Modification of preschool isolate behavior: A case study. *Journal of Applied Behavior Analysis, 3,* 309–314.

Kupersmidt, J. (1983, April). *Predicting delinquency and academic problems from childhood peer status.* Paper presented at the biennial meeting of the Society for Research in Child Development, Detroit.

Ladd, G. W. (1981). Effectiveness of a social learning method for enhancing children's social interaction and peer acceptance. *Child Development, 52,* 171–178.

Ladd, G. W., & Asher, S. R. (1985). Social skills training and children's peer relations. In L. L'Abate & M. Milan (Eds.), *Handbook of social skills training and research* (pp. 219–244). New York: Wiley.

Ladd, G. W., & Mars, K. T. (1986). Reliability & validity of preschooler's perceptions of peer behavior. *Journal of Clinical Child Psychology, 15,* 16–25.

Ladd, G. W., & Oden, S. L. (1979). The relation between peer acceptance and children's ideas about helpfulness. *Child Development, 50,* 402–408.

LaGreca, A. M., & Santogrossi, D. A. (1980). Social skills training with elementary school students: A behavioral group approach. *Journal of Consulting & Clinical Psychology, 48,* 220–227.

Livesley, W., & Bromley, D. (1973). *Person perception in childhood and adolescence.* London: Wiley.

Lochman, J. E., Burch, P. R., Curry, J. F., & Lampron, L. B. (1984). Treatment and generalization effects of cognitive-behavioral and goal-setting interventions with aggressive boys. *Journal of Consulting and Clinical Psychology, 52,* 915–916.

Lochman, J. E., & Curry, J. F. (1986). Effects of problem-solving training and of self-instruction training with aggressive boys. *Journal of Clinical Child Psychology, 15,* 159–164.

Masters, J. C., Felleman, E. S., & Barden, R. C. (1983). Experimental studies of affective states in children. In B. Lahey & A. E. Kazdin (Eds.), *Advances in clinical child psychology* (pp. 91–118). New York: Guilford.

Masters, J. M., & Furman, W. (1981). Popularity, individual friendship selection, and specific peer interaction among children. *Developmental Psychology, 17,* 344–350.

Newcomb, A. F., & Brady, J. E. (1982). Mutuality in boys' friendship relations. *Child Development, 53,* 392–395.

O'Connor, R. D. (1969). Modification of social withdrawal through symbolic modeling. *Journal of Applied Behavior Analysis, 2,* 15–22.

O'Connor, R. D. (1972). Relative efficacy of modeling, shaping, and the combined procedures for modification of social withdrawal. *Journal of Abnormal Psychology, 79,* 327–334.

Oden, S., & Asher, S. R. (1977). Coaching children in social skills for friendship making. *Child Development, 48,* 495–506.

Odom, S. L., & Strain, P. S. (1984). Peer-mediated approaches to promoting children's social interaction: A review. *American Journal of Orthopsychiatry, 54,* 544–557.

Parker, J. G., & Asher, S. R. (1987). Peer relations and later personal adjustment: Are low-accepted children "at risk"? *Psychological Bulletin, 102,* 357–389.

Putallaz, M. (1983). Predicting children's sociometric status from their behavior. *Child Development, 54,* 1417–1426.

Putallaz, M., & Gottman, J. M. (1981a). An interactional model of children's entry into peer groups. *Child Development, 52,* 986–994.

Putallaz, M., & Gottman, J. M. (1981b). Social skills and group acceptance. In S. R. Asher & J. M. Gottman. (Eds.), *The development of children's friendships* (pp. 116–149). New York: Cambridge University Press.

Putallaz, M., & Gottman, J. M. (1982). Social relationship problems in children: An approach to intervention. In B. B. Lahey & A. E. Kazdin (Eds.), *Advances in clinical child psychology* (Vol. 6, pp. 1–39). New York: Plenum.

Rabiner, D., & Coie, J. D. (1987, April). *The role of expectations in the social problems of rejected children.* Paper presented at the biennial meeting of the Society for Research in Child Development, Baltimore.

Rholes, W. S., & Ruble, D. N. (1984). Children's understanding of dispositional characteristics of others. *Child Development, 55,* 550–560.

Rholes, W. S., & Ruble, D. N. (1986). Children's impressions of other persons: The effects of temporal separation of behavioral information. *Child Development, 57,* 872–878.

Richard, B. A., & Dodge, K. A. (1982). Social maladjustment and problem solving in school-aged children. *Journal of Consulting and Clinical Psychology, 50,* 226–233.

Rothbart, M., & Park, B. (1986). On the confirmability and disconfirmability of trait concepts. *Journal of Personality & Social Psychology, 50,* 131–142.

Rubin, K. H., & Krasnor, L. R. (1986). Social-cognitive and social behavioral perspectives on problem solving. In M. Perlmutter (Ed.), *The Minnesota Symposia on Child Psychology, 18,* 1–65. Hillsdale, NJ: Lawrence Erlbaum.

Sherif, M., Harvey, O. J., White, B. J., Hood, W. R., & Sherif, C. W. (1961). *Inter-group conflict and cooperation: The Robbers Cave Experiment.* Norman: Institute of Group Relations, University of Oklahoma.

Sherman, S. J. (1987, May). *Hypothesis-confirmation biases.* Paper presented at the Nags Head International Conference on Social Cognition, Nags Head, NC.

Snyder, M., & Swann, W. B. (1978). Hypothesis-testing in social interactions. *Journal of Personality and Social Psychology, 36,* 1202–1212.

Snyder, M., Tanke, E. D., & Berscheid, E. (1977). Social perception and interpersonal behavior: On the self-fulfilling nature of social stereotypes. *Journal of Personality and Social Psychology, 36,* 941–950.

Strain, P. S., Shores, R. E., & Timm, M. A. (1977). Effects of peer social interactions of the behavior of withdrawn preschool children. *Journal of Applied Behavior Analysis, 10,* 289–298.

Strain, P. S., & Timm, M. A. (1974). An experimental analysis of social interaction between a behaviorally disordered preschool child and her classroom peers. *Journal of Applied Behavior Analysis, 7,* 583–590.

Todd, N. M. (1977). *The effects of verbal reporting and group reinforcement in increasing the interaction frequency of preschool socially withdrawn children.* Unpublished Master's thesis, University of Oregon, Eugene.

Vaughn, B. E., & Waters, E. (1978). Social organization among preschool peers: Dominance, attention, and sociometric correlates. In D. R. Omark, F. F. Strayer, & D. G. Greedman (Eds.), *Dominance relations: An ethological view of human conflict and social interaction* (pp. 359–380). New York: Garland.

Vaughn, B. E., & Waters, E. (1981). Attention structure, sociometric status, and dominance: Interrelations, behavioral correlates, and relationships to social competence. *Developmental Psychology, 17,* 275–288.

Wahler, R. G. (1967). Child-child interactions in free field settings: Some experimental analyses. *Journal of Experimental Child Psychology, 5,* 278–293.

Walker, H. M., & Hops, H. (1973). The use of group and individual reinforcement of contingencies in the modification of social withdrawal. In L. A. Hamerlynck, L. C. Handy, & E. J. Mash (Eds.), *Behavior change: Methodology, concepts, and practice* (pp. 269–308). Champaign, Ill.: Research Press.

Weinrott, M. R., Corson, L. A., & Wilchesky, M. (1979). Teacher mediated treatment of social withdrawal. *Behavior Therapy, 10,* 281–294.

Weissberg, R. P. (1986). Designing effective social problem-solving interventions. In B. Schneider, K. H. Rubin, & J. Ledingham (Eds.), *Peer relationships and social skills in childhood: Vol. 2. Issues in assessment and training* (pp. 225–240). New York: Springer-Verlag.

CHAPTER 14

Children's Strategies for Interpersonal Negotiation with Peers

An Interpretive/Empirical Approach to the Study of Social Development

ROBERT L. SELMAN AND LYNN HICKEY SCHULTZ

Harvard University

TWO WAYS TO GET ALONG: INTERPRETIVE DESCRIPTIONS

In the early afternoon, 6-year-old Jeremy phones his friend Brian from down the block, asking him to come over to play. Brian and Jeremy have known each other for a year and a half, since they started all-day kindergarten together. Here is how their play begins.

When Brian arrives at Jeremy's house, he quickly bursts through the door, throws off his coat, barely stopping to hang it up on an empty coat hook in the downstairs hall, and charges up the stairs with Jeremy in quick pursuit. They head straight for his room. In the middle of the floor stands one of Jeremy's newest acquisitions, recently handed down to him by his older brother. It is a latter-day "boys' dollhouse," called the "Star Wars Death Star Space Station," modeled after the space station in the movie *Star Wars*. This highly visible toy is the immediate object of Brian's attention, and he heads directly for it.

As he does, Brian says, "Now, let's play a little bit here," referring to the space station model. His tone is firm and commanding. He quickly moves to the model, sits on the floor, and begins to work the trash compactor, turning the knob that moves the wall in and out. At almost exactly the same time Brian makes his move, perhaps a moment later, Jeremy anticipating Brian's move, yells out in a somewhat urgent tone, "I'm doing the trash compactor, Brian!" Jeremy then reaches for the compactor knob as he speaks, but his hand arrives at the knob a moment after his friend's. Jeremy's look is questioning, both uncertain and concerned. Brian says with a slight scowl, "You've already played with this, but it's new to me." His tone is more forceful than Jeremy's, perhaps strengthened by the force of his argument, but it does not communicate anger. As Brian says this, he visibly tightens his grip on the compactor knob. Jeremy appears to sit back on his heels for a moment; then he draws back his outstretched arm. He then gets up to move away to the other side of the room, making no active challenge to Brian's assertion and claim, but showing his discontent by withdrawing from the joint involvement. Instead, he rummages through a cardboard box of Star Wars figures, and he pulls out a few of the plastic characters from the movie to play with. He carries a few of them to the floor and fiddles with them somewhat absently with a slight frown. Several seconds later he says aloud, "OK, but next time I get to choose first!" His statement is uttered in a matter-of-fact tone of voice; he apparently assumes it will be accepted with the same force of logic by Brian as Brian's statement was accepted by him. In any event, for whatever reason, he does not even turn around to check Brian's reaction. Indeed, Brian does take Jeremy's last, "equalizer" remark in silence.

After several more minutes of play on the space station with Jeremy, Brian withdraws to a different area of the room. Brian starts to explore some science material and then comes across a shoe box labeled "Creepy Crawlies." These are miscellaneous rubber toy insects and monsters that Jeremy has collected from gumball-like machines at the local supermarket.

"I want to try all the finger ones," announces Brian, referring to the ones that are attached to rings and can be worn on fingers. He picks the box off the shelf and flips it over to let the entire contents spill onto the floor. Excitedly, he then starts rummaging through the pile to find the finger ones, discarding those that do not fit this criterion. As the rummaging continues, Brian gets more stimulated and he throws the discarded vermin more widely to all points of the room. "Look, I've got all the animals on my fingers!" he finally exclaims. Jeremy, who has been watching Brian occasionally from his place at the space station, says with real authority, "You've got to pick them all up. That's the rule here." His remark is made matter-of-factly rather than with anger. This rule to which Jeremy makes reference is one that he has heard many times from his parents, but which he himself usually follows only after threats of some consequence. But as Jeremy did before, Brian now calms down noticeably and starts to pick up the strewn articles with an easy compliance. Jeremy watches Brian for a time and then offers the Star Wars characters, saying, "You can use these if you want. It's okay with me."

When Brian has finished collecting the Creepy Crawlies, he joins Jeremy once again at the space station. Jeremy has added some superhero figures to the arena, and both boys return to a shared fantasy play of good and bad characters in combat with one another. Their play is interactive, animated, with much talking and laughter, yet structured and organized. They pursue this fantasy play for about 15 more minutes, until they get hungry. Jeremy, being a good host, asks Brian if he wants something to eat. When Brian answers affirmatively, Jeremy shouts down the stairs to ask his mother for a snack; this is the first time either one of the boys has addressed an adult since Brian's arrival over a half hour before.

Before considering how we interpret this play session, let us look at another example of peer interaction in which the feeling of the interchange is quite different. The second interaction is between two children who have a history of problematic and unskilled interpersonal functioning. Once we have a comparative feeling of these two instances of peer interaction and an intuition of their relative social maturity, we will outline a set of criteria within a developmental framework for looking at the adequacy of social interactions in general.

The setting in which we find two 9-year-old girls is a small private day school for children with emotional problems. These two children are participating in a joint research and clinical treatment program designed to facilitate social development at the same time that it tries to better understand its complex nature. The two girls are meeting in a room designed to approximate, as much as possible in an institutional setting, the same feeling of safety and supply as Jeremy's room, although it is not expected to duplicate it. Nevertheless, it is a room that is familiar to both girls. They have been meeting there regularly, once a week for 1½ years, with a therapist who has mediated their social interaction in a form of treatment called pair therapy. The adult therapist who usually meets with them for their hour together notes that the last several sessions have gone particularly smoothly and asks the girls whether they would like to be alone to play; one of the goals of pair therapy is to foster each dyad's autonomous capacity to function without the need for adult regulation or direct assistance. Their play begins like this.

Immediately after the therapist has left the room, Tania calls out, "Is there a model? Where's a model for me?" It is not obvious to whom she is directing this inquiry, and her tone is demanding but has a half-kidding quality to it. Janine responds, her voice typically sharp and clipped: "You want to make a model, you can make it out of clay." There is a tough-luck and unsupportive quality to this response. "Take your shoes off, Tania," she barks with a wry, disapproving look. Janine kicks off her own shoes somewhat vehemently and defiantly.

Tania has begun to work with some clay, and Janine joins her at the table. Janine remains standing as she picks up some clay and continues to talk about her shoes. "If this was my room I would just kick them across the room. I don't care who knows. I just kick them as hard as I can. Everything. Pillows too, everything is a mess." Janine is speaking with bravura and smiles in a "So there!" way. Tania stands up to reach across the table and grab half of the still unclaimed clay. She takes no more and no less than half and sits back down to model her growing piece. She has focused on her clay throughout Janine's soliloquy, but occasional glances toward Janine suggest that she has been monitoring Janine's activity. Janine suspiciously eyes Tania's movement toward the unclaimed clay. She appears to contemplate a reaction, some kind of objection, but remains silent. Tania then declares, "Don't talk about yourself. My room's a pigsty." This is said in a manner that suggests a competition has begun. Janine seems willing to enter into the competition. "You know what? I have clothes hanging on my wall right now. That's why my mother threw my toys out." (In a recent session Janine had reported in an "I don't care" manner that her mother had recently thrown away all of her toys because she had refused to pick up her room at home.) Janine ends her claim with a giggly, somewhat artificial and forced laugh. In fact, Janine's mother reported that Janine was furious about the toy incident.

"My cat almost jumped out the window today," she states almost as an afterthought, also in an "I don't care" tone. She continues to fiddle absently with her clay. "Mine almost went out when I was going to my cab," offers Tania. Janine says, "My cab almost left because the cat almost fell out the window." Tania cackles appreciatively at this. "My mother grabbed it by the tail," Janine says giggling, "and pulled it back in like it was a fishing rod." She sits down now and begins to work with the clay more constructively. After a pause Janine says, "She's a fat one, my cabdriver." Tania then throws out a gratuitous insult about her school bus driver. It seems as if the girls are competing to "out-naughty" one another in a battle of malevolence.

The girls' interaction continues in a kind of power struggle between them that never gets resolved. Tania becomes frustrated, bored, restless, and agitated in turn while playing with the clay and asks Janine to play puppets with her. Janine is belligerent but eventually picks up a puppet as if she is doing Tania a big favor. They order each other around, arguing about the puppet show, then about a doll bed, which Janine claims as her own.

Tania says with exasperation, "So, it's your damn bed. I don't care! Now I'm the reporter. Have you seen a huge green monster?" "No!" says Janine, wound up with excitement. "Say 'yes'!" asserts Tania. Janine says, "YES!" very loudly. Then she begins to make monster noises, and Tania screams loudly in response, hopping up and down. Janine changes her monster noises into screams now, and both girls stand with their eyes closed trying to outscream each other. Of course this mayhem succeeds in bringing the therapist into the room. Tania immediately runs over to pull on the adult's arm, saying, "We want to do a play for you. You sit here. C'mon," she says, leading her to a chair. Janine mopes and eyes Tania as the latter is being forceful in getting the adult's attention. Tania runs back to the stage after seating the adult, and she picks up a lion puppet. "C'mon, Janine, let's do a play," she says. She places her lion puppet on the stage to growl at Janine, saying, "I'm going to eat you." Janine then whines a bit frantically, "I need a lion too," her voice rising rapidly in pitch. Janine starts to look through the puppet box, pulling puppets out and dropping them all over the floor.

Tania starts moving impatiently, and she pulls at Janine's sleeve saying "C'mon, this lion of mine isn't in the show anymore," as if Janine shouldn't need one either then. However, Janine jerks her arm away and snaps back, "If you have an animal then I have to have one too." She pulls out a very large puppet.

"You can't have that one!" declares Tania. Janine asserts, "Yes, I can too!" Tania responds with a rising voice, "I'm not using mine. It'll just stay on the stage. I'm not using it!" She sounds almost frantic, but Janine ignores her. Finally Tania throws her lion puppet on the floor and angrily says, "You can take your stupid pet." Janine glares at Tania and then at the puppet at her feet. She returns her glare toward Tania, who stands with a frown, her arms folded and hip stuck out. "I don't want the damn puppet," seethes Janine, and she bolts out of the room before anyone can stop her.

The duration of this whole interaction, from its optimistic start to its disastrous termination, was 12 minutes.

AN INTERPRETIVE/EMPIRICAL APPROACH TO STUDYING SOCIAL REGULATION BETWEEN PEERS

The two dyads in the foregoing examples of peer interaction provide a dramatic contrast in getting along: The relationship between the two boys in the home setting grows and deepens as we watch, that of the two girls in the clinical setting falls apart completely. These differences in tone and outcome are striking, yet it is nevertheless difficult to describe the dynamics of the interactions in a way that illuminates how close peer relationships develop or fail to develop. Despite recent technological advances that have revolutionized the recording and analysis of social interaction data, the conceptual middle step in which a continuous stream of peer interaction is translated into exact yet meaningful data—first into molecular behavioral units and categories and then into molar psychological constructs—remains a difficult and value-laden inferential process (Cairns, 1979; Radke Yarrow & Zahn Waxler, 1979). In this difficult middle step between the recording of social interaction and the statistical or qualitative analysis of coded data, we have taken a nontraditional, interpretive approach that we believe powerfully informs us about why Jeremy and Brian got along and why Janine and Tania did not.

The two opening interpretive descriptions are narratives rather than pure observations. In these accounts the inferential process of selecting and classifying behaviors in ongoing interaction has already begun; clearly, the observer reporting these social interactions had some preconceived ideas that framed his perceptions. This framework derives from a uniting of research and clinical practice informed by developmental theory. For almost a decade we have been involved in a joint venture consisting of descriptive research on social development and the construction of a closely associated clinical practice called "pair therapy." In pair therapy two children or young adolescents with problems in forming and maintaining peer relationships meet regularly with a trained therapist who seeks to establish a context in which the pair can interact in ways that will enhance their capacity to share experience and deal collaboratively with others. The treatment provides a corrective emotional experience because the actual social interaction between the pair, as they choose and implement activities during sessions, is the material used by the therapist to facilitate their social and emotional growth. Clinical, research, and theoretical perspectives mutually enhance each other in this work. The clinical practice provides social interaction data in a context designed to facilitate a naturalistic process of change, thus enabling the research activity to address basic questions of social development. In turn, developmental theory honed in the research provides a road map of what constitutes progress (or regress) in the form and function of peer relationships as they develop during the clinical intervention.

The social regulation processes that enable close interpersonal relationships between peers to develop are basic to the focal treatment of pair therapy and are the object of study of the descriptive research. As the opening vignettes illustrate, emotionally troubled children like Tania and Janine appear to lack the ability to regulate each other in ongoing interactions with their peers and so have difficulty connecting with them and maintaining that connection. In our observations of social regulation processes in peer interaction, undertaken mostly in the context of pair therapy, two complementary themes or types of social regulation have emerged that appear to play a meaningful role in structuring or organizing the course of social relationships: (a) the need for intimacy, sharing, and dyadic community, or self-other integration, and (b) the need for autonomy, agency, and a sense of individual selfhood, or self-other differentiation.

The first of these classes of social regulation involves the developing capacity to experience a sense of connectivity with peers, a sense of common interest or something akin to what Sullivan (1953) called consensual validation. In our research, we have operationalized one aspect of this social regulation process as "forms of shared experience" and have used pair therapy as a context to examine the various forms it takes (Selman & Arboleda, 1986; Selman & Yeates, 1987). In the first of the cases just presented, Jeremy and Brian's fantasy play together with the miniature Star Wars figures (although not described in detail) represents an age-appropriate form of shared experience important for the development of the capacity for connectivity and mutuality. There appear to be opportunities for shared experience in the interaction between Janine and Tania as well, but for reasons that are not apparent or easy to fathom, this potential is realized only on an extremely low-level, primitive form of sharing, with disastrous effects on their interaction.

The second, reciprocal class of social regulation processes facilitates the developing sense of autonomy and serves to help children maintain the necessary boundaries between themselves and their close friends. These social regulation processes are just as necessary for forming and maintaining friendships as are the regulation processes for connectivity. When Brian asserts why he deserves "first shot" at the space station and Jeremy responds with an assertion that he gets first choice next time, this exchange exemplifies the social regulation processes involved in the development of autonomy. We have operationalized one aspect of the developing capacity for autonomy in the construct of "strategies for interpersonal negotiation," and examined the form these strategies take in both interview and observational studies (e.g., Selman, Beardslee, Schultz, Krupa, & Podorefsky, 1986; Selman & Demorest, 1984).

Pair therapists strive to develop children's ability to regulate their peer interactions without adult support, something that seems to come naturally to Jeremy and Brian. When children in pair therapy give evidence of gaining the capacity to use adaptive forms of these social regulations in their interactions with each other under therapeutic supervision, usually after many months or years of pair therapy, the therapist slowly withdraws, occasionally even leaving the therapy room (while continuing to monitor the pair from an adjoining observation room). As the brief report from the case of Janine and Tania demonstrates, members of the pair usually show signs of regression to less functional behavior during those sessions when the therapist first withdraws. But the goal of this form of treatment is that, with time and continued therapeutic work, the two children will be able to recover and to utilize, when they are alone together, the higher level social skills they attained with the therapist's guidance.

In this case, the stress of the new situation (being alone without the therapist) upset the balance of Janine and Tania's newly developing social skills, but Janine's impulsive retreat was only a temporary break in their relationship. She did come back into the room (of her own accord), and the therapist discussed what had happened with the girls, reflecting on the interaction and repairing the relationship by opening up communication with and between them. Thus, pair therapists hold the relationship together when the pair cannot. This continuity in the pair's relationship—the assurance that the pair will keep meeting together whatever may happen in a particular session—provides the children with a novel and unaccustomed connection with a peer. (Of course, the pair therapy could be ended if the therapist decides that the interaction between a pair is so conflictual that the peer relationship is destructive rather than therapeutic.)

The role of the therapist is to provide varying degrees of external structure within which the children are exposed to direct experience with peer interaction, communication, and conflict resolution. The therapist generally sets the stage for, oversees, and reflects on the children's clashes of will, confronting the pair with the fact that there are differing perspectives, which must be brought to bear on a solution that affects them both. The therapist mediates negotiation between the pair by setting limits, encouraging them to reflect on their behavior, facilitating constructive peer feedback, and, through role modeling, suggestions, and theoretical questions, helping them to consider alternate strategies to resolve their conflicts (Lyman & Selman, 1985). In this way the pair therapist helps expand the children's repertoire of negotiation strategies when conflict arises in the ongoing peer relationship that cannot be satisfactorily resolved with their current repertoire. Further-more, in the safety of this unique context children sometimes construct new strategies on their own, either alone (a case in which action leads thought) or in "coconstruction" with the peer. This growth in interpersonal negoti-ation skills in turn sets the stage for more profound shared experience, which leads to a sense of relatedness, consensual validation, and intimacy.

The configuration of an adult intervening with two children in naturalistic interaction seems to be a powerfully effective tool to promote children's social development. Children develop social skills through engagement in deeply intimate exchanges when, motivated by the practical problems of getting along with others, they reflect on and interpret their actions, thus acquiring understanding of actions they already find themselves doing (Packer, 1987). The pair therapist works to establish a context of "peer-like" relations without inherent hierarchical, asymmetrical power and control between the peers. In this way the treatment provides children with an opportunity to learn both sides of social regulation and to begin to experience adult forms of collaboration that involve both assertiveness and intimacy, an experience necessary for an optimal transition from the dependency of childhood to the independence and interdependence of adult social relationships.

Our clinical intervention is informed by a program of research that ex-amines the processes of social regulation within pair therapy sessions. In our efforts to understand social regulation processes in children's peer in-teractions, we have used a method that we label the "interpretive/empirical case study" approach. The consolidation of clinical and research goals in our descriptive work requires the combining of two seemingly polar meth-odologies: positivism and hermeneutics. The positivist approach to obser-vational research has traditionally been employed in the cross-sectional and longitudinal study of group differences in large samples, whereas the her-meneutic approach interprets individual and dyad differences in case studies. Our method consists of a unique integration of traditional observational ("empirical") methodology and intensive, longitudinal study of pairs of chil-dren in therapy using hermeneutic ("interpretive") analysis.

The method we use to study the course of peer relationships is both like and unlike those of traditional researchers studying peer interaction in each of the three "empirical" analytic steps of selecting, coding, and analyzing social behaviors. Most early and current research on peer relationships has studied aspects of autonomy and connection with positivist methods, first selecting molecular behaviors either deductively (most commonly) or in-ductively (e.g., ethologists such as Blurton-Jones & Woodson, 1979) and then coding them into behavioral taxonomies based on some criteria of functional or morphological equivalence—for example, the factors that produce them, temporal proximity, physical appearance, or situational similarity (Hartup, 1979; Menzel, 1979). Finally, the coded behaviors are usually ana-lyzed statistically, often with sequential analyses (e.g., Gottman & Bakeman, 1979). We follow these positivist analytic steps to the extent that we select, code, and interpret molecular behaviors, but we overlay these objective components with hermeneutic, contextual components.

As a number of researchers in developmental psychology and the philosophy of social science have recently articulated (e.g., Gergen, 1985; Packer, 1985; Scarr, 1985), hermeneutic methods examine the structure, organization, and intelligibility of human action in meaningful rather than formal or causal terms. In contrast to traditional positivist approaches to knowledge that aim to elucidate *objective* elements of social action and interchange by analyzing either abstract systems of relations or mechanistic systems of forces and causes, both of which end up decontextualizing—and therefore distorting—behavior, the interpretive approach highlights the importance of context in understanding the *meaning* more than the explanation or cause of social behavior.

This interpretive attitude and focus on personal meaning in longitudinal context is also articulated in clinical theory. Psychoanalysts in the narrative tradition, who reject Freud's metapsychology of natural-science forces, energies, and mechanisms, view persons as agents who construct situations (e.g., Modell, 1984; Schafer, 1983). In this view stimulus and response, situation and action, are not independent: over time agents define situations in ways that imply what they do in them. Furthermore, specific actions are "overdetermined" or have multiple meanings, both conscious and unconscious, and so can be described only selectively and meaningfully, not inclusively and objectively, by agent and observer alike.

The recognition of the intimate relationship between the meaning of an action and the specific context in which it takes place, and the consequent view that these contexts are sociohistorical constructions rather than objective phenomena, is also integral to our approach. Relationships and their history form the context of social interactions, and with our constructionist and contextualist perspective we seek to describe developmental aspects of persons in relationship with one another in addition to the individual's separate psychological processes or states. But if behavior has multiple interpretations, what meaning do we seek in these relationships? Gergen & Gergen (1982) argue that the choice of meaning in explanations of human behavior cannot be established empirically but rather must be based on one's values. In this view, the narrative interpretation one chooses is not a matter of objective truth but of one's sense of valuation. Our quest for developmental meaning in observations of children's peer interactions is closely related to the goals of our clinical practice: We value mutuality and collaboration, and the aim of therapy is to help children generate ways to relate to others more reciprocally and collaboratively, and less impulsively and unilaterally.

The therapeutic goal of fostering collaboration in children's peer relations gets translated into explanations of behavior and clinical interpretations that are very different from—but not contradictory to—the therapeutic goal and value of explicating insight for the child, as in psychodynamically oriented individual therapy. For example, in evaluating the social interaction between

Tania and Janine, we would give a semantic and pragmatic explanation of the social regulation processes that are failing (they can't share or take turns), whereas from the perspective of individual treatment, a thematic explanation could be made instead (each feels needy and depleted and so acts greedily). A content-based inner/dynamic interpretation of the interaction when the two girls are discussing their cats could be that they are really (also) speaking about themselves: They feel trapped, mistreated, and uncared for by their mothers and wish for escape; a more form-based outer/interactional interpretation of the same interchange is that in their search for intimacy/connectedness the girls are colluding in each other's low-level, disorganized, and impulsive expressiveness, and thus fail to regulate one another. These themes and forms of social interaction eventually must be woven together to tell a complete and meaningful story of the interaction.

STRATEGIES FOR INTERPERSONAL NEGOTIATION: A DESCRIPTIVE TOOL FOR THE ANALYSIS OF DYADIC PEER INTERACTION

The children in the two opening vignettes exhibit similar feelings of the sort that are inevitable in close and meaningful relationships at all ages. On the positive side, for both pairs of children there are instances of sharing experiences and fantasy play. On the conflictual side, both interactions contain feelings of frustration, possessiveness, competition, and anger. However, keeping in mind the concept of interpersonal negotiation to maintain equilibrium, we find the two narratives also suggest significant differences in the ability of the peers to regulate their social interaction without adult support. Brian and Jeremy use many orders and commands in trying to subtly negotiate their relative power and control. Yet their interaction progresses as if with checks and balances, as they flexibly respond to each other's needs and intents. They appear to have a number of alternative negotiation strategies and tools for internal and external control that allow their interaction to continue to progress through rough spots back to more balanced states. Our overall impression is they are able to monitor internal disequilibrium with flexibility, to complement each other's asserted wishes, and to maintain interpersonal equilibrium. This is clearly not the case with Janine and Tania. The girls' internal modulation of needs and wishes appears to be very erratic, and their personal and interpersonal equilibrium are altogether destroyed within 12 minutes.

Can the differences in the quality of individual and mutual control in these two sets of peer social interactions be sharpened in a developmental light? The interpersonal negotiation strategies (INS) model we have developed is a descriptive developmental model that allows us to compare, at both a molar level of the general form of the interaction and a molecular level of specific sequences of strategies in particular contexts, the form and function of each pair's conflictual interactions. In the following sections, we will describe the (INS) model and a three-step procedure used to apply the model to actual social interaction. The balance between the positivist (or "objective") and the interpretive (or "subjective") aspects of our model shifts at each of three analytic steps leading from recorded social interaction (e.g., from videotape records) to an interpretive story of interpersonal negotiation and social regulation. New layers of meaning are brought to bear at each step by superimposing interpretive molar information onto the molecular behaviors. We use information successively from different levels of analysis: first, from the *behavioral* context to identify contexts for interpersonal negotiation, then from the *psychological* context to "diagnose" the negotiation strategies (analogous to, but not synonymous with, "coding"), and finally from the *sociohistorical* context to interpret the coded behavior.

Selecting Interactions Defined as Contexts for Interpersonal Negotiation Based on Behavioral Clues

The first task in interpreting social regulation processes with the construct of interpersonal negotiation strategies is to identify negotiation behaviors, or "contexts for interpersonal negotiation," in the ongoing stream of peer interaction. Interpersonal negotiation strategies are the methods by which one person tries to meet personal needs and goals in interaction, and often in conflict, with another person to whom he or she has some degree of emotional attachment. Two criteria define what we call a context for interpersonal negotiation.

First, the interaction must take place in the context of an *ongoing relationship* in which each person cares about the "significant other." Social relationships differ from social behavior per se in several ways important for the process of interpersonal negotiation. Relationships involve the complex influences of interactions on interactions and so have emergent properties not present in component interactions (cf. Hinde, 1979; Sroufe & Fleeson, 1986). In particular, because relationships exist over time, their cognitive/affective psychological aspects transcend their overt behavioral ones. Interactions within relationships are affected by the history of the dyad as well as the complex relational histories of each person. Therefore, ongoing relationships with personal meaning for both social partners are contexts in which mutual expectations are often disrupted and conflicting motivations can be easily aroused. They are also contexts in which caring and investment can powerfully motivate actors to attempt to achieve interpersonal equilibrium.

Second, the relationship must be in *disequilibrium*. This disequilibrium is manifest in both observable outer behavior and inferred inner thoughts and feelings. Interpersonal and internal disequilibrium arise simultaneously from the dyadic context of the interaction—not from within one individual or the other—as aspects of the external situation (including each person's actions) interact with aspects of each person's internal state. Even when subtle, *interpersonal disequilibrium* represents overt behavioral opposition and subsequent mutual effect. For example, when Brian reaches for the trash compactor, Jeremy resists, reaching for the trash compactor himself and calling out, "I'm doing the trash compactor." Then Brian persists forcefully, asserting, "You've already played with this, but it's new to me." Complementing this behavioral disharmony is *internal disequilibrium* or inner conflict over wanting one's own needs met, yet at the same time caring about the other person. In the trash compactor example, Brian is driven by his strong desire to operate the attractive toy, but his resistance to Jeremy's challenge—although forceful—does not communicate anger and is thus respectful of Jeremy's feelings. Likewise, Jeremy's response also reflects internal disequilibrium (although he probably isn't fully aware of it): he relinquishes his claim (from which we may infer that his friend counts with him) but he is discontent (reflecting his own unmet desire to play with it).

In identifying contexts for interpersonal negotiation we use behavioral criteria to define relationships in disequilibrium. The behavioral manifestation of interpersonal disequilibrium is related to the definition of social conflict behaviors discussed in Shantz's (1987) review of research on conflicts between children. Interactions involving interpersonal disequilibrium often fit the traditional positivist notion of two-term social conflict (that actor A does or says something to which actor B objects—e.g., Hay, 1984). Many interpersonal negotiation interactions also meet the three-term criteria for social conflict (occasions when actor A does or says something that influences actor B, actor B resists, and actor A persists—e.g., Shantz & Shantz, 1985). The above example meets the three-term criteria: Brian reaches for the trash compactor, Jeremy resists, and Brian persists, holding firm against Jeremy's challenge.

Negotiation contexts and traditional social conflict episodes are not, however, synonymous; traditional positivist indications of social conflict (behavioral resistance) signal contexts for interpersonal negotiation, but interpersonal negotiation is a more inclusive concept than conflict. In some more subtle negotiations the potential conflict does not become overt because no direct resistance is met; these in essence are "one-term" negotiations. If, for example, Jeremy had wanted to play with the trash compactor but didn't say so or indicate his desire some other way, it would still have been a context for negotiation, but it would have been much more difficult to identify as such because the interpersonal disequilibrium would have been less visible. In such cases, subtle affective cues to inner disequilibrium (i.e, expressions, tones, etc.) are used to identify the interaction as a context for negotiation. Thus, interpersonal negotiation involves potential as well as overt conflict, and very subtle behavioral clues are used to identify contexts in which resistance is not overtly manifest because the actor suppresses his or her own desire for the sake of interpersonal harmony, with consequent (but often almost invisible) internal disequilibrium.

Strategies of different levels and orientations are often employed within one negotiation context as the interaction unfolds and each person's behavior is colored by that of his or her partner (as is the case with the opening gambit of Jeremy and Brian's play). Therefore, when our goal is to understand the process of negotiation in a specific context for negotiation, we examine the sequence of molecular behaviors. Sometimes, however, it is more useful to examine molar patterns, and therefore contexts for negotiation are not always parsed into molecular units but are often summed across interactions and/or relationships. For example, although it was not the case with either the boys or the girls in our examples, a pattern of dominance often gets established early, quickly, and almost unnoticeably in a particular interaction or relationship. In these cases the repeated interactional patterns can be summarized on a more molar level.

In addition, clinical work involves diagnosis and prognosis as well as etiology, and so needs models that are usable at a molar level as a tool for summarizing the multiple and complex interactions that occur in a clinical context (e.g., during an hour of pair therapy, or across several sessions). This summarizing across interactions allows clinical observers to communicate in a relatively simple, but common, easily learned language about their impressions of how the processes of treatment are progressing, as well as how the capacities of the individuals are developing. Thus, we choose contexts for negotiation at molar as well as molecular levels of analysis, depending on our immediate research or clinical purpose. This flexibility permits both microanalytic analyses of the process of negotiation in specific sequences of dyadic interaction and macroanalytic analyses of more general patterns of an individual's negotiation across contexts.

Some negotiation strategies are clear and sharp with respect to beginnings and endings or sequences (e.g., the opening gambit around the trash compactor in Brian and Jeremy's play), but at other times it is not clear at all that negotiation is what is going on (that there is a context for negotiation that clearly can be identified and coded). Negotiation interactions focusing on autonomy issues and interactions focusing on connection probably represent a continuum—instead of a dichotomy—of social regulation process. Hinde (1985) distinguishes between two types of emotional behavior that may help clarify the different role of affect in relation to thought in the two types of social regulation processes we have identified. He views emotional behavior as falling along a continuum from behavior that is more or less purely expressive to behavior concerned primarily with a process of negotiation between individuals (although all emotional behavior involves both). Feelings in social interactions of connection seem predominantly expressive and harmonious, whereas those of autonomy are predominantly negotiative and in disequilibrium. Thus, another major feature of our interpretive procedure is an attention to affective criteria not only in coding and analyzing social interaction but also in identifying the interactions to be interpreted. Because of this attention to behavioral cues of affect management as well as to behavioral opposition, the selection of contexts for interpersonal negotiation is hermeneutic and meaning oriented as well as objective.

Diagnosing Interpersonal Negotiation Strategies in Two Psychological Dimensions: Developmental Level and Interpersonal Orientation

The interpersonal negotiation strategies model provides not only a useful net for catching negotiations as they float down the stream of social interactions in middle childhood and early adolescence, but also a taxonomy for categorizing them into meaningful and useful classes. In the second step of our interpretive/empirical analytic procedure, we diverge from traditional observational research in using psychological instead of behavioral criteria, and thus we "diagnose" rather than "code" the social behaviors.

Instead of using traditional criteria of morphological or functional equivalence to code social interaction, we use developmental criteria based on a heuristic derived from structural-developmental theory. This cognitive-developmental construct is the coordination of social perspectives (Selman, 1980). Social perspective coordination is defined as the developing qualitative capacity to differentiate and integrate the self's and others' points of view through an understanding of the relations between the thoughts, feelings, and wishes of the self and those of other persons. The social-cognitive levels of social perspective coordination integrate two important developmental theories: Mead's (1934) view that role taking is a fundamental process in the socialization of the self, and the Piagetian structural-developmental tradition's focus on the organization and emergence of forms of knowing (e.g., Kohlberg, 1969).

According to the INS model, during the toddler and early preschool years the child's reflective interpersonal understanding is at an egocentric level in which there is no clear differentiation between the social (i.e., intentional) perspectives of self and others (Level 0). At subsequent levels of reflection the child comprehends that another person's subjective thoughts, feelings, and intentions are distinct from the self's (early childhood: Level 1); that the other person can reflect upon and consider as distinct the self's subjective attitudes, feelings, and motives (middle childhood: Level 2); that the self and other can view self's and other's psychological points of view mutually and simultaneously (preadolescence: Level 3); and that there is a more general social viewpoint that transcends individual perspectives and involves a mutual understanding of deeper psychic processes within and between persons (adolescence and adulthood: Level 4).

The perspective coordination model provides a developmental framework for organizing forms of interpersonal behavior, including interpersonal negotiation and shared experience, as well as forms of interpersonal understanding (e.g., friendship concepts). Although the identification of developmental levels of social perspective coordination in interpersonal understanding in our earlier work reflects a positivist and rationalist notion of social-cognitive competence, our use of these levels in studying conduct—in the social regulation processes of interpersonal negotiation strategies and shared experience—takes on a more hermeneutic flavor. This is because in moving beyond the developmental description of the *social-cognitive capacity* to coordinate perspectives when thinking about the social world, so as to understand the child's *social behavior* (in both its molecular and molar forms) from a developmental perspective, we are guided by a social contextual metaphor instead of an individual competence-based metaphor.

What enables us to code specific social-regulative behaviors using the seemingly positivist developmental heuristic of social perspective coordination levels is our reliance on Wernerian orthogenetic rather than Piagetian ontogenetic principles. Werner's (1948, 1957) comparative principle of orthogenesis characterizes development broadly—*wherever it occurs* (i.e., whether in molar processes such as ontogeny or pathogenesis or in a more molecular process of development within a single interaction or relationship known as microgenesis)—as a regulative process proceeding from a state of global undifferentiation to a state of differentiation and hierarchical integration. The orthogenetic principle thus includes not only the structural-developmental principles that describe forms of social-cognitive development, but also other developmental processes that can illuminate the context-dependent dynamics of interpersonal action by taking into account its interrelated emotional and cognitive components.

The coding judgment is made by evaluating the internal disequilibrium that is inferred from the observed behavioral cues that had initially signaled the context for interpersonal negotiation. Observed social action (i.e., the behavioral disharmony that signals interpersonal disequilibrium) is not by itself interpretable developmentally, that is, in terms of the ability to differentiate and integrate the social perspectives of self and other. The developmental diagnosis of overt manifestations of social conflict requires analysis of latent dimensions of the inner disequilibrium—namely, the extent to which the actor in dealing with the experience of disequilibrium appears to understand and coordinate the thoughts, feelings, and motives of both self and other.

The interpersonal negotiation strategies model assumes that the coordination of social perspectives is intrinsic to the process of balancing personal and interpersonal needs in ongoing relationships and that mature negotiation is based on the ability to coordinate (i.e., differentiate and integrate) the perspectives of self and other. The four developmental levels of interpersonal negotiation reflect different levels of sophistication in perspective coordination: "Out of control" impulsive rage or panic reflects no perspective on the negotiation (Level 0); unilateral power through orders and threats reflects a "one-way" perspective (Level 1); self-interested cooperation or psychological manipulation reflects both persons' perspectives (Level 2); and empathic collaboration reflects a third-person perspective (Level 3). But how does one make the plunge from observed social interaction to these deeper levels, each of which represents a uniquely shaped conceptual lens through which self is viewed and understood in relation to other *at the moment of the action?*

Meaningful developmental diagnosis of the ways actors actually deal with themselves and other people to simultaneously balance inner and interpersonal feelings of disequilibrium requires considerable inference about psychological dimensions underlying the observed actions. In evaluating the developmental maturity of conduct it becomes ncessary to study how individuals put emotions as well as cognitions into perspective in ongoing social interaction. Internal motives and feelings and many external factors evoke, inhibit, or otherwise mediate the extent to which individuals actually use their optimal perspective-taking ability as interpersonal conflict evolves out of particular social contexts. In contrast to the traditional coding of children's peer interactions, in which molecular behaviors are usually coded in a "context-free" way by matching each behavior to an item in a behavioral taxonomy that is also more or less molecular ("physical aggression" or "hit"), we use contextual cues to translate the molecular negotiation behaviors into the four molar developmental categories of physical impulsivity, unilateral control, reflective reciprocity, and mutual collaboration.

The INS diagnosing process assesses more than simple motoric behavior and actual words to capture the rich meaning of an interpersonal negotiation in a relatively objective way. The force and style of actions and the tone and volume of phrases are noted in our attempt to assess the cognitions, feelings, and intentions that underlie the observed behavior. Reports of facial expressions (e.g., "a wry disapproving look") and tone of voice (e.g., "threatening tone") reflect interpretations of underlying feeling and intent. Some inferences of feeling and tone are made explicitly from behavior (e.g., "Apparently recovered from his losing skirmish to get first choice, Jeremy stands up to join Brian"). Different impressions of tone and intent make for very different interpretations of negotiation strategies, and this kind of "subjective" information is crucial for translating the observed social conflict interactions into the molar levels of interpersonal negotiation.

The INS model provides four tools to organize the subjective, psychological information that needs to be considered in accurately diagnosing the negotiation behaviors. These tools are in the form of operationalized psychological components inherent in all negotiative acts. Three of the components together represent the developmental dimension of an interpersonal negotiation strategy: (1) a cognitive *construal of self and other* or interpersonal understanding component (the construal of the perspective of self in relation to the perspective of other that operates at the moment of the particular interactive context), (2) an *affective disequilibrium* component (the way the individual perceives and attempts to control emotional disequilibrium arising in that interpersonal context), and (3) a *primary interpersonal purpose* component (the dominant intention or purpose of the actor in that context).

The fourth tool for diagnosing conflictual interactions is the *interpersonal orientation* component of negotiation, which examines the way control is asserted rather than the form of the control. This personalitylike dimension addresses upon whom the actor predominantly acts in attempting to deal with disequilibrium within the self and between the self and other. It classifies social action into one of three modes of control: in the other-transforming mode, the individual primarily attempts to change the thoughts, feelings, and/or actions of the other; in the self-transforming mode, the actor predominantly works on changing his or her own thoughts, feelings, and/or actions to mesh, or at least not to conflict, with the perceived needs of the other. The collaborative mode, integrally connected with the higher developmental levels, integrates self-transforming and other-transforming actions.

The levels of each INS component are logically and psychologically linked in their organization across development because they are based on the same perspective coordination levels, yet the manifestation of perspective coordination at each level can be uniquely described for each component. The developmental components differentiate (in an Wernerian orthogenetic way) with increasing developmental maturity, both from each other and within each component. It is a characteristic of the lowest level that thought, feeling, and intention are not differentiated from each other or from the action itself. At the highest levels an observing self, whose perspective is differentiated from—yet integrated with—that of the other, perceives and tries to sort out the multiple motives and multiple feelings involved in a negotiation, thus accurately representing the complexity of the relationship between self and other.

With respect to interpersonal orientation, at the lower developmental levels where the social perspectives of self and other are either undifferentiated (Level 0) or differentiated but unintegrated (Level 1), each strategy is isolated, rigid, and polarized, at one extreme or the other of a behavioral continuum ranging from physically withdrawing self-transforming strategies to aggressive other-transforming strategies. With developmental maturity, interpersonal orientation becomes more integrated and equilibrated between the two orientations, first either becoming assertively ordering or submissively obedient (Level 1), then either persuasive or deferential (Level 2), and finally collaborative (Level 3). Collaborative actions synthesize differentiated conceptions and perceptions of self and represent a mixture of accommodation and assertion, entailing simultaneous attempts to change self and other. Figure 14.1 illustrates this dependent relation between developmental level and interpersonal orientation.

Although all the components are intertwined in conduct, it is useful to separate them in order to explicate how complex social conflicts are reduced to our four deceptively simplistic levels of interpersonal negotiation. These theoretical tools facilitate the inferential process of "coding" the developmental maturity of interpersonal negotiation (itself in great part characterized by the degree to which actors are able to accurately infer their partners'

LEVEL 3

Third Person/Mutual

Strategies that use both self- and shared-reflection to collaboratively change both Self's and Other's wishes in pursuit of mutual goals

——— LEVEL 2 ———

Self-Reflective/Reciprocal

Strategies that consciously use psychological compliance to value Self's wishes only secondarily to Other's

——— LEVEL 1 ———

Differentiated/Subjective

Strategies that use "will-less" submission to wishes of Other

——— LEVEL 0 ———

Undifferentiated/Egocentric

Strategies that use unreflective, impulsive withdrawal or obedience to protect Self

Strategies that consciously use psychological influence to change Other's mind

Strategies that use willful one-way orders to control Other for Self's way

Strategies that use unreflective, impulsive force to get Self's goal

Social Perspective Coordination Competence

Interpersonal Negotiation Strategies in the *Self-Transforming Orientation*

Interpersonal Negotiation Strategies in the *Other-Transforming Orientation* inner, subjective experience). However, the four components do not represent a traditional scoring system but rather guides for making a clinical judgment of developmental level and interpersonal orientation for a negotiation strategy or series of strategies. The developmental level of a particular strategy is diagnosed by asking a series of questions for each component, which are presented in the Appendix. Because of the logically and psychologically linked nature of the levels across the four components, the responses to these questions converge to define a certain gestalt or tone of a particular negotiation, and the reliability of any particular coding judgment using our model does not depend upon how reliably one can code a particular component (e.g., intent).

Thus, the questions for each component generate dialogues in which we seek converging evidence for our judgments of developmental level and style. We use these questions to make the developmental diagnosis either as individual observers or through consensus among observers and therapists, whether we are coding molecular behaviors in a microanalysis of a particular peer interaction in our roles as researchers or evaluating more molar patterns of repeated behavior (e.g., across pair therapy sessions) in our roles as clinical interventionists. For example, when Janine states to Tania, "You want to make a model, you make it out of clay," we report that her voice is sharp and clipped. Thus we infer a more irritable, angry feeling, a more bossy and controlling intent, and a more competitive perception of the other person than if the exact same words were said in a warm, supportive tone of suggestion. Indeed, in our examples, there is a striking difference in the overall tone of the boys' and the girls' interactions that implies very different personal meanings in the interactions of the two dyads, even for negotiations at the same level and orientation (e.g., orders).

Interpreting Interpersonal Negotiations: Placing Diagnosed Strategies in the Sociohistorical Context

The third step of our analytic procedure—interpreting the diagnosed strategies—places them in the larger social matrix of the relationship. The coded interactions can be analyzed either positivistically or hermeneutically. At the positivistic extreme, our observational diagnostic procedure could be used in a standard systematic research program to analyze coded sequences of dyadic negotiation strategies with sophisticated microanalytic statistical procedures. However, the analyses we have undertaken to date fall much closer to the hermeneutic extreme. We have done some simple formal (statistical) analyses of interpersonal negotiation, but only for small numbers of cases (e.g., Lyman & Selman, 1985). Our analyses are more often qualitative than strictly numerical, reflecting our belief that sequential analyses alone cannot capture the meaning that the sociohistorical context gives to social interactions, even those coded within a psychologically meaningful developmental framework.

Although the settings and goals of the interactions of Brian and Jeremy and those of Tania and Janine are admittedly different in critical ways, the interactions share an important feature from the point of view of a developmental model of interpersonal negotiation. Much of the interaction in both episodes is in the form of orders, sometimes accompanied by impulsive physical behavior. The children often appear to act with a construal of the interaction as a battle of wills, and with the intent of attaining the self's goals alone, not caring—or at least not caring much—about the wants of the other. According to the developmental scheme just presented, these negotiations would fall at Level 1 in an other-transforming orientation. Although both pairs of children appear to use many unilateral, assertively ordering strategies, this way of interacting seems more successfully used by the boys at home than by the girls in the clinic setting. Why does the interaction of the girls go badly and end with what amounts to a total breakdown of negotiation, when the predominant use of orders works so well for the boys?

Negotiation behaviors at the same developmental level and interpersonal orientation have different personal and developmental meanings depending on their context. The act of coding negotiation strategies gives them developmental meaning, but the functional meaning of a negotiation strategy is inherently contextual. To interpret the meaning of a negotiation strategy in terms of its function in regulating the interaction, we must examine its place in the larger social context, that is, in the relationship. Relevant levels of analysis for evaluating contextual meaning include those of the individual (each person's personality style and interpersonal understanding competence level), the dyad (the past history of the relationship and the sequence of events in the present interaction), and the group (each person's relationship history with significant others, which socializes specific relational patterns and group norms).

The two opening narratives provide such a striking contrast in social regulation that we can make a rather rich and illuminating (though incomplete) interpretative description of the different dynamics of the peer interactions by examining only one of the aforementioned relevant factors: the sequence of negotiations occurring in these particular sessions. The sequential unfolding of social interaction is the focus of many traditional quantitative analyses of social interaction, but our analysis is more qualitative and contextual.

We have noted that during their play period the boys negotiated with many orders and commands, frequently in a one-way or unilateral manner that did not call on forms of reciprocity or compromise. Brian commanded Jeremy to yield the trash compactor. Later, with a firm, "Jeremy!", he insisted that his friend calm down. Jeremy ordered Brian to allow "C3PO" to stay on the space station. At another time he asserted that Brian has "got to" pick up the strewn Creepy Crawlies. An adult who views commands as only a negative aspect of social interaction might come away from this interaction thinking it uncooperative and hence unsuccessful, yet the boys seemed to accept each other's commands relatively easily and naturally. Jeremy and Brian were able to use each other's orders as a means or source of external control, alternately regulating each other.

The boys' use of (Level 1) orders and commands often constituted the application of a strategy one level higher than the impulsive behavior of the peer, and it was often offered—and accepted—as a source of control for maintaining self-regulation in the context of the interaction. This regulation often was given in the form of orders (Level 1) addressed to a child who was hinting toward expressive behavior characterized by impulsivity. For example, when Jeremy became almost frenzied in his play with the space station model, finally throwing some model pieces out of the compactor with a shriek, Brian said firmly and angrily, "Jeremy!" Although he was becoming very involved in the fantasy play, and his excitement and agitation were not derived from interaction directly with Brian, Jeremy had started slipping toward a wild expression of aggressive impulses. However, he was able to control these impulses when Brian's firm tone indicated that the equilibrium of their play was in jeopardy. Thus when Brian became disequilibrated (upset) by Jeremy's impulsive expressiveness, their interaction shifted from connection-oriented shared experience to negotiation. Brian's Level 1, other-transforming communication in response to his own discomfort served as a cue to Jeremy to take self-transforming actions to bring himself back into control, and he was able to do so with a little help from his friend. Later these reciprocal roles were reversed. When Brian began to lose control scattering the Creepy Crawlies to the four corners of the room with aroused inner excitement, Jeremy told Brian that he had to follow the rule of cleaning up after himself. Again the expressive interaction turned into negotiation; Jeremy's Level 1, other-transforming strategy, made as a one-way order, served as an external force for Brian, which he was then able to use for self-regulation. He calmed down and reordered the Crawlies.

Not only were the (Level 1) orders offered to a child who was regressing toward (Level 0) impulsivity, in the first exchange the claim with a call to fairness as reciprocity (Level 2) was offered after Level 1 or Level 0 demands for the use of the trash compactor were tried. So the strategies Jeremy and Brian used as declarations and assertions of the need for the other's self-control were often one level above the level where the more disequilibrated child appeared to be functioning. The child who was being "regulated" was able to accept these strategies as "fair" in the sense that he recognized the strategies as more adequate ways of dealing with disequilibrium. Although upset, Jeremy was able to "listen to reason" when Brian claimed that he (Brian) should get to play with the compactor first. In turn Brian was able to accept that Jeremy should have first pick next time. Thus, each child was responsive to later controls for regulating the self's behavior and maintaining fairness. It is also interesting to note that Brian's Level 2 statement also was followed by a classic Level 2, self-transforming strategy and statement from Jeremy—"OK, but next time I get to choose first." Higher (Level 2) strategies seemed to beget higher level strategies in this pair.

With Janine and Tania, however, the orders and grabbing came at a level that was equal to or lower than the level of the other's behavior, and they were competitive and potentially destructive to the relationship, rather than supportive and regulating of it. When either of these two children put forth an assertion of will in Level 1 form, the other matched her, will to will, in a confrontative way. In the very first exchange Tania yelled out with a harsh demandingness, "Where's a model for me?" (Level 1). Janine's response was an irritated, barked order: "You want to make a model, you can make it out of clay" (Level 1). Later as they were planning the puppet show, Tania asserted, "Quick, get on that side, on that side!" Rather than accepting Tania's direction, Janine countered in a Level 1 fashion, "No, don't do that. Do it there." Later, in their interaction around the puppet, Tania declared with building frustration, "You can't have that one!" "Yes, I can too!" Janine growled back. Whereas Brian and Jeremy were able and willing to accept each other's Level 1 or Level 2 assertions of will and postpone or compromise their own needs with self-transforming actions matched in level, Janine and Tania each pulled tighter on the ends of the negotiation rope held between them. When one tugged with Level 1 other-transforming strategies, the other tugged back forcefully *in kind*, as if unwilling to lose even an inch of what they must have as theirs.

Furthermore, each girl reinforced and accentuated the regressive (Level 0) impulsivity of the other, rather than serving as a source of external regulation and control. When either started to lose control, and her impulses began to dictate her actions, the other would collude and join with these chaotic feelings, actually dropping in level, instead of curbing them with helpful, higher level strategies. First, the girls seemed to compete in an attempt to "out-naughty" one another as they talked with increasingly disorganized thoughts about messy rooms and cats escaping or being tortured. On the heels of this "discussion" Tania screamed, "What should I make?" expressing frustration and helplessness about her work with clay. Janine's response reflected this helplessness as she screamed back wildly, "Nothing!" Later Janine threw clay at Tania in an impulsive way, and Tania's response was to screech with surprise. Compare this to Brian's controlling glare at Jeremy when he started to throw materials frantically: Brian's glare served to calm Jeremy down, but surely a screech does not have this effect. As the play evolved, Janine's monster noises led into a screaming competition between the girls. And finally when Tania furiously threw the lion puppet at Janine's feet, spitting out, "You can take your stupid pet," Janine's response was an impulsive (Level 0) physical exit from the scene. Thus, both girls lacked the ability to regulate each other's primitive expressiveness; each got caught up in her partner's loss of control instead of switching the expressive interaction into a negotiative mode with helpful, chaos-curbing orders, as the boys did.

Our model points out that low-level strategies demonstrate less ability to integrate other-transforming and self-transforming orientations within one context for negotiation. Generally speaking, peer interactions at the lower levels can remain mutually satisfying (i.e., the relationship can continue) only if the children can shift from one orientation to the other across different situations during the course of a play session. Brian and Jeremy were able to take turns acting in other-transforming and self-transforming ways. Brian ordered that he have first shot at the trash compactor, trying to make Jeremy change his wants or actions toward using the compactor; Jeremy, however reluctantly, withdrew his pursuit of the compactor. Later Jeremy insisted that Brian not take the "C3PO" from its initial place, and Brian agreed. Janine and Tania, on the other hand, showed a stubborn unwillingness to take any self-transforming action. The girls were rigidly locked into strategies of only one interpersonal orientation, each battling to make the other change for the self. For whatever reason, such a switch probably would have felt to both girls like too much loss of control; such flexible behavior was too unfamiliar for them.

When Tania tried to engage Janine in a game of checkers or in playing with puppets (perhaps because she felt more competent at these activities than at clay modeling), Janine refused to budge from her own interests (perhaps because she felt more secure working with clay). Through the negotiation for working with clay versus puppets, there was no true sense of compromise, even when surface statements or actions took the form of compromise. After Janine adamantly rejected Tania's overture, barking, "No! I'm doing a clay bunny!" Tania called upon a principle of apparent reciprocity. She said, "I did your stupid clay for you," and the form of her words had the artificial appearance of Level 2, calling for a fair exchange, and implying that each should accommodate (self-transform) by spending time doing what the other wanted. However, the tone of Tania's statement conveyed unmasked anger, such that the feeling was not one of mutual sympathy but one of embattled challenge. Tania even undercut her own accommodation (of doing the clay) by calling it "stupid," thus attacking the value of the activity and of Janine's interests. Therefore, although the actual words called for compromise and a transforming of the self's interests, the tone offered an angry battle cry from an unchanging and entrenched self.

Likewise Janine's apparent compromise to join Tania at this point was really a compromise only if viewed at the level of gross motoric behavior (she *did* walk over to the puppet corner), but not if other relevant cues are taken into consideration. The "style" or "tone" of her movement to join Tania was replete with resistance, as she forcefully hurled her work onto the table and clomped stiffly across the room. At the same time she commanded, "Let me finish this," in a tone that seemed to tell Tania to "bug off." In Janine's response, then, we see angry rejection at the same time that she joined Tania's puppet play: Janine strongly undercut her manifest self-transforming action with not-so-latent other-transforming tones and words.

We might conjecture that if either child had carried through consonantly with her self-transforming surface actions, interpersonal equilibrium might have been restored. What if Tania's call to mutual accommodation had been offered with sympathy? What if Janine had joined the puppet play with temporary willingness rather than violent resistance, or had asked to finish the clay in a compromising tone? The girls might not have wound themselves into such distress and disequilibrium. Instead, by the time Janine joined the puppet play, she felt resentful at giving up her own wants, and Tania felt resentful of Janine's rejection. In consequence, both girls tried to order each other and refused to be self-transforming, and both internal and interpersonal affective disequilibrium escalated until Janine finally bolted from the room.

It is important to note, especially following an example such as this session with Janine and Tania, that other-transforming strategy use, in and of itself, is not inherently "bad" or maladaptive. For Brian and Jeremy it presented no problems. That the rigidity and lack of alternatives and flexibility are the problem is brought home by observing that children whose maladaptive social behavior is passive and extremely withdrawn experience equally severe difficulties in their interactions in or out of pair therapy because of being rigidly self-transforming.

The microanalysis of Brian and Jeremy's play shows that both had the capacity to provide regulation to, and accept regulation from, each other. Orders abounded in their interaction, but they were not responded to in kind. In contrast, the responses given by Janine and Tania were matched in level and orientation and seemed to escalate the power struggle or loss of control, whereas Brian and Jeremy gave complementary responses that ultimately checked any escalation. The boys' responses were complementary in level and orientation, and, furthermore, their flexible use of different levels and orientations was cued to the context, that is, to their perception of each other's construal, affect, and intentions. Each boy generally responded to orders from the other either with an accepting self-transforming strategy (presumably when he felt his partner's command was a reasonable suggestion) or with a higher Level 2 other-transforming persuasion (when the other's Level 1 behavior was not found reasonable). Moreover, each boy also used orders when he perceived the other was "losing it" (losing control with impulsivity and lack of perspective). The boys' orders, despite being "only" Level 1, were offered and accepted as helpful controls, intended for keeping behavior controlled or maintaining fairness in the interaction. Their orders resulted in successful maintenance of the interaction rather than in the kind of unyielding competition that Tania and Janine engaged in, which was potentially destructive of the interaction and ultimately of the relationship.

To fill out the interpretation of our direct observations of these two peer interactions, we also need to use information about the children's personalities, their past histories as individuals, and the past history of their particular relationship. For example, if we knew that Brian was much more bossy and controlling at his own home than when at a friend's, this would tell us something about his general interpersonal orientation beyond what we were able to see in one observation. Or, if we knew that Janine usually had a sharp gruff tone in her dealings with most significant others, we would be appropriately wary of attributing to her current behavior a specific anger at Tania or at something that had just happened. Instead it would suggest that generally speaking she construes relationships between the self and other(s) in terms of battles for control of objects, as well as control of others' actions, and she sees these battles requiring orders, threats, and commands, rather than persuasions or collaborations.

One of the most informative contextual factors for interpreting the developmental meaning of peer interactions, and function and dysfunction therein, is a comparison between the children's expected capacity to understand interpersonal relationships and the extent to which they apply that understanding in their social interactions. The (Level 1) ordering strategies are typical and age-appropriate for children of Jeremy and Brian's age and are acceptable forms of interaction to them. At 6 years of age a child may be expected to have developed a reflective awareness of differences in perspective at a concrete level of individual likes and dislikes, needs, and wants. The boys' Level 1 interpersonal understanding was developed to such an extent that they could apply that understanding consistently across situations. Moreover, occasionally Brian and Jeremy used higher, Level 2 negotiations, reflecting their ability to try out the cutting edge of their competence, a level of perspective coordination that was beginning to develop but was not yet integrated. Thus, Brian and Jeremy's modal Level 1 negotiation strategies and occasional Level 2 strategies were matched to their expected level of social-cognitive competence; there was a congruence for both these children between their age-typical level of understanding and their performance.

The girls, however, were older than Brian and Jeremy—9 rather than 6. With these added years we expect to see Janine and Tania use a greater repertoire of strategies in negotiations with peers, reflecting a higher level of interpersonal understanding. We expect the 9-year-olds not only to have acquired a higher level of interpersonal understanding, but also to use that functional understanding of reciprocity in more challenging forms of interpersonal relationships with peers. It is not possible to determine from the narrative we presented whether the two girls had achieved the reciprocal level of social perspective coordination, but (knowing their ages and personal histories) we suspect that the girls probably did have this Level 2 competence; they could probably have demonstrated reciprocal interpersonal understanding in a less personally threatening context (e.g., in a quiet one-to-one interview with an empathic adult about hypothetical social conflicts). Another clue that their competence *was* at Level 2 was their use of the hollow Level 2 statements we described earlier, those whose surface, apparently reciprocal ("I did your stupid clay for you") meaning is belied by their angry tone.

In the 12 minutes of their interaction, Tania and Janine *never* displayed what should be a stably developed level of negotiation, much less "cutting edge" strategies as the boys did (i.e., occasional use of strategies reflecting new, beginning-to-be-developed levels of interpersonal understanding). This discrepancy—the developmental gap—between their actual ways of relating (predominantly at Levels 1 and 0) and their normatively expected capacity of understanding relationships (at Level 2 with perhaps some hints of Level 3) is striking. Chronologically, Tania and Janine no longer inhabited a unilateral (Level 1) world, and orders are no longer enough once reciprocal (Level 2) understanding becomes the norm. Children's "required" roles evolve as they grow up, and the life tasks of 9-year-olds differ from those of 6-year-olds: preadolescence brings tasks that require greater reciprocity of thought and action than the tasks of middle childhood. Therefore, each girl may have wanted and expected reciprocity and sensitivity to her needs, but neither received this from, or offered this to, the other in actual negotiation.

In essence, reciprocal control of affect seems to be one thing friends are for at any age or level. But the reason that the control and mutual regulation worked for the boys yet not for the girls goes beyond this. The 6-year-old boys had something else going for them: a long-standing set of positive shared experiences together, a connection on which to base their mutual social regulations. Moreover, the opportunity for shared experience and expressive emotional behavior—which for 6-year-olds often centers around fantasy play—continued in this session. Tania and Janine didn't get along well enough to be able to begin to play together—their toys (e.g., the puppets) became weapons in their embattled relationship instead of props for the shared experience of fantasy play.

In interpreting specific interpersonal negotiations or series of negotiations we rely heavily on information about the history of the present ongoing relationship. How, for example, do we interpret the lack of reciprocal (Level 2) negotiation in Tania and Janine's play? Because we know that the girls had used reciprocity in their dealings previously (i.e., when the therapist had stayed with them), instead of never, we interpret this particular 12-minute episode as a temporary regression in the service of ultimate progression instead of as a hopeless and complete disaster.

Our interpretation is enriched further by considering the dyad's past individual emotional/relationship histories, a level of analysis that goes beyond the level of meaning-description that we more often engage in to a level of explanation-description. Perhaps the girls couldn't cue themselves to the context of the ongoing peer relationship the way the boys did because they brought too much emotional "baggage" to the interaction from their past relationships. The girls probably didn't expect reciprocity from each other because neither had gotten their needs met with positive emotional responsiveness in their past or present primary relationships. Their negative, distorted construal of the other in all close relationships led them to act in a predeterminedly rejecting way, without taking into account the nature of the details and cues of the particular context and the identity of the other. In contrast, although their responses to each other were also shaped by their idiosyncratic past relational histories, the boys were open to meeting the reciprocal regulation requirements in the ongoing context of their relationship to the extent that their developmental level of social perspective coordination allowed.

CONCLUSIONS

Many researchers who have labored long and hard in the field of observational research have felt it important to come to the contexts of social interaction with as little preformed theoretical bias as possible. We, however, share the constructionist position that such an atheoretical stance is impossible: Knowledge is not merely discovered but socially constructed, and theoretical biases and personal values are inherent not only in the interpretations we make but in the very questions we raise. Our developmental model grows out of our conscious clinical goal to promote growth in children's capacity to deal with peers collaboratively; clinical approaches and applications need models that do more than describe social interaction, they need models to give some direction to the treatment.

The sorting of interpersonal negotiation strategies into the seven bins and boxes representing different levels and orientations depends on inference about the underlying psychological structure that gives the observed behavior its particular developmental form. The core issue in using a developmental model to diagnose (code) observations of social interaction is the utility of the theoretical and methodological tools used to make the inferential leap entailed when coding contexts for interpersonal negotiation into hierarchically ordered categories. In the work presented here, we have attempted to articulate how the perspective coordination model provides an effective framework, or heuristic device, for articulating the cognitive, affective, and motivational factors that give strategies for interpersonal negotiation their developmental quality. Using the four components of interpersonal negotiation as our tools, we take as much care as possible not to misinterpret what we see, that is, not to put an observed strategy in the wrong box because we do not understand the meaning that underlies the interaction. Even more crucial, we try not to build the boxes so rigidly that they cannot change shape, form, and organization as better ways to classify the incoming information might evolve. Our goal is to classify the strategies we observe along the basic dimensions of our levels and orientations, with as much concern as possible for reliable and valid categorization of observed episodes.

We continue to apply the interpersonal negotiation strategies model to clinical cases as well as to large samples because we are not primarily interested in systematic descriptions of the status quo—how interpersonal negotiation varies for different groups (genders, cultures, social classes, young versus old, mentally ill versus healthy) across different situations. Our primary goal in this chapter is to understand how two children in pair therapy learn to get along better (in a developmental sense) with their peers. This interest generates many questions requiring "meaningful" rather than "true" answers. How do new interpersonal negotiation skills develop? What social regulation patterns promote growth? How does the pair get to the next interpersonal negotiation level?

Preliminary answers to these questions must, in our view, come from meaning-oriented case-by-case analysis such as we have presented here. We use our context-dependent interpretations of peer interaction to make generalizations guiding our clinical treatment with pairs of children. Comparisons across our idiographic, hermeneutic case analyses generate nomothetic, positivist hypotheses about what facilitates social development. Particularly compelling generalizations about what configurations of developmental level and interpersonal orientation facilitate children's getting along and growing socially emerge from the extreme differences in the social interactions described in our two interpretive/empirical case studies.

In terms of generalizing about the impact of the relative developmental level of an interacting dyad, it seems that strategies at the leading edge of children's age-appropriate repertoire, such as the reciprocal persuasions of Jeremy and Brian, provide the optimal challenge for growth in a peer relationship. In contrast, the age-inappropriate highest level of the troubled girls in the new context of this particular session—unilateral (Level 1) orders—were not adequate to regulate their interaction. Instead, they seemed to create a context conducive to social chaos, in which both girls degenerated to extremely low-level behavior.

With regard to generalizing about interpersonal orientation, we believe that the kind of alternation of orientation in the play of Brian and Jeremy, in which the boys were complementary in their responses but alternated getting their own way and giving in to each other, is optimal for social development. It may be more common, though, to observe complementarity in orientation in which one child is consistently other-transforming and the other child always self-transforms. This rigid, defensive configuration generally does not seem to be a fertile context for social growth, but at least the dominant/subordinate pattern maintains the relationship. In contrast, the patterning of orientation in Tania and Janine's interaction—both rigidly other-transforming at the same developmental level—destroyed the interaction and probably would have destroyed the relationship itself if the larger context were not that of pair therapy, in which the adult therapist has an opportunity to mediate the impasse.

It is the goal of our interpretive coding procedure—using the cognitive heuristic of social perspective coordination in conjunction with a sensitivity to affect at each successive level of analysis—to capture the complex affective-cognitive interplay in dyadic peer interactions. Using a Wernerian comparative notion of level and the broader developmental principle, we attempt to interpret peer interaction with context-sensitive descriptions of adaptive and maladaptive social regulative behaviors. Our approach to peer research reflects an eclectic blend of world theories (cf. Mueller & Cooper, 1986). It combines goals (descriptive research and clinical intervention), methods (hermeneutic case analysis and positivist generalization), theories (Wernerian comparison and Piagetian structuralism), and levels of analysis (molar and molecular data) in an analysis of social interaction processes in which artificial methodological dichotomies—subject and object, induction and deduction, theory and practice—can begin to be united.

Recognizing that values inhere in both research and clinical intervention enterprises, we present the interpersonal negotiation strategies model with the assumption that peer interaction has many levels of meaning; no one system of observation can hope to provide a complete or even factual record of all the ongoing processes. The more the study of social interaction is seen as a process of interpretation rather than as a set of facts independent of the theories designed to explain them, the more data, method, and theory are intertwined. We have not abandoned positivism, either in theory or practice; rather, we have expanded our epistemological horizons by using those parts of positivist methodology that help illuminate the specific meaning we seek. Where we look, what we see, how we see it, and what it means all become parts of the whole.

Appendix

CODING QUESTIONS FOR DEVELOPMENTAL DIAGNOSES OF INTERPERSONAL NEGOTIATION STRATEGIES

How Is Construal of Self and Other Classified by Level?

The first question we ask is, How does the actor appear to construe the psychological nature of the self and/or other in the context of the negotiation? This cognitive component defines the nature and capacities of the actors involved, as understood at that moment.

> Does the actor appear to construe one or both actors as objects, as objective barriers to each other's quest for a goal, without appearing to consider the self or other as having subjective interests within the context of the negotiation? Does the actor ignore the significant other as having no vested interest or claim whatsoever in the context? If so, then the construal is classified as Level 0. For example, when Tania bolts from the pair therapy room, she totally ignores Janine's internal state and appears to consider her as only a block to obtaining the powerfully felt, but largely uncomprehended, needs of self.

Does the actor appear to construe the other as a separate individual with interests and desires that are viewed as necessarily in direct competition with those of the self for a scarce or limited resource so that only one individual can achieve his or her goal? If so, then the construal would be classified as Level 1. Jeremy's construal of Brian as in competition for the space station represents both self and other as having separate wills and purposes, but each individual's motives are seen in an "either-or," "mine versus yours" light.

Does the actor seem to suggest that each party can consider the other's perspective, at least enough to speak to one another's concerns? Is there a sense that the disequilibrium may be due to conflicting feelings within the self or between self and other, between two individuals who can try to consider each other's needs? If so, then the construal would be classified as Level 2. Brian's subsequent attempt to provide a reason why he should play with the space station shows his recognition that it is possible to change Jeremy's thoughts and feelings through (self-interested) communication.

Does the actor seem to recognize that both parties include as part of their deliberations and as part of their self-interest in the negotiation, the interest of the other as well as the interest of the relationship as it is represented in the specific negotiation under consideration? If so, then the construal would be classified as Level 3. None of the children in our examples exhibit this level of construal because the cognitive capacity to reflect simultaneously on the self, other, and the relationship—and to appreciate the needs of all three as well as the mutual effect within the dyad—does not normally develop until adolescence.

What Is the Actor's Purpose in the Context for Negotiation?

The primary interpersonal purpose component of a strategy is the dominant goal-oriented motivation of the behavior, motivation in the sense of what the individual thinks is his or her reason for attempting to achieve some goal or to deal with the goal achievement of another. Similar to the view of some action theorists, motivation or purpose is used in our developmental analysis as the "forward pull" of a to-be-achieved goal on current conduct rather than as the "from-behind push" of unconscious motivation to explain conduct (e.g., Eckensberger & Meacham, 1984). We use the term "primary intent" because we appreciate that at successive developmental levels, new intents are added while old intents may still be relevant, albeit no longer primary. Immediate goals tend to focus on the allocation of goods, social services, or attention, but longer-term relationship-oriented goals are inherent—though often unattended to—in contexts for negotiation, which involve achieving subjective as well as objective desires (e.g., affection as well as good fortune).

Is the primary purpose to achieve a self-defined goal, without any consideration of the goals or purposes or interests of the other parties involved? Is the actor pursuing immediate physical goals? If so, then the primary purpose would be classified as Level 0. Tania's enraged bolt from the pair therapy room was motivated by her own immediate need to escape a situation she could not control any other way, without reflection on what effect her furious action would have on her in the future, or how her pursued goals, which were undifferentiated from her action, related to Janine's goals.

Is the primary purpose to establish a position of sole power and control in the interaction—be it for self or other—so as to be able to be the one to decide who goes first, gets what, or keeps what, who wins or yields control to the other? If so, then the primary purpose is classified as Level 1. When Jeremy announces, "I'm doing the trash compactor," he is attempting to establish his goals at the expense of, and distinct from, those of Brian. He calls it out as if, since his words will race past Brian and reach the compactor before Brian's hand reaches it, his own claim for the compactor should be respected. This suggests that Jeremy is aware that Brian's perspective is separate from his own, and that he must state his claim and its justification to Brian to give it any social validity and negotiable force.

Is the primary purpose to "make a pact" satisfactory to each party? Is this agreement, however, thought to be achieved either by changing the other to accommodate that person's perspective to the self's or by changing the self's perspective to fit with that of the other instead of by mutual accommodation? If so, then the primary purpose would be classified as Level 2. When Brian explains, "You've already played with this, but it's new to me," he is trying to establish his own goals as more primary and to deemphasize Jeremy's goals by psychological manipulation. He plays up to Jeremy's thoughts to influence his wishes—and ultimately his actions. He does not try to rest merely on a unilateral and physical "I got here first so it's mine" claim; instead he feels the need to provide a rationale for his claim. (However, regardless of his level of justification, we do not expect that Brian would be willing to lighten up his firm grip on the compactor knob.)

Is the primary purpose to have both parties achieve a sense of collaboration, a sense that each person has individual interests as well as mutual interests and that some balance needs to be achieved? Is the goal to resolve conflicts in contexts for negotiation that maintain the balance of the relationship by striving for long-term as well as short-term goals while trying to achieve the particulars? If so, then the primary purpose would be classified as Level 3. Again, none of the children in our examples have attained the capacity to use shared reflection to pursue mutual goals with the understanding that mutuality of outcome and communication in its pursuit are as important as the particular outcome with regard to their initial goal in an interpersonal negotiation.

How Are Perception and Control of Affective Disequilibrium Classified by Level?

The affective component of an interpersonal negotiation strategy attends to the way the individual perceives and attempts to control internal emotional disequilibrium arising in a context for interpersonal negotiation. Three aspects of affective disequilibrium are qualitatively distinct at each developmental level: two aspects of the perception of the upset—its cause (how the disequilibrium came about) and its locus (where the bad or painful feelings reside), and the way the affective disequilibrium is dealt with in the attempt to return to a balanced or calm psychological state.

Does the negotiation context appear to generate in the individual a diffuse, global, and undifferentiated sense of cause and locus? Does the individual appear to experience the disequilibrated feelings as all-encompassing and out of the self's control such that relief must come from some external source of control or authority? If, so, then the affective perception and control would be classified as Level 0. When Tania bolts from the room, ending her interaction with Janine, she makes no conscious attempt to control her enraged, angry feelings through planned action. She cannot deal with these "out of control" feelings; instead, her feelings control and literally propel her.

Does the individual seem to perceive feelings as distinct but *objective* elemental phenomena that can only be changed or soothed if the self's perceived goal is achieved, but in no other way (I will feel badly until I get what I say I want)? Does the actor appear to believe that internal feelings can only be changed through changes in factors external to the self (non-intrapsychic factors)? If so, then the affective perception and control would be classified as Level 1. When Jeremy makes his one-way challenge to Brian's claim on the trash compactor, his tone is urgent and concerned, yet his look is questioning and uncertain. His emotional state appears distinct from his action, yet the feelings are transitory, and he seeks relief from them by trying to change Brian's actions instead of acting directly on his own feelings.

Are the feelings being experienced understood to be subjectively as well as objectively caused? Are they recognized to be due to conflicts within the self (I want that toy, but I also want you to play with me)? Are disequilibrated feelings dealt with by trying to push them out, down, or inside the subjective self? If so, then the affective perception and control would be classified as Level 2. Brian reacts to Jeremy's challenge to his claim to the trash compactor with a tone that is explaining, yet delivered with force and a slight scowl. The combination of reasonableness and force suggests that he recognizes the conflict between his personal and interpersonal needs (getting what he wants, yet not alienating Jeremy) as well as the conflict between his immediate goals and those of Jeremy.

Are disequilibrated feelings experienced as painful but workable, that is, changeable through actions the self can take? Are disequilibrated feelings located in a historical context, viewed as being related to past events, experiences, and relationships, as well as being mutable through future actions? Are feelings managed or controlled through a process of "working through," including the expression of feelings and/or communication and clarification of feelings with a significant other who may be party to their cause? If so, then the affective perception and control would be classified as Level 3. The children in our examples are too young to have achieved the capacity to discriminate the variety of feelings within self and between self and other inherent in a particular context for negotiation, to view their place in the broader historical context of the self and the relationship, and to slowly and reciprocally work to integrate the feelings into the relationship through internal and shared reflection.

How Is Interpersonal Orientation Classified?

Although in practice an individual never acts solely upon the self or upon the other, nor are actions solely derived from within the self independent of the complexity of the interactions between the self and the other, it still remains useful to look upon actions as directed primarily toward the changing of the self or the changing of the other, or, at higher levels, the changing of both. This social action dimension of the model represents an attempt to begin to redefine some classic dichotomies in personality theory within a unified developmental framework—dichotomies such as passive and aggressive, introverted and extroverted, or acting-out and withdrawn. The INS model suggests that neither a self-transforming nor an other-transforming strategy is necessarily less or more mature or pathological; rather it is the rigidity, or lack of differentiation, at the lower levels in contexts where higher-level functioning is both expected and adaptive that determines the degree to which there is normality or pathology, maturity or immaturity. It is often the case, particularly at the lower developmental levels of negotiation, that it is much easier to diagnose orientation than level. Thus, one can use orientation to help determine level.

Does the actor use unreflective physical force to make absolute and impulsive demands or to totally reject or ignore the validity of the other person's needs? If so, then the orientation would be classified as other-transforming at Level 0. Janine's angry bolt from the pair therapy room is an example of such an impulsive and total rejection of the other person in a context for negotiation. Or does the actor show total capitulation (i.e., unreflective and automatic compliance with and acceptance of the wishes of the other person) or impulsive withdrawal? If so, then the interpersonal orientation would be classified as self-transforming at Level 0. If Janine had run from the pair therapy in helpless panic instead of rejecting rage, it would reflect such an unreflective and total withdrawal from her conflict with Tania.

Is the actor observed to be commanding, ordering, or bullying in interactions with others, perhaps even using the threat of force to attempt to change the other's actions so that the self's unilaterally defined goals will be achieved? If so, the interpersonal orientation would be classified as other-transforming at Level 1. Jeremy's announcement that he was doing the trash compactor was delivered with such a commanding, ordering tone. Or does the actor appear to take actions that are submissively obedient to the other, that is, consciously putting the other in a position of control and the self in a weaker or submissive position, quick to withdraw the legitimacy of his or her own recognized will or interest in the arena of negotiation? If so, the interpersonal orientation would be classified as self-transforming at Level 1. Brian's compliance with Jeremy's order to pick up the "Creepy Crawlies" reflected his obedient submission to Jeremy's will.

Does the actor appear to attempt to use psychological influence (e.g., manipulation) or persuasive tactics in order to change the other person's perceived wishes, views, or feelings so that they match, and thus facilitate, the achievement of the self's wishes? If so, the interpersonal orientation would be classified as other-transforming at Level 2. Brian's forceful but reasonable response to Jeremy's challenge to his control of the trash compactor was assertive and persuasive, but it accommodated Jeremy's perspective to the extent that Brian put psychological effort and energy into the process of influence, recognizing the existence if not the full legitimacy of Jeremy's perspective, rather than simply using physical force or the threat thereof. Or does the actor appear to be compliant to the other's wishes, not by negotiating away all the self's interests as at the lower self-transforming levels, but by putting them second, or "on hold," in order to keep the relation with and liking of the other person a high priority? If so, the interpersonal orientation would be classified as self-transforming at Level 2. Jeremy's deferential response to Brian's persistent but reasoned claim to the trash compactor ("OK, but next time I get to choose first") relinquished his immediate claim but made it clear that his own desires, though deferred, were still recognized and valued.

Does the actor appear to try to strike a balance between meeting the self's felt needs and meeting the expressed needs of the other? If so, the interpersonal orientation would be classified as collaborative (Level 3). There are no examples of a collaborative orientation in the two opening narratives because, as we have mentioned, these children have not acquired the capacity for mutual coordination of perspectives (Level 3) necessary to integrate self-transforming and other-transforming actions into more equilibrated action at Level 3 of interpersonal negotiation. Negotiations at this level are more likely to lead to mutually satisfying outcomes because of the balancing of the perspective of self with that of other, or self-agency and assertion with relatedness and accommodation.

REFERENCES

Blurton-Jones, N. G., & Woodson, R. H. (1979). Describing behavior: The ethologists' perspective. In M. E. Lamb, S. J. Suomi, & G. R. Stephenson (Eds.), *Social interaction analysis: Methodological issues* (pp. 97–118). Madison: University of Wisconsin Press.

Cairns, R. B. (1979). Social interaction methods: An introduction. In R. B. Cairns (Ed.), *The analysis of social interactions: Methods, issues, and illustrations* (pp. 1–10). Hillsdale, NJ: Lawrence Erlbaum.

Eckensberger, L. H., & Meacham, J. A. (1984). The essentials of action theory: A framework for discussion. *Human Development, 27,* 166–172.

Gergen, K. J. (1985). The social constructionist movement in modern psychology. *American Psychologist, 40,* 266–275.

Gergen, K. J., & Gergen, M. M. (1982). Explaining human conduct: Form and function. In P. F. Secord (Ed.), *Explaining human behavior: Consciousness, human action and social structure* (pp. 127–154). Beverly Hills, CA: Sage.

Gottman, J. M., & Bakeman, R. (1979). The sequential analysis of observational data. In M. E. Lamb, S. J. Suomi, & G. R. Stephenson (Eds.), *Social interaction analysis: Methodological issues* (pp. 185–206). Madison: University of Wisconsin Press.

Hartup, W. W. (1979). Levels of analysis in the study of social interaction: An historical perspective. In M. E. Lamb, S. J. Suomi, & G. R. Stephenson (Eds.), *Social interaction analysis: Methodological issues* (pp. 11–32). Madison: University of Wisconsin Press.

Hay, D. F. (1984). Social conflict in early childhood. In G. Whitehurst (Ed.), *Annals of child development* (Vol. 1, pp. 1–44). Greenwich, CT: JAI Press.

Hinde, R. A. (1979). *Towards understanding relationships.* New York: Academic Press.

Hinde, R. A. (1985). Was 'The Expression of the Emotions' a misleading phrase? *Animal Behavior, 33,* 985–992.

Kohlberg, L. (1969). Stage and sequence: The cognitive-developmental approach to socialization. In D. A. Goslin (Ed.), *Handbook of socialization theory and research* (pp. 347–480). New York: Rand McNally.

Lyman, R., & Selman, R. L. (1985). Peer conflict in pair therapy: Clinical and developmental analyses: In M. W. Berkowitz (Ed.), *New directions for child development: Vol. 7. Peer conflict and psychological growth* (pp. 85–102). San Francisco: Jossey-Bass.

Mead, G. H. (1934). *Mind, self and society.* Chicago: University of Chicago Press.

Menzel, E. W., Jr. (1979). General discussion of the methodological problems involved in the study of social interaction. In M. E. Lamb, S. J. Suomi, & G. R. Stephenson (Eds.), *Social interaction analysis: Methodological issues* (pp. 291–309). Madison: University of Wisconsin Press.

Modell, A. H. (1984). *Psychoanalysis in a new context.* New York: International Universities Press.

Mueller, E. C., & Cooper, C. R. (1986). On conceptualizing peer research. In E. C. Mueller & C. R. Cooper (Eds.), *Process and outcome in peer relationships* (pp. 3–24). Orlando, FL: Academic Press.

Packer, M. (1985). Hermeneutic inquiry in the study of human conduct. *American Psychologist, 40,* 1081–1093.

Packer, M. (1987, April). *Interpretive research and social development in developmental psychology.* Paper presented at the biennial meeting of the Society of Research in Child Development, Baltimore.

Radke Yarrow, M., & Zahn Waxler, C. (1979). Observing interaction: A confrontation with methodology. In R. B. Cairns (Ed.), *The analysis of social interactions: Methods, issues, and illustrations* (pp. 1–10). Hillsdale, NJ: Lawrence Erlbaum.

Scarr, S. (1985). Constructing psychology: Making facts and fables for our times. *American Psychologist, 40,* 499–512.

Schafer, R. (1983). *The analytic attitude.* New York: Basic Books.

Selman, R. L. (1980). *The growth of interpersonal understanding: Clinical and developmental analyses.* New York: Academic Press.

Selman, R. L. (1981). The development of interpersonal competence: The role of understanding in conduct. *Developmental Review, 1,* 401–422.

Selman, R. L., & Arboleda, C. (1986). Pair therapy with two troubled early adolescents. *McLean Hospital Journal, 10,* 84–111.

Selman, R. L., Beardslee, W. R., Schultz, L. H., Krupa, M., & Podorefsky, D. (1986). Assessing adolescent interpersonal negotiation strategies: Toward the integration of structural and functional models. *Developmental Psychology, 22,* 450–459.

Selman, R. L., & Demorest, A. (1984). Observing troubled children's interpersonal negotiation strategies: Implications of and for a developmental model. *Child Development, 55*, 288–304.

Selman, R. L., & Yeates, K. O. (1987). Childhood social regulations of intimacy and autonomy: A developmental-constructionist perspective. In W. Kurtines & J. L. Gewirtz (Eds.), *Social interaction and socio-moral development*. New York: Wiley.

Shantz, C. U. (1987). Conflicts between children. *Child Development, 58*, 283–305.

Shantz, C. U., & Shantz, D. W. (1985). Conflict between children: Social-cognitive and sociometric correlates. In M. W. Berkowitz (Ed.), *New directions for child development: Vol. 7. Peer conflict and psychological growth* (pp. 3–21). San Francisco: Jossey-Bass.

Sroufe, L. A., & Fleeson, J. (1986). Attachment and the construction of relationships. In W. W. Hartup & Z. Rubin (Eds.), *Relationships and Development* (pp. 51–72). Hillsdale, NJ: Lawrence Erlbaum.

Sullivan, H. S. (1953). *The Interpersonal Theory of Psychiatry*. New York: Norton.

Werner, H. (1948). *Comparative psychology of mental development* (Rev. Ed.). Chicago: Follett.

Werner, H. (1957). The concept of development from a comparative and organismic point of view. In D. B. Harris (Ed.), *The concept of development: An issue in the study of human behavior*. Minneapolis: University of Minnesota Press.

EPILOGUE

Contributions of Peer Relationships to Children's Development

THOMAS J. BERNDT

In planning this volume, our overarching goal was to provide scholars, researchers, and practitioners with an authoritative, comprehensive source-
book on the contributions of peer relationships to children's development.
As the authors prepared their chapters, they were asked to keep in mind
both current knowledge about the impact of peer relationships on psychological development and the gaps in our knowledge that should be the targets
of future research. Even a quick reading of the preceding chapters illustrates,
however, that they are not focused solely on the question of the impact of
peer relationships. Instead, they reflect a broad range of approaches to an
equally broad range of questions about peer relationships in childhood and
adolescence. To differing degrees, each chapter contains evaluative reviews
of recent research, comments and recommendations on research methods,
and theoretical frameworks for the description and analysis of phenomena
associated with peer relationships.

Does this variety across the chapters, and the lack of a single-minded
focus on the question of the effects of peer relationships, constitute a fundamental flaw in the volume itself? Should the authors be chided for failing
to confine themselves to the topic at hand, or the editors be blamed for
failing to restrain the authors' tendencies to ignore the central issue for the
book? I believe that most careful readers will answer these questions in the
negative. To some extent, the contrasts among the chapters were inevitable
and, indeed, highly desirable, because they illustrate the variety of theoretical and methodological approaches in this research area. More importantly,
the contrasts demonstrate the host of issues that must be addressed when
questions about the contributions of peer relationships to children's development are raised. In order to deal adequately with these issues, the authors
of the previous chapters have presented a wealth of information on theories,
methods, and recent findings on peer relationships.

In this concluding chapter, however, I would like to focus on the original
question about the contributions of peer relationships. My main goal is to

identify and compare the different perspectives on this question that are presented in the preceding chapters. The similarities and contrasts between perspectives can be seen most clearly, I would argue, by first examining the various working definitions of peer relationships found in the chapters and then examining the authors' assumptions about the effects of peer relationships.

DEFINING PEER RELATIONSHIPS

Strictly speaking, several of the chapters in this book were focused more directly on peer interactions than on peer relationships. For example, Shantz and Hobart were most concerned with the effects of conflicts between children of the same or roughly the same age. Damon and Phelps were most concerned with the effects of classmates' interactions as they attempted to solve mathematical or spatial problems. Furman and Gavin discussed the impact of structured cooperative activities on the interactions of children placed in the same peer group. In each of these cases, the impact of particular types of interactions was emphasized. The characteristics and the history of the relationships between the interacting children received much less emphasis.

There is a long tradition of research on the special features of interactions between peers as opposed to interactions with parents or other adults (see Hartup, 1983; Youniss & Smollar, this volume). For example, as Piaget (1932/1965) pointed out long ago, peer interaction is more egalitarian than that between individuals who differ markedly in age. Consequently, interactions with peers can be conceived as having distinctive or even unique effects on children's development, regardless of the precise nature of the relationship between the peers who are interacting with each other. In other words, the contributions of peer relationships might be profitably defined in terms of the consequences of specific types of interactions between any pair or group of children or adolescents who are similar in age.

On the other hand, the authors of several chapters emphasized the distinctive features of the interactions between peers who have a special relationship with each other. Hartup, for example, discussed research in which interactions between close friends were compared with interactions between acquaintances. Taking a different approach, Selman and Schultz presented a detailed analysis of the interactions between pairs of children who were either close friends or partners in an extended series of pair-therapy sessions. Selman and Schultz did not present quantitative analyses of the differences between the pairs of each type, but they did argue for the importance of understanding the nature and history of the relationship between a pair of children when judging the meaning of any single interaction between them.

The chapters by Hartup and by Selman and Shultz provide a particularly appropriate contrast to the ones discussed earlier because they all deal to some extent with the issues of peer conflicts and their effects. Hartup argued most explicitly, however, that we need to investigate the special characteristics of the management and resolution of friends' conflicts. In essence, he suggested that different types of peer relationships involve different patterns of interactions. Therefore, we cannot study the features and the effects of conflicts between classmates, for example, and expect to obtain accurate information about the features and effects of conflicts between friends. Actually, Shantz and Hobart suggested the same point when they discussed the distinctive features of conflicts between siblings. Siblings have a special relationship that may make their conflicts different in their patterning and resolution from those of unrelated peers and peers who are close friends. If so, this argument implies, the appropriate focus for research should be the nature of interactions between peers who have a particular type of relationship. Similarly, hypotheses about the effects of peer relationships should, in this view, be stated in terms of the effects of interactions between peers who are friends, siblings, classmates, or have some other specified relationship, rather than in terms of the effects of peer interactions in general.

The authors of other chapters focused not on the characteristics of specific interactions between peers, but on more abstract qualities of relationships. Bukowski and Hoza, for example, described a model for assessing children's friendships that referred first, to whether a child has any close friends, second, to how many close friends the child has, and finally, to various features of these friendships such as their intimacy and the friends' support for the child's self-esteem. Youniss and Smollar discussed the importance for adolescents of having close friendships based on mutual respect and a balance between connectedness and separateness. Both sets of authors referred primarily to research in which the qualities of friendships were judged from children's or adolescents' responses to interviews or questionnaires. Although these verbal reports can and have been related to evidence from observations of the friends' actual interactions with each other (e.g., Berndt, Hawkins, & Hoyle, 1986), the full meaning and significance of intimacy or mutual respect cannot be captured by behavioral observations in a single situation or even a number of situations. In terms of Hinde's (1979) taxonomy, features such as intimacy and mutual respect refer to emergent qualities of relationships that reflect a complex combination of overt behaviors, attitudes, and emotions.

Naturally, researchers who emphasize the importance of the emergent qualities of relationships assume that these qualities are most critical for understanding and predicting the effects of relationships on children's development. Bukowski and Hoza, for example, examined the effects of the qualities of children's friendships on their self-concepts. Youniss and Smollar considered the influence on parent-child relationships of the changes in the qualities of friendships during adolescence. In short, these authors treated the relationship as the unit of analysis in their descriptions and their hypotheses.

A final set of authors concentrated on a level of analysis more general and more abstract than either specific types of interactions or particular kinds of relationships. These authors emphasized an individual's position in a larger social group. The measure of social position with the longest history in developmental research is popularity, or sociometric status. Not surprisingly, many of the chapters in this book include reviews and critiques of research on sociometric status (e.g., Furman & Gavin; Lewis & Feiring; Price & Dodge, Rowe). Bukowski and Hoza perhaps point out most explicitly, however, that systems for classifying children's sociometric status reflect an abstraction by researchers. These systems focus on one facet of a child's social position in a group and do not provide any precise information about the qualities of the child's relationships with members of that peer group. Similarly, measures of sociometric status are related to observational data on the child's interactions with peers (e.g., Masters and Furman, 1981), but sociometric status is not itself an index of peer interaction. The same is true for other indicators of social position such as the measure of crowd membership discussed in Brown's chapter.

There is ample evidence that a child's social position in the peer group is significantly related to concurrent and subsequent measures of psychological adjustment and development (see Parker & Asher, 1987). Moreover, there is suggestive evidence that interventions designed to improve the social position of rejected or isolated children can also foster improvements in their adjustment (Furman & Gavin; Price & Dodge, this volume). Thus the abstractness of such measures, as well as their lack of direct connections to measures of interactions and relationships, does not translate into a lack of theoretical or practical importance. On the contrary, these measures appear to be among the most powerful and practically significant of all measures of adjustment to the social world of peers.

In sum, researchers investigating the broad area of peer relationships have created and employed measures that represent four different levels of analysis. The first level includes measures for particular types of interactions with peers, without regard to the relationships among the peers who are interacting. Measures of a child's frequency of conflicts or positive interactions with any and all peers would fall at this level. The second level includes measures for types of interactions between peers who have a specified relationship. Measures of conflicts with close friends would fall at this level. The third level includes measures of relationship qualities that are not linked (and may not be easily linked) to any single, specific type of interaction. Measures of intimacy or mutual respect between friends or parents would fall at this level. The fourth and final level includes measures of an individual's position in a particular peer group. Measures of sociometric status are the best-known exemplars of this level of analysis.

Distinguishing between measures of peer relationships that reflect different levels of analysis may be heuristically valuable in several ways. First, simply making the distinctions may increase the clarity and specificity of theoretical and empirical writings. It seems clear, for example, that Youniss and Smollar attach different meanings to the notion of conflict than do Shantz and Hobart. Part of the difference may derive from Youniss and Smollar's use of the term *conflict* to describe a quality of relationships whereas Shantz and Hobart consistently use the term to describe a particular type of interaction. Similarly, hypotheses about the effects of peer relationships would be easier to test if they were stated explicitly in terms of a specified level of analysis. We might ask, for example, whether the negative consequences of peer rejection (e.g., Price & Dodge, this volume) are intrinsically related to a child's low position in the peer group or reflect the continuity of the negative interaction patterns that led to that low position in the first place (cf. Parker & Asher, 1987).

Second, once the different levels of analysis are distinguished, the benefits of research on the connections between them can be seen. Research that focuses on particular types of interactions, for example, is conceptually and operationally simpler than research on particular types of interactions between individuals who have a particular type of relationship. Hartup argued that the more complex design of research on interactions in relationships is necessary for understanding the contributions of peer relationships. This conclusion holds, however, only if the patterning of peer interactions differs markedly for individuals who have different types of relationships. Hartup presents evidence that this patterning does differ for friends and nonfriends, at least for episodes of conflict management. Across a broader range of types of interactions, however, the differences between friends and nonfriends are noticeable but not always substantial or statistically significant (Berndt, 1987). Thus adding the additional level of complexity required for examining the differences between the nature and consequences of interactions with different classes of peer partners may not always be necessary.

Currently, there is an even more pressing need for research on the connections between a child's social position and the qualities of his or her close peer relationships. In particular, little is known about the relations between measures of popularity and friendship quality. The existing data (e.g., McGuire & Weisz, 1982) suggest that measures at these two levels of analysis may be relatively independent. Their independence would call into question intervention programs (e.g., Oden & Asher, 1977) designed to increase children's popularity by teaching them strategies for making friends. On the other hand, the demonstrated success of these interventions raises questions about correlational data that suggest little connection between children's position in a social group and the qualities of their friendships.

Ideally, researchers would attempt to chart all of the connections and the disjunctures between the different levels of analysis of peer relationships. Researchers could then move more confidently through the entire network of constructs and measures with a clear picture of the overall terrain. Until that point is reached, researchers are likely to see apparent contradictions— or apparent consistencies—in findings that are not strictly comparable. They are also likely to draw inaccurate conclusions about the contributions of peer relationships to children's development.

JUDGING THE CONTRIBUTIONS OF PEERS

On the whole, the authors of the preceding chapters argued for largely positive contributions of peer relationships to children's and adolescents' behavior, adjustment, and development. Bukowski and Hoza reported evidence consistent with the hypothesis that the quality of students' close friendships influenced their feelings of general self-worth. Damon and Phelps summarized the results of a long-term experimental study that demonstrated the benefits of collaborating with peers in learning mathematical and spatial concepts. Furman and Gavin discussed various techniques such as cooperative peer contact that have positive influences on children's social behavior. These and other authors also referred to the well-known hypotheses of Piaget (1932/1965) and Sullivan (1953) regarding the impact of peer relationships on children's social and moral development. In addition, the authors of several chapters provided an overview of their own recent theories about the positive effects of peer relationships on psychological development (e.g., Parker & Gottman; Youniss & Smollar; Selman & Schultz).

Many reasons for the emphasis on positive effects of peer relationships could be given. As already noted, the theoretical traditions best known to developmental psychologists, those of Piaget and Sullivan, stress the positive effects of peer relationships more than potential negative effects. In addition, there is little doubt that peer relationships become closer and more important to children with increasing age (Hartup, 1983). Developmental psychologists normally assume that "older is better," so it is natural for them to assume that the more mature pattern of close, significant peer relationships that emerges in adolescence is a completely positive phenomenon. Even evidence of an effect of peer influence on deviant behavior in adolescence can be reinterpreted so that it is consistent with this viewpoint. For example, Youniss and Smollar suggested in their chapter that peer contributions to deviant behavior may, in a broader view, be part of the process of reconstruction in parent-child and peer relationships that is one of the key tasks of adolescence.

Of course, one important reason for the emphasis on positive contributions of peer relationships is that the bulk of the research findings are consistent with this emphasis. As noted already, data from correlational, longitudinal, and experimental studies indicate that peers can and do have positive effects on children's personality, social behavior, and academic achievement. By contrast, warnings about the negative effects of peer influence (e.g., Bronfenbrenner, 1970; Coleman, 1961) tend to be unsupported by data or, more commonly, are supported by data that seems best interpreted in other ways. Bronfenbrenner's original research suggested, for example, that peer influence fostered antisocial behavior by adolescents in American society, but it seemed to foster the inhibition of antisocial behavior in Russian society. Similarly, Coleman argued that the norms of peer groups in most American high schools favor social or athletic success over academic achievement. He and other researchers (e.g., Ball, 1981) have noted, however, that under certain conditions peer-group norms place a higher value on academic achievement than on achievement in other domains.

The more even-handed position that peer influence can lead to desirable or undesirable behavior provides a better fit to the data than either unequivocally positive or unequivocally negative views of peer influence. In this volume, Epstein, Rowe, and Brown all reviewed evidence that demonstrates the variability in the outcomes of peer influence. Their explanation for this variability in outcomes can be summarized in a brief, common sense proposition: How you are influenced by your friends depends on the friends that you have. For example, Epstein described research that showed positive effects of friends' influence on the measured achievement of students with high-scoring friends and negative effects of friends' influence on the achievement of students with low-scoring friends. Rowe presented comparable findings regarding friends' influence on delinquent behavior.

The proposition that peer influence can be either positive or negative is also consistent with several important and well-supported theories. A social-learning theorist, for example, would argue that peers may affect children's or adolescents' behavior by reinforcing certain behaviors and punishing other behaviors. The behaviors reinforced by peers may not always be socially desirable; the behaviors punished by peers may not always be socially undesirable. For example, peers can and often do reinforce sex-stereotyped behaviors that limit the behavioral alternatives available to boys and girls (see Hartup, 1983). Similarly, peers may affect one another's behavior through the models that they provide for one another. Because both desirable and undesirable behaviors may be modeled by peers, both types of behaviors may be learned from peers.

Nevertheless, to say that peer relationships can have either a positive or a negative impact on social behavior and psychological development is ultimately unsatisfying. This conclusion leaves at least three important questions unanswered. First, does every child or adolescent have the same amount of influence on friends or other peers? If not, who are the peers who are more influential, and who are the ones who are more susceptible to influence? Writers who express concern about the negative effects of peer influence assume that those children or adolescents whose attitudes, values, and behaviors are most at odds with those of adult society typically have the most influence in the peer group. By contrast, other writers such as Damon and Phelps in this volume have adopted the Piagetian view that children and adolescents who express more mature or cognitively sophisticated arguments typically have more influence on their peers. The data relevant to this issue are limited to a few studies in a narrow range of situations and settings. The general question is an especially intriguing one because, since Piaget (1932/1965), researchers have accepted the assumption that peer relationships are fundamentally egalitarian. Our general question, therefore, is how to conceptualize and investigate the possibility of asymmetrical influence in fundamentally egalitarian relationships.

Second, are there any facets of peer relationships that under most conditions have clearly positive effects—or clearly negative effects? To answer this question, a look at the research on parent-child relationships is useful. A great number of studies have examined the impact of warmth, acceptance, or nurturance on children's behavior and development (Maccoby & Martin, 1983). In this vast literature, cases in which warmth has negative effects on psychological development are difficult to find. Nearly all studies indicate that warm relationships between parents and children contribute positively to children's development. In the same way, close and supportive friendships may contribute positively to virtually all aspects of psychological development. In other words, the impact of specific qualities of peer relationships may be more uniform and more predictable than the impact of the influence of specific peers.

Third, how much do peers and peer relationships contribute to children's behavior and development? Neither specific theories such as those of Piaget and Sullivan nor the propositions found in social learning or other general theories provide much guidance in answering this question. One way to address the question is to ask: How much—compared to what? Several authors in this volume provided partial answers to the latter question. Most often, these partial answers referred either to other sources of influences on psychological development or to factors that have a causal influence on peer relationships themselves. Rowe, for example, presented a strong case for the proposition that an individual's genotype has important effects on the individual's personality and his or her ultimate social position in the peer group. Similarly, Lamb and Nash argued that a general disposition toward sociability may account for individual differences in social relationships with peers as well as parents. Feiring and Lewis also considered the impact of constitutional factors on children's formation of peer relationships.

In addition, children's development seems almost certainly influenced by their relationships with parents and with teachers or other significant adults. Lamb and Nash extensively discussed the currently popular hypothesis that parent-child relationships have a major impact on children's success in the peer group. Although these authors concluded that the data taken as confirming the hypothesis are indirect and incomplete, other data with older children and adolescents more strongly suggest that parent-child relationships have significant effects on peer relationships and other aspects of development (Berndt, 1983; Hartup, 1983; Maccoby & Martin, 1983). In this volume, Epstein summarized a large body of research indicating the effects of school characteristics on the formation and maintenance of children's friendships.

Increasing our knowledge of genetic influences and family and school influences on peer relationships in childhood and adolescence should be a high priority for future research. Without this knowledge, researchers risk exaggerating or misinterpreting the effects of peer relationships on development. More importantly, the ultimate goal of researchers is to understand the interplay of multiple influences on children's development. Specifying the position of peer relationships in regard to this multitude of influences is likely to be more rewarding, in the long run, than a single-minded focus on peer relationships themselves.

CONCLUSION

Even though there are important gaps in our current understanding of the contributions of peer relationships, recent research has convincingly established that these relationships play a significant role in the development of children and adolescents. Numerous illustrations of the impact of interactions or relationships with peers were presented in the preceding chapters. For example, Damon and Phelps showed that collaborative exchanges between classmates working on academic tasks to improved children's ability to solve mathematical and spatial problems. Children's and adolescents' selections of close friends were shown by Epstein to influence subsequent changes in their academic achievement. Lamb and Nash reviewed research showing that infants' interactions in a playgroup with peers influenced later interactions with their own mothers. Furman and Gavin summarized a large body of literature on the positive effects of cooperative learning and other interventions that involve peer interaction. These and other examples demonstrate not only that peer relationships can make a positive contribution to children's development, but also that programs that rely on peers as change agents are currently being used in schools and other settings. In other words, the application of knowledge about the contributions of peer relationships has already begun. As Price and Dodge point out, many other strategies for utilizing peer influences in intervention programs could be implemented. Testing and evaluating these programs, while continuing basic research on the processes and outcomes of peer relationships, should be high priorities for future research.

REFERENCES

Ball, S. J. (1981). *Beachside comprehensive*. Cambridge, UK: Cambridge University Press.

Berndt, T. J. (1983). The peer relationships of children with working parents: A theoretical analysis and some conclusions. In C. D. Hayes & S. B. Kamerman (Eds.), *Children of working parents* (pp. 13–43). Washington, DC: National Academy Press.

Berndt, T. J. (1987). Conversations between friends: Theories, research, and implications for sociomoral development. In W. M. Kurtines & J. L. Gewirtz (Eds.), *Moral development through social interaction* (pp. 281–300). New York: Wiley.

Berndt, T. J., Hawkins, J. A., & Hoyle, S. G. (1986). Changes in friendship during a school year: Effects on children's and adolescents' impressions of friendship and sharing with friends. *Child Development, 57,* 1284–1297.

Bronfenbrenner, U. (1970). *Two worlds of childhood.* New York: Sage.

Coleman, J. S. (1961). *The adolescent society.* New York: Free Press.

Hartup, W. W. (1983). Peer relations. In E. M. Hetherington (Ed.) & P. H. Mussen (Series Ed.), *Handbook of child psychology: Vol. 4. Socialization, personality, and social development* (pp. 103–196). New York: Wiley.

Hinde, R. A. (1979). *Towards understanding relationships.* New York: Academic.

Maccoby, E. E., & Martin, J. A. (1983). Socialization in the context of the family: Parent-child interaction. In E. M. Hetherington (Ed.) & P. H. Mussen (Series Ed.), *Handbook of child psychology: Vol. 4. Socialization, personality, and social development* (pp. 1–101). New York: Wiley.

Masters, J. C., & Furman, W. (1981). Popularity, individual friendship selection, and specific peer interaction among children. *Developmental Psychology, 17,* 344–350.

McGuire, K. D., & Weisz, J. R. (1982). Social cognition and behavior correlates of preadolescent chumships. *Child Development, 53,* 1478–1484.

Oden, S., & Asher, S. R. (1977). Coaching children in social skills for friendship making. *Child Development, 48,* 495–506.

Parker, J., & Asher, S. R. (1987). Peer acceptance and later personal adjustment: Are low-accepted children at risk? *Psychological Bulletin, 102,* 357–389.

Piaget, J. (1965). *The moral judgment of the child.* New York: Free Press. (Originally published 1932)

Sullivan, H. S. (1953). *The interpersonal theory of psychiatry.* New York: Norton.

Author Index

417

Subject Index